UNMASKING TERROR
IV

The JAMESTOWN
F O U N D A T I O N

A Compendium of Articles from
The Jamestown Foundation's *Terrorism Monitor*

Edited By
Dr. Andrew McGregor

Jamestown's Mission

The Jamestown Foundation's mission is to inform and educate policy makers and the broader policy community about events and trends in those societies which are strategically or tactically important to the United States and which frequently restrict access to such information. Utilizing indigenous and primary sources, Jamestown's material is delivered without political bias, filter or agenda. It is often the only source of information which should be, but is not always, available through official or intelligence channels, especially in regard to Eurasia and terrorism.

Origins

Launched in 1984 after Jamestown's late president and founder William Geimer's work with Arkady Shevchenko, the highest-ranking Soviet official ever to defect when he left his position as undersecretary general of the United Nations, The Jamestown Foundation rapidly became the leading source of information about the inner workings of closed totalitarian societies.

Over the past two decades, Jamestown has developed an extensive global network of experts – from the Black Sea to Siberia, from the Persian Gulf to the Pacific. This core of intellectual talent includes former high-ranking government officials and military officers, political scientists, journalists, scholars and economists. Their insight contributes significantly to policymakers engaged in addressing today's new and emerging global threats, including that from international terrorists.

THE JAMESTOWN FOUNDATION

Published in the United States by
The Jamestown Foundation
1111 16th St. N.W.
Suite 320
Washington, DC 20036
http://www.jamestown.org

For more information on this book or The Jamestown Foundation, email pubs@jamestown.org.

ISBN 978-0-9816905-1-3

Cover photos by Getty Images

Contents

Iraq

Part III: Africa

Part IV: South Asia

Afghanistan

Part V: The Caucasus and Central Asia

United States

Acknowledgements

A s with each volume of Unmasking Terror, the list of those who have contributed to this publication is quite extensive. We owe our gratitude primarily to the writers, analysts and security professionals who are at the core of Jamestown's program of research and analysis. Integral to this research are the many analysts who reside in Eurasia and Africa and provide us with the penetrating insights from those societies that have given Jamestown global recognition for its terrorism coverage. This group represents a truly global network of research and analysis that extends to over fifty different countries and makes our terrorism publications an important source of information to the U.S. policymaking community. No acknowledgement is complete without an expression of gratitude to those who read our publications and draw upon our research for their work. To all the persons above, Jamestown owes its thanks for helping us continue to offer a diverse array of perspectives on conflict and instability unlike those found in the mainstream Western media.

A special note of thanks is due to Andrew McGregor, the editor of the latest volume of Unmasking Terror, who labored many hours indexing the volume, liaising with Jamestown staff in putting this latest volume together and patiently interacting with the hundreds of writers who have contributed to Jamestown's flagship publications, *Terrorism Monitor* and *Terrorism Focus*. In the final analysis he has raised the standard and quality of our terrorism research to an even higher level of quality for which no words of acknowledgement will ever be enough. A special round of thanks also is due to our Jamestown staff anchored by Russell Hsiao, who devoted many hours to compiling this volume and oversaw the tedious job of copy-editing the nearly five hundred pages of text, assisting with the creation of the cover page and running endless interference for us in making this volume come to fruition. Supporting him in this effort was Adrian Erlinger, who assisted with the proof reading of the final edited document, as well as Will Carlson, who found the *Time* magazine photo used for the cover page and designed the cover art. Last but not least, I want to thank our talented interns Brooke Callahan and Andrew Parker, who labored many hours creating the important names index that was a vital tool in producing this volume.

I would like to thank The Jamestown Board of Directors, in particular our outgoing Chairman, James G. Gidwitz, for his support and direction of our terrorism program. For more than twenty years he has guided this organization through prosperity and turbulence, both as a long-standing board member and chairman of the board. Replacing him will be Willem de Vogel, who will offer this organization a new source of energy and dedication as the foundation continues to grow and expand.

Finally, The Jamestown Foundation owes its gratitude to our generous donors who have made the work of our terrorism program possible. Without their support, our research would simply not be possible. Lastly, we would like once more to thank the readers of Jamestown's publications for their continuing support, feedback and encouragement.

Glen E. Howard
President, The Jamestown Foundation
November 2008

Unmasking Terror IV: Introduction

Terrorism is a tactic, but fear is a tool. As terror creates fear, it is important to remember the warning given over 250 years ago by British statesman and philosopher Edmund Burke: "No passion so effectually robs the mind of all its powers of acting and reasoning as fear." Fear is born of our dread of the dark corners, the places where understanding is absent and our gravest misgivings are given life. Welcome to the pages of the Jamestown Foundation's Unmasking Terror IV – an effort to cast light on the dark corners of the world of terrorism.

Unmasking Terror IV is the latest anthology of analytical articles drawn from Jamestown's biweekly *Terrorism Monitor* publication. They represent, unfortunately, only a selection from a larger number of articles, all of which deserved publication within these pages.

With presidential elections in the United States bringing a change in America's leadership, the War on Terrorism is about to enter a new phase in which we are likely to witness a shift in emphasis from Iraq to Afghanistan and the possible opening of a major new front in the volatile North-West Frontier Province of Pakistan.

In a world of ideas so often dominated by partisan publications, politicized media, lobbyists, advocacy groups and ideologically-driven commentary, The Jamestown Foundation plays a vital role in delivering objective and unfiltered analysis of a range of important security issues related to the world of terrorism. Energy security, demographic shifts, military developments, national strategies, tactical innovations and the role of religion in politics and international security are just a few of the elements that form the spectrum of ideas examined in the pages of *Terrorism Monitor*.

A diverse and broadly based group of analysts ensures that Jamestown's terrorism publications never become stale. From locations across the world, Jamestown's analysts draw on a variety of skills, specializations and backgrounds as academics, journalists and veterans of military and intelligence affairs to tackle security issues from a variety of viewpoints. Though based in Washington D.C., Jamestown provides a truly international forum for timely and critical analysis of events in the often murky spheres of terrorism and counterterrorism. The articles presented in *Terrorism Monitor* rely deeply on indigenous and frequently overlooked or difficult to obtain sources of information, such as the statements and manifestos of insurgent groups, foreign intelligence reports and interviews with individuals at the center of the various crises that Jamestown focuses on.

The articles found in *Terrorism Monitor* and its sister publication, *Terrorism Focus*, typically contain a wealth of detail without losing their readability. This attention to detail reflects the true complexity of the myriad of trends, motivations, personalities and national objectives gathered so roughly under the framework of the "War on Terrorism." It also gives these reports a lasting usefulness as a reference tool for a wide range of security professionals.

Terrorism Monitor articles rely primarily on open-source information, a vital yet surprisingly underused resource. Despite its importance and value as raw information, open-source material is often neglected by policy-makers in search of "secret" intelligence in the misguided belief that only documents marked "secret" can have any value. In the hands of experienced analysts such as those found here, indigenous open-source material can provide a wealth of insights. Jamestown's writers go to great lengths to expose poorly known but extremely important sources, such as the many obscure jihadist websites that carry the views, plans and intentions of terrorists and would-be terrorists.

There are many who are eager to exploit the War on Terrorism's cycle of violence for their own ends, partly through the delivery of misinformation or disinformation. *Terrorism Monitor* analysts penetrate the issues and latest developments in the War on Terrorism, using local sources in a host of languages. Not surprisingly, the analyses developed through this method often differ substantially from the slogans and assumptions that currently permeate much of the debate surrounding terrorism issues. The aim is not to render complex issues simple, but to make difficult issues easier to understand when examined in their context.

The importance of this kind of work to policy-makers is evident. Stripped of political motivation, inclusive rather than "cherry-picked," *Terrorism Monitor* offers policy-makers a critical source of information essential for developing realistic approaches to today's security challenges. Widespread reproduction of Jamestown's *Terrorism Monitor* articles in print media and on the internet is a testimony to the relevance and importance of these works, while giving Jamestown an international presence that goes far beyond its own website.

Though al-Qaeda and its many permutations are regularly examined by Jamestown's analysts, the work presented here goes far beyond bin Laden's al-Qaeda to include rival Islamist groups, variant forms of political Islam and even examinations of those who have recanted Islamist violence.

As editor of Jamestown's Global Terrorism Analysis publications, I must express my thanks to the many men and women who work so diligently to produce these reports, sometimes at risk to their own personal safety. The sum of Jamestown's efforts at Understanding Terrorism is well expressed in the late Eric Hoffer's maxim: "You can discover what your enemy fears most by observing the means he uses to frighten you."

Andrew McGregor
Editor, *Terrorism Monitor*
and *Terrorism Focus*

Part I

Jihadi Doctrine and Methods of Terrorism

AL- QAEDA

Al-Qaeda's Caucasian Foot Soldiers
By Hayder Mili

In the West, Islamic terrorism is a threat traditionally associated with Middle Eastern men whose faces are easily perceived as "alien" and who present a suitable profile around which to organize law enforcement monitoring. Recent events have again shown that this profile is outdated. The July 7, 2005 London bombings and the further discovery of other operational cells in Britain and Canada included several converts, such as 25-year-old Hindu-Canadian convert Steven Chand and Germaine "Jamal" Lindsay, the young Briton who not only participated in but led the four-man suicide bombing cell on July 7, 2005. The activities of converts, or rather those who adopt a militant ideology inspired by Salafi-Jihadi interpretations of Islam, have become increasingly important in executing terrorist attacks. The incorrect perception of the "face of terror" risks obscuring our understanding of how terrorist groups operate. In monitoring and preventing terrorist activity, law enforcement agencies need to move beyond the current profile and react to the empirical reality.

Blue-Eyed Emirs

That empirical reality has been apparent for some time, particularly in France. The logistical support cell involved in the Algerian Armed Islamic Group's (GIA) 1995 bombing campaign in France included two converts, David Vallat and Joseph Raime, who had been converted to Salafi-Jihadism while in prison by GIA "emir" and Afghan veteran Ahtmane Saada. Beyond logistical support, French law enforcement also found operational converts when they investigated the ultra-violent jihadi-gangster Roubaix Gang (*Terrorism Monitor*, January 12, 2006). Notably, the gang was composed of Algerians led by two ethnic Frenchmen, both veterans of the war in Bosnia.

In another French example, the "blue-eyed emir" Pierre Robert, who was apprehended by authorities, was the recruiter and leader of several Salafi-Jihadi cells involved in the Casablanca suicide bombings of May 2003 (*La Gazette du Maroc*, February 4, 2004). Other converts were involved at different levels in this operation, including Andre

Abu Musab al-Zarqawi had called for "an army of 'white-skinned' militants, men born in Europe and America who can convert to Islam and become harder for the authorities to detect."

Rowe, a Briton of Afro-Caribbean origin who was a Bosnian war veteran linked to the Roubaix Gang (*The Telegraph* [London], July 9, 2005). In the latter examples, French and Algerian cultural/historical enmity had no effect on cooperation. Easily bypassing racial and ethnic divides, the French converts were cell leaders whose faith, commitment and legitimacy were not questioned on account of their ethnic or cultural background. In fact, conversion may help to strengthen perceptions of devotion in some cases.

Beyond France, the participation of converts in al-Qaeda activities has been visible at all levels of operations. German national Christian Ganczarski, accused of involvement in the Djerba synagogue attack along with another white convert Daniel Morgenej, was asked for a religious blessing by young suicide bomber Nizar Nawar moments before he struck a Tunisian synagogue (Agence France-Presse, April 20, 2002). Not only was he respected enough as a religious ideologue to offer such a blessing, but he had maintained a close personal relationship with al-Qaeda's inner circle, including Khalid Sheikh Mohammed and Osama bin Laden himself, indicating a high-level of trust from the secretive organization. Not simply foot soldiers, Australians Shane Kent and Jack Roche also met bin Laden personally and, as reported by terrorism analyst Trevor Stanley, Roche was given a mission to create a "Caucasian Cell," highlighting what appears to be a tactical shift for al-Qaeda. Other reports seem to support this. According to the *London Times* on June 7, 2006 Abu Musab al-Zarqawi had called for "an army of 'white-skinned' militants, men born in Europe and America who can convert to Islam and become harder for the authorities to detect."

Converts are fully trusted to carry out attacks, lead cells and to lend logistical, financial and even ideological support. It was a Jamaican convert, Trevor William Forest, imam at the Brixton mosque in Britain, who radicalized Zacarias Moussaoui as well as converts Xavier Jaffo and Richard Reid. This is an issue that contemporary counter-terrorism officials need to take into account in order to prepare themselves for terrorists who do not fit the nationality profile.

Propaganda

The use of converts in al-Qaeda videos is a further sign of their growing symbolic importance for al-Qaeda's legitimacy and for increasing recruitment efforts aimed at Muslims and non-Muslims. In August 2005, an Australian East Timor veteran Mathew Stewart appeared in a propaganda video exhorting jihad. Most recently, al-Qaeda member Adam Pearlman (known as "Azzam the American") appeared for the third time in a broadcast inviting Americans to convert to Islam. Al-Qaeda may presume that English language propaganda will attract more Westerners to Salafi-Jihadi ideology.

Beyond al-Qaeda's strategy or tactics, much of the phenomenon revolves around the nature of the ideology itself. There is still a misconception in the general public that the al-Qaeda movement is Arab-centrist when in fact it effectively transcends ethnic differences, rejecting Arab nationalism (and any other nationalism) and stressing the supremacy of the Muslim Ummah. A good example is the conflict in Chechnya, where "Chechen" field commanders are from various ethnic and cultural backgrounds, including ethnic Russians like Vitali Smirnov. The Islamist website Kavkaz Center frequently claimed that many disaffected Russian soldiers—captive or otherwise—had joined the ranks of the Chechen fighters and there is some evidence to support this. On June 11, 2000, ex-Russian soldier Sergey Dimitriyev conducted a suicide mission in Khankala, Chechnya [1]. This was not an isolated case; another ex-soldier, Pavel Kosolapov, was recruited by warlord Shamil Basaev prior to his involvement in several bomb attacks and, as reported by The Jamestown Foundation, one of the Beslan ringleaders and perpetrators of several bomb attacks in southern Russia was an ethnic Ukrainian convert and veteran of Chechnya, Vladimir Khodov (Newsru.com, May 13, 2005).

While "profiling" measures in Russia (especially in Moscow) are particularly stringent, Russian law enforcement authorities are at a loss when trying to deal with a threat generally associated with people of Middle Eastern or North Caucasian ancestry. In Dagestan, ex-Russian soldier Sergei Tiunov, who was arrested in November 2001, had allegedly been commissioned—along with two other accomplices—by the warlord Khattab to assassinate Russian Prosecutor General Vladimir Ustinov (Vesti7.ru, November 18, 2001). More recently, it was disclosed that the February and August 2004 Moscow subway blasts are believed to have been organized by mostly Slavic converts led by ethnic Ukrainian Nikolai Kipkeyev (Gazeta.ru, August 31, 2005). The "Karachai Jamaat" network, as it calls itself, is also thought to be behind several deadly explosions in Krasnodar, Russia.

The phenomenon of conversions to Islam, however, needs to be separated from the conversion to a destructive ideology such as Salafi-Jihadism, which is a violent revolutionary strain of fundamentalist Islamism. As illustrated by the case of Franco-Algerian Khaled Kelkal (who converted to Salafi-Jihadism in prison), there are in effect two types of converts: those who convert to Islam and those, both Muslims and non-Muslims, who gravitate toward Salafi-Jihadi ideology. A good example of the significance of this distinction is in Central Asia. In that region, governments and clergy are pitting local traditional Islam against imported Salafi-Jihadism, denouncing the latter as a deviancy in media and speeches and warning against converting to "alien ideologies." It is telling that the only documented terrorist act attempted in Kazakhstan was by an ethnic Russian convert, Andrey Mironov, arrested in January of this year for attempting to blow up a public administration building he had infiltrated as an employee (Kompromat.kz, January 6, 2006).

Conflict Zones and Virtual Recruitment

What has continued to be more important than nationality in security profiling is personal history, especially engagement with radical preachers (often veterans of past jihads) and/or exposure to Islamicized conflict zones. With regard to the latter, war in Muslim countries and the associated loss of lives are heavily exploited in extremist propaganda to attract recruits. A central component of this effort is the presentation of injustices—real or perceived—on graphic videos posted on the internet. Converts such as French terrorist Lionel Dumont and David Vallat have testified that footage of the Bosnian genocide or the Chechen conflict was a primary catalyst in their radicalization (*La Croix*, December 16, 2005; *L'Humanité*, December 3, 1997).

Al-Qaeda's ideology is undoubtedly gaining legitimacy in the current international context, which it tries to frame as a war on Islam and Muslims through propaganda concocted by media-savvy jihadi groups. In Romania, Florian Les was preparing a car bomb attack in the city of Timisoara when arrested by Romanian security services. His stated intent was to "teach a lesson" to Romania for its involvement in Iraq and

Afghanistan and to avenge "his brothers in Chechnya and Bosnia" [2]. Authorities believe that he was radicalized after exposure to jihadi literature and videos on the internet, which also enabled him to forge links with jihadi fighters around the world, just as Wyoming native Mark Robert Walker had done in his efforts to provide material assistance to al-Ittihad al-Islami in Somalia (News365.ro, June 27, 2006). The impact and effectiveness of this "virtual recruitment" can also be seen in the failed attempts of former U.S. National Guardsman Ryan Anderson to assist al-Qaeda, as well as young Dutch convert R. Maik who discovered Salafi-Jihadism and Takfir ideology on the internet, subsequently building a home-made bomb and sending death threats to controversial Dutch politicians (*De Volkskrant*, November 7, 2005).

The Magnet

Conflict zones are also a destination of choice for jihadis and converts who wish to undergo military and ideological training. Afghanistan has, for a long time, been such a destination. Australian Jack Thomas is but one of many Westerners suspected of having trained in the country and it is telling that three of the nine Britons arrested in Afghanistan and detained in Guantanamo are catholic-to-Islam converts. Kosovo was a training ground for Australian David Hicks, and Chechnya (like Bosnia) attracted a number of Westerners, including American Aqil Collins and French convert Xavier Jaffo, a propagandist for the jihadi site Azzam.com who was killed in 2000 (CNN, July 3, 2002). Beyond Europeans and North Americans, many jihadi converts from the post-Soviet states also travel to the North Caucasus (in part for geographic but also linguistic reasons), such as in the case of the Belarusian and alleged chemical weapons expert Sergei Malyshev who was recently arrested in Spain for his involvement in a recruitment network for Iraq (Regnum.ru, December 20, 2005). Somewhat bewildering, in August 2002 Hiroshi Minami, a Japanese convert who had fought in the war-torn republic, was arrested with a Chechen militant trying to cross the Georgian border into Chechnya. Interestingly, Palestine has remained relatively free of this phenomenon, with the possible exception of Stephen Smyrek, a German convert who was arrested in Israel in November 1997 (*Al-Ahram Weekly*, August 26-September 1, 1999). An admitted member of Hezbollah, he had allegedly been trained in southern Lebanon to carry out a suicide attack in Tel Aviv.

Iraq has now become a magnet for jihadis. While the majority of foreigners in Iraq are still from the Arab world, there is evidence that converts are at least involved in logistical support and recruitment in Europe. The recently arrested Spaniard José Antonio D.M. is one of 18 men charged in relation to a cell supplying volunteers to Iraq. At the operational level, Peter Cherif, the young French convert who was arrested in Iraq by U.S. forces, had been radicalized and incited along with other young Frenchmen by Afghan veterans (*El Pais*, December 21, 2005; *Le Figaro*, May 21, 2005). These examples further showcase the "egalitarian" non-ethnic nature of many of the jihadi networks; these networks are increasingly non-Arab as a result of the first Afghan jihad generation dwindling in numbers and veterans of other conflict zones entering the arena.

The tightening of security measures, particularly profiling, may put more pressure on the networks to rely on individuals who would otherwise be able to pass the first security "screening" with more ease, mainly Caucasian men but also women. The latter would prove to be even more of an interdiction nightmare. As French anti-terrorism Judge Jean Louis Bruguière has long warned, al-Qaeda is also interested in recruiting women. The case of 35-year-old Belgian female Muriel Degauque's successful suicide attack against a U.S. convoy in Iraq should therefore not be viewed as an anomaly. In May, for example, Der Spiegel reported on a foiled suicide bombing plot in Iraq involving a German female convert. It is interesting to note that convert Pascal Cruypenninck, the alleged head of the Belgian network sending suicide bombers to Iraq, was preparing a similar operation with another female convert named Angelique when he was apprehended by authorities (*La Dernière Heure*, December 2, 2005). Just as unsettling, in March, Australian Jill Courtney was arrested on terrorism charges, while in the Netherlands Martine Van Den is alleged to have had strong links to the Dutch Islamist militant organization the Hofstad Group (which also included several Dutch converts) (*De Volkskrant*, July 6, 2005).

Conclusion

Where conversion involves an adoption of violent ideologies, traditional profiling techniques may be inadequate. Nevertheless, it is clearly a mistake to simply expand the profile to include all converts. Law enforcement monitoring faces a clear challenge in creating a suitable filter to inform this distinction and the existence of this endogenous threat should not feed the fantasies of a "fifth column." Many converts and born Muslims are at the forefront of the anti-jihadi struggle. For example, it was friend and fellow convert Ibrahim Fraser who first alerted police about Australian Jacke Roche's obsession with jihadi ideology. Similarly, the El Fath Mosque in Amersfoort threw out the Walker brothers, who were members of the Hofstad Group, and also informed the authorities of their extremist tendencies.

Recent arrests in Britain involving at least five converts (of Afro-Caribbean origin) training to become suicide bombers—as well as the arrest of Dhiren Barot, a convert plotting a dirty bomb attack in the United States—indicate that this trend is on the upswing, reflecting both the globalization and growing appeal of Salafi-Jihadism and a tactical adjustment to Western security and profiling measures on the part of al-Qaeda and its affiliates. It also underscores the truly transnational and cross-cultural nature of the threat, against which profiling may not provide an adequate defense.

Originally published in *Terrorism Monitor*: Volume 4, Issue 21 on November 2, 2006.

Notes

1. International Policy Institute for Counter-Terrorism, June 20, 2000.
2. See http://www.roumanie.com/Justice-Un_homme_converti_islamisme_soupconne_de_terrorisme-A1250.html.

Al-Qaeda Adapts its Methods in Iraq as Part of a Global Strategy
By Abdul Hameed Bakier

For the last few months, reports from Iraq have been indicating a tangible decline in insurgency and terrorist operations. For the first time since 2003, the Iraqi people are enjoying a sense of security in the streets of Iraq, although skeptics claim it is the calm that precedes the storm. The stabilizing security situation comes amid claims that al-Qaeda has been defeated or at least has been seriously crippled in Iraq (Alerhab.net, November 24, 2007). Has al-Qaeda actually been defeated and subjugated by the coalition forces in the Iraqi arena? Taking al-Qaeda's past and current behavior into account while monitoring Iraq's jihadi websites, one is presented with strong indications that al-Qaeda is adapting to the new realities on the ground while avoiding direct confrontation with the coalition forces. The global strategy of al-Qaeda since 9/11—as posted in al-Qaeda's internet forums—sheds further light on the terror plans it has designed to lure and engage Americans in various fronts in the region (Alboraq.info, March 10, 2007).

Al-Qaeda: Defeat versus Retreat

The discourse concerning al-Qaeda's possible defeat in Iraq comes as a result of the relative drop in violent operations in the so-called "Sunni triangle." The decrease in al-Qaeda activity is attributed to many different factors, the most important of which is the mistake it made by targeting other Sunni jihadi groups such as the Islamic Army of Iraq, Iraqi Hamas and al-Rashideen Army. In August 2007, Iraqi Hamas was accused of helping Coalition forces in Diyala province against al-Qaeda. Al-Qaeda did not understand the Iraqi mentality and tried to lead the community by establishing the Islamic State of Iraq, instead of coexisting with the different Iraqi groups. The targeting of Shiites and their shrines aggravated the Sunnis Iraqis as much as it did the Shiites because it upset the precarious balance between the Sunnis and Shiites. These blunders were exploited by the Iraqi government and Coalition forces, leading to the establishment of the successful Sunni Majalis al-Sahwa, or "Awakening Councils" (Emirate Centre for Strategic Studies and Research, December 9, 2007).

The Majalis al-Sahwa are paramilitary groups comprised of Sunni tribes formed to fight al-Qaeda. Contextually, Sunni wrath directed at the Coalition veered towards al-Qaeda, depriving it of much needed Sunni support. In the same way, the spokesman of the Islamic Army of Iraq (IAI), Ibrahim al-Shamari, says:

"The decline in jihadi operations against the occupier is due to the fact that they are engaged by al-Qaeda in the worst struggle that could exist among fellow Muslims. The attacks of al-Qaeda, in some cases, took a form of full-scale war extending from north of Babel to Latifia area and from north and west Baghdad to Samarra. In this big area of its operations against IAI, al-Qaeda didn't target a single American, Shiite militia or the Shiite police" (Hanein.info, December 15, 2007).

Conversely, the impression that al-Qaeda has been defeated in Iraq is challenged by the continued violent attacks occurring daily in Iraq. Al-Qaeda operatives are adapting to the new situation in the Sunni triangle imposed by the Majalis al-Sahwa by moving to northern Iraq, especially to the city of Mosul where they found a new ally. The Maghawir al-Tai Mujahideen in Mosul began a year ago as a small group operating in the industrial area in Mosul. They have since grown larger and decided to join al-Qaeda in the Islamic State of Iraq, consequently providing a safe heaven for al-Qaeda to launch its new tactics.

Before 2001, al-Qaeda devised a new strategy to fight the crusaders and Zionists what they call the "far enemy." To achieve victory over the enemy, al-Qaeda deemed it necessary to engage the enemy on many fronts in the region away from its bases.

Jihadi forum chatters from Iraq claim that over 2,000 jihadis from Mosul have already joined al-Qaeda (hanein.info, December 15, 2007). It seems that a new application of the tactics of guerrilla warfare in other provinces is succeeding. These tactics include indirect confrontation, or "open grave tactics," that include road bombs, hit-and-run operations and car bombs, together with al-Qaeda attempts to take advantage of the differences between Sunni tribes on the issue of cooperation with Coalition forces. Al-Qaeda is also leaving behind sleeping operatives in the cities they flee, awaiting the right circumstances to reactivate. Evidence of this may be found in the recent bomb attacks in Diyala province that killed over 20 civilians and injured many others (Almalafpress.net, December 10, 2007).

The jihadi websites responded indirectly to the reports on al-Qaeda's defeat in Iraq by posting reports and video of al-Qaeda attacks on Coalition forces, especially in areas where the Iraqi government says al-Qaeda has fled. In addition some websites re-posted al-Qaeda's future global strategy (Alboraq.info, March 10, 2006). Moreover, al-Qaeda second-in-command Ayman al-Zawahiri commented on the new developments in Iraq in general and al-Qaeda defeat in particular in a December 2007 interview published by Sahad, the media production house of al-Qaeda. According to Al-Zawahiri: "The jihadi situation is good in general, but setbacks are inevitable in jihad. The latest reports from Iraq indicate an increase in mujahideen strength and deterioration of the American situation regardless of their desperate efforts to delude by false propaganda. British withdrawal proves they are lying. Claiming victory over ISI through the collaboration of the Sunni tribes is mere cover for their big failure."

In summary, al-Zawahiri called upon the mujahideen to continue hit-and-run attacks, eradicate the hypocrites and traitors that infiltrated the mujahideen ranks, expose the traitors, call upon Muslims to stop supporting the pro-U.S. armed groups, concentrate on jihadi media and propaganda mainly through the internet and build upon what has already been achieved by establishing the ISI. Al-Zawahiri also called for the mujahideen to unite around monotheism and reconcile with the rest of the jihadi groups, especially with Ansar al-Sunna, headed by Sheikh Abu Abdallah al-Shafi'i. On the political side, al-Zawahiri said, "After the victory of the Islamic State of Iraq, it will endeavor to establish the Islamic caliphate from ocean to ocean" (Sahab.net, December 16, 2007).

Al-Qaeda's Global Strategy

The conflict in Iraq forms only part of a larger al-Qaeda plan. Before 2001, al-Qaeda devised a new strategy to fight the crusaders and Zionists what they call the "far enemy." To achieve victory over the enemy, al-Qaeda deemed it necessary to engage the enemy on many fronts in the region away from its bases. 9/11 was the spark that would bring U.S. forces to al-Qaeda's battlefield. According to jihadi forums, al-Qaeda's global confrontation strategy comprises seven phases:

• The Awakening (2000-2003): This phase ended with the U.S. invasion of Iraq. The Salafi ideologues believe that the Islamic Umma (nation) has been dormant in the 19th and 20th centuries because all the strategies implemented by the Muslims for resurrection have failed. Therefore, al-Qaeda planned to strike a blow to the enemy to induce an uncalculated reaction. 9/11 was the bait that provoked the crusaders and lured them to attack the Muslim nation.

• Eye Opening (2003-2006): By occupying Baghdad in April 2003, the Muslim nation awoke to the bitter realities of occupation. Al-Qaeda's objective in this phase was to keep the U.S. forces engaged in a fight against al-Qaeda until 2006. Regardless of the results, the ability to maintain constant clashes with the enemy was considered a victory in itself.

• Resurrection (2007-2010): In this phase, al-Qaeda will be capable of mobilizing jihadis productively, exploiting unrest in different hot areas to keep the U.S. forces occupied in a war of attrition that will weaken its resolve and pave the way to directly attack Jews in Palestine and elsewhere.

• Recuperate and Attain Power (2010-2013): This phase will concentrate on overthrowing the infidel Muslim regimes by direct confrontation. The United States will be exhausted and unable to support all the infidel regimes in the region, hence, al-Qaeda will become more powerful and eligible to replace these regimes.

• Declaration of an Islamic state (2013-2016): At this point, the Western grip on the region will loosen, paving the way for the establishment of an Islamic state that will regain control of the Muslim nation, rebuild it and utilize the nation's wealth in creating an international deterrent to foreign intervention as well as expediting the demise of corrupt and tyrant regimes.

• Massive Confrontation: 2016 will witness the onset of an all-out war between the forces of good and evil with, of course, final victory for the Islamic state.

• Achieving Multiple Victories: Any victory achieved by al-Qaeda opens the door for more recruits to work with al-Qaeda in many different domains. Those who cannot join directly will establish their own centers based on similar radical Islamist theory and ideology. Al-Qaeda believes there is a direct proportion between multiple victories and repelling U.S. and Jewish aggression [1].

Jihadis typically corroborate this scenario by citing verses from the Quran for every phase of the plan and believe that God will facilitate the victory of the Muslim nation.

Conclusion

Although the success of the United States and its partners in exterminating notable numbers of al-Qaeda leaders has significantly reduced its ability to perpetrate terror operations, it has not ended the al-Qaeda phenomenon. Rather, it has led to the creation of unpredictable, incoherent and scattered groups adhering to the Salafi-Jihadi ideology. These decentralized formations will attempt to attack soft targets and wait patiently for any slackening of security on the hard targets. A complete defeat of al-Qaeda is unlikely to come about in the near future. Iraq—like other countries in the region—will suffer from al-Qaeda terrorism long after the withdrawal of the coalition forces.

Originally published in *Terrorism Monitor*: Volume 5, Issue 24 on December 20, 2007.

Notes

1. Sources for the seven phases of al-Qaeda's global confrontation strategy are drawn from alboraq.org; al-ekhlaas.net/forum; alhesbah.com/v; alridaws.org/vb.

Three Explanations for al-Qaeda's Lack of a CBRN Attack
By Chris Quillen

The evidence of al-Qaeda's interest in conducting a terrorist attack with chemical, biological, radiological, or nuclear (CBRN) weapons appears compelling. As early as 1998, al-Qaeda leader Osama bin Laden declared the acquisition of CBRN weapons a "religious duty" for Muslims [1]. He followed up in 2003 by asking for and receiving a fatwa from Saudi Sheikh Nasir bin Hamid al-Fahd that condoned the use of CBRN weapons by Muslims against infidels [2]. Combined with the multitude of warnings from al-Qaeda associates that a CBRN attack against the West is not only forthcoming but also long overdue, the Muslim "duty to warn" has been firmly established. In al-Qaeda's opinion, no further justification is needed and no additional warnings are required [3].

These words have also been backed up by deeds. In the early 1990s, al-Qaeda began its efforts to acquire radiological and nuclear materials [4]. While no evidence exists that these efforts have succeeded, there is little doubt that al-Qaeda continues to pursue this capability today. Prior to the fall of the Taliban, the training camps in Afghanistan taught recipes for the manufacturing of poisons and toxins including cyanide and botulinum. A video recovered by CNN in Afghanistan in 2002 clearly demonstrates that al-Qaeda had some success in manufacturing chemical weapons in the form of a poisonous gas capable of causing death. The WMD Commission reported that al-Qaeda had similar success with biological weapons, including the acquisition of at least small quantities of the virulent strain of "Agent X" which has been widely reported to be anthrax [5]. While some technical hurdles remain for al-Qaeda to weaponize and effectively employ CBRN weapons on a mass-casualty scale, the terrorist group clearly is capable of conducting small-scale, low-tech CBRN attacks.

Given this stated desire and apparent capability to conduct a CBRN terrorist attack, why has al-Qaeda not yet launched an attack with such weapons? This analysis explores three possible explanations for this lack of a CBRN attack: disruption, deterrence and, most disturbingly, patience.

Disruption

An encouraging explanation is that al-Qaeda's efforts have thus far been disrupted through a combination of stepped-up counter-terrorist efforts after 9/11 and possibly the simple luck enjoyed by government authorities. Clearly, the al-Qaeda CBRN programs that existed in Afghanistan under the Taliban were at least temporarily disrupted by the 2001 U.S.-led invasion and subsequent need to move to safer locales. According to this explanation, al-Qaeda's CBRN programs have yet to recover from this significant setback.

Several specific CBRN attack plots have apparently been disrupted, although none advanced far beyond the initial planning stages. In May 2002, Jose Padilla arrived in the United States, reportedly planning a "dirty bomb" attack, but never got much beyond the idea stage. Similarly, Dhiren Barot (also known as Issa al-Hindi) was arrested in the

United Kingdom in 2004, carrying relatively detailed plans for conducting a Radiological Dispersal Device (RDD) attack, but had not yet acquired the necessary materials [6]. Given that an RDD attack is widely considered the CBRN attack most likely within al-Qaeda's capabilities, these disruptions could be especially significant.

Al-Qaeda's chemical and biological plots have not fared much better. In 2003, UK police arrested a group of Algerians with recipes and materials for creating ricin and cyanide, although stories conflict about whether any actual poisonous material was recovered (BBC, April 13, 2005). A 2004 chemical plot against multiple targets in Jordan had apparently advanced to the point of acquiring vehicles and materials, selecting targets and assigning duties (Al Jazeera, May 2, 2004). It remains unclear whether the materials recovered were for the manufacture of conventional explosives or chemical gases [7].

At the same time as these arrests, however, al-Qaeda succeeded in launching devastating conventional attacks in Egypt, Turkey, Tunisia, Indonesia, Jordan, Spain, the United Kingdom, Pakistan, Afghanistan and Iraq. Thus, while al-Qaeda has suffered some setbacks in its CBRN efforts, these disruptions alone do not appear sufficient to have prevented al-Qaeda from conducting a CBRN attack given its other successful attacks.

Deterrence

Another possible explanation for al-Qaeda's apparent restraint is the threat of massive retaliation. Although an intriguing possibility, the complications of deterrence theory may offer more questions than answers.

Al-Qaeda's initial rationale for pursuing CBRN weapons was the desire to deter enemies such as the United States from attacking the organization [8]. In 2001, bin Laden specifically warned, "We have [chemical and nuclear] weapons as a deterrent" (*Dawn*, November 10, 2001). While this particular strategy clearly failed after the September 11, 2001 attacks, al-Qaeda may still be using its CBRN efforts as part of its deterrence strategy [9].

Traditional deterrence theory indicates that terrorist organizations are less susceptible to deterrence strategies because they lack the defined territory that can be held hostage to a retaliatory attack. Al-Qaeda's strategy, however, has long been to acquire just such territory. In his book *Knights Under the Prophet's Banner*, Ayman al-Zawahiri described this goal when he wrote, "Confronting the enemies of Islam and launching jihad against them require a Muslim authority, established on a Muslim land." Al-Qaeda is no doubt aware of the risks of acquiring territory. Previous efforts to establish al-Qaeda authority in Sudan, Afghanistan, Somalia, Pakistan and Iraq have all resulted in U.S. attacks. Nevertheless, al-Qaeda is an organization that requires territory to operate and carry out its mission and is clearly willing to accept this risk to achieve its stated goals.

Today, al-Qaeda is heavily dependent on its safe haven in the tribal areas of Pakistan. This dependency may have driven al-Qaeda to compromise its immediate desire to launch CBRN attacks against the United States for the longer-term goal of establishing their authority in a Muslim land as a stepping stone to future attacks and ultimate victory. In particular, al-Qaeda may assess that a significant CBRN attack against the West (or, for that matter, another major attack on the U.S. homeland) would invite a U.S. invasion of the tribal areas. The Pakistani government—always staking a position somewhere between Washington's and al-Qaeda's interests—may have even warned al-Qaeda's leadership that such an attack will lead to U.S. troops on Pakistani soil (with or without Islamabad's consent) and the subsequent end of al-Qaeda's safe haven. The U.S. occupations of Afghanistan and Iraq, not to mention the presence of thousands of U.S. troops across the border in Afghanistan, make the threat of an American invasion more than credible.

Of course, al-Qaeda is not the only combatant being deterred in this war. In fact, the United States and al-Qaeda appear to have settled into a pattern of violence acceptable to both sides. While al-Qaeda continues to launch terrorist attacks around the world, the terrorist organization appears to be deterred from launching another major attack on the U.S. homeland or a significant CBRN attack against U.S. interests by the threat of a U.S. invasion of Pakistan. Meanwhile, the United States occasionally launches missile strikes against al-Qaeda targets on Pakistani territory, but is reportedly deterred from sending ground troops into Pakistan due to the possibility that the Musharraf government would fall and an even more dangerous Islamic terrorist threat would rise from the ashes. Al-Qaeda may very well assess that a CBRN attack would upset this delicate balance.

Patience

A final possibility is that al-Qaeda simply is waiting for the right time to launch a CBRN attack. Bin Laden has often been described as an exceedingly patient man, willing to wait for the right moment to act. Major terrorist attacks such as 9/11 were in the works for years before the final order was given. Al-Qaeda's leaders reportedly view their struggle against the United States as a long one, likely to continue well after they have left this world. In this view, the attacks on September 11, 2001 were only one battle and the final destruction of the United States may take generations to complete.

Under this scenario, al-Qaeda is building its capabilities in anticipation of a great victory and will not rush to act just for the sake of acting. The planned attack on the New York City subway system with the "mubtakkar" improvised chemical device may be an example of such patience. Al-Zawahiri reportedly called off the attack because it was not an adequate follow-up to

Bin Laden has often been described as an exceedingly patient man, willing to wait for the right moment to act. Major terrorist attacks such as 9/11 were in the works for years before the final order was given.

September 11, 2001 [10]. Al-Qaeda apparently wanted an even more devastating attack for its second wave. Given the carnage of 9/11, it is hard to imagine al-Qaeda wreaking even more havoc, but a CBRN attack—including the physical, psychological and economic impacts—could certainly fit the bill.

It is possible that al-Qaeda's success with the September 11, 2001 attacks has set the bar too high for its current CBRN capabilities. Al-Qaeda may be concerned that a CBRN attack that "only" kills dozens of people would be perceived as a relative failure and demonstrate its weakened position relative to its pre-9/11 stature. The organization may prefer to wait until its CBRN capability has matured to the point where its chances of success are greater and its capability for destruction has increased [11]. Given the fact that there is no indication that al-Qaeda has abandoned its pursuit of CBRN weapons, the possibility of a patient al-Qaeda is a disturbing possibility worth remembering.

Conclusion

Many of the traditional reasons why terrorist groups do not attempt CBRN attacks do not exist for al-Qaeda. The organization has clearly demonstrated its willingness to engage in indiscriminate killing on a massive scale without fear of losing the support of its followers. Al-Qaeda has also shown it is willing to take on the technical challenges involved and has had some successes in developing lethal materials including cyanide, anthrax and especially the mubtakkar device. Unfortunately, this combination of continuing interest, growing capability and demonstrated patience may one day pay off for al-Qaeda.

Originally published in *Terrorism Monitor*. Volume 5, Issue 3 on February 15, 2007.

Notes

1. Interview with Jamal Isma'il, December 1998 and re-broadcast on Al Jazeera, September 2001.
2. Sheikh Nasir bin Hamid al-Fahd, "A Treatise on the Legal Status of Using Weapons of Mass Destruction Against Infidels," May 2003.
3. Michael Scheuer, *Imperial Hubris: Why the West is Losing the War on Terror* (Washington, DC: Potomac Books Inc., 2004), 155-156.
4. Jamal Ahmad al-Fadl, Testimony before the U.S. District Court, Southern District of New York, United States vs. Osama bin Laden et al., February 2001.
5. Commission on the Intelligence Capabilities of the United States Regarding Weapons of Mass Destruction, Report to the President, March 31, 2005, 269-270.
6. See, in particular, Dhiren Barot, "Final Presentation," posted by the London Metropolitan Police Service at http://www.met.police.uk/pressbureau/rhyme/index.htm.
7. *Al-Sharq al-Awsat*, April 26, 2004; *Al-Hayat*, April 16, 2004. Abu Musab al-Zarqawi admitted to planning a conventional bomb attack, but called the allegations of a chemical plot "fabrications" in an audio statement posted on the al-Ansar Forum, April 29, 2004.
8. According to Abu Walid al-Masri in his book *The Story of the Afghan Arabs: From the Entry to Afghanistan to the Final Exodus with Taliban*, published in *al-Sharq al-Awsat*, December 8, 2004. See also Robert Wesley, "Al-Qaeda's WMD Strategy Prior to the U.S. Intervention in Afghanistan," *Terrorism Monitor*, October 7, 2005 and Sammy Salama and Lydia Hansell, "Does Intent Equal Capability?: Al-Qaeda and Weapons of Mass Destruction," *Nonproliferation Review* 12, no. 3 (November 2005): 625-626.

9. For another discussion of al-Qaeda's deterrence strategy, see Lewis A. Dunn, "Can al-Qaeda Be Deterred from Using Nuclear Weapons?" Occasional Paper 3, Center for the Study of Weapons of Mass Destruction, July 2005.

10. Ron Suskind, *The One Percent Doctrine: Deep Inside America's Pursuit of its Enemies Since 9/11* (New York: Simon and Schuster, 2006) 218-220.

11. See also Lewis A. Dunn, 15. "The fact that no single attack has yet occurred may simply indicate that preparations for a more spectacular multi-attack effort are under way."

JIHAD

The Ideological Voices of the Jihadi Movement
By Chris Heffelfinger

It is news to few observers that thousands, even millions, of young Muslims are influenced—to some extent—by jihadi literature circulating on various Islamist websites and discussion forums. The mujahideen's use of the internet for communication, indoctrination, recruitment and public relations has been well demonstrated. Through this medium, a field of preachers and ideologues compete for the vast audience of young Muslims, attempting to sway their opinion and bring them to the "correct" practice and understanding of Islam. Those backing the global jihadi movement have succeeded in capturing this audience—perhaps more so than other contenders—and have gained a wide following of careful but loyal readers. This phenomenon was studied in-depth by the recent *Militant Ideology Atlas* published at the Combating Terrorism Center at West Point [1]. The study examined the most popular texts read online from one of the websites most frequently used by al-Qaeda to host their literature—http://tawhed.ws. The literature is critical because it provides deeper motivation to the believer, who seeks ideological backing before taking action. According to the study, a group of Muslim scholars—Abu Muhammad al-Maqdisi, Abu Basir al-Tartusi, Abu Qatada al-Filistini, 'Abd al-Qadir bin 'Abd al-'Aziz and a few other Saudi clerics—are the primary Salafi opinion-makers guiding the jihadi movement. These scholars are relied upon for their credibility since they have either been imprisoned or exiled by their home countries. They are also perceived as being true to Islam and putting the interests of Muslims before themselves, making them sincere, legitimate and incorruptible. For the mujahideen, they are portrayed as scholarly authorities and the source for doctrinal legitimacy.

Surprisingly, the study found that al-Qaeda leaders Osama bin Laden and Ayman al-Zawahiri are not highly cited in jihadi literature. They are not considered authorities in Islamic law or looked to as the ideological force behind the jihadi movement. Indeed, in the world of Salafi-Jihadi ideology, they are relatively minor players. One possible reason for this is that the two are figureheads, pioneers in carrying out successful attacks against one of the enemies of Muslims. This suggests that there is a role for charismatic leaders to bring Muslims to jihad, as soldiers to the battlefield, but there is a separate role for these Salafi scholars in setting the broader goals for the movement, the limits and terms of engagement and selecting valid and legal targets. They are, in essence, creating the Islamic legal framework for this struggle so that the basis upon which it is waged will be sound. It is then left to strategists and mujahid leaders to conduct successful campaigns within this framework.

Sharia and the Larger Debate

There is no single governing body for determining Islamic law in the Muslim world. Movements tend to center around persuasive and influential scholars that can grant them legitimacy in the eyes of other Muslims. This has been the case for the Salafi movement, including militant Salafis who form the global jihadi movement. Although the mujahideen are not held accountable to their constituency, they understand the need for their fellow Muslims to support their actions, provide them with funding and safe haven and ultimately be able to mobilize them when needed. Accordingly, the advice and writings of Salafi scholars carry much weight with the mujahideen and Muslim readers—regardless of their affiliation. This can clearly be seen by the readership that websites like tawhed.ws and revivingislam.com receive.

For the most influential scholars of the Salafi movement, such as Abu Muhammad al-Maqdisi, Abu Qatada and Abu Basir, the end goal is never jihad itself. The objective is to bring Muslims to a Salafi reading of Islam and then to deliver salvation to the global Muslim community. As such, the primary element of the literature is the meaning and implementation of the shaira. The scholars first bring their interpretation of Islamic law on various political and social issues and present their advice on the appropriate action. The common ground among the scholars behind the jihadi movement is their rejection of Muslims living under apostate laws and political systems governing outside what God has decreed. The required response—for all, but to differing degrees and with differing tactics—is resistance.

This drive to instill Islamic law into Muslim society, and ultimately recreate that society under their interpretation of the law, often translates into an endorsement for violent jihad as practiced by bin Laden and others. While there are many Muslim scholars who call for these sources of law to be the primary factors in how Muslims live, the important distinction lies in how one should confront political systems that rule by law other than sharia. The debate over law and society is critical in jihadi literature. It establishes the framework through which young Muslims should struggle; for these scholars, it is clear their aim is not jihad, but the creation of such a society through jihad, an obligatory struggle for the believer.

In this larger debate, militant Salafi scholars have a much different role than the mujahid leaders. A prime example of this is that of the late Abu Musab al-Zarqawi, a student of al-Maqdisi from their shared time in a Jordanian prison; al-Maqdisi, however, publicly disapproved of his former student's tactics that targeted innocent Muslims. For them, the disagreement was a result of al-Maqdisi's understanding of the sharia and the best interests of Muslims. Examining such relationships can allow one to understand how the internal debates among the mujahideen are framed and directed, how limits on targets are created when scholars strongly condemn a certain act (such as al-Zarqawi's hotel bombings in Amman) and how the various jihadi groups can work together under the ideological umbrella of one militant Salafi scholar, even though that scholar is not involved operationally in the groups' actions.

The debate over law and society is critical in jihadi literature. It establishes the framework through which young Muslims should struggle; for these scholars, it is clear their aim is not jihad, but the creation of such a society through jihad, an obligatory struggle for the believer.

The Key Thinkers and their Positions

The main authors identified in the West Point study are all considered reliable sources for the mujahideen and their supporters when they seek a ruling on a given issue. They are generally careful and diligent in investigating questions put before them, regarding jihad or other matters, and write in a scholarly, but authoritative tone, unlike the rants heard by many mujahid leaders. In this backdrop, the scholars establish the principles for carrying out jihad—what is lawful and unlawful in their operations, and what broader goals should be kept in mind by those Muslims who answer the call to jihad. This process more often determines what course of action should be avoided, not only based on the Quran, hadith and the earliest generation of Muslims, but also based on lessons learned from past jihadi endeavors and their failings.

'Asim Tahir al-Barqawi, better known as Abu Muhammad al-Maqdisi, is one of the most prolific contemporary jihadi ideologues and a classically trained scholar. He was born in Nablus in 1959, but has been imprisoned intermittently since the 1990s by the Jordanian authorities for his criticism of the government and calls for jihad. Al-Maqdisi is regarded as one of the highest living authorities in Islam for Salafis, jihadis and other conservative Sunni Muslims who share elements of his program. His imprisonment, however, seems to have had little effect on his scholarly output. As part of the aforementioned study, he was the most frequently cited living Salafi scholar, indicating the wide range of jihadis (from strategists to mujahideen to fellow scholars) that cite his writings.

Al-Maqdisi is well traveled; he spent time in Saudi Arabia (with the scholars of the Saudi establishment) as well as in Pakistan and Afghanistan, where he spent time with and observed various mujahideen groups. He returned to Jordan in 1992, having formed his views in the previous years' travels, and denounced the rule of the royal family as being in contradiction to sharia. Al-Maqdisi's texts are frequently aimed at the youth in Jordanian prisons and similar Muslims around the world that are encouraged to hold steadfast to the path of jihad in accordance with the principles of Islamic law detailed in his texts. To be sure, the legal arguments are lost on many of his students who lack formal Islamic legal training, but he provides contemporary examples to buttress his points. Many of his texts are in response to criticisms of jihad by other Salafi clerics, typically from the Gulf states or Saudi Arabia. Other writings include the education of the next generation of leaders, numerous issues relating to resistance to tyrannical regimes and the need to uphold the sharia and one of his most-widely read works, the Creed of Abraham, on monotheistic faiths (which is highly critical of contemporary Christians and Jews) [2].

Through his writings on tawhed.ws, al-Maqdisi sets out the "correct" agenda for the various mujahideen groups to follow, what their intentions and objectives should be as they enter jihad, what preparation is required and what they should avoid (such as hasty actions that make the mujahideen look inept, inexperienced, or indifferent to killing innocent Muslims). There are more nuanced discussions of espionage, defining apostasy, takfir (labeling another Muslim an unbeliever), different examples of interaction with tyrannical rule and explanations of when resistance is obligatory for the believer. Yet, in the end, a clear direction is set out for the mujahideen and those who support their cause on how best to proceed. Al-Maqdisi's calls for unity are respected because of the scholarly weight behind his name and reputation. This also exposes one of the movement's weaknesses, and the shortcomings of governments confronting jihadi ideologues: a blow to his standing or a publicly lost debate would likely do much more to damage the unity of the jihadi movement than would his imprisonment.

Abu Basir al-Tartusi is another prolific contemporary scholar of Syrian origin. He is a slightly more moderate Salafi ideologue who resides in London, more often criticizing past jihadi mistakes and urging caution and selective action. His tone is due in large part to the scrutiny he was put under following the 2005 London train bombings. He has provided scholarly arguments to back armed resistance to tyrannical rule (by employing jihadi tactics), also prefaced on the importance of Muslims living by the sharia.

Abu Qatada al-Filistini, born in 1960 in the West Bank, is another example of a Palestinian-born cleric who encourages jihad against apostate rule in accordance with the shaira and is among the most frequently cited authors in the study. He is alleged to be a member of al-Qaeda's Fatwa Committee and is currently fighting extradition from the United Kingdom to Jordan [3]. His writings contend that, according to the shaira, it is every Muslim's individual obligation to overthrow and expel any secular government from Muslim lands by bombing, sabotage, coup, or other means available to them that would advance the implementation of shaira in that land.

Conclusion

These Salafi scholars play a critical but not widely observed role in the global jihadi movement. Ideology is often overlooked and is considered separate from the strategic and operational aspects of Islamist militancy. Yet, the scholars behind the jihadi movement set the framework for debates and provide direction that is by and large adhered to, or is at the least a determining factor in the planning of attacks. By better understanding their role in the movement, governments combating terrorism can attempt to intervene earlier in the radicalization process and ultimately work toward undermining their influence.

Originally published in *Terrorism Monitor*: Volume 4, Issue 24 on December 14, 2006.

Notes

1. The author was one of the researchers and compilers of the study. He spent ten months cataloging the most widely read and downloaded Arabic-language texts related to jihad from tawhed.ws and conducted a citation analysis of the data. The views in this paper are those of the author, they do not represent the United States Military Academy, the Department of the Army, or the Department of Defense, or any other agency of the U.S. government.
2. See William McCants, ed., *Militant Ideology Atlas* (West Point, NY: Combating Terrorism Center, 2006) 28-29.
3. According to testimony of Jamal al-Fadl in Southern District Court of New York in February 2001.

Al-Suri's Doctrine for Decentralized Jihadi Training – Part 1
By Brynjar Lia

The evolution toward smaller, more autonomous and decentralized organizational structures has been identified as a key trend in jihadi terrorism during the past few years [1]. Confronting amorphous structures and networks, which lack clearly identifiable organizational linkages and command structures and in which self-radicalization and self-recruitment are key elements, is a formidable challenge for security services [2]. The jihadi decentralization trend is clearly a result of counter-terrorism successes. These "defeats" have been scrutinized and digested in the writings of key jihadi theoreticians during the past few years. New roadmaps and operational concepts are being explored as the jihadis search for effective ways to operate in the much less permissive security environment of the post-9/11 era.

Among the new literature on future jihadi strategies, the writings of the Syrian-born, al-Qaeda veteran Mustafa bin Abd al-Qadir Setmariam Nasar have received considerable attention, both in jihadi circles and in Western media and scholarship. Using his most common pen names—Abu Mus'ab al-Suri and Umar Abd al-Hakim—he has written a 1,600 page treatise, *The Call to Global Islamic Resistance*, which is among the most frequently mentioned jihadi strategy books. It has been featured on numerous jihadi websites since its release in January 2005. The core ideas of this voluminous work are presented in chapter eight, in particular the section on "military theories" and the subsequent two sections on "organizational theories" and training doctrines. This two-part article outlines and discusses al-Suri's training doctrine and briefly assesses its potential importance for the new generation of jihadis. Hopefully, it will be a contribution to improving understanding of how jihadi groups are adapting their training doctrines in the face of a harsher and less permissive operative environment.

How to train and prepare recruits for armed jihad is a topic that has preoccupied al-Suri throughout his entire jihadi career until his capture in late 2005. During his participation in the Islamist uprising against the Syrian regime in the early 1980s, Abu Mus'ab al-Suri received significant military and security training. He quickly rose to become a military instructor in the Syrian Muslim Brotherhood's camps in Iraq and at the organization's safe houses in Jordan. Combining his newly acquired military skills with his previous training in mechanical engineering at the Faculty of Engineering at the University of Aleppo, he co-authored a handbook in explosive engineering, which was then his specialty. Al-Suri claims that this handbook, which became known as "The Syrian Memorandum," was later used in the Arab-Afghan camps in Afghanistan. In July 1987, al-Suri met with Abdullah Azzam, the godfather of the Arab volunteers in Afghanistan, and was quickly enlisted as a military instructor. His intellectual ambitions, however, were greater than teaching explosive engineering and basic guerrilla warfare principles. Following the publication of his 900 page treatise *The Islamic Jihadi Revolution in Syria*, published in Peshawar in May 1991, he gradually emerged as a jihadi writer and theoretician of some stature. In his treatise, he debated the lessons learned from the failed Islamist uprising against Hafez al-Asad's regime [3]. The book was a frontal attack on the Muslim Brotherhood and was in many ways a Syrian parallel to Ayman al-Zawahiri's *The Muslim*

Brothers' Bitter Harvest in Sixty Years, which appeared at the same time. Both works were part of the intellectual foundation for the radical jihadi trend that emerged as a considerable force inside the Arab-Afghan movement after Azzam's death in November 1989.

The Demise of the Revolutionary Tanzims

As opposed to many other jihadi writers, al-Suri always strived to maintain a practical and "operative" perspective, emphasizing the need to learn from past mistakes and devise new practical "operative theories" (*nazariyat al-'amal*) for future jihadi campaigns [4]. In his most important works, he focused on explaining how jihadi groups should operate in order to survive in the new post-Cold War context characterized by enhanced international anti-terrorism cooperation and the progressive elimination of terrorist sanctuaries and safe havens. Even though he himself had been a member of a typical *tanzim* (organization), the Syrian "Combatant Vanguard Organization," and continued to maintain very close contact with other tanzims, especially the Egyptian Islamic Jihad and the Libyan Islamic Fighting Group, all of al-Suri's operative theories are built on the premise that the tanzim model—the centralized hierarchical and regional secret jihadi organization—has outlived its role. Their Achilles' heel was their hierarchical structure, which meant that if one member was caught, the whole organization would be at peril.

Another factor which has made the revolutionary tanzims less relevant in al-Suri's eyes is the progressive Western "occupation and usurpation of Muslim land" (Palestine, Saudi Arabia, Afghanistan, Iraq, etc.). This transition from "indirect" to "direct occupation," which began in earnest around 1990 (Operation Desert Shield and Desert Storm), obligates a reorientation: the current war must be aimed at "repelling the invading intruders and assailants" from Muslim lands. The traditional goal of attaining an Islamic revolution in one country or one geographical area has to be postponed. Al-Suri, therefore, recommends that future jihadi warfare should be concentrated around other forms, namely the "jihad of individual terrorism," practiced by self-contained autonomous cells in combination with jihadi participation on "Open Fronts," wherever such fronts are possible.

Al-Suri, therefore, recommends that future jihadi warfare should be concentrated around other forms, namely the "jihad of individual terrorism," practiced by self-contained autonomous cells in combination with jihadi participation on "Open Fronts," wherever such fronts are possible.

In al-Suri's parlance, this term refers to conflict areas with an overt presence of mujahideen, permanent bases, open battle lines, or guerrilla war from those fixed positions [5]. Given the difficulty of opening such fronts, al-Suri concludes that "the jihad of individual terrorism" becomes, in reality, the only option for most jihadis.

Hence, the practice of "individual terrorism" is a core theme in al-Suri's most recent writings, and it is rooted in his most famous slogan: *nizam, la tanzim*—system, not organization [6]. In other words, there should be "an operative system" or template available anywhere for anybody wishing to participate in the global jihad either on one's own or with a small group of trusted associates, and there should not exist any "organization for operations." Hence, the global jihadi movement should discourage any direct organizational bonds between the leadership and the operative units. Leadership should only be exercised through "general guidance," and operative leaders should exist only at the level of small cells. The glue in this highly decentralized movement is nothing else than "a common aim, a common doctrinal program and a comprehensive (self-) educational program" [7].

The same goal of decentralization is applied in al-Suri's training doctrines; training should be moved to "every house, every quarter and every village of the Muslim countries" [8]. Al-Suri caricatures the jihadi training doctrine of the past as not much more than an invitation to Afghanistan: "calling the Islamic nation to the camps." His answer is to do the opposite; one should strive to "plant training camps across the Islamic nation, in all her houses and quarters" [9]. For al-Suri, the issue is not only that of decentralization, but also of transforming the jihadi cause into a mass phenomenon. One of al-Suri's oft repeated slogans is that "the resistance is the Islamic nation's struggle and not a struggle by the elite" [10]. This is an ambition many revolutionary theoreticians of all ideological stripes have nurtured without much success.

Determination to Fight

The decisive factor for successful jihadi training is the moral motivation and the desire to fight, not knowledge in the use of arms, al-Suri asserts. If the ideological program is not fully digested and the mental preparation is absent, weapons training is of no use. In an audiotaped interview in the late 1990s, al-Suri recalled how he had second doubts about the training that many Arab volunteers received in Peshawar and in Afghanistan, especially those hailing from the Gulf countries, since they more often than not failed to share his radical ideological platform:

"I am not prepared to train [people] in shooting practices because I think they will fire back at us justifying this by the fatwas of the Muslim Brothers and the Azhar clerics…People come to us with empty heads and leave us with empty heads…They have done nothing for Islam. This is because they have not received any ideological or doctrinal training" [11].

Partly based on this experience, al-Suri therefore came to insist that purely military disciplines should never form the dominant part of jihadi training.

Al-Suri finds the religious foundation for jihadi training in two Quranic verses, namely verse 60 of Surat al-Anfal and verse 46 of Surat al-Tawbah. The former is perhaps the most frequently cited Quranic verse among jihadis. It contains an injunction to prepare for "striking terror in the hearts of the enemies" [12]. It has therefore been a point of departure for a considerable number of jihadi writings on the legitimacy of "terrorism" in Islam [13]. Verse 46 of Surat al-Tawbah, "And if they had wished to go forth they would assuredly have made ready some equipment, but Allah was averse to their being sent forth and held them back and it was said (unto them): Sit ye with the sedentary," demonstrates, according to al-Suri, God's disgrace over the hypocrites who fail to prepare for war [14]. He concludes from reading these two verses that there are three stages in the performance of jihad: "will ... preparation ... launch." In other words, preparation cannot come without sincere will and firm determination, and an armed campaign cannot be launched without thorough preparation.

As opposed to many Salafi writers, al-Suri is not averse to comparisons with and citations of Western and non-Islamic sources to support his conclusions: "All military schools agree that a will to fight and moral strength of the fighter is the basis for victory and good performance" [15]. While this determination to fight is important in regular armies, it is "the fundament for the guerrilla fighter in general and the jihadi resistance fighter in particular" [16]. Al-Suri's writings are also characterized by a willingness to practice self-criticism, sometimes in a relatively sharp and satirical language. When writing about the moral and ideological prerequisites for proper jihadi training, al-Suri ponders the fact that many of those tens of thousands who trained for an armed jihad in Afghanistan under the first Arab-Afghan phase in 1986-1992, as well as during the second "round" under the Taliban regime in 1996-2001, returned to their homes without any intention to fight. They obviously "had the will to prepare [for armed jihad], but at the same time they intended to avoid jihad. They wanted to willfully and premeditatedly desist from jihad!" [17]. In al-Suri's eyes, jihad should be practiced not only in Afghanistan, but also in the wider global arena against the "Western Crusaders" and their "Arab collaborationist regimes." If this ideological platform is not fully embraced by the jihadi recruits, military training could easily become a double-edged sword.

Originally published in *Terrorism Monitor*: Volume 5, Issue 1 on January 18, 2007.

Notes

1. The author would like to thank his colleagues Petter Nesser, Thomas Hegghammer and Anne Stenersen at the Norwegian Defense Research Establishment (FFI) for valuable comments and feedback on this article.
2. See, for example, "The Changing Face of Terror: A Post 9/11 Assessment," Testimony Before the Senate Committee on Foreign Relations by Ambassador Henry A. Crumpton, Coordinator for Counter-terrorism, Washington, DC, June 13, 2006, http://www.state.gov/s/ct/rls/rm2/68608.htm.
3. The full title of the two volume book was Umar Abd al-Hakim, *The Islamic Jihadi Revolution in Syria, Part I. The Experience and Lessons (Hopes and Pains)* and *The Islamic Jihadi Revolution in Syria: Part II. Ideology and Program (Research and Foundation in the Way of Armed Revolutionary Jihad)* [in Arabic], (Peshawar: May 1991).4. Umar Abd al-Hakim, *The Islamic Jihadi Revolution in Syria, Part I*, 9.
5. As examples of such "Open Fronts," al-Suri refers to: "The First Afghani Jihad, Bosnia, Chechnya, and The Second Afghani Jihad in the Era of Taleban," in *The Call to Global Islamic Resistance*, p. 1361 (pdf-version).
6. The term is introduced by al-Suri in Chapter 8.4 and 8.5 in his *The Call to Global Islamic Resistance*, p. 1379, 1395 and 1405.

7. *The Call to Global Islamic Resistance*, 1407. For more on this, see Brynjar Lia, "Abu Mus'ab al-Suri: Profile of a Jihadist Leader," Paper and presentation given at the King's College Conference, *The Changing Faces of Jihadism*, London, April 28, 2006.

8. The "training theory" is presented in Chapter 8.6 of *The Call to Global Islamic Resistance*, 1414-1428.

9. Ibid., 1425.

10. Ibid., 1425.

11. See Chapter 4 of Brynjar Lia, *Architect of Global Jihad: The Life of Al Qaeda Strategist Abu Mus'ab Al-Suri* (New York: Columbia University Press, 2007).

12. Translation from Pickthal, via Search Truth: Search in the Quran and Hadith website, http://www.searchtruth.com.

13. See, for example, a booklet by the now deceased Sheikh Hamual

14. Translation from Pickthal, via Search Truth: Search in the Quran and Hadith website, http://www.searchtruth.com.

15. *The Call to Global Islamic Resistance*, 1420.16. Ibid.

17. Ibid., 1421.

Al-Suri's Doctrines for Decentralized Jihadi Training – Part 2
By Brynjar Lia

Training jihadi recruits in the post-9/11 world is increasingly about finding a safe place where training is possible rather than discussing curricula, facilities, selection of recruits, instructors and related tasks [1]. In his voluminous treatise *The Call to Global Islamic Resistance*, published on the internet in January 2005, the Syrian-born al-Qaeda veteran Mustafa bin Abd al-Qadir Setmariam Nasar, better known as Abu Mus'ab al-Suri and Umar Abd al-Hakim, examines five different methods for jihadi training based on past jihadi practices [2]:

1. Secret training in safe houses.
2. Training in small secret camps in the area of operations.
3. Overt training under the auspices of states providing safe havens.
4. Overt training in the camps of the Open Fronts [3].
5. Semi-overt training in areas of chaos and no [governmental] control.

Secret training in safe houses has been extremely important in terrorist training in all jihadi experiences, according to al-Suri. He considers this method "the very foundation" in preparing jihadi cadres, even though it only allows for live training in the use of light weapons and some lessons in the use of explosives [4]. Al-Suri himself had hands-on experience with this type of training in Jordan from the early 1980s, and he emphasized, in particular, successes in educating cadres "in doctrinal and ideological courses" using this method [5].

Training in small, secret mobile camps has also been frequently used by jihadi groups during the past decades. This type of training may take place in remote regions such as in mountains, forests and distant rural areas, and the number of persons involved should be in the range of 5-12. Slightly more advanced training, such as setting up ambushes and organizing assassinations, is possible in such camps. Al-Suri suggests that live training in the use of explosives can be practiced inside caves or near places where the sound of explosions would not attract attention, such as in the proximity of stone quarries, fishing areas and related locations.

Although al-Suri acknowledges that jihadi organizations in the past have derived great short-term benefits from establishing overt training camps in states providing safe havens, he finds that the results have ultimately been mostly disastrous: "Experience has proven that this is strategically a mortal trap" [6]. Safe haven states tend to constrain, exploit and may eventually sacrifice the jihadi organizations to further their own interests [7]. Moreover, after 9/11 "it is no longer possible for countries to open safe havens or camps for the Islamists and the jihadis" [8].

Al-Suri is more positive about overt training in the camps of the "Open Fronts," based mainly on the Afghan and Bosnian experiences. The comprehensiveness of the training opportunities on these fronts, and the absence of "political and ideological constraints," makes this a better option [9]. He nevertheless cautions that training on the "Open

Fronts" is not always effective, partly because of the presence of many competing jihadi and Islamist groups. The conditions do not allow for the kind of tight ideological indoctrination that is possible in safe houses. Furthermore, the economic costs involved in dispatching volunteers to camps in distant countries are very high. More importantly, crossing several national borders to reach the areas of the "Open Fronts" involves too many security risks [10].

As for semi-overt training in areas of chaos and where there is no governmental control, al-Suri points out its benefits in the past: in locations such as the tribal areas in Yemen, Somalia, the Horn of Africa, the tribal areas in the border regions of Pakistan and the great Saharan countries in Africa, both local and non-local jihadi groups have been able to set up semi-overt camps. The low cost of weapons, ammunition and space in these regions is an advantage [11]. He finds, however, that the prospect for exploiting these black holes is rapidly declining as a result of the U.S.-led war on terrorism and the new geopolitical situation:

"The areas of chaos are on the verge of coming under American control and being closed … the only [training] methods which remain possible for us now, in the world of American aggression and international coordination to combat terrorism, are the methods of secret training in houses and mobile training camps" [12].

In other words, only the first two models are viable options in the post-9/11 era. Al-Suri clearly believes that the formation of large-scale overt camps similar to the al-Qaeda camps in Afghanistan must be postponed until some point in the distant future [13].

Devising Jihadi Training in a Harsh Security Environment

Al-Suri's training doctrine is heavily informed by his acute awareness of the military weakness of the jihadi movement. The current situation in which the enemy "is dominating air, ground and sea" imposes very strict security precautions on jihadi training opportunities [14]. From this point of departure, al-Suri offers five building blocks for jihadi training: 1) mental and ideological preparation and developing the desire to fight and moral strength; 2) jihadi guerrilla warfare theory; 3) spreading the ideological, theoretical and military training programs across the Islamic Nation by various means; 4) secret training in houses and in limited, mobile training camps; 5) developing fighting competence through jihadi action and through participation in battle [15].

Not surprisingly, ideological indoctrination comes first, but no less important is the emphasis on studying guerrilla warfare theory adapted to the jihadi struggle. This has been a topic of intense study by al-Suri. In fact, three of al-Suri's most well-known audiotaped lecture series deal specifically with this topic. One of them was held in Khost in 1998 and consists of 32 audiotapes in which he reads and comments on *War of the Oppressed*, an American book on guerrilla warfare that has been translated into Arabic. Al-Suri strived to modify and adapt leftist guerrilla warfare literature to the Islamic context and planned to turn these lectures into a book entitled *The Basis for Jihadi*

Guerrilla Warfare in Light of the Contemporary American Campaigns [16]. Finding very few works in the Arab library on jihadi guerrilla warfare, al-Suri called upon his followers to transcribe his lectures in order to make them available to the broadest possible audience; in September 2006, his request was apparently heeded, as several of these lectures appeared on jihadi websites in Arabic PDF-formatted transcripts [17].

The widest possible distribution of jihadi training materials is clearly a cornerstone of al-Suri's training doctrine. One needs the "spread of culture of preparation and training ... by all methods, especially the internet" [18]. This recommendation has been followed up by jihadis in recent years. Not only have numerous, comprehensive training manuals and encyclopedias, such as the 700 MB size *Encyclopedia of Preparation for Jihad* (*mawsu'at al-i'dad*), been made available online in text and picture formats, but also sleek, professional, video-formatted, instructional materials detailing various explosive manufacturing recipes have begun to circulate widely during the past two years, and at least 22 separate audio-visual jihadi manuals are now in circulation on the web. Furthermore, 29 WMV-formatted files of al-Suri's videotaped lectures, recorded in August 2000 at his own training camp, called *mu'askar al-ghuraba* (The Strangers' Camp), in Karghah near Kabul, have been available to download from multiple sites since January 2005.

The widest possible distribution of jihadi training materials is clearly a cornerstone of al-Suri's training doctrine.

The last building block in al-Suri's training doctrine, namely training through action and fighting, is derived directly from his experience in the Syrian Islamist uprising in 1980-82. Al-Suri did not intend to allow untrained recruits to undertake complicated operations, which would contradict his principle of sequence: "Will ... preparation ... launch." Rather, he described how a gradual introduction of untrained recruits into an operative role can take place to allow "expertise [to] develop through battle" [19]. Recruits should first participate in action only as bystanders or witnesses. Later, they will serve in a minor auxiliary function without directly intervening. Finally, when deemed qualified, they will operate directly in main operations under the command of senior members [20].

Although al-Suri does not go deeply into the details of jihadi training, he presents what he terms "a light program which can be implemented by the simplest cells...operating under the most difficult circumstances of security and secrecy" [21]. The program is characterized by training activities that do not involve serious security risks, but are still relevant to a jihadi. The elements of the program range from physical exercise and studies of explosive manuals to practicing explosive manufacturing using dummies, shooting practice with compressed air guns, practicing procedures for secure communication and studies of all kinds of relevant military- and weapons-related handbooks. Only when the time is right should the group proceed to find a proper secret location to undertake live practice shooting and use of explosives.

Conclusion

The danger of al-Suri's training doctrine lies in its very realistic assumptions about the jihadis' military weakness. His doctrine seems to be cleanly and pragmatically tailored to the security situation in the Western world of the post-9/11 era. It emphasizes training and fighting at home or in the country of residence (which for many al-Qaeda sympathizers means the Western world), not overseas, using whatever means are available and always maintaining security precautions as the number one priority. This hard-hitting realism differs greatly from the main body of jihadi literature. Although al-Suri stands out as one of the sharpest theoreticians in the jihadi movement, he is rarely quoted in the wider and more religiously oriented Salafi-Jihadi literature [22]. Lacking the stature of a religious scholar, his writings probably have a limited, but important audience among the more intellectually oriented jihadis. Al-Suri is emblematic of the rise of a new generation of jihadi strategic study writers, who are still a tiny minority, but whose writings are informed by pragmatism, presented in a rational-secular style and emphasize a willingness to put political effectiveness before religious dogmas [23].

Originally published in *Terrorism Monitor*: Volume 5, Issue 2 on February 1, 2007.

Notes

1. The author would like to thank Petter Nesser, Anne Stenersen and Thomas Hegghammer at the Norwegian Defense Research Establishment (FFI) for valuable comments and feedback on this article.
2. When al-Suri discusses the training options, especially the last three models, he appears slightly ambiguous and self-contradictory, although his conclusion is clear. This probably reflects the fact that *The Call to Global Islamic Resistance* was written over a long period of time. After the United States announced a $5 million bounty on his head, the book was hastily released before he had time to double-check and finalize the manuscript. See introduction in *The Call to Global Islamic Resistance*.
3. For an explanation of the term "Open Fronts," see *Terrorism Monitor*, Volume 5, Issue 1, January 18, 2007.
4. *The Call to Global Islamic Resistance*, 1414.
5. Ibid., 1417.6. Ibid.
7. Ibid., 1416.8. Ibid., 1419.9. Ibid., 1416.
10. Ibid., 1418.
11. Ibid., 1416.
12. Ibid., 1419.
13. Ibid., 1424.
14. Ibid., 1423.
15. Cited in Ibid.
16. Ibid., 1424.17. These lectures were "The Management and Organisation of Guerrilla Warfare," Khost, 1998; "Explanation of the Book 'War of the Oppressed,'" Khost, 1998; and "Lessons in Guerrilla Warfare Theories," Jalalabad, 1999. See posting on muntadayat al-firdaws al-jihadiyyah, September 21, 2006, at http://www.alfirdaws.org, accessed October 2006.
18. *The Call to Global Islamic Resistance*, 1424.
19. Ibid., 1426.

20. Ibid., 1424.
21. Ibid., 1427.
22. See William McCants, ed., *The Militant Ideology Atlas* (West Point, NY: Combating Terrorism Center, 2006), http://www.ctc.usma.edu.
23. For one such strategic study, see Brynjar Lia and Thomas Hegghammer, "Jihadi Strategic Studies: The Alleged Al Qaida Policy Study Preceding the Madrid Bombings," *Studies in Conflict and Terrorism* 27, no. 5 (September-October 2004): 355-375.

The New Issue of *Technical Mujahid*, a Training Manual for Jihadis
By Abdul Hameed Bakier

The al-Fajr Information Center, a jihadi organization, recently published the February 2007 issue of *Technical Mujahid*, a magazine released once every two months that is available online. The release marks the second issue of the publication. The various jihadi websites have posted links to different locations to download the publication, that way stifling any attempts by outside forces to remove the document from the web (Arabteam2000-forum.com, March 13, 2007). According to the editor-in-chief of *Technical Mujahid*, Abu al-Mothanna al-Najdi, the objectives of the magazine are to eradicate the phobia and anxiety suffered by those who refrain from participating in jihad because they erroneously believe that intelligence services are monitoring their every move. Additionally, the publication aims to spread a sense of security, vigilance and self-confidence, in a scientific way, among members of jihadi forums by educating them in jihadi propaganda and enhancing their knowledge of field operations. To achieve these objectives, the magazine is organized into six sections of technical training that are aimed at helping the mujahideen carry out certain tasks.

Section 1: Covert Communications and Hiding Secrets Inside

Secure communications, a significant and important tool for any underground group, is the first training subject in the magazine, authored by Abi Musab al-Jazayri, "the Algerian." After a brief historical account of the evolution of secret communications from the use of secret ink to Morse code to binary 256 bit and 2048 bit encoding, al-Jazayri launches into the body of his training article with "the thing that scares the FBI most is the use of secret communication techniques, by jihadis, known as the concealment science." The training article outlines steganography, which is the art of hidden messages; steganalysis, the art of detecting hidden messages; and the merits of hiding data in innocuous-looking images. Al-Jazayri appears to be an expert on the subject judging from the details he included such as image pixels, mathematical equations to prevent distortions in pictures used to hide data and the disadvantages of encryption software available on the market like Ezstego, S-Tools and Hide and Seek, which can all be easily deciphered using hexadecimal editors. He explains that a good program to use is the "Secrets of the Mujahideen" software application because it is a dual system that hides encrypted data in a picture and compresses the files to nullify steganalysis methods. He then provided an example of hiding 20 communiqués of the Islamic Army in Iraq in a 100 x 50 pixel picture. His example highlights the necessity of applying steganalysis before choosing a picture to hide data. Al-Jazayri concludes the training by warning jihadis not to use ineffective encryption programs in their secret communications, reiterating that the best encryption uses multiple concealment techniques such as compression, encoding and concealment or uses communication-engineering techniques such as Spread Spectrum.

Section 2: Designing Jihadi Websites from A-Z

The second section, prepared by Abu Dojaina al-Makki, simply explains the steps of designing websites and uploading them to the internet via a host company. There is nothing unusual about this training except that the writer recommends hiring foreign website host companies because Arabic companies are incompetent, have "attitude" problems and break down frequently. To jihadis, experience in website development is important since the web is one of their key communication venues across various theaters of conflict. It also provides a recruitment opportunity for jihadi operations.

Section 3: Smart Weapons, Short Range Shoulder-Fired Missiles

The training magazine recommends two types of short range shoulder-fired missiles for the jihadis as the most appropriate anti-aircraft weapons: the U.S.-made Stinger and the Russian-made Igla missiles. Abi al-Harith al-Dilaimi, the writer of the smart weapons section, included many details about the specifications of the missiles, operating manuals and the electronic heat-seeking control systems of the missiles. The section is very thorough and even includes pictorial illustrations. Al-Dilaimi does not fail to brag about the recent downing of U.S. aircraft using these missiles, saying "The best example we can give about these missiles is the downing of ten helicopters in one month in Iraq such as the Apache, Black Hawk, Chinook and even an F-16 supersonic fighter jet that was shot down in al-Karma area west of Baghdad by the Islamic State of Iraq mujahideen in cooperation with the Mujahideen Army on November 27, 2006."

Furthermore, the training touches on the types of supersonic aircraft, helicopters and slow military cargo planes and missile counter-measures employed by these aircraft, such as heat flares that can throw off-course heat-seeking missiles and infrared missile repelling systems. The Russian-made Igla is an exception as it has a nitrogen-cooled heat seeking system capable of resisting the heat flares and identifying the real target among the decoy targets. The section also includes Igla and Stinger specification lists and a table of the English equivalents of the technical terms used in Arabic. Al-Dilaimi ends the training with a note saying, "we would like to assert that the mujahideen have proven skillful use of these weaponry by inflicting heavy loses on the colonizing U.S. forces in Iraq and Afghanistan."

Section 4: The Secrets of the Mujahideen, an Inside Perspective

Also mentioned in other jihadi publications, the "Secrets of the Mujahideen" is a computer program for internet communications. According to the security section of the Global Islamic Media Front, who wrote this training section, it is the first Islamic encryption software. The section on the program affirms the necessity of creating Islamic encryption tools due to the currently ineffective programs available on the market. In general, the section talks about the following five topics: 1) encryption and correspondence through the internet; 2) encrypting personal emails; 3) the degree of encryption and the symmetric, 128 bit, and asymmetric, 1024 bit, encryption keys; 4) public encryption keys and pass phrases that protect them; and 5) private encryption keys and decryption keys.

The authors claim that the Secrets of the Mujahideen program offers the highest level of encryption in asymmetric encoding that furnishes safe transfer of public encryption keys over the internet. The keys, which use "key prints" to identify the recipient, can be advertised in the jihadi forums. In general, the strength of the jihadi encryption program lies in the following: the use of the best five algorithms in encryption science; strong symmetric encryption; private and public asymmetric 2048 bit keys; strong compression of data; use of stealthy encryption keys and algorithms; secure deletion of files, elimination of retrieval possibilities; and the ability to run it from a flash disc, i.e. the program does not have to run from a computer hard drive. The encryption training section is extremely detailed and explains all the technical implications of the program. The writers claim that the program surpasses all international symmetric encryption systems.

Section 5-6: Video Technology and Subtitling Video Clips

This is the second lesson in a series of training that will be included in future issues of the magazine. Although very technical, there is nothing unusual about the video training as it talks about signal reception, sample rates and vertical video samples. In the same context, the training explains how to dub video clips with subtitles and background voiceovers. Video skills are clearly needed by jihadis for their propaganda campaigns. *Clearly, the Technical Mujahid is not a magazine for the common jihadi since it contains many scientific details. To comprehend and apply the training the magazine offers, the jihadi has to have a certain level of education and specific academic background or be tutored by an expert in training camps or safe houses.* One well known example would be the videos released of the "Baghdad Sniper" (*Terrorism Focus*, February 14, 2007). Abu al-Hassan al-Magribi, the writer of this section, concludes by stressing the importance of translating jihadi propaganda into as many foreign languages as possible.

The Conclusion of the Magazine

The editor-in-chief ends the magazine with an article calling upon jihadi forum participants to contribute technical information to the magazine, saying:

"Haven't you thought that you might have some knowledge that would assist your brothers in our nascent Islamic state of Iraq? My technical jihadi brother, this magazine gives you the opportunity to share whatever scientific knowledge you have with tens of thousands of jihadis frequenting the Islamic forums. Half of the efforts we exert in our battles against enemies of God occupying our land in Iraq, Palestine, Chechnya and Somalia lie in the media that will enlighten our fellow Muslims with facts about the crusaders."

He reminds the readers of the al-Qaeda in Iraq leader Abu Hamza al-Muhajir's call to Muslim scholars and scientists to utilize their knowledge for the benefit of jihad. Finally, the magazine instructs willing participants to send their technical articles to http://www.teqanymag.arabform.com. That website contains a welcoming note from the board of editors of the magazine and a contact form where participants can send in their technical articles.

The next issue of *Technical Mujahid* is set to contain the following subjects: jihadi forums and secure surfing on the internet; smart weapons such as night vision and thermal imaging; and information on how intelligence agencies can bug cellular phones. Also, al-Fajr Information Center has announced the release of an interview with a jihadi leader in Afghanistan that will be posted soon. Clearly, the *Technical Mujahid* is not a magazine for the common jihadi since it contains many scientific details. To comprehend and apply the training the magazine offers, the jihadi has to have a certain level of education and specific academic background or be tutored by an expert in training camps or safe houses. Nevertheless, it is another example of how the internet is used to train fellow mujahideen in topics ranging from weapons training to secure communications.

Originally published in *Terrorism Monitor*: Volume 5, Issue 6 on March 29, 2007.

GIMF Develops Defensive and Offensive Software for Jihadi Operations
By Abdul Hameed Bakier

In July 2007, jihadi forums announced the creation of a new computer program called the "Secrets of the Mujahideen," version 1.0. The objective of the program—which was published and distributed by the Global Islamic Media Front (GIMF) through many jihadi websites—is to replace the old and unreliable PGP Corporation encryption tools that jihadis had used in the past. Since the release of the program, jihadi websites, especially the GIMF, are instructing their subscribers to communicate using the program's encryption keys (Ebnseren.modawanati.com, March 22, 2007). Furthermore, al-Qaeda operatives are using Secrets of the Mujahideen in an attempt to avoid U.S. eavesdropping operations against them (El-bilad.com, July 6, 2007).

Separately, and on the offensive front, jihadi hackers have also invented their own programs to steal data off other computers, part of a larger "Electronic Jihad." Some of the Islamic hackers' targets are computers attached to cameras transmitting live videos from intersections and other busy areas. They claim that these videos can be used to case potential targets.

This article will elucidate the documentation of the Secrets of the Mujahideen, in addition to providing information on the ongoing Electronic Jihad.

The Secrets of the Mujahideen

The GIMF claims that the development of the Secrets of the Mujahideen started years ago to replace PGP encryption programs that apparently have multiple security breaches. According to the GIMF, the new program relies on the "highest standards" attained by encryption science, digital communication engineering and source codes developed after studying research published by the best encryption scientists.

According to the program's documentation, it is the first Islamic software that offers the highest level of 2048-bit asymmetric and 256-bit symmetric encryption. The program combines the highest level of data compression and uses a new technique call the "stealth cipher" that permits the program to change the random encryption algorithm every time a file is encrypted. The program uses five different algorithms. Furthermore, the program explains how encryption keys are managed and how the software creates files.

The Secrets of the Mujahideen's characteristics include: encryption using the best five algorithms in cryptography, also known as the Advanced Encryption Standard (AES); strong symmetric 256-bit encryption keys; asymmetric 2048-bit encryption keys; Zlib software library used for data compression; stealth cipher technique that uses variant keys and algorithms; cipher auto-detection; file shredder without possible retrieval of deleted files; single file program that does not require setup and can run from a flash card.

Keys Management and Program Options

In cryptography, keys management is the art of inventing secret keys and distributing them to the relevant parties. Keys management must contain security protocols that generate, exchange, store, safeguard and replace old or compromised secret keys to ensure protection of data.

Therefore, keys are the first important element in cryptography. The jihadi program illustratively explains, in-depth, the different stages of public and private key generation. The program generates two types of keys after the user chooses a username and a pass phrase for the two keys. One key is called the public key, which is the one the users exchange in the jihadi forums and use for ciphering, and the second is called the private key, which is used for deciphering. Both keys have the extension ".AkF" (Acrobat Key File). Depending on the strength of the computer's microprocessor, the program takes 2-5 minutes to generate the two encryption keys. The keys are automatically saved in the main folder and imported to the active database. Separately, there are a number of other features included with the program, such as:

File Compression: The user can choose the degree of selected file compression prior to data encryption. Users are advised to use high compression in text files and low compression in large audio files because the latter is already compressed. The program has 1,000-fold compression capability for text files.

File Shredder: According to the program, the user can shred files up to ten times making it impossible to retrieve them with any currently available software.

Ciphering Files Using a Public Key: Once the needed file and recipient user ID are selected, clicking on the "encrypt" button will automatically determine the decryption key for the recipient. Additionally, if the "stealth cipher" is selected, the encryption algorithm is randomly chosen; otherwise, the user can choose from five types of encryption algorithms.

Deciphering Using a Private Key: Once the ciphered file, using a public key with the extension ".enc," is received, the recipient simply presses decrypt and enters his or her password phrase. Thereafter, the program produces a decrypted file with the extension ".dec." The software recommends that the pass phrase be between 20-36 characters long.

The GIMF, which designed the Secrets of the Mujahideen, assures forum users that the program is a secure way of communicating over the internet because it uses all globally used symmetric encryption techniques with the distinct feature of stealth encryption using five algorithms. The capability of the file shredder in the program is also essential because the first step security forces take when they confiscate jihadis' computers is to retrieve and undelete every possible piece of data that might have been on the computers.

Software Files

After activating the program, the following additional files are created by the program:

AsrarKeys.db: an encrypted database that contains the active keys inserted in the program. This file is created automatically after program activation where the keys are inserted using the "import key" feature from the file manager.

Asrar.ini: this file holds user settings and is created only if the users choose to change the default settings.

Publicxxxxxxxx.akf: holds the public key and privateyyyyyyyy.akf for the private key. Both files are created after generating the "key pair."

According to the GIMF, the Secrets of the Mujahideen is a high-level encryption tool that outperforms other internationally used symmetric encryption software. Finally, GIMF dedicates the software to global al-Qaeda operations and mentions 11 more Salafi-Jihadi groups operating inside and outside Iraq. The dedication states: "This program is dedicated to all those who stood up and raised the ummah's head against the demon soldiers, the Jews and crusaders, and their Islam-grudging Shiite allies."

The Electronic Jihad

On the offensive front, jihadi users are exchanging computer programs that they claim are designed to hack into enemy computer systems to obtain intelligence or inflict economic damage. One such program used for these purposes is al-Mojahid al-Electroni. The program was created by an Islamist nicknamed al-Aqrab al-Aswasd (Black Scorpion), and it appears as "actskn43.ocx" and works on Windows XP and 98 systems. The program, Islamists claim, can take screen shots of hacked computers; steal passwords; record all typed material; and fully control the victim's files. Furthermore, they claim that the program is undetectable and destroys anti-virus programs.

Separately, and on the offensive front, jihadi hackers have also invented their own programs to steal data off other computers, part of a larger "Electronic Jihad." Some of the Islamic hackers' targets are computers attached to cameras transmitting live videos from intersections and other busy areas. They claim that these videos can be used to case potential targets.

Another jihadi forum user, nicknamed Qaheer al-Fors, posted a search phrase (intitle:liveapplet inurl:LvAppl) that helps locate many cameras connected to the internet in different countries. Even though these cameras can be easily accessed by ordinary internet users, taking interest in the video feeds and the details of the places they are mounted at is an indication of the mujahideen's future intentions. Al-Fors says, "by virtue of God, I was able to bring you the codes that you can use to watch some countries in the world through the cameras, those countries mounted to servile people," but he does not include these codes in his post. It is possible, however, that al-Fors passed these codes through encrypted e-mails using Secrets of the Mujahideen (Hanein.info, July 20, 2006).

Although al-Fors did not specify the countries where he claims to have hacked into their public cameras, a forum moderator nicknamed al-Fedayee (The Commando) posted active links to cameras in Israel. The cameras are for traffic purposes and can be accessed via the links al-Fedayee posted, some of which are cameras mounted in Israel's Herzliya intersection, Shalom intersection, Holon intersection and eight others (Hanein.info, July 20, 2007). Al-Fedayee says, "Mujahideen, as you do in your jihad against the occupying Zionists, here we are presenting you with this simple gift that was a personal effort to transmit to you live feeds from the Occupied Territories. After hard work, almighty God helped us in penetrating the internal system of the Zionist traffic ministry. We call upon you to take the needed measures and benefit from it because the enemy will soon change the codes of these cameras." The posting is signed, "Your brother, the son of Aladamia. A gift from the great Iraqi sons to those stationed in the battle fields of Palestine."

Conclusion

Almost all jihadi websites and forums devote whole sections to computer and internet information. These sections include many different computer programs downloaded from legal websites, cracked and made available for jihadi brothers for free. Certainly, the jihadis concentrate on internet secure communication and hacking programs.

Regardless of the accuracy of the mujahideen's cyber competence claims, the labeling of internet violations as "jihad" is attracting some Muslim internet users to join the so-called Electronic Jihad. Although few forum users question the ability of this particular Electronic Jihad software, Islamic forum users almost unanimously approve intrusion attempts against Western websites. The perseverance and continuous efforts of Islamic forum members to harm Western internet-based interests could, inevitably, mount to a serious threat in the future.

Originally published in *Terrorism Monitor*: Volume 5, Issue 18 on September 27, 2007.

Is There a Nexus between Torture and Radicalization?
By Chris Zambelis

A great deal of debate surrounds the factors driving the brand of radical Islam in the Middle East that inspires some individuals to commit acts of violence. A recurring theme in extremist discourse is opposition to incumbent authoritarian regimes in the Middle East. For radical Islamist groups such as al-Qaeda, unwavering U.S. support for the autocracies that rule Egypt, Jordan, Saudi Arabia and elsewhere in the region tops a list of grievances toward what amounts to pillars of U.S. foreign policy in the region. In addition to al-Qaeda, however, most Muslims in the Middle East also see these regimes as oppressive, corrupt and illegitimate. Authoritarian regimes in the region are also widely viewed as compliant agents of a U.S.-led neo-colonial order as opposed to being accountable to their own people. Ironically, having realized that most of al-Qaeda's leaders and foot soldiers received their start in radical opposition politics in their home countries, including U.S. allies Egypt and Saudi Arabia, the United States identified the persistence of authoritarianism in the Middle East as a critical factor in the spread of radicalization in its call for greater political liberalization and democratization in the region after the September 11, 2001 attacks [1].

Radical Islamist discourse highlighting the scourge of authoritarianism in the Middle East takes on many forms. One subject in particular, however, receives a great deal of attention in militant literature, communiqués, and discussions on radical Islamist chat room forums: The practice of systematic torture by the ruling regimes, especially that which occurs in prisons. Brutal and humiliating forms of torture are common instruments of control and coercion by the security services in police states intent on rooting out all forms of dissent. Previously the domain of human rights activists, researchers investigating the many pathways toward radicalization in the Middle East are increasingly considering the impact of torture and other abuses at the hands of the state during periods of incarceration in an effort to better understand the psychology of the radicalization process. Many researchers see these kinds of experiences as formative in the path toward violent radicalization [2].

There is ample evidence that a number of prominent militants—including al-Qaeda deputy commander Dr. Ayman al-Zawahiri and the late al-Qaeda in Iraq leader Abu Musab al-Zarqawi—endured systematic torture at the hands of the Egyptian and Jordanian authorities, respectively (*Terrorism Monitor*, May 4, 2006). Many observers believe that their turn toward extreme radicalism represented as much an attempt to exact revenge against their tormentors and, by extension, the United States, as it was about fulfilling an ideology. Those who knew Zawahiri and can relate to his experience believe that his behavior today is greatly influenced by his pursuit of personal redemption to compensate for divulging information about his associates after breaking down amid brutal torture sessions during his imprisonment in the early 1980s [3]. For radical Islamists and their sympathizers, U.S. economic, military, and diplomatic support for regimes that engage in this kind of activity against their own citizens vindicates al-Qaeda's claims of the existence of a U.S.-led plot to attack Muslims and undermine

Islam. In al-Qaeda's view, these circumstances require that Muslims organize and take up arms in self-defense against the United States and its allies in the region.

Torture in Extremist Discourse

Radical Islamist literature and discourse is replete with references to torture. The infamous al-Qaeda training manual "Military Studies in the Jihad against the Tyrants," more commonly referred to as the "Manchester Document," includes references to the oppression and torture endured by Muslims at the hands of "apostate" rulers whose prisons are "equipped with the most modern torture devices" [4]. Al-Zawahiri's public statements often contain references to torture by the Egyptian regime and others in the region. In addressing the nature of U.S.-Egyptian relations during a May 2007 statement, Zawahiri criticizes what he labels "American hypocrisy, which calls for *Explicit references to accounts of torture in the region by al-Qaeda and other militants helps sustain the narrative that Muslims and Islam as a whole are under siege by a hostile U.S.-led campaign. These messages also resonate with wide segments of society in U.S.-backed authoritarian regimes in the region.* democracy even as it considers [Egyptian president] Hosni Mubarak to be one of its closest friends, and which sends detainees to be tortured in Egypt, exports tools of torture to Egypt and spends millions to support the security organs and their executioners in Egypt, even as the American State Department, in its annual report on human rights, criticizes the Egyptian government because it tortures detainees!" [5].

Following the July 11, 2007 suicide bombing claimed by al-Qaeda in the Islamic Maghreb (AQIM) against a military barracks in Lakhdaria, Algeria, two members of a radical Islamist chat room forum with seemingly intimate knowledge of Algerian affairs refer to the attack as an act of vengeance and provide insights into the possible motivations of the attackers:

"Revenge has come 13 years after the massacre of Lakhdaria perpetrated by members of the base who kidnapped, tortured, and slaughtered 35 Muslims and strew their torn bodies in the streets. Their blood-thirstiness reached the extent of slaughtering an old sheikh (Muhammed Moutadjer) like a sheep after torturing him. There is also a mansion (a villa) which they use as a center (or laboratory as they call it) for brutal torture. This place is called the "Villa Copawi," established by the French during the period of direct colonialism for the same mission (torture, killing, violation of honor); this place is known to all near and far …"

"What about the women that were raped inside the barracks in front of their husbands and sons? What about the little girls, no more than ten years old, who were tortured inside the barracks in front of their fathers …? My brother, you have forgotten about all this, but we have not forgotten and will never forget. This is a day of judgment for the Pharaoh of Algeria and his soldiers" [6].

Explicit references to accounts of torture in the region by al-Qaeda and other militants helps sustain the narrative that Muslims and Islam as a whole are under siege by a hostile U.S.-led campaign. These messages also resonate with wide segments of society in U.S.-backed authoritarian regimes in the region.

Torture and Social Control

In the Middle East, the use of torture is not reserved for violent militants. On the contrary, authoritarian regimes regularly resort to draconian measures against moderate democratic reform-minded Islamists such as the Muslim Brotherhood in Egypt, secular and liberal opposition dissidents, or even student protesters to eliminate challenges to their rule. These measures are often carried out in the name of maintaining stability or protecting national security. In reality, they are about regime survival. Many observers are convinced that this vicious cycle of systematic abuse has the potential to radicalize dissident activists, leading some to join the ranks of violent militants to avenge their ordeal. At the very least, these practices vindicate the claims of extremists regarding the conduct of regional governments.

The accounts of abuses at Abu Ghraib prison in Iraq shocked Americans and the international community. In the Middle East, however, the extent of the abuses uncovered at Abu Ghraib was not out of the ordinary. In many ways, the events at Abu Ghraib were emblematic of what many have grown accustomed to in their own countries. Severe beatings, electric shocks, sexual humiliation and abuse, sleep and food deprivation, and threats against family members and associates, among other things, are common tactics used by authoritarian regimes to attack their opponents. By perpetuating a climate of fear, authoritarian regimes are able to engender a kind of tacit obedience among citizens.

Addressing the prevalence of torture, let alone the nexus between torture and radicalization, remains a taboo in the Middle East. Due to fears of reprisals by the authorities, many researchers and journalists in the region practice a form of self-censorship when addressing the topic. As a result, there is a dearth of primary source research on the topic. At the same time, a number of organizations and opposition dissidents are beginning to raise the issue, despite fears of reprisals by the authorities [7]. The disclosure of a graphic video of Egyptian police officers beating and sexually abusing Emad al-Kabir—who was held by police officers at a police station in the Boulaq el-Dakrour section of Giza in Greater Cairo for apparently resisting authorities during a January 2006 incident when he attempted to mediate a dispute between the officers and his cousin—caused outrage in the Middle East. The abusers filmed the ordeal and forwarded the footage to the cell phones of the detainee's friends to humiliate their victim (*Daily Star Egypt*, May 22, 2008). Al-Kabir was neither an Islamic militant nor a political dissident. Nevertheless, graphic scenes from the video appeared amid firsthand accounts of similar experiences endured by ordinary citizens and political dissidents in the Middle East during a lengthy videotaped statement by Zawahiri released in July 2007. Zawahiri devoted a segment of his presentation to the issue of torture in the Middle East in a savvy effort to reach out to a mainstream audience [8].

This controversial subject was also brought to the forefront of debate with the publication of the widely popular Egyptian novel *Imarat Yacoubian* (The Yacoubian Building) by Alaa al-Aswany [9]. The book treats the nexus between torture and radicalization through the character of Taha al-Shazli, a disaffected young man who joins an Islamist opposition group in Cairo. After being detained for taking part in a public demonstration, Taha is subject to extreme forms of torture by the hands of the Egyptian security officials, including severe beatings and sexual abuse, in an attempt to extract information about his political affiliations and the identities of his associates. Taha, angry and humiliated at his ordeal, is eventually released by his captors but is never the same. Bent on exacting revenge on his tormentors, Taha's disaffection with the Egyptian regime evolves into a visceral hatred that can only be satisfied through violence. Al-Aswany's fictional account of Taha's experience provides a glimpse into one aspect of the radicalization process in the Middle East that is too often ignored.

Conclusion

Based on the discourse of al-Qaeda and other radical Islamist organizations, the current trajectory of U.S. foreign policy in the Middle East will continue to serve as a battle cry for militants to take up arms against the United States. The prevalence of systematic torture and the persistence of authoritarianism in countries the United States counts as loyal allies will facilitate this process. These conditions will also provide al-Qaeda's highly-effective media and propaganda wings with ample material to implicate the United States in the activities of regional security services. Regardless of political sensitivities, this subject requires far more attention from serious researchers examining the paths toward political radicalization.

Originally published in *Terrorism Monitor*: Volume 6, Issue 13 on June 26, 2008.

Notes

1. Chris Zambelis, "The Strategic Implications of Political Liberalization and Democratization in the Middle East," *Parameters* 35, no. 3 (Autumn 2005): 87-102.
2. Thomas Heghammer, "Terrorist Recruitment and Radicalization in Saudi Arabia," *Middle East Policy* 13, no. 4 (December 2006): 39-60.
3. Dr. Ayman al-Zawahiri's experience in an Egyptian prison and the torture endured by his associates is chronicled in Montasser al-Zayat, *The Road to Al-Qaeda: The Story of Bin Laden's Right-Hand Man* (London: Pluto Press, 2004), 31-32.
4. See Part I of "Military Studies in the Jihad against the Tyrants," at http://www.usdoj.gov/ag/manualpart1_1.pdf.
5. "Interview with Sheikh Ayman al-Zawahiri," Al-Sahab Media, May 5, 2007.
6. Quoted from "Al-Qaeda in the Lands of the Islamic Maghreb/The Suicide Bomber Suhaib Pulverizes a Barracks" [in Arabic], July 18, 2007 at www.tajdeed.org.uk [no longer accessible].
7. In Egypt groups such as the Egyptian Organization for Human Rights (EOHR) are at the forefront of shedding light on the prevalence of torture by the security services and advocating on behalf of victims. For more details, see http://www.eohr.org. For more

graphic accounts of torture in Egypt and elsewhere in the Middle East, see www.tortureinegypt.net.

8. See excerpts from Dr. Ayman al-Zawahiri's July 4, 2007 statement addressing the issue of torture in the Middle East, entitled "The Advice of One Concerned" at http://www.youtube.com/watch?v=2a_K2sxgRKk . The entire video is available at http://video.google.com/videoplay?docid=-7664209432789370243&hl=en .

9. Alaa al-Aswany, *The Yacoubian Building* (Cairo: American University of Cairo Press, 2004).

Part II

Middle East

IRAN

The Hidden Hand of Iran in the Resurgence of Ansar al-Islam
By Lydia Khalil

Ansar al-Islam, an Islamic militant group based in the Kurdish mountains that briefly housed Abu Musab al-Zarqawi, was at the height of its power in 2002-2003. They controlled the areas of Bayarah and Tawilah along the Iranian border and operated with impunity. Yet, during the 2003 invasion of Iraq, Ansar al-Islam was driven out of the areas it had occupied for the past year in only five days. Operations by U.S. and Kurdish forces virtually annihilated it as an organized force, yet it is unclear to where its members fled. Some postulate that they were appropriated by other emerging insurgent groups such as Ansar al-Sunnah and Al-Qaeda in Iraq. A number of their members either retired from insurgent activity or fled to Iran and Europe to work in logistics and financing networks. Ansar al-Islam did not, however, disappear entirely. Many of its members went into hiding across the border. With the recent increase in insurgency activity in the Kurdish areas, Ansar al-Islam has reemerged as an organized force, likely as part of a new arm of al-Qaeda, the Kurdistan Brigades. The "Ansar al-Islam" title has been mentioned consistently in Kurdish and regional reports regarding recent violent attacks in the Kurdish region. It appears that Ansar al-Islam elements are not solely operating as part of the Kurdistan Brigades, but also as a viable, independent group once again. Newspapers and analysts from the region postulate that Ansar al-Islam and associated al-Qaeda elements are operating, as they had before, along the Iran-Iraq border and possibly with the acquiescence of Iran.

Iran's Potential Role

During the past month, Kurdish leaders have made frequent trips to Iran. Both Kurdistan Democratic Party (KDP) and Patriotic Union of Kurdistan (PUK) officials have summoned Iranian consuls to the Kurdish region to discuss Ansar al-Islam's border activity (*Awene*, May 1, 2007). Kurdish officials, like many others who reside along the border areas, express concern that Iran has perhaps played a role in Ansar al-Islam's resurgence. Various regional newspapers have reported on Iran's involvement with Ansar al-Islam, and some have leveled this accusation since 2004. One of Kurdistan's weekly independent papers, Hawlati, issued a series of reports on the matter. In a July 2004 article, Hawlati wrote that that "Italaat," the Iranian Secret Service, and al-Qaeda elements are training Ansar al-Islam along the eastern border of Kurdistan (*Hawlati*, July 2004).The Hawlati report posits that Iran is supporting Ansar al-Islam elements against the Iraqi Kurdish parties in order to separate Iraqi and Iranian Kurds and stave off any potential cooperation. In more recent news coverage, an anonymous Kurdish source said:

"In fact, there is an organized campaign to recruit young Iranian Kurds in ideological and military training courses during which the recruit is paid a salary ... Along with these training courses, the recruit goes through other military activities most of which are of a terrorist nature. These courses are held in Iranian camps spread in various regions of Iran" (*Elaph*, April 27, 2007).

Not only has Iran been indicted with recruiting Iranian Kurds, it has also been accused of offering training and support to al-Qaeda-affiliated elements harbored in the Hamrin Mountains. Reports suggest that al-Qaeda is training in a camp near the city of Marivan in Iran and elsewhere along the vast border area (*Elaph*, April 27, 2007). Several anonymous sources have claimed that Iran offers a monthly stipend of $1,500 to each recruit, although this has not been independently verified.

Kurdish journalists have speculated that Iran allows Ansar al-Islam to operate along its borders as a way to reinforce and advance its influence in the Kurdistan Regional Government (KRG). Iran has been a long-standing benefactor and player in Iraqi Kurdish politics when the KDP and PUK administered Kurdistan under the No Fly Zone. Iran wielded an enormous amount of influence and the two main Kurdish parties were largely at the mercy of Iran's benevolence. In response to the intrusion of the United States, Iran has seen its influence wane, although it is still a factor in the region. The Sulaymaniyah paper Aso

Is Iran willing to jeopardize its relatively good relationship with Kurdish authorities by either actively supporting Ansar al-Islam or by failing to crack down on these elements operating along its border area?

states, "In light of a number of changes following the war, Iran no longer has an economic [and political] impact as before. That is why now Iran, through using Ansar al-Islam, wishes to create security problems for the Kurdistan region the same as it tried to impose its own political agenda on Kurdistan through using the majority of the Islamist parties of Kurdistan prior to the Iraqi war" (*al-Sulaymaniyah Aso*, April 24, 2007). This refers to groups such as the Islamic Movement of Kurdistan that were the precursors of Ansar al-Islam.

Offering an alternative perspective, Sulaymaniyah's new security director, Hassan Nuri, recently said in an interview: "I do not think that Iran will allow them to be active on the border" (*Awene*, May 15, 2007). By "them," Nuri referred to militant Islamists. Iranian representatives stated in a paper circulated during a conference in Sharm el-Sheikh that fighting al-Qaeda, and Ansar al-Islam specifically, was a priority. A major goal in the Iranian working paper was to cooperate with Sunni and Kurdish elements to "draw up a plan to control the activity of groups that are close to al-Qaeda ... specifically Ansar al-Islam" (*al-Hayat*, May 5, 2007).

Reports, nevertheless, continue to suggest an Iran and Ansar al-Islam connection. One report states that Ansar al-Islam and other associated al-Qaeda groups have taken over abandoned garrisons of the Mojahedin-e-Khalq, an Iranian dissident group that had been supported by Saddam Hussein against the Islamic Republic of Iran. These former garrisons lie only 25 kilometers from the Kurdish controlled areas. Two Ansar al-Islam leaders, Aso Kirkuki and Rahwan Sabir, are reportedly in charge of the fighters in this area. They are allegedly working with a previous Ansar al-Islam leader, Hiwa Kwer, who was arrested but later released as part of a prisoner exchange (*Awene*, April 10, 2007).

Ansar al-Islam has extended its operations outside of traditionally PUK controlled areas along the Iranian border into the heart of Kurdish territory in Irbil. According to PUK sources, an Ansar al-Islam squad appeared in the city of Taqtaq in Irbil before the attack on the Ministry of Interior on May 9. A shepherd spotted the strangers moving between the villages of Homar Gomt and Smaqah (PUKMedia, May 11, 2007). It is possible that Ansar al-Islam elements were responsible for the Kurdistan Brigades attack. According to Sulaymaniyah's new security director, al-Qaeda appoints an amir to all of their areas of operation. The amir of Sulaymaniyah, Irbil and Dohuk is a man by the name of Swara who was first a member of the Islamic Movement of Kurdistan and then of Ansar al-Islam, like many of his counterparts (*Awene*, May 15, 2007). Ansar al-Islam has also conducted sophisticated attacks against KRG border guards. In April, they planted a roadside bomb and detonated it via remote control. Insurgents opened fire after the initial blast (Kurdsat TV, April 15, 2007). Kurdish authorities have become extremely concerned about insurgent infiltration along the Iranian border and have closed six checkpoints (*Hawlati*, April 27, 2007). Prior to the April attack, Ansar al-Islam forces ambushed a customs checkpoint and a cell phone tower in the city of Bashmagh. The insurgents were wearing traditional Kurdish garb and attacked with light and heavy weapons (*Awene*, March 27, 2007).

Ansar al-Islam is using its bases along the borders to conduct attacks in the Iraqi province of Diyala as well. Diyala residents are fearful that the border area will turn into a "new Kandahar" (*al-Mustaqbal*, April 30, 2007). Ansar al-Islam and other al-Qaeda elements are setting up recruitment and training camps and are trying to impose a strict shaira code in the province. Iraqi security services confirmed the reports of Diyala residents and said that there are Afghan, Arab and even Western foreign fighters present along the border area.

Although Ansar al-Islam is recently resurgent, they have been present in the Hamrin Mountains since 2004, when they were ousted from Kurdish controlled areas. Not only were they active around the city of Marivan, but also near the Iranian cities of Sanadaj, Dezli and Orumiyah, among others (*Hawlati*, July 15, 2004). Since the recent surge in Baghdad and the resistance from the Anbar Salvation Council in its traditional stronghold, however, al-Qaeda and its associates have shifted their operations elsewhere—namely in Diyala and in KRG territory (*Terrorism Focus*, June 5, 2007).

Contradictions Remain

It may seem counter-intuitive for Iran to associate with Kurdish Islamic extremists such as Ansar al-Islam and militant Salafi groups like al-Qaeda. Al-Qaeda is deeply opposed to Iranian involvement in Iraq, and Iran has had problems with its own Kurdish autonomy movements. Iran, furthermore, has traditionally supported the KDP and PUK, first against Saddam and afterwards when they set up their own administration under the No Fly Zone. Is Iran willing to jeopardize its relatively good relationship with Kurdish authorities by either actively supporting Ansar al-Islam or by failing to crack down on these elements operating along its border area?

It appears that Iran is primarily concerned with maintaining its influence over its neighbors, no matter how counter-intuitive the mechanisms. Destabilizing the Kurdish region would serve as a way for Iran to reassert its influence. The United States has replaced Iran as the Kurds' primary benefactor. Dabbling with insurgent groups while also maintaining ties with Kurdish authorities is a complicated method of maintaining its influence. Iran has concerns over its own Kurdish population, which it hopes will not attempt to mimic the Iraqi Kurds' successful autonomy framework. Iran's foreign policy principle, especially with its Kurdish neighbors, can perhaps best be described as "one hand gives, while the other hand takes away."

Originally published in *Terrorism Monitor*: Volume 5, Issue 11 on June 7, 2007.

Iran's Challenges from Within: An Overview of Ethno-Sectarian Unrest
By Chris Zambelis

Iran continues to face international pressure over its nuclear program and heightening tensions with the United States regarding its role in Iraq and Afghanistan. A pillar of U.S. strategy in the Middle East after the fall of the shah has been to check Iranian power in the Gulf region and Eurasia through a policy of strategic encirclement. U.S. support for Iraq during the Iran-Iraq war is widely perceived as the first salvo in this plan. Fearing Iran's territorial ambitions and the spread of its revolutionary Islamism, Saudi Arabia and other Gulf monarchies followed the U.S. lead by helping to finance Iraq's war effort. Meanwhile, the United States built a formidable presence in Arab Gulf states in the form of bases and security pacts. In addition to the robust U.S. military footprint in Iraq and Afghanistan and the deployment of carrier battle groups in the Gulf, Iran is flanked on its frontiers by pro-U.S. Azerbaijan, major non-NATO U.S. ally Pakistan and NATO member Turkey. A nuclear-armed Israel is also perceived as a threat in Iran. Another factor contributes to Iran's anxiety about U.S. strategy in the Middle East. Tehran is convinced that the United States and other foreign powers are actively exploiting Iran's diverse ethnic and sectarian society by supporting violent secessionist and insurgent movements—including terrorist groups—in an effort to destabilize the ruling government (Islamic Republic News Agency, July 27, 2006).

The Domestic Threat

Iran believes that a marked increase in domestic unrest orchestrated from abroad will precede any future U.S. attack. Indeed, Tehran attributes the steady rise in incidents of violence and terrorism across the country by ethnic Baloch, Arab and Kurdish minority rebel groups and signs of growing ethnic Azeri and Turkmen dissent to foreign meddling in its internal affairs by U.S. and other foreign intelligence services. Iranian security forces are currently engaged in low-intensity counter-insurgency operations across the country against an array of nationalist and terrorist groups.

In principle, the United States supports political opposition groups seeking an end to clerical rule. Some American proponents of a U.S. attack against Iran have gone as far as to call for enlisting the People's Mujahideen of Iran (PMOI), also known as Mujahideen-e-Khalq (MEK)—a bizarre militant group cited by the U.S. Department of State as a foreign terrorist organization whose ideology combines a mix of leftist and Islamist discourse with a fanatical cult-like veneration for its leaders—as an armed proxy in a future invasion. Under Saddam Hussein, Iraq provided MEK with arms, training and bases on Iraqi soil, such as Camp Ashraf located near the Iraq-Iran border. MEK units were disarmed and remain under the watch of U.S.-led forces. Tehran, nevertheless, worries that they may still be mobilized to serve as a proxy ground force in a future confrontation with the United States (*Terrorism Monitor*, February 9, 2006). Although not an ethnic or sectarian-based movement, MEK is affiliated with the National Council of Resistance of Iran (NCRI), an umbrella organization of anti-regime movements based in Iran and the diaspora that include ethnic and sectarian minority-led groups agitating for an end to the Shiite Islamist regime (Ncr-iran.org).

Given this background, Tehran has cause for concern, as U.S. planners are likely to use the threat of aiding active insurgent groups as an effective lever over Iran, especially as a response to allegations of passive and direct Iranian support for insurgents in Iraq and, more recently, Afghanistan. Iran, however, has long been plagued by domestic instability and tensions rooted in minority grievances due to what is widely viewed as a failure or refusal by the ethnic Persian-dominated Shiite Islamist regime to integrate minority communities into the fabric of society. This includes respect for minority rights and the preservation of unique cultural identities. Ethnic Kurds, Baloch, Arabs, Azeris and Turkmen in Iran also share ethnic, linguistic and cultural links with their kin in neighboring states such as Iraq, Pakistan, Afghanistan, Azerbaijan and Turkmenistan. This leaves them susceptible to the influence of social and political currents outside of Iran, especially nationalism.

The shifting geopolitical landscape in the Middle East following the U.S.-led invasion of Iraq, which propelled traditionally oppressed communities such as Shiite Arabs and Kurds to unprecedented positions of power and influence in the country, has also emboldened Iranian minorities to agitate for greater cultural rights and political representation. The debate over the proposed federalization of Iraq along ethnic and sectarian lines is inspiring similar calls in Iran and from a sophisticated network of activist groups advocating on behalf of Iranian minorities from abroad. The Congress of Iranian Nationalities, an association of Iranian opposition groups based in the diaspora representing ethnic Kurds, Arabs, Azeris, Turkmen and Baloch, called for the federalization of Iran along ethnic lines in a joint manifesto issued in February 2005 [1]. In other cases, armed rebel groups representing ethnic Kurdish, Baloch and Arab interests in Iran have taken up arms, while communities such as the Azeris and Turkmen have staged protests in an effort to assert themselves.

> *The shifting geopolitical landscape in the Middle East following the U.S.-led invasion of Iraq, which propelled traditionally oppressed communities such as Shiite Arabs and Kurds to unprecedented positions of power and influence in the country, has also emboldened Iranian minorities to agitate for greater cultural rights and political representation.*

The Demographic Picture

Iran's Farsi-speaking, ethnic Persian community comprises only a slim majority of the total population of an estimated 70 million, of whom nearly all are Shiites. Ethnic Azeris, who are estimated to number between 15 and 20 million and are also Shiites, constitute the second largest minority. Ethnic Kurds represent the third largest ethnic group, with a population between four and seven million, and are mostly Sunnis. Ethnic Baloch, the majority of whom are Sunnis, number between one and four million. Ethnic Arabs number between one and three million and are predominantly Shiites. Turkmen number between one and two million and are mostly Sunnis. Iran is also home to Gilakis, Mazandaranis, Bakhtiaris, Lurs and Qashqais, most of whom are Shiites, as well as Bahais, Zoroastrians, Armenian Christians and Jews [2].

Violence and Rebellion

Kurdish insurgents are among the most prolific militants operating in Iran. Most Iranian Kurds inhabit the mountainous region of northwestern Iran, where the borders of Turkey, Iraq and Iran meet, while smaller communities reside in Iran's northeastern region of Khorasan. Like their kin elsewhere in the region, they face widespread discrimination by the ethnic Persian-dominated Shiite clerical regime. As Sunni Muslims with a proud sense of cultural and national identity, they do not identify with the Shiite Islamist regime and efforts by the state to suppress their culture and identity. Iran's Kurdish regions have experienced growing violence in recent months between the Party for a Free Life in Kurdistan (PJAK), a group alleged to have ties to the Kurdistan Workers Party (PKK) in Turkey, and Iranian security forces (*Terrorism Monitor*, June 15, 2006). Iran claims that PJAK operates in Kurdish-controlled northern Iraq and receives support from the United States (Islamic Republic News Agency, July 14, 2007). On the political front, groups such as the Democratic Party of Iranian Kurdistan (DPKI) and the Komoleh-Revolutionary Party of Kurdistan advocate for Iranian Kurdish rights in the diaspora (Pdki.org; Komala.org).

Iranian Baloch nationalist groups such as Jundallah (Soldiers of God), also known as People's Resistance Movement of Iran (PRMI), have orchestrated a series of high-profile attacks against Iranian security forces dating back to 2003. Ethnic Baloch inhabit Iran's impoverished and desolate southeastern province of Sistan-Balochistan, a lawless region and smuggling crossroads. Sistan-Balochistan is a frequent target for Iranian security forces. As a fiercely independent tribal society that has been neglected by a highly-centralized state, ethnic Baloch have always felt a sense of alienation from Tehran. Despite a lack of evidence, Iranian authorities often label Baloch militants as agents of al-Qaeda and the Taliban in an effort to tarnish the group's reputation due to their Sunni faith (*Terrorism Monitor*, June 29, 2006). Ethnic Baloch animosity toward Tehran runs so deep that they look to their kin in Pakistan's neighboring province of Balochistan, who are engaged in their own secessionist struggle, and the Baloch community in Afghanistan in what Baloch nationalists label as "Greater Balochistan." Iran accuses the United States of supporting Jundallah from Pakistani territory (Islamic Republic News Agency, April 18, 2007). Baloch nationalists are represented by the Balochistan People's Party (BPP) and a host of other groups abroad (Ostomaan.org).

The southwestern province of Khuzestan located on the Iran-Iraq border is home to most of Iran's ethnic Arab population known as the Ahwazi (Ahvazi in Farsi). Khuzestan contains much of Iran's oil and gas wealth, yet remains one of the country's least developed regions. This is partly a legacy of the devastation it endured as the frontline for much of the Iran-Iraq war and, according to many Ahwazis, a deliberate policy by Tehran to ensure that the region remains underdeveloped and impoverished. Despite the fact that most Ahwazis are Shiite Muslims and speak Farsi, they maintain close tribal and cultural links with their Shiite Arab kin in southern Iraq and maintain a strong sense of Arab identity. The region was the scene of a number of bombings and attacks against government targets in recent years. Tehran blamed Ahwazi militants, including the obscure Hizb al-Nahda al-Arabi al-Ahwazi (Ahwazi Arab Renaissance Party) and other groups as acting on the behest of U.S. and British intelligence (Al-mohamra.nu). Ahwaz nationalists are represented in the diaspora by the Democratic Solidarity Party of Ahwaz, Ahwaz Revolutionary Council, Ahwaz Study Center (ASC) and British-Ahwazi Friendship Society (Alahwaz-revolutionary-council.org; Ahwaz.org.uk).

Tensions in the ethnic Azeri community boiled over in May 2006 when a state-run newspaper published a cartoon they believed likened them to cockroaches. The publication inspired widespread protests in ethnic Azeri-dominated regions of northern Iran and communities in Tehran. Despite their Shiite faith, ethnic Azeris mobilized in protest against what they saw as the ethnic Persian and Farsi chauvinism of the clerical regime and to agitate for greater cultural and linguistic rights (Oursouthazerbaijan.com).

Although the publishers of the cartoon were quickly reprimanded and their actions were condemned by officials in Tehran, the spontaneous outburst of anger among ethnic Azeris, Iran's largest ethnic minority that shares close links to the Turkic peoples of the Caucasus and Central Asia, especially their kin in former Soviet Azerbaijan, is another example of the nascent domestic tensions that could ignite violence and unrest in Iranian society. Iranian officials blamed outside agitators, namely pan-Turkic nationalists acting on the behest of the United States, for inciting the riots (Islamic Republic News Agency, May 25, 2006). The ethnic Azeri cause in Iran is represented by the Federal Democratic Movement of Azerbaijan and South Azerbaijan Human Rights Watch (Achiq.org; Hr.baybak.com).

Iran's ethnic Turkmen community, a predominantly Sunni population that inhabits northern parts of Iran along the border with Turkmenistan, appears to be following the lead of other Iranian minorities and raising its voices in protest against what it sees as a deliberate policy to stifle its cultural identity and rights, especially in regards to religion, language and education. Ethnic Turkmen are also emboldened by the plight of their kin in Iraq and their attempt to return to oil-rich Kirkuk, where they were expelled along with other minorities as part of the former Baath regime's "Arabization" program. Tehran accuses foreign elements based in Iraq and the wider Turkic world of supporting Turkmen dissent in Iran. Iranian Turkmen are represented by the Organization for Defense of the Rights of Turkmen People and the Turkmensahra Liberation Organization (Azatlyk.net).

Conclusion

The issues inspiring minority ethnic and sectarian-based dissent in Iran are the result of a multiplicity of factors, only one of which can be attributed to acts of foreign intervention by outside powers. Deep-seated grievances rooted in practical issues, such as Iran's inability to integrate entire communities into its social, political and economic fabric, is a case in point. Iran also has to adapt to the changing geopolitical landscape in the region that is seeing the rise of new centers of power and influence, such as Iraqi Kurdistan, which will reverberate well beyond their borders by serving as an inspiration to underserved communities to assert themselves, even through violence.

Originally published in *Terrorism Monitor*: Volume 5, Issue 15 on August 2, 2007.

Notes

1. See "Manifesto of the Congress of Iranian Nationalities for a Federal Iran," February 9, 2005, http://www.ahwaz.org.uk/congress-manifesto.pdf. The manifesto's signatories included the Balochistan United Front, Federal Democratic Movement of Azerbaijan, Democratic Party of Iranian Kurdistan, Balochistan People's Party, Democratic Solidarity Party of Ahwaz, Organization for the Defense of Rights of Turkmen People and Komoleh-Revolutionary Party of Kurdistan.
2. The demographic data were amalgamated from a variety of sources. It is important to note that demographic figures for Iran, especially as they relate to ethnic and sectarian minority representation, are frequently used to bolster and/or diminish a given community's presence for political reasons. This is often the case for data provided by official government sources or activists and parties based abroad representing ethnic and sectarian minority interests. For more information on the ethnic and sectarian breakdown of Iran, see Eliz Sanasarian, *Religious Minorities in Iran* (Cambridge: Cambridge University Press, 2000). Also see Massoume Price, *Iran's Diverse Peoples: A Reference Sourcebook* (Santa Barbara: ABC-CLIO, 2005).

PJAK Faces Turkish-Iranian Storm
By James Brandon

The year 2007 has seen a steady increase in violence between Turkey and the Kurdish Workers' Party (PKK). On October 21, 2007 a group of PKK fighters killed 12 Turkish soldiers and captured eight others in an attack in southeastern Turkey. Since then Turkey has called on the United States, the Kurdish Regional Government and Iraq's government in Baghdad to take actions against the 3,000 PKK members based in Iraqi Kurdistan. Simultaneously Turkey has built up its military forces on Iraq's border in apparent preparation for an incursion into northern Iraq to root out the PKK militants based there and to destroy related camps and training facilities.

Analysis of this increasingly tense stand-off has largely focused on how U.S.-Turkish relations will be affected and how the leaders of Iraqi Kurdistan will react to Turkey's increasingly shrill ultimatums. Overlooked in this complex equation is the role that the estimated 1,500 members of the PKK's Iranian sister organization, the Party for a Free Life in Kurdistan (PJAK), will play in any conflict.

In order to understand PJAK's attitude towards Iraqi Kurds, Turkey, Iran and the PKK— as well as the group's likely response to any moves against the PKK—it is necessary to appreciate the group's origins. PJAK was founded as a civil society movement in Iran in the late 1990s, partly inspired by the PKK, to promote Kurdish nationalism among Iran's roughly five million-strong Kurdish minority. Within a few years, however, the group's increasing success and its sporadic acts of violence against Iran's security service provoked a government crackdown. This forced its leadership to move to Iraqi Kurdistan where the group began to work closely with the PKK, basing itself in the PKK's main camp on the sides of Mount Qandil on the border between Iraq and Iran. Following this move, the group became increasingly militant, discarding much of its student activism and receiving military training and logistical assistance from the PKK.

Since 2004, PJAK has profited from access to the PKK's military and organizational expertise. The group's attacks on the Iranian military have become increasingly effective, killing around 100 Iranian troops and security forces a year since 2005. At the same time, however, PJAK's comparatively youthful leadership has made the group relatively immune to the lethargy, indecision and in-fighting that has on occasion plagued the PKK. Compared to the PKK, which was involved in an intermittent conflict with Iraqi Kurds through much of the early and late 1990s, PJAK's relationship with Iraq's Kurds has been less tense. At the same time, however, PJAK leadership remains heavily indebted to the PKK—not only because the group relies on the PKK's logistical apparatus and battle experience but also because substantial numbers of the PJAK's older members had been in the PKK before PJAK's formation in the late 1990s. Despite this, however, PJAK has repeatedly attempted to distance itself from the PKK when reaching out to Western governments in the hope of receiving military or economic aid to help it fight against the Iranian government.

Growing strength but uncertain future

Consequently PJAK is in a strong position. The last few years' uneasy equilibrium in Iraqi Kurdistan have allowed it to remain on good terms with Iraq's Kurds and the PKK while also continuing to carry out attacks in Iran and bidding, both covertly and overtly, for Western support. These strong foundations—and a solid recruiting base in Iran—should allow PJAK to face the storm gathering on the borders of Iraqi Kurdistan with some confidence.

In military terms, 2007 has been PJAK's most successful year so far. Although the PKK's attacks against Turkish targets achieve much greater coverage, PJAK's activities in Iran appear often to be of only a marginally smaller size and scope. On September 1, 2007, a press release purportedly issued by the group claimed that PJAK had killed 113 Iranian troops this year and destroyed six vehicles [1]. In addition the group has possibly begun to access more advanced weaponry. For example in February, PJAK members shot down a helicopter belonging to Iran's Islamic Revolutionary Guards Corps (IRGC) near the town of Khoy in southwestern Iran, although it remains unclear whether the aircraft was brought down by rocket or small-arms fire (*Today's Zaman*, August 20, 2007). Fars, the Iranian state news agency, reported that a senior IRGC commander, Saeed Ghahari, was killed in the crash (Al Jazeera, February 24, 2007).

Consequently PJAK is in a strong position. The last few years' uneasy equilibrium in Iraqi Kurdistan have allowed it to remain on good terms with Iraq's Kurds and the PKK while also continuing to carry out attacks in Iran and bidding, both covertly and overtly, for Western support.

Comparing the relative strengths of the PKK and PJAK is fraught with difficulties, however. The Iranian military is less organized and modern than the Turkish army and therefore presents an easier target. Critically, Iranian forces are less able to mount the swift counterattacks that the Turkish army has used to great success following PKK raids. In particular the Iranian forces are hampered by a lack of helicopters—although the Iranian military does have around 40 modified Cobra attack helicopters purchased from the United States before 1979. Balanced against this, however, is that Kurds in Iran make up less than 10 percent of the total population compared to over 20 percent in Turkey. As a result, PJAK has not only a smaller absolute pool of potential recruits than the PKK but also operates in a relatively less sympathetic milieu.

There is reason to believe that—not counting a Turkish invasion of Iraq—PJAK will become a greater irritant to the Iranian forces in southwestern Iran. For example, in the last year the PKK has begun making extensive use of IEDs in Turkey (*Terrorism Focus*, June 26, 2007). As yet there is no evidence that this technology has been transferred to PJAK. Given the close links between the two groups, however, the use of similar IEDs by PJAK over the coming months is probably all but inevitable. In Turkey such IEDs have already inflicted considerable damage—against less modern Iranian equipment their effect would be multiplied.

Since mid-2006, PJAK has also shown a growing awareness of the importance of a media strategy for building local and international support, even granting interviews to Western media outlets such as *The New York Times* [2]. Between the late 1990s and early 2006, in comparison, the group did not carry out a single interview with the Western press, although this change may reflect the group's increasing profile outside Kurdistan. In addition, the group has begun filming attacks and their aftermath in the manner of other Middle Eastern insurgent groups. According to Fars, some members of PJAK have even been arrested for filming the funerals of Iranians soldiers killed by these attacks (Fars, March 4, 2007); other videos have appeared on YouTube. Some of these take the form of formal press conferences, others commemorate PJAK's "martyrs," others again are more overt recruitment videos with pro-independence Kurdish songs, including Kurdish rap played over footage of young PJAK members training in the Qandil Mountains. Some of the media productions emphasize the group's ideological debt to Abdullah Öcalan, the jailed leader of the PKK, while others do not, perhaps suggestive of the group's own uncertainty over their relations with the PKK. All the group's videos emphasize the prominent role of women in the group and their equality with male fighters. This presentation aims to contrast PJAK's attitude to women against the policies of the Iranian government, which many Kurds regard as an assault on their relatively liberal traditions.

Prospects

Any Turkish military action will be closely coordinated with Iran, which regularly shells PKK and PJAK bases in the Qandil mountain range from its military bases four miles away on the nearby Iraqi-Iranian border (PUKmedia, October 25, 2007). Turkey and Iran already have long-standing agreements to cooperate against Kurdish militants. As early as July 2004, for instance, Turkish Prime Minister Recep Tayyip Erdoğan visited Tehran to develop a joint strategy against Kurdish militants (Iran Press Service, July 28, 2004). Iran regularly hands over captured Turkish Kurds to Turkey. Ankara in return delivers Iranian Kurdish insurgents to the Iranian military where they face torture and execution. For example, in early 2006 Iran sent 30 suspected PKK members to Turkey (*The New Anatolian*, February 25, 2006). In any military assault on the Qandil Mountains, Iranian forces would probably aim to block PKK attempts to flee into Iranian Kurdistan and perhaps even enter Iraqi Kurdistan to attack PJAK bases in the confusion caused by a Turkish assault.

In the event of such an invasion, much would hinge on whether Iraqi Kurds resisted or stood by. If they were to resist, PKK and PJAK members would almost certainly disregard past differences with the Iraqi-Kurdish leadership and join them. If Iraqi Kurds stood aside, however, PKK and PJAK forces would have to choose between making a last stand or attempting to blend into the local population and escape. In either case, the two Kurdish groups would probably feel honor-bound to help each other. They would also seek to rally local people to their side and would probably use force against anyone who did not cooperate. Providing PKK/PJAK did not alienate ordinary Kurds (as they did spectacularly in the 1990s in both Iraq and Turkey), they would likely receive a high degree of tacit and open support from Iraqi Kurds, including members of the security forces.

If, as seems most likely, Turkey puts economic pressure on the Iraqi Kurds to force them to either arrest PKK leaders or prevent future PKK operations, PJAK would have time to relocate itself away from the Qandil region and to re-distribute its forces around Kurdistan in a way that the PKK would be unable to do. This would disrupt PJAK's training and operations but would allow the group to survive in the long-term relatively unscathed. Even in the event of a massive Iranian-Turkish-U.S. strike on its PKK-linked bases, PJAK would still survive. It has well-developed recruiting and an infrastructure already in place in Iran and a funding network in Europe (particularly in Germany). There is no doubt PJAK would use the heightened profile created by such an attack to attract new recruits and funding from Kurds in Iran and elsewhere.

Originally published in *Terrorism Monitor*: Volume 5, Issue 21 on November 8, 2007.

Notes

1. The press release may not be authentic. It can be accessed at http://www.cl-netz.de/read.php?id=22422.
2. Richard A. Oppel Jr., "In Iraq, Conflict Simmers on a 2nd Kurdish Front," *The New York Times*, October 23, 2007.

Insurrection in Iranian Balochistan
By Chris Zambelis

Issues of dissent and rebellion amongst Iran's elaborate patchwork of ethnic and sectarian minority communities are receiving increasing international scrutiny. Many advocacy organizations representing Iranian minorities accuse Tehran of operating a policy of cultural subjugation aimed at erasing identities distinct from Iran's dominant Persian culture and Shiite brand of Islam. In some cases, these grievances have led to unrest and bloodshed. The latest round of violence between ethnic Baloch nationalists led by Jondallah ("Soldiers of God") and Iranian security forces in the province of Sistan-Balochistan is indicative of this wider trend in Iranian society. The shadowy Jondallah group emerged sometime in 2003 to advocate on behalf of Baloch rights. It has been known to operate under other monikers as well, including the People's Resistance Movement of Iran (PMRI).

Tehran has implicated Jondallah in a series of high-profile terrorist and guerrilla attacks against the security forces and symbols of the regime in Iranian Balochistan. Bold operations—such as the June 2005 abduction of Iranian military and intelligence personnel along the Iranian-Pakistani border and the February 2007 car bomb attack against a bus transporting members of the elite Islamic Revolutionary Guards Corps (IRGC) just outside of the provincial capital of Zahedan that left 11 dead and scores injured—have become a Jondallah signature (*Terrorism Focus*, February 27, 2007).

Iranian government sources reported a series of clashes in recent weeks between Jondallah rebels and the IRGC and provincial police forces in Iranian Balochistan. On December 13, 2007, Iranian security units reported killing 12 men belonging to Jondallah and arresting others affiliated with the group in the city of Iranshahr. Security officials also reported the discovery of a weapons cache that included automatic rifles, ammunition, detonators and explosives material, as well as communications equipment and what were described as "important internal documents." They also claimed that the detainees confessed to being part of a cell planning a series of bombings across the province in an effort to foment ethnic and sectarian unrest (Islamic Republic News Agency, December 13, 2007).

Subsequent reports alleged that Jondallah leaders and four men directly implicated in previous terrorist attacks were among those killed and detained by Iranian security forces (Voice of the Islamic Republic TV, December 19, 2007). In a December 14, 2007 interview, Jondallah's young leader Abdulmalak Rigi disputed the official casualty count, and claimed that only one member of his group was killed in the battle. Rigi, who is reported to be in his mid-twenties, also claimed that Iranian forces killed civilians during the skirmishes—including women and children—and that his forces killed 26 IRGC officers. He vowed to "take revenge for the women and children who were killed" (Voice of the Islamic Republic TV, December 19, 2007).

In another sign of escalating tensions, Iran hanged two Baloch men convicted of armed robbery and drug smuggling on December 31, 2007 in a Zahedan prison and amputated the right hand and left foot of five others convicted on armed robbery and kidnapping charges a few days later (Iranian Students' News Agency, January 6, 2008; Balochpeople.org, January 7, 2008). Baloch activists accuse Tehran of systematically harassing dissidents in the province by accusing them of false criminal charges in an effort to intimidate opposition elements. In a January 3, 2008 incident, Baloch sources reported that Iranian security forces opened fire against a vehicle delivering drinking water to a wedding ceremony on a busy street in Zahedan. Witnesses videotaped the alleged incident and the ensuing chaos and posted it online [1].

Nationalism and Rebellion in West Balochistan

The Baloch national question has been a source of simmering tensions for decades. Iran's approximately one to four million-strong Baloch community inhabits the southeastern province of Sistan-Balochistan [2]. This desolate and underdeveloped region is one of Iran's poorest provinces. Unlike most Iranians, the Baloch are predominantly Sunni Muslims. Violent crackdowns and repression by security services in the economically backward province have engendered deep-seated animosity toward the Shiite Islamist regime among the fiercely independent and proud Baloch people.

Iranian Baloch identify with their kin in neighboring Pakistan's southwestern province of Balochistan—home to the region's largest Baloch population at approximately four to eight million—and the smaller Baloch community in southern Afghanistan. The Pakistani Baloch are engaged in their own long-running struggle for greater rights and independence through a violent insurgency against Islamabad. The sum of these circumstances imbues the Baloch national consciousness with a sense of historic persecution at the hands of imperial powers that left *The Pakistani Baloch are engaged in their own long-running struggle for greater rights and independence through a violent insurgency against Islamabad.*
the Baloch nation divided and without a state of its own. Baloch nationalists see the unification of their people in an independent "Greater Balochistan" as a historical right. The plight of Iranian Balochistan, referred to as "West Balochistan" by Baloch nationalists, is a pillar of the wider Baloch nationalist cause [3].

Despite a lack of evidence, Tehran accuses Jondallah of serving as an affiliate of both al-Qaeda and the Taliban, claims the group emphatically denies (*Terrorism Monitor*, June 29, 2006). Jondallah does, however, rely on religious discourse to highlight its grievances against the Shiite Islamist regime. This most likely represents an effort to highlight the Iranian Baloch position as an oppressed ethnic and sectarian minority within the Shiite Islamist clerical regime. Nevertheless, there are no indications that the group has ties to radical Sunni Islamists. Iran also links Jondallah to other Iranian opposition groups—including the radical People's Mujahideen of Iran (PMOI), more commonly referred to as the Mojahedin-e-Khalq (MEK), and the affiliated National Council of Resistance of Iran (NCRI)—in an effort to tarnish its reputation. Tehran also accuses Jondallah of harboring secessionist aspirations. Abdulmalak Rigi has stated on numerous occasions that his group's goal is not secession, but the achievement of equal rights for his people in a reformed Iran. Essentially, Jondallah frames its campaign as a war of self-defense. At the same time, Rigi has gone so far as to declare himself an Iranian and Iran as his motherland (Roozonline.com, May 10, 2006). This is a position held by other Iranian Baloch dissident groups advocating on behalf of greater Baloch rights. Organizations such as the Balochistan United Front and the Balochistan National Movement coordinate closely with other ethnic and sectarian-minded opposition groups agitating for greater rights and representation in Iran, including the Congress of Nationalities for a Federal Iran [4].

Iranian authorities often describe the group as Pakistani-based in an apparent effort to implicate outside forces in the insurgency, especially the United States. Iran also occasionally accuses Pakistan of turning a blind eye to Jondallah activities, despite a strong record of Iranian and Pakistani cooperation in suppressing Baloch nationalism on both sides of the border. Iran also suggests Jondallah is a creation of the CIA, an allegation strongly denied by Rigi himself. Iran believes that the United States and other hostile forces are providing moral, material and financial support to ethnic and sectarian-based secessionist movements—including insurgent and terrorist organizations—to undermine the Islamic Republic. Tehran is convinced that any potential U.S. attack against Iran stemming from tensions over its nuclear program or alleged support for insurgents in Iraq and Afghanistan will include a campaign to destabilize the Islamic Republic from within. Groups such as Jondallah would figure prominently in such a strategy (*Terrorism Monitor*, August 2, 2007).

There is no concrete evidence that Jondallah maintains a formal operational base in Pakistan. The difficult terrain that characterizes the Iranian-Pakistani border region is, however, a major crossroads for drug and arms smuggling between locally-based gangs. The porous border also facilitates links between Baloch families and tribes on both sides of the border. In a testament to the extent of Iranian and Pakistani Baloch links, a controversial proposal by Islamabad to construct a wall along the border inspired vocal protests from Pakistani Baloch leaders who labeled the initiative the "anti-Baloch wall" (*The News International* [Karachi], May 28, 2007). Given this background, it is likely that Jondallah maintains contacts over the border in Pakistan, possibly with Baloch insurgent groups operating there, such as the Baloch Liberation Army (BLA). There is no evidence, however, of formal operational links between the two groups, as both appear committed to furthering their respective causes separately within the Iranian and Pakistani contexts.

The recent assassination of two-time Pakistani Prime Minister and opposition leader Benazir Bhutto raises questions about the trajectory of the Baloch insurgency in Pakistan and—by extension—Iran. As a center of Baloch nationalism, events in Pakistani Balochistan have a profound impact on the Baloch cause in Iran. In an effort to win support in Pakistani Balochistan for her campaign to oust incumbent President Pervez Musharraf, Bhutto promised that her Pakistan People's Party (PPP) would implement a general amnesty for Baloch prisoners and rebels and immediately enter into negotiations with local leaders to help settle the conflict. She also criticized Islamabad's heavy-handed approach in dealing with the Baloch insurgency, accusing Musharraf of exacerbating regional tensions (*Dawn*, December 21, 2007); her assassination was strongly condemned by Baloch activists. Ironically, tensions between Pakistani Baloch and the state during her father Zulfiqar Ali Bhutto's tenure as prime minister in the mid-1970s were high. The senior Bhutto used brutal tactics—as well as direct material and military support from the Shah of Iran that included helicopter gunships and armored vehicles—to quell the armed Baloch uprising [5]. The history of Iranian-Pakistani cooperation in jointly repressing Baloch nationalism—a trend both countries see as a potential threat to their respective territorial integrity and stability—suggests that Iranian accusations of Islamabad's support for Jondallah in Iran are unfounded.

Bhutto's assassination is not likely have a major impact on the situation in Iranian Balochistan, at least not directly. Despite expressions of solidarity and what is most likely limited contact, ethnic Baloch rebels in Iran and Pakistan will continue to devote their efforts to pursuing local agendas, essentially focusing on furthering the Baloch cause in Iran and Pakistan, respectively. Although Bhutto's amnesty proposal may have set an interesting precedent for relations between Tehran and Iranian Balochistan had she lived to implement it, it is unlikely that Islamabad will pursue a similar course of action in the foreseeable future.

Conclusion

The simmering tensions and violence in Iranian Balochistan will continue to characterize Tehran's interface with its Baloch minority. The social, political and economic grievances of the Iranian Baloch will remain a source of resentment toward the clerical regime until Tehran commits to integrating minorities into the fabric of society. Despite Iranian claims, there is no conclusive evidence that the United States is providing material support to Jondallah. It is likely, however, that the group calculates its activities and operations to correspond with periods of tension between the United States and Iran. This enables Jondallah to maximize the effect of its campaign. At the same time, Iran does have cause for concern, as the United States could consider the possibility of supporting active insurgencies as a means to pressure Iran during any potential conflict.

Originally published in *Terrorism Monitor*: Volume 6, Issue 1 on January 11, 2008.

Notes

1. See "Iranian Security Forces Shooting at Furious Baloch Demonstration," Balochistan News, January 1, 2008. For footage of the alleged incident, see the official website of the Baloch People's Party (BPP), a Baloch nationalist organization based in Sweden: www.balochpeople.org.
2. Demographic figures related to ethnic and sectarian minority representation in Iran tend to be heavily politicized, hence the wide ranging estimates.
3. The Baloch national cause is bolstered by a sophisticated network of activists in the diaspora and online advocating for their kin in Iran and Pakistan.

4. The Congress of Nationalities for a Federal Iran includes Kurdish, Azeri, Ahvazi (Arab), Turkmen, Baloch and other organizations advocating the federalization of Iran along ethnic and regional lines.
5. Stephen Philip Cohen, *The Idea of Pakistan* (Washington, D.C.: Brookings Institution, 2004), 219-221.

Is Iran's Mujahideen-e-Khalq a Threat to the Islamist Regime?
By Chris Zambelis

The People's Mujahideen of Iran (PMOI), more commonly known as the Mujahideen-e-Khalq ("people's mujahideen"; MEK), is one of the most organized and controversial Iranian opposition groups. Although it maintains an armed wing—known as the National Liberation Army (NLA)—and numerous front organizations, it derives its greatest strength from the slick lobbying and propaganda machine it operates in the United States and Europe. The MEK also boasts extensive support within U.S. government and policy circles, including many of the most vocal advocates of a U.S. invasion of Iran [1].

The MEK remains on the list of banned terrorist organizations in the United States and European Union (EU). Both parties have indicated no intention of reconsidering their positions. The May 7 decision by the United Kingdom's Court of Appeal to overrule the British government's inclusion of the MEK on its list of banned terrorist organizations, however, may pave the way for both the United States and EU to reassess their positions regarding the MEK down the line. Given the MEK's history of violence and its willingness to act as a proxy force against Iran, such a move would represent a major escalation in hostilities between the United States and Iran, with consequences in Iraq and beyond.

Ideology

The MEK is an obscure organization with a long history of violence and opposition activities. It emerged in the 1960s, composed of college students and leftist intellectuals loyal to Prime Minister Mohammad Mossadeq; the popular leftist nationalist prime minister was deposed by a U.S.- and U.K.-backed coup in 1953 that restored Mohammad Reza Shah to power. Its revolutionary zeal combined aspects of Marxist and Islamist ideologies in pursuit of its goal to overthrow the U.S.-backed shah through armed resistance and terrorism. Its primary targets in the 1970s included ranking officials and symbols of the shah's regime, both within and outside of Iran. The regime responded in kind with brutal repression through SAVAK, the shah's notorious domestic intelligence apparatus. Thousands of members and associates of MEK were killed, tortured and jailed during this period. Consequently, like many Iranians at the time, the MEK viewed the Islamist opposition as a positive force for change. The MEK supported the revolutionary forces and the 1979 seizure of the U.S. Embassy and subsequent hostage crisis led by student activists in Tehran. The group's unique brand of Marxism and Islamism, however, would bring it into conflict with the rigid Shiite Islamism espoused by the post-revolutionary government. The failure of a June 1981 coup attempt intended to oust Ayatollah Khomeini elicited a massive crackdown by the regime against the MEK, forcing the group's leaders and thousands of members into exile in Europe. When France ousted operational elements of the group in 1986, many made their way to Iraq, where they joined Saddam Hussein's war effort against Iran and enjoyed a safe haven [2].

Massoud and Maryam Rajavi, a charismatic husband and wife team that fled into exile in

Europe, lead the MEK. From her base in France, Maryam Rajavi currently holds the position of "President-Elect of the National Council of Resistance of Iran (NCRI)" after her husband's disappearance sometime in 2003. He is presumed to be in hiding [3]. The Rajavis enjoy a fanatical cult-like following among MEK members and supporters [4]. The group's cult-like character was displayed when 16 followers of the Rajavis staged dramatic public acts of self-immolation over a period of three days in June 2003 across major European and Canadian cities. The protests followed the arrest of Maryam Rajavi and 160 of her followers after a French court ruled that the MEK and its numerous front groups constituted a terrorist organization. According to former members of the group, the MEK's "human torches" are a testament to the stranglehold the Rajavis have over their followers and the extent to which members are brainwashed and manipulated psychologically into blindly following them. The MEK is reported to maintain a list of volunteers ready and willing to perform acts of self-immolation on the orders of the leadership [5]. Like other cults, MEK members are often separated from their children and families and discouraged from maintaining contact with individuals outside of the group. Former members who defected from the MEK describe the Rajavis as autocrats who demand unquestioned loyalty from their followers (pars-iran.com, January 30, 2006).

Women make up a significant contingent of the MEK's ranks, especially in its armed wing. In addition to its Marxist and Islamist pedigrees, the rise of the Rajavis to the group's leadership led to the introduction of feminist ideologies into the group's discourse. This aspect of the MEK's ideology indicates their attempt to tap into local grievances and international sympathy regarding the position of women in the Islamic Republic [6]. In this regard, the MEK presents itself as a liberal and democratic alternative to the rigid brand of Islamism espoused by the ruling clerics, an image it has cultivated in U.S. and Western policy circles to great effect [7]. The U.K. court based its ruling on the premise that the MEK has renounced violence and terrorism, and that it currently maintains no operational capability to execute future acts of violence.

Violence and Terrorism

The MEK's long history of violence and terrorism includes the abduction and assassination of ranking Iranian political and military officials under the shah in the 1970s, as well as attacks against the clerical establishment throughout the 1980s. Foreign-based MEK operatives also targeted Iranian embassies abroad in a series of attacks. MEK militants struck diplomatic officials and foreign business interests in Iran under both the shah and the Islamists in an effort to undermine investor confidence and regime stability. Furthermore, the MEK targeted and killed Americans living and working in Iran in the 1970s, namely U.S. military and civilian contractors working on defense-related projects in Tehran (Mkowatch.com). The group has never been known to target civilians directly, though its use of tactics such as mortar barrages and ambushes in busy areas have often resulted in civilian casualties.

In addition, the MEK's repertoire of operations includes suicide bombings, airline hijackings, ambushes, cross-border raids, RPG attacks, and artillery and tank barrages.

Saddam Hussein exploited the MEK's fervor during the Iran-Iraq war. In addition to providing the group with a sanctuary on Iraqi soil, Saddam supplied the MEK with weapons, tanks and armored vehicles, logistical support, and training at the group's Camp Ashraf in Diyala Province near the Iranian border and other camps across Iraqi territory. In a sign of the group's appreciation for Saddam's generous hospitality and largesse, the MEK cooperated with Iraqi security forces in the brutal repression of uprisings led by Shiite Arabs, Kurds and Turkmens in 1991 [8]. MEK members also served alongside Iraq's internal security forces and assisted in rooting out domestic opponents of the regime and other threats to Baathist rule.

Despite its history of high-profile attacks, the MEK never posed a serious threat to the Iranian regime. The group never enjoyed popular domestic support, despite its claims to the contrary. Many Iranians actively oppose the clerical regime and sympathize with segments of the opposition. At the same time, most Iranians also regard the MEK as traitorous for joining the Iraqi war effort against Iran and resent its use of violence and terrorism against Iranians at home and abroad (Mkowatch.com).

Approximately 3,500 members of the MEK remain in Camp Ashraf. Following an agreement with U.S.-led Coalition forces, MEK units allowed Coalition forces to disarm the group. Decommissioned MEK units are currently under surveillance in Camp Ashraf. Their future status, however, remains a point of controversy. Despite their demobilization, Iran believes that the United States is holding on to the group as leverage in any future confrontation with the Islamic Republic (*Terrorism Monitor*, February 9, 2006).

Political Activism

Although it has been disarmed, the MEK retains the capacity to remobilize, especially if it gains a state sponsor. Nevertheless, it is the MEK's lobbying and propaganda machine in the United States and Europe that enables it to remain a relevant force in Middle East politics and a key factor in U.S.-Iranian tensions. The MEK's political activism falls under the auspices of the National Council of Resistance of Iran (NCRI)—an MEK political front organization that also serves as an umbrella movement representing various Iranian dissident groups. These efforts persist despite the fact that U.S. authorities ordered NCRI offices in Washington to shut down in 2003 (*New York Observer*, June 5, 2007).

Although it has been disarmed, the MEK retains the capacity to remobilize, especially if it gains a state sponsor. Nevertheless, it is the MEK's lobbying and propaganda machine in the United States and Europe that enables it to remain a relevant force in Middle East politics and a key factor in U.S.-Iranian tensions.

From Iran's perspective, the U.S. position on MEK is both ambiguous and at times hypocritical. On the one hand, the MEK remains on the U.S. State Department's list of banned terrorist organizations, yet the group remains on Iraqi soil, albeit disarmed and under surveillance by Coalition forces. The MEK has cultivated a loyal following among an outspoken network of U.S. politicians, former and active government officials, members of the defense establishment, journalists and academics advocating violent regime change in Tehran. The MEK is even credited in some of these circles for disclosing aspects of the Iranian nuclear program [9]. At the same time, it is accused of fabricating intelligence information to boost its profile in the United States (Asia Times, March 4, 2008). With their call for regime change in Iran and pleas for international support, media-savvy MEK representatives based in the United States appear regularly on the cable news show circuit and other forums in Washington, DC in a campaign reminiscent of the one led by Ahmed Chalabi and the network of Iraqi exiles who mustered American support for the Iraq war [10]. The MEK has also gained legitimacy as a liberal and democratic force for positive change in Iran, despite evidence to the contrary.

Conclusion

The MEK will continue to capitalize on the ongoing tensions between the United States and Iran by enlisting the support of elements in Washington seeking a bargaining chip against Tehran. It is important, however, to see this bizarre organization for what it is; that is, to see through the façade of liberalism, democracy and human rights that it purports to represent through its propaganda. The well-documented experiences of scores of former MEK members are reason enough to consider this group and any of its claims with a healthy dose of skepticism.

Originally published in *Terrorism Monitor*: Volume 6, Issue 11 on May 29, 2008.

Notes

1. See Iran Policy Committee, "U.S. Policy Options for Iran," February 10, 2005, http://www.nci.org/05nci/02/IranPolicyCommittee.pdf.
2. For a historical narrative of the MEK's formative years, see Ervand Abrahamian, *The Iranian Mojahidin* (New Haven: Yale University Press, 1992). For an insider's perspective on the history of the MEK from a former member, see the website of Massoud Khodabandeh at http://www.khodabandeh.org.
3. See the official website of the National Council of Resistance of Iran (NCRI) at http://www.ncr-iran.org/ and the official website of Maryam Rajavi at http://www.maryam-rajavi.com.
4. See "Cult of the Chameleon," an Al Jazeera documentary on the MEK (broadcast October 17, 2007) at http://www.iran-interlink.org/?mod=view&id=3384. For an insider's perspective on the cult-like character of the MEK, see the website of the Dissociated Members of the People's Mojahedin Organization of Iran at http://www.pars-iran.com.
5. For an overview of the events of 2003, including graphic photographs of the acts of self-immolation, see "MKO Human Torches" at http://www.mojahedin.ws/art_pdfs/MKO-HUMAN-TORCHES.pdf.

6. For an overview of the MEK's position on women, see Shahin Torabi, "Women in the Cult of Mojahdin," March 5, 2003, http://mojahedin.ws/article/show_en.php?id=653 and Sattar Orangi, "The Strives [sic] for the Freedom of Women," March 13, 2008, http://mojahedin.ws/news/text_news_en.php?id=1601.

7. A. Ashfar, "The Positive Force of Terrorism," October 10, 2006, http://mojahedin.ws/news/text_news_en.php?id=842.

8. See "MKO and Massacre of Kurd and Turkmen Iraqis," April 19, 2006, http://pars-iran.com/en/?mod=view&id=664.

9. See "U.S. Policy Options for Iran," 7.

10. For more details on the MEK's political activities in Washington, DC see "Ali Reza Jafarzadeh, Front Man for the MEK and NCRI in Washington," February 2004, http://pars-iran.com/en/?mod=view&id=851.

IRAQ

The Shiite Zarqawi: A Profile of Abu Deraa
By Lydia Khalil

Depending on whom you ask, Abu Deraa is either considered a Shiite hero or the Shiite version of Abu Musab al-Zarqawi. The legendary militant, notorious for his brutal tactics and hatred for Sunnis, is known to operate out of Sadr City, yet he remains a mysterious and elusive presence. He is feared by many Iraqis because of his reputation for cruelty as a death squad leader. The U.S. military has launched numerous operations recently to capture or kill Abu Deraa, but have so far come up empty-handed. Nevertheless, while Abu Deraa's fable is great, the facts on him are slim.

"Abu Deraa," his *nom de guerre*, means "Father of the Shield"; his real name is Ismail al-Zerjawi. Other than his name, little else is known about him or his whereabouts. It is believed that Abu Deraa was a refugee who came to Sadr City from the southern marshes where he had worked as a fishmonger. During the rule of the Baath Party, Saddam Hussein drained the marshes and destroyed Shiite villages as punishment for their uprising after the first Gulf War—this caused many Shiites, like Abu Deraa, to move to the Sadr City slum in Baghdad. Abu Deraa is allegedly in his forties and is married with two children.

Many of the tidbits of information on Abu Deraa used for this report were gleaned from various Western and Arab news reports covering the practices of Iraq's Shiite militias. The Iraqi media have remained largely silent on Abu Deraa. He has granted no interviews nor released any statements to the Iraqi or foreign press, preferring to remain elusive and have his legend speak for itself. Any member of the Iraqi press that conducts too many inquiries about Abu Deraa would likely suffer a fate similar to his victims. His associates and the Shiites he lives amongst are protective of him.

Until recently, his appearance was disputed, but oddly enough a video clip surfaced of him on the popular file-sharing website YouTube (see: http://www.youtube.com/watch?v=qV1qA_4v6u8). Short, stocky and bearded, Abu Deraa is pictured feeding a baby camel. His bodyguards were reported as saying that the video of Abu Deraa and the camel was a message to Iraqi Vice President Tariq al-Hashemi. According to his bodyguards, when Abu Deraa captures and kills al-Hashemi, he will sacrifice this new camel. The accuracy of the video cannot be confirmed.

Abu Deraa's Operations

Iraqi Sunnis accuse Abu Deraa of killing thousands of Sunnis, not just political figures and militant Salafists, but ordinary civilians as well. One of his associates recounted to an Australian newspaper how Abu Deraa lured Sunni men to their deaths. The associate explained how Abu Deraa commandeered a fleet of ambulances and drove them into a Sunni neighborhood in Baghdad calling on all young men to come and give blood, announcing on a loud speaker that "the Shiites are killing your Sunni brothers" (*The Age*,

August 22, 2006). The young men went to the ambulances and were trapped and killed. According to one of the many rumors circulating around the country, Abu Deraa offers his victims a choice in their murder—suffocation, shooting or being smashed to death with cinder blocks. Many of the murdered victims have been found in the al-Seddah sector of Sadr City, an area which Iraqis have nicknamed the "Happiness Hotel." Victims are found in shallow graves, many with signs of torture.

Yet Abu Deraa has also captured and killed high-value targets. A video recorded on a telephone camera and circulated in Shiite areas shows a man believed to be Abu Deraa conducting the kidnapping and assassination of Saddam Hussein's lawyer Khamis al-Obeidi. The video shows al-Obeidi emerging from a private residence, where he was undergoing interrogation, into a narrow alleyway. Al-Obeidi pleaded with his captors on the video, saying that he would lie beneath their feet and do whatever they wanted. Abu Deraa then tied al-Obeidi's hands behind his back and placed him in the back of a white Toyota pickup truck. Al-Obeidi was paraded through Sadr City, where the crowd threw stones at him and taunted him with Shiite slogans. He was hit on the back of the neck, an extreme insult in Arab culture. After being paraded through the slum, the vehicle stopped and Abu Deraa fired three shots into al-Obeidi's skull (*The Age*, August 22, 2006). Abu Deraa is also thought to be responsible for the July abduction of female Sunni MP Tayseer Najah al-Mashhadani. Unlike al-Obeidi, she is still believed to be alive.

The Sunni leadership is understandably nervous. Last summer, an anonymous letter was distributed to Sunni mosques in Baghdad, titled "The Reaper of al-Rusafa." It warned Sunnis living in the area about Abu Deraa. The letter reads, "His name is Abu Deraa and he is a professional killer who is not any less dangerous than al-Zarqawi ... Some of the Sadr City police force works under his command and under the *"His name is Abu Deraa and he is a professional killer who is not any less dangerous than al-Zarqawi ..."* command of other forces from Moqtada al-Sadr ... Everyone in Sadr City knows this madman but they do not say his name; it is whispered in Sadr City when they wake up to the news of the blindfolded dead bodies thrown out at al-Seddah ... which the Interior Ministry officially made as a place for Abu Deraa's victims."

Connections to Shiite Militias

Reportedly, Abu Deraa was a forger during Saddam's rule, but he now makes his living doing the dirty work of Shiite militias and political parties, whose leadership publicly disavow him. His connection to Moqtada al-Sadr's Mahdi Army is unclear. He may have, at one point, taken orders from al-Sadr, or alternatively played up his connection to the Mahdi Army for his own legitimacy and standing within the Shiite community. Either way, he is most likely now working as a free agent whose actions are publicly denounced by the Shiite leadership but who privately are not altogether unhappy about the "justice" he is inflicting on the Sunni community. Since he mostly operates out of Sadr City and neighboring Shula, he must have at least the tacit approval of al-Sadr since the latter's organization regulates human traffic in the entire area (*al-Sharqiyah*, November 3, 2006).

Abu Deraa has mostly been associated with the al-Sadr trend, but it is also rumored that he is supported by Iran (Tehran, not knowing who will emerge as the dominant Shiite group in Iraq, has been supporting all of the Shiite parties). It is also possible that he is supported in some way by the Supreme Council for the Islamic Revolution in Iraq (SCIRI), a powerful party within the United Iraqi Alliance (UIA). SCIRI and the Mahdi Army are rival Shiite groups that are competing for dominance in the UIA. SCIRI has a powerful backer in Iran and is a strong proponent of federalism based on three large regional blocs. SCIRI's power base is mostly in southern Iraq, while al-Sadr is more powerful in Baghdad. Al-Sadr is a nationalist and is opposed to the strong federalization of Iraq. Although he has recently flirted with Iran, his group's connection to Iran is not anywhere near as strong as is SCIRI's.

Yet, where does Abu Deraa fit into this picture? There is much confusion about the labyrinth of connections and competing interests among Shiite political parties and Abu Deraa is a piece of that puzzle. Abu Deraa is married to the sister of Hadi al-Amari, the SCIRI Badr Corps commander (author interview, senior Iraqi advisor, November 6, 2006). It is not altogether clear what other connection between Abu Deraa and SCIRI exists beyond family ties, but it is safe to assume that the SCIRI's Badr Corps commander is at least aware of Abu Deraa's actions and whereabouts. SCIRI has publicly condemned the sectarian killings conducted by Shiite gangs and militias, despite incidents committed by their own Badr Corps. It is in SCIRI's interest to have Abu Deraa associated with the Mahdi Army. This connection damages the Mahdi Army's and Moqtada al-Sadr's reputation by associating them with such a ruthless figure. It also keeps the political heat on al-Sadr and the Mahdi Army and away from SCIRI. SCIRI is also aware that the U.S. military has been intent on capturing or killing Abu Deraa, and it has not raised any public criticism against these operations.

Nevertheless, for both al-Sadr and SCIRI, Abu Deraa is a useful tool because he remains a disposable one. If he is killed or captured, as will likely happen sooner or later, he will have served his purpose in avenging Shiite deaths without tainting the more established political parties, especially SCIRI and Da'wa. For Moqtada al-Sadr, it is in his interests to maintain a murky connection to the death squad leader. The Shiite community applauds Abu Deraa's actions against their former oppressors, making it important for al-Sadr to appear on Abu Deraa's side; at the same time, al-Sadr must distance himself from Abu Deraa's distasteful methods so as not to damage his growing political reputation.

Al-Sadr understands that the U.S. military seeks to capture or kill Abu Deraa. He has calculated that it is not in his interests to stick out his neck for Abu Deraa and has ordered his followers to avoid confrontation with U.S. troops in Sadr City. Al-Sadr's spokesman said on al-Sharqiyah television on November 3, 2006 that "Al Sayed Moqtada al-Sadr and the jihadist al-Sadr trend distance themselves from the deeds that were committed, and are being committed, and which are attributed to the al-Sadr trend."

Abu Deraa has been reportedly pushed further and further out of Sadr City. Previously based out of the Lost 70s area of Sadr City—a desolate, largely abandoned area of the poor slum—military operations have forced him to go to the al-Amin district, according to some sources. Others have even speculated that Abu Deraa crossed the eastern border into Iran. Military forces conducted two recent raids targeting Abu Deraa, one in July 2006 and most recently on October 25, 2006. He escaped in both instances, but in October his son and an associate were killed (Al Jazeera, October 30, 2006). Abu Deraa may be able to evade capture for a period of time, but the pressure on him is intense. That same pressure is also on his tacit Shiite backers. Nevertheless, the established Shiite parties, particularly al-Sadr's movement, are still unwilling to take action against him. Al-Sadr, for example, recently released a list of blacklisted members of his party and individuals he claims are acting on his behalf but are not associated with the Mahdi Army—Abu Deraa is not on that list.

Conclusion

Abu Deraa, however, is only a small part of the larger issue facing Iraq—the splintering of militia groups into uncontrollable gangs. The Mahdi Army may have unleashed Abu Deraa and others like him, but now they are unable to rein him back in, even if they had the will to do so. This development is a serious threat to al-Sadr. Al-Sadr's movement is considered the only legitimate, national, grassroots movement to have emerged out of Iraq since the fall of Saddam Hussein. Having criminal gangs and individuals like Abu Deraa not only associated, but uncontrolled by al-Sadr, marks a serious danger to his legitimacy. If this trend continues, then Moqtada al-Sadr will no longer be viewed as an Iraqi nationalist, but as another partisan Shiite leader beholden to Iran.

Originally published in *Terrorism Monitor*: Volume 4, Issue 22 on November 16, 2006.

Harith al-Dari: Iraq's Most Wanted Sunni Leader
By Lydia Khalil

According to Iraqi President Jalal Talabani, Harith al-Dari has "nothing to do but incite sectarian and ethnic sedition." Al-Dari, the leader of the Association of Muslim Scholars (AMS), has been an outspoken critic of the Shiite-led Iraqi government and is rumored to be affiliated with the 1920 Revolution Brigades, an indigenous Iraqi insurgent group. In November, the Iraqi Interior Ministry issued a warrant for the arrest of the controversial Sunni leader for "inciting terrorism and violence among the Iraqi people." The Iraqi government has been critical of him in the past and it is unclear what finally triggered the Interior Ministry to issue a warrant for his arrest. Al-Dari's published statements and numerous interviews, however, give us a clear window into his attitudes and actions regarding the insurgency. He is certainly a supporter of what he labels the "resistance" and what others label as "terrorism."

Arrest Warrant Issued

Harith al-Dari was believed to be in Jordan when the arrest warrant was issued on November 16, 2006. The surprise announcement of the warrant was made by Jawad al-Bolani, Iraq's Shiite interior minister. He stated that it is "the government's policy that anyone who tries to spread division and strife among the Iraqi people will be chased by our security agencies ... We have to prove to everyone that the government...is going forward with major steps to achieve security." Al-Bolani even stated that the government was asking international police to arrest al-Dari if he does not return to Baghdad. Yet, according to al-Dari and his supporters, the arrest warrant has nothing to do with the Interior Ministry's desire to achieve security in Baghdad, but rather it was an attempt to silence and marginalize the cleric. The AMS, which al-Dari leads, issued a formal statement on its website on November 17, 2006. The statement read: "The warrant issued by the Interior Ministry against Dr. Harith al-Dari ... is clear evidence that this government has lost its balance and declared its bankruptcy." Al-Dari flatly denied the accusation of inciting terrorism. He speculated that the timing of the arrest warrant had to do with his visit to Saudi Arabia, which angered Shiite members of the Iraqi government. He has also repeatedly challenged the legitimacy of any government that was formed "under the occupation," which has further encouraged the government to come out against him.

The political timing of the announcement for his arrest is certainly controversial. It has elicited a strong backlash among Iraq's Sunni community. Faced with overwhelming evidence implicating Shiite militias attached to the government with sectarian violence, the arrest warrant was viewed as a sectarian attack by a biased government—regardless of the objective justifications for the arrest warrant. After the initial outcry against the Interior Ministry's announcement, the ministry quickly softened its stance and announced that the government did not issue an "arrest warrant" but an "interrogation warrant" (al-Arabiya, November 17, 2006). Harith al-Dari remains outside of Iraq, traveling in the region. He was last seen in Syria.

There is no doubt that Harith al-Dari has made public statements against the government and called on all Iraqis to resist the occupation and its Iraqi partners. He is also reported to have ties to certain groups that make up the indigenous Iraqi insurgency such as the 1920 Revolution Brigades and the Islamic Army in Iraq. The question, however, is whether he has directly supported or directed the violent insurgency, rather than simply made public statements encouraging resistance. Is he a vociferous advocate of Sunni rights and anti-sectarian tendencies? Or is he a rejectionist with links to the insurgency, as many U.S. and Shiite leaders claim? Who is Harith al-Dari? Where did he come from and can he claim to represent Sunni and Iraqi interests?

Al-Dari's Past and the Role of the AMS

Harith al-Dari was born in Baghdad in 1941 and hails from a prominent Iraqi family of the al-Dari clan. He is considered Iraq's most notable Sunni scholar with degrees from Cairo's al-Azhar University. He is related to the famous Sheikh Dari who became a national hero when he killed a British officer in 1920, sparking a revolution. He spent much of his adult life teaching Islamic law and history at various Arab universities. Harith al-Dari organized the AMS, also referred to as the Muslim Ulema Council or Muslim Scholars Association, on April 14, 2003 as an anti-occupation movement, as a nationalist force and as a nucleus for Iraq's Sunni religious authority (al-Manar al-Yawm, September 5, 2004).

The AMS is largely a response to the marginalized role of the Sunni community. It has a strong nationalist bent but its message mostly resonates with Iraq's disenfranchised Sunnis. It is a clerical body, but has been vocal on political issues and has provided religious cover for the resistance. Yet, because of its refusal to fully enter the political fray due to al-Dari's opposition to the occupation and the U.S. sponsored political process, the AMS' political influence is limited. The coalition has tried repeatedly to negotiate with the AMS, but it has remained adamant that it will not engage substantively with the United States while the military occupation remains. It did, however, negotiate in ending the siege of Fallujah in 2004. The fact that Harith al-Dari has mediated with certain insurgent groups for the release of hostages and mediated to end the siege of Fallujah suggests that he has strong ties to elements in the insurgency. Nevertheless, he insists that "we did not negotiate or mediate because we have no links to those parties. We only appealed to them and our appeals succeeded in freeing the hostages" (al-Dustur, November 2, 2004).

Harith al-Dari's son, Muthana Harith al-Dari, is also an active member of the AMS. He serves as the organization's spokesman. He is reported to be the leader of the 1920 Revolution Brigades, but he publicly denies this. The AMS, through both father and son, has been an enthusiastic supporter of the Iraqi resistance and has defended Iraqis' right to resistance and has even stated that it is a religious duty that needs no fatwa for justification (al-Manar al-Yawm, September 5, 2004). The AMS has repeatedly called on the government to resign. Al-Dari has made a link between occupation and sectarianism in Iraq—two developments that have weakened the position of the Sunni minority. Since he has rejected political participation, however, all that is left is promoting the resistance. It is this support of the resistance that prompted the arrest warrant.

While promoting resistance, al-Dari has also discounted the political process in all its forms. He has rejected the constitutional process, boycotted elections and disparaged participation in government. Al-Dari has stated, "The political process, irrespective of the way they describe it, has brought nothing good to Iraq ... they have divided Iraq on a sectarian and ethnic basis ... Iraq today belongs to the occupation, to those who benefit from it, who serve it and who are collaborating with it to oppress their Iraqi brothers" (Al Jazeera, November 25, 2006).

The Islamic Army in Iraq, the Islamic Front for Resistance and the 1920 Revolution Brigades have all condemned the arrest warrant against Harith al-Dari, all groups that the Iraqi government claims he supports. It is not clear whether he directly leads or supports Iraqi insurgent groups, but al-Dari is certainly an articulate spokesman for their cause.

Resistance or Terrorism

Harith al-Dari has made an effort to establish a clear distinction between resistance and terrorism—which he claims the Iraqi government, the United States and the media have lumped together to further their aims. According to al-Dari, "The resistance is the party that targets the occupation, the occupation alone. It has not harmed any Iraqis because it is a rationalized resistance and is defending something called the liberation of Iraq" (al-Quds Press Agency, April 26, 2006). Terrorism, on the other hand, is something entirely different according to al-Dari. He blames the occupation and the ineffective Iraqi government's security policies for terrorist activity. During an interview published earlier this year on Egypt's Muslim Brotherhood's website, al-Dari outlines which Iraqi groups he considers part of the resistance and which he does not. He divides the resistance into several groups, the most important of which he says are the Islamic Army, the Islamic Resistance Movement, the Mujahideen Army and the Islamic Resistance Front.

Harith al-Dari has made an effort to establish a clear distinction between resistance and terrorism—which he claims the Iraqi government, the United States and the media have lumped together to further their aims.

He also classifies the Mujahideen al-Shura Council, an umbrella group of al-Qaeda affiliated groups, as part of the legitimate resistance. Other groups which he labels as part of the legitimate resistance are the Iraqi Mujahideen and the al-Rashidin Army, among others. He explains, "I must point out that these factions attack the occupation forces and do not target the civilians because it is a resistance that broke out immediately at the beginning of the occupation. These factions do not receive support from any foreign party" (Ikhwanonline, March 6, 2006). He has gone so far as to say that actions known to be taken by Sunni insurgent groups—such as the attack on an Egyptian diplomat and violent bombings that killed Iraqi civilians—were not the responsibility of the insurgency, but instead the work of intelligence agencies (Ikhwanonline, March 6, 2006).

He also believes that the bombing of the United Nations headquarters in Baghdad in 2004 was either the work of the "occupation" or groups they encouraged.

He has admitted that members of the resistance have made mistakes, but is more forgiving of their actions and blames "media exploitation" for the distorted image of the resistance. He has stated that tactics like kidnapping and car bombings were exploited especially by the U.S. media to tarnish the resistance (*al-Misri al-Yawm*, July 9, 2005). In an article published in the Baghdad newspaper *al-Zawra*, he writes, "Some Iraqi resistance factions have made mistakes that gave a faulty impression about the resistance as a whole. This is not strange. What is strange is to expect the resistance to be perfect and free from error at all times. No resistance movement has succeeded in doing that."

Al-Dari has tried to avoid characterizations of him as a spokesman for the resistance, preferring to be considered as a representative for national Iraqi interests. "The voice of the Association is not a voice that speaks on behalf of the resistance. It is the voice that speaks on behalf of all of Iraq and on behalf of all those that reject the occupation." He also states, however, that he seeks recognition of the resistance. "The resistance should not be disregarded. It should be recognized as an effective party that has its weight in Iraq. The problems of Iraq cannot be resolved without listening to the resistance and involving it in the affairs of the country" (*al-Sharq al-Awsat*, May 13, 2006).

Al-Dari has given religious cover to many insurgent tactics. He has justified kidnappings by saying, "Many scholars, including [Yusuf] al-Qaradawi, have issued fatwas sanctioning the kidnapping of combatants in times of war because it is permitted by religion and according to the practices of the Prophet Muhammad." He asserts that kidnappings are akin to taking prisoners of war and that their killing is justified if the "commander of the people deems those prisoners war criminals and sentences them to death" (*al-Dustur*, November 2, 2004). Even though al-Dari has recognized the legitimacy of the Mujahideen al-Shura Council, he has also stated that Abu Musab al-Zarqawi's importance, when he was alive, was exaggerated by the United States to justify its occupation of Iraq. Al-Dari accuses the United States and the Iraqi government of building a myth around al-Zarqawi in order to hijack the resistance, attributing it only to al-Qaeda so that when al-Zarqawi was killed, they could claim they killed off the resistance (*al-Dustur*, November 2, 2004).

Conclusion

Al-Dari's ability to unify the Sunni community in a constructive way has certainly been hampered by the arrest warrant and by his own tactics. He has alienated an important tribal constituency—the al-Anbar tribes who are now committed to fighting against al-Qaeda and the insurgents. They have even gone so far as to ask the AMS to remove him as leader. They have even filed a lawsuit against him. In an announcement on al-Iraqiyah television, "In the name of the al-Anbar Chieftains Council, we tell Harith al-Dari that if there is a bandit, it is you. If there is a murderer or kidnapper, it is you." While some other Iraqis have rallied around him, he is not in Iraq to lead them and has rejected government participation. His voice is limited by the arrest warrant since this prevents him from returning to Iraq, unless he is willing to face arrest, and by his own refusal to support the government so as to change its policies from within.

Originally published in *Terrorism Monitor*: Volume 4, Issue 24 on December 14, 2006.

The Sadr-Sistani Relationship
By Babak Rahimi

One of the oddest developments in the recent history of Iraq has been the growing connection between the young firebrand cleric, Moqtada al-Sadr, and the highest-ranking Shiite cleric, Ayatollah Ali al-Sistani. Earlier in 2003, the erratic politics of al-Sadr, with his mix of Arab nationalism and militant chiliastic ideology, was considered to eventually collide with al-Sistani's quietist form of Shi'ism, which advocates that clerics should maintain a clear distance from day-to-day state politics. Since 2004, however, an unlikely alliance has gradually taken form between the former adversaries, which is bound to reshape Iraqi Shiite politics in the years to come.

By and large, the relationship between the two clerics has been one of asymmetrical partnership, in which al-Sistani plays the superior partner, guiding the younger and less experienced al-Sadr in his quest for becoming a legitimate leader of the Iraqi Shiite community. In doing so, al-Sistani has tried to tame al-Sadr by bringing him into the mainstream Najaf establishment in order to form a united Shiite front against extremist Sunnis and the United States. In return, al-Sadr, who lacks religious credentials, has been using al-Sistani's support to legitimize his religious authority and expand his influence in southern Iraq. The relationship is mutually opportunistic, but also pragmatic, since the two clerics have not been able to ignore each other.

In broad terms, such an alliance signals two significant changes: first, a dramatic shift in the balance of power in Shiite Iraq in terms of the revival of the Hawza, as a cluster of seminaries and religious scholarly institutions in Najaf, and, second, an increase of tension between Shiites and Sunnis in Iraq. Moreover, the growing alliance between al-Sadr and al-Sistani also underlines another vital feature tied to the Shiite ascendancy in Iraq: the rise of Iran as a regional power. Iran has been playing a crucial role in the shaping of Sadr-Sistani relations, since any alliance between Shiite leaders is intertwined with the Qom-Tehran nexus and Iranian politics in the greater Middle East.

Against the Najaf Hawza: 2003-2004

Since the U.S.-led invasion of Iraq, the Sadrist movement, mainly dominated by Moqtada al-Sadr, has emerged as one of the most populist and grassroots currents in the post-Baathist era. Yet the militant movement has also posed the most serious threat to clerical orthodoxy and its conservative and quietist tradition, best embodied by Ayatollah al-Sistani.

Much of the "heterodoxy" of the Sadrist movement lies in its early (2003–04) rejection of clerical monopoly, led by some young clerical students and followers of al-Sadr who accused al-Sistani of transforming the shrine city of Najaf into a "sleeping house of learning." The heretical tendencies of the Sadrist movement entailed rejecting the religious authority of a living, high-ranking cleric in favor of the rulings of a deceased *marja* (religious scholar), a blasphemous idea according to the orthodox thinking that al-Sistani and his Hawza represent. Yet there is also the factor of Arab nationalism.

Ideologically, the Sadrists are Arab nationalists and resent the presence of any non-Arab cleric in Iraq, especially those of Iranian descent, like al-Sistani, who have been residing in the shrine-cities for decades.

The origin of the movement dates back to the early 1990s, when Ayatollah Muhammad Sadeq al-Sadr, the father of Moqtada, led an anti-quietist campaign by accusing al-Sistani and other leading clerics in Najaf of abandoning ordinary people and allowing Baathist oppression to take place [1]. When Moqtada emerged as the leading figure in the movement four years after the assassination of his father by Saddam's regime in 1999, he continued his father's legacy and expanded his anti-quietist movement in the slums of Baghdad and southern Iraq. In spring 2003, al-Sadr refused to accept al-Sistani's leadership, and declined his invitations for a meeting [2]. Tensions between the outspoken al-Sadr and the quietist al-Sistani were at their highest when the cleric followers of al-Sadr criticized the grand ayatollah for his Iranian origin and even urged him and other quietist clerics to leave Iraq [3]. The conflict between al-Sadr and al-Sistani culminated in the August 2004 showdown between the Mahdi Army and U.S. troops in Najaf, when al-Sistani saw the clash as an opportunity for the eradication of his young rival [4].

Nevertheless, eventually al-Sistani decided to intervene and offer protection to al-Sadr and his followers. After three weeks of intense fighting between the Mahdi Army and U.S. and Iraqi forces around the Imam Ali Mosque in Najaf, al-Sistani was finally able to broker a cease-fire deal with al-Sadr in late August 2004 [5]. Although his change of position was partly aimed at ending the destruction of the shrine complex and protecting Najaf's inhabitants, al-Sistani saw the Mahdi Army as a major asset in dealing with anti-Shiite Sunni groups and U.S. forces in Iraq. Due to the encouragement from Hezbollah and Tehran, the agreement signaled an opportunity to tame al-Sadr and his Mahdi Army, militarily weakened by U.S. forces, by bringing his troops closer to the mainstream Shiite establishment [6].

Post-2005 Elections and the Iran Factor

The 2004 deal signaled a tipping point in Sadr-Sistani relations, bringing the two leaders closer together with the aim of advancing Shiite interests in the democratic arena. Despite a period of tension with the Supreme Council for the Islamic Revolution in Iraq (SCIRI) and the Badr Organization, the largest Shiite militia that backed al-Sistani, al-Sadr finally joined forces with a Shiite-led political party approved by al-Sistani, the United Iraqi Alliance (UIA), in the December 2005 elections. The move advanced a new stage in Sadr-Sistani relations, which underlined how the two clerics saw the importance of a centralized democratic government as a means to solidify Shiite power in a country with a long history of Sunni-dominance.

Since 2004, al-Sadr and al-Sistani have met a number of times to discuss issues related to elections, including a major meeting in mid-September 2004 that included Abdul Aziz al-Hakim, al-Sadr's main rival [7]. In early September 2004, in a potentially explosive incident, al-Sistani helped al-Sadr by asking the Iraqi police to end the siege of his office in Najaf [8]. Al-Sistani's growing relations with al-Sadr continued to evolve when he appealed to Abdul al-Saheb-e al-Khoei to delay the search for his slain brother, Sayyid Abdul Majid al-Khoei, who was allegedly murdered by al-Sadr's followers in 2003 [9]. This was a major move by al-Sistani since it basically extricated al-Sadr of any wrongdoing in the case of al-Khoei's murder.

After the January and December 2005 elections, al-Sistani refused to call for the disarming of the Mahdi militia. This decision was made in connection with the rise of sectarian tensions unleashed after the bombing of the Shiite al-Askari Shrine in Samarra in February 2006. With the absence of a strong centralized government in Baghdad, al-Sistani considered al-Sadr's militia as a major force to protect the Shiite community and its sacred shrines against Sunni extremist attacks. He even used al-Sadr to negotiate with the Sunni clerics about the looming problem of sectarian violence. After a major meeting in March 2006, al-Sistani dispatched al-Sadr to discuss the escalation of Sunni-Shiite tensions with a number of Sunni clerics at the Azamiyah mosque in Baghdad [10]. At this stage, al-Sistani appeared to have gained considerable influence over al-Sadr, while his Mahdi Army was gradually breaking into subgroups, challenging their former leader for his compromising stance toward the Sunnis and the Americans—perhaps partly due to al-Sistani's influence.

In an important meeting in early January of this year, al-Sistani persuaded al-Sadr to end his boycott of the UIA and return to the parliament [11]. Al-Sadr agreed, and his followers returned to the parliament later that month. In another major meeting mid-February, al-Sadr sought the counsel of al-Sistani about attacks and death threats he was receiving from his own militia [12]. Following al-Sistani's advice, al-Sadr reportedly left Iraq for Iran and he is now staying at his cousin's house, Jafar al-Sadr, in Qom [13]. This final meeting highlights the growing dependence of al-Sadr on al-Sistani's religious and intellectual authority, which has increased considerably since the toppling of Saddam's regime. For now, al-Sistani appears to have tamed al-Sadr, especially by helping him in becoming a major figure to advance an anti-sectarian platform.

Both al-Sadr and al-Sistani share the common interest of protecting the Shiite community against the ongoing sectarian war and, simultaneously, promoting a unified Iraq governed by a centralized government in Baghdad. In this sense, the two are against a federalist

Although al-Sadr and al-Sistani do not want Iranian influence in Iraq, they also realize that Tehran cannot simply be ignored.

system of government, particularly the sectarian-provincial model of federalism advocated by Abdul Aziz al-Hakim. This common objective has brought them closer together, while facing opposition from pro-federal factions, such as the Iranian-backed SCIRI, which continue to push a sectarian agenda in the revised version of the constitution expected to be proposed by the constitutional committee in mid-May 2007.

Here the role of Iran in the making of such an alliance should not be ignored. Although al-Sadr and al-Sistani do not want Iranian influence in Iraq, they also realize that Tehran cannot simply be ignored. Both clerics recognize that Shiite empowerment in Iraq can only be ensured by Iranian support, and challenging Tehran could only lead to the consolidation of Sunni power, with the backing of the United States, in Iraq and the region.

Given the fact that the financial center of his religious network is based in the Iranian city of Qom, al-Sistani has been careful not to upset the Iranian authorities. He refuses to challenge the authority of Ayatollah Khamenei, despite their differences in theological outlooks. For instance, al-Sistani has so far declined to declare a fatwa on the production of a nuclear bomb since he wants to avoid a confrontation with Tehran [14]. Al-Sistani has also criticized the student reformist movement in Iran for its disregard of Iranian national interests and warned the students against foreign influences [15]. He has even praised the Iranian president, Mahmud Ahmadinejad, for his travels to local regions in Iran and getting involved in the daily problems of his constituency; he has urged Iraqi officials to follow in Ahmadinejad's footsteps in Iraq [16]. Like al-Sadr, al-Sistani considers the backing of Iran as something necessary in a period of foreign aggression (i.e. Israel and the United States) and increasing anti-Shiite currents in the Sunni world. Iran, too, recognizes the influence of the Najaf Hawza and the Sadrists in Iraq, and continues to ride the rising tide of the Shiite revival. Tehran knows that al-Sadr and al-Sistani can play a major role in advancing Iran's interests in Iraq and the region in case the United States decides to attack Iran's nuclear facilities.

Implications of Sadr-Sistani Ties

The changing relationship between Moqtada al-Sadr and Grand Ayatollah Ali al-Sistani signals a dramatic shift in the political landscape of the Shiite Iraqi community since the fall of the Baathist regime in 2003. While new conflicts have emerged between Shiite groups, especially between the opposition groups that left the country (Dawa and SCIRI) and those who stayed in Iraq under Saddam's reign (Sadrists), old adversaries are now becoming new partners as a result of the sectarian conflict engulfing the country.

There are two main implications involved. First and foremost, despite theological and ideological differences between Shiite groups and leaders, sectarian identity is playing a major role in the shaping of future alliances and conflicts in Iraq. It is an undeniable truth that with the rise of Salafi Sunni attacks against Shiites, rivalry among Shiite groups subsides, and loose alliances are formed to protect the community. Yet while creating such alliances, each rival group also prepares to protect its own particular economic and political interests in various localities throughout Baghdad and southern Iraq [17]. In short, Shiite relations in Iraq should be considered as both political and sectarian. Theological and ideological differences play an important role, but not a prominent one, as Sadr-Sistani relations best demonstrate.

Such a dramatic shift, however, also underlines the unpredictable political situation in the country, signaling certain unforeseen challenges that may arise in the years to come. In this sense, it is hardly an overstatement to claim that with the death of Ayatollah al-Sistani, who is 76, new unforeseen problems will likely emerge in the form of competition among leading Shiite groups to control the Shiite community. Since the grand ayatollah has not yet appointed a successor according to the traditional clerical succession process, it remains unclear what sort of political vacuum his death could create. Nevertheless, a political vacuum will certainly be created. No other cleric in the post-Baathist era has had so much authority in Iraq, and it is very likely that his absence will be deeply felt.

The leading candidate to replace al-Sistani is the Afghan-born, Najaf-based Grand Ayatollah Muhammad Ishaq al-Fayadh. He is an old seminary student friend of al-Sistani since the 1950s and a staunch ally since 1992. Ayatollah al-Khoei, the mentor of al-Sistani, reportedly recognized al-Fayadh as one of his most trusted and loved students, and it is likely that al-Sistani will soon appoint him as his successor. As a successor, al-Fayadh is more likely to deal directly with the United States and get involved in the transition process; however, he is also likely to antagonize the Sadrist nationalists, who view him as an Afghan foreigner who should not have a say in Iraq's politics. Two other Najaf-based clerics, the grand ayatollahs Bashir Hussein al-Najafi and Muhammad Said Hakim, are also potential candidates. It is unlikely that they will be the successors, however, because they are considered lesser scholars than al-Fayadh, who is highly respected by many Shiite Iraqis, particularly by the tribal chieftains of Najaf.

With the vacuum of authority in Najaf, new conflicts between Shiite groups will certainly come to light, especially in the oil-rich province of Basra, where SCIRI and the Sadrists, especially the Fadhila Party, compete for territorial control. With spawned rivalries among various Shiite groups (and subgroups), Iraq may also see an increase of sectarian conflict as anti-Shiite Salafi groups begin to increase their attacks on Shiites with the aim of creating more chaos in a community devoid of a central religious authority. Tehran can also extend its religious network in Najaf in order to establish the authority of Ayatollah Khamenei in the Najaf Hawza [18]. Khamenei's increase of influence in southern Iraq could seriously jeopardize the independence of the Hawza. These scenarios could also cause major problems for a transitional government in Baghdad that is seeking to establish authority in southern Iraq.

Therefore, what are the implications of a Sadr-Sistani partnership? First and foremost, the United States should be aware of the unpredictable politics of the Shiite community. The swing of alliances merits serious attention, despite the fact that sectarian identity will play a central role in the intra-Shiite relations in years to come. Second, the United States should also recognize the enduring authority of the Najaf Hawza and its sphere of influence in Shiite Iraq. This influence is so significant that even the defiant al-Sadr failed to challenge the establishment, let alone muster enough support to lead the Shiite community among the poor and the youth for his anti-occupation and nationalist image.

It was the common consensus in the academic and policy communities that after the Samarra bombing of 2006, al-Sistani had become a marginal figure. Despite his brief diminishing influence as a result of the rise of sectarian tensions, al-Sistani now appears to be back with even greater authority. He is supported by centuries of traditional authority and backed by an extensive financial and religious network that reaches beyond

Iraq and Iran. Both Tehran and al-Sadr know that al-Sistani should not be ignored. The United States should certainly do the same.

Originally published in *Terrorism Monitor*: Volume 5, Issue 6 on March 29, 2007.

Notes

1. International Crisis Group, "Iraq's Muqtada al-Al-Sadr: Spoiler or Stabilizer?" 3-6.
2. Ibid.
3. Author interview with an al-Sistani representative, Najaf, Iraq, August 7, 2005.
4. Vali Nasr, *The Shi'a Revival: How Conflicts within Islam Will Shape the Future* (New York: Norton, 2006), 194.
5. According to al-Sistani's representative in Najaf, Hamed Khafaf, the deal also included the disarming of the Mahdi Army, Baztab, "Moafeqat-e Moqtada va Dowlat-e Moaqat ba Pishnahade Ayatollah al-Sistani," September 3, 2004, http://www.baztab.com. The disarmament of the militia was never fully enforced.
6. Author interview with an al-Sistani representative, Najaf, Iraq, August 7, 2005. See also Nasr, 194.
7. Baztab, "Jalas-e Moshtarak-e Hakim va Moqtada al-Sadr ba Ayatollah al-Sistani," September 15, 2004, http://www.baztab.com.
8. Ibid.
9. The reason behind this call was mainly to show Shiite solidarity in the January 2005 elections. See Baztab, "Inetaf-e Marjayat Shi'I dar Moqableh Al-Sadriha baraye Vahdat-e Shiaan-e dar entekhabat," November 12, 2004, http://www.baztab.com.
10. Baztab, "Didar-e Moqtada al-Sadr va Ayatollah al-Sistani," March 29, 2005, http://www.baztab.com.
11. Hussain al-Kabi, "al-Sadr Yahath Mowaqf al-tiyar al-Sadri beshan al-Hukumat wa al-barleman ma al-Sistani," *al-Sabaah*, January 9, 2007.
12. Al-Sistani is reported to have advised al-Sadr the following: "You have two options: bear the consequences, on you and the Shiites in general, or withdraw into a corner," see Rod Nordland, "Silence of the Sadrists," *Newsweek*, March 12, 2007, 38.
13. Reported by Diyar al-Umari on al-Arabiya TV, February 19, 2007.
14. Author interview with a seminary student of al-Sistani in Qom, Iran, December 23, 2005.
15. Abdul al-Rahim Aghiqi Bakhshayeshi, *Faqihe Varasteh* (Qom: Novid Islam: 2003), 202.
16. Baztab, "Ayatollah al-Sistani: Az Amalkard Ahmadinejad Ulgo Begirid," November 11, 2006, http://www.baztab.com.
17. The case of Sadrist and SCIRI relations since 2003 merits serious attention.
18. The control of Najaf has been one of the primary objectives of the Iranian government in Iraq since the fall of Saddam's regime in 2003. In the last four years, Ayatollah Khamenei has established a center in Najaf, which pays the highest salary to the seminary students in the city. The extent of Tehran's influence in Najaf, however, is still limited, as al-Sistani and three other high-ranking clerics remain the most revered and influential religious authorities in the shrine city.

Divisions within the Iraqi Insurgency
By Lydia Khalil

With so many actors in the Iraqi insurgent theater, it is hard to keep track of the various permutations of militant Islamic groups and their alliances. It is going to become all the more difficult given recent splits and conflicts between and within indigenous Iraqi groups and al-Qaeda affiliates. The violence in Iraq has not abated, but the cohesiveness of the insurgency is certainly challenged. Iraqi insurgents are concerned about this given the recent fissure of a prominent indigenous group, the 1920 Revolution Brigades, and the fighting between al-Qaeda and their former allies within the Sunni Arab tribes. All militant groups within Iraq have been frantically calling for unity and insisting that recent splits are amicable, while al-Qaeda has been aggressively and violently demanding allegiance from all involved. Despite their best efforts, the Iraqi insurgency continues to splinter.

1920 Revolution Brigades Splits over Islamic State of Iraq

The most obvious example was the mid March announcement by the 1920 Revolution Brigades that they have split into two groups—one retaining the name of the 1920 Revolution Brigades, and the other calling itself Hamas-Iraq. The division was not just the result of internal disputes within the organization, but also accelerated by disagreements over the group's relationship with al-Qaeda (*al-Hayat*, March 31, 2007).

On March 27, for example, the leader of the 1920 Revolution Brigades, Harith Dhahir Khamis al-Dari, was killed by al-Qaeda for his reported negotiations with the government and his refusal to pledge allegiance to al-Qaeda's Islamic State of Iraq (Mohajroon.com, March 27, 2007; *Terrorism Focus*, April 10, 2007). While members of his tribe and the 1920 Revolution Brigades denied that he had any dealings with the government, it turns out that the off-shoot organization, Hamas-Iraq, is advocating more political activity, perhaps even modeling itself after the original Palestinian organization Hamas (Mohajroon.com, April 2007). The 1920 Revolution Brigades, however, denounced strongly Hamas-Iraq's advocacy of political participation and defended the Islamic State of Iraq. The recent debate in Iraq mirrors the larger disagreement that Ayman al-Zawahiri had with the Palestinian Hamas, in which he criticized their participation in elections (Muslim.net/vb, March 12, 2007).

Islamic Army in Iraq Ridicules Al-Qaeda

The elements of the 1920 Revolution Brigades that are now Hamas-Iraq are not the only ones to have quarreled with al-Qaeda's Islamic State of Iraq. The Islamic Army and Baathist elements within the insurgency, along with tribes making up the al-Anbar Salvation Council, have also conflicted with al-Qaeda (*Terrorism Focus*, March 28, 2006). The Islamic State of Iraq has come out so forcefully against those who have not submitted allegiance to its leader Abu Omar al-Baghdadi that it has created a backlash within indigenous elements of the Iraqi insurgency who resent al-Qaeda co-opting their indigenous struggle for global Islamic goals in which they do not necessarily believe.

In a lengthy statement posted on their website in April, the Islamic Army accused al-Qaeda of killing many of its members and of being behind attempts to discredit the Islamic Army within the insurgency. They even accused al-Qaeda of operating outside the *The Islamic State of Iraq has come out so forcefully against those who have not submitted allegiance to its leader Abu Omar al-Baghdadi that it has created a backlash within indigenous elements of the Iraqi insurgency who resent al-Qaeda co-opting their indigenous struggle for global Islamic goals in which they do not necessarily believe.* bounds of Islamic law and robbing and killing innocent Sunni civilians. They refuted Abu Omar al-Baghdadi's claim that the Islamic State of Iraq is the most powerful force operating in the insurgency and claimed that al-Qaeda has killed members of other insurgent groups like Ansar al-Sunna and the Mujahideen Army (Iaisite.info).

The Islamic Army's posting states that al-Qaeda rushed to label fellow Muslims as infidels without clear proof and calls on the "leaders of al-Qaeda, especially Osama bin Laden...to purify his faith and honor...it is not enough to declare disavowal of these deeds, but to correct their path" (http://iaisite.info). It is significant that the Islamic Army, after remaining silent about its disputes with al-Qaeda, is now choosing to go public. It even defended its position of being open to negotiating with the coalition under certain circumstances. In fact, the Islamic Army has become so disenchanted that it is now reported by Iraqi government sources that it is also bringing in other insurgent groups like the al-Rashidin Army, the Umar Brigades and the Black Banners to join the fight against al-Qaeda (*al-Quds al-Arabi*, April 2, 2007).

Baathist elements of the insurgency have also come out against al-Qaeda in Iraq. On March 18, 2007, Al Jazeera carried an interview by Dr. Abu Mohamed, spokesman for the Baath Party in Iraq. On Al Jazeera, Mohamed denied any relationship with al-Qaeda, saying, "their doctrine, vision and strategy differ from those of the Baath Party and remaining national resistance factions." The Baath Party has quarreled publicly with the Mujahideen Army and the Islamic Army in Iraq, who resent the Baath Party inflating their role within the insurgency. Both groups have issued statements on their websites and on jihadi forums diminishing the role of the Baath Party and their relationship to it, prompting a rebuttal by Baath leaders (al-Basrah.net, March 24, 2007).

Cohesion Challenged

Ansar al-Sunna, a powerful group within the insurgency and with past ties to al-Qaeda, has cautioned the insurgent groups against airing their disagreements publicly, warning Iraqis that reports of division are a new deceptive tactic by the Iraqi government and coalition forces (*Terrorism Monitor*, December 20, 2005). Abu Abdullah, a leader within Ansar al-Sunna, stated that the U.S. and Iraqi governments "found they were left with no other option but to resort to deception, misguidance and playing with words through the media" (Islamic Renewal Organization, March 30, 2007). At the same time, Ansar al-Sunna has responded to recent statements that it has allied with the Islamic State in Iraq and denied reports that it has joined a "coordination group" made up of other insurgent elements. Ansar al-Sunna's message is inconsistent in that it calls for unity, while it has fiercely retained its independence from other groups operating in the Iraqi theater.

Elements of the Iraqi insurgency routinely deny their contacts with the government and downplay the significance of splits within their respective organizations, saying they are for operational expediency. It is in their interest to maintain a public front of unity in many regards. Firstly, many insurgent groups deny contacts with the government so as not to jeopardize their jihadi credentials. Secondly, while divisions within the insurgency are very real, they do not want to air out their dirty laundry in public, believing that it will weaken their position vis-à-vis the government and coalition forces if they are believed to be capitulating. Critical statements of other groups are often couched under the banner of "advice." Thirdly, insurgent groups, regardless of their internal differences, want to portray reports of their splits as coalition propaganda attempts, revealing the Iraqi government's weak position, not their own. Nevertheless, divisions within the insurgency cannot be denied and present a critical opportunity for both the Iraqi government and coalition forces to exploit these divisions effectively.

Originally published in *Terrorism Monitor*: Volume 5, Issue 7 on April 12, 2007.

A Shiite Storm Looms on the Horizon: Sadr and SIIC Relations
By Babak Rahimi

Post-Baathist Iraqi politics is undergoing a dramatic change, and the Sadrists and the Supreme Islamic Iraqi Council (SIIC), formerly known as the Supreme Council for the Islamic Revolution in Iraq (SCIRI), are leading the way by bringing a major shift in the balance of power. With the gradual decomposition of Prime Minister Nuri al-Maliki's National Unity Government, mainly dominated by Shiite and Kurdish parties, Iraq is entering a new political era. As splintered political factions, such as the Sadrists, seek to form a new coalition made up of Sunni parties, formerly exiled Shiite groups like Da'wa and the SIIC are facing new challenges in maintaining a dominant political bloc in Baghdad.

Moqtada al-Sadr's call to create a "reform and reconciliation project," which would also include Sunnis, is a radical departure from his sectarian base which was formed with the United Iraqi Alliance (UIA) and under the spiritual leadership of Grand Ayatollah Ali al-Sistani in 2004 (*al-Hayat*, May 8, 2007). In addition, al-Sadr's move is a direct challenge to his main Shiite rival, the SIIC, which has posed the most serious threat to al-Sadr's political prestige and leadership in Iraq since 2003. For the most part, limited political mobility in the UIA and the al-Maliki government itself were the sources of frustration for the Sadrists, and most of the blame was directed at the SIIC for its political tactics to tame the Sadrist movement in the government. SIIC leader Abdul Aziz al-Hakim's May 13, 2007 call to change the name of the party from the Supreme Council for the Islamic Revolution in Iraq to the Supreme Islamic Iraqi Council, dropping the word "revolution" from the name, also brings to light a key move by Iraq's leading Shiite politician in preparing for the post-coalition era (*al-Hayat*, May 13, 2007). As the leader of Iraq's largest party, backed by possibly the largest militia in the Middle East, al-Hakim's

Due to the failure of the constitutional drafting process, tensions over key political issues, such as federalism and the distribution of oil, are paving the way toward a major Shiite-on-Shiite conflict.

new strategy also includes a renewed pledge of allegiance to Grand Ayatollah Ali al-Sistani and his Najaf-based religious organization (Al Jazeera, May 13, 2007; *Terrorism Monitor*, November 7, 2003). The reason for this symbolic reaffirmation of the party's political position is clear. Al-Hakim aims to distance his party from its exiled past when the party was based in Iran from the early 1980s to 2003, and reconstruct a Shiite Iraqi identity by aligning with the Najaf clerical authority. The call was also an attempt to establish distance from the Iranian shrine city of Qom, where Ayatollah Khamenei has considerable power over the religious and political institutions (Historiae.org, May 12, 2007).

Both factions are taking new positions in a shifting political landscape. Due to the failure of the constitutional drafting process, tensions over key political issues, such as federalism and the distribution of oil, are paving the way toward a major Shiite-on-Shiite conflict. The two parties appear to expect some sort of a political confrontation over the constitution after the future collapse of the al-Maliki government. What these new strategies also indicate is how the weakening of the Iraqi government is forcing Sadrists to expand their military prowess for control over cities and regions that are at the moment dominated by the SIIC's militia group, the Badr Organization. A major clash between the two Shiite parties can be expected in the future, and only a viable political solution can prevent a full outbreak of conflict.

Arch Rivals

The early history of Sadrist-SIIC conflict dates back to the competition between the al-Hakim and al-Sadr clan families over influence in the Da'wa party since its inception in 1959. When Ayatollah Baqir al-Sadr, the uncle of Moqtada, emerged as the most prominent leader of the Da'wa movement, Ayatollah Muhammad Baqir al-Hakim, as an active member of the party, was eclipsed by al-Sadr. Energetic, contemplative and charismatic, Baqir al-Sadr's impact as a political leader was so deep that after his assassination in 1980 he continued to inspire a cult-like following among the Shiite Iraqis. However, a major split in Shiite politics occurred when al-Hakim formed SCIRI (al-Majlis al-A'la lil Thawra al-Islamiya fil Iraq) in Tehran on November 17, 1982, with the help of Iran's Islamic Revolutionary Guard Corps. The formation of SCIRI in Iran was perceived by many Shiite Iraqis, including Moqtada al-Sadr's father, Ayatollah Sadeq al-Sadr, who later formed the Sadrist movement in the 1990s, as an Iranian intervention in the native Shiite Islamic politics, which was believed to remain a homegrown movement. Since its inception, SCIRI has been perceived as an alien, foreign agent by most Sadrists.

With the failure of the Badr Brigade's (Faylaq Badr) military venture against Saddam's army during the Shiite uprising in 1991, SCIRI's chance to win the popular support of the Shiite population was reduced considerably. The death of Ayatollah Khoi, the country's most senior cleric, in 1992 opened the way for the formation of alternative native Shiite movements to energize Shiite aspirations for freedom from Saddam's tyrannical rule, and Ayatollah Sadeq al-Sadr emerged as a leading candidate.

Sadeq al-Sadr's power base was so deeply grounded in the plebian Shiite population, especially in eastern Baghdad, that still four years after his assassination by Saddam's regime his movement continued to expand. On entering Iraq after more than 20 years of exile in Iran in 2003, al-Hakim witnessed the rise of a major Shiite political rival, a young cleric named Moqtada al-Sadr, who would publicly question his bravery and Iraqi credentials for not only failing to stand up to Saddam, but also for being a foreign agent backed by the Iranian government.

Violence has frequently erupted between the Mahdi Army and the Badr Organization since 2004 in cities like Baghdad, Basra and Diwaniya, and all of these clashes have their roots in this complicated historical setting. Yet such tension also reflects how each of these two parties aim to control the future of the country. Domination of the oil production in Basra and military control of major southern Iraqi provinces, especially in eastern Baghdad, is the key problem to this growing dilemma. There is also a major ideological rift: the envisaged future of Iraq as a nation-state by the two parties.

Although Sadrists are staunchly Shiites, they are, however, fervidly opposed to al-Hakim's August 2005 call for the formation of a nine-province Shiite region, with Basra as the major governmental center. As Iraqi nationalists, Sadrists are highly suspicious of a federalist model for Iraq and consider al-Hakim's proposal as one that would snatch away economic and political power from supporters of al-Sadr based in Baghdad. Al-Hakim, on the other hand, opposes al-Sadr's call for an alliance with Sunni Arabs and since 2004 has been hesitant to accept a deadline for a U.S. troop withdrawal from Iraq (Baztab, February 2004). Al-Hakim is worried that once U.S. forces leave Iraq, the Badr militia would have to confront the Mahdi Army and al-Sadr's young followers in Baghdad and Basra. Distrust of the adversary remains a major problem.

Iran and the al-Sistani Factors

In the middle of this conflict lies Iran and al-Sistani. By and large, both have a significant stake in this subtle standoff between two of Iraq's major political factions. Since an outbreak of conflict between the rival groups could harm their authority and influence in Iraq, Najaf and Tehran are doing their best to prevent a clash. Iran is desperately attempting to muster enough Shiite support for both expanding its influence in Iraq and protecting itself from potential U.S. attacks against its interests in the region. Al-Sadr could be a huge asset for Iran's regional ambitions, but he could also be a liability. For Tehran, al-Sadr is an independent Shiite voice who needs to be tamed and brought into the Qom-based Shiite power base with Khamenei recognized as the main source of authority.

Al-Sistani, however, shares al-Sadr's vision of a united, non-sectarian nation-state, but he vehemently opposes his youthful aspiration for power in Iraq. For al-Sistani, al-Sadr should be tamed and brought into the Najaf-based Shiite power base with al-Sistani and the other leading Shiite clerics recognized as the main sources of authority. SIIC's recent pledge of allegiance to al-Sistani, then, could be viewed as a shrewd way to create a rift between Najaf and al-Sadr by forcing al-Sistani to choose sides between them—even though al-Sistani would most likely refuse such factional politics. Despite al-Sadr's growing relationship with al-Sistani since the summer of 2006, al-Hakim knows that al-Sistani views al-Sadr as a potential threat to the Najaf orthodoxy (*Terrorism Monitor*, March 29, 2007). Therefore, SIIC's tactic is to indirectly force al-Sadr to become estranged from Najaf by renewing the party's allegiance to al-Sistani; at this crucial stage of the political game, it appears that alienating al-Sadr from Najaf remains a high priority for al-Hakim.

Yet, al-Hakim's political strategy is two-fold. By getting closer to al-Sistani, SIIC is building alliances with both Najaf and Tehran. Yet, he also appears to be expanding Khamenei's influence in Najaf, where the Badr Organization is controlling the shrine city, a symbol of Shiite power. Regardless of Tehran's involvement in al-Hakim's recent change of tactics, SIIC realizes that al-Sadr is a major threat to the party's influence, and that with the rapid rise of his popularity since 2006, both al-Sistani and Iran could play a major role in backing al-Hakim's party in case of a major eruption of conflict.

Policy Implications

The potential descent into an intra-sectarian civil war poses a serious danger to Iraq and the region. This sort of civil war could contribute to the formation of new Shiite groups, destabilization of the Iraqi government and the southern provinces, especially Basra, and lead to serious humanitarian catastrophes. Although such intra-sectarian conflict is essentially a political one, it also includes a significant religious component. Iraq is undergoing a shift in the balance of power among Shiite militant groups, and the best Washington can do is to hope for the victory of the orthodox Shiite institution in Najaf. It is with the authority of al-Sistani that fighting between these two militia groups can best be prevented.

The most practical strategy that the United States could adopt at this stage is to prevent the meltdown of the Iraqi government into a state of political factionalism; in reality, Iraq's worst enemy at this moment is the Baghdad government itself. The reason is that with the absence of a relatively centralized state, militias (regardless of their ethnic and sectarian associations) are bound to expand and continue to fight among themselves (and Iraqi and U.S. troops) for power. This general strategy also means that Washington should recognize the pivotal role of political integration, rather than military operative tactics (like the troop surge), against the radicalization of Shiite groups.

Regardless of the success or failure of the surge, the post-coalition era would need to see the formation of inter-sectarian political parties. In light of his recent call for the creation of a "reform and reconciliation project," al-Sadr could possibly lead the country to a new post-Baathist political era, in which Shiite and Sunni nationalists, who remained in Iraq during Saddam's reign, could unite against former exiled Shiite and Kurdish parties like the SIIC and the Kurdistan Democratic Party. The United States should encourage such political coalitions, despite its obvious anti-occupation (or anti-American) fervor. Nevertheless, although this new coalition can lessen sectarian tensions, it will not, however, do away with the Shiite militia competition over power and prestige. An SIIC-Sadrist clash looms ahead, and the best Washington can do is to contain it through an already fragile Iraqi government.

Originally published in *Terrorism Monitor*: Volume 5, Issue 10 on May 24, 2007.

The Surge, The Shiites and Nation Building in Iraq
By Reidar Visser

For some time, analysts have been suggesting that the Bush administration's "surge" strategy may have achieved a measure of success in certain parts of Iraq. Many highlight the tendency on the part of local tribes in the Sunni-dominated areas to stand up against al-Qaeda, in that way emphasizing their own "Iraqiness" as well as their unwillingness to join in an all-out war against Western civilization. The number of attacks against U.S. forces has declined in many of these areas, and there are signs that al-Qaeda has been forced to relocate to new areas and to choose new targets.

Perhaps the most convincing indicator of a degree of "surge" success is one that has gone largely unnoticed. Reports out of Baghdad suggest that the Sunni politicians who for the past two years or so have worked with the Americans through participating in government and parliament are now becoming increasingly nervous about internal Sunni competition from the newly emerged anti-jihadist tribal leaders of their "own" community, for example in places like the Anbar governorate [1]. In terms of Iraqi nation-building, this is a healthy sign. There was always a degree of doubt with regard to the true representativeness of the Sunni parties that emerged as "winners" in their fields in the heavily boycotted 2005 parliamentary elections. The fact that these parties are now worried about internal competition means that more Sunnis are interested in participating in the system, and that a group of politicians firmly attached to the vision of a unified Iraq but also enjoying solid popular backing in their core constituencies may be on the way up, assisted by the "surge." At the same time, foreign-sponsored groups, such as al-Qaeda, and office seekers whose popular legitimacy is in doubt (for instance, some members of the Tawafuq bloc) are coming under pressure or are even being weeded out.

South of Baghdad, the logical corollary to this kind of "surge" policy would have been to build local alliances with those Shiite groups that have a historical record of firm opposition to Iran and are unequivocal in their condemnation of Iranian interference in Iraq. The principal aim would be to create a counter-balance to the most pro-Iranian factions inside the system, such as the Supreme Islamic Iraqi Council, which is now known as the Islamic Supreme Council of Iraq (ISCI, formerly the Supreme Council for the Islamic Revolution in Iraq, SCIRI) and their Badr Brigades—organizations that since 2003 have been successful in obtaining a disproportionate degree of formal political power in the Iraqi political system and are currently profiting from their role in the Nuri al-Maliki government to consolidate their position further [2]. In the south, there is a vast array of groupings with a long record of hostility to Iran, above all the various Sadrist factions like Fadhila and the "mainline" followers of Moqtada al-Sadr (some of whom have even served jail sentences in Iranian prisons in the past), but also independent Shiite tribal groups that are fiercely proud of their Arab heritage [3]. These groups also distinguish themselves from ISCI in that they maintain that any kind of clerical rule in Iraq under the principle of *wilayat al-faqih* (the rule of the jurisprudent) should have as its point of departure Iraqi clerics and not Iranian ones [4].

Actual U.S. policy south of Baghdad is the exact opposite of this. Pro-Iranian ISCI and its friends in the Badr Organization (now powerful in the Iraqi security forces) are being supported by the United States in their efforts to bulldoze all kinds of internal Shiite opposition, as seen for instance in the large-scale battle against an alleged cultist movement at Najaf in January 2007, as well as in the ongoing operations against the Sadrist Mahdi Army and its splinter factions. Indiscriminate mass arrests have often accompanied these incidents, with the al-Maliki government's wholesale designation of its enemies as "terrorists" apparently being taken at face value by U.S. forces, and with the persistent complaints from those arrested about "Iranian intrigue" being ignored. Today, apart from isolated rural enclaves, the sole remaining bastions of solid Shiite resistance to ISCI outside Baghdad are Maysan and Basra (which happen to be located outside direct U.S. control, in the British zone in the far south), but here too change may be underway: ISCI has worked for more than one year to unseat the Fadhila governor of oil-rich Basra (he remained in office by early September 2007 despite an order by al-Maliki to have him replaced), and the Badr Brigades are reportedly influential within the security forces in Maysan. Ironically, long-standing enemies of Iran like the Fadhila party are now feeling so isolated that they see no other recourse than to upgrade contacts with their erstwhile foes in Tehran, if only tentatively [5]. The apparent U.S. rationale for letting all this happen is the idea that the Sadrist Mahdi Army somehow constitutes their worst opponent in Iraq, and that some Mahdi Army factions are even being supplied with arms from Tehran.

An alternative reading is that Iran could be deliberately feeding weaponry to marginal (or splinter) elements of the Sadrists precisely in order to weaken the Sadrist movement as a whole, and to make sure that Sadrist energy is combusted in clashes with U.S. forces. Right now, from Tehran's point of view, the implementation of the "surge" south of Baghdad could not have been more perfect. Today, U.S. forces are working around the clock to weaken Tehran's traditional arch-enemy in Iraq's Shiite heartland—the Sadrists—while Iran's preferred and privileged partner since the 1980s, SCIRI/ISCI, keeps strengthening its influence everywhere. Back in the United States, think tanks concentrate on the ties between Sadrists and Iran and consistently overlook those factions that have truly close and long-standing ties to Tehran, whereas the recently released National Intelligence Estimate was devoid of initiatives to bring the Shiites into a more reconciliatory mode—suggesting that few ideas exist in Washington about alternative Shiite policies. The U.S. mainstream media also make a contribution: after having first demonized Ibrahim al-Jaafari for alleged ties to Iran back in 2005, U.S. newspapers are now using big headlines every time there is the slightest hint about some kind of connection between Iran and Moqtada al-Sadr. On top of all this, the U.S. military itself is exposed to a significant irritant through its constant encounters with militia splinter groups and the low-level conflict that comes with them—no doubt another factor that works to Tehran's advantage.

The great irony in this is that, from the historical perspective, the neo-conservative working assumption that Iraqi Shiites can be trusted to resist Iranian domination is generally sound—with the sole exception of the particular faction on which Washington has fixed its eyes as its special partner in the country. In the 1980s, SCIRI was designed by Iran to maximize Tehran's control of the unruly Iraqi opposition. Throughout its history, it has stressed the importance of subservience to Iran's leaders, first Khomeini and later Khamenei [6]. In the mid-1990s, its leader Muhammad Baqir al-Hakim became one of the first Shiite intellectuals to produce an elaborate plan for the political unification of the Shiites from Iran to Lebanon in a federal system under the leadership of Tehran, and as late as 1999 one of SCIRI's key figures, Sadr al-Din al-Qubbanji, angrily attacked the Sadrists for daring to suggest that the Iraqi Shiite opposition could operate independently of Khamenei [7]. Close scrutiny of SCIRI's highly publicized name change and supposed "ideological makeover" in May 2007 shows that none of this heritage has been annulled in a convincing manner: the new and much trumpeted "pledge" to Grand Ayatollah Ali al-Sistani is in reality nothing more than a non-committal expression of general praise, and there is no renunciation of a decades-long policy of subordination to Khamenei [8]. It is suspicious that ISCI and Iran still hold virtually synchronized views on the sacrosanctity of the al-Maliki government and the 2005 constitution. Both tend to describe the idea of challenging al-Maliki as "subversive coup activity," and they are unified in rejecting challenges to the constitution by what they describe as neo-Baathists [9].

The problem is that Washington's "surge" is framed as a straightforward counter-insurgency operation in which the nation-building component is in the far background. "The enemy" is defined on the basis of a myopic interpretation of who is directly hostile to U.S. forces while the historical dimension of alliance patterns between Iran and Iraqi Shiite factions is overlooked. This prevents Washington from fully understanding who is friend and foe in Iraq. It is conceivable that ISCI may assist Washington in temporarily reducing the amount of noise out of Iraq, and this may well be what the Bush administration is looking for right now. Yet, even if its members are more genteel and well-behaved than the Sadrists, it is highly unclear what kind of "moderation" ISCI is really capable of delivering in Iraq, especially in terms of a political system based on true reconciliation between Shiites and Sunnis [10]. For that to be brought about, many Iraqis, regardless of sectarian affiliation, will require unequivocal answers from ISCI on certain key questions: Does its leadership still believe in the principle of the rule of the jurisprudent (*wilayat al-faqih*) and the idea of a supreme Shiite leader (*wali amr al-muslimin*), and if so,

> *The problem is that Washington's "surge" is framed as a straightforward counter-insurgency operation in which the nation-building component is in the far background. "The enemy" is defined on the basis of a myopic interpretation of who is directly hostile to U.S. forces while the historical dimension of alliance patterns between Iran and Iraqi Shiite factions is overlooked.*

whom do they consider to be the current holder of this leadership role? Are they prepared to reject, squarely and explicitly, any possible role for Iran's Khamenei in shaping their policies? Can they offer reassurances to the Iraqi people that the Iran-dominated pan-Shiite federation scheme laid out by Muhammad Baqir al-Hakim in 'Aqidatuna in the 1990s is now null and void? After all, the futility of an approach based on vague ideas about "moderate, pro-U.S. personalities" and private assurances to U.S. officials ("Iraq will never become a carbon copy of Iran") is particularly pronounced in the strictly hierarchical Shiite context. All orthodox Shiites who are not themselves qualified theologians (mujtahids) will have to defer to the higher clergy on important issues. None of the Shiite operators in Iraq with whom Washington has been dealing is a recognized mujtahid.

Clarification of these issues would help ISCI enormously and could assist the party in finding a much more constructive role as a key mainstream, truly "moderate" player in Iraqi politics. But until answers from ISCI are forthcoming in a very public way (rather than in hazy name changes and in private meetings with U.S. special envoys), many Iraqis will remain ambivalent about the organization's ties to Iran. In that situation, the "surge" will be doomed to fail unless it can be redefined to include a credible nation-building component aimed at areas south of Baghdad: the Iraqi nationalist Shiites will remain on the margins, and the alliance of ISCI and the two Kurdish parties will feel that they can safely continue to ignore the Sunnis, secularists and independent Shiites and their calls for a more substantial constitutional revision (and true national reconciliation). Even the main Sadrist parties, which have invested considerable energy in presenting themselves as "made in Iraq" and ridiculing ISCI for its ties to Iran, could end up as ironic Iranian clients unless Washington starts dealing with them in a more constructive way.

Still, if the United States is willing to rethink some of its fundamental assumptions about Iraqi politics, several options for policy adjustments remain. Washington could, for instance, take a more open-minded approach to the ongoing efforts to create a more broadly based coalition in opposition to the al-Maliki government—such as, for instance, the latest efforts by Ibrahim al-Jaafari and Iyad Allawi to engineer cross-sectarian coalitions, and as seen in the recent decision by the legal committee of the Iraqi parliament to condemn al-Maliki's decision to sack the Basra governor [11]. In theory, these kinds of alliances could be capable of compromises on issues where consensus has eluded the al-Maliki government (like the oil law and federalism), and whereas the United States should certainly refrain from backroom machinations (which would only taint any alternative government), it could focus on simply recalibrating its own policies—including its "surge"—so as to ensure that the newly improved participation of the Sunni community within the system is accompanied by parallel positive developments among the Iraqi Shiites. That, in itself, could be enough to help the Da'wa party move back to its Iraqi nationalist ideals, and thereby nudge the al-Maliki government into a more conciliatory mode. Conversely, if Washington continues to conceive of "the Iranian threat" in Iraq as exclusively a matter of security in the most palpable sense—meaning "Sadrist terrorists"—then Tehran and its ISCI allies seem set for easy sailing in Iraq.

Originally published in *Terrorism Monitor*: Volume 5, Issue 17 on September 13, 2007.

Notes

1. Author interview with a member of the Iraqi National Security Council, June 2007.

2. According to a formal statement dated July 31, 2007, the party henceforth wishes to be referred to in English with the abbreviation ISCI; e-mail from Karim al-Musawi of the ISCI Washington office dated August 11, 2007. Separately, for a critical perspective on SCIRI's level of popular support in the December 2005 elections, see Reidar Visser, "SCIRI, Daawa and Sadrists in the Certified Iraq Elections Results," February 11, 2006, http://www.historiae.org/sciri.asp.

3. An excellent source on the historical roots of the long-standing enmity between the Sadrists and Iran is Fa'iq al-Shaykh Ali, *Ightiyal sha'b* (London: Al-Rafid, 2000).

4. Recent examples of such attitudes include an article penned by Fadhila member Abu Taqi, "Muqarina bayna al-nizam al-dakhili li-hizb al-fadila al-islami wa-wilayat al-faqih," January 7, 2007, with a note of approval by Muhammad al-Ya'qubi dated 20 Dhi al-Hijja 1427 (January 10, 2007). The article clearly refers to a specifically Iraqi rather than an Iranian context. See also 'Adil Ra'uf, *Muhammad muhammad sadiq al-sadr: marja'iyyat al-maydan* (Damascus: Al-Markaz al-'Iraqi li-a-I'lam wa-al-Dirasat, 1999), 53–57.

5. Fadhila's move to open offices in Tehran has been particularly conspicuous; see press release from the Fadhila party dated October 22, 2006.

6. The cliché that Iran had no ambition about acting as overlord in Iraq in the 1980s lacks a sound empirical basis. SCIRI leaders like Muhammad Baqir al-Hakim and Sadr al-Din al-Qubbanji wrote frequently about the need for ultimate subordination to Khomeini even if a façade of Iraqi separateness might be retained; see for instance Liwa' al-Sadr, April 28, 1982, p. 8, and Liwa' al-Sadr, October 4, 1987.

7. Muhammad Baqir al-Hakim, *'Aqidatuna wa-ru'yatuna al-siysiyya*, a pamphlet published at the Hakim website (http://www.al-hakim.com) before 2003 but removed soon after the start of the Iraq war. Also, Al-Muballigh al-Risali, February 15, 1999.

8. SCIRI/ISCI, *"Al-bayan al-khatami li-mu'tamar al-dawra al-tasi'a li-al-hay'a al-'amma li-al-majlis al-a'la al-islami al-'iraqi,"* May 12, 2007.

9. See for instance comments by Hasan Ruhani quoted in *E'temad*, April 26, 2006.

10. Characteristically, supporters of the ISCI scheme to create a single federal Shiite entity have been among the most prominent critics of the (Shiite) Fadhila party's dialogue with Sunni politicians; see open letter from Ahmad al-Shammari to Nadim al-Jabiri, January 2006, http://www.nahrainnet.net/news/51/ARTICLE/6968/2006-01-21.html.

11. See *al-Hayat*, August 7, 2007. Letter from the legal committee of the Iraqi parliament to Nuri al-Maliki dated July 30, 2007.

Sufi Insurgent Groups in Iraq
By Fadhil Ali

The mystical approach to Islam known as Sufism has deep roots in Iraqi society. Adherents to Sufism normally stress prayer, meditation and the recitation of the various names of God as part of their effort to create a mystical communion between themselves and Allah. Yet at various times and places—such as 19th century Africa or the 19th and 20th century North Caucasus—Sufi orders have formed the core resistance to colonial and imperial occupation efforts. Heavily criticized within Iraq during the first two years of the current U.S. occupation for focusing on spiritual matters rather than resistance, Iraq's Sufis have begun to take up arms against Coalition forces.

In the early days of Islam, Sufis tended to be lone ascetics known for wearing suf (rough wool garments), but gradually they began to organize around spiritual leaders known as sheikhs, or pirs. One of the greatest Sufi orders, the Qadiria, was founded in Baghdad by Abd al-Qadir al-Jilani, who lived from 1078 to 1166. The second most prominent Sufi order in Iraq is the Naqshbandia, introduced to Iraq from India by Sheikh Khalid Naqshbandi in the early 13th century. Despite the common perception that Sufism is a strictly non-violent form of Sunni Islam, there are at least three insurgent groups in Iraq today that claim to be Sufi:

• Jaysh Rijal al-Tariqa al-Naqshbandia (The Men of the Army of al-Naqshbandia Order, or JRTN) is the largest Sufi insurgent group. The group announced its formation in December 2006, right after the execution of Saddam Hussein.

• Katibat al-Sheikh Abd al-Qadir al-Jilanin Al-Jihadia (The Jihadi Battalion of Sheikh Abd al-Qadir al-Jilani) was announced in August 2006.

• The Sufi Squadron of Sheikh Abd al-Qadir al-Jilani was founded in April 2005.

For hundreds of years the founders and leaders of various tariqas (Sufi orders) developed special rituals, chants and even dances to pursue the spiritual dimension of Islam and praise God and his prophet Muhammad. Sufis have been frequently criticized by Salafist Muslims for syncretism with pre-Islamic religious practices, innovation in methods of worship and the veneration of their sheikhs and their burial places, which tend to become places of pilgrimage.

In Iraq, the Qadiria—both Arab and Kurd—are divided into several branches. The largest branch, the Kasnazania, is headed by Sheikh Muhammad Abd al-Karim al-Kasnazan, who lives in the city of al-Sulaimania. The Naqshbandia is led by Sheikh Abdullah Mustafa al-Naqshbandi, who lives in the city of Erbil. A third important group is the al-Rifa'ia order, whose branches do not acknowledge the leadership of a single sheikh. According to Nehru al-Kasnazan—son of Sheikh Muhammad al-Kasnazan—there are currently three million adherents to the various Sufi orders in Iraq (al-Arabiya.net, August 23, 2005).

The Sufis enjoyed many freedoms when Saddam Hussein was in power. Ezzat Ibrahim al-Douri, his vice-president and the current head of the banned al-Baath party, is a well-known Qadiri Sufi. The former sheikh of the Iraqi Qadiria, Muhammad al-Hallab, was strongly criticized by other members of the order for the haste with which he advanced al-Douri through the spiritual teachings of the order without adequate preparation (*Mafkarat al-Islam*, August 24, 2006).

Reaction to the Collapse of the Baathist Regime

After the fall of the Baathist regime in April 2003 and the development of a large-scale Sunni insurgency, none of the leading Sufi groups called for violence during the first years of the occupation. Sufis watched the insurgency being dominated by their historical opponents, the Salafis. Militant groups affiliated to al-Qaeda have attacked Sufis and their sacred places—including the demolition of tombs of Sufi saints—but on one remarkable occasion Sufis and Salafis fought together in the battles for Fallujah in 2004. The insurgents were under the leadership of Sheikh Abdullah al-Janabi, who is an adherent of a minor Sufi order called al-Nabhania. Al-Janabi was the head of the Mujahideen Shura Council, which controlled the Sunni city until December 2004. The Council was an umbrella organization of Salafi, Sufi and Baathi groups.

With the escalation of Sunni-Shiite sectarian violence in post-invasion Iraq, Sufis started to complain of attacks by Shiite militias. The Kasnazani Qadiris called for civil peace through a fatwa proclaimed on their website, television station and the Mashriq newspaper. Other Qadiris had a different response to the growing violence. In April 2005 the Sufi Squadron of Sheikh Abd al-Qadir al-Jilani announced their formation as an anti-American armed group. According to statements in jihadi websites and forums, the group is especially active in and around the northern city of Mosul, where it is involved in setting road-side improvised explosive devices (IEDs) and sniper attacks against U.S. forces. Statements issued directly by the group are issued by the authority of the "General commanding the jihadi armed forces" and are published by the Baath website, www.al-basra.net.

A few months later the creation of the Jihadi Battalion of Sheikh Abd al-Qadir al-Jilani was announced in the town of al-Haweeja near the northern city of Kirkuk (Mafkarat al-Islam, August 23, 2006). The Qadiri Sufi lodge in Kirkuk has both Kurdish and Arab members. The head of al-Qadiria in Kirkuk, Sheikh Abd al-Rahim al-Qadiri, ordered his followers to suspend their usual Sufi rituals and practices to form a battalion to fight U.S. troops, Iraqi

Heavily criticized within Iraq during the first two years of the current U.S. occupation for focusing on spiritual matters rather than resistance, Iraq's Sufis have begun to take up arms against Coalition forces.

government forces and the Shiite militias of Badr Corps and al-Mahdi Army. Al-Qadiri disappeared several days before the announcement was made, though it is believed that he may have gone underground to lead the combat operations of his followers. Little activity from this group has been observed since their leader's disappearance, but the area in and around Kirkuk is still one of the most volatile in Iraq.

Formation of the JRTN

On the same day as the hanging of Saddam Hussein on December 30, 2006, the Men of the Army of al-Naqshbandia Order (JRTN) announced their formation. The JRTN is clearly the most organized of the three aforementioned groups. In a sign typical of Baathist and Arab nationalism—but one that contradicts the pan-ethnic nature of Sufism—the main page of the JRTN's website is headed by a map of the Arab homeland of 22 countries stretching from the Middle East to North Africa. The terminology used on the website also indicates that the JRTN is a Baathist-dominated organization that reflects a growing trend within the party towards Islamism since the early 1990s. This trend is represented today by the wing led by Ezzat Ibrahim al-Douri more than the rival wing led by Muhammad Younis al-Ahmad, which is hosted and sponsored by Syria and its secular Baathist regime.

The target of the JRTN attacks is the Coalition forces, "the unbeliever-occupier" as they are referred to in the group's doctrine. The following principles form the JRTN canon:

• The individuals, equipment and supplies of the Coalition forces are to be targeted anytime and anywhere in Iraq.
• Iraqis have not been and will not be targeted unless they fight with the Coalition.
• There will be no confrontations with other jihadi groups; the JRTN will cooperate with them as long as they remain committed to "the legitimate constant principles and the national agenda," which likely means the Baath agenda and policies.
• Funding is accepted from Muslim supporters, but not from any other external resource that might apply conditions.
• Secrecy is a vital principle in planning and implementing operations.
• There will be no participation in the political process in Iraq under the occupation.

The al-Naqshbandia website and the monthly online magazine regularly release videos of the group's military operations as well as statements outlining their military and political positions (*Terrorism Focus*, January 8, 2008).

According to the JRTN website, the backbone of the militant formations is the followers and supporters of the Naqshbandia order, who follow operational doctrines formed during the first week of the 2003 invasion by a gathering of Naqshbandia clerics, military men and professionals.

The lightly-equipped JRTN have used guerrilla tactics to launch a long war of attrition against Coalition forces armed with the most developed weapons and communications systems. During the early stages of combat, the fighters arranged themselves in small groups of 7-10 fighters, each with a local *amir* (commander). There were commanders in every province, each connected to the "Amir al-jihad," who was the grand sheikh of al-Naqshbandia. Military staff worked under the sheikh. These jihadi groups used light and medium rifles, road-side bombs and anti-tank RPG-7 grenade launchers in urban warfare against the Coalition. They were involved in the first battle of Fallujah in April 2004, where a number of Naqshbandia clerics were among the JRTN casualties.

Mortar and rocket assault groups were formed to attack Coalition bases at the Baghdad airport and the Green Zone, in addition to air bases in al-Anbar, al-Tameem, Ninawa, Salah al-Din and Diyala provinces. The JRTN also claim responsibility for a series of bombing operations, including the October 2003 attack on the Green Zone's al-Rasheed hotel by a rocket array during a visit by then Deputy Secretary of Defense Paul Wolfowitz. They also claim attacks on the headquarters of the Ministry of Oil and hotels used by foreign companies operating in Baghdad.

After two years of using small-group tactics, the commanders of JRTN formations decided after strategic study to reorganize their units to form a corps based on the standards of the old Iraqi Army. These preparations are being taken to prepare for a coming battle to control Baghdad and eventually the whole of Iraq. This transformation brought the following benefits:

• The range of operations has been expanded with the help of other small local groups.
• It has become possible to implement brigade-size operations, according to plans set by commanders assisted by military staff.
• It has become possible to launch division-wide maneuvers to deploy troops through any sector for support purposes or to implement a joint operation in another sector.

The JRTN also indicates that they have the skilled personnel and workshops needed to maintain, develop and modify different types of weapons and ammunition. The group has lately joined The Supreme Command for Jihad and Liberation, a Baathist umbrella group. On the Supreme Command's website, the JRTN is listed first of the 22 affiliated insurgent groups.

Conclusion

Joining the insurgency was not the decision of the recognized leaderships of Iraqi Sufi orders. The pressure of attacks by Salafis and Shiite militias appears to have played a major role in convincing Sufis in some areas to defy the non-violent doctrine of their traditional leaders. In response to sectarian violence and military occupation, few of the Sufis turned to Salafist groups like al-Qaeda in Iraq, but those who decided to fight joined the more familiar Baathist-led resistance.

Al-Douri's wing of the Baath Party continues to wield its traditional influence on the Sufis. Many Sufis were originally Baathists, so it was not difficult for the party to recruit them. In most areas of Iraq, Sufi insurgents are either Baathists or controlled and directed by al-Baath. Efforts to take the Sufis out of the insurgency will have little success without first breaking the bond between the Sufis and Ezzat al-Douri's organization. Easing the Shiite-Sunni sectarian conflict would be a significant step toward removing the Sufis from the frontlines.

Originally published in *Terrorism Monitor*: Volume 6, Issue 2 on January 24, 2008.

Becoming an Ayatollah: The New Iraqi Politics of Moqtada al-Sadr
By Babak Rahimi

As a political and military force, Iraq's Shiite Sadrist movement has undergone a number of radical transformations since 2003, when its leader, Moqtada al-Sadr, surprisingly emerged as a leading political figure. Al-Sadr's recent decision to continue with his seminary studies and graduate as an ayatollah at the conservative seminary school of Najaf underpins a major change in the movement's structure that could have serious repercussions for the future of Iraq. Against the backdrop of changing political alliances between Kurds and Sunnis, al-Sadr is transforming his movement into a new political phenomenon with implications for the country's political structure and security dynamics. The consequences are also immense for Shiite Iraq, posing serious challenges to the conservative clerical establishment in Najaf.

Al-Sadr's attempt to become an ayatollah follows his earlier call to suspend operations by his militia, the Jaish al-Mahdi (The Mahdi Army, or JAM) in the summer of 2007. Together with his decision to study in Najaf, this has marked a decisive new beginning in the organizational structure and leadership dynamics of the Mahdi militia. The decision to suspend JAM was made largely because of the outbreak of violence between Mahdi forces and the rival Badr Organization in Karbala in August 2007 (*Aftab-e Yazd* [Iran], August 30, 2007). The incident was a major embarrassment for al-Sadr, who had been seeking the support of Ayatollah Ali al-Sistani, Shiite Iraq's grand cleric, and the conservative establishment in Tehran against the rebellious splinter groups within his own militia since 2005. The suspension, which came in August 2007, was a way to ensure his Shiite partners that he was willing to restructure his forces for the sake of Shiite unity at a time when US—or Israeli—forces seemed to be on the brink of starting a major military conflict with Iran.

The call was welcomed by al-Sistani, who had been encouraging al-Sadr to arrive at such a decision since January 2007 [1]. The two met in June to discuss the problem of JAM splinter groups (*Aftab-e Yazd*, June 14, 2007).

Najaf and Tehran both share an interest in containing al-Sadr and his militia, as well as bringing his paramilitary organization—and other shadowy anti-Najaf movements—under the control of the Shiite clerical establishment. For Najaf and Tehran, the best way to tame al-Sadr is to chip away at his popular base through the electoral process and intra-Shiite negotiations, such as the October 2007 cooperation pact with rival Shiite leader Abdul Aziz al-Hakim (Fars News Agency, October 6, 2007). This would, accordingly, diminish his status as a charismatic militant leader defiant of existing institutions.

Al-Sadr's decision to become an ayatollah, along with his suspension of JAM, is an indicator of more complex transformations occurring within the Sadrist movement. Al-Sadr is not merely trying to gain religious legitimacy by becoming an ayatollah, but also access to a major source of religious and financial capital that is primarily under the control of high-ranking Shiite clerics in Najaf. Since his family legacy alone would not entitle him to what his father had acquired as a senior jurist (*marja taqlid*, or "source of imitation") in the 1990s, becoming an ayatollah would guarantee al-Sadr access to religious capital that has been solely in the domain of high-ranking clerics for centuries. The attainment of religious credentials through the traditional seminary complex can provide al-Sadr with enhanced authority over spiritual matters, such as the ability to issue a fatwa (religious verdict) and control religious taxes, powers he now lacks as a junior cleric. If successful, al-Sadr could extricate himself from the authority of Najaf with its strict hierarchical set of power relations and close familial ties to Iran and beyond. It could also help him get rid of the influence of Iranian-born clerics by refusing al-Sistani's mentorship, instead studying under an Afghan-born senior cleric, Grand Ayatollah, Shaykh Ishaq Fayyaz (*Shahrvand-e Emrooz* [Tehran], December 30, 2007).

Al-Sadr's New Political Strategy

How could these developments impact Iraq's security politics? First off, with an inflated religious authority, al-Sadr could wield greater power in regions where he lacks influence. In Basra especially, al-Sadr prepares to tackle his most powerful rival, the Badr Organization, by propagating his new image in tribal and urban regions of the province [2]. In a significant sense, al-Sadr wants legitimacy in places where he is mostly viewed as a young cleric of low-ranking scholarly status. By flexing his muscle as a high-ranking spiritual leader, Basra may witness a new series of conflicts between rival Shiite groups with equal claim to religious legitimacy in the traditional Shiite sense.

But al-Sadr also aims to consolidate his power by bringing together his followers and identifying himself as their sole spiritual leader. This would ultimately undermine al-Sistani's influence among his younger followers who may revere al-Sadr but obey al-Sistani on matters of religious and potentially political importance. By further consolidating power in terms of attaining religious authority, al-Sadr is preparing to revitalize his organization as a new religious-political movement with a highly centralized military branch. Under this new leadership, the political branch of the Sadrist movement will most likely be strengthened and the unruly JAM subordinated to the civilian—i.e. clerical—leaders of the movement.

Second, al-Sadr's rise to the rank of ayatollah will reinforce his Iraqi identity. The move towards nationalism should be seen as a way to challenge the transnationalism of Najaf by creating a new form of Shiite politics free from non-Iraqi influence. Aside from their plans to centralize control over oil reserves, one of the reasons al-Sadr and his parliamentarian representatives have sided with the secular National List of former Prime Minister Ilyad Allawi and Sunni leader Salah al-Mutlak's National Dialogue Front is to create a new parliamentary bloc to challenge Najaf and its influence over the four-party alliance of Nuri-Maliki by carving out a new political front of nationalist parties (Al Jazeera, January 14, 2008). Al-Sadr is playing a delicate game of balancing his position between nationalism and sectarianism, though his appeal to Shiite factionalism is mainly aimed at bolstering his base where he is now seeking a new constituency and a more centralized political movement.

The focus on a nationalistic leadership strategy can also be attributed to the ongoing political transformation of Sunni politics on the parliamentary level. The new agreement signed between the Patriotic Union of Kurdistan (PUK), the Kurdistan Democratic Party (KDP) and the Sunni Iraqi Islamic Party (IIP)—which led to the formation of a new Kurdish-Sunni alliance (*Terrorism Monitor*, January 11, 2008)—can further push al-Sadr to the nationalist camp. With the possibility of Ninawa province and the city of Mosul coming largely under the administrative control of Iraqi Kurdistan—as one of the key points of agreement between IIP leader Tariq al-Hashimi and the Kurdish parties and the ascendancy of Kurdish nationalism marked by symbolic events like the display of a Kurdish flag by the regional parliament of Kurdistan (*al-Sabaah*, January 16, 2008)—al-Sadr and his followers are bound to move to the nationalist and anti-federalist camp of the Iraqi parliament.

In this altered political setting, the new JAM could emerge as a powerful militia, a fully organized, disciplined paramilitary force, vying not only for domination over other Shiite militias in the southern regions, but possibly challenging the Kurdish militias in Baghdad and northern Iraq. Due to the shadowy network apparatus of the militia, the military might of the new JAM should not be underestimated. It may help to better understand how the new JAM may emerge as a new military force by briefly reviewing its formation since 2003.

By further consolidating power in terms of attaining religious authority, al-Sadr is preparing to revitalize his organization as a new religious-political movement with a highly centralized military branch.

The Transformation of a Militia

When dozens of young Shiite volunteers responded in June 2003 to a fiery call by the maverick cleric to join JAM, the U.S. administration and the Coalition authorities dismissed the new paramilitary force as nothing more than a nuisance. The militia, the Coalition Provisional Authority (CPA) argued, would disappear—along with the insurgency—once the Coalition troops completed the process of de-Baathification and the institutionalization of democracy in the country. But this was a major understatement. In reality, al-Sadr's armed forces were not just a "gang," but a newly formed unit of militants drawn largely from former Shiite infantry from Saddam's army and downtrodden unemployed young people based in the slums of Sadr City.

Surprisingly, the militia grew into a sizable force of more than 6,000 nearly a year after the U.S.-led invasion of Iraq. Its expanding network of operatives grew in parts of the country where Coalition and Iraqi security forces failed to protect civilians against insurgent attacks and criminal activities. To many military analysts who truly realized the growing importance of the up-and-coming militia, JAM represented a complex set of social and religious currents in Shiite Iraqi society that were largely forced underground during the Baathist era. Its appearance after the fall of Saddam's regime underlined the formation of a momentous social movement with real and legitimate grievances that merited serious attention at a time when Iraqi politics was undergoing major transformations under the occupation.

From late 2003 to spring 2004, JAM quickly grew in size and strength. From 2005 to 2006, JAM's rapid expansion in size and influence astonished even those observers who correctly predicted the rise of the Sadrists as a major military force in the post-Baathist era. By December 2006, JAM had an estimated membership of 60,000 armed men, constituting a major military force competing for power in the streets of Iraq.

The two main reasons for JAM's initial success can be identified as follows. First and foremost, the Sadrist armed forces were effective in providing security for the local population in exchange for loyalty and allegiance to the movement. In the neighborhoods of Sadr City, where the militia's headquarters is based, JAM is revered as a vigilant public institution that operates to safeguard the economic, legal and political interests of the Shiite community. In light of the bombing of the Sammara shrine in 2006, which unleashed a new wave of sectarian violence in the country, JAM gained even more prestige among the Shiite inhabitants of the slums for their ability to protect the community against Wahabi militants. The Sadrist militias were also able to provide security for the Shiite population in diverse places around the country, especially during religious festivals in shrine cities like Karbala and Najaf when members of the Badr Organization were primarily busy protecting officials of the Supreme Islamic Iraqi Council (SIIC).

Second, under the leadership of its politically shrewd leader, JAM was successful in combining its populist ideology with social programs aimed at supporting the lower-income strata of the Shiite population. The Sadrists are avid advocates of social justice and try to represent the more economically disenfranchised Shiite Iraqis, who make up a considerable portion of the southern urban regions and parts of the capital city. The Sadrist militants are inspired by the apocalyptic teachings of Moqtada al-Sadr's father, Grand Ayatollah Muhammad Muhammad Sadiq al-Sadr, whose execution by Saddam in 1999 elevated his prestige to a cultic figure of immortal status. The core of these teachings is a belief in the millenarian notion of the return of a messianic figure, in this case the twelfth Imam and Mahdi, Muhammad ibn Hassan (born in 868 C.E.), whose reappearance—as he is already on earth but concealed from view—will establish justice in a world infected by sin and oppression. The spiritual mission of the militia is to hasten the Imam's return through various heroic enactments of self-sacrifice, though at times these acts may merely mean offering selfless service to the Shiite public. In this ideological spirit, JAM is known to operate both as a military unit and a charity group.

The New JAM(s)?

Although it remains to be seen whether JAM will re-emerge as a more disciplined militia under the full control of al-Sadr, February 2008 will most likely witness the rise of a new JAM with a better trained military corps, a centralized command apparatus and tightly watched areas of operation. Iran's Revolutionary Guards—or perhaps Lebanese Hezbollah—may play a more direct role in the organizational restructuring process, though much of this may depend on the future of U.S.-Iranian relations. With Hezbollah of Lebanon serving as a model for the new JAM, the result could be an impressive, newly equipped and armed military force, unlike its origin as a populist militia with limited abilities (*Shahrvand-e Emrooz*, December 30, 2007).

But this new development contains the danger of upsetting many Sadrists who may feel left out from the reorganized militia, inflating the number of existing splinter groups. Those members of al-Sadr's militia who are desperately seeking new leadership from a charismatic leader who can bravely uphold the movement's nationalist and anti-establishment ideology have the greatest risk of splitting from the existing militia. The new JAM unveiled in early 2007 may give way to an upsurge of new Sadrist movements, all claiming to represent the authentic ideals of al-Sadr's father, though all differing in the ways in which they operate in the militia-ridden landscape of Shiite Iraq.

All in all, al-Sadr's choice of strategy is significant. It signals a new era of Iraqi politics that will likely revolve around control over resources—i.e., oil—and territorial domination—i.e., militia power—rather than identity politics of the ethnic and sectarian sort witnessed in the earlier years of the post-war period. Although the decline of sectarianism is certainly good for Iraq, the rise of a new factional struggle for control over resources may only breed new forms of militia politics. The appearance of the new JAM may serve as a sign of an ominous future.

Originally published in *Terrorism Monitor*: Volume 6, Issue 3 on February 7, 2008.

Notes

1. Author interview with a representative of Ayatollah al-Sistani, Qom, August 29, 2007.
2. Author interview with a seminary student of Ayatollah al-Sistani, Qom, August 28, 2007.

The Ansar al-Mahdi and the Continuing Threat of the Doomsday Cults in Iraq
By Fadhil Ali

On January 18, 2008, a day before the annual Shiite festival of Ashura, most of the concerns in Iraq revolved around possible attacks by Sunni extremists against the Shiites. What happened was unexpectedly different—the attacks came from the little-known Shiite cult of Ansar al-Mahdi (Helpers of the Expected One). Gunmen of the cult—believing that a Shiite Messiah was coming to help them—launched simultaneous attacks against Iraqi forces in the cities of Basra and Nasiriya in Shiite-dominated southern Iraq. The attacks came a month after British forces handed over security responsibilities in Basra to Iraqi security forces. During the clashes in Basra and nearby Nasiriya, 97 members of Ansar al-Mahdi were killed and about 500 arrested. Among these were doctors, engineers and other respected professionals (*al-Hayat*, January 30, 2008).

The media mistakenly referred to the group as the Soldiers of Heaven, another small Shiite cult with similar beliefs. By the end of the second day of fighting, Iraqi forces succeeded in restoring order in the two cities, but the mystery of Ansar al-Mahdi was not completely solved—especially with the disappearance of the leader of the group, Ahmad al-Hassan, better known as Shaykh al-Yamani. It is possible, as some suggest, that al-Yamani commands the allegiance of as many as 5,000 followers.

Development of the Post-Invasion Doomsday Cults in Iraq

The apocalyptic radicalism of the Ansar al-Mahdi derives from a militant interpretation of the "Twelver School" of Shiite theology. Twelver Shiites await the return of a Mahdi (Expected One) in the form of the twelfth Shiite Imam, Muhammad ibn Hassan ibn Ali, born in 868 A.D. It is believed that the Imam is still alive, but has been hidden by God from mankind—a process known as "occultation"— until the appointed time of his return. The Imam will help the Nabi Isa (Prophet Jesus) to defeat al-Masih al-Dajjal (the false Messiah—an Anti-Christ figure) and establish social justice on earth prior to the Day of Judgment. Mahdism is not unique to Shiite Islam, though many orthodox Sunnis frown on the concept as being unsupported by Quranic tradition. The most notable Sunni "Mahdi" was Muhammad Ahmad al-Mahdi—who lived from 1844 to 1885 and led a successful revolt against Turco-Egyptian rule in the Sudan during the 1880s.

It is important that the Iraqi government not underestimate the threat of such cults; the Shiite-led government must avoid being affected by its historical relationship with Iran if Iranian forces are indeed behind these cults.

During the January 2007 Ashura festival, a millenarian cult known as the Jund al-Samaa (Soldiers of Heaven, or SoH) engaged in severe clashes with Iraqi government forces in southern Iraq's Shiite holy city of Najaf. The SoH were led by Dhia Abdul Zahra al-Gar'awi, or the Judge of Heaven as he is known among his followers. According to the Iraqi government, hundreds of gunmen of the SoH were about to implement a plan to assassinate the top Shiite clerics. The SoH believed that killing those clerics who are followed by the majority of Iraq's Shiite population would pave the way for the return of al-Imam al-Mahdi (the Shiite Messiah). The Iraqi government announced that it had uncovered the plot. Coalition-backed Iraqi forces surrounded the SoH in a rural area and attacked them—263 of the SoH members, including al-Gar'awi, were killed and a further 500 arrested.

Al-Mahdi Army

The radical Shiite cleric Moqtada al-Sadr and his followers in the Jaysh al-Mahdi militia might not believe in an imminent return for the Mahdi, but their ideology still gives the impression that his return is close. Whenever al-Sadr or other leading members of the movement are asked about the possibility of disbanding the militia, they reply that only the Imam al-Mahdi (the returned savior of mankind) could do this and no one else, including militia founder Moqtada al-Sadr.

The Sadrists deny any connection with Ansar al-Mahdi. Some media reports mentioned that Sadr's men were fighting with the Iraqi army against Ansar al-Mahdi, but an anti-Sadrist web forum suggests that Ansar al-Mahdi is merely a group of al-Mahdi Army. There are reports that former members of the Baathist Fedayeen Saddam militia have joined the Ansar al-Mahdi and al-Mahdi Army in an effort to regain their old power and influence (Shababeek, January 19, 2008).

Al-Yamani and the Ansar al-Mahdi

Ahmad al-Hassan al-Yamani—whose real name is Ahmad Ismail Gat'a—was born near Basra to a well-known and well-respected Shiite family. One of his brothers had a doctorate in nuclear technology and worked as an assistant to General Hossam Ameen, the spokesman of Saddam's nuclear program. Another brother of al-Yamani was a colonel in the former Iraqi Army. The strong family ties to the regime could not help al-Yamani when he was sent to jail in the 1990s for unknown reasons. After the 2003 Coalition invasion, al-Yamani—who already had a college degree in civil engineering—enrolled as a scholar in the Shiite religious institutes of Najaf and became a cleric. In 2004 he participated in the Najaf battle between Coalition forces and Moqtada al-Sadr's al-Mahdi Army. Eventually al-Yamani led his followers to his home town of Basra and the adjacent Nasiriya and Emara areas where they established their own mosques and offices. The mission expanded quickly in the poor Shiite far south of Iraq (al-Malaf, February 2007).

In 2006, the Ansar al-Mahdi started to increase their propaganda efforts in Basra and Baghdad with slogans like "Every solution has failed but the solution of al-Mahdi" or "Democracy is the people's rule but al-Mahdi is Allah's rule." On August 28, 2007, the first issue of the group's newspaper al-Sirat al-Mostakeem was published to express the policy and ideology of the cult. Intellectual adherents of al-Yamani were placed in charge of editing the paper.

Al-Sirat al-Mostakeem was mostly devoted to the cult's propaganda, but the editorials had a clear anti-American position. In the October 13, 2007 issue, there was an article about "jihad by words and swords" based on Jihad is the Gate of Heaven, a book written by al-Yamani. In the January 25, 2008 issue, there was a statement by al-Yamani—allegedly answering a Christian woman—declaring that America would fall by Imam al-Mahdi's hands. The United States is customarily referred as al-Masih al-Dajjal (the "Grand Imposter" or "False Messiah," a personality comparable to the Anti-Christ). In the same issue, al-Yamani writes that the Americans—whom he cursed—supported the enemies of Islam, like the apostate rulers of the Gulf countries. He claims that Osama bin Laden was raised up by U.S. support and says elsewhere in the same issue that the campaign against the followers of Moqtada al-Sadr is intended to clear the ground for U.S. occupation.

In a video released on YouTube, al-Yamani stresses his role as a representative and deputy of Imam al-Mahdi while challenging other Shiite clerics to a debate. Al-Yamani has made this challenge many times, but while the traditional senior Shiite clerics have not responded, some junior members of the Shiite movement have offered to take up al-Yamani's challenge. The top Shiite spiritual leader in Iraq, Ayatollah Ali al-Sistani, has urged the government to address those who spread defective views on religion. The Sadrists blame the Iraqi government for the emergence of "spoiling movements" like that of al-Yamani, claiming that while the national army was busy tackling al-Sadr's al-Mahdi army, more dangerous extremist groups were proliferating in southern Iraq.

An Iranian Role?

The Iraqi government first accused neighboring countries of sponsoring the extremist millenarian Shiite groups. Later on, government spokesman Ali al-Dabbagh stated that there was no evidence that the cult was supported by any party from outside Iraq (al-Sharqia, January 28, 2008). In an interview with al-Hurra TV, an arrested senior member of Ansar al-Mahdi admitted that there were foreign individuals but no states involved in the financial support of the cult. Unnamed political and security sources took a different view by telling the Iraqi press that "the interrogations with Ansar al-Yamani showed that they are agents of Iranian intelligence and some of them were trained by the Iranian Revolutionary Guards. The weapons and ammunition of the cult's fighters were Iranian made" (al-Malaf, February 6, 2008).

Conclusion

Although the Iraqi forces succeeded in putting down the Ansar al-Mahdi rebellion in two days, the danger is still present. Cult leader Ahmad al-Hassan al-Yamani managed to escape and might return to launch other attacks against the Iraqi government or the Coalition. The possibility of attacks outside Iraq cannot be ruled out. Militant cults like Ansar al-Mahdi and the SoH have an international agenda as they believe that al-Imam al-Mahdi is coming back to liberate the entire world and defeat the unbelievers. It was a worrying sign that one of the SoH had a British passport.

The clashes at Basra and Nasiriya occurred a month after the security handover between the British and the Iraqis in the south and a month before the end of the six-month suspension of al-Mahdi Army activities. The Iranians have expressed many times that they are willing to be involved in the security arrangements in Iraq and fill what they describe as a security vacuum that will exist after the Coalition withdrawal. A connection between Ansar al-Mahdi and Iranian intelligence could explain the clashes—even partially—as an unusual means for Iran to send a message about potential instability in Shiite Iraq.

The followers of al-Sadr ascribed the violence in southern Iraq to the government's crackdown on their militia. By accepting al-Yamani's call for a debate, the Sadrists are apparently trying to gain the political benefits of negotiating on behalf of the Iraqi government or being a mediator. They are likely thinking of bringing the cult back to its wider Shiite environment and more specifically to al-Mahdi Army.

It is important that the Iraqi government not underestimate the threat of such cults; the Shiite-led government must avoid being affected by its historical relationship with Iran if Iranian forces are indeed behind these cults. Dealing with radical Shiite groups is complicated by the delicate internal balance between the different Shiite parties that form the government. Whether al-Yamani is captured or remains on the loose, the danger of the doomsday cults could linger for years, even after the backbone of the movement has been destroyed.

Originally published in *Terrorism Monitor*: Volume 6, Issue 4 on February 22, 2008.

Uncertainty Facing Iraq's Awakening Movement Puts U.S. Strategy at Risk
By Ramzy Mardini

As Iraq's security situation deteriorates in the midst of resurgent violence, an increase in internal and external pressures facing the Awakening (Sahwa) Movement may jeopardize the prospects and goals set forth in the U.S. counter-insurgency strategy created by U.S. General David Petraeus.

The formation of the Awakening Councils seemed a promising linchpin to the "surge" strategy, which has shown concrete signs of improving Iraq's security sector. Though the rise of the Awakening movement contributed substantially in limiting al-Qaeda in Iraq in the short term, its forces face uncertain and problematic long-term challenges. If the dilemmas confronting the Awakening members continue to be marginalized by Prime Minister Nouri al-Maliki's government, Iraq's improved security situation is likely to revert back to sectarianism and civil war-like conditions.

Formation of the Awakening Councils

The Awakening movement began in al-Anbar province in 2006. The governorate was then described as "an impregnable garrison" of al-Qaeda in Iraq (*Azzaman*, January 3, 2008). The terrorist organization, then led by the late Abu Musab al-Zarqawi, suppressed the local population and killed thousands of tribal members in an effort to impose an Islamic authority over the province. Though many of the members representing the Awakening today were at one time or another part of the insurgency killing U.S. soldiers, al-Qaeda's use of vicious intimidation tactics eventually led tribal leaders to shift their allegiances by cooperating with the U.S. military.

Since 2005, the Sahwa has spread outside al-Anbar province, with fighters joining or forming Awakening councils across the country. With the support and nurturing of the U.S. military, the Awakening has grown to at least 80,000 members, with Sunnis representing four-fifths of the force (*Al-Sharq al-Awsat*, January 23, 2008). The movement represents one of the main components of U.S. counter-insurgency strategy and one of the very few Iraqi success stories. But in September 2007, al-Qaeda assassinated Shaykh Abdul Sattar Abu Risha, the charismatic leader of the Awakening movement (*Aswat al-Iraq*, January 14, 2008). Killed just days after meeting with President Bush, Abu Risha's death promoted uncertainty as to what would come of the Awakening movement without the shaykh's leadership and credibility.

> *Though many of the members representing the Awakening today were at one time or another part of the insurgency killing U.S. soldiers, al-Qaeda's use of vicious intimidation tactics eventually led tribal leaders to shift their allegiances by cooperating with the U.S. military.*

Security/Political Dilemmas

Though the Sahwa councils are credited to a large extent for the decline in the total number of Iraqi casualties, all three of Iraq's major political groupings—Shiites, Sunnis and Kurds—are wary of the Awakening's role in state affairs.

The Kurdistan Regional Government (KRG) is opposed to the formation of Awakening Councils in its region and areas subject to Article 140 of the Iraq Constitution, which calls for a reversal of the Baathist "Arabization" process in Kirkuk and other disputed areas (*Kurdish Globe*, January 23, 2008). The Sunni Arab makeup of the Awakening forces conflicts with Kurdish interest in sustaining security autonomy, especially in Kirkuk and parts of Ninawa province. The major concern for Sunni Arab leaders such as Iraqi Vice President Tariq al-Hashimi and Iraq Accordance Front (IAF) leader Adnan al-Duleimi is that the Awakening Councils will gain political power at the expense of Sunni politicians. The increasing influence of the Awakening tribesmen has begun to challenge the Sunni bloc for a share in political power—a prospect many Sunni leaders want to avoid. The boycott by IAF ministers of al-Maliki's government last August prompted rumors that the Awakening Council would nominate candidates to replace them (*Al-Sharq al-Awsat*, November 29, 2007).

A dilemma has emerged in the current relationship between the United States and the Awakening Council concerning the prospect of integrating Sahwa tribesmen into Iraqi security and police forces. The Shiite political community is uneasy with what they perceive as U.S. control over the Sunni-dominated militia. The Awakening forces are autonomous and unaccountable to the Iraqi government. Depending on their rank, members are paid from $300 to $1,200 every month by the U.S. military (*Independent*, January 28, 2008). The Sahwa leaders are demanding that they be integrated into Iraq's national defense forces, assuming permanent positions with permanent payrolls.

In addition to the suspicion of the Sahwa held by Iraq's Shiites, the Awakening leaders have a reciprocal mistrust of the Shiite-dominated government, often defining it as a puppet of Iran. But concern over the Awakening Council's political agenda is perhaps not necessarily the major reason why some Sunni and Shiite lawmakers have been reluctant to embrace the movement. Rather it may be suspicions over the past history of Sahwa members. According to Shaykh Harith al-Dari, head of the Sunni Association of Muslim Scholars: "Many of those who have joined the Sahwa Councils have been members in al-Qaeda. They joined al-Qaeda in the first place for the sake of money, and when more money became available in a different direction, they rushed to it" (*Aswat al-Iraq*, January 9, 2008).

Many of the Sahwa fighters are former insurgents, Baathists and al-Qaeda terrorists. The rapid growth of the tribal coalition has led many in the Shiite government to assume that the Awakening Councils could not possibly have inspected every member thoroughly—suggesting the organization suffers from mass infiltration. Rumors of infiltration have lately been advanced through a series of Shiite newspaper articles. Even the idea of infiltration helps discredit the Awakening Councils in the eyes of Iraqi officials. Prime Minister al-Maliki said in an interview: "We, as a government, have intelligence information: the Baath party has ordered its members to join the Awakening Councils, and al-Qaeda has ordered its members to infiltrate the Awakening Councils" (*Al-Sharq al-Awsat*, January 5, 2008).

Threat from the Shiite Militias

The secular and Sunni-oriented makeup of the expanding Awakening Movement has led to deep anxiety in Shiite circles in southern Iraq. Referring to Iraq's powerful Shiite religious leaders, the current Sahwa commander, Kamal Hammad al-Muajal Abu Risha, said in an interview that Islam has "an active role in our society but we reject clerics' interference in politics. The power of the clerics should not exceed the mosques nor affect the political decision-making process" (*Aswat al-Iraq*, January 14, 2008).

Statements like this have produced anxiety in powerful Shiite clerics such as the anti-American firebrand Moqtada al-Sadr and Abdul Aziz al-Hakim, leader of the Supreme Islamic Iraqi Council (SIIC). Though the men are intense rivals for the Shiite sphere of influence, the two share a mutual concern for the Awakening's increasing threat to Shiite Iraq. Al-Hakim and al-Sadr lead the two most powerful militias in Iraq: the Badr Brigade and the Jaysh al-Mahdi (JAM), respectively. Both organizations are Iranian-backed and trained by the Islamic Revolutionary Guards Corps (IRGC).

The formation of a secular and Sunni-dominated force of 80,000, spread out across Iraq, supersedes both JAM and the Badr Brigade—effectively defining them now as second-class militias. While both Shiite militias are forced to work covertly in their funding and armament activities, the Sahwa profits from being openly supplied and backed by the U.S. military.

Terrorist Pressures

The Awakening Councils have received threats from outsiders for their collaboration with U.S. forces. In November 2007, Syrian Shaykh Abd al-Munim Mustafa Halima—also known as Abu Baseer al-Tartousi—condemned the Iraqi tribesmen for cooperating with the U.S. occupiers. Residing in London, al-Tartousi is considered one of the leading theoreticians of the Salafi-jihadist trend in Islam. He writes that "the so-called Awakening Councils [Majalis al-Sahwa], which preferred to join ranks with the invaders and aggressors against the jihad fighters, should be called the Councils of Stupor and Oblivion." When addressing the suggestion that the Councils' collaboration is a reaction to al-Qaeda's brutal tactics against their members, al-Tartousi suggests that "one injustice does not justify a greater injustice" (MEMRI, January 15, 2008).

In late December 2007, Osama bin Laden also condemned those joining the Awakening movement, claiming that "they sold out their religion in return for a mortal [monetary] world" (RFE/RL, January 4, 2008). Since this statement was made, there has been an exceptional spike in al-Qaeda's attacks against members of the Awakening Council. In the month of January, the tribal coalition experienced the loss of well over a hundred members, including the assassinations of at least six senior Awakening leaders.
Awakening Returning to Insurgency?

The U.S. military and intelligence community is alarmed by the possibility of the Awakening Council strategy backfiring, essentially leading to an unfortunate path similar to that experienced in Afghanistan. This is the likely scenario if the United States is unable to keep paying the Awakening members and/or the central government fails to meet their demands. U.S. officials are concerned over the recent increase in killings of Sahwa members and the possibility that some Sahwa fighters might rejoin the insurgency:

"If the Americans think they can use us to crush al-Qaeda and then push us to one side, they are mistaken," says Abu Marouf, the commander of 13,000 fighters who formerly fought U.S. soldiers. As a member of the powerful Zubai tribe, he was part of al-Qaeda's defeat in the stronghold of Fallujah. While discussing his demand for the integration of his fighters into official Iraqi forces, Abu Marouf stated: "If there is no change in three months there will be war again." According to local sources, Abu Marouf is a former commander in the insurgent 1920 Revolution Brigades (*Independent*, January 28, 2008).

Many politicians recognize a return to insurgency as a possible consequence if terrorist pressures continue. Senior Sunni politician Omar Abdul Sattar warned that if the Awakening Councils were disbanded, the security situation in Iraq will "deteriorate precipitously" (*Azzaman*, January 3, 2008). Unfortunately, despite the risk of reversing Iraq's security progress, there is no apparent urgency in al-Maliki's government to integrate Awakening members. U.S. officials point to Shiite politicians as the main source of obstruction to the integration program. According to Brig. Gen. Jim Huggins, of the 3,000 recruits of the Awakening Council he sent to a Shiite leader's office to apply for integration, only 400 names received approval—all Shiites (*USA Today*, February 1, 2008).

Prospects: al-Sadr and Iran

To add to the dilemma plaguing the U.S. counter-insurgency strategy, the rise of the Awakening councils may risk reigniting the Jaysh al-Mahdi. Since August 2007, Moqtada al-Sadr's self-imposed ceasefire has contributed tremendously to the decline of violence throughout Iraq. On February 22, 2008, the ceasefire was extended for another six months. But if the Awakening movement becomes too powerful or rejoins the insurgency due to unsatisfied demands, al-Sadr may be inclined to end the ceasefire or concede further fragmentation of the Jaysh al-Mahdi. Rogue factions within the Shiite militia have already targeted Sahwa fighters, especially in Baghdad.

The Islamic Republic seems to be reasserting itself in Iraq. Reports published by the Iraqi Islamic Party and the pro-Baathist website "Quds Press" cited unidentified intelligence sources stating that brigades comprised of rogue JAM elements were being formed by the Iranian Quds Force to assassinate Awakening Council members (RFE/RL, January 4, 2008). This was later corroborated by sources belonging to the Awakening Councils: "Special groups supported by the Iranian Quds have started armed activities against elements of the Awakening forces in various parts of Baghdad" (Al-Sharqiyah TV, January 28, 2008).

The success of the counter-insurgency strategy is contingent on elements of the security situation that the United States has little control over. One of the major factors contributing to recent security improvements is the Awakening's formation. Another major part of the success story is Moqtada al-Sadr's ceasefire. However, the security and political dilemmas facing the Awakening Councils may lead these organizations to fragment, split and rejoin the insurgency. This would effectively force al-Sadr to reinstate an active Jaysh al-Mahdi—a prospect likely to diminish security progress, even to the point of reverting back to pre-surge status.

Originally published in *Terrorism Monitor*: Volume 6, Issue 4 on February 22, 2008.

Confronting the Sadrists: The Issue of State and Militia in Iraq
By Fadhil Ali

On April 26, 2008, Iraqi Shiite leader Muqtada al-Sadr stood down from his threat to wage an all-out war against the Iraqi government and the coalition. A week before, the anti-American cleric had issued a statement threatening to declare an open war if the security crackdown by the Iraqi and U.S. forces against his loyalists was not called off. Al-Sadr said that he was giving a final warning to the Shiite-led Iraqi government to "take the path of peace and stop violence against its own people." Al-Sadr's statement went on: "If [the Iraqi government] does not stop the militias that have infiltrated the government, then we will declare a war until liberation" (Al Jazeera, April 19, 2008).

The statement was read out in the mosques of Sadr City, a largely Shiite district of Baghdad. There were calls for jihad against the U.S. forces and calls for the Iraqi government to release detainees and end the siege on the poor district of eastern Baghdad. Sadr City is populated by more than two million people and is a main stronghold of Muqtada's Jaysh al-Mahdi militia (JAM).

Neither the Iraqi government of Prime Minister Nuri al-Maliki nor the U.S. forces showed any intention of submitting to al-Sadr's threat. The Iraqi-American joint operations continued, with over 1,070 people killed in Iraq in April, most of them in the violence between Shiite militias and government/Coalition forces (Agence France-Presse, April 30, 2008).

Major General Rick Lynch, the commander of the U.S. Army in central Iraq, threatened to hit back if al-Sadr launched war: "If Sadr and Jaysh al-Mahdi become very aggressive, we have got enough combat force to take the fight to the enemy." General Lynch also called on al-Sadr to play a positive role: "I hope Muqtada al-Sadr continues to depress violence and not encourage it" (*Kuwait Times*, April 21, 2008). Al-Sadr, currently pursuing theological studies in the Iranian city of Qom, made his open war threat while his followers' strongholds in southern Iraq were falling and Sadr City and other Shiite neighborhoods in Baghdad were under military pressure.

On February 22, 2008, al-Sadr renewed the six-month suspension of JAM activities. The suspension was initially imposed by al-Sadr after inter-communal clashes during a religious festival in the holy Shiite city of Karbala were blamed on the JAM. The decision to renew the suspension was not opposed but many figures from al-Sadr's movement were ready to end the ceasefire as they claimed they were increasingly targeted by government forces.

Days after this decision, al-Sadr announced that he had retired and admitted that he had failed to achieve his main goals: "What made me retire is the continuing presence of the occupation … I have succeeded neither in liberating Iraq nor in making it an Islamic society; it might be my dereliction, it could be society's or it could be both … Many of those who were close to me have left me for worldly reasons, and a dominant independent trend was one of the secondary reasons behind my isolation" (*al-Sharq al-*

Awsat, March 8, 2008). Al-Sadr also revealed that he was thinking seriously of reconstructing his movement but did not clarify how he would do so while isolated in Qom. He indicated that he had undertaken advanced religious studies to become a senior Shiite cleric (*ayatollah*), which will give him great spiritual and institutional influence (*Terrorism Monitor*, February 7, 2008).

The Assault of the Nights

Basra is the second largest city in Iraq. Being the only Iraqi port and enjoying a rich oil-producing industry, it became the scene of a power struggle among the various Shiite militias and factions after the invasion. By the end of 2007 the British Army handed over security responsibilities to the Iraqi government.

On March 25, 2008 al-Maliki himself was in Basra, where he launched "The Assault of the Nights," a security operation intended to disarm the illegal militias. It was clear that the JAM was the main target. On the threshold of the operation, the main powers in Basra, in addition to the JAM, were the Islamic Supreme Council of Iraq (ISCI), led by Abdul Aziz al-Hakim, and al-Fadhila (Islamic Virtue Party), led by Ayatollah Muhammad al-Yaqubi. The influential mayor of Basra, Muhammad al-Walili, is a member of al-Fadhila Party.

The ISCI is the main rival of al-Sadr's movement in Shiite Iraq. Thousands of members of the Badr Organization—the military wing of the ISCI—have joined Iraqi government forces in post-invasion Iraq, especially when Bayan Jabur Solagh, a senior member of the ISCI, was Minister of the Interior (May 2005 – June 2006). The ISCI and the Badr Organization also influence other affiliated armed groups. The ISCI currently dominates the provincial councils in central and southern Iraq as most Sadrists boycotted the previous election in January 2005.

After the Operation

The fighting in Basra stopped when al-Sadr called on his followers to lay down their arms and clear the way for an exchange of prisoners and a cessation of government raids against his followers (*Terrorism Focus*, April 1, 2008). 600 were killed and 2,000 injured after a week of fighting which rapidly extended from Basra to Baghdad and other parts of central and southern Iraq. Despite the call for a ceasefire, the fighting continued, with mortar and rocket attacks on Baghdad's "Green Zone." The JAM was still armed: "We are committed to [al-Sadr's] orders but we will not hand our weapons over as they are for resisting the occupation," said Hazim al-Arako, a senior aide of Muqtada (*al-Hayat*, April 1, 2008). The Iraqi and U.S. forces did not release any detainees and kept raiding al-Sadr's strongholds throughout the country.

Many looked at the operation as a victory for al-Sadr after he had shown that he still had control of his militia. Iran also appeared as another winner as the settlement for the crisis was agreed upon in the Iranian city of Qom, where al-Sadr studies (*al-Sharq al-Awsat*, April 5, 2008). Hundreds of Iraqi soldiers and officers surrendered to the JAM, including some who did so in front of TV cameras. In his testimony before Congress, General David Petraeus, commander of the U.S. Army in Iraq, described the operation as not adequately planned (BBC, April 8, 2008).

Muqtada under Pressure

Though al-Maliki could not prove himself a remarkable military leader in the field in Basra, he nevertheless gained political support when he returned to Baghdad. The Political Council for National Security, made up of leading Shiite, Sunni and Kurdish politicians, backed al-Maliki and called on all parties to disband their militias or risk being barred from participating in political life. Al-Maliki had the council's full support in the campaign against the militias and the outlaws (al-Hayat, April 6, 2008). Next al-Maliki presented al-Sadr with a difficult choice: "The decision was made that [the Sadrists] no longer have the right to participate in the political process or take part in the upcoming election unless they end al-Mahdi Army" (CNN, April 7, 2008). Moreover the Sunnis decided to rejoin al-Maliki's government—they withdrew in August 2007—and urged al-Maliki to take action against the Shiite militias they blamed for sectarian killings.

Despite the political progress, the fighting continued. On April 11, 2008, Muqtada's right hand man and brother-in-law, Riyad al-Nuri, was assassinated in Najaf. Al-Sadr called for calm and blamed the "occupier and its tails"—referring to the Americans and the Iraqi government—though al-Nuri might have been killed by his own people (Alalam, April 12, 2008). On April 19, 2008, the Arab newspaper al-Sharq al-Awsat published a letter allegedly written by al-Nuri asking al-Sadr to purify the movement and disband the JAM; a source close to al-Nuri accused extremists from the movement of the assassination. The head of al-Sadr's parliamentary bloc neither denied nor confirmed the allegations. No matter who killed al-Nuri, it was a blow to al-Sadr and his followers and it raised the possibility that Muqtada himself might be next. Al-Qaeda's second-in-command Ayman al-Zawahiri mocked al-Sadr, describing him as a dissembler who was being used by Iranian intelligence (AKI, April 18, 2008).

The Iranian ambassador to Iraq, Saeed Kazemi Qomi, denounced the American operation in Sadr City saying that it led to the killing of innocent people, but added that Iran supported the Iraqi government in its operation in southern Iraq. In Sadr City, alleged field commanders from the JAM said that the militia is now unified under the command of al-Sadr. They added that Iran had stopped sending weapons to the JAM but the weapons they already had are sufficient for a year of continuous fighting. For the first time, al-Maliki warned Iran from intervening in Iraq's internal affairs (al-Arabiya, April 25, 2008).

Al-Maliki's Four Conditions

Al-Maliki set four conditions for the JAM in order to bring an end to the military operations:

- Heavy and medium weapons must be turned in to government security forces;
- The militia must cease interference in state affairs and institutions;
- The militia must cease interference in the army and security forces;
- Wanted individuals must be turned over and lists compiled of those involved in violence (al-Arabiya, April 25, 2008).

The next day the U.S. army issued a statement announcing that U.S. and Iraqi forces had taken control of Hay Hiteen, the last stronghold of al-Sadr in Basra. At the same time Iraqi forces backed by U.S. air support were raiding the last stronghold of the JAM in the southern city of al-Kut (BBC, April 26, 2008). U.S. forces were barely involved in the opening round of the operation, but by this time they had become heavily involved after some Shiite units proved unreliable in fighting the Shiite militias.

Despite these setbacks, al-Sadr refused to submit to al-Maliki's conditions (Radio Sawa, April 27, 2008), though he did retract his open war threat and called for an end to the bloodshed. In a statement, al-Sadr said that his threat was directed to the occupier—i.e. the U.S.-led Coalition—while calling on Iraqis not to use arms against fellow Iraqis, not to use violence to impose law and not to divide Iraq. Significantly al-Sadr called on the resistance not to use the cities as military operational fields against the *occupier (al-Sharq al-Awsat*, April 26, 2008). It is not clear if al-Sadr meant to make an essential change of his tactics; since the invasion, all JAM battles have been fought inside the cities and residential neighborhoods. As al-Sadr rejected al-Maliki's four conditions, the Iraqi prime minister responded: "The Iraqi government will not retreat until the JAM and other Sunni groups are disarmed and until al-Qaeda is destroyed." Al-Maliki accused JAM of using civilians in Sadr City as human shields (BBC, April 30, 2008). Baha'a al-Araji, an MP and member of al-Sadr's movement, suggested the Iraqi presidency act as a mediator and a guarantor between the Sadrists and al-Maliki. This would be preferable to Iran, which hosted the initial peace deal in the beginning of the fighting.

As al-Sadr rejected al-Maliki's four conditions, the Iraqi prime minister responded: "The Iraqi government will not retreat until the JAM and other Sunni groups are disarmed and until al-Qaeda is destroyed."

The Crisis Continues

The first days of the anti-JAM operation revealed the poor performance of some Iraqi government units and a lack of coordination with the Coalition forces, demonstrating that any major campaign in the future should be well prepared politically and militarily.

The Iraqi government can bar al-Sadr's movement from participating in the upcoming provincial election but it cannot change the fact that millions of Iraqis are sincere followers of Muqtada al-Sadr. The cleric might have declined pursuing "open war" at the moment, but he is still capable of waging a popular uprising that would raise the number of casualties on both sides. April became the deadliest month for the U.S. Army in Iraq since September 2007 (BBC, April 30, 2008).

The ban on militias has focused on the Sadrists. The peshmerga militias of the two major Kurdish parties and the ISCI Badr Organization have found their way into the Iraqi forces while the poor Shiites who are the raw material of the JAM are still suffering from unemployment and negligence. The same applies to the Sunni fighters of the Awakening movement who have been trying in vain to join the Iraqi forces. A program of rebuilding the Iraqi forces on a base of national loyalty is essential to reduce violence. There may be steps in this direction—al-Maliki recently called for the recruitment of 25,000 Shiite tribesmen to the Iraqi security forces (*al-Hayat*, April 6, 2008). To fight extreme ideologies, the Iraqi government must direct greater efforts and funding to development and reconstruction projects in impoverished Shiite areas; otherwise, the crowded slums will continue to produce extremists and criminals.

Originally published in *Terrorism Monitor*: Volume 6, Issue 9 on May 1, 2008.

The Militia Politics of Basra
By Babak Rahimi

Basra, the second largest and the richest city in Iraq, is at the brink of a major economic and political meltdown. Unless Baghdad succeeds in reaching a compromise over the country's governmental apparatus (especially over the issue of federalism), the southern city may become the greatest threat to the future of post-Baathist Iraq. Such a threat lies mainly in a struggle for power between Shiite militias and tribal forces who compete for control over oil resources, territorial domination and public capital (hospitals and schools), which are all leading to an erosion of security in a city that is the source of Iraq's economic life. Although much of this turmoil is a reflection of the unstable nature of the transitional process, the current situation in Basra may represent a future scenario for Iraq that is made up of political factionalism and devoid of a functional government [1].

At the center of Basra's meltdown lies the ongoing conflict between different Shiite factions, mainly vying for control over Basra's energy industry and oil smuggling. Domination over local governance through confrontation, and at times violence, has become the routine method of conducting politics in a city that appears to be breaking apart into territories governed by different militias. Such political conflict, however, also includes competing visions of post-Baathist Iraq, as each Shiite militia advocates a particular ideological agenda (regionalist, nationalist and sectarian), while seeking popular support from various segments of the Shiite community in Basra and other southern cities.

The Fadhila Party

The Fadhila Party (Virtue Party) is a case in point. An offshoot of the original Sadrist movement in the mid-1990s, when Moqtada al-Sadr's father, Ayatollah Sadeq al-Sadr, led a nativist Shiite movement to oppose clerical traditional authorities in Najaf and the Baathist regime in Baghdad, Fadhila emerged as a major Shiite party in Basra in 2003. With its own militia and support from the city's professional class sympathetic to the Sadrist millenarian ideology, the party managed to win local elections and gained the allegiance of smaller Shiite parties, such as Wifaq and Harakat al-Dawa, for the control of the provincial council in January 2005.

On the level of religious ideology, Fadhila is a millenarian nativist movement and the party has many supporters among Basra regionalists who envision an autonomous Basra province that includes Maysan and Dhi Qar governorates. Ayatollah Muhammad Yaqubi, a student of Sadeq al-Sadr and the head of Fadhila, who is based in Karbala, opposes al-Sadr and sees him as a rogue cleric who is taking advantage of his father's legacy to gain power. Yaqubi also opposes Iranian influence in Shiite Iraq—even the authority of Grand Ayatollah Ali al-Sistani, an Iranian-born cleric based in Najaf. Since 2003, Yaqubi has tried to form a strong alliance with Grand Ayatollah Kadhim Haeri, based in the Iranian city of Qom, who is regarded by some Sadrists as the successor to the late Ayatollah Sadeq al-Sadr, the main rival of al-Sistani throughout the 1990s [2]. The move can be recognized to highlight Fadhila's attempt to strengthen native Iraqi clerics in order to counterbalance Iranian influence in the province.

In January 2005, Fadhila moved up the political ladder in the United Iraqi Alliance (UIA) in the interim government, but only to face major obstacles from the Nuri al-Maliki-led government later in 2006. Under Ibrahim al-Jaafari, the party was in charge of the oil ministry, but when al-Maliki's government came to power the Fadhila minister was replaced by Hussein al-Shahristani, a prominent Shiite politician and scientist with no ties to the militia politics in Basra. When Fadhila withdrew from the unity government in May 2006, the party began to concentrate on local politics as a way to maintain control over the oil industry and trafficking. It was at this juncture that conflict with other rival Shiite groups, including tribal forces, began to escalate (*Azzaman*, May 16, 2006).

Fadhila Challenges Legitimacy of the SIIC

Realizing the influence of the Supreme Islamic Iraqi Council (SIIC), which was also present in the city council and the police force, Fadhila sought ways to challenge the legitimacy of the rival group. As journalist Juan Cole described, the governor of Basra and member of Fadhila, Muhammad Misbah al-Wa'ili, accused the chief of police of allowing the continuation of political assassinations [3]. The accusation was made in a way to discredit the Badr Corps, the SIIC's militia, which had maintained influence in the city's police force through the Interior Ministry. Tensions between local groups and the SIIC grew when a major tribesman was assassinated in May 2006. The Karamishah Marsh Arabs attacked the SIIC's headquarters, accusing the Badr Corps of carrying out the assassination. Immediately after the event, followers of the SIIC and militia groups linked to the Badr Corps, namely Tha'r Allah (Revenge of God), formed demonstrations against the governor [4]. With the rise in tension between Shiite militias and tribal rivals, al-Maliki quickly stepped in later in May to establish security by declaring a month-long state of emergency in the city (Baztab, May 30, 2007). At present, frictions in the Basra government continue to grow, especially between Fadhila and the SIIC, as nativist political parties (such as Harakat al-Dawa) accuse the Badr militiamen of being agents of Tehran and advancing Iranian interests in Basra.

Fadhila and al-Sadr Compete for Basra

With the reemergence of al-Sadr on the political scene in spring 2006, Fadhila faced another Shiite contender. Although conflict between the two groups dates back to spring 2003, al-Sadr failed to establish a strong base in Basra. After the 2004 uprising against the United States that led to the destruction of Najaf, the Sadrists lost even more support in the city, especially among the professional class who saw al-Sadr as an uneducated, unruly cleric. When al-Sadr began to rise as a major political figure in the UIA in 2005 and Basra began to experience greater economic hardship because of corruption in the oil industry, many younger Iraqis from the poorer parts of the city, in places like the northern district of al-Hayani-e, started to support al-Sadr [5].

Fadhila-Sadr relations are as complex as Shiite Iraqi politics. Although the two parties rely on the legacy of Sadeq al-Sadr to legitimize their prestige, they both compete for greater influence in southern politics—in the case of Fadhila, this is limited to Basra. They also share a nationalist interest, however, to curtail the influence of SIIC leader Abdul Aziz al-Hakim, who envisions a nine-province federal state, in which Basra would be the capital of the Shiite-dominated southern region. Fadhila, however, rejects al-Sadr's tendency for a tightly centralized government based in Baghdad (or Sadr City). Fadhila believes that Basra should become an autonomous regional power with the oil revenues under the control of the city, while distributing the wealth to the other parts of the country [6]. Competing visions of a future Iraqi government are the fundamental elements of the Fadhila-Sadr conflict.

There are also accusations of corruption and mayhem, however, which the two parties use to discredit each other. Fadhila's control over the oil industry has been a major problem for the Basra-based party. Wa'ili, the governor, functions as the head of Iraq's Southern Oil Company, which administrates the province's oil industry (*Azzaman*, April 30, 2007). He is also well connected to wealthy oil traders [7]. Al-Sadr accuses Wa'ili and his party of involvement in oil trafficking that creates shortages of oil for the country, especially in Baghdad and the Sunni provinces in western Iraq (United Press International, April 17, 2007). Accordingly, members of the Mahdi Army are accused of infiltrating the police force, which has been blamed for political assassinations since 2005 (*Azzaman*, March 27, 2007). In reality, the followers of al-Sadr also operate in the oil smuggling business, controlling Abu Flus port, which is a major center for the export of crude oil sold on the black market (*The Guardian*, June 9, 2007). Amidst such rivalry, Wa'ili's provincial government faced a major defeat when in April the provincial parliament—which included smaller Shiite groups like Master of All Martyrs and Hezbollah (an offshoot of the Da'wa party)—almost unseated him and challenged Fadhila authority in the local parliament (*International Herald Tribune*, April 28, 2007). The blow to Fadhila's power has allowed al-Sadr to increase his influence in Basra's provincial parliament and expand his popularity among the urban poor, who view Fadhila as corrupt.

As al-Sadr attempts to widen his influence in Baghdad, the two rival factions have grown more confrontational in Basra. In March, after British forces departed the city, the headquarters of the Fadhila party was destroyed, later leading to urban clashes between the Mahdi and Fadhila militias (Voices of Iraq, March 23, 2007). The two parties have tried to play down their differences, but in reality the Sadrists will continue to push for domination over oil commerce and Fadhila will most certainly fight to retain its tenacious hold on the Southern Oil Company (*Azzaman*, March 27, 2007).

Seen in this context, the Fadhila-SIIC-Sadr feud has been largely over control of local politics. Provincial politics, especially in terms of control over territorial domination in what can also be called the politics of "fiefdom," have been central to the balance of power between vying Shiite militia groups. Basra is now undergoing a militarization of local politics as a weakened Baghdad government loses control of its southern provinces. Such militarization processes, however, are also linked to oil trafficking, as profit made from smuggling helps the militias and preserves the factional politics of the city.

Other Factors Destabilizing Basra

Other major factors will play a role in the destabilization of Basra. One problem concerns tribe-militia relations. Many tribes face major challenges from urban militias, especially formerly exiled Shiite groups such as the SIIC, as competition over territorial domination and oil trafficking grows with the expansion of militia power. The increase in Shiite-Sunni conflict also represents a major factor. Since the Samarra bombing in February 2006, Sunni communities continue to face the wrath of Shiite militias (Baztab, June 20, 2006). In May 2007, for example, nearly 170 Sunni mosques were closed for security reasons in response to the assassinations of a number of Sunni clerics (Baztab, May 27, 2006). With a long history of religious movements, Basra is also witnessing the rise of new millenarian currents, namely the movement led by Karbala-based Ayatollah Mahmud al-Sarkhi al-Hassani, who has gained support from disgruntled Sadrists. All of these developments could trigger further instability in a city devoid of a functioning government.

What is Iran's role in this complicated political landscape? For the most part, Iran's influence in Basra has been significant yet limited. Since the 1950s, Basra has been a major hub for Iraqi nationalism (mainly the version advocated by non-Baathist nationalists like Abdul Karim Qasim), and many Shiites (including nativist parties like Fadhila) are highly suspicious of any Iranian presence in the city. As numerous attacks on the *Cultural and economic ties between Basra and Iran have grown strong since 2003. Farsi is now spoken as a second language, and many Iranian goods are sold in the Basra markets. The Iranian toman is a major currency in the Basra banking system, and many use it in the open markets of the city.* Iranian consulate in the city indicate, anti-Iranian sentiments run high in Basra despite Tehran's efforts to create new alliances with local Shiite factions, especially with the Sadrists (Baztab, June 14, 2006).

This does not mean, however, that Iran is absent from Basra's socio-economic life. Cultural and economic ties between Basra and Iran have grown strong since 2003. Farsi is now spoken as a second language, and many Iranian goods are sold in the Basra markets (Baztab, May 23, 2007). The Iranian *toman* is a major currency in the Basra banking system, and many use it in the open markets of the city. As for oil, the importation of Iranian (refined) oil has increased from 8 million to 11 million liters a day, and some Iraqi crude oil is also refined in the Abadan and Kermanshah refineries (RFE/RL Iraq Report, September 2006). As for military operations, Iranian intelligence officers are reported to reside in the city (some of them have dual citizenship), and they travel freely between the two countries through the Shalamcheh border crossing [8].

Implications

Although Iran's impact on the daily life of Basra cannot be ignored, the internal politics of Basra remain critical to the stability of the city. Overall, the problem in Basra is a localized conflict with ties to Baghdad's political process. The rapid recovery of Basra from militia politics would require the following:

1. On immediate terms, the Basra oil industry (production and distribution) should come under the direct control of Baghdad, ideally under the supervision of Basra natives who have no links to any of the militia groups. This move is crucial, as militia jurisdiction over the production and distribution of oil plays a central role in the consolidation of militia power in the city.

2. Accordingly, the containment of militia politics will depend on the strong presence of an Iraqi force trained in Baghdad and comprised of non-militia forces with no ties to local militia groups. Although a major undertaking, this could help bring some stability to the city by replacing officials linked to militia with non-militia officers who would receive their orders directly from the prime minister.

3. Baghdad should not only rely on the clerical circles in Najaf to contain the militias since much of the infighting between militant factions in Basra regards the control of local politics. Although Najaf may influence the SIIC and the Sadrists (although not necessarily enough to disarm the militias), it will most likely fail to persuade Fadhila, which is suspicious of the "quietist" school of thought advocated by leading Najaf clerics. In a significant sense, the Basra Shiite religious community, a major part of which is comprised of Fadhila, can be described as largely regional-nationalist in contrast to the conservative orthodoxy based in Najaf or the transnational Islamists led by Tehran. This point should be kept in mind as anti-Najaf millenarian movements continue to grow in southern provinces (especially in Karbala) and anti-Iranian sentiments remain strong in Basra.

The opinion regarding the U.S. and British role in the political order of Basra is clear: it is dangerous to become involved. One of the gravest mistakes made by the British since 2003 was their overwhelming reliance on the Badr Corps to impose order on the city and its suburbs. By taking sides, Britain has (unintentionally) shifted the balance of power by allocating too much authority to the Badr Corps. Although British forces have contributed to most of the security in the city since 2003 (despite the argument that they have also failed to do so because of their inability to quash the militias), the stability of Basra will largely depend on a multi-sectarian Iraqi army administered from Baghdad, not an occupied force or a militia faction. Furthermore, the main problem with overtly (or clandestinely) strengthening or arming one of the factions is that it could entail unintended consequences that most likely would harm the country rather than contribute to its stability.

Conclusion

For the time being, Baghdad remains Basra's worst enemy. The lack of a stable and relatively centralized government, at least in this transitional stage, is at the heart of the problem. Without a stable government, Basra is destined to experience the sort of violence that Beirut suffered two decades ago. A major civil-militia war in Basra seems imminent, and the consolidation of a centralized Iraqi government (including administrative and non-sectarian federated features) may possibly be the country's best solution. Basra's meltdown could well foretell the future of Baghdad as a failed state. Even worse, it could mean the unraveling of a dysfunctional city that may threaten the stability of the Gulf region and beyond.

Originally published in *Terrorism Monitor*: Volume 5, Issue 13 on July 6, 2007.

Notes

1. For a recent study of Basra that argues this point, see International Crisis Group, "Where Is Iraq Heading? Lesson From Basra," no. 67, June 25, 2007.
2. The alliance was never formed, perhaps, as a follower of al-Sadr suggests, due to Haeri's close ties to the Iranian government. Author interview, Najaf, Iraq, August 7, 2005.
3. See Markus E. Bouillon, David M. Malone and Ben Rowswell, eds., *Iraq: Preventing A New Generation of Conflict* (Boulder: Lynne Rienner Publishers, 2007).
4. Ibid.
5. Including al-Amarah, some of the Basra branch of the Mahdi Army is based in this northern district, where Abu Qadir, a major officer in al-Sadr's militia, was killed in early June 2007 by British forces. Baztab, June 5, 2007.
6. Reider Visser, *Basra: The Failed Gulf State: Separatism and Nationalism in Southern Iraq* (Münster: New Brunswick, 2005).
7. In fact, he comes from an affluent family of oil merchants. Author interview, Basra, Iraq, August 13, 2005.
8. Author interview, Basra, Iraq, August 13, 2005.

If Iran's Revolutionary Guards Strike Back: The Case of Iraq
By Hussain Mousavi

The recent move by the U.S. government to designate Iran's most powerful military unit, the Islamic Revolutionary Guard Corps (IRGC), as a terrorist organization reflects a tougher U.S. stance towards Tehran in response to its controversial nuclear program and military reach in the Middle East. Though largely aimed at weakening the IRGC's global business operations and financial network, the new sanctions are the most aggressive form of U.S. policy in confronting Iran's growing influence in Iraq, where U.S. military officials accuse the Guard of supplying weapons and military expertise to Shiite militias (The Associated Press, September 24, 2007). With the IRGC as the first national military organization sanctioned by the United States, Washington and Tehran have now moved another step closer to a possible military showdown.

In light of the unfolding crisis, it remains unclear what could happen in a military conflict between Iran and the United States. A basic scenario involves a comprehensive U.S. attack on Iran's nuclear facilities, naval forces, information and technology support system (especially those linked to nuclear sites in Bushehr, Isfahan and Tehran) and finally the bombing of IRGC ground force units stationed near the strategic cities of Abadan, Ahvaz, Chah Bahar, Dezful, Hamadan, Khoramshahr and Mashahd. The United States, possibly with the help of Israel, could help stave off Iranian retaliation by destroying Iran's command air base where Iranian fighter jets are kept on daily readiness against potential attacks by U.S. forces.

Assuredly, these military operations will be followed by a severe Iranian retaliation. In the words of the Guard's commander, General Muhammad Ali Jafari, the IRGC will unleash its most sophisticated conventional armed forces against the U.S. military in the event of any attack on Iranian soil (Fars News Agency, November 1, 2007). To what degree the Guard will use unconventional means of response remains unclear. So far, most of the discussion in academic and policy circles has focused on the Guard's connection with various Iraqi Shiite militia groups, particularly the Badr Organization, the military wing of the Supreme Islamic Iraqi Council (SIIC) that originally received training and funding from the IRGC in the early 1980s. Yet such a straightforward assessment reads too much into the historical connections between the two military units and ignores the highly complex relationship between post-Baathist Shiite militias and IRGC forces.

Shiite Militias and Sunni Insurgents

A common perception in the intelligence community is that the IRGC and its intelligence operations branch, the Qods Brigade, have their greatest influence with Shiite militant organizations like the Mahdi Army (whose operations were suspended for six months in August by Shiite leader Moqtada al-Sadr). According to General David Petraeus, the Qods Brigade is already engaged in a proxy war with U.S. forces by providing the most radical Shiite groups ammunition and shaped explosive charges to wage guerrilla warfare in the cities of Iraq (Voice of America, October 23, 2007).

While conclusive evidence for Iran's activities in Iraq has yet to be presented by the U.S. army, a direct connection between the IRGC and politically established Shiite militant groups remains somewhat unlikely. The military wings of a number of major Iraqi Shiite parties are already implanted in the country's political establishment and these organizations will most likely avoid any risky involvement in a proxy war that would link them with a foreign army, especially one which was largely responsible for the death of many Iraqis (including Shiites) in the 1980s.

Since 2003, Shiite leaders like Abdul Aziz Hakim and Moqtada al-Sadr have been doing their best to be perceived by the Iraqi population as leaders of indigenous movements, independent from any foreign entities, especially Iran. Any direct attempt to collaborate with the Iranian government, particularly the IRGC with its infamous reputation among many Shiite and Sunni nationalists as the sworn enemy of Iraq, could jeopardize the long-standing objective of politically active Shiite groups to secure their parties' interests in the country's unstable democratic process.

Much of the rhetoric behind al-Sadr's support for Iran should be viewed therefore as the tactics of political opportunism rather than an actual plan of military cooperation with Tehran. In the case of the Badr Organization, this professional militia is fully under the control of the political elites of the SIIC and integrated within the party's political structure. The chances of the militia splintering away from the political party and collaborating with the IRGC, while at the same time continuing to seek the support of the U.S. military against potential attacks from the Mahdi Army and Sunni insurgents, remains unlikely.

In Iraq's unstable political situation, the IRGC will most likely seek the alliance of non-politically established Shiite militants, like the many splinter groups of the Mahdi Army. Many former Mahdi Army commanders are willing to strike an alliance with the Guard in their fight against U.S. domination over Shiite territories. Here ideology may play a more decisive role than mere military or political opportunism. Many high-level IRGC militants, especially veterans of the Iraq-Iran War, are admirers of the revolutionary ideology advocated by Ayatollah Sadeq al-Sadr, who is a source of authority and reverence for his followers. The ideological affinity between the IRGC and various Sadrists militants, especially those who see Moqtada al-Sadr as a traitor for joining the Iraqi political establishment under the U.S. occupation, may bring about a dangerous alliance between the two Shiite factions, despite their different agendas.

A less likely but still conceivable scenario involves the emergence of a military alliance between the IRGC and Sunni insurgent groups. Sunni insurgent groups may be a source of support for the IRGC as the Qods Brigade moves to provide advance explosive devices and intensive training for assassination and kidnappings of U.S. personnel and Iraqi collaborators. In the event of a U.S. attack on Iran, the Guard could supply arms and military technology to various non-Baathist, non-Salafist Iraqi Sunni militant groups, though such a move remains unlikely since many Sunni Iraqis are Arab nationalists unwilling to cooperate with Persian Iran.

Tactics of Retaliation

It goes without saying that in the case of a U.S. attack on Iran the Shiite population in Iraq would be largely supportive of Tehran's retaliatory military actions. It remains unclear, however, as to the extent to which the Shiite clerical establishment would be willing to give allegiance to the Iranian leadership, who historically have rejected the Quietist ideology of the Iraqi Shiite seminary at Najaf and its conservative stance against revolutionary uprising. By holding that a cleric should advise and teach rather than rule, Quietism is at odds with the late Ayatollah Khomeini's belief that those most knowledgeable in Islamic law should rule.

The Shiite clerical establishment of Iraq could declare its opposition to U.S. military operations, particularly if civilian casualties resulted from an attack. This would be reminiscent of the time when Grand Ayatollah Ali al-Sistani gave a stark warning to Israel during the summer war of 2006 when many Lebanese civilians (especially Shiites) were the victims of Israeli air attacks. Ayatollah Sistani could call on ordinary Shiite Iraqis to rise up against the U.S. occupation with the IRGC finding fertile new ground for recruitment in its military attacks against U.S. forces inside Iraq.

The IRGC's most effective means of combating U.S. forces in Iraq will revolve primarily around unconventional war tactics and intelligence gathering, namely suicide terrorism and espionage intelligence through an effective system of native informants. The deadliest weapon that the IRGC can employ against U.S. forces in Iraq will be the "live bomb." It is well-known that the IRGC originally carried suicide strategies to Hezbollah militants in Lebanon in the early 1980s; the IRGC and Hezbollah even deployed joint suicide operations against Israeli and U.S. forces.

Undoubtedly, the younger generation of the IRGC would be more willing to commit acts of suicide terrorism as a way to reenact the heroic days of the Iran-Iraq War. The older, more experienced generation of the Guard could operate in Iraq as covert military instructors to Shiite militants for suicide operations. With porous borders between the two countries, many IRGC militants trained in suicide tactics could find bases in a number of southern Iraqi cities where they could recruit volunteers for suicide missions from the younger population of Shiite Iraq, especially in places where anti-occupation sentiments run high, like Diwaniya and Sadr City.

Although most of the IRGC's military operations rely on conventional forces based in Iran, like the special Muharram 10 Brigade with combined training in ground and air defense (Fars News Agency, October 31, 2007), IRGC operatives in Iraq could make car bombs a central feature of counter-attacks on U.S. forces. Similar to Lebanese Hezbollah tactics against Israeli and U.S. forces, explosive-laden vehicles driven by radicalized Iraqi Shiites could be crashed into military targets.

The Fifth Column

The most significant advantage that the IRGC has in Iraq is the support of military operatives working within the U.S.-trained Iraqi police and army units in Baghdad and elsewhere. According to a former Iranian agent deployed during the Iraq-Iraq War, the IRGC's operatives were fully embedded members of the Baathist army while collaborating with the Guard's intelligence center [1]. In a similar way, these military personnel, who have been entrenched in the Iraqi military and police force since 2003, can provide valuable information for the IRGC's Qods Brigade. At the time of conflict between Iran and the United States, the task of the Qods Brigade would be to transfer critical tactical and military operations information from Iraq to the Committee on Foreign Intelligence Abroad (CFIA), an IRGC intelligence agency in Tehran.

Evaluating the Threat

The most dangerous development that could occur in the period prior to a military conflict between the United States and Iran is the development of an alliance between non-political Shiite organizations, like the Mahdi splinter groups, and the IRGC. The formation of such alliances could be prevented by encouraging the Iraqi government (with the possible assistance of al-Sadr and his militia) to find ways to locate, negotiate and incorporate these splinter groups into the Iraqi electoral process and governmental institutions. There is a further threat of acting on bad intelligence from Iranian sources like the terrorist group Mojahedin Khalq Organization (MKO), who may provide information to the coalition forces designed to expand a military conflict between the United States and Iran for their own political interests.

A crisis of legitimacy has already been in process in Iran since the election of Mohammed Khatami in 1997. What a policy of engagement consists of is not the "appeasement" of the Iranian government but its recognition as a regional power, and the understanding that the best way to contain Iran would depend not on external forces of pressure ...

Conclusion: Defusing the Revolutionary Guards

The notion that direct negotiations with the Islamic Republic of Iran legitimize its authority is to ignore the basic truth that the fundamental source of legitimacy of the Iranian regime lies with the Iranian people. A crisis of legitimacy has already been in process in Iran since the election of Mohammed Khatami in 1997. What a policy of engagement consists of is not the "appeasement" of the Iranian government but its recognition as a regional power, and the understanding that the best way to contain Iran would depend not on external forces of pressure (e.g. UN sanctions or military attacks), but the weakening of the most radicalized faction of the IRGC, which seeks to keep Iran isolated for its own economic interests. In this sense, the most effective way to chip away at the IRGC's power is to vigorously integrate it into the global economic and political system rather than isolate it.

Similar to the Chinese military, the IRGC is now a major financial enterprise, but its economic power is unevenly distributed among its members. Many lower-ranking Guard militants come from the low-income sector of Iranian society and have leanings toward the reformist camp. Offering younger IRGC officers an opportunity to participate in regional and global markets could create division between senior and middle ranks within the Guard's economic community. An obsession with force threatens to unite the IRGC against a common enemy and brings the younger, more impoverished generation closer to the older, wealthier generation. As the sound of the drum-beat of confrontation increases, the call for unity within Iran also gets louder. The consequence of the policy of disengagement is that Iranian influence in Afghanistan and Iraq is enhanced by the growing military threat on Iran; this accordingly follows the empowerment of Iranian hardliners in the country's domestic political circles with the looming threat of an invasion by a foreign force already occupying two of Iran's neighbors. The irony of the U.S. policy of disengagement is that the more it aims to weaken IRGC through sanctions, the more it strengthens its military influence, and hence increases the chance of conflict in a region the United States has sought to stabilize for many years.

Originally published in *Terrorism Monitor*: Volume 5, Issue 22 on November 26, 2007.

Notes

1. Author interview with a former IRGC intelligence officer of the Iran-Iraq War, October 10, 2007.

Looking to the Levant: Internationalizing the Iraqi Insurgency
By Pascale Combelles Siegel

A number of Iraqi insurgents are increasingly turning their guns outward—rhetorically at least—toward the Levant (Jordan, Gaza, the West Bank, Israel and Lebanon) in general and Israel in particular. It is no secret that Osama bin Laden has renewed calls for the destruction of Israel and the liberation of Palestine, and has also stepped up efforts to set up bases of operations around the Levant in its attempt to restore the Caliphate over every former territory of Islam, from Spain to Iraq. At a time when al-Qaeda is enhancing its Israeli-Palestinian agit-prop and is developing networks in Lebanon and Palestine, the rhetoric of Iraqi insurgents—whether involuntarily or by design—might play into the hands of al-Qaeda's master plan for the region.

Iraq a Cornerstone for al-Qaeda's Expansion Toward the Levant

Since 2003, Iraq has become the main front of al-Qaeda's war against the West. Iraq has served as a recruiting poster for would-be jihadis from all over the world and as a training ground for thousands of foreign and Iraqi fighters. Maybe more importantly, it appears clear now that al-Qaeda has skillfully exploited the situation in Iraq to establish a base in the heart of the Middle East—something it had never accomplished before—a conveniently located stepping-stone from which to launch the liberation of Jerusalem through the infiltration of operators into the Levant and the spread of its brand of Salafist-Jihadist ideology.

In his July 2006 commentary on Israel's war against Lebanon, al-Qaeda ideologist Ayman al-Zawahiri said:

"By Iraq being near Palestine it is an advantage; therefore the Muslims should support its mujahideen until an Islamic Emirate of jihad is established there. Subsequently it would transfer the jihad to the borders of Palestine with the aid of Allah, then the mujahideen in and out of Palestine would unite and the greatest conquest [i.e. that of Israel] would be accomplished" [1].

In May 2007, al-Zawahiri reinforced the same point:

"The jihad in Iraq today, by the grace of Allah, is moving from the stage of defeat of the Crusader invaders and their traitorous underlings to the stage of consolidating a mujahid Islamic Emirate which will liberate the homelands of Islam, protect the sacred things of the Muslims, implement the rules of the sharia, give the weak and oppressed their rights back, and raise the banner of jihad as it makes its way through a rugged path of sacrifice and giving toward the environs of Jerusalem, with Allah's permission" [2].

Al-Qaeda in Iraq Calls for Jihad in Palestine

Al-Qaeda in Iraq (AQI) logically appears to be al-Qaeda's greatest ally in its plan to subvert the Levant. The group, echoing al-Qaeda's leaders and ideologues, has consistently claimed the suffering of the Palestinians epitomizes the suffering of Muslims around the world, treating their plight as a symbol of the so-called Western war on Islam. Consequently, AQI has made it clear that its enterprise in Iraq was one of the struggles that will lead to the liberation of Jerusalem. In an April 2006 speech, Abu Musab al-Zarqawi declared: "In Iraq we are very close to al-Aqsa Mosque of the Messenger of Allah, so we fight in Iraq and our eyes are on Jerusalem which can only be restored by the guiding Quran and sword of victory" [3].

More importantly, AQI's development in Iraq seemed to follow the path outlined by al-Qaeda's leaders. After al-Zawahiri announced that the mujahideen should unify and create an emirate in Iraq, AQI formed the Islamic State of Iraq, an emirate designed to unify all the mujahideen fighting in Iraq under the banner of Islam [4]. When al-Zawahiri called on Iraq to become a consolidating base from which to launch the liberation of all Muslim lands last May, the leader of the Islamic State of Iraq, Abu Omar al-Baghdadi, made similar references while emphasizing the duty of Iraqi Muslims to join the ranks of the mujahideen and reject the Coalition's engagement mechanisms—such as Awakening Councils, political parties and local concerned citizen groups [5].

Al-Qaeda and the Islamic State of Iraq in Collusion

The rhetorical and operational collusion between the two plans has become even more apparent in recent months. First, al-Zawahiri has repeatedly condemned the Palestinian factions—Fatah and Hamas—for either endorsing negotiations to achieve a two-state solution (Fatah) or for engaging in the democratic political process (Hamas). Al-Zawahiri contends that these actions are a betrayal of jihad and true Islamic tenets. Second, Osama bin Laden reminded his supporters:

"I reassure my people in Palestine specifically that we will expand our jihad, Allah willing, and will not acknowledge the Sykes-Picot border, nor the rulers installed by colonialism … if [America] and its agents are defeated in Iraq, then hopefully not much will remain before the mujahideen from Baghdad, Anbar, Mosul, Diyala and Salah al-Din will go to liberate Hittin [6] for us—Allah willing—and we will not acknowledge the Jewish state's existence on one inch of Palestinian land like all the Arab rulers did when they accepted the Riyadh initiative years ago."

During remarks on the Israeli blockade of Gaza, ISI leader al-Baghdadi expressed views perfectly congruent with al-Qaeda's leadership: "Our conversation today is our view of terminating the struggle with the Jews in the Land of Congregation and Resurrection [Palestine]." According to Baghdadi, because Israel is a religious state and because there is "no difference between Judaism and Zionism," Israel has no claim to statehood. Like al-Zawahiri, he heavily criticizes Fatah and the secularist-nationalist Palestinian leadership who he says has achieved nothing after years of lying. Like al-Zawahiri, he repudiates Hamas as betraying Islam and the *ummah* (Islamic community) [7].

Maybe more worrisome, anecdotal evidence suggests that both al-Qaeda and the ISI have moved beyond the motivational phase and into a more operational one. A document calling for the implementation of a three-year plan to move from Iraq into the Levant recently surfaced on the web. The document calls for the establishment of Salafist-Jihadist cells in Jordan, Palestine and Lebanon (Al-boraq.info, January 28, 2008). Meanwhile, al-Baghdadi is recommending actions that fit within that plan. In particular, he calls for the creation of a Salafist creed and belief group in Palestine and advises the Izzedine al-Qassam Brigades—Hamas' military wing—to secede from Hamas and act on its own according to sharia principles. Finally, U.S. military commanders have recently noticed that several ISI leaders are leaving Iraq in response to the increased U.S. military pressure there (Agence France-Presse, February 11, 2008). Although their whereabouts and future plans remain unknown, their escape from Iraq at a time when al-Qaeda/AQI have established the liberation of Jerusalem as their ultimate goal begs the question of their potential role in making this happen.

Are Nationalist and Islamist Insurgents Joining the International Jihad?

At the same time, non-al-Qaeda-affiliated insurgents in Iraq have increasingly commented on international issues and affairs as they relate to Islam or the Palestinians. In effect, these groups are using selected events to show that Islam is under existential attack and/or that the West does not care about Muslim suffering. For example, the Islamic Army in Iraq (IAI), a large insurgent group which has cooperated temporarily with the United States on the ground in Iraq, recently delivered a vitriolic indictment of Western policies in the Middle East, accusing the United States of seeking to control the economic wealth of Muslims, facilitating Western cultural domination and enabling the establishment of a "Greater Israel" that would include Iraq [8]. A larger alliance that includes the IAI along with more nationalistic movements—such as the Islamic Front of the Iraqi Resistance and the Mujahideen Army—the Political Council of the Iraqi Resistance (PCIR) condemned Denmark for the re-publication of cartoons that seemed to equate the Prophet with terrorism. The group says that retaliatory strikes are to be expected [9]. Central to al-Qaeda's strategy, such stories reinforce the idea that the West in general and the United States in particular are seeking to dominate and subjugate the Islamic world.

> *Maybe more worrisome, anecdotal evidence suggests that both al-Qaeda and the ISI have moved beyond the motivational phase and into a more operational one. A document calling for the implementation of a three-year plan to move from Iraq into the Levant recently surfaced on the web. The document calls for the establishment of Salafist-Jihadist cells in Jordan, Palestine and Lebanon.*

The continuously stalled peace process between Israel and the Palestinians as well as Israel's deadly incursions into Gaza and the month-long Israeli blockade all figure prominently in the nationalist and Islamist insurgents' propaganda. In late January, the Reformation and Jihad Front, Hamas-Iraq and the Islamic Front for the Iraqi Resistance (JAMI) strongly condemned the Israeli blockade of Gaza [10]. Meanwhile, the Jihad and Change Front (JACF), along with al-Furqan Army, the Conquering Army, the Brigades of Martyrs in Iraq and the Army of Ansar al-Mujahideen issued a statement of support to the Palestinians, claiming that they "will strike the occupier on our land [i.e. the United States] and give him a taste of defeat and shame" while their "eyes are on al-Aqsa" [11]. Recently, the IAI released a documentary equating the U.S. occupation of Iraq with the Israeli blockade of Gaza [12]. The visuals are well done and professional and their subtext speaks to all—Arab and non-Arab, Muslim or non-Muslim—who view what Israelis do in Gaza and what Americans do in Iraq as oppression. The visuals can be both interpreted within a secular/anti-imperialist framework—most common in Europe and parts of Asia—or within an Islamist framework—most common in the Middle East. However, the speech accompanying the images, in Arabic, calls for jihad against the infidels and vows to liberate Palestine from Israeli aggression.

This use of radical Islamist rhetoric by nationalist and Islamist Iraqi insurgents will most probably have a pernicious effect in the future. Whether the leadership of these groups actually intends to transform their operations into international jihad is not yet known. However, regardless of the intentions of these leaders, their use of such rhetoric, their focus on the resemblance between Iraq and Palestine and their use of religious justifications to examine the "crimes" committed by the West against Muslims play exactly into the hands of al-Qaeda's plan for the Middle East.

Originally published in *Terrorism Monitor*: Volume 6, Issue 5 on March 7, 2008.

Notes

1. Dr. Ayman al-Zawahiri, "The Zio-Crusaders' War on Gaza and Lebanon," As-Sahab Media Production Company, July 27, 2006.
2. "Third Interview with Dr. Ayman al-Zawahiri," As-Sahab Media Production Company, May 5, 2007.
3. Abu Musab al-Zarqawi, "A Message to the People," Mujahideen Shura Council, April 25, 2006.
4. The Mujahideen Shura Council in Iraq, "Announcing the Establishment of the State of Iraq," October 15, 2006.
5. See for example, "Between Perversion of Creed and Tenets of Jihad," Statement by the Islamic State of Iraq, August 27, 2007.
6. The former Palestinian town of Hittin was the site of Salah al-Din's 1187 victory over the crusaders that allowed the re-conquest of Jerusalem.
7. Abu Omar al-Baghdadi, "Religion is Sincere Advice," Islamic State of Iraq, February 14, 2008.
8. "A message from the Islamic Army leader/Bush and Sarkozy ... Political alliance or wealth and power share," Islamic Army in Iraq, January 25, 2008.
9. "Response to Denmark," Political Council of the Iraqi Resistance, February 18, 2008.
10. "Formation of a campaign of the Iraqi resistance to support Gaza," Political Council of the Iraqi Resistance, January 21, 2008.
11. "Start of the Campaign of the 'Twins' Operation in support for our brothers in Gaza and All of Palestine," Joint statement by the Furqan Army, the Conquering Army, the Brigades of Martyrs in Iraq and the Army of Ansar al-Mujahideen, January 23, 2008.

12. The video is available on the video-sharing website LiveLeak: http://www.liveleak.com/view?i=a8f_1202716268.

The Mahdi Army: New Tactics for a New Stage
By Fadhil Ali

Iraqi radical Shiite cleric Muqtada al-Sadr has issued a statement describing a new strategy for attacking Coalition forces (Alkufanews.com, June 13, 2008). The statement follows a year of intense military pressure against his Jaysh al-Mahdi (JAM) militia and a series of confusing and sometimes contradictory decisions. The hard-line cleric, who has not been seen in public for months, issued orders to reorganize his militia into a civilian branch and a small but select armed wing commissioned to fight Coalition forces. Only three months earlier al-Sadr had announced his retirement and admitted failure in his efforts at "liberating Iraq" (*Terrorism Monitor*, May 1, 2008).

Muqtada's statement was proclaimed in the mosques by his aides during the weekly prayer of his followers on Friday, June 13, 2008 (Almanar.com, June 13, 2008). A written copy—signed the previous day—was published on a pro-Sadr web site: "Everyone knows that we will not abandon the resistance against the occupiers until liberation or death, but you individuals in Jaysh al-Mahdi should know, and this is an obligation on you, that the resistance will be restricted to a group which will be authorized by a written statement by me soon. Those will be people with experience, management, awareness and sacrifice. They would have a prior permission—firstly from the religious ruler through their appointed command and secondly from the supreme command—through secret and private structures. Hereby weapons will be only for them and they will direct the weapons to the occupiers only, every other usage of weapons will be prohibited. The other part of Jaysh al-Mahdi with its thousands and millions will struggle against western secular ideology and emancipate the heart and minds from domination and globalization. They will be under a cultural, religious and social title and will be prohibited from carrying and using weapons..." (Alkufanews.com, June 13, 2008).

Since the foundation of the militia shortly after the invasion in 2003, the fighters of JAM have not hesitated to fight in large formations and initiate confrontations in their strongholds. They were involved in severe clashes with the U.S. military in major uprisings inside the poor Shiite neighborhoods in Baghdad and southern Iraq in 2003 and 2004. The fighting against Iraqi forces in Basra last March provided a clear example of JAM tactics. JAM also has the ability to recruit thousands when necessary and sometimes shows them in military parades. Until the government intensified its crackdown against JAM starting in late 2007, Iraqi Sunnis were complaining of JAM's coordination with Iraqi security forces to commit acts of sectarian violence. As part of the al-Sadr movement, JAM was a popular organization rather than a secret one, with

The announcement of the new strategy came after JAM suffered successive setbacks in the continuing crackdown by the Iraqi government, but al-Sadr had also launched a protest movement against the security pact now under negotiation between the American administration and the Iraqi government.

regional offices in every Shiite neighborhood. These features are about to change in Muqtada's reorganization.

The announcement of the new strategy came after JAM suffered successive setbacks in the continuing crackdown by the Iraqi government, but al-Sadr had also launched a protest movement against the security pact now under negotiation between the American administration and the Iraqi government. Al-Sadr called his followers to rally against the agreement, which aims to legalize and organize the American military existence in Iraq after its UN mandate ends in 2008. Al-Sadr called on Iraqis to "protest against the deal every week after the Friday prayer until the agreement is called off." He announced in a statement that the protests will continue until the government agrees to hold a public referendum on the American military existence in Iraq. In response to his call, thousands of al-Sadr's followers marched in Baghdad, Basra and other parts of southern Iraq protesting the long-term security agreement. American flags and an effigy of Iraqi Prime Minister Nuri al-Maliki were burned (Al Jazeera, May 31, 2008).

New Tactics for a New Stage

Dr. Asma'a al-Mossawi, a senior member of al-Sadr's political movement, explained the link between the new tactics and the U.S.-Iraqi security pact. In an interview one day after al-Sadr announced the new plan she said:

"It is not a reaction—Muqtada's new order—but a new strategy to deal with the current situation in Iraq considering the pressures that will lead to the signing of the security agreement with the American forces without the approval of the Iraqi people ... We believe that in the coming period of time there will be new moves against the American forces. During the last five years there were painful operations against them while they were among the Iraqi people. [In] the next period the American forces will be in their bases—this requires preparing a trained force from al-Mahdi Army, a force that should be experienced and works secretly guided by intelligence information to execute tasks quickly and return."

Dr. Mossawi did not rule out coordination between other insurgent groups and the new JAM military wing, which will be chosen and led by Muqtada (*Asharq al-Awsat*, June 14, 2008).

A Way around the Ban

In a sign that they insist on having their own militia, the followers of al-Sadr announced that they would not participate in the regional election that is supposed to be held later this year, but they would support other candidates: "We will not contest [the election] as an independent party but we will coordinate with other parties that serve the same national goals ... it will be impossible to bar us from the election, we have plenty of options on how to participate." The Sadrists have been negotiating lately with former Prime Minister Ibrahim Jafari, who was expelled from the Dawa Party of current Prime Minister Nuri al-Maliki after forming his own National Reform Movement. The Sadrists went further and said that they might even support their old opponent, former secular Prime Minister Iyad Allawi in the upcoming poll (*al-Hayat*, June 16, 2008). In April 2007, Nuri al-Maliki offered the Sadrists the choice of disbanding their militia or being denied participation in the election and political life (*Terrorism Monitor*, May 1, 2008).

The Beginning of the Campaign

It seems that the propaganda campaign of al-Sadr has started in the province of Babil, south of Baghdad, where leaflets are distributed daily urging people to store weapons and fight the U.S. army. The local police believe that in addition to JAM other insurgent groups are involved. Saddam Hussein's Ba'ath party and the extremist Shiite cult of the "Soldiers of Heaven" are among the suspect groups (*Terrorism Monitor*, February 22, 2008). The leaflets carry slogans like: "The national resistance is the only choice for the Iraqi people to drive out the occupiers and their agents." They also urge people to store ammunition, follow what is published on the internet about "the armed Iraqi revolution" and get ready for the zero-hour (*al-Hayat*, June 23, 2008).

Babil province is one of the areas where the Iraqi forces have not yet launched any major operation against the JAM. Shiites are the majority there, except in the northern part adjacent to Baghdad where there is a concentration of Sunnis. The Sadr movement has grown further from the governing Shiite coalition and looks more open to coordinate with non-sectarian parties. Many former members of the pro-Saddam Fidayeen militia are believed to have infiltrated JAM after the fall of Saddam, providing the possibility of coordination against the common enemy, the Iraqi government.

Conclusion

Iran and many Iraqi Shiites, especially Ayatollah Kadhum al-Ha'iri—an influential pro-Iran cleric and patron of al-Sadr—have condemned the prospective security deal between Washington and Baghdad (Iraqshabab.net, May 21, 2008; *Terrorism Focus*, June 18, 2008). Al-Sadr and his followers will most likely concentrate their efforts against any kind of U.S.-Iraq agreement; after a year of setbacks they will try to gain a new momentum based on the legitimacy of the support of senior Shiite clerics. In this way and by claiming to restrict their attacks on the Coalition forces only they will try to gain national support. To succeed, the long-term security deal must be handled by both the American and Iraqi governments carefully and not overshadow the recent security progress in Iraq. With the Kurds supporting the agreement and the Sunnis saying it is necessary, the big mission is to convince the Shiite majority. Unlike Iranian religious leaders, influential Iraqi Shiite clerics like Grand Ayatollah Ali al-Sistani have not put a veto on the deal in principle. After meeting al-Sistani, Abdul Aziz al-Hakim, head of the Islamic Supreme Council of Iraq (ISCI), said that the Grand Ayatollah indicated that the agreement should consider four points:

1. Recognition of the national sovereignty of Iraq
2. Transparency
3. The formation of a national consensus

4. Ratification by the Iraqi parliament (Elaph.com, June 4, 2008)

Sistani's blessing for any major political deal has become a must in post-war Iraq, let alone a situation like the current one where Iran and many leading Shiite clerics are openly against the agreement. Sistani's position appears to be negotiable, but the parties involved will need to work to gain his approval. On the other hand, August 22, 2008 will mark the renewal date for al-Sadr's six-month suspension of JAM's military activities. This might provide a suitable benchmark for al-Sadr and his reorganized JAM to launch a new page of the insurgency.

Originally published in *Terrorism Monitor*: Volume 6, Issue 13 on June 26, 2008.

Al-Qaeda's Palestinian Inroads
By Fadhil Ali

When al-Qaeda invited journalists and the people at large to direct questions by internet to al-Qaeda's second-in-command, Dr. Ayman al-Zawahiri, one of the most frequent questions was: "Why does al-Qaeda not launch operations in Palestine?" Al-Zawahiri responded with an audio message published on al-Sahab, the media wing of al-Qaeda, threatening Israel and Jewish interests. He endorsed "every operation against Jewish interests" and promised to "strive as much as we can to deal blows to the Jews inside Israel and outside it, with Allah's help and guidance." Al-Zawahiri also advised "the people of Palestine to perform jihad, jihad and jihad." He added, "I expect the jihadi influence to spread after the Americans' exit from Iraq and to move toward Jerusalem" (*Al-Sharq al-Awsat*, April 4, 2008).

The Palestinian issue has been a big challenge for the propaganda of al-Qaeda. Most Muslims around the world look at Israel as a hostile occupier and sympathize with the Palestinians. At any level of the Israeli-Palestinian conflict, Muslims obviously consider Israel as their enemy, yet al-Qaeda activity within Israel has been strikingly non-existent.

Al-Qaeda Front in Gaza?

In early March Israel ended a week-long offensive in Gaza in an attempt to stop Palestinian militants from firing rockets against the nearby Israeli cities of Ashkelon and Sderot. The Israeli assault killed more than 120 people, including many civilians. Three Israelis were also killed (Al Jazeera, March 13, 2008; The Associated Press, March 24, 2008). During the weeks following the operation, al-Qaeda released two audiotapes by bin Laden, one of which addressed the situation in Gaza and the Palestinians (Al Jazeera, March 20, 2008). Al-Zawahiri also appeared in an audiotape, which arrived shortly after bin Laden's March 20, 2008 release:

"Today there is no room for he who says that we should only fight the Jews in Palestine. Let us strike their interests everywhere, just like they gathered against us from everywhere … Let [the Americans] know that they will get blood for every dollar they spend in the killing of the Muslims, and for every bullet they fire at us, a volcano will turn back on them … They cannot expect to support Israel, then live in peace while the Jews are killing our fugitive and besieged people (al-Sahab, March 24, 2008)."

Bin Laden called for the use of "iron and fire to end the siege of Gaza" and accused what he called the "Zionist-Crusader alliance" of implementing the siege on Gaza, which came on the heels of the U.S.-hosted November 2007 Annapolis Conference, intended to revive the peace process in the Middle East. "This killing siege has started after the support of the Arabs of Annapolis to America and the Zionist entity (Israel); by that support they are partners in committing this horrible crime." Bin Laden identified jihad as the only way to support the Palestinian people, but urged Muslims to join "the mujahideen brothers in Iraq" to support the Palestinians rather than going to Palestine to fight:

"Iraq is the perfect base to set up the jihad to liberate Palestine ... Palestine and its people have been suffering from too much bitterness for almost a century now at the hands of the Christians and the Jews. And both parties didn't take Palestine from us by negotiations and dialogue, but with arms and fire, and this is the only way to take it back (Al Jazeera, March 20, 2008)."

After Hamas took over Gaza and drove out rival Fatah fighters and security services, the Palestinian president and leader of Fatah, Mahmoud Abbas, accused Hamas of protecting al-Qaeda and allowing it to gain a foothold in Gaza (*Haaretz*, July 10, 2007). Abbas renewed his accusations this year, alleging that al-Qaeda militants had infiltrated the Gaza strip and were receiving assistance from Hamas to establish a base of operations there. He also declared that an alliance had formed between al-Qaeda and Hamas (*al-Hayat*, February 25, 2008). Hamas denied the accusations, but

Abbas renewed his accusations this year, alleging that al-Qaeda militants had infiltrated the Gaza strip and were receiving assistance from Hamas to establish a base of operations there.

interestingly it seems that Hamas used the specter of al-Qaeda in Gaza during their talks with Egypt right before taking over Gaza. Khalid Meshaal, the head of the political bureau of Hamas, told the Egyptians that if Hamas lost its battle with Fatah over Gaza, "al-Qaeda will be your neighbor." The delegation told the Egyptians clearly that only Hamas was capable of securing the borders and curbing the cells of al-Qaeda. In retrospect it appears Meshaal wanted to neutralize Egypt before his approaching battle with Fatah in Gaza (Masrawy, June 18, 2007).

New Extremist Groups Emerge in Gaza

The propaganda of jihad has been spreading for years among the youth in Gaza, with stores making big profits selling the recordings of bin Laden and Abu Musab al-Zarqawi, the late leader of al-Qaeda in Iraq—killed by a U.S. air strike in June 2006. The Gaza strip borders with Israel and Egypt and is approximately 25 miles long and six miles wide. It is populated by only about 1.3 million Palestinians, most of whom live in poverty and suffer from both unemployment and neglect—an ideal environment for extreme ideologies to spread. Gaza has been a stronghold of the Muslim Brotherhood-rooted Hamas since its formation in the late 1980s.

After the Israeli withdrawal from Gaza in 2005, Gaza became a land of political confusion and lawlessness. The conflict between Hamas and Fatah elements was escalating and under these circumstances the name of al-Qaeda appeared in Gaza. On May 8, 2006, a group called al-Jaysh al-Quds al-Islami (The Islamic Army of Jerusalem) announced its formation: "With Allah's help the Islamic Army of al-Quds (Jerusalem), which follows the organization of al-Qaeda in the land of Ribat (i.e., Palestine), has been formed, basing [itself] on the words of Shaykh Osama bin Laden, Shaykh Ayman al-

Zawahiri and Shaykh Abu Musab al-Zarqawi." The group added that it would target every enemy of Islam: "We will explode with our bodies all of their locations and shake the land under their feet" (*Al-Watan*, May 24, 2006).

Later in 2006 another allegedly Palestinian group released a videotape. Calling itself Qaedat al-Jihad Wilayat Palestine (The Base of Jihad – Palestine region), the group started the tape with an excerpt from bin Laden's well known speech that followed the 9/11 attacks: "To America, I say to it and its people: I swear by God, who has elevated the skies without pillars, neither America nor the people who live in it will dream of security before we live in Palestine" (Al Jazeera, October 7, 2001). The video also included al-Zarqawi saying: "We fight in Iraq with our eyes on Jerusalem which cannot be regained without the sword" (al-Asr, November 2, 2006).

A Gaza group called Suyuf al-Haq (The Swords of Righteousness) proclaimed its existence with attacks on Internet cafes, music stores and women not wearing Islamic dress. Churches and Christian bookshops were also targeted. The group did not introduce itself as part of al-Qaeda but seemed to have similar Salafist beliefs. Khalid Abu Hilal, spokesman of the Palestinian Ministry of the Interior, said that he did not believe there was a link between the Palestinian extremists and the international organization of al-Qaeda, but a security source said that some al-Qaeda-affiliated extremists might have succeeded in entering Gaza through the border with Egypt the previous year (al-Naba, June 6, 2006).

On March 12, 2007, BBC reporter Alan Johnston—the only Western journalist based in Gaza—was kidnapped. A group called Jaysh al-Islam (Army of Islam) claimed responsibility and released a video of Johnston. The group demanded the release of Abu Kutada, who is believed to be al-Qaeda's spiritual leader in Europe and is currently jailed in Britain. After Hamas took power in Gaza, Johnston was turned over to Hamas forces (BBC, October 25, 2007).

The Jaysh al-Islam, which is believed to be headed by Mumtaz Daghmash, was also linked to the kidnapping of Israeli soldier Gilad Schalit. In an operation launched on June 25, 2006, Jaysh al-Islam joined with two other groups: the Izz al-Din al-Kassam brigades—the military wing of Hamas—and the Salah al-Din brigades, who are closer to Fatah. Three Israeli soldiers were killed in the operation and corporal Schalit captured. The statement of the Army of Islam garnered a lot of attention; it was their first appearance and the operation indicated the organization's ability to coordinate with other active armed groups or with extremist elements within them, creating new strategic possibilities in the Israeli-Palestinian conflict (al-Arabia, July 7, 2006).

Conclusion

As al-Qaeda endures continuing difficulties in Iraq due to the success of the Awakening (al-Sahwat) movement in Iraq, it has become crucial for the supreme leaders of al-Qaeda to revive their appeals for support, with the miserable conditions and ongoing conflict in Gaza providing a propaganda opportunity. Bin Laden and al-Zawahiri indicated that the way to Jerusalem passes through Iraq, so despite the new messages, the main front for al-Qaeda is clearly still Iraq. At the same time, Palestine has been and always will be an essential part of the ideology of al-Qaeda and the situation in Gaza has presented an opportunity for al-Qaeda to examine opening a presence in the Palestinian territories. Muslim extremist groups in Gaza like the Army of Islam might not have a direct link to the international organization of al-Qaeda but it seems that Mumtaz Daghmash and his followers have succeeded in operating outside the control of Fatah and Hamas. The Army of Islam will likely try to launch other operations in the region.

The existence of al-Qaeda in Gaza was used by Fatah and Hamas as part of their internecine conflict, both trying to gain political benefits by raising the issue. There is a danger in the Palestinian leaders using al-Qaeda as a propaganda prop while ignoring the reality of the issue and its possible consequences.

Originally published in *Terrorism Monitor*: Volume 6, Issue 8 on April 17, 2008.

Jordan's Jihad Scholar al-Maqdisi is Freed from Prison
By James Brandon

On March 12, 2008, Abu Muhammad al-Maqdisi—born Isam Muhammad Tahir al-Barqawi in 1959—was released from a Jordanian prison after almost three years imprisonment without trial (*Al-Sharq al-Awsat*, March 13, 2008). Maqdisi has long played a pivotal role in defining jihadist ideology. After taking part in the Afghan jihad of the 1980s, he refined the ideology of declaring takfir against other Muslims—i.e. defining them as apostates and thus deserving of death—leading to the creation of jihadist groups in Jordan and 1995 attacks in Saudi Arabia—whose government he had denounced as un-Islamic as early as 1989. Between 1995 and 1999, Maqdisi was imprisoned in Jordan, during which time he expanded his ideas and built new radical networks with the help of his right-hand man, Abu Musab al-Zarqawi. From 1999, Maqdisi has spent most of his time in Jordanian prisons, reemerging briefly in 2005 before being re-imprisoned for giving an interview to Al Jazeera television in which he criticized Zarqawi's attacks on civilians while reiterating his support for a broader jihad against the West and "un-Islamic" governments. Despite his long prison terms, however, Maqdisi has written and distributed several accessible books addressing key issues such as democracy, takfir and jihadist tactics, giving him an almost unmatched influence over the evolution of jihadist theory.

Maqdisi's Influence

Maqdisi's latest release from prison—apparently on grounds of ill-health—was reported extensively on radical Islamic websites. Significantly, even Islamic extremists outside the Arab world reacted euphorically to the news of his release. For example, a senior member of the islamicawakening.com forum, a prominent English-language Salafi website, responded to news of his release by writing: "Allahu Akbar! Allahu Akbar! Nothing describes the happiness of the *mu'mineen* [faithful] all around the world this day. Allahu Akbar! Our beloved Shaykh is released!" Similarly, on islambase.co.uk, the online home of many British extremists, one member described his release as "the best news in ages." Their attitude suggests that despite the death of Zarqawi and his own long imprisonment, Maqdisi's teachings—a mixture of bigotry and pragmatism—are still seen as relevant. Indeed, Maqdisi's correct predictions in 2004 and 2005 that Zarqawi's attacks on Muslim civilians would undermine support for al-Qaeda both in Iraq and abroad may have further boosted his standing among Islamic extremists worldwide. In light of Maqdisi's influence and popularity it is worth examining his key ideas in detail.

Maqdisi on Takfir

Like many jihadis, Maqdisi's ideology depends on declaring takfir against his Muslim rivals in order to permit violence against them. However, he repeatedly says that declaring takfir should not be undertaken lightly; in his 1997 book *This Is Our Aqeedah* (creed), he frequently quotes Qadi Iyad, a 12th century judge from Grenada, as saying:

"Declaring the blood of those who pray, who are upon tawhid [belief in the unity of God], to be permissible is a serious danger" [1]. Maqdisi adds that takfir should only be pronounced against those who have abandoned tawhid. He says a Muslim abandons tawhid, and hence Islam, if their actions show allegiance to un-Islamic entities by aiding them or participating in their legislation. In other words, he says only those who actively support non-Islamic governments or oppose jihadis should be targeted. Unlike many al-Qaeda members, Maqdisi repeatedly warns on both moral and strategic grounds against pronouncing takfir—and hence carrying out attacks—against ordinary Muslims, saying that in the absence of an Islamic state, it is understandable that many Muslims are unable to perfectly practice Islam. In his July 2004 book, *An Appraisal of the Fruits of Jihad* (Waqafat me'a themerat al-jihad), he writes contemptuously of jihadis who "start bombing cinemas or make plans to blow up recreation grounds, sports clubs and other such places frequented by sinful Muslims." Similarly, in *This is Our Aqeedah*, he criticizes extremists who kill for small infractions of Islamic principles: "The shaving of the beard and imitation of the *kuffar* (infidel) and other forms of disobedience like it is a general affliction that is spread far and wide. It is not suitable by itself for evidence of takfir."

On Democracy

A large proportion of Maqdisi's writings is devoted to the discussion of democracy, which he regards as one of the main threats to Islam. Maqdisi does not object to democracy as a form of representative government, however, but because legislators deliberately create man-made laws to replace or supplement the sharia (Islamic law). Maqdisi's arguments stem from his belief that a Muslim's faith is not complete unless he lives under sharia law. As he wrote in his early 1990s book, *Democracy is a Religion* (Al-Deemoqratiyya Deen): "Obedience in legislation is also an act of worship" [2]. Maqdisi consequently argued that anyone seeking to create legislation to replace the sharia is effectively seeking to take the place of God. From this, he concludes that "anyone who seeks to

A large proportion of Maqdisi's writings is devoted to the discussion of democracy, which he regards as one of the main threats to Islam. Maqdisi does not object to democracy as a form of representative government, however, but because legislators deliberately create man-made laws to replace or supplement the sharia (Islamic law).

implement legislation created by someone other than Allah, is in fact a polytheist." Yet his dislike for democracy is not absolute; he accepts that consultation (shura) between a Muslim ruler and his subjects is a valid Islamic principle—but says that this principle has been hijacked by secularists to legitimize the legislative aspect of democracies. Unlike many al-Qaeda fighters, however, Maqdisi says that the illegitimacy of legislative elections does not necessarily permit attacks against anyone who votes, since some people vote only "to choose representatives for worldly living" rather than to subvert the sharia [3].

On Jihadi Tactics

Maqdisi believes that violent jihad against non-Muslims is a core part of Islam which can be carried out by individuals at any time or place. In an interview with al-Nida magazine in 1999, he described jihad as an "act of worship that is permissible any time" [4]. He also says that jihad is not dependent on living in an Islamist state or having a Caliph, nor is it restricted to battlefields or places of open conflict. Despite this, however, Maqdisi criticizes would-be jihadis whose enthusiasm for glory blinds them to political and religious realities. In *An Appraisal of the Fruits of Jihad*, he mocks the "youths moved by their zeal." He continues:

"[They] have studied neither the sharia nor reality. They have newly begun practicing the religion and have not yet rid themselves of the arrogance, pride, and tribalism of their pre-Islamic days, such that some of them even consider it shameful, cowardly, and disgraceful to be secret and discrete. Others proclaim that they are carrying automatic weapons or bombs that they roam about with in their cars here and there, showing them to this person and that person; they think it is a trivial matter to blab to everyone about how they dream and hope to kill Americans and destroy the American military bases in their lands. They then become astonished at how the enemies of Allah ask him about these things when they interrogate him, and he wonders how they knew about it?!" [5]

Maqdisi also complains that many jihadist attacks are not carried out for strategic benefit but because such attacks are easy:

"There are other young enthusiasts who oppose us by attacking churches or killing elderly tourists, or relief agency delegates—and other such trivial targets—whereby they do not consider what will benefit the da'wah [call to religion], jihad or Islam, nor do they give preference to what will cause most injury to the enemies of Allah. Rather, their choice is only based on the easiest target." Maqdisi describes the best mujahideen as those who are "looking for targets that will bring down the enemy combatants and defy them—such as nuclear weapons, or intelligence centers and political posts, or centers of legislation and economy in the land of the polytheists" [6].

Maqdisi also criticizes those who attack Shiite Muslims, objecting to the attacks on both theological and practical grounds. In a 2005 interview with Al Jazeera, he said that ordinary Shiites could not be held responsible for their beliefs: "The laypeople of the Shiite are like the laypeople of the Sunna, I don't say 100 percent, but some of these laypeople only know how to pray and fast and do not know the details of the [Shiite] sect" [7]. This pragmatism does not contradict his intellectual hatred for Shiite teachings, saying in *This Is Our Aqeedah*: "We declare our hostility toward the path of the Rawafid [the Shiites] who hate the companions of the prophet and curse them."

On the West

Maqdisi frequently writes that hating non-Muslims is an Islamic duty. In his 1984 book, *The Religion of Abraham* (Millat Ibrahim), he says that this hatred "should be shown openly and declared from the outset." In *An Appraisal of the Fruits of Jihad*, he writes that any attacks on non-Muslims are theologically justified regardless of whether they result in any progress toward creating, or "consolidating," an Islamic state and regardless of changing political circumstances: "Any fighting done for the sake of inflicting injury upon the enemies of Allah is a righteous, legislated act, even if it brings about nothing more than inflicting this injury, angering the enemy [and] causing them harm." Simultaneously, however, he argues that for strategic reasons the mujahideen should at present concentrate their efforts on trying to establish a pure Islamic state in the Muslim world, saying that "one of the greatest tragedies of the Muslims today is that they do not have an Islamic state that establishes their religion on the earth." He also says that "the mammoth, accurately planned operations that were carried out in Washington and New York, despite their size, they do not amount to more than fighting for injury"—i.e. that they were justified only because they killed non-Muslims but had no strategic benefit. Importantly, however, he also says that if such attacks make it harder for the mujahideen to consolidate and build a true Islamic state, they should be avoided.

Outlook

Through his writings, which simultaneously justify both extreme violence and tactical pragmatism, Maqdisi has gained an iconic status in radical circles at a time when many jihadis—perhaps including even Osama bin Laden and Ayman al-Zawahiri—are becoming increasingly discredited. As a result, a public retraction of his more extreme views would send shockwaves through the jihadist community; on the other hand, a systematic recalibration of jihadist theory focusing attacks on Western military installations and secularists in the Arab world could reinvigorate the jihadi movement and perhaps win it new followers. Given that Jordan has reportedly forbidden Maqdisi from speaking publicly as part of the conditions of his release, it seems unlikely that his views have changed while in prison (*Dar al-Hayat*, March 13, 2008). A poem allegedly written by Maqdisi in May 2007 tellingly describes a conversation between himself and the prison authorities in which they tell him: "Renounce [your views]; many shaykhs have... Renounce and you will be generously rewarded with material [benefits]. In return, you shall [have freedom to] speak" [8]. Maqdisi records his response as "Prison is sweeter to me ... My suffering for the sake of religion is sweet." If Maqdisi has indeed remained loyal to his ideals, much will depend on how much freedom Jordan's government gives him to propagate his ideas; Maqdisi has consistently shown himself willing to continue promoting jihadist ideology regardless of the personal consequences.

Originally published in *Terrorism Monitor*: Volume 6, Issue 7 on April 3, 2008.

Notes

1. See the English translation of *This Is Our Aqeedah* (Al-Tibyan Publications) at http://ia341232.us.archive.org/2/items/sep2007tib/This-is-our-aqeedah.pdf.
2. Taken from Abu Muhammad al-Maleki's English translation of *Democracy is a Religion* which is available on the islambase.co.uk website.
3. From *This Is Our Aqeedah*.
4. *An edited transcript of the interview is included in the introduction to* This Is Our Aqeedah.

5. From *An Appraisal of the Fruits of Jihad*. An English translation of the book is serialized on the pro-jihadi website http://tibyan.wordpress.com.

6. From the chapter "Let the Expert Sharpen the Bow," in *An Appraisal of the Fruits of Jihad*.

7. Cited in Nibras Kazimi, "A Virulent Ideology In Mutation: Zarqawi Upstages Maqdisi" in *Current Trends in Islamist Ideology*, vol. 2 (Hudson Institute, 2005): 67.

8. Middle East Media Research Institute, "A Poem by Al-Maqdisi on the Occasion of His Father's Death," *Islamist Websites Monitor*, no. 105, May 31, 2007.

KUWAIT

Kuwaiti Cleric Hamid al-Ali: The Bridge Between Ideology and Action
By Chris Heffelfinger

Hamid bin Abdallah al-Ali is an influential Salafi cleric in Kuwait. He is designated by the U.S. government as a global terrorism financier and supporter, yet his website is registered in Vancouver in Washington state. Figures such as al-Ali are critical to the education and doctrine of Salafis—especially those that join the armed resistance of the jihadi movement—yet they often fall under the radar while they continue to radicalize thousands of followers. Part of the reason behind the lack of attention that clerics like al-Ali receive in the West is due to the pronounced cultural differences between opinion-makers in the United States and in the Muslim world. It would be hard to imagine a leading public figure in the United States composing lines of poetry, for example, in response to a security or political development.

Yet, among Arabs—and true as well of Salafi-Jihadis—poetry remains a respected form of expression and one lauded by the elite. One of al-Ali's poems, entitled "These Lines Were Composed By the Sheikh upon Hearing the News of Iran's Nuclear Announcement," published on http://h-alali.net on April 10, 2007, was read by more than 6,300 users. The poem offered al-Ali's historical perspectives on Iran's potential rise to power (in a fashion typical of his strong position against Shiite Muslims). However, the dense religious rhetoric typical of Salafi clerics, more than anything, prevents the West from understanding the message and importance of these individuals.

As one of the leading public Salafi personas in the Arab and Muslim world, al-Ali frequently comments—and sways Muslim opinion—on a variety of critical issues. He is outspoken about Iraq and the direction in which jihadi groups are moving the country; he regularly calls for unity among Salafi and jihadi groups; and he encourages the mujahideen to adhere strictly to the doctrine of the Salafiyya. His fatwas, articles and sermons have been received by hundreds of thousands of Arabic-speaking Muslims. Yet, he is perhaps most famous for his fatwa, issued in early 2001, sanctioning suicide bombings—and specifically the flying of aircraft into targets during such operations [1].

Al-Ali's Rise to Prominence

Born in 1960, al-Ali is married with five children [2]. He was a primary education teacher in Kuwait, where he taught Islamic studies. He studied sharia (Islamic law) at the Islamic University of Medina from 1979 until 1988, receiving a Masters degree in tafsir (exegesis) and Quranic studies. This university, along with Umm al-Qura' University in Mecca and Imam Muhammad bin Sa'ud University in

In his writings, [al-Ali] is most concerned with the proper implementation of the Sharia, and the doctrine and program of the Salafiyya being instilled upon the new generation of Muslims, as well as the mujahideen.

Riyadh, is among the most prestigious Salafi educational institutions in the world. The curriculum of these universities provides the fundamentals of Salafi doctrine, and easily transitions from the clerics in U.S.-allied Saudi Arabia to those like Hamid al-Ali, who call for jihad against Americans as well as any Arab governments who support U.S. "aggression."

After returning to Kuwait, al-Ali served as a professor of Islamic studies at Kuwait University for several years. He rose to the position of general secretary of al-Harakat al-Salafiyya fil-Kuwait (The Salafi Movement of Kuwait) by 1991, a position he maintained until 1999. A controversy arose in late 1999, when the Kuwaiti daily al-Siyassa was suspended for a week after publishing comments from al-Ali critical of Kuwait's relationship with the United States. The tension with the Kuwaiti emirate escalated after he published fatwas declaring Kuwait and other governments *kuffar*—disbelievers and lawful targets for the mujahideen—for supporting non-Islamic countries' aggression against the Muslim world. Following his arrest and a suspended sentence, al-Ali was officially banned from teaching or speaking in any institution under the auspices of the emir. Despite that, he has since become an even more prolific writer and speaker, well known in Kuwait and throughout the Arab world. He has since also become one of the leading voices of the jihadi movement.

Al-Ali maintains his highly popular website—http://h-alali.net—on which he posts a wide array of jihadi materials. His articles are also distributed on jihadi forums like http://elshouraa.ws, and Islamist websites like http://islamtoday.net. In his writings, he is most concerned with the proper implementation of the shaira, and the doctrine and program of the Salafiyya being instilled upon the new generation of Muslims, as well as the mujahideen.

Ties to al-Qaeda and the Global Mujahideen

In January 2005, arrests by Kuwaiti security forces uncovered a Kuwaiti al-Qaeda cell planning attacks within the country. The arrests also led to evidence that al-Ali had been actively recruiting Kuwaiti youth for jihad in Iraq and in his home country [3]. The U.S. Treasury Department also maintains that al-Ali provided funds to training camps in Kuwait and posted technical assistance on explosives making and other training materials to his website. Yet, the specific acts of support to local terrorist groups pale in comparison to the effect he has had on countless Muslims guided by his teachings. His rulings and commentary on current events and political issues—like his contemporaries Abu Muhammad al-Maqdisi and Abu Basir al-Tartusi—frame the debate among Salafis, and between them and other Muslims. Even if temporarily silenced by the imposition of an official government ban, the writings of such individuals will live on into the indefinite future, reposted on various Islamist websites and discussion forums.

The doctrine of the Salafi movement instructs Muslims on all aspects of life, from the mundane to societal and political. Salafis, more so than traditional Sunni Muslims, restrict individual interpretation or consensus among scholars as sources of law, relying instead on the accounts of the first three generations of Muslims (the Salaf al-Saliyeen, or righteous predecessors, for which the movement is named). With their desire to return to the Islamic purity of seventh century Arabia, the movement leaves no room for disagreement or compromise in its doctrine. Competing ideas are labeled *bida'* (innovation), *kufr* (disbelief), or *shirk* (polytheism, in particular as it applies to loyalty to a democratic regime and man-made laws).

This ideology is perpetuated largely through extensive funding from the Kingdom of Saudi Arabia and other Gulf states that are predominately Salafi (the movement originated in the late 1700s in the Najd, present-day eastern Saudi Arabia). Under this rubric, many Salafi teachings often condone jihad as a legitimate response to the military, political and economic aggression of the West.

Al-Ali's Teachings

An article by al-Ali published on April 17, 2007, republished widely across Islamic websites, such as islamicnews.net, declared that Iraq has been "a demonstration to the occupiers ... the Americans and Safavids [Iranians]." His extreme distrust of Shiites and their "true" agenda is persistent throughout his writings. Yet, more surprising, the same comments were made in an interview with islamonline.net, a widely popular Islamic website under Yusuf al-Qaradawi. Clearly, his views and teachings have found an audience outside the relatively narrow ranks of the Salafi-Jihadis.

Another recent article, "What Will Follow the Coming War," argues that the United States has brought and instilled ignorance along with its occupation, an intentional plan to corrupt the people of Iraq and the region (the period before Islam in Arabia is known as the age of ignorance). Similar to al-Ali's own long-range strategic thinking, he sees the U.S. war as aimed at achieving two developments: the uprooting of Islam from society and the dividing of Iraq into pieces to be controlled by Iran, Israel and the United States. Accordingly, the only response to this aggression is for Muslims to join the jihad against these forces.

A fascinating parallel exists between al-Ali's call for a war against the occupiers of Iraq with that of ibn Abd al-Wahhab (the founder of the Salafi/Wahhabi movement) and his ideological justifications for war against the foreign occupiers, the Ottoman Turks. Both called for jihad against fellow, non-Arab Muslims. In al-Ali's case, it was a call to jihad against the Shiites of Iran; in ibn Abd al-Wahhab's, it was the Sufi-practicing Sunni Turks. Although clearly a religious movement, one cannot discount that it is an Arab-led movement, whose discourse and literature are almost exclusively in Arabic (indeed, in the classical Arabic tongue of Arabia, where it was born). Other such instances have occurred, like ibn Taymiyya's famous fatwa against the Mongols (the 13th century scholar who inspired much of ibn Abd al-Wahhab's movement), declaring his fellow Muslims unbelievers for being insincere in their Islam, and hence lawful enemies.

Conclusion

Despite his clear ties to al-Qaeda and mujahideen in Kuwait, al-Ali is presented to thousands of Muslims as simply a senior Kuwaiti cleric. He enjoys this prestige, as do other Salafis, due to the juxtaposition of the Salafi movement with the two holiest sites in Islam, Mecca and Medina. To many, especially those less-educated Muslims who fulfill their Hajj duties, Salafi Islam is simply pure, or highly conservative Islam. Its exclusive reliance on the holy texts of Islam, seen by many as a return to the basics of the religion, obscures its true doctrine. It is thus seen not as a 17th century movement, arising largely out of the drive to expel Turkish Ottomans and their forces from Arabia, but Sunni Muslims who enjoy among the highest authority in Islam. Given this climate—and the view toward the Salafi movement by Muslims, Arabs and the West—it is unlikely that figures like Hamid al-Ali will cease the education and indoctrination of young Muslims into jihad.

Originally published in *Terrorism Monitor*. Volume 5, Issue 8 on April 26, 2007.

Notes

1. See William McCants, ed., *Militant Ideology Atlas* (West Point, NY: Combating Terrorism Center, 2006).
2. Biographical data from "al-sira al-dhatiyya bi-fadhilat al-Shaykh Hamid bin Abd Allah al-Ali" (Curriculum Vitae of Sheikh Hamid bin Abd Allah al-Ali), on http://h-alali.net.
3. U.S. Treasury Department Press Release, "Treasury Designations Target Terrorist Facilitators," December 7, 2006.

LEBANON

Hassan Nasrallah and the Strategy of Steadfastness
By Sherifa Zuhur

When speaking about Hezbollah leader Hassan Nasrallah's political strategy, it is necessary to study the organization as a whole. According to Hezbollah's leaders, the party was born as a resistance movement, not as a political party in the classic sense. Nasrallah emphasizes the collective nature of Hezbollah's leadership and its decision-making process [1]. This explanation makes Hezbollah similar to the post-Tunis PLO, a non-monolithic organization with a non-elitist self-construction. Nasrallah has become the voice of an organization rather than just another za'im (political leader). This leadership method bolsters Hezbollah's argument that it is more than just another Lebanese political party, and is instead a genuine resistance movement. Beginning as an alliance between Islamic Amal, al-Jihad al-Islami and Ummat Hezbollah, the party transformed itself into a much larger Islamist movement resisting Israeli incursions, surviving civil war and intra-sectarian strife (with the Amal Party) and providing developmental, educational and charitable assistance in the areas where the party operates. According to Hezbollah, this status means that it is not simply a militia, and therefore is not obligated to disarm as ordered by UN Resolution 1558.

In keeping with this history, Nasrallah welcomed all Lebanese who supported Hezbollah at its September 22, 2006 victory rally and characterized the movement as follows: "We are neither a disorganized and sophistic resistance, nor a resistance pulled to the ground that sees before it nothing but soil, nor a resistance of chaos. The pious, God-reliant, loving and knowledgeable resistance is also the conscious, wise, trained and equipped resistance that has plans. This is the secret of the victory we are today celebrating, brothers and sisters" (al-Manar TV, September 22, 2006). This explanation and his abilities of clear, understandable political and strategic analysis has positioned Nasrallah differently than Sayyid Muhammad Hussein Fadlallah, whom many regard as Hezbollah's spiritual inspiration and who promoted the Lebanonization of Hezbollah [2]. Alongside some friction between more radical or accomodationist party elements, Fadlallah wanted Hezbollah to create local interests for itself. Since these early years, the organization pursued these interests and achieved a Lebanese identity. Nasrallah's political statements that Hezbollah defends Lebanon are complemented by Fadlallah's fatwa that the believer is obliged to come to the defense of others who are not "capable of warding off danger to themselves or their property," or who are "not aware of the danger," even if the consequence is loss of life [3].

Since the latest conflict with Israel, Nasrallah is now arguably the most popular man in the Arab Muslim world (al-Ahram, July 20-26, 2006; CNSNews.com, July 31, 2006). Songs are dedicated to him and babies are named for his Truthful Promise summer campaign. Certain Lebanese, Americans and Israelis hope to diminish his stature, although these Lebanese still criticize Israel's military response. These critics include Samir Geagea and the anti-Syrian March 14, 2006 coalition. Washington likens Hezbollah to the "irregular challenge" that it faces in Iraq and some Israelis are still claiming their own victory in the latest conflict, while others are criticizing their army for not waging more destruction to Hezbollah and Lebanon.

Nasrallah's September 22, 2006 victory speech marked the continuities in Hezbollah's strategy and called for assessment and reflection during a peaceful Ramadan. Hezbollah as "Lebanon's defender" has always been a major Nasrallah theme, and the war with Israel played into Hezbollah's hands that Lebanon is in dire need of a defensive force (Arab News, September 5, 2006). Defense of the weak is the foundational narrative of Hezbollah itself. Israel's invasion of 1978, Operation Litani, set the stage, and the huge Lebanese, Palestinian and Syrian loss of life in 1982 and the devastation and occupation of southern Lebanon served as the party's raison d'être until 2000. When in 1997 Hezbollah waged a small victory with the deaths of 12 Israelis, Nasrallah proclaimed this as the first event in the party's restoration of dignity to the region [4]. Now he dates recovery from 2000 when Israel withdrew from Lebanon.

Post-war, Nasrallah shows the interaction of strategy, politics and discourse in highlighting that the steadfastness of a few thousand fighters against "40,000 Israeli troops" was reflected in the people's support for the party, and that the enemy was unable to sow political divisions between the two.

Nasrallah's Post-War Strategy

Nasrallah's post-war strategy is related to his war strategy. Moving from methodological analysis into the broader regional stage, he has summarized Hezbollah's military and political elements with ease. Nasrallah knows his enemy, and he has stressed that this war was planned by Israel and if this particular incident had not served as an excuse for an Israeli attack, another would have been found within months (Al Jazeera, July 22, 2006). Just like other movements of the "new jihad," Hezbollah provides sober self-assessments and self-critiques, earning popular respect for its honesty [5]. Nasrallah accurately compared Israel with its overwhelming airpower to his own smaller, less powerful force. He regarded Hezbollah's ability to remain steadfast (here is another similarity with Palestinian discourse) in the face of heightened Israeli attacks in July as a military victory. He pointed out that while the Israelis first spoke of destroying Hezbollah, his command structure remained intact, and Israel was forced to make a rhetorical shift to claiming that they were just attempting to degrade Hezbollah's capabilities. According to Nasrallah, their claim to have destroyed 50 percent of Hezbollah's rockets is inaccurate (Al Jazeera, July 22, 2006).

Hezbollah has iterated a deterrent and resistance strategy for some time. Nasrallah explained some years ago that the party used Katyushas only when Israelis attacked Lebanese, not as an ongoing tactic [6]. In his July interview, after defending Hezbollah's capture of Israelis and denying any foreknowledge of the plan on the part of Syria or Iran, Nasrallah explained that the differential in damage was due to the difference between an offensive and a deterrent arsenal, which remains at "20,000 rockets" (Al Jazeera, July 22,

2006). By this, he defended the party against Lebanese or Arab critics who said that Hezbollah's actions had caused the Lebanese to suffer for the sake of its own goals.

Post-war, Nasrallah shows the interaction of strategy, politics and discourse in highlighting that the steadfastness of a few thousand fighters against "40,000 Israeli troops" was reflected in the people's support for the party, and that the enemy was unable to sow political divisions between the two. The population of south Lebanon and the southern districts of Beirut returned to their homes at the party's directive, thereby outdoing the government when the party more swiftly and effectively offered aid to the people. Nasrallah catalogued this event as a political victory as well (al-Manar TV, September 22, 2006).

As virtually every publication asked who "won" the conflict, and in line with the party's tone, Nasrallah clarified his idea of "victory." Just as during the war, it meant steadfast defense. Hezbollah's tenacity surprised Israel. According to Nasrallah, victory did not mean the territorial liberation of Palestine, since that is the task of the Palestinians; victory is, rather, a perception that should be celebrated, but not in a sectarian or partisan manner (al-Manar TV, September 22, 2006).

Nasrallah's Current Political Strategy

His current political strategy is tied in with his critique of external forces that had accused the party of being an Iranian and Syrian tool. He ridiculed this charge, pointing out that he had not even informed Damascus or Tehran of his summer operation. Nasrallah criticized the passive Arab governments and decried U.S. support of Israel as well as the U.S. refusal to call for a cease-fire, saying "we should today stress that this war was an American war in terms of decision, weapons, planning and desire, and by giving several deadlines for the Zionists; one, two, three and four weeks" (al-Manar TV, September 22, 2006). He also denounced the U.S. plan for a "new Middle East" in general, and the rally crowd agreed. As for the alleged cause of the July hostilities and others since 2000, the party will only informally negotiate a prisoner release if it is an exchange, and it retains its claim to the Shabaa Farms and the Kfar Shouba Hills [7]. Nasrallah does not reject the idea of disarmament, saying, "We don't want to keep our weapons forever and they will never be used against anyone inside Lebanon." He suggests, however, that the causes of the conflict between Israel and Lebanon must first be addressed before any such disarmament takes place [8].

As for the UNIFIL force, he cautioned the Lebanese Army not to serve merely to catalogue arms violations, for that is not its real function; here, Nasrallah is suggesting that its function is to protect Lebanon, thus rendering Hezbollah's military force unnecessary. UNIFIL forces will not be resisted if they support the Lebanese Army, but if they are part of a broader strategy to transform the balance of power within Lebanon, resistance may form. Thus, Hezbollah's political strategy, despite the new element of UNIFIL forces and the Lebanese Army in the south, appears to be steadfastness to its own principles.

Nasrallah explains that political division but not simply sectarianism can be healed by a new Lebanese national unity government and more fair electoral laws. He warns Lebanese with reference to their own terrible civil war of the past and to Iraq, saying that "any talk in Lebanon about partition is Israeli talk; any talk in Lebanon about federalism is Israeli talk; and any talk in Lebanon about cantons is Israeli talk" [9].

Nasrallah is not the only leader to criticize the current Lebanese government or to call for national unity. The Free Patriotic Movement of Michel Aoun, the Lebanese Forces of Samir Geagea and the Future Movement of Saad Hariri have done the same. It may be that Hezbollah will now concentrate on the Lebanese internal situation, calling as Nasrallah has for a "clean" and accountable government [10]. Additionally, and in contrast with Lebanon's other political factions, Nasrallah has argued that this government should also have the ability to defend the Lebanese people in case Israel's resting period proves more brief than the party hopes. If the government is incapable of doing that, then Hezbollah will step in to defend Lebanon since, as stated in his July 14, 2006 speech, they are the party that made good on threats to strike Haifa and beyond.

Originally published in *Terrorism Monitor*: Volume 4, Issue 19 on October 5, 2006.

Notes

1. Farid Assaf, dir. *Lebanese Political Parties: Hezbollah* [in Arabic], Lebanese National Broadcasting Company, 2003.
2. Fadlallah and Hezbollah have denied any organizational connection. See Amal Sayed Ghorayeb, *Hizbu'llah: Politics and Religion* (London: Pluto Press, 2002), 6. Also see: A. Nizar Hamzeh, "Lebanon's Hezbollah from Islamic Revolution to Parliamentary Accomodation," *Third World Quarterly* 14, no. 2 (1993).
3. Sayyid Muhammad Hussein Fadlallah, "Rules of Self-Defense: Defending Other People," Fatawa, http://www.bayynet.org.
4. *Lebanese Political Parties: Hezbollah.*
5. S. Zuhur, "New Strategy for a New Jihad," Wilberforce Quarterly 1, no. 1 (Summer 2006): 8-14.
6. *Lebanese Political Parties: Hezbollah.*
7. For a more detailed description, see Sami Hajjar, *Hezbollah, Terrorism, National Liberation or Menace?* (Carlisle Barracks: SSI, 2002), 25-35; and
Ann Zwicker Kerr, *"The Murder of American Values in Lebanon,"* The Christian Science Monitor, *August 14, 2006.*
8. Ibid.
9. Ibid.
10. Some interpret this as a threat. See *Daily Star*, September 26, 2006.

Shifting Alliances in the Salafi Movement After the Lebanon War
By Abdul Hameed Bakier

The recent war in Lebanon could become a significant factor leading to a transformation within the Salafi movement in the Arab world. The conflict may also have a similar impact on Salafis as did the Gulf War of 1991. Transformations within the Salafi movement tend to create divisions and cause new splinter groups to form. When the new splinter groups emerge, they generally are more radical in nature and closer to Salafi-Jihadi extremist ideology. This article explores the early fractures in Salafi ideology, examines the controversial arguments among Salafis in the wake of the war in Lebanon, and attempts to understand how the recent war in Lebanon may affect the Salafi movement as a result of the increasing sectarian conflict in the Arab world and the acute divisions over the perspectives of Shiite Hezbollah.

Origins of Modern Salafi Factions

On the eve of Iraq's invasion of Kuwait in 1991 and the eruption of the Gulf War, the Arab-Islamic world witnessed severe internal divisions. The presence of U.S. troops in the region was a source of internal disagreements in the Salafi movement about the justification of the U.S. presence on the Arabian Peninsula. As a result of these disagreements, the Salafi movement splintered into two factions: the "traditional faction" and what can be labeled as the "center-wing faction." A third faction—the Salafi-Jihadis—was formulating in Afghanistan at the time and would remain concentrated in Osama bin Laden's al-Qaeda network.

The traditional Salafi faction expressed Saudi Arabia's and the Gulf States' approved government perspective of Islam and justified the presence of foreign forces in the region, particularly on the Arabia Peninsula.

The second faction, however, formed what became the first modern Salafi political opposition. This new Salafi orientation can be labeled as the center-wing faction or the al-Sorour faction, an attribution to Syrian Sheikh Mohammad bin Sorour Zinalabdeen. Sheikh Salman al-Odeh and Sheikh Safar al-Hawali were the two prominent clergymen of the center-wing faction and were considered unique in the history of Salafi movements because they politicized the movement to a degree that had not been seen previously. This Salafi faction was opposed to the U.S. military's presence in the region and against other political issues in Arabia such as government corruption and the mounting influence of the liberal movement in the Arab world.

The influence of the center-wing spread across the Arab world and the lectures of the "two sheikhs of resurgence," al-Odeh and al-Hawali, circulated throughout the Muslim community. Some of these lectures included, "Why They Fear Islam" by al-Odeh, and "Kissinger's Promise" by al-Hawali. The Salafi movement, even though not fully mature, emerged as a popular political movement. The imprisonment of both al-Odeh and al-Hawali from 1994 to 1999 by Saudi authorities made them symbols of that movement.

After the events of September 11, 2001, the center-wing and the Salafi-Jihadi factions witnessed deep discord, especially when the two sheikhs were released from prison. These divisions occurred because after the two sheikhs were released, they were less radicalized and less willing to irritate the Saudi government. They became especially conservative on the use of violence. The disagreements between both factions exacerbated over time. These differences were manifested when a prominent Salafi-Jihadi, Yousef al-Ayyiri, released an article criticizing Saudi religious reformists by calling them weak and accusing them of begging the West to spare the Muslim world [1]. In a message to Sheikh Safar al-Hawali, in response to al-Hawali's declaration to the umma entitled "Message to Bush" released in November 2002, al-Ayyiri commenced by describing al-Hawali's declaration as "a scholar's slip of tongue that should not dishonor him"; nevertheless, he criticized al-Hawali for not having a clear position regarding the mujahideen, governments that do not apply shaira and Western culture. Al-Ayyiri insinuated that al-Hawali was using the mujahideen to pressure the government without participating in jihad himself [2].

After the events of September 11, 2001, the center-wing and the Salafi-Jihadi factions witnessed deep discord, especially when the two sheikhs were released from prison.

The deep dissidence between the center-wing and the Salafi-Jihadis was further manifested in another message by al-Ayyiri to representatives calling for Islamic reforms on the eve of the inauguration of al-Hawali's "Global Campaign for Aggression Resistance" [3]. Al-Ayyiri rejected the campaign and accused al-Hawali of becoming a pro-government intellectual and of removing the duty of jihad from Islam [4]. Further, he says that al-Hawali does not support jihad, citing an interview that the latter gave to al-Majd Islamic television declaring his disapproval of jihad in Afghanistan and calling upon the Taliban to hand over Osama bin Laden to stop the bloodshed there [5]. Al-Ayyiri also criticized al-Odeh for altering his previous perspectives that were more in-line with center-wing and Salafi-Jihadi ideology. This was a significant development in the Salafi movement because al-Ayyiri was once a major supporter of al-Odeh and al-Hawali.

In the Salafi-Jihadi publication Sawt al-Jihad, a writer by the name of Mohammad bin Salem wrote an article that said fatwas issued by some Saudi religious scholars prohibiting suicide bombings were gifts for Jews [6]. He criticized al-Odeh for forbidding the mujahideen to travel to Afghanistan to fight U.S. forces. The writer accused Safar al-Hawali of turning Ali al-Faq'asi al-Ghamidi into the authorities; al-Ghamidi was on the Saudi most wanted list of 19 terrorists issued in 2003. Al-Ghamidi, however, surrendered to the authorities himself and is still in prison.

From the aforementioned, we notice the state of antipathy and escalation that culminated between the two factions that started from admonitions, arguments, ideological queries, acquiescence and ending with accusations that center-wing Salafis were collaborating with the state.

The Impact of the Lebanon War

To understand the impact of the Lebanon war on the Salafi movement, there are three developments to be considered. First, the traditional Salafis that represented the state's opinion argued that it was permissible to sign a truce with Israel. The argument was presented by Sheikh Abdul Mohsen al-Obeikan who strayed from the traditional norms of Salafis and said "min al-Siyasah Ala Natdakhal bel Syasah" (it is good policy to quit policy). This sanctioned a truce with Israel by citing Islamic historical practices toward Jews. He said that "resorting to peace, reconciliation or political and peaceful solutions with the Jews is needed at this time for the lack of Islamic might to liberate by force what is righteously theirs" (*Asharq al-Awsat*, July 27, 2006).

Second, the Shiites' glory and increasing popularity after the Lebanon war in the Arab world caused concern among Salafi-Jihadis. They were afraid that they would lose the lead role in the global jihad. Salafi-Jihadis have expressed many times that they are leading the global Islamic liberation war. Consequently, the analogies drawn between Hezbollah chief Hassan Nasrallah and al-Qaeda leader Osama bin Laden in the Arab street were in favor of Nasrallah. The analogy was that Nasrallah is a nationalist leader with political legitimacy who is fighting the direct enemy Israel; bin Laden, on the other hand, is a global leader who is fighting the indirect enemy, the United States, without credible political justifications (CNN Arabic, September 16, 2006). The Salafi-Jihadi fears of losing the lead role were expressed by Ayman al-Zawahiri, who on September 11, 2006 threatened to take revenge on Israel and called upon the Muslim nation to fight the "Zionists and Crusaders." Al-Zawahiri added that "al-Qaeda cannot standby and watch missiles fall on our people in Palestine and Lebanon," a statement perceived by many as an attempt by al-Qaeda to pull the rug from underneath Hezbollah.

Third, the center-wing faction became divided during the conflict in Lebanon. While this division started with the release of al-Odeh and al-Hawali from prison, it culminated when the Lebanon conflict began. After their release from prison, both sheikhs became more traditional and less radical. This caused elements of the center-wing faction to move further away from al-Odeh and al-Hawali, yet not all the way into the Salafi-Jihadi camp. These new elements can be labeled the "conservative" center-wing faction and they have been led by Nasser al-Omar, who replaced the ailing Safar al-Hawali. The conservative center-wing faction has refused to support Hezbollah and the Shiites, while the more traditional center-wing faction has supported Hezbollah in its latest conflict with Israel. The division in the center-wing was manifested in a fatwa issued by Nasser al-Omar prohibiting support for Hezbollah. On the other hand, al-Odeh, who represents the traditional center-wing, called for the postponement of internal Islamic struggles—such as Sunni-Shiite violence—promising to debate these issues at a later stage (*al-Hayat*, August 25, 2006).

Conclusion

In the wake of the divisions over the Lebanon war, the proclamations of the conservative center-wing faction are in concurrence with Salafi-Jihadis. In the September 2006 issue of *al-Bayan* magazine, published in London, an article was published warning of the rise of the Shiites after the Lebanon war. In an article entitled "Lets be Frank, Salafi is the Last Defense Line," the writer indicated that Hezbollah is active in upholding the interests of Iran, Syria and the Shiites, therefore the victory of Hezbollah serves an Iranian expansionist policy that aims to strengthen Shiite penetration and dissemination of Shiite ideology through fueling minorities and sectarian disputes among Sunnis. The writer calls upon world Salafis to unite. Furthermore, he reiterates the need to develop genuine political rhetoric so that Salafi ideology appeals to more Muslims.

With each new conflict in the Middle East, the Salafi movement has experienced divisions, which have created new strains within the movement. Yet, as each new strain forms, it becomes more radical in nature and closely resembles the ideology of the Salafi-Jihadis. The conflict in Lebanon furthered this trend, and the intensifying sectarian violence in Iraq between Sunnis and Shiites is also playing an important role that will only increase tension over time. It is likely that this increase will result in added strength to the Salafi-Jihadi movement and this may cause severe security problems for the Gulf States when these veteran Salafi-Jihadis begin returning to their home countries.

Originally published in *Terrorism Monitor*: Volume 4, Issue 20 on October 19, 2006.

Notes

1. Yousef al-Ayyiri, "Fadlan Inbatiho Siran" ("Please Lie Down Secretly"), 2002, http://www.albatar.org.
2. Yousef al-Ayyiri, "Letter to Safar al-Hawali, " 2002, http://www.albatar.org.
3. The campaign was an effort to explain the righteousness of Islamic causes. It primarily consisted of a website at http://www.qawim.org. Its general secretary was al-Hawali.
4. Ibid.
5. Ibid.
6. *Sawt al-Jihad*, no. 5, 34-35.

SAUDI ARABIA

Jailing Jihadis: Saudi Arabia's Special Terrorist Prisons
By Christopher Boucek

Saudi Arabia is nearing completion of new purpose-built prison facilities for its program of rehabilitation and counseling for Islamist militants. Under this program five new specialized prisons have been built in Riyadh, Qassim, Abha, Dammam, and Jiddah over the span of approximately nine months. These new facilities have been designed to facilitate the dialogue process while at the same time housing individuals assessed to be significant security risks. These five new prisons are each designed to hold up to 1,200 prisoners [1].

The decision to build specially-dedicated facilities in which to focus on the counseling program was based upon a number of considerations. First and foremost was the fact that the existing prison facilities were not designed to promote dialogue and it was determined that successful advancement of the rehabilitation program could best be done through new specially-designed facilities. Furthermore, these new facilities would make the classification and segregation of detainees easier [2]. The classification of detainees into those more predisposed to dialogue, and then separation of them from other more militant prisoners, would encourage and facilitate the work of the Advisory Committee, the Ministry of the Interior body that runs the rehabilitation program.

Typically in Saudi Arabia, there are eight to ten prisoners held in a cell at one time [3]. In other detention facilities up to 30 individuals may be housed together in a single group cell. In the new facilities, prisoners will be housed in individual cells or perhaps sharing with another inmate [4]. Saudi officials are now careful to sort petty criminals from those that may harbor extremist or takfiri beliefs, in an attempt to prevent further radicalization while in prison. Although it was never practice to house suspected militants or violent extremists with common criminals, it is known that some offenders have left detention in Saudi Arabia with a greater knowledge of criminal logistics [5]. There have also been reports that some prisoners have sought to impose their strict religious interpretations and practices on others.

Rehabilitation and the Counseling Program

Approximately four years ago, in the aftermath of a series of domestic terrorist attacks, Saudi officials launched a comprehensive program designed to engage security detainees in psychological counseling and a series of religious dialogues (*Terrorism Monitor*, August 16, 2007). Through discussion, education, and observation, the counseling program seeks to de-radicalize and demobilize extremists and militants held in Saudi prisons. By demonstrating that detainees' religious and ideological justifications for their beliefs and actions are based upon corrupted versions of Islam, the Saudi government has sought to delegitimize and invalidate the theological underpinnings in what they have termed the "war of ideas."

Much of the Interior Ministry's rehabilitation program takes place within the prison system. The scholars and sheikhs that dialogue with detainees visit prisons and spend considerable amounts of time speaking with program participants. After significant progress is made in the rehabilitation process and after a prisoner's sentence has been completed, then the process can continue in other settings, such as at the Care Rehabilitation Center outside Riyadh.

Inside the new al-Ha'ir prison

The Riyadh facility was built outside the city at the site of a pre-existing prison at al-Ha'ir, located approximately 25 miles south of Riyadh [6]. The complex is made up of several existing facilities, including one for common criminals and another specially designated to house security offenders. A number of reported al-Qaeda figures are held at the maximum security facility at al-Ha'ir and it has been said that this has made the prison a tempting target for militants. The new facility at al-Ha'ir *A number of reported al-Qaeda figures are held at the maximum security facility at al-Ha'ir and it has been said that this has made the prison a tempting target for militants.* is set off from the other pre-existing structures at the site and is surrounded with its own sophisticated security, including perimeter walls and fences, buried seismic cables and microwave detection systems [7].

The new al-Ha'ir prison is comprised of two sections with different types of cells: one section of the prison has small group cells designed to house up to six prisoners, while the other section is made up of smaller individual cells. The individual cells can accommodate up to two people. The facility also includes ten handicapped cells and ten larger single occupancy cells with desks and other amenities to facilitate advanced study. In total, there are 320 cells at the new facility at al-Ha'ir [8]. In addition to the detainee and prisoner processing and intake areas, there are 32 individual interrogation rooms, as well as a prison infirmary.

There are cameras throughout the new facility, including one in every cell and interrogation room. The video feeds first to the prison headquarters, then to the *mabahith* ("General Investigations," the Saudi internal security service), and ultimately to the Ministry of the Interior in Riyadh [9]. This is intended to provide accountability and to prevent instances of abuse through the knowledge that no act of mistreatment will go unseen.

Each cell is designed in large part to be self-contained, each equipped with toilets, showers, sinks, and windows. This was intended to reduce the need for prisoners to be leaving their cells more than is necessary and lessening the level of interaction between guards and prisoners. The cells were also constructed to prevent inmates from communicating between cells; in older prisons inmates were able to use the pipes to speak with each other [10]. Food is prepared centrally in the prison kitchen and then delivered to the each cell [11]. After meal services, inmates can purchase tea and other sundries from someone who goes cell-to-cell.

Intercoms in each cell allow prisoners to communicate with the guard posts. Each corridor of cells has a dedicated and contained outdoor area for prisoner exercise or in the event of fire evacuation. In September 2003 there was a major fire at al-Ha'ir in which 67 inmates died and at least 20 more were injured. The furnishings and mattresses used in the cells are now fire proof [12].

Rehabilitation within prison

Each cell is equipped with a television set, mounted within the wall above the cell door behind Plexiglas. The televisions are centrally controlled from guard posts at the end of each corridor. In addition to regular television broadcasts, these can also be used to transmit lectures and special programs designed or selected by the advisory committee.

One of the factors that differentiate these new facilities from other prisons in the kingdom is the inclusion of special purpose-built space dedicated to the counseling program. This is centered on a large lecture hall and classroom space designed to accommodate up to 50 persons. This large space can be further divided into smaller rooms for more private discussion, as well as to accommodate female visitors. Lectures from here can be broadcast to individual cells in order to increase the reach of the clerics and scholars that come to work in the prison beyond the physical capacity of the hall, but also to engage with those prisoners who may not yet be ready to interact with others. An important aspect of the Saudi rehabilitation program is that it does not just consist of religious lectures; dialogue and discussion is encouraged. To facilitate this, prisoners are able to ask questions via the intercom system in their cells. Networking the prisons together now allows lectures, sermons, and presentations to be broadcast simultaneously throughout the entire Saudi prison system.

Off of the lecture hall there are a number of smaller counseling rooms, each with windows and separate toilets. Elsewhere in the building there are a series of other spaces for families to accommodate visits and facilitate the inclusion of a detainee's family and larger social network in the rehabilitation process. This also includes rooms for conjugal visits for married prisoners, who are allowed several hours with their spouses [13]. One of the keys to the Saudi program is that it does not just treat the individual, but involves a detainee's whole family. Greater family involvement, such as through extended family visitations, shared meals, and other sessions with scholars creates opportunities for a detainee's family to learn about the plight of their loved one. Furthermore, it also allows the committee to learn more about a prisoner's unique social situation, data which in turn is used to help support the detainee's family while he is in custody and to help support his reintegration upon release.

Promoting cooperation

Another essential aspect of the rehabilitation program is to demonstrate that cooperation with the authorities will result in a suspect being treated well. It is understood that this is needed not just to facilitate dialogue, but also to encourage others to take advantage of this and other programs offered by the government. As such it crucial to dispel rumors of abuse and to guarantee a program participant's welfare—these are vital steps in building the rapport and trust that the counseling process will eventually build upon.

Instances of torture and abuse have previously been documented in the Saudi prison system (U.S. State Department Country Reports on Human Rights Practices, 2006). A recent video recorded on a mobile phone showing a guard beating a prisoner at al-Ha'ir raised further concerns. As a result, the government has a high desire to portray positive conditions for cooperating suspects. Previous examples of this have included government sponsored testimonies of suspected terrorists jailed at al-Ha'ir praising the conditions of their incarceration and statements encouraging others to cooperate with *authorities (al-Sharq al-Awsat*, December 15, 2004; *al-Youm*, January 5, 2005). These measures sought to combat the perceptions of mistreatment and to promote participation in periodic amnesties. These new prisons are part of the effort to demonstrate the compassion that will result from cooperation.

While Saudi officials readily admit that building new prisons is never a good sign, the construction of facilities such as that at al-Ha'ir demonstrates a commitment to continue pursuing rehabilitation and engagement strategies in dealing with takfiri militants. The continued institutionalization of the counseling program reveals Riyadh's determination to win the "war of ideas." To be sure, soft counter-terrorism efforts alone will not be sufficient, and the new prison construction program is a unique hybrid of multiple strategies. Moreover, this construction effort is also very useful as it gives us an insight into the size and scope of the prison rehabilitation program envisioned by Saudi authorities for the foreseeable future.

Originally published in *Terrorism Monitor*: Volume 6, Issue 2 on January 24, 2008.

Notes

1. Author interview with HRH Prince Mohammed bin Nayef, Assistant Minister of Security for Security Affairs, Riyadh, Saudi Arabia, October 2007.
2. Based in part on author interview with Dr. Abdulrahman al-Hadlaq, Advisor to HRH Prince Mohammed bin Nayef, Assistant Minister of Security for Security Affairs, Riyadh, Saudi Arabia, November 2007.
3. Author interview with HRH Prince Mohammed bin Nayef, October 2007.
4. Ibid.
5. Based in part on author's conversations in Saudi Arabia, October and November 2007.
6. Data in this section is based upon a site visit to al-Hair prison in November, 2007, and discussions with prison and Ministry of Interior officials, al-Hair prison, Saudi Arabia.
A journalist with CBC News recently visited the facility and her story includes some photos of the new prison. Nancy Durham, "Where Saudi Arabia Will Send Their Most Dangerous," CBC News, December 18, 2007,
http://www.cbc.ca/news/reportsfromabroad/durham/20071218.html.

7. Based on author interviews with Major General Youssef al-Mansour, Investigative Division, Ministry of Interior, Lieutenant Colonel Mohammed al-Zahrani, Engineering Director of al-Ha'ir project, and an unindentified project engineer.

8. Author interviews with Major General Youssef al-Mansour, Investigative Division, Ministry of Interior, and Lieutenant Colonel Mohammed al-Zahrani, Engineering Director of al-Ha'ir project, al-Ha'ir Prison, Saudi Arabia, November 2007.

9. Author interview with HRH Prince Mohammed bin Nayef, Assistant Minister of Security for Security Affairs, Riyadh, Saudi Arabia, October 2007.

10. Ibid.

11. According to prison administrators, camel is said to be a favorite of detainees and is served about once a week.

12. Author interview with Lieutenant Colonel Mohammed al-Zahrani, Engineering Director of al-Ha'ir project, Riyadh Saudi Arabia, November 2007.

13. Author interview with HRH Prince Mohammed bin Nayef, Assistant Minister of security for security affairs, Riyadh Saudi Arabia, October 2007.

Yemen's Al-Iman University: A Pipeline for Fundamentalists?
By Gregory D. Johnsen

The recent arrests of 23 men, including four Europeans and three Australians, have once again raised questions about Yemen's al-Iman University and its possible links to extremism. Initial reports suggested that the European and Australian suspects, who were accused of smuggling weapons to Islamist militias in Somalia, were students at al-Iman; this claim, however, was quickly denied by the university's president and founder Sheikh Abd al-Majid al-Zindani (*al-Sharq al-Awsat*, November 1, 2006). Al-Zindani, who was listed as a "specially designated global terrorist" by both the United States and the United Nations in 2004, has often used this ploy to distance himself and the university from students suspected of terrorist activities [1]. This time, however, his claim was defended by Yemeni President Ali Abdullah Saleh, who paid a surprise visit to al-Iman on November 12 (Saba News, November 12, 2006). An analysis of the university itself displays how it is both an institution of higher learning and a pipeline for fundamentalist activity.

President Saleh's Defense of al-Iman

Saleh's recent comments marked the second time in three months that he has publicly defended the university against its critics. The first time was on August 21, 2006, when Saleh was the keynote speaker at the graduation ceremony of al-Iman's third group of graduates. He claimed on that occasion that Western governments had been sending students to the university in an attempt to ascertain the university's curriculum, but that they had "failed because the university taught only the Quran and Sunna" (*al-Sharq al-Awsat*, August 22, 2006). He said that this sort of behavior has caused the university's students to "live in a corner of fear" from Western security infiltration (*al-Sharq al-Awsat*, August 22, 2006). Saleh went further in his November defense of the university, not only claiming that al-Iman did not produce extremists, but also praising al-Zindani as a "leading soldier in the Yemeni Revolution and an enlightened academic soldier" (*al-Hayat*, November 13, 2006). Saleh flatly denied the allegation that al-Iman produced terrorists. "That is a lie," he said in his speech. "If this is a nest of terrorists, then what is the president of the country doing here?" (*al-Hayat*, November 13, 2006).

Saleh has defended al-Zindani before, most notably in March, 2006, when he told U.S. Ambassador Thomas Krajeski: "Sheikh al-Zindani is a rational, balanced and moderate man and we know him well and the Yemeni government guarantees [his actions] and I guarantee his character" (*al-Quds al-Arabi*, March 12, 2006). His speech at al-Iman came only days before Saleh was scheduled to head a delegation to a donor's conference in London, signifying once again that Saleh is not willing to trade al-Zindani for economic aid.

Regardless of Saleh's defense, al-Iman University is not the terrorist producing institute that the United States thinks it is, but then neither is it the misunderstood religious college that Yemen claims it to be; the problem is that the university is a complex mix of the two, which is what makes it so difficult to define. The university, which sits on the outskirts of Sanaa, is best known in the United States as the place where American Taliban John Walker Lindh studied before leaving for Pakistan and later Afghanistan. In Yemen, it is famous for producing students such as Ali al-Jarallah and Abed Abdul al-Razak Kamal, who were responsible for the murder of an opposition politician and three Baptist missionaries in late 2002. Over the years, al-Zindani has issued separate statements claiming that none of these students, except for al-Jarallah, ever attended the university. In a 2005 interview with the Lebanese journalist Hazim al-Amin, al-Zindani said that al-Jarallah only studied at al-Iman for a year and a half before leaving out of frustration over the lack of religiosity at the university (al-Hayat, October 12, 2005). Nevertheless, like his carefully worded and ambiguous statements about the nature of his relationship with Osama bin Laden, al-Zindani's denials appear more contrived than concrete.

The Makeup of the University

Al-Zindani established the university in 1993, the same year that he took up a post on the five-man presidential council, although the university did not start classes until 1994. The university, which initially operated outside of government control, relied on donations and the support of wealthy benefactors. The Yemeni government, under Saleh's instructions, donated the land, while Saudi Arabia and a host of private groups from around the Islamic world contributed financial capital. It is often assumed that bin Laden was among these donors, as he was fairly close to al-Zindani during the 1980s when both men spent a great deal of time in Afghanistan and Pakistan. Musa al-Qarni, a Saudi scholar, told al-Hayat in March that the two, along with Abdullah Azzam, were the most prominent men at the absentia trial of Ahmad Shah Masoud (al-Hayat, March 8, 2006). Despite these ties, however, al-Zindani has denied that bin Laden was a source of funding for al-Iman (al-Sharq al-Awsat, June 3, 2001). Ever since al-Zindani was listed as a "specially designated global terrorist," he has become even more reticent to discuss the university's sources of funding. In his interview with al-Amin, al-Zindani said that if he revealed the university's donors, they would come under international pressure to end their support for al-Iman (al-Hayat, October 12, 2005).

Ever since al-Zindani was listed as a "specially designated global terrorist," he has become even more reticent to discuss the university's sources of funding.

Despite government support—Saleh laid the cornerstone for the university—al-Iman has not led a trouble-free existence. In the aftermath of the September 11, 2001 attacks, the university was closed down temporarily and scores of foreign students were deported. It has also been accused of fostering a military wing by the ruling General People's Congress' newspaper, al-Mu'atammar. Al-Zindani wasted little time in putting out a statement emphatically denying this, saying that the very claim was designed to help foreigners accuse al-Iman of supporting terrorism (Al Jazeera, January 6, 2005). This denial, like his many others, did little to convince al-Zindani's numerous critics within the government. Yet while al-Zindani's enemies maintain a significant amount of power, he has always been protected, when it mattered most, by President Saleh.

On a number of occasions, the United States has, in fact, made a similar claim that the university has a military wing, but the accusation is usually dismissed out of hand by the Yemeni government. In 2005, Mansur al-Zindani, Abd al-Majid's brother and a member of parliament, laughed off the suggestion in his interview with al-Amin, saying that maybe the U.S. government could not read their own satellite pictures. "There is a military camp (the 1st Armored Division) next to the university, and maybe the Americans can't see the border, and maybe they think the soldiers are actually on university grounds" (*al-Hayat*, October 12, 2005).

Given al-Zindani's status and the rumors about al-Iman, it has always been extremely difficult to get inside the walls of the university. Nicholas Kristof, a columnist for *The New York Times*, was turned away at the gate by armed soldiers in 2002. Even the Arabic press has had difficulties getting access, but in the past two years al-Zindani has granted passes to two journalists, al-Amin for *al-Hayat* and Arafat Madabish, a Yemeni stringer writing for *al-Sharq al-Awsat*. Both men have published lengthy reports on the university, which represent a great deal of what outsiders know about the institution. Al-Amin describes the university center as a "town within a town," as it has an internet café, restaurant, laundromat, grocery store, telephone center and other small shops. He divides the students at al-Iman into two categories according to their dress. Some of the students wear traditional Islamic clothes, while others wear normal street clothes (*al-Hayat*, March 12, 2005). This division of the students can also be seen in their political inclinations. The vast majority of them are quietists, but there is a significant group that tends toward extremism and violence.

The university currently has an enrollment of 4,650 students; 3,750 males and 800 females (*al-Sharq al-Awsat*, July 21, 2006). Like other universities, there are dorms available for the students, although no women live on campus and most Yemeni students live with their families or stay with friends in Sanaa. The vast majority of these students are serious-minded young scholars; they almost have to be, as a full course of study in one of al-Iman's four schools takes seven years, which is why the university has only graduated three groups of students since it started offering classes in 1994. Al-Iman offers degrees in the schools of sharia (or Islamic jurisprudence), Arabic, Islamic preaching and human sciences. There is a small contingent of students that veer away from the quietist trend of their colleagues. They tend to be foreign students that are drawn to al-Iman by al-Zindani's radical reputation, while the Yemeni students are attracted by the overt religiosity of the university. These categories are not, of course, concrete. Some Yemeni students are inclined toward political violence, while some foreigners are interested only in knowledge. Yet, generally speaking, the categories hold true.

Al-Iman's enrollment numbers and experience bear this out. While the university has students from more than 50 countries—including the United States, Somalia, Kosovo, Indonesia, Albania and most European countries—the actual number of these students is quite small, hovering around 150. These students are also inclined to be more interested in contemporary politics than in completing their studies, which is why al-Zindani has some wiggle room in refusing to call people like Lindh and Kamal students, as neither of them ever finished a degree. The foreign students also work as a convenient scapegoat for the Yemeni government. They can be expelled from the university at a much greater rate than the Yemeni students, partly out of their self-selecting nature as being more politically active, and partly because the government does not have to deal with the tribes and families of these students. This allows Yemen to look like it is being tough on potential terrorists at al-Iman, while not suffering domestically for its actions.

Conclusion

Al-Iman will continue to straddle this divide as a legitimate religious institution and as a fundamentalist pipeline for as long as it is given cover by the Yemeni government. Saleh's recent speeches at al-Iman suggest that this support will not end soon. Periodically, the government will be forced to crack down on extremists attending the university, but this will continue to be tempered by al-Zindani's denials, which will be supported by Saleh. Al-Iman's legitimate practices will allow the Yemeni government to defend it, which will provide the university with the political space to carry out its more nefarious actions.

Originally published in *Terrorism Monitor*: Volume 4, Issue 22 on November 16, 2006.

Notes

1. For a detailed profile of Sheikh al-Zindani, see *Terrorism Monitor*, Volume 4, Issue 7, April 6, 2006.

Yemen and the U.S.: Different Approaches to the War on Terrorism
By Andrew McGregor

Following the introduction of a new two-year plan to eliminate religious-based political extremism in Yemen, President Ali Abdullah Saleh made an official visit to Washington from April 30 to May 3, 2007. While in the United States, President Saleh discussed security and counter-terrorism efforts with President Bush, FBI Director Robert Mueller, Secretary of State Condoleezza Rice, Secretary of Defense Robert Gates, CIA Director Michael Hayden and members of the House of Representatives Intelligence Committee. The visit marked an enormous change in U.S.-Yemeni relations since the dangerous days following the September 11, 2001 attacks, when a U.S. attack on Yemen seemed imminent. At the conclusion of his stay, President Saleh thanked the United States for its support of Yemen's counter-terrorism efforts, while President Bush spoke of Yemen's continuing cooperation in bringing "radicals and murderers" to justice. Nevertheless, while the sometimes-tempestuous U.S.-Yemeni alliance carries on, there are serious differences between the Yemeni and U.S. approaches to counter-terrorism.

Reforming Terrorists with Islam

The most unusual aspect of Yemen's counter-terrorist efforts is a broad effort to reform religious extremism (both Shiite and Sunni) and replace it with a moderate approach to Islam. This task (rooted in traditional Yemeni methods of conflict resolution) has been handed to Yemen's recently appointed Minister for Endowments and Religious Guidance, Judge Hamoud Abdulhamid al-Hitar, who states, "The strategy will be an important factor in treating their mistaken ideas" (*Yemen Observer*, April 30, 2007). As the leader of Yemen's Dialogue Committee, al-Hitar developed a policy of confronting incarcerated militants in debates designed to expose their misinterpretations of Islamic doctrine and challenge the legitimacy of al-Qaeda-style jihadism. Using "mutual respect" as a basis for the discussions, al-Hitar points to numerous successes in reforming the views of extremist prisoners, some of whom later provided the security apparatus with important intelligence. Hundreds of terrorism suspects have passed through the program. Recidivism is untracked, however, and there are reports that some of those released went to Iraq to fight U.S.-led coalition forces. The list of graduates is closely guarded, and ex-prisoners are warned not to discuss their participation in the dialogues, thus allowing a degree of deniability should graduates return to terrorism.

Within Yemen, al-Hitar is widely believed to be a member of the feared Political Security Organization (PSO). When 23 terrorism convicts escaped from a PSO prison in the national capital of Sanaa last year, their tunnel emerged in al-Hitar's mosque. The mass escape was clearly assisted by some PSO agents. The fact that the escapees included several convicted of bombing the USS *Cole* placed a severe strain on U.S.-Yemen relations.

For two years, the Ministry of Endowments and Religious Guidance has kept a close watch on unlicensed Quranic schools suspected of promoting political violence, although none have been closed so far. A corps of "religious guides" (both men and women) has been tasked with promoting "the noble values of Islam" and to establish the principles of moderation and tolerance in areas where the government fears extremism is feeding on a lack of religious knowledge (Saba News Agency, April 25, 2007). Saleh has challenged the country's religious scholars and preachers to "clarify the facts" of Islam for the Muslim community, especially in rebellious Sa'dah province, where preachers have a "religious, moral and national duty" to eradicate sedition.

Steps Toward Disarmament

On April 24, 2007, Yemen's cabinet took the unusual measure of ordering the closure of Yemen's many arms shops and markets, finally acknowledging that the proliferation of weapons and their common use to resolve all types of disputes are continuing barriers to much-needed foreign investment. Heavy weapons are to be confiscated, while possession and sales of sidearms and assault rifles will be subject to licenses and registration. With some 50-60 million weapons in circulation in a country of 21 million people, the cabinet's order represents only a first step toward changing Yemen's ubiquitous arms culture. At the moment, there are 18 major arms markets and several hundred gun-shops in Yemen. Some shops will be allowed to reopen for the sale of personal arms under government control (IRIN, April 26, 2007). Yemen continues to be an important regional transit point for arms shipments of all types, a lucrative trade that benefits leading members of the regime.

Legislation to regulate the possession of arms continues to be opposed by a number of members of parliament who, like most of their constituents, regard holding one or more weapons as a traditional right. Some of the larger tribes possess stockpiles of heavy weapons that they will be reluctant to part with, given the 22 tribal clashes recorded last year alone. The tribes also regard their weaponry as a means of protecting themselves from government malfeasance.

Reforming the Security Apparatus

Apart from the military, Yemen's security is handled by three civilian agencies, at least two of which are believed to include Salafi and Baathist sympathizers at the highest levels. Most important of these is the PSO. A number of PSO officials have been dismissed in the last few years in an attempt to eliminate corruption and Islamist sympathizers from the organization as it is reshaped to take the lead in Yemen's counter-terrorism effort. The PSO reports directly to the president and its upper ranks are composed exclusively of former army officers. The Ministry of the Interior runs the Central Security Organization (CSO), a paramilitary force of 50,000 men, equipped with light weapons and armored personnel carriers. The smaller National Security Bureau (NSB), founded in 2002, reports directly to the president as well. The NSB may be designed to be in competition with the PSO. The United States currently offers counter-terrorist training to members of Yemen's security forces and is involved in helping build a new national Coast Guard (a project that also includes contributions from the United Kingdom and Australia).

The CSO's elite Counter-Terrorism Unit (CTU) is trained jointly by the United States and the United Kingdom. As a relatively new organization formed in 2003, the CTU is expected to apply innovative strategies to counter-terrorism work, while avoiding the corruption ingrained in more senior security groups. The Interior Ministry is also engaged in a campaign to decrease the size of both official and unofficial corps of bodyguards employed by public figures in Yemen. Some groups of bodyguards now approach the level of private militias, enforcing the will of local sheikhs and tribal leaders (*Yemen Observer*, April 24, 2007).

Arbitrary arrests and extended detentions without charge or trial continue to be preferred methods of the security services. The PSO, CSO and many tribal sheikhs operate their own extra-judicial detention centers. Relatives of militants are routinely imprisoned to put pressure on wanted individuals to surrender. At a recent judicial symposium, it was suggested that there are as many as 4,000 innocent citizens being held in the prisons of the security services (*Yemen Observer*, April 28, 2007). Regular use of torture in Yemen's prisons and other judicial abuses have been documented in the U.S. Department of State's annual report on human rights (*Yemen Times*, March 14, 2007).

The ongoing rebellion in Sa'dah province has the advantage, at least, of keeping the army busy while Saleh attempts to repair relations with Washington. Many in the officer corps were trained in Baathist Iraq and deeply oppose the U.S.-led intervention there. Dissatisfaction in the ranks has not yet become disloyalty, however, and Saleh has placed a number of family members in crucial command roles to ensure that it stays that way. These include his son Ahmad (a possible presidential successor and presently commander of the Republican Guard and the Special Forces), his brother Ali Saleh al-Ahmar (commander of the Air Force) and half-brother Ali Mohsin al-Ahmar (commander of the northwest region and a long-time Salafi sympathizer). Two of the president's nephews serve as commanders of the CSO and the NSB.

U.S. diplomats in Yemen have frequently been targeted by Salafi extremists, although Yemen's security services have preempted several such operations. Typical of the "revolving door" approach to terrorism prosecutions that irks the United States is the case of two Yemenis convicted of trying to assassinate U.S. Ambassador Edmund James Hull (an important official in U.S. counter-terrorism efforts) in 2004. Only days after Saleh's return from Washington, the two convicts had their sentences reduced from five years to three on appeal (Agence France-Presse, May 7, 2007).

Yemeni Prisoners in the United States

During his visit to Washington, President Saleh asked for the repatriation of Sheikh Muhammad Ali Hassan al-Moayyad, a Yemeni religious scholar extradited from Germany to the United States (along with his assistant Muhammad Za'id), where he is serving a prison term after being convicted of supporting Hamas (but acquitted of supporting al-Qaeda). Yemeni human rights organizations are agitating for the sheikh's release on the grounds of declining health. The head of a national committee to free al-Moayyad (who is popular in Yemen for his charitable work) notes that, since "Europe and the whole international community are (now) dealing with Hamas as an independent entity, why is it forbidden for al-Moayyad?" (*Yemen Observer*, April 25, 2007).

Saleh also discussed the case of Yemeni citizens held in Guantanamo Bay. Although official Yemeni sources claim that Saleh requested the release of all the Yemeni Guantanamo Bay prisoners, there are signs that Yemen's government is not overeager for their repatriation. In a March, 2007 visit to Yemen, Marc Falkoff, a lawyer for 17 of the Yemeni detainees, revealed that he had obtained documents from the Pentagon showing that many of the Yemeni prisoners had been eligible for repatriation as far back as June 2004. The Yemeni government justifies its inaction by claiming that the citizenship of some of the Yemeni detainees is under question. According to Falkoff,

> *Although official Yemeni sources claim that Saleh requested the release of all the Yemeni Guantanamo Bay prisoners, there are signs that Yemen's government is not overeager for their repatriation.*

"Fully one-third of the Saudis are back in Saudi Arabia, more than half of the Afghanis are home with their families and every single European national has been released from Guantanamo. Yet, more than 100 Yemenis remain at the prison—sitting in solitary confinement on steel beds, deprived of books and newspapers, slowly going insane" (*Yemen Times*, March 11, 2007).

U.S. officials claim that there are 107 Yemeni prisoners at Guantanamo, while human rights activists cite as many as 150, but there is no doubt that Yemenis form the largest single group of foreign nationals detained at the facility. Although the government may be in no hurry for their return, reports of alleged torture practiced on Yemeni detainees in U.S.-run detention centers have inflamed anti-American sentiment in Yemen.

The Case of al-Zindani

Saleh also requested that the U.S. drop Yemen's controversial Sheikh Abd al-Majid al-Zindani from its list of designated terrorists. Believed by U.S. intelligence services to be an important link to bin Laden and al-Qaeda, the sheikh's terrorist designation has been an unrelenting irritant to U.S.-Yemeni relations. The sheikh is a powerful member of the Islamist Islah Party and has close ties to Saleh's administration. Yemen's parliament recently rescinded a decision to join the International Criminal Court (ICC) system, largely because of the fear of Islah Party MPs that the ICC could be used as a tool to extradite and try al-Zindani on terrorism charges (*al-Thawri*, May 2, 2007). Apparently, Sheikh al-Zindani has lately joined the call for religious scholars to correct the mistakes in Islamic interpretation that promote dissension and political violence (*Yemen Observer*, May 2, 2007).

Conclusion

Security issues and concerns with government reforms led donor states to suspend economic aid to Yemen in 2005, but President Saleh's reform efforts appear to have regained the confidence of the international donor community. Despite the detention of political activists and opposition candidates during the 2006 election campaign, Saleh's new seven-year term as president is regarded as a sign of stability. European aid is flowing once again, and in February 2007 the Bush administration announced that Yemen was once more eligible to receive funds from the Millennium Challenge Account (MCA) tied to progress in governance. Of the $94 million released by the MCA, $59 million is dedicated to the military and security sector (Saba News Agency, May 3, 2007). The aid represents vital assistance to Yemen's weak economy. Unemployment persists at about 40 percent, there is little development and Yemen's small petroleum industry does not enjoy the bountiful reserves found in its prosperous Arabian Peninsula neighbors.

While Saleh cannot ignore the general discontent within Yemen regarding U.S. foreign policy, he also recognizes that cooperation with the United States is the best method of ensuring the survival of his regime. Methods such as the "dialogue with extremists" and the "revolving door" of the judicial system allow Saleh to keep a lid on Sunni radicalism, while at the same time posing as a vital ally of the United States. Despite the apparent success of Saleh's visit to Washington, there is still much to concern the United States in its relationship with Yemen. Reforms to the security services have notably involved purges of al-Qaeda sympathizers at only the lowest levels. Yemeni extremists continue to join anti-coalition forces in Iraq and have been involved in terrorist operations in several countries as President Saleh continues his search for a "third option" in the war on terrorism.

Originally published in *Terrorism Monitor*: Volume 5, Issue 9 on May 10, 2007.

Tracking Yemen's 23 Escaped Jihadi Operatives – Part 1
By Gregory D. Johnsen

In mid-September 2007, Yemeni President Ali Abdullah Saleh issued a stern warning to the Wa'ilah tribe in northern Yemen: turn over the six al-Qaeda suspects you are sheltering or face serious repercussions (*al-Wasat*, September 12, 2007). The six men that Saleh believes have found refuge with the tribe near the Saudi border are the remnants of a group of 23 prisoners that escaped from a Yemeni political security prison on February 3, 2006. The prisoners escaped by tunneling out of their cell and into a neighboring mosque, which has since been detailed in a lengthy narrative written by one of the escapees and published by the Yemeni paper al-Ghad. The escapees included a number of prominent al-Qaeda militants, among whom were individuals convicted of carrying out attacks on the USS *Cole* in 2000 and on the French oil tanker *Limburg* in 2002.

Six of these suspects have since been killed in clashes with Yemeni or U.S. forces, 11 have either turned themselves back in to authorities or have been recaptured and six of the suspects remain at large. Many of these individuals have continued to fight for al-Qaeda since their escape, and one of them, Nasir al-Wuhayshi, has since been named the new head of Al-Qaeda in Yemen.

Despite differences of age and background, the 23 men who were being held in the cell were linked together through shared experiences. Nearly half of the escapees, 11, were born in Saudi Arabia to Yemeni parents. Several of the men were arrested in late 2002 after a series of bombings in Sanaa and Marib. Seven of these men were part of a 15-man cell that was later charged with planning to attack five foreign embassies as well as to assassinate the then U.S. Ambassador Edmund Hull. Three of the men were convicted of being part of an 11-man cell that was charged with plotting to carry out attacks in Yemen and abroad. Among the escapees, there are also two sets of brothers, Hizam and Arif Mujali and Mansur and Zakariya al-Bayhani, who are themselves brothers of Ghalib and Tawfiq al-Bayhani, who are currently in U.S. custody in Guantanamo Bay. Two other escapees, Qasim al-Raymi and Fawaz al-Rabay'I, also have brothers in Guantanamo.

This two-part series presents a biographical sketch of each escapee, along with his current status.

The Dead

Umar Sayd Hasan Jarallah (1979-2006): Jarallah was from the Red Sea port city of Hudaydah. Jarallah was also known as Abdullah al-Gharib and Ibn Hafiz. He was sentenced to ten years in prison in February 2005 for his role in the attack on the *Limburg*. Along with al-'Umda, Huwaydi and Zayd, Jarallah was hidden for one month following their escape by Muhammad Hajir (*22nd May*, April 29, 2007). He killed himself along with Ahmad Muhamad al-Abiyad in a failed suicide attack on an oil facility in Marib on September 15, 2006. One guard was killed in the attack on the Safir facility (*al-Sharq al-Awsat*, September 21, 2006).

Shafiq Ahmad Umar Zayd (?-2006): Zayd was born in Saudi Arabia to Yemeni parents and is known by the *kunya* Abu Abdullah. He was extradited to Yemen from Saudi Arabia along with two other individuals in 2003. He was part of an 11-man cell, which was charged with forging passports, weapons and explosives possession, planning to travel to Iraq and forming an armed gang to carry out attacks in Yemen. Along with Mansur al-Bayhani and Abdullah al-Wada'i, he was convicted only of forging passports. Ibrahim al-Muqri, who was part of the same trial, was cleared of all charges (*Yemen Times*, March 24–27, 2005). All of the men, however, remained in prison until they managed to escape in February 2006. As was mentioned above, Zayd was sheltered by Muhammad Hajir for one month following his escape. He killed himself along with Hashim Khalid al-'Iraqi in a failed suicide attack on an oil port in Hadramawt on September 15, 2006.

Fawaz Yahya Hasan al-Rabay'i (1979-2006): Al-Rabay'i was born in Saudi Arabia, the third of four brothers and four sisters (News Yemen, October 9, 2006). He is also known by the *kunya* Furqan al-Tajayki (*al-Ghad*, October 2006). He attended al-Falah school in Saudi Arabia, where he learned to recite the Quran. Along with nearly one million Yemenis, the family was expelled from Saudi Arabia in 1990 as a result of Yemen's support for Saddam Hussein following his invasion of Kuwait. His mother is known as Umm Hasan, after her oldest son. Hasan is a bus driver with six children. According to his family, Hasan is no longer close to them, as he was arrested on two separate occasions in order to put pressure on his younger brothers. Hasan complained that his brothers were trouble makers, and that when he was in jail his children went hungry.

Six of these suspects have since been killed in clashes with Yemeni or U.S. forces, 11 have either turned themselves back in to authorities or have been recaptured and six of the suspects remain at large. Many of these individuals have continued to fight for al-Qaeda since their escape, and one of them, Nasir al-Wuhayshi, has since been named the new head of Al-Qaeda in Yemen.

The second brother, Abu Bakr, is currently awaiting sentencing in Yemen for his role in a series of al-Qaeda plots. The youngest brother, Salman, is being held by the United States in Guantanamo Bay (News Yemen, October 9, 2006). According to his father, he was sent to Afghanistan by his family to search for Fawaz, and was subsequently arrested and turned over to the United States. His father denies that either Abu Bakr or Salman have any links to al-Qaeda (News Yemen, October 9, 2006).

During the late 1990s, al-Rabay'i took a job in the personnel department in the presidential office in Yemen. In early 2000, he traveled to Afghanistan with two other men, including a former agent in Yemen's Political Security Organization (News Yemen, October 9, 2006). Like many young men who head off to fight in Afghanistan or Iraq, al-Rabay'i did not tell his family where he was going. Later, he called his father, Yahya, to tell him that he was in Afghanistan. The family claims that they knew nothing of his activities in Afghanistan, although he did mention to his father that his salary contradicted Islamic law and that his goal was to die as a martyr (News Yemen, October 9, 2006). According to one source, al-Rabay'i trained with Abu Musab al-Zarqawi in an al-Qaeda training camp in Afghanistan (*al-Ghad*, October 2006). He is also known to have spent time with at least two of the September 11, 2001 hijackers, Muhammad Atta and Zayd Jarah (*al-Ghad*, October 2006).

Al-Rabay'i spent one year in Afghanistan before returning to Yemen in 2001, as the head of a 12-man cell (News Yemen, October 9, 2006). In 2002, the United States asked Yemen to arrest him on the suspicion of belonging to al-Qaeda. He escaped security forces two separate times that year before finally being captured in 2003. In August 2006, he managed to escape a raid on his house in Sanaa dressed only in his *pajamas (al-Sharq al-Awsat*, October 2, 2006). The raid did result in the death of one member of his cell, Samir al-Hada'. He also escaped from a security checkpoint, when the car he and Hizam Mujali were traveling in was stopped in the southern governorate of Abyan. Instead of allowing their car to be searched, the two shot one of the two soldiers, Hamid Khasruf, manning the checkpoint and fled (*Yemen Times*, April 7–13, 2004). The pair was later arrested in March 2003 in Marib (BBC, April 5, 2003). During the time that al-Rabay'i was on the run, he was sheltered by different tribes in Marib and Abyan.

On August 30, 2004, al-Rabay'i was sentenced to ten years in prison for attacking a Hunt Oil helicopter in November 2002, which was reportedly done with the authorization of Abu Ali al-Harithi (*Yemen Times*, May 31–June 2, 2004). He was also fined 18.3 million Yemeni riyals—roughly $99,450—for his role in a 2002 attack on the Civil Aviation Authority building in Sanaa (News Yemen, October 1, 2006). Six months later, in February 2005, al-Rabay'i was again on trial for his role in the attack on the French oil tanker, Limburg, and for killing a soldier. The court sentenced him to death on these charges. During his trial, al-Rabay'i frequently alleged that he was being tortured by Yemeni security officers (*Yemen Times*, December 27–January 2, 2004–2005). He did, however, find time during his trial to arrange to be married to a daughter of Yahya Salih Mujali, the brother of Hizam and Arif (News Yemen, October 9, 2006).

Following his escape from the security prison in February 2006, he was charged with planning the dual suicide attacks in Marib and Hadramawt on September 15, 2006. This operation was partially funded by four million Saudi riyals that al-Rabay'i received from Bandar al-Akwa through Said al-'Akbar. Both al-Akwa and al-'Akbar are currently awaiting sentencing for their roles in the attack (*22nd May*, April 29, 2007). During this time, he also paid a visit to his father, Yahya, who was in the hospital. According to reports that surfaced after his death, al-Rabay'i did not wear a disguise when he made the visit (News Yemen, October 9, 2006). Al-Rabay'i was killed on October 1, 2006 along with Muhammad al-Daylami during an early morning shoot-out with Yemeni security forces in the Bani Hashish region just north of Sanaa. In a story about the escapees, the Yemeni newspaper al-Ghad mentioned that some sources claim that al-Rabay'i was murdered in "cold blood" after he surrendered himself to soldiers (*al-Ghad*, June 25, 2007). Security forces also arrested three individuals it claimed had assisted the pair (*al-Sharq al-Awsat*, October 2, 2006).

Muhammad Ahmad Abdullah al-Daylami (c.1978-2006): Al-Daylami was charged with participating in the November 2002 attack on a Hunt Oil helicopter, planning to attack five foreign embassies and a 2003 plot to assassinate Edmund Hull, the U.S. ambassador in Yemen. He was sentenced to five years in prison in February 2005. In October 2006, he was killed along with Fawaz al-Rabay'i in a shootout with Yemeni security forces in the region of Bani Hashish.

Yasir Nasir Ali al-Hamayqani (c.1978-2007): Al-Hamayqani was also known by the kunya Abu Khalid. He was charged with traveling to Iraq. Al-Hamayqani was killed in clashes with Yemeni security forces in the Sabah district of the southern governorate of Abyan on January 15, 2007 (*al-Sharq al-Awsat*, January 17, 2007). According to a security official, al-Hamayqani was in possession of a machine gun and two hand grenades when he was surrounded by security forces. He managed to wound two officers before he was killed (*al-Sharq al-Awsat*, January 17, 2007).

Mansur Nasir 'Awadh al-Bayhani (1974-2007): Al-Bayhani was born in 1974 in the city of Tabuk in Saudi Arabia to a Yemeni migrant worker from al-Rida'a in the governorate of al-Baydha. He took his *kunya*, Abu 'Assam al-Tabuki, from his boyhood home. Mansur's brother, Zakariya, was also among the escapees. Additionally, both his older brother Tawfiq (b. 1972) and his younger brother Ghalib (b. 1980) are currently in U.S. custody in Guantanamo Bay. Al-Bayhani made his way to Afghanistan via Pakistan in the 1990s, where he joined the Taliban. Later that decade, he was part of Samir Salih Abdullah al-Suwaylim's Arab brigade that fought in Chechnya against Russian forces. During their time in Chechnya, al-Suwaylim, who was better known as al-Khattab, was poisoned by Russian security forces, while al-Bayhani was wounded in the right eye. Following the death of Suwaylim, he traveled back to Afghanistan to fight U.S. forces, before returning to Saudi Arabia where he was arrested and extradited along with five companions, including his brother Zakariya, to Yemen.

Al-Bayhani was eventually brought to trial, along with ten others, on charges of forging passports, weapons and explosives possession, planning to travel to Iraq and forming an armed gang to carry out attacks in Yemen. He was acquitted in March 2005 of all charges save for forging Saudi, Iraqi and Yemeni passports (*Yemen Times*, March 24-27, 2005). Shafiq 'Umar and Abdullah al-Wada'i were also convicted of forging passports. Ibrahim al-Muqri, who was part of the same trial, was acquitted of all charges. All of the men, however, remained in prison until they managed to escape in February 2006. Al-Bayhani later turned himself in to Yemeni authorities, and was later released following a security guarantee. Mansur eventually made his way to Somalia, where he was killed in a U.S. naval strike by the USS *Chafee* on June 2, 2007.

Originally published in *Terrorism Monitor*: Volume 5, Issue 18 on September 27, 2007.

Tracking Yemen's 23 Escaped Jihadi Operatives – Part 2
By Gregory D. Johnsen

The first part of this series offered a biographical sketch of each escapee who is now deceased (Terrorism Monitor, September 27, 2007). This second part of the two-part series presents a biographical sketch of each escapee who is still at large or has surrendered.

At Large

Qasim Yahya Mahdi al-Raymi (b. 1977): Al-Raymi is from Sanaa, and was also known by the kunya Abu Hurayrah al-San'ani. His younger brother, Faris, who fought in Afghanistan and Iraq, was killed in mysterious circumstances in Sanaa in June 2007 after leaving his house in the company of Zakariya al-Yafa'i, another escapee. Another brother, Ali, is listed as being in U.S. custody at Guantanamo Bay. Al-Raymi was arrested in connection with a series of explosions in the al-Qadasayah district of Sanaa in 2002. He was charged with being part of the cell that was planning to attack five embassies in Sanaa. During his trial in 2004, al-Raymi threatened to cut off the leg of Said al-Akil, the public prosecutor. Al-Akil's house was subsequently attacked with a hand grenade later that week. Al-Raymi was sentenced to five years in prison on August 30, 2004, which was later upheld by a superior court in February 2005.

Following his escape, al-Raymi was sheltered for a while by Yahya Muhammad al-Shara'i, who has since been apprehended and is currently awaiting sentencing (*22nd May*, April 29, 2007). On June 21, 2007, al-Raymi posted an audio statement to an Islamist website announcing that fellow escapee Nasir al-Wuhayshi was the new head of Al-Qaeda in Yemen. On August 2, 2007, Yemeni authorities announced that al-Raymi was part of the ten-man cell that was responsible for the July 2, 2007 suicide bombing in Marib, which killed eight Spanish tourists and two Yemeni drivers (*Terrorism Focus*, August 14, 2007). That same week, on August 5, 2007, al-Raymi posted another audio message to an Islamist forum, once again warning his colleagues in al-Qaeda against negotiating with the government (*al-Sharq al-Awsat*, August 6, 2007). Three days later, al-Raymi was rumored to be killed in an early morning raid on his hideout in the al-Suhaym region in the governorate of Marib. That report proved to be premature, as al-Raymi had left the hideout the night before the attack. Instead, later reports revealed that Ali bin Ali Jaradan, Abd al-Aziz Jaradan and Ali Nasir Duha were killed in the raid (al-Arabiya, August 8, 2007). All three were linked to the July 2, 2007 suicide attack in Marib. The trio was also wanted for their involvement in the assassination of Ali Mahmud Qasaylah, the chief criminal investigator in Marib, in March 2007 (*Terrorism Focus*, May 22, 2007).

Ibrahim Muhammad Abd al-Jabar Huwaydi (b. 1982): Huwaydi is from the Red Sea port city of Hudaydah. He was arrested in the wake of the 2002 bombings in the neighborhood of al-Qadasayah in Sanaa. He was charged with planning to attack foreign embassies as well as plotting to assassinate Edmund Hull, the U.S. ambassador in Yemen. He was sentenced to five years in prison in February 2005. During his trial, Huwaydi claimed that he attempted suicide on two different occasions as a result of torture (*Yemen Times*, December 27, 2004–January 2, 2005). Along with Muhammad al-'Umda, 'Umar Jarallah and Shafiq Zayd, Huwaydi was hidden for a month by Muhammad Hajir, who has since been captured and is currently awaiting sentencing (*22nd May*, April 29, 2007). Hajir claimed in his confession that he was worried that the men would kill him if he did not hide them. Huwaydi has yet to be recaptured.

Muhammad Sa'd Ali Hasan al-'Umda (b. 1981): Al-'Umda is from the Yemeni city of Taiz and is known by the kunya Abu Ghrayb al-Taizi. He was charged with being involved in the 2002 attack on the Limburg, and in February 2005 was sentenced to ten years in prison. Al-'Umda, as was mentioned above, was sheltered for one month by Muhammad Hajir (*22 May*, April 29, 2007). Al-'Umda is still at large.

Jamal Muhammad Ahmad Ali al-Badawi (b. 1966): Al-Badawi is originally from the southern port city of Aden, and is also known by the *kunya* Abu Abd al-Rahman. He is charged with being involved in both the attack on the USS *Cole* and the one on the *Limburg*. Prior to his escape in February 2006, al-Badawi also escaped, along with nine others, from a political security prison in Aden on April 11, 2003. He was sentenced to death by Najib Muhammad al-Qadari in 2004, although this was later reduced to a sentence of 15 years by Said Naji al-Qata' in February 2005 (News Yemen, May 12, 2007). He is wanted by the United States and is still at large.

Nasir Abd al-Karim Abdullah al-Wuhayshi (b. 1976): Al-Wuhayshi, who is also known by the *kunya* Abu Basir, is from the southern governorate of al-Baydha. During the late 1990s he worked as a secretary to Osama bin Laden in Afghanistan (*al-Ghad*, June 25, 2007). Following the U.S. attack on the Taliban and al-Qaeda in Afghanistan in late 2001, he escaped across the border to Iran where he was arrested. Iran later extradited al-Wuhayshi and eight others back to Yemen in November 2003 (*Yemen Times*, November 2003). The Yemeni government never officially brought charges against him, although he remained in prison until he escaped in February 2006. In June 2007, he was named the new head of Al-Qaeda in Yemen in an audiotape that was posted to an Islamist website. He is still at large. On August 2, Yemen announced that he was part of the ten-man Marib cell, which was responsible for the attack that killed eight Spanish tourists and two Yemeni drivers (*26th of September*, August 2, 2007).

Hamza Salim Amar al-Qayti (b. 1969): Al-Qayti was born in Saudi Arabia to a family from Mukalla in the eastern Yemeni governorate of Hadramawt. He is also known by the kunya Abu Samir. He was extradited to Yemen from Saudi Arabia in 2003. Al-Qayti was never officially charged with any crime, although he remained in prison until he escaped in February 2006. In March 2007, al-Wasat reported that al-Qayti was injured during a car chase after the Land Cruiser he was riding in with seven others in the southern governorate of Abyan refused a request to be searched at a military checkpoint (*al-Wasat*, March 21, 2007). Officials later found weapons and anti-aircraft missiles in the vehicle. On August 2, 2007, Yemen announced that he was part of the ten-man Marib cell (*26th of September*, August 2, 2007).

Surrendered

Fawzi Muhammad Abd al-Qawi al-Wajayhi (b. 1982): Al-Wajayhi was born in Saudi Arabia to Yemeni parents. His family is from the same neighborhood in Taiz as is Muhammad al-'Umda's family. Both men took *kunya* that reflect this link, Abu Musab al-Taizi and Abu Ghrayb al-Taizi, respectively. Al-Wajayhi spent time in Afghanistan during the 1990s as a bodyguard to Osama bin Laden (*Washington Post*, July 4, 2007). When he returned to Saudi Arabia in the aftermath of the U.S. attacks on the Taliban and al-Qaeda in Afghanistan, he was arrested and extradited to Yemen along with two other men. He was charged with involvement in the *Limburg* attack, and was part of the 15-man cell that was sentenced on August 30, 2004. Al-Wajayhi was given ten years for his role in the attack. Following his escape, he turned himself back in to Yemeni authorities as part of a security arrangement, which allowed him to remain under loose house arrest in exchange for his not taking part in any illegal activities. In Yemen, this process is usually sealed by a security guarantee, which often involves both the money and reputation of the mediator.

Abdullah Yahya Salih al-Wada'i (b. 1978): Al-Wada'i was born in Saudi Arabia to Yemeni parents from Sanaa. He is also known by the *kunya* Marwan al-Hashidi. Al-Wada'i was arrested in Saudi Arabia upon his return from Afghanistan, and later extradited to Yemen along with five others, including Mansur al-Bayhani and Ibrahim al-Muqri. He was part of the 11-man cell that was brought up on charges in February 2005 of belonging to an armed gang intent on carrying out criminal attacks in Yemen and abroad, as well as of fighting in Afghanistan and Iraq and possessing forged travel documents. Al-Wada'i was eventually cleared by the court of all charges save forging passports, but was never released from prison. Following his escape, he turned himself back into authorities and is currently free on a security guarantee.

Khalid Muhammad Abdullah al-Batati (b. 1982): Al-Batati was born in Saudi Arabia and is also known by the *kunya* Abu Sulayman. His family is from Sanaa. He was extradited to Yemen from Saudi Arabia. In early 2005, he was accused of being part of an eight-man cell formed by Anwar Jaylani, an Iraqi, that was planning to attack the British and Italian embassies as well as the French Cultural Center in Sanaa. The group was also accused of planning to assassinate a number of prominent Yemeni officials, including then Prime Minister Abd al-Qadir Bajammal and Minister of Interior Rashid al-Alimi. Al-Batati was sentenced to three years and two months in prison in August 2005. Following his escape, he turned himself back into security forces in late April 2006 (*26th of September*, April 23, 2006).

Abd al-Rahman Ahmad Hasan Basurah (b. 1981): Like his companion al-Batati, al-Basurah was also born in Saudi Arabia to a Sanaani family. Basurah, who is also known by the *kunya*, Abu Ghrayb, was also extradited to Yemen from Saudi Arabia and was also charged with being part of the cell formed by Anwar Jaylani in 2005. Basurah's role was apparently collecting information on the French Cultural Center, which was one of the targets in the plot (*Yemen Times*, March 31–April 3, 2005). He also confessed to making a sketch of the British Embassy (*Yemen Times*, June 9–12, 2005). During the trial,

Basurah admitted that one of the military uniforms seized by security forces was his, but that he had bought it in order to impersonate Saddam Hussein in a student *play (Yemen Times*, June 2–5, 2005). Later during the trial, Basurah claimed he had been duped by al-Jaylani, and that the leader had exploited his feelings and absconded with his money (*Yemen Times*, June 9–12, 2005). He was sentenced to three years and four months in prison. He later turned himself in alongside Jamal al-Badawi on May 15, 2007. He is currently free on a security guarantee.

Abdullah Ahmad Salih al-Raymi (b. 1977): Al-Raymi is originally from the city of Taiz. He spent time fighting in Afghanistan, before returning to Qatar where he was arrested. Qatar later extradited him to Yemen in May 2005. Yemeni authorities charged him with forging documents for travel to Afghanistan. He was sentenced to four years in prison. Following his escape from prison, al-Raymi was re-captured in a joint raid by Yemeni security forces and a local counter-terrorism unit in the governorate of Marib on May 5, 2006 (News Yemen, May 11, 2006). He was later released.

Zakariya Nasir Awadh al-Bayhani (b. circa 1977): Like his brother Mansur, Zakariya was born in the northern Saudi city of Tabuk to Yemeni parents. Both his older and younger brothers, Tawfiq and Ghalib, are currently in U.S. custody in Guantanamo. Following his return to Saudi Arabia from Afghanistan, he was arrested and subsequently extradited to Yemen. In Yemen, he remained in prison although no charges were ever brought against him. Along with his brother Mansur, he turned himself in to Yemeni authorities in late 2006. Both were later released in accordance with a security guarantee.

Zakariya 'Ubadi Qasim al-Yafa'i (b. 1973): Al-Yafa'i was born in Saudi Arabia, and his family is from the village of Yaf'a in the southern Yemeni government of Lahj. Saudi Arabia extradited him to Yemen along with two other men in 2003. He was never charged with any crime, although he was kept in prison until he escaped in February 2006. He was re-captured by security forces in a raid on a house in the Shumayla neighborhood of Sanaa on April 17, 2006 (*al-Wasat*, April 19, 2006). According to reports, he did not resist arrest. Al-Yafa'i was later released on a security guarantee. Following his release from prison, he was involved in the death of Faris al-Raymi, the younger brother of Qasim al-Raymi, who is still at large. According to a report in the Yemeni newspaper al-Ghad, Zakariya agreed to take Faris to see his brother in early June 2007. The two left al-Raymi's house in Sanaa at 7:30 in the morning. Four hours later, Faris' father, Nasir, received a call from a surgical team at the German hospital in Sanaa saying they had removed seven bullets from Faris' head, chest and hands. Faris remained alive for another week, but never regained consciousness. The reason for his killing remains a mystery.

Jabir Ahmad Salih al-Banna (b. 1966): Al-Banna, who holds dual U.S.-Yemeni citizenship, is also known as Abu Ahmad. His family is from the village of Yahir in the governorate of Dhall'a. Al-Banna *According to the United States, al-Banna was an admirer of Kamal Darwish, a veteran fighter who was killed along with Abu Ali al-Harithi in missile attack by a CIA-operated drone in November 2002.*

was linked to the Lackawana Six, and is still wanted by the United States, which has offered a $5 million reward for information leading to his capture. According to the United States, al-Banna was an admirer of Kamal Darwish, a veteran fighter who was killed along with Abu Ali al-Harithi in missile attack by a CIA-operated drone in November 2002. Al-Banna traveled to Afghanistan on May 14, 2001 to participate in an al-Qaeda training camp along with Mukhtar al-Bakri, Sahim Alwan, and Yahya Goba. Before crossing the border from Pakistan into Afghanistan, al-Banna took up residence for a short time at a guesthouse in Kandahar, which was visited by Osama bin Laden. Later, along with his friends, he received military training at an al-Qaeda camp in Afghanistan. Unlike the others, al-Banna never returned to the United States. One of his former companions, Sahim Alwan, described him as very eager to fight the Northern Alliance and as someone who was actively seeking to become a martyr (PBS, July 24, 2003). He eventually made his way to Yemen, and surrendered himself in Taiz in late 2003, following a lengthy mediation effort headed by a "high-ranking member" of the ruling GPC party (al-Ghad, June 25, 2007). Among the guarantees that al-Banna was given was a promise that he would not be extradited to the United States. Al-Banna received a similar pledge from the Yemeni government in May 2007 when he once again turned himself into Yemeni forces along with Abd al-Rahman al-Basurah. He is currently under loose house arrest.

Hizam Salih Ali Mujali (b. 1980): Hizam is the older brother of Arif Mujali. He is from the governorate of Sanaa. Yemeni forces arrested him along with Fawaz al-Rabay'i in late 2003. The two resisted arrested, and fired at the security forces, killing one soldier, Hamid Khasruf. Hizam, like his younger brother, Arif, was part of the 15-man cell that went on trial in 2004. Hizam was charged with attacking a Hunt Oil helicopter and for participating in the attack on the Limburg. On August 30, 2004, he was sentenced to death for killing Khasruf. This sentence was upheld by a higher court in February 2005. Both Hizam and Arif turned themselves into the government in August 2006 (al-Wasat, August 30, 2006). Their surrender was orchestrated by Sheikh Hadi Dalqim, a tribal leader from Marib, who served as a mediator between the government and the brothers. It is unclear whether Mujali's sentence was commuted as a result of the negotiations.

Arif Salih Ali Mujali (b. 1984): Arif is the younger brother of Hizam Mujali, and is also known by the kunya Abu al-Layth al-San'ani. As his kunya indicates, he is from Sanaa. Another brother, Yahya, is also active in jihadi circles, and had agreed to marry his daughter to Fawaz al-Rabay'i. He was part of the 15-man cell and was charged with involvement in the November 2002 attack on the Hunt Oil helicopter, planning to attack five embassies, and for planning to assassinate then U.S. Ambassador Edmund Hull. He suffered from an injured leg, which he claimed was the result of torture, during his 2004 trial (Yemen Times, August 19–22, 2004). In the weeks following his escape from prison in February 2006, security forces managed to corner Arif and three companions in a building in the Musayk neighborhood of Sanaa, which has become known over the past few years as a haven for Islamic militants. The four men were able to escape, and eventually made their way to Marib. Sheikh Dalqim eventually persuaded both Arif and Hizam to surrender themselves to the government in August 2006 (al-Wasat, August 30, 2006). Arif is free as part of this arrangement.

Ibrahim Muhammad Abdu al-Muqri (b. 1972): Like many of his fellow escapees, al-Muqri was born in Saudi Arabia to Yemeni parents from Hudaydah. He has two known *kunyas*, Abu Muhammad and Abu Musab. Al-Muqri was arrested in Saudi Arabia upon his return from Afghanistan and later extradited to Yemen. He was then kept in a political security prison until he was brought up on charges in February 2005, along with ten other defendants. The men were charged with forming an armed gang intent on carrying out criminal acts both in Yemen and abroad. The 11 defendants were also charged with training in al-Qaeda camps in Afghanistan between 1998 and 2002, as well as possessing forged travel documents. Also indicted in the case were: Mansur al-Bayhani, Abdullah al-Wada'i and Shafiq 'Umar. Al-Muqri was cleared of all charges in March 2005, but was not released, and instead remained in prison until he escaped in February 2006. He surrendered himself to authorities a few months after his escape. As part of the deal, he was released but kept under surveillance. Al-Muqri, however, evaded Yemeni security forces and made his way to Somalia. Later, as he was crossing the border into Kenya, he was arrested along with two companions. He is currently in prison in Kenya.

Originally published in *Terrorism Monitor*: Volume 5, Issue 19 on October 11, 2007.

Yemen's Three Rebellions
By Brian O'Neill

Politics in Yemen has always been a violent affair. Two of its four presidents have died unnaturally—one in a hotel room surrounded by drugs and prostitutes; his successor, suddenly and absurdly, by an exploding briefcase. The next man to take office, a young tank commander named Ali Abdullah Saleh, was not expected to fare much better.

He did, though, and is approaching his thirtieth year in power. He survived and, through his intimate knowledge of Yemen's tribal politics, consolidated his rule. He oversaw the unification of his country with the formerly socialist South Yemen, and then crushed the south in a civil war. He never fully expanded his government's writ over the chaotic, tribal north, but he stayed in power and kept his country together better than anyone could have predicted.

Until now. President Saleh faces three separate rebellions: A tribal, sectarian battle in the north, economic and social riots in the south, and a pervasive enemy in a younger and more brutal generation of al-Qaeda. These are happening while Yemen faces crushing demographic and natural pressures, from its exploding population to its dwindling water supplies to its aging leadership. Saleh has held his country together, but the fragile, violent quilt-work that makes Yemen is now threatening to come quickly apart.

The Believing Youth of the North

Tribal rebellions have never been rare in Yemen, but the al-Houthi rebellion, now in its fourth year, seems to be a different, lingering animal. It has transformed itself from Saleh's persistent headache into a long and catastrophic war that has claimed thousands of lives and threatens the tribal and sectarian balance, which the president has meticulously massaged over the years.

The rebellion started in 2004 when Hussein Badr al-Houthi, a sheikh of the Zaidi sect of the Shiite branch, proclaimed that Saleh's government had become too aligned with the United States and Israel. Longing to reestablish the Zaidi Imamate (1918-1962), al-Houthi led his Shabab al-Mu'mineen (Believing Youth) into battle. This came after government crackdowns on the shaykh's unlicensed mosques.

Shaykh Hussein Badr al-Houthi was killed in September of that year and was jointly replaced as commander by his son and son-in-law, while his father took the reins as spiritual leader. There were back-and-forth negotiations, stall tactics, cease-fires, and more battles over the years. The government accused the rebels of receiving aid and training from co-religionists in Iran, which may have been true or may have been a way for Saleh to link his domestic concerns with the broader Arab fear of the emerging "Shiite Crescent" (and thus to obtain more outside assistance). None of these allegations have been proven.

Then, on May 2, 2008, a motorcycle-borne bomb exploded in a mosque in Sa'ada, killing over a dozen people and wounding scores more (*Yemen Times*, May 5, 2008). Immediately, the violence began again as accusations flowed from both sides. More than 50 people were killed in a battle near the town of Dafaa (ArabianBusiness.com, May 5, 2008). Both sides in this war have accused the other of targeting non-combatants, with the Sa'ada governor claiming the al-Houthis "kill innocent people and set fire to their farms" (News Yemen, May 5, 2008). This bombing, though, marked a new and spectacular level of violence.

Immediately, speculation rose as to the identity of the slaughter's architect. Abd al-Malik al-Houthi—brother of Hussein Badr al-Houthi—was quoted as saying: "The renewed tension is due to the repeated aggressions of the army ... which is using tanks and other weapons in unjustified operations" (ArabianBusiness.com, May 5, 2008). While he stopped short of saying the government planted the bombs, his calls for a fair and legitimate investigation leads one to believe he is not discouraging that speculation.

But this rebellion has hurt the Saleh government, and renewed fighting is not in its interests. Cynically, one could say that a planted bomb that looks like an al-Houthi attack would hurt the rebellion, but Saleh knows his country. The north has never fully accepted the government of Sanaa, and continued fighting only helps further delegitimize his regime. This leaves a previously unknown faction or al-Qaeda as suspects in the attack. This would be a difficult but not impossible operation for al-Qaeda given the security in Sa'ada. Their motivations for doing so will be dealt with below.

> *Civil wars rarely seem to happen along an east-west axis; similar climates help produce similar economies and ideas—it is typically when different regions are yoked together that violence is produced. So it is with Yemen.*

The Restless South

Civil wars rarely seem to happen along an east-west axis; similar climates help produce similar economies and ideas—it is typically when different regions are yoked together that violence is produced. So it is with Yemen. North and South Yemen have had different histories, colonial experiences, and economies. Though it seems antithetical to the romantic idea of an ancient, eternal Yemeni state, it could be argued that having two separate countries made more sense.

Following the fall of the Soviet Union, the socialist south, known as the People's Democratic Republic of Yemen, was faced with a failed economy and little external support. It had also never recovered from a brutal internecine war of its own during the 1980s. So it turned toward the north, and unification with the Yemen Arab Republic.

Speeches of brotherhood were given; promises were made. But the speeches never translated into reality, as Saleh squeezed out southern politicians and attempted to make the south part of his extended patronage network. Eventually, in 1994, civil war broke out. Saleh used his superior army and, more importantly, veterans of the Afghan jihad to crush the godless south. Aden, which had been an open and secular city—where mini-skirts were far more popular than the hijab—fell under the harsh rule of victorious jihadis. It would be an exaggeration to say that sharia had been implemented, but the typical southern way of life had been disrupted [1].

Beside the difficulties of the new way of life, the south chafed in other ways. Its economy never improved and many blamed the north for lack of interest in helping out its rival. The influence of the jihadis was felt. Though it seems insignificant, the destruction of the city brewery marked a dramatic change of daily rhythm, and the buildings became cold and gray concrete hulks. More strikingly, terrorism began to hit the south, with both the al-Qaeda variety and homegrown groups such as the Aden-Abyan Islamic Army influenced by returning jihadis.

Commodity shortages have been hitting the south, including a severe diesel shortage (NewsYemen, April 23, 2008). While these shortages intensified, dissatisfaction with a number of issues strengthened. In January of this year, citizens were killed during a riot protesting the lack of "rights and benefits" accorded to citizens of the south. The rally was held in Aden during the Forum for Forgiveness and Reconciliation, an attempt to get past the divisiveness of the civil war (Al Jazeera, January 13, 2008). Instead, it sharpened the divide. Youths complained they were not allowed into the army; army retirees claimed they were not getting their benefits (Al Jazeera, April 1, 2008). In April 2008, hundreds were detained following a massive protest two days after a government soldier was killed (*Yemen Times*, April 8, 2008).

Perhaps most threatening of all was the re-entrenchment of old players and the reopening of old wounds. On April 8, 2008, the *Yemen Times* reported that demonstrators were in "Al-Dhale's main street chanting 'Get out, Colonialization,' and 'Revolution, Revolution South.' " Ominously, a former president of the south, Ali Naser Mohammed, signaled his approval of the riots, demonstrations and discontent (*Yemen Observer*, April 5, 2008).

It seems clearer than ever that the tenuous grafting of north onto south never really fit. It is far from too late to fix the situation—a little more aid, a more just hiring procedure and a reining in of Islamist interference would make southerners feel less colonized in their own country.

The Pervasive Threat

In the last year, a new generation of al-Qaeda has taken over from Yemen's old guard. This group has been hardened by the battles in Iraq and shared experiences in prison. The leaders and primary soldiers escaped from a Yemeni prison in 2006, and have since consolidated their own power while seeming driven to unravel Saleh's.

Their first big blow was against Spanish tourists in July 2007. They have since attacked foreign and local interests, including the U.S. Embassy and the Customs Office (*Terrorism Focus*, April 16, 2008). Al-Qaeda seems immune to the standard Yemeni tactic of negotiation and compromise that Saleh has used with the older generation. Though it seems contrary to ideas of justice to let the bombers of the USS *Cole* walk free, Saleh has to balance domestic concerns and local passions to avoid letting his country slip into the abyss.

But that seems to be the exact strategy of the hard new guard of al-Qaeda. They are working at undermining tourism revenue and shaking any faith people have in the government with attacks on foreigners and random violence against citizens. A recent statement proclaimed their desire to "control Yemen's waterways" by organizing attacks on "commercial, tourist and oil tankers" (News Yemen, April 30, 2008; *Terrorism Focus*, May 13, 2008). This will eat away at another source of revenue and further weaken Saleh.

In the Middle, Nearing the End

Ali Abdullah Saleh has held his country, and his office, for a staggeringly long time. But events seem to be swirling faster now. The history of Yemen is catching up with his efforts, and demography is working to accelerate these damning trends. Using jihadis to fight his secular war may have irretrievably poisoned unification. Buying time with northern tribal leaders allowed him to shift focus from sectarian discontent, which led to the al-Houthi rebellion. Making deals with al-Qaeda emboldened a new generation.

All of these decisions made sense at the time and even in retrospect one feels the hands of the government were tied. Governing Yemen is a series of ad hoc decisions, assuaging the immediate concern while punting other issues down the road. President Saleh is getting older, and a new generation of leaders is waiting its turn. It is unknown whether new leaders will be able to save the waterless, booming population from fragmenting into a failed state. But now, near the end of his tenure, President Saleh has to make decisions to save his new/ancient country from both its short-term difficulties and the catastrophes that loom over the near horizon.

Originally published in *Terrorism Monitor*: Volume 6, Issue 10 on May 15, 2008.

Notes

1. Joseph Kostiner, *Yemen: The Tortuous Quest for Unity, 1990-94* (London: The Royal Institute of International Affairs, 1996).

Part III

Africa

Oil Industry at the Heart of the Zaghawa Power Struggle in Chad
By Andrew McGregor

It was only a few years ago when the African nation of Chad was being promoted as a groundbreaking example of a new model of transparent oil revenue distribution that would relieve poverty and initiate development. Tribalism and kleptocratic rule would no longer be part of the familiar equation of vanishing oil wealth in other parts of Africa. Instead, only a few weeks ago, the world witnessed blood running in the streets of the Chadian capital of N'Djamena as rival factions of the minority Zaghawa tribe battled for the right to empty Chad's ever-growing coffers. This unwelcome instability only adds to a downward spiral of violence in a region already beset by political and ethnic violence in neighboring Darfur and the Central African Republic (CAR).

Chad is host to hundreds of thousands of refugees from Darfur and the Central African Republic, as well as Chad's own internally displaced peoples. Most Chadians live in grinding poverty overseen by a political and administrative structure routinely viewed as one of the most corrupt in the world. Despite this, the February 2–3, 2008 attack on N'Djamena by 300 armed pick-up trucks full of rebels had less to do with righting these glaring inequities than with replacing President Idris Déby's Zaghawa faction with other Zaghawa factions eager to take control of Chad's sudden oil wealth.

Role of the French

Formed as a territory of France after the conquest of a number of small sultanates and the expulsion of the Libyan Sanusis in the early years of the 20th century, Chad gained independence in 1960. There is a strange relationship between Chad and France that began in 1940 when Chad, through its governor, Felix Aboué—actually from French Guiana—was the first overseas territory of the French Empire to declare for Free France. General Leclerc had the first Free French military successes in Chad before marching into southern France, together with thousands of Chadian troops. In the process Chad became inextricably tied with the mythology surrounding the creation of modern, Gaullist, post-war France. In practice this often translates into seemingly inexplicable French support for the government of the day in Chad, regardless of corruption or inefficiency.

The French military presence in Chad is officially referred to as Operation Epervier (Sparrowhawk), which began in 1986 as a means of supplying French military assistance in the form of troops and warplanes to the regime of President Hissène Habré as the Libyan army tried to seize the uranium-rich Aouzou Strip in northern Chad. When General Déby overthrew the increasingly brutal Habré in 1990 the French looked on. Though the dispute with Libya was settled in 1994, the French military mission stayed on as a "deterrent." Today it includes about 1,200 troops, six Mirage aircraft and three Puma helicopters (*Le Figaro*, April 19, 2006). Typically the French supply the regime with intelligence and logistical assistance. France has limited commercial interests in Chad and is largely uninvolved in the nation's oil industry.

Rebel leader Mahamat Nouri notes that Chad and France share a "community of interests in history, religion, blood and culture," while adding that the French government—and not the people of France—have befriended Déby against the people of Chad (TchadVision, February 27, 2008).

Chad's Oil Industry

Crude oil was first discovered in Chad in the late 1960s, but development of a local industry was delayed due to the remoteness of the land-locked country, lack of infrastructure and political instability. The oil boom changed all that, and today a consortium run by ExxonMobil, ChevronTexaco and the Malaysian Petronas operate Chad's oil industry. Three oil fields in the Doba Basin are currently in operation, with estimated reserves of 900 million barrels (Afrol News, December 22, 2004).

A 2000 deal between Chad, the World Bank and a consortium of oil companies called for the construction of a $3.7 billion pipeline from Chad's oilfields to the Cameroon port of Kribi on the Gulf of Guinea. Three years later 160,000 barrels per day were running through the pipeline, gradually growing to the peak capacity of 225,000 barrels per day. The agreement called for 70 percent of Chad's revenues from the project to go toward infrastructure development and poverty relief. Transparency and accountability were to be the key in avoiding the widespread corruption of other oil-rich African countries.

In practice very little of this new affluence trickled through the hands of the regime. Increased spending on weapons began almost immediately while electricity remains unknown outside of the capital. A failed rebel assault on the capital in April 2006 led a shaken President Déby to begin diverting an even greater share of oil revenues toward arms purchases for the army and the Republican Guard. Unfortunately for Déby, the World Bank had already suspended roughly $125 million in grants and loans and payment of an equal amount of royalties in January after the president unilaterally changed the terms of the 2000 agreement. Déby simply threatened to turn off the taps and things suddenly began to swing his way. Under pressure to keep the oil flowing in Chad, the World Bank offered a new deal doubling the amount of oil revenues going directly to the government for unsupervised spending to 30 percent. With oil having now crashed through the $100 a barrel barrier, there is suddenly enormous and unprecedented wealth available to whatever faction can seize and control it. The Sudanese may be training and supplying the Chadian rebels, but they do not need to give them a reason to fight.

The government is actively encouraging new exploration in the promising Lake Chad Basin as only the existing Doba Basin oil fields are subject to the oversight and supervision terms of the 2000 agreement. The distribution of all new revenues from the industry will be completely unsupervised by outside agencies. Unfortunately the industry has created very little local employment, most of which is menial and low-paying.

The Zaghawa and the Chadian Power Structure

The struggle for Chad and its oil industry is part of the growing commercial and political strength of the non-Arab Zaghawa in Chad and Sudan. The Zaghawa are a small indigenous semi-nomadic tribe that once controlled a string of petty sultanates running across what is now northern Chad and Darfur. Despite their small numbers, they have become politically and economically powerful and are challenging the dominance of Sudan's Jallaba (Nile-based Arabs) over Darfur. Déby's support for Zaghawa-dominated rebel groups in Darfur has led to reciprocal Sudanese support for Zaghawa factions seeking to depose Déby.

Traditionally the Zaghawa are divided into several groups, including the Zaghawa Kobe, Zaghawa Tuer and Zaghawa Kabka. They are closely associated with a similar tribe, the Bidayat. Their growing strength in the region does not necessarily imply unity—the Zaghawa are heavily factionalized. The president of Chad, Idris Déby, is a Zaghawa, but his strongest opposition is formed from other groups of Zaghawa, many of them led by his relatives. It is some measure of the growing power of the Zaghawa that, despite comprising only two percent of Chad's population, they are still able to divide their forces in a struggle for power to the exclusion of every other ethnic group in the nation. Déby is kept in power by the Zaghawa-dominated Armée Nationale Tchadienne and the Garde Républicaine (largely Zaghawa Kobe).

In neighboring Darfur, the strongest of the anti-Khartoum rebel groups is the Justice and Equality Movement (JEM). The leadership is strongly Zaghawa and is supported by Chad, though there have been disputes over JEM recruiting from the ranks of the Chadian army. Sudanese sources claim that a leading JEM commander was killed while assisting Chadian troops against the rebels in N'Djamena (Sudan News Agency, February 4, 2008). Darfur's National Movement for Reformation and Development (NMRD) is drawn mostly from the Zaghawa Kabka and includes former leading members of Chad's Garde Républicaine and the state intelligence service. The National Redemption Front (NRF) is another Zaghawa-dominated rebel movement that receives military support from N'Djamena.

Chadian Opposition

The Chadian opposition takes the form of a bewildering array of acronym movements that shift, merge and realign almost daily. The rebel movements are largely defined by tribal rather than ideological differences and operate from bases inside Sudan (Agence France-Presse, January 8, 2008). Sudanese support for the rebels has been an effective way to delay the undesired deployment of the European Union peacekeeping mission to Chad and the Central African Republic

The leading rebel groups have developed a unified military command. These groups include the Union des Forces pour la Démocratie et le Développement (UFDD), the Rassemblement des Forces Démocratiques (RAFD), and the UFDD-Fondamentale. The UFDD are mostly Gura'an from the Tibesti region—the tribe of Déby's predecessor,

Hissène Habré—and are led by Mahamat Nouri, the former Chadian ambassador to Saudi Arabia. The RAFD is a coalition led by twin brothers Tom and Timane Erdimi, who also happen to be Déby's nephews and former cabinet ministers in his government. Most RAFD fighters are Zaghawa defectors from the Garde Républicaine. The UFDD-Fondamentale is led by an Arab, Abdul-Wahid Makaye.

The Rebel Assault

Like an earlier assault on N'Djamena in April 2006, the rebels were eventually driven off, but only after severe fighting in the streets of the capital. Rebel tactics typically draw on the highly mobile land cruiser-based tactics perfected in the 1980s by Zaghawa and Tubu fighters against Libyan troops in northern Chad. There are reports that the 300 Toyota Land Cruisers used in the assault were purchased by Khartoum, while the entire operation was planned by Salah Gosh—head of Sudan's National Security and Intelligence Service—and the Sudanese defense minister, Lt. General Abdelrahim Muhammad Hussein (*Al-Sudani*, February 7, 2008; Sudan Tribune, February 7, 2008).

Chad often refers to the rebels as radical Islamists in an effort to garner international support and has accused Saudi Arabia of recruiting mercenaries associated with al-Qaeda to fight alongside the rebels, going so far as to make an official complaint to the UN Security Council (*Al-Wihda*, May 5, 2007; Agence France-Presse, November 30, 2006; Reuters, December 1, 2006). As one rebel spokesman has noted: "We have no Islamist ideology ... It is now a fashion in the world to call one's enemy an Islamist or a terrorist" (*Al-Wihda*, November 26, 2006). After the assault on N'Djamena, the Chadian Interior Ministry put over 100 prisoners on display for the press, describing them as "Sudanese mercenaries, Islamic militants and members of al-Qaeda" (Reuters, February 13, 2008).

Chad often refers to the rebels as radical Islamists in an effort to garner international support and has accused Saudi Arabia of recruiting mercenaries associated with al-Qaeda to fight alongside the rebels, going so far as to make an official complaint to the UN Security Council.

The defeat of the rebel attack even as it reached the presidential palace in N'Djamena was more likely due to poor training and coordination on the part of the rebels than to French intervention. The timing of the assault reflected Khartoum's urgency in deposing Déby and ending Chadian support for Darfur's rebels before the arrival of the European Union peacekeeping force made this a practical impossibility.

France provided logistical and intelligence support to the president's forces during the fighting. The French Defense Ministry confirmed that it arranged for ammunition for Chad's Russian-built T-55 tanks to be flown in from Libya for use against the rebel offensive (Reuters, February 14, 2008). Oddly enough, the Chadian prime minister accused Libya of supporting the rebel attack (Sudan Tribune, February 7, 2008). Other reports that French Special Forces participated in the fighting in N'Djamena have been denied by Paris (*La Croix*, February 8, 2008; *L'Humanité*, February 9, 2008).

Chadian Reaction

Following the assault, President Déby instituted a State of Emergency, set to last until March 15, 2008. Déby's forces are fortifying the capital to deter similar attacks. Armed vehicles will no longer be able to strike across the savanna into N'Djamena with the construction of a three-meter deep trench around the city that will force all traffic to go through fortified gateways. The trees that offer the only refuge from N'Djamena's blistering heat are also being cut down after rebels used some cut trees to block roads during the raid (Reuters, March 3, 2008; BBC, March 4, 2008). The regime is also seeking to buy half a dozen helicopter gunships from Russia or other East European sources.

French President Nicolas Sarkozy visited Chad in late February 2008 in a show of support for President Déby that included a call for a more effective democratization process (TchadVision, February 28, 2008; African Press Agency, February 27, 2008). Earlier, Sarkozy had declared his intention to make a clean break with French neo-colonialism in Africa, but his quick reversal on Chad demonstrates the deep roots of the French government's "FrançAfrique" network that seeks to preserve commercial and strategic interests in the former colonies. Despite Sarkozy's visit, France may already be preparing for the post-Déby era by granting asylum to Chadian opposition leader Ngarlejy Yorongar. Full details are lacking, but Yorongar is reported to have been arrested on February 3, 2008, held in a secret N'Djamena prison—probably in the headquarters of the state intelligence service, the Direction des Renseignements Generaux—and finally dumped in a cemetery on February 21, 2008 before finding his way to Cameroon. Another opposition leader, Ibni Oumar Mahamat Saleh, was arrested at the same time but has not been seen since (Agence France-Presse, March 4, 2008; Al-Wihda, March 6, 2008). Former Chadian President Lol Mahamat Choua was also detained, but was later released.

European Union Peacekeeping Force in Chad (EUFOR)

A 14-nation EU peacekeeping force began deploying in February but is not expected to be fully operational until the end of March 2008. The majority of the 3,700 troops will be French, with the second largest contingent of 450 troops coming from Ireland. EUFOR is commanded from France by Irish Major General Pat Nash and in Chad/CAR by French Brigadier Jean-Philippe Ganascia.

EUFOR deployment was delayed by the rebel strike into N'Djamena which came at precisely the same time deployment was set to begin. EUFOR allows the French to expand France's military presence in traditional overseas areas of influence like Chad and the CAR in a way that would raise eyebrows if done unilaterally. Though it has said little publicly, France is worried about the growing U.S. military encroachment into Africa through the establishment of AFRICOM and various counter-terrorism training programs, including one in Chad. The spokesman for the rebels' unified military command, Abderahman Koulamallah, describes the EUFOR deployment as "a low maneuver by the French government to try and rescue Déby" (*Al-Wihda*, March 7, 2008). Other rebels speak of EUFOR as a French commitment to "liquidate" the opposition (TchadVision, February 16, 2008).

Conclusion

Following mediation from Senegal, Chad and Sudan have agreed to sign another in a series of peace agreements on March 12, 2008 at the Organization of the Islamic Conference summit in Dakar (Agence France-Presse, March 6, 2008). There is little reason to hope that this agreement will be any more effective than those that have preceded it. Rebel leader Mahamat Nouri has denied reports of negotiations with the Déby regime, claiming the president "treated us as nobodies. He has no intention at all to negotiate while we have been demanding national dialogue, round-table meetings, etc., for 20 months in order to resolve our problems permanently. But we never received any response" (Radio France Internationale, February 21, 2008).

In an effort to retain power, President Déby has purged the general staff several times in the last few years and has lost many of his most powerful supporters in the military. The president is seriously ill and would like to be succeeded in the presidency by his son Brahim, but this is unlikely to happen. Far from becoming the hoped for example of a way out of the factionalism and corruption that has tended to accompany the discovery of oil reserves in Africa, Chad has developed a bloody intra-tribal struggle for control of oil revenues with little hope for stability and progress in sight.

Originally published in *Terrorism Monitor*: Volume 6, Issue 5 on March 7, 2008

Egypt's Muslim Brotherhood: Political Islam without al-Qaeda
By Chris Zambelis

The September 11, 2001 attacks inspired an unprecedented upsurge of interest in Middle East and Islamic studies within academic, policymaking and security circles in the United States. Now, more than ever, Americans are seeking to understand the circumstances that culminated in the worst terrorist attacks on American soil, especially the rise of radical Islam and political Islam as a whole. Despite this newfound curiosity, however, much of the commentary on Islamism is ill-informed by generalizations that fail to distinguish between moderate Islamists advocating political liberalization and democratization and their violent militant counterparts. Indeed, many observers continue to see political Islam through a Cold War lens: a monolithic movement akin to the Soviet Union that threatens the United States. Ironically, during the Cold War, the United States viewed Islamists of all stripes as allies against the spread of Soviet influence and Arab nationalism.

In reality, an overwhelming majority of Islamists, including influential groups such as Egypt's al-Ikhwan al-Muslimeen (The Muslim Brotherhood)—the largest and most organized Islamist movement in the world—do not harbor violent agendas and are actually outspoken against terrorism. The Brotherhood in Egypt, for instance, renounced violence in the 1970s and has since demonstrated its pragmatism by participating in electoral politics and other formal institutional bodies, essentially abiding by the established rules of the game despite being banned by the authorities [1]. In contrast, violent militants constitute only a tiny minority within the larger Islamist trend, a fact that is often overlooked. The implications for recognizing the nuances and complexities within political Islam—the dominant current shaping society and politics in the contemporary Middle East and Muslim world—are profound. This is especially true for those seeking to understand the trends and events in the Middle East that gave rise to al-Qaeda.

The Rise of Political Islam

In general terms, political Islam—or Islamism—is based on the premise that Quranic scripture, theology and inspiration should shape society and politics. Political Islam emerged as an influential force in the Middle East in the late 1960s and 1970s during a period when Muslims began to seek new solutions to the deep-seated social, political and economic problems affecting the region. The failure of Western ideologies (such as the secular socialist pan-Arab nationalism espoused by Egyptian President Gamal Abdel Nasser) to address these concerns and to restore regional power and pride drove many to search for answers from within their own societies. Israel's invasion of Egypt, Syria and Jordan in 1967 and eventual occupation of Arab land confirmed the failure of the status quo in Muslim eyes. The ouster of the U.S.-backed shah of Iran in 1979 by Shiite Islamists coupled with the Soviet invasion of Afghanistan in the same year also helped galvanize a sense of transnational Muslim consciousness in the Middle East, lending further legitimacy to the idea that Islam was the solution [2].

This critical period also saw authoritarian regimes in the region suppress liberal and secular political dissent. Ruling autocrats determined to root out any perceived threats to their control used widespread repression, torture and other draconian measures, such as the assassination of outspoken Islamists and the outlawing of subversive political elements. Great efforts were also made to co-opt the opposition in order to fracture and weaken dissent. These tactics contributed to the radicalization of some Islamists and even former secular activists, driving some to take up arms against the state in the name of Islamic revolution. As a result, the regimes in places such as Egypt, Jordan and Saudi Arabia—all staunch U.S. allies—are widely viewed by their people as illegitimate, tyrannical, inept and agents of U.S. imperialism. It is also worth noting that many of al-Qaeda's ranking members, including Osama bin Laden and Ayman al-Zawahiri, got their start in domestic opposition politics in their home countries of Saudi Arabia and Egypt, respectively, before shifting their ire towards the United States [3].

Political opposition was resilient in the face of sustained government pressure. The absence of free political space and public venues for association and debate drove the resistance underground, as activists sought alternative channels of dissent in order to circumvent government controls. As a result, mosques and religious associations emerged as vibrant hubs of social, political and economic protest, a trend that continues today. This was the case even in countries where the regimes appointed clerics and infiltrated religious congregations. The resurgence of Islam as a political force also gained a boost from the marked increase in outward religious observance in what would represent a collective assertion of identity. Some observers characterize this trend as a form of Islamic nationalism; by calling for the restoration of Muslim pride and glory, Islamists play a role analogous to that of traditional populists and nationalists in the West (*The Future of Political Islam*, 20-23). The actions and discourse of Islamists resonate among the masses because Islam represents a tradition that is familiar and a product of local culture, as opposed to a foreign ideology inherited from the colonial period.

> *The absence of free political space and public venues for association and debate drove the resistance underground, as activists sought alternative channels of dissent in order to circumvent government controls. As a result, mosques and religious associations emerged as vibrant hubs of social, political and economic protest, a trend that continues today.*

It is against this background that Islamists such as the Muslim Brotherhood emerged as the most organized form of political opposition in the Middle East. The failure of sitting governments in the region to meet the demands of their citizens elevated political Islam as a promising alternative. The popularity of Islamists cannot, however, be attributed to their religious credentials. The Brotherhood, for instance, is at the forefront of democratic opposition politics in Egypt. It is a vocal critic of the regime on tangible issues such as state repression, corruption, unemployment and foreign policy. It also provides vital social services such as health care and education where the regime is absent, bolstering its reputation as an agent of action [4]. This refutes the argument that the Brotherhood's political reform-minded agenda is merely a façade meant to conceal a radical agenda. Similarly, radical Islamists also back up their words with action of a different kind, using violence and terrorism to get their message across.

Like other political movements, the Brotherhood's membership in Egypt is diverse and includes followers who hold diverse and often conflicting views on any number of topics. What members do agree on, however, is the group's opposition to violence. Although members of the organization have been implicated in violence in the past, it renounced the use of force in the early 1970s. As a result, the Brotherhood resents comparisons to al-Qaeda and other violent militants [5]. The same holds for local branches of the group elsewhere in the region, who should be considered independent actors with unique and local interests as opposed to being formally part of a larger movement.

Radicals vs. Moderates

Radical Islamist organizations such as al-Qaeda despise their moderate counterparts, including the Muslim Brotherhood in Egypt, a reality that is often ignored in studies of Islamism. Al-Qaeda views them as traitors who have abandoned their revolutionary calling by participating in inherently flawed elections and other aspects of social and political life in countries where they face severe repression. In contrast, the Brotherhood regularly condemns al-Qaeda, devoting a section on the English-language version of its website to the topic [6]. Despite their often common origins and shared opposition to U.S. foreign policy and incumbent authoritarian regimes in the Middle East, the goals of moderate groups such as the Muslim Brotherhood share little in common with their extremist counterparts.

Nevertheless, Arab regimes in the Middle East frequently label moderate Islamists as affiliates of al-Qaeda in an effort to justify systematic crackdowns against dissent. For example, Egypt has stepped up its attacks against the Brotherhood in 2007 in response to the group's increasingly vocal opposition to what appears to be President Hosni Mubarak's goal to have his son Gamal succeed him as leader. This strategy is also meant to counter international pressure to implement political reform and improve domestic human rights conditions (*Foreign Affairs*, March/April 2007). The regimes in question often argue that political liberalization and democratization will allow radicals to gain power through legal means, before reneging on their commitment to uphold democratic principles once elected to office [7].

Despite their non-violent platform, moderate Islamists pose a threat to radicals. Although much of al-Qaeda's discourse resonates strongly with Arabs and Muslims—principally its vocal opposition to U.S. foreign policy in the Middle East—the group does not enjoy popular support among Muslims. In contrast, groups such as the Muslim Brotherhood can count on a wide base of support in critical countries such as Egypt, especially among youth and student activists (*Middle East Report*, Winter 2007). Policymakers should pay close attention to this reality, especially while moderates continue to face harassment by the state. Moreover, undermining the efforts of moderate Islamists emboldens the position of radicals with violent agendas. Despite their opposition to many aspects of U.S. foreign policy in the Middle East, moderate Islamists have demonstrated that they are prepared to seek pragmatic dialogue with the West and constructive engagement with the United States, an opportunity that should not be missed.

Conclusion

Political Islam, in all of its manifestations, will remain a dominant force in the Middle East in the foreseeable future. It has been over six years since the September 11, 2001 attacks, and it is critical that observers of the region finally take the time to acknowledge the profound differences between Islamist groups, especially the differences between the various moderate and radical currents. A genuine understanding of the nature of political Islam is crucial for informing an effective foreign policy, as well as distinguishing between potential threats and prospective partners.

Originally published in *Terrorism Monitor*: Volume 5, Issue 22 on November 26, 2007.

Notes

1. Despite being officially banned in Egypt, the Muslim Brotherhood enjoys a sizeable representation in the Egyptian parliament. Affiliates of the group have participated in elections as independents since the 1980s, thus circumventing official government controls.
2. The slogan "Islam huwa al-hal" (Islam is the solution) is often used by the Muslim Brotherhood and other Islamists to characterize their perspective on key issues affecting society and politics.
3. Prior to the emergence of al-Qaeda, radical Islamists focused their attention on attacking incumbent regimes in the Arab and Muslim world. In this regard, al-Qaeda's decision to target the United States directly represented a revolutionary shift among radical Islamists. For an analysis of the reasons behind al-Qaeda's decision to strike the United States, see Fawaz A. Gerges, *The Far Enemy: Why Jihad Went Global* (New York: Cambridge University Press, 2005).
4. In an example of its public outreach and organizational capacity, the Muslim Brotherhood launched its own campaign to help contain the spread of bird flu in Egypt and to assist farmers and businessmen affected by the ban on the sale of poultry. The Brotherhood was strongly critical of the government's handling of the crisis.
5. One member of the Brotherhood compared the decision by the group and that of other moderate Islamists in the region to abandon violence to the U.S. decision to abolish slavery, racial segregation and other historic injustices, in that the same U.S. institutions that upheld these policies in the past have since overturned them and have remained staunchly opposed to their reinstatement ever since. In this regard, the Brotherhood resents the fact that the image of moderate Islamists continues to be judged by incidents that occurred decades ago, as well as the failure of many Western observers to distinguish between moderate and radical Islamists. Based on author's interview with a member of the Egyptian Muslim Brotherhood, Cairo, March 2006.

6. The English-language version of the Muslim Brotherhood website is http://www.ikhwanweb.com/.

7. This same concern is shared by many in U.S. foreign policy circles. See Chris Zambelis, "The Strategic Implications of Political Liberalization and Democratization in the Middle East," *Parameters* 35, no. 3 (Autumn 2005): 87-102.

Imprisoned Leader of Egypt's Islamic Jihad Challenges al-Qaeda
By Abdul Hameed Bakier

The Salafi-Jihadi ideology, the doctrine and constitution of al-Qaeda's terrorists, is being re-evaluated by prominent Salafi-Jihadi ideologues. The same ideologues that previously sanctioned terrorist operations are now having second thoughts about the ideology behind many heinous terrorist acts. In November 2007, Sayed Imam Abdulaziz al-Sharif, a founder of the Egyptian Jihad organization and a prominent jihad theoretician better known as "Doctor Fadl," released a new ten-part document called *Tarshid al-amal al-jihadi fi misr wa al-alam* ("Rationalizing the jihadi action in Egypt and the world") (Islamtoday.net, November, 2007). The treatise is expected to have a major influence on Salafi-Jihadi operatives in general and al-Qaeda in particular (Aljarida.com, November 21, 2007).

The Path of a Jihadi

The 57 year-old Dr. Fadl was born and raised in the city of Bani Suwayf, 72 miles south of Cairo. He is married to two women and has four boys and three girls. Dr. Fadl's family (who are, according to Dr. Fadl's son Ismail, descendents of the Prophet Mohammad) was ardent in their religious faith. This was reflected in Dr. Fadl's upbringing as a pious grade-A student who graduated from high school as one of the top students in Egypt in 1968, rendering him eligible to enroll in Cairo's faculty of medicine. After graduating in 1974 he worked in the faculty's surgical department. During his years in the university, Dr. Fadl devoted much of his free time to the study of Salafist literature, never quite trusting contemporary Islamic commentaries. Consequently, he formed his first jihadi group in 1968 with his friend, fellow physician Ayman al-Zawahiri (now second-in-command of al-Qaeda). In 1978 Dr. Fadl finished a graduate program in plastic surgery and worked at Suez Canal University until 1981.

After the assassination of Egyptian president Anwar Sadat in 1981 and the consequent arrest of al-Zawahiri, Dr. Fadl fled Egypt to the United Arab Emirates, working there until 1983, when he moved to Peshawar in Pakistan in order to offer medical services to the mujahideen. Dr. Fadl was also tried in absentia in the Sadat assassination case but was acquitted in 1984. After their release, Ayman al-Zawahiri and several other Egyptian militants traveled to Pakistan and reorganized the Egyptian Islamic Jihad group (EIJ) with Dr. Fadl as the leader of the group (Aljarida.com, November 27, 2007). Even though Dr. Fadl was the emir of the EIJ, he kept a low profile and led the group ideologically, whereas al-Zawahiri, the second-in-command, was more active in the group's daily activities to the point where members of the group thought he was the actual leader and pledged allegiance to him (*Almasry Alyoum*, November 18, 2007). In 1993 the group had a major setback when Egyptian authorities arrested over 1,000 members of the group's military wing, Tali'at al-fatah (The Liberation Vanguard). After the arrests, the leadership of the group moved to Sudan, except for Dr. Fadl, who refused to relocate in Sudan or accept responsibility for the group's setback. As a result, he was forced to resign and al-Zawahiri took charge of the group. In 1993 Dr. Fadl moved to Yemen and worked in the hospital of Ebb. In 1999 Egyptian authorities again tried Dr. Fadl in absentia and sentenced him to life in prison on terrorism charges in a case known in Egypt as "The Returning Albanian Arabs" (*Al-Sharq Al-Awsat*, March 9, 1999). After the 9/11 attacks, Yemeni authorities arrested Dr. Fadl and extradited him to Egypt to serve his life sentence.

Revising the Salafi-Jihadi Ideology

Prior to writing "Tarshid al-amal al-jihadi fi misr wa al-alam," Dr. Fadl published, among other books, his influential 1988 document "Al-omda fi eddad al-edda" (The Master in Making Preparation [for Jihad]) under the name Abdul Qadir bin Abdulaziz. A comparison of the two works highlights the changes and retractions Dr. Fadl has made in jihadist ideology.

"Al-omda fi eddad al-edda" is considered a global manifesto for jihadi groups; since its initial publication it has been translated into English, French, Turkish, Farsi, Urdu, Kurdish, Spanish, Malay and Indonesian. The book treats, in detail, jihadi recruitment, training and the religious justification for conducting jihad. Written in Peshawar during the war against the Soviets, the book supplies a code of conduct for the activities of jihadis everywhere. In takfiri fashion, Dr. Fadl terms Arab-Islamic autocrats infidels if they fail to implement sharia law. Rulers who fail to bring in Islamic law should be overthrown by violent means, killing them and everyone that works for them. The near enemy of the Salafi-Jihadis is any Arab-Islamic country that does not rule according to Islamic theology.

In comparison, Dr. Fadl commences his new work by saying that some jihadis have misunderstood his first book and committed infringements on sharia. The main points of the new manifesto are as follows:

• Islam is mandatory for all. Islam is submission to sharia, which includes jihad as one of its divine precepts.
• Duty is dependent on comprehension and the ability to perform.
• There is a difference between disseminating the "science of sharia" and imposing fatwas (religious decrees).
• Piety is a duty, especially in blood and money feuds.
• Religious decrees must rely on sharia evidence.

Dr. Fadl reiterates that before practicing jihad (as with performing any other religious duty), certain prerequisites have to be met:

• The jihadist must be not only physically capable, but also financially capable. It is impermissible to practice jihad if the jihadi cannot provide for his dependents while performing this duty.
• The parents' permission must be obtained by minors. God does not accept jihad without parental consent.
• The lives and property of Muslims must be preserved.
• Jihad against the leaders of Muslim countries is not acceptable.

• It is forbidden to harm foreigners and tourists in Muslim countries.
• It is treachery to kill people in a non-Muslim country after entering that country with its government's permission (i.e., a legal visa).
• Single individuals should not try to conduct jihad by themselves.
• Using fraudulent means to fund jihad is a sin punishable by Islam.

Dr. Fadl also retreats from his takfiri ideology, citing the many constraints that should be considered before designating an individual as an infidel.

Reaction from the Salafi-Jihadis

One of the strongest criticisms of Dr. Fadl's document came from Hani al-Sibai, a London-based Egyptian political refugee who runs the Almaqreze Centre for Historical Studies (http://hani.phpnet.us, November 18, 2007). Al-Sibai says "the so-called rationalizing Jihad document that was released with unprecedented media coverage lacks credibility because Dr. Fadl wrote it under duress in prison in return, perhaps, for visiting privileges or a reduction of his sentence." Al-Sibai underlines many other reasons that render the document unreliable, such as Dr. Fadl's repeated claim that he was not forced to write the document. Another strong reply to Dr. Fadl came from Muhammad Khalil al-Hukayma, leader of the al-Qaeda in Egypt group, who refutes Fadl's arguments in numerated points (Pal-hacker.com, November 29, 2007). Although Osama bin Laden hasn't directly commented on Dr. Fadl's document, sources say that al-Zawahiri directed Hukayma's reply because Hukayma is closer to bin Laden and al-Zawahiri than al-Sibai; al-Qaeda also considers Hukayma the legitimate representative of Egypt's al-Gama'a al-Islamiya, which split over Hukayma's efforts to unite the group with al-Qaeda.

Regardless of all the negative responses to Dr. Fadl's initiative by Salafi-Jihadi leaders, calls by Egyptian Gama'a al-Islamiya leaders on bin Laden and al-Qaeda to seriously consider Dr. Fadl's document are likely to have a major impact on al-Qaeda.

For weeks after the release of his book, al-Zawahiri attacked Dr. Fadl without naming him, sending a message that al-Qaeda no longer considers Dr. Fadl a legitimate ideologue (Islamonline.net, November 20, 2007). In the same context, jihadi forum chatters posted short comments on the document. A chatter nicknamed Asad bin Hashim declared, "The Fatwa of the coerced is unacceptable"; another said, "It sounds like the Sheikh is forced to write the document or lacks accurate information. When did Muslims kill anyone because of his or her skin or hair color? May God free him from prison."

In addition, a third chatter posted this question to Dr. Fadl: "Why didn't you write this before 2004 when all the big events were happening such as the Manhattan attack and the occupation of Iraq?" Dr. Fadl's answer came through a chatter nicknamed Abu Anwar al-Muslim, saying, "It's not right to prematurely reject the document on the pretext that I'm in prison. I didn't claim to be a religious authority nor do I impose my opinions on anybody. I also don't claim to be religiously eligible to issue fatwas. I'm only an Islamic theology conveyer. Everything I wrote is based on shaira attestation" (Muslim.net November 19, 2007).

Conclusion

Regardless of all the negative responses to Dr. Fadl's initiative by Salafi-Jihadi leaders, calls by Egyptian Gama'a al-Islamiya leaders on bin Laden and al-Qaeda to seriously consider Dr. Fadl's document are likely to have a major impact on al-Qaeda. Furthermore, the document will have a long-term influence on second-level and new generations of Salafi-Jihadi leaders because Egypt's Gama'a al-Islamiya has always been a major ideological authority in the Arab and Islamic world. Osama bin Laden's October 2007 audio and Ayman al-Zawahiri's November 2007 announcement that the Libyan Islamic Fighting Group has joined al-Qaeda show al-Qaeda's grim concern over Dr. Fadl's ideological "deviation." Rather than becoming involved in a public religious debate, al-Qaeda is expected to respond by releasing new publications that counter Dr. Fadl's arguments.

Originally published in *Terrorism Monitor*: Volume 5, Issue 23 on December 10, 2007.

LIBYA

Libyan Fighters Join the Iraqi Jihad
By Alison Pargeter

Despite Libyan leader Muammar al-Qaddhafi's uncompromising stance toward Islamist activism, a number of Libyan volunteers have traveled from Libya to join the Iraqi jihad. From the information that is beginning to emerge about some of these militants, it would seem that they are not part of any organized Islamist group, but rather have their own particular reasons and motivations for joining the jihad. The Libyan government is wary of returning fighters who could stir up the pot back at home, yet, at the same time, factions within the Libyan government and in the state-run media continue to dramatize the Iraqi "resistance."

Libyan Volunteers

Right from the start of the Iraq war, Libyans were keen to defend Saddam Hussein. This was not surprising given that many Arabs considered Iraq to be the eastern gate of the Arab world and the protector against Persian expansionism. As such, defending Saddam against imperialist forces was as much about Arab nationalism as it was about Islam. It would seem, however, that some of the Libyans who went to defend the Baathists at the outset of the conflict were largely unaware of the complexities of the sectarian and ethnic dynamics at play in Iraq. The fact that Iraq is composed of Shiites as well as Sunnis seems to have come as a shock to some of the volunteers and many returned to Libya disillusioned by what they had discovered. One taxi driver in the eastern city of Benghazi, for example, recounted how some of his friends had gone to defend Iraq, but had been disappointed to discover that some Iraqis did not want Saddam to stay in power. They could not understand why their offer of "brotherly support" had been rejected, and they returned home puzzled [1].

In spite of this, other volunteers continue to join the jihad. Nevertheless, not just any Libyan takes up the call to arms. The vast majority of those who have gone to fight in Iraq have come from the east of the country from in and around Benghazi. These fighters include jihadis such as Khalid Buisha who was killed in Fallujah in 2004 and Muhammad Abd al-Hadi Muhammad who was arrested in Iraq around the same time [2]. The fact that most of the Libyan volunteers have come from the east is no coincidence. Benghazi has traditionally been a center of rebellion against the al-Qaddhafi regime. It is a highly conservative area that has been kept purposefully underdeveloped, and for this reason it has developed into the main center of Islamic activism in the country. It represented the core of the militant Islamist groups that appeared on the Libyan scene in the 1980s and 1990s, including the Libyan Islamic Fighting Group (LIFG).

Libyans from other cities have also gone to Iraq. A number of militants from Sirte, which is in the center of the country and from the area that al-Qaddhafi originates, were reportedly killed in Iraq this summer. They included Mansour Busharada who allegedly came from al-Qaddhafi's own tribe, although this may be pure speculation [3].

Nevertheless, it is the eastern regions, encompassing Benghazi and other smaller cities such as Derna and al-Bayda, which have made-up the Libyan contingent fighting in Iraq.

From the limited information available, it would appear that those Libyans who have gone to Iraq from Libya itself are not part of any particular group or organization and are certainly not part of al-Qaeda. Indeed, the regime has kept such a tight lid on the Islamist movement since the shock of the 1990s that there is practically no space for any organized group to operate, least of all one with international connections. As such, these jihadis appear to have gone to Iraq as individuals rather than as part of any organized militant group. That is not to say, however, that there are not informal networks operating in the region around the mosques. Indeed, Muhammad Abd al-Hadi Muhammad, for example, who had joined the jihad in Fallujah, but who was captured by Iraqi forces, explained how a number of Libyan sheikhs in the mosques of Benghazi issued fatwas telling people it was their duty to fight in Iraq (Memri TV, January 24, 2005). This was also confirmed by the same Benghazi taxi driver who explained how the local imams had encouraged people to join the jihad in Iraq [4].

This kind of support for the idea of martyrdom clearly had an impact on men, such as Ali Attia Mohamed Bujafool Zwai from Benghazi who was killed in Iraq in 2006 during Ramadan and was 26 years old (*Libya al-Youm*, October 7, 2006). According to Ali's father, as a child he was brought up on his grandmother's stories about the heroic members of his own tribe who had become martyrs fighting against the Italian occupiers. Ali reportedly used to dream of becoming a martyr himself to defend the honor of his particular branch of the tribe. After leaving school, Ali, who had no interest in politics, went on to study electronic engineering, but soon became bored by the subject. His father suggested he study the Quran instead and Ali went first to Benghazi and then to Zliten to attend courses in Quranic studies. At some point, Ali managed to get a good job with the government, but this clearly did not satisfy his cravings for heroic adventure. In 2006, Ali telephoned his family to say that he had made it to Baghdad and had joined the resistance. Days later, his family received news of his death.

Perhaps more extraordinary than the story of this young man was the way his family and neighbors reacted to his killing. Ali's father recounted how the whole family began celebrating when they heard the news and they distributed drinks and sweets among the neighbors. His father explained how he was extremely proud and particularly happy that Ali had been martyred during the holy month of Ramadan and one of Ali's brothers, Ahmed, declared, "We all wish for martyrdom." Family support for joining the jihad is not unique. In fact, in some instances several members of the same family have taken it upon themselves to fight in Iraq. For example, in July 2006, news emerged about three youths from the Ishkal family from Sirte who had been killed in Iraq (Libya Focus, July 2006). Similarly, three brothers from the eastern city of Derna—Hamza, Abdulrahman and Bilal Aqila Bin Khayal—were all killed in Iraq [5]. The eldest, Hamza, had reportedly gone to Iraq even before the war had started. He was caught and imprisoned for two years. By this time, his younger brother, Abdulrahman, who was 21 years old, traveled to join him. Shortly after Hamza left prison, Abdulrahman contacted the family back in Libya to tell them that his brother had been killed. This news convinced the youngest brother, Bilal, who was just 16 years old, that it was also his duty to go to Iraq. Both Abdulrahman and Bilal, however, met the same fate as their older brother. It was reported that the three sons had been encouraged to fight by their father who was keen for them to defend their honor in Iraq [6].

Figures such as the Aqila Bin Khayal brothers clearly came from deeply religious families who believed that it was their Islamic duty to fight in Iraq. For others, the motivation appears to have been more haphazard and mundane. The Arab media seems to have been a key motivating factor for some of the volunteers. Muhammad Abd al-Hadi Muhammad, for example, who had joined the jihad in Fallujah but was captured by Iraqi forces, explained that the "media is what brought me [to Iraq]. The pictures of Abu Ghraib ... the Al Jazeera and al-Arabiya channels and other TV channels like al-Shariqa and others" (Memri TV, January 24, 2005). For such young men who have limited educational opportunities and who live in places such as Benghazi where life offers little hope, few prospects or any sense of fulfillment, it is easy to see how such images and messages could be persuasive.

Moreover, there is a degree of acceptance about the merits of jihad and martyrdom among some sections of the broader population. There have been numerous reports of martyrdom "wedding" festivities taking place in Libya for those who have been killed in Iraq. For example, in May 2005, celebrations were held to mark the deaths in Iraq of three young Benghazi inhabitants. This support, however, is not only the domain of militants. Even the tightly controlled state-run mosques are promoting the cause of martyrdom. In March, 2006, for example, the imam at the Ahmed Pasha Mosque in Tripoli told his congregation during Friday prayers, "Bravo to the martyrdom for the sake of Allah. Bravo to the martyrdom for elevating the word of Allah. Bravo to martyrdom for elevating the word of truth" [7]. This idealizing of the heroism of sacrifice arguably creates a permissive environment that encourages desperate young men to give their lives for a battle being fought many miles away from home.

Double Talk

Despite the fact that Colonel al-Qaddhafi has displayed a completely intolerant attitude toward political Islamists of any hue, the Libyan regime has proved to be as ambiguous in its attitude toward the whole Iraq crisis as others in the region. On the one hand, it has been anxious to ensure that Iraq does not become a repeat of the Afghanistan experience with returning veterans ready to wage war against the state. In a speech in March 2005, al-Qaddhafi warned about potential returnees and stated, "We cannot be more Iraqi than the Iraqis themselves" (BBC, March 4, 2005). The regime has also taken more direct measures. It was reported that Khalid al-Zayidi returned to Benghazi in October 2005 after he had fought in Iraq to undergo surgery for a wound on his leg that he sustained on

Despite the fact that Colonel al-Qaddhafi has displayed a completely intolerant attitude toward political Islamists of any hue, the Libyan regime has proved to be as ambiguous in its attitude toward the whole Iraq crisis as others in the region.

the battlefield [8]. Shortly after his return, the Libyan internal security service killed him as he tried to escape arrest after he had protested the attempts by the security services to arrest his friend and fellow Islamist, Hatem Busnina [9]. The regime has also launched pre-emptive arrests, such as in November, when it was reported that a number of young men who were showing Islamist tendencies were arrested in Bani Walid after it had been discovered that some individuals from the Saadat, Jamila and Fladna tribes had gone to Iraq.

At the same time, however, the regime has not shied away from praising the Iraqi resistance. Al-Qaddhafi's daughter Aisha, who was a member of Saddam Hussein's legal team, has repeatedly supported those fighting in Iraq. In September 2005, she exclaimed, "We salute proudly the fighters of the Iraqi resistance who were able to break the American dream" (UPI, September 28, 2005). Al-Qaddhafi himself has been more reticent in his praise of the fighters as he has to keep an eye on his newly restored relations with the United States. The tightly controlled state media, however, continues to use the term resistance and regularly reports on the killings of U.S. troops in Iraq.

Some have gone as far as to suggest that the regime was content to allow Libyans to fight in Iraq. Indeed, at the end of 2004 the Iraqi media accused Libya of allowing the former Iraqi Embassy in Tripoli to recruit for the Iraqi jihad. These reports have not been confirmed. In October 2004, the London-based Maqreze Center announced that it had received a letter from inside Libya which stated, "All these people went to Iraq with the blessing of the regime because it wanted Iraq to win, not because it liked the Iraqis, but out of fear that it may lose power. But ... when some of these young people returned, the regime started liquidating them" [10].

Therefore, while the regime has been alert to the prospect of its own citizens returning to Libya with the aim of bringing down the regime, it has also maintained an ambivalent attitude toward the conflict. Al-Qaddhafi, however, should be concerned that while still relatively few in number, there are Libyans who are desperate and angry enough to die as martyrs in Iraq, and perhaps more worryingly, there is still a degree of support for such acts among sections of the population, especially in the troubled and embittered east.

Originally published in *Terrorism Monitor*: Volume 4, Issue 23 on November 30, 2006.

Notes

1. Conversation between author and Libyan taxi driver, Benghazi, June 2005.
2. "Kaima bi asma'a shuhada bilad al-rafidain min al-Muhajirine wa al-Ansar bi'ithnilah" (A List of Martyrs from Mesopotamia from al-Muhajirine and al-Ansar, if Allah Permits), http://majdah.com/vb/showthread.php?t=8239; Memri TV, January 24, 2005.
3. "Libi min sirte dahiyat al-Kital fi al-Iraq" (A Libyan from Sirte is a Victim of the Fighting in Iraq), http://www.akhbar-libya2.com/index.php?option=com_content& task=view&id=134&Itemid=51.
4. Conversation between author and Libyan taxi driver, Benghazi, June 2005.
5. See http://majdah.com/vb/showthread.php?t=8239.

6. Ibid.

7. Excerpts from a Friday sermon at Ahmed Pasha Mosque, Tripoli, Libya, aired on Libya TV on February 3, 2006.

8. See http://www.libya-alhora.com/forum/showthread.php?t=3575.

9. Arabic Network for Human Rights Information, October 28, 2004.

10. See http://almaqreze.com/bayanat/artcl022.html.

The Reconstituted Al-Qaeda Threat in the Maghreb
By Andrew Black

In the first week of January 2007, the Moroccan government announced the dismantling of an alleged 62-person terrorist cell (*Gulf Times*, January 5, 2007). According to statements made by the government, this cell had "ideological links with and financial and logistical support for international terrorist groups" including al-Qaeda and the Salafist Group for Call and Combat (GSPC). Although details are still emerging about the cell and its connections with the GSPC and al-Qaeda, its alleged activities are emblematic of the new paradigm in the Maghreb. As a result of two mergers, one among the various Maghrebi groups and the other between the GSPC and al-Qaeda, the terrorist threat to the region has become an increasingly unified system that provides substantial support to the Iraqi jihad and which will increasingly challenge local security services as mujahideen return from Iraq.

The Mergers

On September 11, 2006, as the world's thoughts were on the fifth anniversary of the 9/11 terrorist attacks, al-Qaeda deputy leader Ayman al-Zawahiri issued a statement announcing the merger of his group and the GSPC. Previously, the GSPC had declared its support for al-Qaeda in 2003 under the leadership of Nabil Sahraoui; however, this marks the first time that the two groups formally merged. The importance of this momentous event was underlined by the fact that the merger was first announced not by the GSPC, but by al-Zawahiri. Demonstrating the significance of this merger to the Algerian jihad, local security services have already remarked that al-Qaeda's support appears to have bolstered the GSPC's morale, and the December 10, 2006 roadside bomb attack on Halliburton subsidiary Brown & Root-Condor in Algeria carried many al-Qaeda hallmarks.

As a curious side note, GSPC leader Abu Mus'ab al-Wadoud issued a statement in October 2006 in which he declared that his group "joined the real Islamist organization under the leadership of our brother and supreme chief Ayman al-Zawahri" (*El-Khabar*, October 8, 2006). Although Osama bin Laden featured prominently on the GSPC website (Almedad.com/jama3a) prior to its removal, it was not until January 8, 2007 that al-Wadoud made specific, public reference to the al-Qaeda leader. In this statement, al-Wadoud named bin Laden as the group's amir and said he was awaiting bin Laden's instructions for the next phase (al-Bawaba, January 8, 2007). Considering al-Zawahiri's August 5, 2006 announcement of al-Qaeda's merger with the Egyptian al-Gama'a al-Islamiyya (EIG), this indicates that al-Zawahiri may be the one responsible for al-Qaeda's recent unification efforts.

Prior to the September merger, however, reports surfaced that al-Qaeda had made inroads in forming a pan-Maghreb group along the lines of the now infamous Tanzim Qaidat al-Jihad fi Bilad al-Rafidayn (The al-Qaeda Organization of Jihad in the Land of the Two

Rivers) (*Asharq al-Awsat*, December 8, 2005). Reportedly, this new group, dubbed "Qaedat al-Jihad in the Arab Maghreb Countries," was to be led by the GSPC and would bring together jihadi groups from Algeria, Tunisia and Morocco. In support of this, a Spanish intelligence report, quoted by local media in late November 2006, claimed the group would also include the Libyan Islamic Fighting Group (LIFG). By January 26, 2007, al-Wadoud officially declared that the new name for his organization would be "The al-Qaeda Organization in the Islamic Maghreb," a name which is strikingly reminiscent of al-Qaeda's affiliate in Iraq (Al Jazeera, January 26, 2008).

Considering these two mergers together, the result is a broad network falling under the regional leadership of the GSPC, which in turn is aligned under al-Qaeda. Al-Qaeda has clearly taken a renewed interest in reconstituting its Maghrebi affiliates with the dual intent of supporting the Iraqi jihad and bolstering its operational assets around the region. In effect, by consolidating its affiliated groups in the Arab Maghreb, al-Qaeda has established a North African extension with assets that reach not only into Iraq, but also well into Europe. As veteran fighters begin emigrating from the Iraq theater, these mergers effectively establish a conduit and structure for these individuals to continue their jihad in other venues.

The Path To and From Iraq

As part of these reports, it has become apparent that al-Qaeda has a number of strategic intentions for its North African network. Integral to these plans is the formation of an extensive training cycle, which in essence provides the means by which al-Qaeda can move fighters between Iraq and the Maghreb. This training cycle, which first came to light from sources in Morocco, begins with regional fighters participating in training provided by the GSPC, presumably at one of the group's *In effect, by consolidating its affiliated groups in the Arab Maghreb, al-Qaeda has established a North African extension with assets that reach not only into Iraq, but also well into Europe.* mobile training camps in the Sahara desert. Following completion of this phase of their training, fighters will move on to fight alongside the GSPC against the Algerian government. In this phase, jihadis gain operational experience, which will serve them well in the next stage of the cycle: the Iraq jihad. Once they have been smuggled in through one of Iraq's neighboring countries (likely Syria), fighters will participate in terrorist and insurgent activities and potentially conduct martyrdom operations. For those select few who complete this stage and survive, they are to return to the Maghreb to await operational orders from al-Qaeda *(Asharq al-Awsat*, December 8, 2005).

Aside from providing GSPC operatives with mission critical training, the GSPC's mobile training camps have functioned as the primary catalyst in forming and strengthening the organizational bonds among the Maghrebi groups. These training camps arguably constitute the backbone of the GSPC's networking efforts in North Africa. Indicative of this, according to General Kip Ward of U.S. EUCOM, the group has succeeded in assembling "militants from as far afield as Nigeria, Tunisia or Morocco" (Sudan Tribune, October 16, 2006).

As the groups in the Maghreb coalesce, the role of the GSPC's mobile training apparatus will be of vital importance in coordination and inter-group cooperation. As seen with the training camps in Afghanistan in the 1990s, the experiences shared by mujahideen in the camps can have a lasting impact through the establishment of an *esprit de corps*, which subsequently leads to high levels of trust and a willingness to cooperate. These camps will also be vital in feeding the flow of mujahideen traveling to Iraq to participate in the insurgency there. Although there are training facilities in Iraq for foreign fighters, efforts to prepare fighters prior to their departure for Iraq will alleviate some of the burden placed on the Iraqi jihadi training system.

The Result

Although it is still too early to accurately assess the cumulative affects of this reconstituted threat, there are indications of the means by which it will impact the threat environments of both the Maghreb and Europe. Bearing in mind the criticality of the aforementioned training cycle—both in terms of raising operational proficiency and in facilitating the flow of fighters between the Maghreb and the Iraqi jihad—this organizational restructuring provides al-Qaeda and its constituents with the means to perpetuate the jihad against North African governments and the West. For those jihadis who participate in and survive the training program (including the Iraqi phase), they will return with extensive operational experience to a reconstituted Maghrebi network that extends well into the West and has the capability of raising requisite operational resources for large-scale attacks. Providing such a structure prior to the injection of these jihadis is vital to ensuring the smooth and rapid transition from fighting in Iraq to executing attacks in the western Mediterranean region.

Considering the Maghreb's proximity to Europe and also bearing in mind Spain's African enclaves—Ceuta and Melilla—the reconstituted Maghrebi threat has direct implications for Europe. In early December 2006, Spanish police interrupted a plot targeting a trade fair and an explosives depot in Ceuta (*El Pais*, December 13, 2006). During the investigation, the Spanish press released details of an intelligence report compiled by four European Union countries: Spain, France, Germany and the United Kingdom (*El Pais*, December 17, 2006). Although the number of Europeans who have participated in the Iraq insurgency is thought to be few, this report lists roughly 200 individuals residing in Europe who have undergone training and who have fought in Iraq. The majority of those listed are of North African origin. Although this alone does not conclusively indicate a role of North African groups, it does demonstrate the need for the al-Qaeda network to establish an organizational link between the Iraqi theater and Europe.

Operationally, this network has already exhibited a number of alterations that demonstrate the influence of both al-Qaeda and Iraqi veterans. As shown with the high profile attack on Halliburton subsidiary Brown & Root-Condor in early December 2006, this network, led by the GSPC, has shifted its targeting tendencies to focus on assets symbolic of foreign, primarily Western, influence. This was demonstrated in a video of the attack released by the GSPC on January 22, 2007, in which al-Wadoud clearly identifies Halliburton as the target of the operation. As an indication that this trend is likely to continue, the GSPC's amir, al-Wadoud, issued a vitriolic statement in early January in which he specifically vilified France and the United States for their activities in the Maghreb and for stealing the oil and natural gas of the *ummah*.

Tactically, Maghrebi operations will likely shift to conform with al-Qaeda hallmarks, and during the past year there have been indications that this shift is already occurring. Maghrebi groups have previously conducted suicide operations, yet this tactic has not featured prominently in regional campaigns. In his January 8, 2007 statement, al-Wadoud specifically notes the willingness of his cadres to perpetrate martyrdom operations.

By consolidating the Maghrebi groups, al-Qaeda has, in effect, created the conduit through which jihadis can migrate among Iraq, North Africa and potentially Europe, while also establishing the organizational structure in the Maghreb to pursue the global jihad. Reorganizing the Islamist groups in the Maghreb provides al-Qaeda the means not only to perpetuate the Iraqi jihad while leveraging its gains from that conflict, but also to undermine regional regimes and promote attacks on their Western supporters.

Originally published in *Terrorism Monitor*: Volume 5, Issue 2 on February 1, 2007

Islamist Infiltration of the Moroccan Armed Forces
By Matthew Chebatoris

At the end of July 2006, Moroccan authorities dismantled Ansar al-Mahdi, a previously unknown terrorist group, and made initial arrests of 44 people. The number of arrestees later grew to 56 and spanned multiple cities in northern Morocco. The group itself was unique and included an eclectic mix of drug traffickers, wives of Air Maroc pilots and members of the armed forces reportedly led by Hassan al-Khattab—a known Salafi-Jihadi aspirant who was imprisoned for two years in 2003 following the Casablanca bombings (*La Gazette du Maroc*, August 21, 2006; *L'Expression*, August 13, 2006). Unlike previous terror cells, which were predominantly comprised of members from the poor working class, appearances suggest this organization transcended social barriers in its quest to recruit members. Moreover, while Moroccan authorities have disrupted numerous terrorist cells in recent years, the disclosure that members of the Moroccan military had been recruited into a terror cell with the intent of conducting attacks against government and tourist targets in Morocco could signify a new stage in Morocco's efforts to combat the influence of radical Islamists.

Origins of Moroccan Salafism

Salafi-Jihadism, which was blamed by Moroccan authorities for the Casablanca bombings, is best characterized as an amorphous movement comprised of like-minded individuals who adhere to a radical interpretation of Salafism, which, in their eyes, sanctions violence. While the movement lacks an overarching command structure, the origins of Moroccan Salafism can be traced back to the network of Saudi-trained imams who discarded traditional apolitical Salafi beliefs in exchange for politically charged rhetoric and a willingness to engage in violence. Beginning in the 1960s, the government of King Hassan II began to encourage Islamists, particularly those from Saudi Arabia, as a natural bulwark against the pan-Arab social nationalist policies of Egyptian leader Gamal Abdel Nasser. Whatever skepticism Morocco may have had of Salafism, broader strategic considerations at the time—such as the relationship between Morocco and Saudi Arabia vis-à-vis the United States, and Saudi support for Morocco's conflict with Western Sahara—took precedent [1]. Many of the imams who were originally sanctioned by the Moroccan government set out to establish ad hoc mosques in the slums on the outskirts of Morocco's cities. It was here that their influence began to take hold among the poor and socially disenfranchised residents of the vast shantytowns known in Morocco as *bidonvilles*.

Prior Unrest in the Armed Forces

The Moroccan military has not always served as the guardian of the Moroccan crown. During the early 1970s, the military was involved in two failed coup attempts against King Hassan II, the father of Morocco's current ruler. In contrast to the current environment, these coup attempts were led by military officers and were not Islamist in nature. Moreover, they were directed solely at the regime and not the Moroccan public. The acknowledgement by Moroccan authorities that Ansar al-Mahdi had penetrated the ranks of the armed forces is the first time a threat of this nature has been admitted publicly and may be a sign of its seriousness.

There are conflicting reports surrounding the identities of the military members belonging to Ansar al-Mahdi. Most point toward the involvement of five soldiers deemed to have expertise in explosives (*La Gazette du Maroc*, August 14, 2006). *L'Expression*, an Algerian daily, claimed on August 13, 2006 that the soldiers were working at the airbase in Sale. Interestingly, a Western media outlet interviewed the family of Mohamed Khalouki, one of the five soldiers arrested, who claimed Mohamed and his four colleagues were merely members of the military band and had nothing to do with the alleged terror group (ABC News, September 29, 2006). Little more regarding the background of the soldiers has been publicly disclosed, giving scant insight into the depth that Salafi-Jihadi ideology has penetrated the armed forces. Fortunately, available information does not point toward the involvement of military officers in the terror cell, which would be an indicator of wide penetration as the officers are in a position to influence the lower ranks. Nor does information suggest the involvement of elite units, which could make their specialized skills and training available to radical Islamists.

The inclusion of military members in Ansar al-Mahdi is but one of the differences between this round of arrests and previous actions by the security services. While Moroccan authorities have disrupted Salafi-Jihadi cells in the past, the cells have lacked the structure of traditional terrorist organizations. Hassan al-Khattab's Ansar al-Mahdi, on the other hand, appears to have had a more traditional framework, possibly indicative of an evolution in the shape of Moroccan terror organizations, with the added muscle of military expertise to assist in the training of members. *La Gazette du Maroc* on August 14, 2006 characterized Ansar al-Mahdi as a military organization with separate members in charge of Islamist indoctrination and operations. Notably, al-Khattab appears to have built a hierarchical organization where members were not only aware of one another, but also worked together in a coordinated effort, which marks a contrast with the past shape of Salafi-Jihadism in Morocco.

Indeed, given Morocco's social inequalities and the susceptibility of low paid soldiers to corruption and outside influences, on the surface the armed forces give the appearance of an organization vulnerable to the influence of radical Islamists. Made up of three services (Army, Air Force and Navy), the Moroccan armed forces are comprised of roughly 196,000 active personnel, among which there are between 75,000-100,000 conscripts, and a reserve force of 150,000. The seemingly high number of conscripts is somewhat misleading since roughly 353,377 Moroccan men become eligible for the draft each year. Moreover, many voluntarily remain in the military where they have the ability to earn a steady, albeit low, monthly income comparable to Morocco's minimum monthly wage of $223.30.

Implications for the Future

As of late January 2007, the trials of al-Khattab and Ansar al-Mahdi members have been postponed until appropriate legal representation can be agreed upon for all defendants.

While officials have disclosed few details on the extent of the Islamist infiltration, the actions taken by the Moroccan government in the wake of the Ansar al-Mahdi arrests provide observers with the most telling signs as to the seriousness of the Islamist threat vis-à-vis the armed forces. On August 31, 2006, the government ended conscription in the armed forces, a move undoubtedly aimed at mitigating the vulnerability of the lower ranks to the influence of radical Islamists. Young men aged 18 were previously required to enter military service for a compulsory period of 18 months. Most were deployed to serve in Western Sahara—which is territorially administered by Morocco—in what has become an increasingly unpopular policy decision by Rabat and desertions were not uncommon. The end of mandatory service, however, was but one of the wide-sweeping changes felt across the Moroccan security services. Changes also occurred at the top of the ranks with the dismissal of General Hamidou Laanigri, head of the General Office of National Security (Direction Generale de la Surete Nationale, DGSN), and General Mohammed Belbachir, head of the Military Intelligence Service (Direction de la Surveillance du Territoire, DST) (*Le Journal Hebdomadaire*, September 23–29, 2006). Furthermore, the palace relieved 12 lower officials, predominantly from regional elements of the various security services, of their duties. Notably, many were replaced by civilians with personal ties to the king (*La Gazette du Maroc*, September 18, 2006).

This far reaching purge of the security services suggests the degree of Islamist infiltration has perhaps been greater than previously disclosed by the Moroccan government. Nevertheless, it remains unlikely that units of the armed forces have been co-opted to the extent that they have the ability or the popular support to overthrow the Moroccan government and establish an Islamic state as witnessed during the Iranian revolution. The move to an all volunteer force is a positive step and should have the effect of reducing the appeal of radical Islamic ideology in the military by removing the most susceptible layer from the ranks. Ending conscription is unlikely to significantly impact manning levels in the armed forces and will allow the kingdom to focus on developing all-volunteer, professional military services.

Indeed, given Morocco's social inequalities and the susceptibility of low paid soldiers to corruption and outside influences, on the surface the armed forces give the appearance of an organization vulnerable to the influence of radical Islamists.

Morocco's official unemployment rate is a mere 7.7 percent; however, this calls into question the level of "underemployment" across the kingdom. As a result, the benefit of a steady monthly income offered by the armed forces will likely remain appealing to many young Moroccan men. From a purely security perspective, while Algeria remains a regional rival, Morocco does not face an external military threat to its security that would necessitate the need for mandatory military service. Additionally, a permanent resolution of the dispute over Western Sahara would likely serve to alleviate some of the strain on the armed forces and boost morale.

In many ways, the Casablanca bombings served as a wake up call for the Moroccan government, which has begun to take measures to alleviate the socio-economic pressures affecting the majority of Moroccans. Importantly, the demographic makeup of Ansar al-Mahdi appears to have eroded the often held belief that socio-economic pressures alone are driving Morocco's internal Islamist movement. Despite the violence of the Casablanca bombings in May 2003, Morocco does not have a history of Islamic terrorism. In contrast to other North African countries, such as Algeria and Egypt, Morocco has remained relatively immune from the plagues of violence. The kingdom's ability to incorporate democratic reforms and not allow security concerns to drive all facets of government policy will prove to be crucial in combating the future threat of terrorism in Morocco.

Many of the changes related to the recent events are transparent to ordinary Moroccans and have not resulted in an overtly large security presence in popular tourist areas such as the Djemma al-Fna in Marrakesh. Additionally, despite the implication of wives of Air Maroc pilots, airport security is not at a heightened level [2]. The recent reorganization of the security services is an important step toward dismantling the powerful *makhzen* (governing elite), who have remained influential in guiding Moroccan politics during Mohammed VI's reign. In addition to these changes, continuing efforts must be made to improve the prospects of those in the lower echelons of the armed forces in order to mitigate the ideological influence of radical Islamists and maintain the honor of an important institution.

Originally published in *Terrorism Monitor*: Volume 5, Issue 3 on February 15, 2007.

Notes

1. Howe, Marvine, *Morocco: The Islamist Awakening and Other Challenges*, (Oxford: Oxford University Press, 2005).
2. Observations by the author from November 2006 travel to Marrakesh, Ouarzazate and Zagora.

AQIM's Threat to Morocco's Tourism Sector
By Matthew Chebatoris

As with most North African countries, Morocco's tourism sector is vulnerable to fluctuations as a result of terrorism and political developments. Recent incidents such as the panicked detonation of a suicide bomber's vest in an internet cafe in April and the subsequent, albeit possibly unrelated, occurrences involving individuals with suicide belts, including the detonations near the U.S. Consulate and cultural center in Casablanca, reinforce the unfortunate reality that, despite modest economic progress, the underlying root causes for terrorism in Morocco persist (MAP, April 12, 2007; MAP, April 14, 2007). The number of foreign tourists visiting the kingdom dipped after the September 11, 2001 attacks in the United States and remained relatively stagnant through 2003. These numbers have been bolstered as of late, however, due to an increase in the number of Moroccans living abroad who regularly return home. In 2005, tourism comprised roughly 10 percent of the country's GDP, with commerce and import duties, a related sector, making up the largest figure at 22.1 percent (Economist Intelligence Unit, 2005). Additionally, 2005 saw the implementation of the "Open Skies" agreement between Morocco and the European Union, which opened Morocco's airline industry to competition from low-cost European carriers. The proliferation of Europe-based discount airlines such as Ryan Air and Easy Jet has made travel to Morocco increasingly cost effective for European holiday travelers. Furthermore, the search for new markets has pushed developing countries such as Morocco to the forefront of Western tourism markets and made them fashionable travel destinations.

The Effect on Tourism

Morocco's close geographic proximity to Europe, abundance of sunshine and rich cultural heritage has made the kingdom an increasingly popular holiday destination for European travelers. This is particularly true among French citizens who share a common language and maintain historic ties to the Maghreb. In marked contrast to neighboring Algeria, Morocco's tourism industry is thriving and is regularly cited as one of the hallmarks of the kingdom's openness. In January 2001, King Mohammad VI of Morocco embarked on "Vision 2010," a national plan to increase Morocco's infrastructure to accommodate ten million tourists by the end of the decade. As an indication of its commitment to this endeavor, the government recently allocated more than $2.2 billion toward the development of seaside resorts (MAP, May 11, 2007). The underlying goal of these development initiatives is to increase the percentage of the tourism sector's contribution to the national GDP to 20 percent by 2010 (MAP, May 11, 2007). Understandably, terrorism ranks at the top of political risks to Morocco's desire to attract foreign investment in order to fuel the

While Western venues have been targeted in the past, attacks have not struck major hubs for the Moroccan tourism industry ... Nor does travel to Morocco appear to be affected by the tenacity of the political violence in neighboring Algeria, as the sector has enjoyed sustainable growth during the first decade of the 21st century.

country's economic development. Even in the absence of attacks, the mere perception of the threat of terrorism can be enough to deter travelers, thus starving local merchants of income and, as a result, challenging the resilience of related sectors such as transportation and commerce.

While Western venues have been targeted in the past, attacks have not struck major hubs for the Moroccan tourism industry such as the seaside resort of Agadir or the cultural centers of Fez and Marrakech. In fact, Morocco's tourism industry actually grew by 17 percent in 2003—the year of the Casablanca bombings [1]. Nor does travel to Morocco appear to be affected by the tenacity of the political violence in neighboring Algeria, as the sector has enjoyed sustainable growth during the first decade of the 21st century. Indeed, according to figures provided by the Moroccan Ministry of Tourism, the tourism sector continues to experience growth, posting a 16 percent increase in the number of visitors to the country in the first trimester of 2007 during the same period in 2006 (Moroccan Ministry of Tourism, 2007). Therefore, absent a sustained terror campaign or a catastrophe along the lines of the 1997 massacre of German tourists outside of Luxor by Gammat al-Islamiyya, the number of tourists visiting the kingdom will likely increase in the near future.

Mitigating the Threat

Physical security is the most effective deterrent employed to directly mitigate the risk of terrorism to both hard and soft targets, including venues frequented by tourists. Throughout popular tourist locations in Morocco, the security presence is visible but not overbearing. In order to reduce the threat of car bombings, most resort hotel complexes primarily catering to European visitors have constructed natural barriers such as large steps leading up to the hotel lobby or palm groves throughout the complex. Most are also encompassed by high walls and gate guards to provide an added level of comfort and security [2]. Moreover, in an effort to manage tourist concerns about the risks of using local transportation (i.e. kidnapping, overcharging and general vagaries of the local system), many hotels and *riad* (traditional Moroccan Bed and Breakfast) operators arrange taxis both to and from popular tourist sites, as well as direct couriers to the local airport. Importantly, terrorists and Islamic fundamentalists alike have not benefited from a level of grassroots support among the Moroccan populous [3].

While clamping down on Islamists, particularly those deemed to share affiliation with the Salafi-Jihad, Moroccan authorities are striving to strike a balance between the legitimate need for security and the more oppressive policies of the past. In this regard, it is essential for the Moroccan government to avoid coming across as too heavy-handed as it cracks down on domestic Islamist militants. Overly intensive efforts to eradicate the roots of Salafi-Jihadi ideology, if left unchecked, could lead to a return to the previous era of political persecution and human rights abuses in Morocco. A successful domestic security policy will recognize the nuances within Islamic thought and not apply a blanket approach to dealing with the kingdom's opponents. Social inequalities, such as the income gap, are exceedingly stark in Morocco and are considered a symbol of the government's neglect of its people. This was undoubtedly one of the motivating factors for the individuals who conducted the Casablanca bombings, and it is cited by at least one government opposition group as a factor in the incidents in Spring 2007 (*El-Khabar*, April 11, 2007). Fatallah Arslane, a spokesperson for al-Adl wal-Ihsane (Justice and Charity)—a political party banned from participating in elections—cited the Moroccan government's failure to adequately address the needs of its people as a contributor to the recent spate of suicide bombings in Casablanca (*El-Khabar*, April 11, 2007). Arslane stated that, "Overcoming the phenomenon of violence requires a comprehensive remedy which is not restricted to security measures. This remedy has to go beyond security measures to include lifting injustice and improving people's economic, political and social conditions" (*El-Khabar*, April 11, 2007).

As a result of these inequalities, the need to address social issues like unemployment and the income gap is seen as a critical front in Morocco's war on terrorism. Embarking on this path, Morocco has set out to mitigate the economic and social factors contributing to terrorism by undertaking a series of social welfare programs. For example, in October 2003, the government initiated an education campaign aimed at tackling the high illiteracy rate in the country. Conscious of the growing disparity between the rich and poor, the government recognizes that with increased education its citizens will become more able to gain employment and move out of the slums and their cycle of poverty.

Acting on the assumption that domestic issues contribute to acts of terrorism, Morocco submitted a proposal for a $150 million housing sector development loan to the World Bank in June 2005. Morocco hopes that a judicious implementation of the World Bank's loan will contribute toward eradicating the bidonvilles successfully, viewed increasingly as simmering pots of Salafi-Jihadi ideology, and improve the overall living conditions for the poor by increasing the availability of low-cost urban housing. The loan, approved on June 31, 2005, will also result in an increase in construction and development, thus creating some forms of temporary employment.

Conclusion

The makeover of the tourism industry is but one part in the process of broader democratic and economic reform being undertaken by the kingdom in which the Moroccan government must tread carefully given the present atmosphere of increased popular resentment with the West and prescient concerns surrounding the intentions of Al-Qaeda in the Islamic Maghreb to export terror beyond Algeria. Success will largely hinge on how the government proceeds on the path of democratic reform. To date, the incidents in Casablanca, Morocco's economic center, have not altered the flow of tourists to the country, and no cancellations of foreign tourist or business delegations have been noted (*al-Hayat*, April 27, 2007). Violent Salafism, nevertheless, remains a key ideological underpinning where al-Qaeda and related movements continue to draw additional followers by mobilizing Moroccan residents through a process in which local grievances are increasingly viewed through the prism of the global Salafi-Jihad. The government's continued success in disrupting terror plots, as well as the vigilance and bravery exhibited by ordinary Moroccans in the face of terrorism, i.e. the actions of the Casablanca internet cafe owner, indicates that the risk environment, for now, remains secure.

Originally published in *Terrorism Monitor*: Volume 5, Issue 11 on June 7, 2007.

Notes

1. Dermot Davitt, "The War on Tourism," *Travel Retailer International*, December 2004/January 2005, 8-9.
2. Observations by the author from travel to Marrakesh, Ouarzazate and Zagora in November 2006.
3. Ibid.

Splits Revealed Inside Al-Qaeda in the Islamic Maghreb
By Geoff D. Porter

During an August 14, 2007 news conference organized by Algerian authorities for a select group of Algerian reporters, Benmessaoud Abdelkader, a former Salafist Group for Call and Combat (GSPC) regional commander, confirmed that there was deep disagreement within the former GSPC over national commander Abdelmalek Droudkel's decisions first to merge with al-Qaeda in September 2006 and then later to rename the group the Al-Qaeda Organization in the Islamic Maghreb (AQIM) in January 2007 (*Liberté*, August 21, 2007). The split appears to have diminished the terrorist group's logistical capacity and reduced its overall size, but has also made the al-Qaeda affiliate more desperate and determined to demonstrate its continued effectiveness and relevancy. The rift in Algeria has also likely split GSPC/AQIM's numerous cells in Europe. While this means that there are probably fewer European cells supporting AQIM than previously thought, these cells have likely mutated to embrace a wider range of targets than their GSPC precursors and in that sense represent a heightened risk for European security. Similarly, possibly orphaned GSPC cells could eventually merge with other Islamist terrorist cells, such as the group behind the plot to attack the Frankfurt International Airport and the nearby U.S. Ramstein Air Base in Germany that was thwarted on September 4, 2007.

Splits within AQIM

The current split is due to two related disagreements: should the group try to redefine its struggle as part of a global jihad, or should it remain focused on overthrowing the secular government of Algerian President Abdelaziz Bouteflika? Second, is it legitimate to attack civilians, or is the government the only permissible target? Droudkel's AQIM wants to expand throughout North Africa and join forces in neighboring countries along the Mediterranean coast and in the Sahel. In his worldview, anyone who is not AQIM is against it and therefore a legitimate target. The September 6 , 2007 attack on a crowd awaiting the arrival of President Bouteflika that resulted in at least 15 civilian deaths is a case in point (*Le Quotidien d'Oran*, September 6, 2007). The GSPC's grievance was with the government that scuttled an Islamist electoral victory in 1991. It drew a clear distinction between the government and the populace at large.

The GSPC's evolution has significant ramifications for Droudkel and the AQIM's continued viability. Benmessaoud was the commander of the GSPC/AQIM's Zone IX, a long corridor down the middle of the country stretching from the high plateaus in the north to a large swath of Sahara Desert along Algeria's borders with Mali and Niger. Benmessaoud took over the position after its previous incumbent, Mokhtar Belmokhtar, entered into negotiations with the Algerian government (through interlocutors in Tamanrasset) to surrender and decamp to Mali where his wife and children live (*El Watan*, June 16, 2007). Zone IX has historically been critical for the viability of GSPC/AQIM activities in the north of the country. Through contraband smuggling, drug-running and weapons sales, Belmokhtar and Benmessaoud funneled funds and guns to the group's northern zones. With Belmokhtar's resignation and Benmessaoud's surrender, however, Droudkel is deprived of this key source of money and arms.

Benmessaoud also said that Droudkel responded repressively to a spate of defections following the alliance with al-Qaeda. According to Benmessaoud, Droudkel's trouble retaining recruits prompted him to forbid new AQIM members from straying out of sight of trusted veteran fighters. In a private conversation, Algerian security chief Ali Tounsi surmised that that the three car bombs used in the April 11, 2007 attacks in Algiers were wired with remote detonation devices in addition to the detonation devices triggered by the drivers because Droudkel feared that the bombers would abort their missions. The attempted assassination on August 14, 2007 of a former chief of the now defunct Islamic Salvation Front's (FIS) armed wing, Mustapha Kertali, has intensified new recruits' fear of being killed themselves should they attempt to abandon the organization and try to return to their civilian lives (Temoust, August 16, 2007).

The loss of Zone IX, in conjunction with a tremendously intensified military campaign, has left Droudkel restricted to Zone II, his personal fiefdom in the mountainous Boumerdes region several hundred kilometers to the southeast of Algiers. Deprived of southern smuggling revenue, Droudkel and his supporters have come to depend more heavily on kidnap and ransom operations to generate money. As communications break down between zones and the group is eliminated from certain regions entirely, Droudkel has been compelled to explore new means of maneuvering throughout the country. The latest method is to charter coastal fishing boats to move men and materiel along Algeria's Mediterranean coastline (*El-Chourouk el-Youmi*, August 15, 2007).

The schism instigated by Droudkel's decision to ally with al-Qaeda has likely prompted Droudkel to step up attacks in order to dispel any perception that his group has been weakened. AQIM has carried out two deadly attacks in the last week. On September 6, 2007 the group tried to assassinate President Abdelaziz Bouteflika in Batna, but the bomber was discovered and he blew himself up before the president arrived. The explosion killed more than 20 civilians. Three days later, AQIM drove a truck full of explosives into a Coast Guard base in the eastern city of Dellys, killing 30 Coast Guard members and destroying several of the base's buildings. It bears mentioning that despite the devastation of the attacks, they both occurred in AQIM's Zone II, or that zone to which Droudkel is most restricted. It is likely that AQIM will try to sustain its offensive, but its limited room for maneuver as well as its disrupted supply chain may prevent it from doing so.

Implications for Europe

The implications for the former GSPC/AQIM cells in Europe are less obvious, even if they are arguably more troubling to markets and investors than what happens to the group in Algeria. The question is whether the cells remain committed to the GSPC's Algerian goals or if they have become AQIM satellites in Europe—with all that implies for potential attacks throughout the continent.

The fact that the GSPC has cells in Europe is well known. In fact, the GSPC's parent organization, the GIA, took credit for the bombing of a Paris Metro station in 1995 and assassinated numerous Algerian intellectuals who had sought refuge in Paris. Yet ties between the GSPC in Europe and al-Qaeda were weak. Those ties that did exist were significantly disrupted with European successes countering al-Qaeda operations, especially after September 11, 2001 and March 11, 2004. Since 2004, most remaining Algerian cells became dormant, having been forced under by tough and effective continental European anti-terror laws. According to Europol, the European Law Enforcement Organization, most people arrested with ties to Islamist terrorism in Europe throughout 2006 were North Africans and the majority of those were Algerians or of Algerian origin (EU Terrorism Situation and Trend Report, 2007).

As a result of the organization's cellular structure, it is likely that remaining European cells have divided themselves along the lines of their Algerian contacts. European cells that support members of the GSPC who have resisted Droudkel's changes also likely resist the al-Qaeda affiliation. It is likely that they are still committed to trying to destabilize Algeria's secular government.

European cells that support Droudkel and his efforts to transform the GSPC into AQIM have likely embraced al-Qaeda's violent "jihadis-versus-Crusaders" *It is likely that Droudkel's AQIM cells* mentality. In addition to being *throughout Europe are channeling funds* hostile to France, AQIM cells may *and providing logistical support to non-* broaden their ire to include any *Algerian jihadi groups in Europe and* government deemed either non-Islamic or insufficiently Muslim. *smuggling North African fighters to Iraq.* This includes the United States and United Kingdom, historically not high on the GSPC target list, if at all, as well as Morocco and Tunisia.

European cells may provide logistical support to their colleagues in Algeria, but it is not at all clear which side of the strategic and tactical divide the continental cells stand. In Algeria, for example, the fact that French landmines were used in Algerian attacks suggests that European cells may continue to support Droudkel's AQIM, but for the most part the roadside bomb attacks in Boumerdes target soldiers—or what pre-al-Qaeda GSPC members would view to be legitimate victims. In addition, recently resolved conflicts in Francophone sub-Saharan Africa and the monetization of sub-Saharan arsenals mean that the landmines may not necessarily come from France. It is possible that remnants of Belmokhtar and Benmessaoud's smuggling networks remain intact and are furthering the objectives of the GSPC Algerianists.

It is likely that Droudkel's AQIM cells throughout Europe are channeling funds and providing logistical support to non-Algerian jihadi groups in Europe and smuggling North African fighters to Iraq. It is yet to be seen whether those fighters are making their way back to Algeria and Morocco. This, however, is something that the GSPC also did in Bosnia and Chechnya prior to the U.S. invasion of Iraq, so the AQIM's connection to Iraq cannot necessarily be interpreted as a new group characteristic.

The implication of the GSPC's evolution into AQIM for Europe is also unclear. French counter-terrorism analysts reacted with alarm to the transformation of the GSPC into AQIM and anticipated an increased risk of terrorist attacks in European countries with large North African—and especially Algerian—populations. For example, while French security services were well attuned to the GSPC's strategy, tactics and methods, the April 11, 2007 attacks in Algiers changed France's assessment of the danger posed by the evolved GSPC to European targets.

France's caution appeared to be justified with the May 24, 2007 announcement from AQIM that a heretofore unknown Abou Hafs Abdelouadoud has been named head of the Kata'ib el-Mouhadjirine (Emigrants' Regiments). What made the report especially worrying was that it suggested that Abou Hafs would be in charge of entire regiments or divisions instead of just disparate cells. On closer inspection, however, the announcement's authenticity is questionable. Abou Hafs' declaration did not appear on any conventional al-Qaeda associated websites and the declaration itself was riddled with inaccuracies about the operations AQIM had undertaken in Algeria under Droudkel's leadership (*La voix de l'Oranie*, May 24, 2007).

Conclusion

In spite of inconclusive evidence, it would be prudent to assume that the GSPC/AQIM evolution split in Algeria has been replicated among cells in Europe. On the other hand, it is possible that the GSPC's European cells did not survive the organization's mutation into AQIM in Algeria and have been orphaned by the eviscerated GSPC in Algeria. Neither scenario augurs well for European security. The first instance would suggest that there are fewer cells in Europe that embrace al-Qaeda's worldview than had been anticipated after the organization began mutating into AQIM in September 2006, but those cells that do survive pose a greater threat to a broader array of European targets than did the fully constituted network of GSPC cells. The second instance—that of the possibly orphaned, dormant GSPC cells that did not evolve into AQIM cells—is potentially a net positive for European security. Deprived of their raison d'etre, the GSPC cells may dissolve. It is also possible, although less likely, that at some point the isolated GSPC cells become the nuclei of new cells allied with new violent Islamist organizations. This, however, has yet to take place and it remains to be seen whether AQIM could connect with the GSPC remnants or form completely new cells.

Originally published in *Terrorism Monitor*: Volume 5, Issue 17 on September 13, 2007.

Recasting Jihad in the Maghreb
By Andrew Black

It has been a little over one year since Ayman al-Zawahiri announced the official merger between al-Qaeda and the Salafist Group for Call and Combat (GSPC), and since that time the jihad in the Maghreb has passed through a tumultuous and dynamic period. On the one hand, it has been characterized by an increase in bombings—particularly in public settings—the use of suicide attackers, and the targeting of foreign nationals and assets. Yet, on the other hand, Al-Qaeda in the Islamic Maghreb (AQIM), the successor to the GSPC, has more recently exhibited signs of internal fissures, largely resulting from recruitment issues and the actions of its amir, Abu Musab Abd al-Wadoud (*Liberte*, September 18, 2007; *Terrorism Monitor*, September 13, 2007). Recent reports allege that al-Wadoud has been replaced by Ahmad Haroun, a claim refuted on the AQIM website (Qmagreb.org, October 6, 2007; *El-Khabar*, October 3, 2007). Despite the operational successes of the past year and al-Wadoud's apparent ability to recast the regional jihad, the divisiveness within the organization has made its future somewhat precarious.

The Changing Landscape

In late July, AQIM released a statement noting that it had succeeded in restructuring and reforming the agenda of the Algerian jihad (MEMRI, July 25, 2007). The extent of these adjustments encompasses matters from strategy, such as targeting foreigners, to tactics, such as the use of suicide operatives. At the broadest level, this reform has led the Algerian jihad to shift from a nationalist to a regionalist movement, as exhibited in January 2007 when al-Wadoud announced that the GSPC would be changing its name to Al-Qaeda in the Islamic Maghreb, a name more reflective of the organization's expanding purview (*Terrorism Monitor*, February 1, 2007).

Operationally, AQIM has recently been linked with numerous activities outside of Algeria. Although the GSPC had been known to conduct operations throughout the Maghreb and into sub-Saharan Africa—notably exhibited in a June 2005 attack on the Lemgheity military barracks in northeastern Mauritania—since the merger there are signs that AQIM has placed greater emphasis on recruiting and perpetrating attacks in each of the states in the Maghreb. A prime example of this is a disrupted plot in Tunisia, which would have initially targeted the U.S. and UK embassies in Tunis around the New Year, followed by smaller attacks on tourist sites throughout the country. Significant information came to the attention of Algerian and Tunisian security officials that the plot was closely linked with the GSPC and included a Mauritanian member of the Algerian group. His involvement in the plot and more recent reports of non-Algerians operating under the AQIM banner are a testament to al-Wadoud's ability to not only recruit foreigners, but also to deploy them throughout the region (*Liberte*, August 7, 2007; *El-Khabar*, August 21, 2007). Other recent examples of AQIM's regional operations include the group's links with a disrupted plot in Morocco, as well as a September report that Egyptian authorities were investigating AQIM's attempts to procure forged passports for its members traveling to Iraq (MAP, October 20, 2007; *Elaph*, September 4, 2007).

Beyond this, efforts in the public relations arena have grown dramatically under al-Wadoud's leadership. Stretching back to the summer of 2004 when he became amir of the GSPC, al-Wadoud has placed great emphasis on the organization's information operations (*Terrorism Focus*, May 15, 2007). In an attempt to eliminate the near information blackout his predecessors had cast on the organization—and no doubt heeding al-Zawahiri's advisement that the jihadi movement must not become isolated from the populace—al-Wadoud began to engage the Algerian people and the outside world through an enhanced information campaign [1]. Though clumsily executed at first, the GSPC/AQIM media apparatus has become comparable to those found in other jihadi venues. AQIM now disseminates regular videos of attacks, such as the "Under the Shadow of the Swords" series, as well as statements from al-Wadoud through a variety of affiliated forums, which is largely due to the inconsistency of the group's website [2].

Style of Attack

Militarily, al-Wadoud has gone beyond the minimalist strategies of his predecessors and enacted a multifaceted campaign blending guerrilla attacks in eastern Algeria with publicity grabbing bombings in urban areas. Whereas the GSPC had previously relegated itself to engaging the government in rural, mainly northeastern Algeria, al-Wadoud has chosen to expand the campaign to include increasing urban attacks like the April 11, 2007 dual bombings in Algiers.

Fundamental to AQIM's campaign is target selection, often an important indicator of an organization's ideological leanings and grand strategy. In the GSPC/AQIM case, this target set is diverse but has remained largely unchanged since 2004, although priorities within this set have clearly been altered. The key themes include a virulent hatred of foreigners alleged to be supporting the "apostate regimes" and pillaging North African resources. France, in particular, has featured prominently in the organization's rhetoric—famously highlighted in al-Zawahiri's quote from his September 11, 2006 speech that the GSPC be a "a bone in the throat of the American and French Crusaders" (*Le Monde*, September 18, 2007; *Libération*, September 19, 2007; *Terrorism Focus*, August 7, 2007). Specifically, AQIM's leadership has identified France's cultural influence, which is palpable throughout Morocco, Algeria and Tunisia, as being a source of corruption within the region. The previous day, AQIM injured two Frenchmen and an Italian in a bombing near Lakhdaria (Echorouk Online, September 21, 2007). Al-Zawahiri addressed the issue in a September 20, 2007 speech calling for AQIM to purge "the Islamic Maghreb of the French and the Spanish who have returned there" (MEMRI, September 20, 2007). Consistent with the jihadi narrative, AQIM has named both the United States and United Kingdom as legitimate targets, whose embassies were targets in the aforementioned Tunis plot. Finally, there are indications that AQIM is looking to target the region's tourist and energy sectors, arguably the backbone of the Maghrebi economies [3]. Although terrorism has not had a significant impact on regional economies in recent history, there is concern among regional governments that a revived terrorist threat could be a drain on their economies, particularly given the reliance on revenue from these sectors (*Dar al-Hayat*, April 27, 2007).

Al-Wadoud's efforts to alter both the ideology and strategy of the organization have also manifested in the use of suicide bombers in Algeria, such as the April 11, 2007 attacks and the September 2007 bombings in Dellys and Batna. Although suicide attacks have previously been committed in the region and Algerians have even perpetrated martyrdom operations in other jihadi venues, this tactic has not been featured in the Algerian context despite the country's long and brutal civil war. In addition to the obvious tactical benefits that martyrdom operations bring—which are a critical component of the narrative of the global Salafi-Jihad—they are powerful symbols of the vitality of an organization's struggle and are also an important legitimizing mechanism for its cause. As seen in the aftermath of the April 11, 2007 bombing, each suicide operative is lionized as a hero, his symbolic death effectively declaring the organization's cause to be worth giving oneself up for. In the case of AQIM—an organization attempting to congeal support while mobilizing and recruiting additional members—martyrdom is a potent addition to the attack repertoire. Although al-Wadoud's decision to employ suicide operations has brought criticism from within and without his organization, the AQIM amir has received support for his decision from key figures in the global jihadi movement, most notably from Abu Yahya al-Libi (Echorouk Online, August 12, 2007; MEMRI, August 17, 2007). However, insofar as AQIM can encourage Iraqi veterans to return to the Maghreb and fight or recruit under its banner—and there are signs that this has occurred—the employment of suicide operations will likely increase (El-Watan, September 12, 2007).

The Threat to the West

Well before the merger between the GSPC and al-Qaeda, North Africans had weighed heavily on Western European security, as noted by French Interior Minister Michele Alliot-Marie (Agence France-Presse, September 23, 2007). While perpetrating attacks on the continent was arguably not a core objective of the Maghrebi groups, it is now a part of AQIM's objectives. With this in mind, much of the rhetoric surrounding the merger specifically identified attacking Western countries, particularly France, as central to AQIM's strategy (*Terrorism Focus*, September 26, 2006; *Terrorism Focus*, August 7, 2007).

One must also not overlook the implications this may potentially have for North America. Although it must be plainly stated that the perceived threat from AQIM to the United States is low, there are indications that North African groups continue to maintain networks in North America and that there is a potential, albeit remote, for these networks to become operational. This gains credence remembering the case of Ahmed Ressam, an Algerian national and the so called "Millennium Bomber," who was based in Montreal and who had plans to bomb Los Angeles International Airport on New Year's Eve in 1999 [4]. To make this network operational, al-Wadoud and his organization must find a narrative that sufficiently resonates within this network, an onerous task and one potentially made more difficult with the recent leadership troubles (*Terrorism Monitor*, September 13, 2007).

Conclusion

In sum, while AQIM's ascent has raised the specter of a revitalized and expansive jihad in North Africa—one which may include coordinated operations throughout the region and the West—the unsteadiness in the group's leadership among other factors have cast doubt on AQIM's future prospects. Regardless of his fate as the leader of AQIM, it appears the reformation process al-Wadoud enacted has fundamentally recast the Maghrebi jihad by altering both the character of his Algerian movement and the structure of the regional jihad at large. As evident from the high number of attacks and casualties in September, AQIM is becoming increasingly active and lethal, and the group has demonstrated a willingness to perpetrate large-scale, suicide bombings in urban environments. These attacks and the proliferation of media material over the past year have bolstered AQIM's relevancy in the regional counter-terrorism discourse and reinserted the North African arena into the conscience of the global Salafi-Jihad.

Originally published in *Terrorism Monitor*: Volume 5, Issue 20 on October 25, 2007.

Notes

1. See Ayman al-Zawahiri's book *Knights Under the Prophet's Banner*.
2. The group's recent website, http://www.qmagreb.org, has been shut down multiple times, but usually reappears a few days later.
3. For an assessment of Morocco's tourist industry and its capacity to overcome a terrorist attack, see *Terrorism Monitor*, June 7, 2007. Separately, energy targets are a popular theme in the jihadi narrative, and have featured strongly in the writings of Abu Musab al-Suri, Ayman al-Zawahiri and several other strategists linked to the North African arena.
4. For an examination of this network, see Marc Sageman, *Understanding Terror Networks* (Philadelphia: University of Pennsylvania Press, 2004).

Morocco's Resistance to Regional Jihad
By Matthew Chebatoris

As 2007 draws to a close, the one year anniversary nears of the Salafist Group for Preaching and Combat's (GSPC) official rebranding of itself as al-Qaeda in the Islamic Maghreb (AQIM) following its merger with Osama bin Laden's group. With the change in name came the stated desire to move the group beyond its nationalistic goal of initiating regime change within Algeria to a broader regional movement which ostensibly covers, as the new name implies, the entire Maghreb region—Libya, Tunisia, Algeria, Morocco and Mauritania. The merger with al-Qaeda has likely been a contributing factor in the evolution of AQIM's tactics over the past year, the most notable example being the dual suicide bombings in Algiers on April 11, 2007 (*Terrorism Monitor*, October 25, 2007). Though there has been a clear change in tactics and a departure from the GSPC's strategy of limiting civilian casualties, AQIM has yet to convincingly demonstrate the capability to project itself as a true threat to the stability of the region. This is perhaps most evident in Algeria's neighbor Morocco, a country by no means immune to acts of Salafi-Jihadi-inspired terrorism, but whose population has thus far largely rejected the notion of lending widespread domestic support to AQIM's desire for regional jihad.

AQIM's first year coincided with a handful of disrupted and clumsy attempts to conduct terror attacks in Morocco. While far from insignificant, the attacks and disrupted plots pale in comparison to the sophisticated and highly lethal operations perpetrated by AQIM in Algeria (Maghreb Arabe Presse, August 23, 2007). The disparity in the technological prowess of the Moroccan attackers compared to the events in Algeria suggests any ties to AQIM were likely inspirational at best. While regional media outlets have cited anecdotal cases of Moroccans suspected of attempting to enter Algeria to undergo training at AQIM camps, these reports are difficult to fully assess without first hand insight into the true intentions of those in custody (*La Tribune*, August 4, 2007). Contrary to the view espoused at times by the current U.S. administration, the absence of an attack, in this case in Morocco, is by no means an accurate measure of an organization's effectiveness as most successful mass casualty attacks take months—if not years—of planning. Nonetheless, despite Algeria and Morocco's common language, culture and (to a lesser degree) experiences under colonialism, the factors motivating AQIM in Algeria are not automatically transferable to Morocco.

Youth Culture in Morocco

Human factors analysis is an often overlooked strategy in examining the critical question of what motivates individuals to turn to terrorism. Techniques of this type have recently received greater attention as a result of the counter-insurgency initiatives championed by U.S. General David Petraeus in Iraq. Considering this approach, one factor which may play a role in mitigating the development of a level of grassroots support for AQIM in Morocco is the burgeoning youth culture there. This is perhaps best symbolized by King Mohammed VI himself who, in a departure from tradition, married a middle class woman and has been photographed in a leather jacket and sunglasses. The king has distinguished himself from autocratic dictatorships in Tunisia and Libya by acknowledging the abuses of power that took place during his father's reign, thereby endearing himself to the people. In a valuable study on the youth culture in Morocco, polling data solicited by German political scientist Sonja Hegasy suggest Moroccan youth are active participants in the process of globalization [1]. Far from advocating the rigid principles of sharia or a rejection of Western cultural influences, the majority of respondents cited both the positive as well as the negative aspects of increased globalization in Morocco. Even more telling was the answer to a question as to the main basis of the king's authority, where the response "his youthful spirit" polled the highest out of ten possible choices.

Corroborating the insight into the Moroccan psyche highlighted above is data collected by World Public Opinion.org in March 2007 indicating 76 percent of Moroccans felt attacks on civilians in pursuit of political goals are either "weakly justified" or "not justified at all," while 8 percent responded such attacks were either "justified" or "strongly justified". Only 9 percent of Moroccans indicated they support al-Qaeda's attacks on Americans and share its attitudes towards the United States, and 62 percent hold a positive view of globalization (World Public Opinion.org, April 24, 2007). Voter turnout in Morocco's recent parliamentary elections was low, a clear indication of voter discontent, but recent protests against the rising cost of living and government policies were conducted peacefully and lacked any signs of a turn toward radical religious fervor (*Al-Ahdath al-Maghribiya*, September 27, 2007). Those who have engaged in terrorism are looked down upon and are viewed as criminals on the fringes of society.

Security Cooperation in the Maghreb

Human factors are by no means the only deterrent to the expansion of AQIM's Algeria-centric jihad into Morocco. Moroccan security services are capable, a fact demonstrated by the past disruption of terror plots. Multilateral cooperation across the Maghreb also facilitates the rapid exchange of threat information and enhances the collective security environment. In late April 2007, five Maghreb countries (Morocco, Mauritania, Algeria, Tunisia and Libya) concluded a round of talks in Tripoli and agreed to implement a new multilateral mechanism to share intelligence on what they view to be a common terrorist threat to the region (*al-Hayat*, April 30, 2007). The meeting of the Arab Maghreb Union came on the heels of the devastating suicide car bombings in Algeria by AQIM and the multiple incidents in Casablanca involving the use of suicide belts by locals. Although the occurrences of suicide terrorism in the two countries lack direct operational ties with one another, the comparatively loose collective of Salafi-Jihadists in Morocco are undoubtedly inspired by their ideological "big brother" next door in Algeria. More importantly, taking a cue from international observers of the terrorist threat, governments in the Maghreb appear to have recognized that the threat posed by Islamic-inspired insurgencies is indeed "part of a much bigger picture" (*Terrorism Focus*, April 3, 2007).

Until now, trans-Maghreb collaboration has been difficult to achieve and Tripoli has historically played a divisive rather than binding role in enhancing regional cooperation. Other salient security concerns, such as Algerian support to Polisario's bid for independence for Western Sahara, have created long-lasting fissures between potential partners (Maghreb Arabe Presse, May 12, 2007). The potential for individuals to transit the region and participate in mobile training camps run by AQIM presents a credible threat to the security of the region. Therefore, the renewed desire to work together is timely and is the right choice for governments across the region to make in light of the nature of the current threat.

Outlook

A successful security strategy should recognize not only the commonalities of the region's languages, culture and geopolitical interests, but also be aware of the differences that exist between the countries of the Maghreb. To date, Morocco has been largely successful in resisting the broad call of the global Salafi jihad, inasmuch as AQIM has not been able to establish a foothold in the country, nor has a "domestic" group been able to construct a viable strategy to bind together the disparate cells of Moroccan Salafi-Jihadi aspirants. This is not to suggest that individual cells, regardless of size and composition, do not pose a threat; but rather to highlight the distinct nature of the threat from Salafi-Jihadi-inspired terror in Morocco.

To date, Morocco has been largely successful in resisting the broad call of the global Salafi jihad, inasmuch as AQIM has not been able to establish a foothold in the country, nor has a "domestic" group been able to construct a viable strategy to bind together the disparate cells of Moroccan Salafi-Jihadi aspirants.

Abbas el-Fassi, Morocco's newly appointed prime minister, acknowledged in a recent interview that while incidents have occurred, no country has been safe from terror. He expanded by championing his country's stability and continued growth of foreign investment, highlighting the fact Morocco has received seven million tourists this year compared to only two million in 2002 (Al-Arabiya, November 9, 2007). Morocco has at times been depicted as being rife with terrorists, an image fostered not only by incidents in Morocco, but also by attacks and disrupted plots in Europe. Assessing risk on the number of incidents or the body count alone is not an accurate measure—if this method were to be used it would place countries such as Spain and the United Kingdom far ahead of Morocco in terms of risk from attack. Terrorism remains a form of political violence with ideological root causes. Prime Minister el Fassi concluded his remarks by stating his country's priority is on enhancing employment, housing and education to discourage terrorism (Al-Arabiya, November 9, 2007). To that list should be added reformation of the political party structure in order to encourage increased participation in future elections, thus giving Moroccans the confidence in their government they deserve.

Originally published in *Terrorism Monitor*: Volume 5, Issue 23 on December 10, 2007.

Notes

1. For a more in-depth study of Moroccan youth attitudes, see Sonja Hegasy, "Young Authority: Quantitative and Qualitative Insights into Youth, Youth Culture, and State

Power in Contemporary Morocco," *Journal of North African Studies* 12, no. 1 (March 2007) 19-36.

The Ideological Struggle Over al-Qaeda's Suicide Tactics in Algeria
By Andrew Black

On January 29, 2008 a lorry laden with 1,400 lbs of explosives and driven by a member of al-Qaeda in the Islamic Maghreb (AQIM) was detonated in the town of Thenia, east of Algiers, killing four and wounding an additional 23 people. The target of the attack was the police barracks in the center of town, and among the dead was a police officer who has been heralded for preventing the bomber from detonating at his targeted location (Magharebia, February 1, 2008). While this attack did not result in the high casualty figures seen in AQIM's previous suicide attacks, such as the December 11 bombing of the United Nations and Constitutional Court in Algiers, this attack constitutes yet another in an unpopular series of suicide bombings conducted by AQIM that have resulted in casualty figures not seen since Algeria's civil war. In a subsequent statement issued by AQIM on January 30, the group claimed responsibility for the attack and addressed the ideological and societal tension brewing over the group's continued use of this tactic in Algeria. Despite the unpopularity of suicide bombings in Algeria and the development of an appealing counter-narrative by members of the ulema (body of Islamic scholars), it appears AQIM is positioned to carry on with its suicide bombing campaign, particularly as the group absorbs fighters returning from Iraq.

The Perspectives of the Debate

The debate over the legitimacy of suicide operations in Algeria was triggered by AQIM's April 11 dual bombing in Algiers, an event that stood as the group's proclamation that it had indeed fallen in line with al-Qaeda's tactical doctrine. Immediately following this and subsequent suicide attacks, several key elements within Algeria displayed their disdain for the new path that the group's amir, Abu Mus'ab Abd al-Wadoud, had cut for his group. Still scarred from a lengthy and profoundly bloody civil war in the 1990s, the general public has shown an unwillingness to return to a period of high casualty conflict. However, this ideological schism has been most prominently displayed in the opposing views of martyrdom posited by AQIM and Islamic jurisprudents both within and without Algeria.

In late January, five Muslim scholars from Algeria, Saudi Arabia and Syria issued scathing fatwas (religious verdicts) condemning AQIM's use of suicide bombings (Le Jeune Independent, January 27, 2008). Although this was not the first time members of the ulema had condemned AQIM's suicide campaign, this event did pick up on an important trend. The opinions on martyrdom of these five scholars generally fall in line with the classical view and stand diametrically opposed to the modern interpretation propagated by al-Qaeda [1]. One scholar in the group, Shaykh Abu al-Harith Abu al-Hassan, denounced suicide operations as having "no religious basis or valid pretext, but instead [are based] on the desires and the ravings of their own architects." Still another scholar, Shaykh Ali Hassan Abdelhamid, blamed AQIM's use of suicide bombers for "only increasing the number of Muslims' difficulties." That these men, recognized as leading experts of Islamic law, condemned the use of suicide operations as being both illegal and onerous for the general Muslim population might prove vital in erecting a counter-narrative to undermine the legitimacy of AQIM's use of this tactic [2].

On the other side of this debate is AQIM, supported by leading members of the global Salafist jihad who have lent their voice to AQIM's cause [3]. Repudiating the aforementioned scholars, AQIM's January 30, 2008 statement pointedly sought to attack their credibility by pejoratively labeling them as "Bush's scholars" and "mouthpieces of the tyrants." Doing so not only undermines the validity of these condemnatory fatwas, but also exculpates AQIM from incurring blame for violating Islamic law. Defending its decision to employ suicide operations, AQIM claimed legitimacy for its actions on the premise of careful timing and target selection. Referring to the Thenia attack, the AQIM statement notes how the group limited civilian casualties through precise timing and targeting of the police barracks:

[The Thenia attack] denies the fabricated and deceitful boasting of the enemy who claims that the mujahideen are targeting innocent Muslims, for those who perished today are part of the apostate police force and the choice of the mujahideen for this target was clear. Also, the precise timing of the operation is clear proof to those who inquire into the lies of the apostates and the hypocrites and their allegations and of the truthfulness of the mujahideen (al-Fajr Center, January 30, 2008).

Despite these attempts to assert the legitimacy of its suicide bombing campaign, it appears that AQIM's defense cannot mask the fact that these attacks have been ill received even by many within the organization. In late July 2007, Abdelkader Ben Messoud (alias Abu Daoud), a leading member of AQIM who had recently surrendered to the Algiers government under amnesty, depicted an organization divided against itself as a consequence of al-Wadoud's strategic decision to employ suicide bombers. The divisions appear to roughly comport with those stemming from al-Wadoud's decision to merge the organization with al-Qaeda in 2006. Many of the nationalist old guard who oppose suicide attacks, such as Abu Daoud, feel that the tactic is counterproductive and inevitably causes an undesirably high number of innocent casualties. This point was picked up by former members of AQIM who have likened al-Wadoud to the leaders of the Armed Islamic Group (GIA), which terrorized Algeria in the early 1990s before AQIM's predecessor organization—the Salafist Group for Call and Combat (GSPC)—split from it (Echorouk [Algeria], August 22, 2008). This point has more recently been restated by a group, reportedly born out of former GSPC members, calling itself the "Protectors of the Salafist Call" (Dar al-Hayat, June 6, 2007; Echorouk, February 5, 2008). It appears, therefore, that a consequence of the use of suicide attacks has been to create potentially debilitating acrimony and splintering within the ranks of AQIM.

Over the long term, the durability of the group will be determined by its ability to attract new members and enhance its broad appeal across a constituent element within Algerian society.

Counter Narratives and Recruitment

Although the leadership schisms depicted above may prove to be detrimental for the organization, the criticisms AQIM has endured from Algerian society will likely have a more potent impact on the group's sustainability over the long term. This point is borne out by AQIM's ability to decentralize its operations, placing less emphasis on central command and control functions, thus making the group more resilient to leadership turmoil [4]. Over the long term, the durability of the group will be determined by its ability to attract new members and enhance its broad appeal across a constituent element within Algerian society.

This factor also has indirect operational implications with regard to suicide operations. In order for AQIM to sustain its suicide bombing campaign, there must continue to be a steady flow and retention of new recruits willing to martyr themselves for the group's cause. Reports from this past summer that noted AQIM's personnel troubles illuminate this point (*Terrorism Monitor*, September 13, 2007). AQIM's own statements indicate the importance the group places on maintaining its broad appeal to those willing to perpetrate these attacks. For instance, in May 2007, al-Wadoud released a video, entitled "Where are those who are committed to die?" that included an unabashed call for volunteers to offer their lives for the group. Many of the attacks AQIM perpetrates are named after fallen members of the organization, hence lionizing them as martyrs and enhancing the appeal of committing one's life to the path of jihad. However, if public criticism and the growing counter-narrative discussed above succeed in demonizing AQIM's activities and alienating the group from its pool of recruits, the effect would be to diminish AQIM's ability to perpetrate suicide bombings. While it would appear that for the time being such an effect has not been witnessed in Algeria, the prospects for such an outcome are hopeful.

Past as Prologue?

Despite public and clerical condemnation of the use of suicide operations, it seems likely at this point that AQIM will continue to escalate its campaign. Indeed, it appears AQIM is poised to continue its suicide bombing campaign for the foreseeable future, as seen in the activities of a cell near Algiers that was responsible for the December 11 bombings. Local media have noted that three of the bombers were building contractors and one was a computer scientist for Brown & Root Condor, a joint venture of the Algerian state energy company and a Halliburton subsidiary (*El Khabar*, February 7, 2008). The cell had reportedly already procured the necessary materiel for a future attack (al-Watan, January 29, 2008). Moreover, this incident highlighted AQIM's sophisticated methodology for deploying suicide operatives as well as the group's enduring appeal among the educated parts of Algerian society. This point is made especially salient in light of the recently released records of foreign fighters entering Iraq through Syria [5]. These captured documents indicate that a greater number of North Africans are actively engaged in the Iraqi insurgency than previously thought. With leading figures in the global jihadist movement already looking to the post-Iraq period (*Terrorism Focus*, January 22, 2008), it stands to reason that these individuals will seek to return to their home countries. Provided they are able and willing to return to the Maghreb—two assumptions that must not be overlooked—they will carry with them a wealth of skills and experience in conducting a suicide bombing campaign.

Although the looming specter of returning veterans could have a significant impact on Maghrebi—and more precisely Algerian—security, the ideological schism which has developed due to the use of suicide bombers is potentially auspicious for counter-terrorism efforts. As noted earlier, if the ulema are capable of undermining the legitimacy and appeal of AQIM's activities through the construction of an equally appealing and legitimate counter-narrative, then the use of suicide operatives will likely diminish. Given the high success rate of such operations, losing the capacity to implement this tactic would no doubt hinder AQIM's lethality and destructiveness.

Originally published in *Terrorism Monitor*: Volume 6, Issue 3 on February 7, 2008.

Notes

1. For an excellent depiction of the classical view of martyrdom versus the contemporary interpretation espoused by al-Qaeda and other jihadis, see David Cook, *Martyrdom in Islam* (Cambridge: Cambridge University Press, 2007).
2. The notion of building a narrative to counter the radicalization process has been discussed by numerous authors. For a summary, see Jeffrey Cozzens, "Identifying Entry Points of Action in Counter Radicalization," Danish Institution for International Studies, Working Paper no. 6, 2006.
3. Abu Yahya al-Libi, a native of Libya and a leading figure in al-Qaeda, issued a rebuttal in July 2007 to Muslim scholars who had condemned AQIM's April 11 suicide bombings in Algiers (see *Terrorism Focus*, July 31, 2007; *Terrorism Focus*, August 14, 2007).
4. For a description of AQIM's networked operations, see Noureddine Jebnoun, "Is the Maghreb the 'Next Afghanistan?' Mapping the Radicalization of the Algerian Salafi Jihadist Movement," Center for Contemporary Arab Studies, Georgetown University, Occasional Paper, December 2007.
5. Joseph Felter and Brian Fishman, "Al-Qa'ida's Foreign Fighters in Iraq: A First Look at the Sinjar Records," Combating Terrorism Center, U.S. Military Academy, West Point, 2007.

Guide to the Armed Groups Operating in the Niger Delta – Part 1
By James Briggs

During the course of the last year in Nigeria's oil-rich but turbulent Niger Delta region, armed men kidnapped more than 150 foreigners, killed unknown numbers of Nigerian armed forces personnel, crippled the oil production of Africa's largest oil exporter by nearly a quarter and detonated five car bombs. There is a bewildering variety of armed groups operating in the delta, ranging from community vigilantes to armed political movements to criminal gangs. The groups, whose aims and members often overlap, are involved in activities that include kidnapping, theft of crude oil, attacking oil infrastructure, extortion, bombings, murders and rigging elections. Without adequate equipment or political will, the military cannot tackle the problem effectively. Unrest in the Niger Delta can be traced back to the beginning of oil exploration, when impoverished communities were exploited and polluted, while billions of dollars were extracted from underneath their feet (*Terrorism Monitor*, August 10, 2006). In many cases, however, criminal elements and corrupt politicians have exploited the expression of legitimate grievances and armed many of these groups for their own ends. The emergence of modern militant groups is closely related to politics, corruption and bad governance in the delta. Both the 2003 polls and the April 2007 elections have strengthened pre-existing armed groups.

For the purposes of clarity, this two-part analysis focuses on militias and gangs—with part two focusing exclusively on the Movement for the Emancipation of the Niger Delta (MEND)—and discusses the existence of community groups within that framework. It also explains their leadership structures and links to politicians. In reality, the distinctions are somewhat arbitrary. The gunmen and the government are as tangled together as the mangrove roots of the swamps in the Niger Delta.

History of Militancy

The term "militants" refers to gunmen who make political demands, including the release of imprisoned leaders, cash reparations for communities, change of electoral candidates and a greater share of oil revenues, among other issues. These political demands distinguish them, albeit tenuously, from criminals who simply kidnap people for money. Militants are also distinct from disaffected communities, whose people may perform kidnappings or attacks in the hopes of getting a clinic, school or cash, but have no overall political aims. It is a very blurred line—a person may be a community activist one day, then a militant and then a criminal the next. Nevertheless, it is a line worth noting.

Militancy against oil companies in the delta can be traced back a long way, but the general agreement is that the turning point from peaceful activism to armed resistance came after the execution of Ken Saro-Wiwa and eight other Ogoni leaders in 1995. The Nigerian government had responded with lethal force to the justified anger of the local people over corruption, underdevelopment and lack of political representation. Dictator

Sani Abacha's government continued to contain any real challenges with severe brutality until the 1999 elections.

Democracy was a disappointment for the people of the delta, as the corrupt government provoked widespread anger by failing to deliver basic social services. Oil companies stoked the problem by failing to clean up their oil spills, flaring gas (which produces acid rain that damages fishing grounds and crops), failing to ensure their police treated local people with respect, executing poorly conceived "development" projects and doling out cash payments that set communities against each other. Communities then began to occupy oil platforms and hold protests, which were often violently dispersed by the police. Moderate demonstrations were met with violence, the debate became polarized and criminal gangs began to use the protesters' rhetoric to excuse their own activities. By 1999, notable figures such as Prince Clark Igodo (declared wanted by the police in March) began to carry out kidnappings for ransom. Igodo, who lost one hand to an explosion during clashes between different cult groups, was originally a gang leader, but had positioned himself as an important ransom negotiator, so it was difficult to arrest him.

Asari, Ateke and Politicians in Rivers State During the 2003 Elections

During the 2003 elections, politicians sought to arm various groups in return for helping to rig the polls. The problem with this policy, however, was explained by human rights lawyer Anyakwee Nsirimovu in 2004 in a private interview: "Once you give someone a gun, you cannot take it back. After the elections were won, the men turned to crime." At that time, the now-infamous Alhaji Dokubo-Asari (he later changed it from "Alhaji" to "Mujahid") occupied a leading role within the Ijaw Youth Council, a forum set up in 1998 by Ijaw activists who wrote the Kaiama Declaration, a manifesto for resource control after which many subsequent militant groups modeled their demands [1]. One Rivers State official, Sara Igbe, has said Governor Peter Odili initially armed Asari. Although Igbe has subsequently refused to discuss this statement, he does not deny it [2]. Asari has denied helping to rig elections. Asari, a Muslim convert, later fell out with Odili over the government's neglect of the delta region and over negative comments Asari made about President Olusegun Obasanjo. Asari then formed the Niger Delta People's Volunteer Force (NDPVF), which consisted of a loose alliance between several local gangs known as "cults" [3]. Asari was not a gang leader himself, but was able to convince various other groups such as the Greenlanders, Bush Boys, Elegant Face and Deegbam to cooperate under his leadership.

It should be stressed that many of the young men involved in the gangs turned to crime because of a complete lack of alternatives after the government failed to invest in education, employment schemes and infrastructure.

It should be stressed that many of the young men involved in the gangs turned to crime because of a complete lack of alternatives after the government failed to invest in education, employment schemes and infrastructure. Although Asari, the son of a judge and brother of a university professor, articulated complex arguments for self-determination and resource control, many of his followers were simply fighting because they had lost a struggle with another local gang leader, Ateke Tom, and had been pushed out of their territory in Okrika in Rivers State. Asari, however, retained his links to many people in the government. When this analyst visited his militia camps in 2004, several of his mobile and satellite phones rang with tip-offs from senior military figures when they were planning to attack. He funded his struggle through tapping crude oil pipelines and wellheads, a practice that nets hundreds of millions of dollars worth of crude in Nigeria each year and requires the collusion of senior figures in the military, particularly in the navy, to escort the barges out to tankers waiting at sea.

After Asari retreated to the swamps and formed the NDPVF, the state government armed Ateke, who led a rival gang called the Icelanders. Ateke has also referred to his armed followers as the Niger Delta Vigilantes [4]. According to Amnesty International, more than 500 people died before a truce was negotiated between the two groups. After several months of living undisturbed in Port Harcourt, Asari's calls for greater resource control and the rejection of the federal government finally led to his arrest in 2005. He is currently in prison on trial for treason and his release is a key demand of many militant groups. Despite accusing him of involvement in a string of kidnappings and bank robberies, the government continued to have links with Ateke for many months. "During his traditional marriage with his wife on January 15, 2005, the governor gave [Ateke] 15 million naira," said Ateke's nephew Akinaka Richard [5]. Richard also says that Abiye Samuel Sekibo, the former national transportation minister seen as Odili's political patron, has strong links with Ateke. Both men come from Okrika. Yet in 2006, Ateke fell from favor and was chased into hiding. His nephew and spokesperson, Richard, however, has declared that his uncle is unhappy with the gubernatorial candidates of Delta and Rivers States and if there is no acknowledgment over their complaints, it is possible the fighters will reband, although their numbers will probably be reduced.

FNDIC, Smaller Groups and the 2003 Elections in Delta State

The Federated Niger Delta Ijaw Communities (FNDIC) was originally an ethnic militia. It grew out of the conflict between the Gbaramatu and Egbema clans (part of the Ijaw, Nigeria's fourth largest ethnic group and the dominant tribe in the delta region) and the much smaller Itsekiri, which began in 1998 and culminated at the end of the 2003 elections, when hundreds died and thousands were displaced in a fight over the delineation of a local government boundary [6]. The fight began over communities competing for control over the headquarters of Warri South West Local Government and for the privilege of "host status" for an oil facility, which meant that they were given preferential treatment in development projects and jobs, among other benefits. It was fueled by local politicians who wanted control of the lucrative territory [7]. A heavy-handed government response opened up a third front in the fighting.

When the conflict (known locally as a war) ended, many of the fighters turned to bunkering (the theft of crude oil) and kidnapping. Senior members of FNDIC, such as former leader Bello Oboko, were co-opted into the state government to negotiate between oil companies, the government and their fighters. Many FNDIC members and their families also set up "security companies" to provide "protection" for oil majors. The organization has a formal, elected leadership, although it is often factionalized.

Bayelsa State

Bayelsa contains many armed groups organized around a strong local leader or a community such as Nembe or Brass. The smaller groups have recently begun to form alliances with larger groups, which are dissolved or shifted with great frequency. Since the state lacks a large community of expatriate oil workers, it has not seen the same level of violence as Delta or Rivers, although in 1999 government troops massacred scores of villagers at Odi after the murders of seven policemen. Frequent and indiscriminate reprisals by the military throughout the delta help win the militants tacit approval from villagers who could otherwise inform authorities of their activities.

According to various interviews, several militant fighters say that Bayelsa State is where the leadership of the largest and best organized militant group is based, the MEND, which will be profiled in part two of this analysis.

The delta militants are eager to exploit publicity and frequently issue threats by e-mail. Some of the groups known through email include the Joint Revolutionary Council (through Cynthia Whyte), the Coalition for Militant Action in the Niger Delta (COMA) and the Martyr's Brigade. None have ever proved their existence through providing proof of hostage taking (such as photos) or pre-warning of attacks.

The Government

There is a fault line between Nigeria's federal government, which seeks to prevent militants from interfering with foreign oil workers and production, and state governments, which benefit from it in several different ways. Anyakwee Nsirimovu, the human rights lawyer, explained in a 2006 interview that state governments under investigation for corruption are able to shift attention onto hostages and get a reprieve by insisting that only state officials can handle negotiations. While Nsirmovu does not accuse state governments of actively encouraging hostage taking, officials ensure they benefit from the publicity by always bringing released hostages to the Government House for a photo opportunity with the governor.

State officials also pay ransoms from "security budgets" [8]. In Rivers State, the five billion naira fund is not accountable to any oversight. In at least one instance, government officials who had been given a 20 million naira ($170,000) ransom only showed up with four million ($34,000), claiming that the balance had been stolen from their car. An angry argument ensued in front of the foreign hostage, and the officials later returned with more money [9]. One Rivers-based militant said that government officials typically take over half of the ransom [10].

The military is also compromised. Senior officials are correct when they say that the militants have faster, smaller boats and outmaneuver the navy in the swamps, which they know far better than enlisted men from outside the area (*Terrorism Focus*, October 17, 2006). Senior commanders and some politicians, however, also benefit from the militants' trade in stolen crude oil, which is transported through the mangroves in large, slow and unwieldy barges. Lastly, but most importantly, officials also benefit from the ability to call on organized and armed gangs to rig themselves into power during election time [11]. Brigadier General Samuel Salihu, the second-highest ranking officer in the Joint Task Force, has said that some of the armed groups are being protected by vested political interests [12].

Conclusion

The number and the background of the various militant groups in the delta underscore the difficulty in solving this problem. The militant groups in the delta are connected to the communities, in addition to the local and state governments. Unless both state and federal governments seriously tackle the problems of pollution, poverty, underdevelopment and corruption, low-level conflict in the delta will continue. Part two of this analysis will focus on the most prolific of the delta militant groups, the Movement for the Emancipation of the Niger Delta.

* Part Two of this article will discuss the Movement for the Emancipation of the Niger Delta (MEND).

Orginally published in *Terrorism Monitor*: Volume 5, Issue 7 on April 12, 2007.

Notes

1. The full declaration can be read at http://www.dawodu.net/kaiama.htm. The IYC, intended as a united forum for discussion and negotiation, was infiltrated by the government and subsequently wracked by infighting, according to former member and human rights lawyer Dimieari von Kemedi. In a March 28, 2007 phone interview, he said, "The lack of a credible forum ... has helped the militias to come on strong."
2. Author interviews with Sara Igbe, former Rivers State official, in 2004 and 2006.
3. According to face-to-face author interviews with two cult leaders in 2006, cult groups are primarily urban gangs. Like the militants, they were originally formed to protest social injustice. Wole Soyinka founded the first one, the Pyrates, while attending university, to protest the brutalities of military rule. These days, they have spread far beyond the universities and have been taken over by criminal elements that use the gangs to sell drugs, rig elections, fight each other, among other activities. Unlike the NDPVF or MEND, once an individual joins a cult, they are in that cult for life, barring exceptional circumstances. All cults have secret initiation ceremonies, which include elements varying from theft to beatings to the murder of a member of your own family. Cults are rigidly hierarchical.
4. Author interview with Ateke Tom, 2006.
5. Author interview with Akinaka Richard, 2007.

6. Author interview with Patrick Naagbanton, a researcher on gangs and militants, 2007.

7. In the vacuum left by a corrupt government, oil companies are typically expected to be service providers throughout the delta. For an in-depth examination of government corruption, see "Chop Fine: The Human Rights Impact of Local Government Corruption and Mismanagement in Rivers State, Nigeria," Human Rights Watch, 2007.

8. Author interview with Emmanuel Okah, Rivers State spokesman, 2006.

9. Author interview with an oil company employee, 2006.

10. Author interview, militant affiliated with Asari, 2006.

11. Author interview, gang leader, 2007.

12. Author interview, Samuel Salisu, second-highest ranking officer in the JTF, 2007.

Guide to the Armed Groups Operating in the Niger Delta – Part 2
By James Briggs

The Movement for the Emancipation of the Niger Delta (MEND) first burst onto the international stage in December 2005, when it blew up Shell's Opobo pipeline in Delta State. It followed with several high profile group kidnappings, further bombings and attacks on oil installations that left many dead. Apart from its devastating impact on Nigerian oil production, the initial bombing garnered attention because the militants had carried out an action that did not benefit them directly financially—unlike kidnappings or oil bunkering. MEND's strategic placement of the bombs, which took out nearly a quarter of Nigeria's oil production, showed an intricate knowledge of the thousands of miles of pipelines that may well have been gathered in previous bunkering operations.

Structure

There are no card-carrying militant members of MEND. Like most of the groups with long, politically idealistic names—the Niger Delta People's Volunteer Force (NDPVF) or the Niger Delta Freedom Fighters—it draws on the same pool of fighters from communities across the delta, ethnic militias in the west and cults (partially absorbed into the NDPVF or the Niger Delta Vigilantes) in the east. It does, however, use recognized leaders to control each of the three main states and each leader has a deputy. MEND's flexible structure allows it to channel arms and funds across the delta to regions where it is concentrating operations. It differs from the cults and the ethnic militias because its kidnappings appear primarily motivated by publicity rather than ransom (although money often changes hands) and by placing its struggle in a social rather than ethnic context [1].

For example, "Mike" from Gbaramatu can fight for MEND one day, rig an election for his local government chief the next, kidnap a foreigner for ransom and get in a cult clash on Saturday. He can be, but is not necessarily, a militant, a political enforcer, a criminal and a gang member all at the same time. He can be motivated by money, a sense of injustice, reprisals against his community by the military, or fear of attack from a rival gang. All of these loyalties overlap, meaning that his political patron will protect him from the police when he kidnaps a foreigner, and he can call on his brothers in the cult to come and fight with him for MEND. He can fight for MEND one day and the Federated Niger Delta Ijaw Communities (FNDIC) the next. This is the source of a lot of the confusion over conflicting MEND statements.

Case Study

When 24 Filipinos were abducted from the Bacoliner ship earlier this year and threatened with execution in Delta State, many were confused by apparently conflicting statements both claiming and denying that the attack was conducted by MEND. The MEND leader, known by his nom de guerre Jomo Gbomo, disclaimed the attack from a recognized e-mail address. "We do not attack cargo vessels, issue ultimatums nor do we execute hostages in our custody without good reason," he said. Another MEND spokesman, however, appeared using another email address, claiming that the attack had been carried out by members of MEND and threatened to execute the hostages.

A close study of the demands issued by the second spokesman, which included the replacement of the ruling party's gubernatorial candidate, reveals that they were far more politically specific demands than previously issued by Gbomo. The demands echoed a series of advertisements and interviews taken from Nigerian newspapers by local chiefs, including Ijaw Chief Edwin Clark, demanding Delta state Governor James Ibori's cousin Emmanuel Uduaghan step down as the gubernatorial candidate (*Vanguard*, March 6, 2007). Clark has often called for more oil revenues to be diverted to the Ijaw people and was frequently linked to members of FNDIC. The articles and advertisements pointed out, correctly, that the corrupt Delta government had failed to provide even the most basic services for its citizens during the last eight years. The signatories protested that Uduaghan would probably continue the tradition.

Thus, the Bacoliner attack was carried out using FNDIC affiliated fighters who had previously fought for MEND. They may have called themselves MEND because that has greater resonance with the media and perhaps because MEND supplied the weapons. Certainly, the CNN report that was shown in February was filmed with these fighters. The report helped spark a warning from the U.S. Embassy of further attacks, which drove up oil prices by more than a dollar when it was released. The effect of the report on oil prices underlines the ability of the militants to manipulate the media and oil prices merely by making threats. The fighters subsequently claimed to have seized explosives (actually destined for commercial use) from the boat. They said they were destined for political use. Despite public assurances to the contrary, security sources say that a large ransom was paid [2].

Modus Operandi

MEND's masked fighters in matching body armor are better organized and more disciplined than Alhaji Dokubo-Asari's flip-flop wearing boys, and their spokesman Jomo Gbomo is far more skilled at media manipulation [3]. He issues e-mail messages to confirm or deny attacks and occasionally to warn of an impending bomb. MEND set off five car bombs in 2006—one at a refinery, one at a military barracks (which killed two people), one at a state government house and two in the car parks of oil companies. "Bombs ... were triggered by

The effect of the report on oil prices underlines the ability of the militants to manipulate the media and oil prices merely by making threats.

cell phone and were a cocktail of military and commercial explosives ... The operative in one location reported a concentration of civilians at his location and that bombing was aborted at the very last minute to prevent loss of innocent lives," the group said [4].

MEND has repeatedly stressed that their aim is not to kill civilians or even Nigerian armed forces personnel, but to force oil companies to leave the delta and to economically paralyze Nigeria, forcing reform. The December car bombs appeared to use about five pounds of explosives each, enough to destroy the car, but not to cause much damage to the surroundings. They appeared to be parked out of the way of normal civilian traffic.

Militants have said that the deaths of two people at the military camp were caused by the car bomb detonating prematurely.

Most fighters are issued a Kalashnikov or another assault rifle, although there are also plenty of General Purpose Machine Guns (GPMGs) and Rocket Propelled Grenades (RPGs). A researcher who tracks weapons from the delta says that significant quantities of new and heavier arms are being distributed throughout the delta [5]. Several researchers in Port Harcourt believe that MEND simply provides money and weapons for specific operations to pre-existing groups and brokers alliances between them [6].

MEND typically holds hostages longer than most other groups and kidnaps more people at a time. The initial batches of four and nine oil workers were held for several weeks; the latest ended with the release of two Italian hostages last month who had been held for 99 days, a record for Nigeria. Gbomo frequently issues press releases and photos of the hostages to ensure they are kept in the news. He denies that MEND solicits ransoms, although he admits to "confiscating" over half a million dollars offered by oil company Agip during the most recent kidnapping and that his fighters "freelance" when not engaged on MEND missions [7]. He also says that MEND encourages the proliferation of smaller, criminal gangs that take hostages for purely financial reasons, saying that the actions of such gangs help MEND in their quest to make the delta "ungovernable" [8].

Expansion

After Asari was put in prison and rival gang leader Ateke Tom was declared wanted, Ateke's former number two, Soboma George, stepped in to fill the power vacuum. Soboma leads a large breakaway faction of the Icelanders known as the Outlaws [9]. He fell out with Ateke after he was charged with murder and Ateke did not do enough to help him. He subsequently escaped from jail and began to work against his former boss. In January 2007, Soboma was arrested for a traffic violation. Police later admitted that they had no idea whom they had detained and it appears unlikely that Soboma would have been arrested if they had [10]. Within hours, more than 50 heavily armed militants stormed the prison, which lies in the heart of Port Harcourt and is minutes from the main police station and military camp. They appeared to face little resistance as most of the buildings around the prison were not marked by heavy gunfire.

After Soboma's release, MEND issued a statement saying that he was a "senior commander" in the movement [11]. Subsequently, foreign journalists met with Soboma, senior militants and a government official on the outskirts of Port Harcourt. Many believe factions within the state government are seeking to use Soboma against Ateke just as they used Ateke against Asari. Police say that Soboma is heavily involved in crime, including kidnappings, gang warfare and narcotics [12]. Prior to his arrest, however, he was able to move around the city relatively freely, despite the outstanding murder charge. Former gang members say the alliance between MEND and the Outlaws (and defected Icelanders) is significant because it has a deliberate strategy of infiltrating urban areas with fighters who have traditionally been based in the creeks.

Conclusion

Before the April elections, MEND said that the polls would not affect their ultimate aim of resource control. While that may be true for their main spokesman, it is obvious that several of the groups that MEND collaborates with had a vested interest in the Nigerian election. Money or weapons supplied by MEND for other operations may have been turned against political opponents and their supporters during the polls.

It remains to be seen whether or not MEND will be a long-term force in the delta. So far, it has bequeathed local groups with heavier weapons, better organization and more sophisticated tactics, as well as linking up smaller groups that previously operated independently. In the mercenary world of Niger Delta fighters, such alliances are always subject to change and it is likely that the government will continue its tactics of co-opting senior militants with cash payments or positions and sending the *MEND's relatively small leadership structure means it is vulnerable to changes in top personnel. If that happens, however, it is common to subcontract fighters, meaning that several heavily armed militias will remain, ready to fight for the next would-be leader.* military after those who will not submit. MEND's relatively small leadership structure means it is vulnerable to changes in top personnel. If that happens, however, it is common to subcontract fighters, meaning that several heavily armed militias will remain, ready to fight for the next would-be leader. If MEND disappears, another would-be umbrella organization will eventually take its place in the same way that MEND replaced the NDPVF. As long as the delta remains underdeveloped and corrupt, increasingly bloody battles will be fought over the oil industry since it is the only source of funds.

Originally published in *Terrorism Monitor*: Volume 5, Issue 8 on April 26, 2007.

Notes

1. Author e-mail correspondence with Jomo Gbomo, spokesman for MEND, 2006.
2. Author interview with private security contractors, Lagos, 2007.
3. Author interview with MEND militants, 2006; author interview with Alhaji Dokubo-Asari, 2004.
4. Author e-mail correspondence with MEND spokespeople, 2006.
5. Author interview with a Geneva-based organization, 2007.
6. Author interview with a local conflict resolution organization headquartered in Port Harcourt, 2007.
7. Author e-mail correspondence with MEND spokespeople, 2006.
8. It should be noted that despite frequent complaints over lack of clean water, schools, clinics and rhetoric about redistributing wealth, there is not a single recorded instance of a militant group ever spending money on a project to develop their own community.
9. Author interview a with former senior Icelander commander, 2007.
10. Author interview with an officer from the station in which Soboma was held, 2007.

11. Author e-mail correspondence with MEND spokespeople, 2007.
12. Author interview with Police Commissioner Felix Ogbaudu, 2007.

Weapons of War in the Niger Delta
By Bestman Wellington

The Niger Delta region of Nigeria, home to large oil and gas operations, is awash with dangerous small arms and light weapons (SALW). The explosion in activities of non-state armed groups poses a serious threat to residents, the security of the Nigerian state and the booming petro-business in the region. Prominent among the armed groups operating in the oil- and gas-rich, but poverty stricken and under-developed enclave, are the Niger Delta People's Volunteer Force (NDPVF), the Bush Boys and the Movement for the Emancipation of the Niger Delta (MEND). Some of these groups are political militant groups, demanding an equitable distribution of oil resources, justice and development of the Niger Delta region, while others are gangs and criminal syndicate groups, also called cults or confraternities in Nigeria. All of them tap into the vibrant gun and gang culture in the delta.

Weapons Flood the Delta

From various police and military raids of the groups' armories and hideouts, or the government initiated disarmament or cash-for-arms programs, weapons have been uncovered in droves. The weapons vary from AK-47s, Czech SAs, light machine guns, Czech Model 26s, Sten MK 2s, Rocket Propelled Grenades (RPG), MAT-49s, MG 36s, Berettas, HK G3s, FN-FALs, home-made guns, pump-action shot guns, G3s, among others [1]. The sophisticated European-made assault rifles and explosives are in the hands of the militant groups like MEND and the Martyrs Brigade. The groups also possess a few M-16s, which are made in the United States. Russia, Germany, Belgium, Serbia, Czechoslovakia, the United States and China are all sources for Nigerian arms (*Niger Delta Standard*, March 5, 2006).

These weapons—so called SALWs—are brought into the delta from various locations. Most of the assault rifles—such as the Russian AK-47, the German G3, the Belgian FN-FAL, the Czech machine-guns and the Serbian RPGs—are supplied by illegal dealers and sellers. Some of the illegal gun dealers are Nigerians. In October 2006, for example, the Rivers State police command arrested Chris Ndudi Njoku, a 45 year-old businessman who specialized in importing prohibited firearms into Nigeria. In his possession were hundreds of G3s, AK-47s and Beretta automatic rifles [2]. There are also European dealers involved in the trade, but, unlike their Nigerian counterparts, they almost always escape the arm of the law, in some cases due to their connections with powerful figures in various governments (*This Day*, February 18, 2003).

Nigeria has porous borders on both its land and sea edges, allowing gun smuggling from a variety of African countries. Many of the weapons also come from war-torn countries in Africa. Additionally, poorly paid Nigerian soldiers who have served in peacekeeping missions in other African countries, such as Liberia and Sierra Leone, often return home and sell their weapons to combatants or gun dealers [3]. According to one arms researcher, Babafemi Ojudu, many of the arms smuggling rings operate out of Equatorial Guinea, Gabon, Cameroon and Nigeria (IRIN, May 2006). The smugglers use speed boats to connect with ships on the high seas, and then ferry the arms back to shore. Jailed militant leader Alhaji Dokubo-Asari confirmed this method to reporters in 2005, stating: "We are very close to international waters, and it's very easy to get weapons from ships" (IRIN, May 2006). Some of the weapons in the armed groups' stockpiles are acquired after attacks on police and military outposts. During such attacks, the militant groups break into the police or military armories and cart away arms. There are many cases in which armed groups conduct well-coordinated attacks and kill Nigerian security officials, carting away their weapons. On July 12, 2006, for example, MEND combatants killed four naval personnel and injured three soldiers who were escorting a Chevron oil tanker along Chonomi creeks in the Warri South West Local Government Area of Delta State and in turn confiscated their weapons (The Punch, July 13, 2006). Just this year, in Port Harcourt, the capital of Rivers State, on the eve of the Governorship and House of Assembly elections on April 14, armed militants attacked the Mini-Okoro Elelenwo police stations and carted away recently-arrived AK-47s, killing many police officers during the attack (The Midweek Telegraph, April 18-24, 2007). Corrupt security officials also sell weapons to militants. Before the April 2007 elections, for example, politicians in Niger State imported massive amounts of arms for their "security detachments" (which also likely went to thugs hired to help rig the elections) (*Vanguard*, April 13, 2007).

Oil money is a significant force behind the proliferation of weapons in the region. Major bunkering groups also supply gangs with weapons and have them act as armed guards while they travel along the waterways and bunkering routes looking for pipelines from which to pilfer oil.

Additionally, armed groups thrive on the local oil boom. They carry out oil bunkering (theft) operations, often exchanging bunkered oil for weapons or selling oil and then purchasing guns. Oil money is a significant force behind the proliferation of weapons in the region. Major bunkering groups also supply gangs with weapons and have them act as armed guards while they travel along the waterways and bunkering routes looking for pipelines from which to pilfer oil. Politicians also hire gangs and criminal groups to have them provide security and, during election season, to help intimidate voters to vote a certain way. Many of the politicians purchase their weapons from illegal dealers, helping to fuel the trade.

Apart from the above weapons sources, there are local underground arms manufacturing industries in Awka, the capital of Anambra State in eastern Nigeria. There, local blacksmiths produce weapons popularly called, "Awka made." The Awka guns cannot be classified as automatic weapons because the quality of the weapons is so poor. Nevertheless, the gun can inflict serious injury or even death on its target at close range.

Attacks in the Delta

The armed groups of the Niger Delta have carried out deadly and paralyzing attacks on oil and gas facilities with their weapons. They have shut down oil production and massacred scores of security officials guarding the facilities and infrastructure. The groups are fighting in familiar terrain which, despite the fact that the security forces are armed, gives the armed groups the upper-hand. They have also taken foreign oil workers hostage—sometimes releasing them only after huge ransoms are paid. The groups often use the ransom money to support their insurrectionary campaigns. These latter activities are always associated with the political-militant groups like the NDPVF, MEND and the Martyrs Brigade.

The success of the militant operations hinges on two factors: the ingenuity of the militant boat drivers who are familiar with the terrain of the creeks' complex web of streams, and the popular support among the people of the region that the many years of neglect and under-development of the Niger Delta area have fostered.

The armed groups in the delta often conduct their attacks using outboard-engine motorized fiber boats. Some of the speed boats are imported, while some are locally crafted. Most locally-manufactured speed boats are smaller compared to the foreign-made, yet the former can also travel the rough seas. Despite the employment of sophisticated gunboats by the Nigerian military taskforce, insurrectionary campaigns by the militant groups are almost always successful. The success of the militant operations hinges on two factors: the ingenuity of the militant boat drivers who are familiar with the terrain of the creeks' complex web of streams, and the popular support among the people of the region that the many years of neglect and under-development of the Niger Delta area have fostered.

To reduce the number of weapons in the Niger Delta, there is a need to prevent the flow of weapons from other countries into illegal hands in Nigeria. The local police bureaus must also live up to their responsibility of curtailing the inflow of these illicit guns into the delta. The government should run a credible and transparent security system that, by providing residents with their basic security needs, will discourage them from forming or joining cults or militant formations that are proliferating dangerous SALWs throughout Nigeria

Originally published in *Terrorism Monitor*: Volume 5, Issue 10 on May 24, 2007.

Notes

1. Nicholas Florquin and Eric G. Berman, "Armed and Armless; Security in the ECOWAS Region," Small Arms Survey, Geneva, 2005. The above weapons are not exhaustive of the guns in the hands of the various groups.
2. "Soldiers, Police Seize High Caliber Rifles in Rivers," Human Rights News, Centre for Environment, Human Rights and Development (CEHRD), Ogale-Nchia, Eleme, Rivers State, Nigeria, October, 2006.
3. Florquin and Berman.

Nigeria and the Threat of al-Qaeda Terrorism
By Bestman Wellington

Not long ago, Mike Mbama Okiro, Nigeria's inspector general of police, raised an alarm over threats by al-Qaeda to launch an attack using time-bombs on Nigerian soil. Okiro's warning generated much attention in local and international media. Islamic groups in Nigeria, including the Supreme Council for Sharia in Nigeria (SCSN), held several press conferences debunking such claims, and labeled Okiro a "liar." The police chief did not give more details about his allegation, but said his warning was based on intelligence reports. An SCSN spokesman said: "The police know where the terrorists are and Muslims should not be referred to as terrorists. The militants are terrorists for kidnapping and killing people and the police should go there and stop tagging Muslims as terrorists" (*Nigerian Tribune*, May 21, 2008).

Later a Nigerian newspaper quoted a statement from the police high command asking Nigerians to disregard recent media reports on the purported threats from al-Qaeda: "For the avoidance of doubt, the Inspector General of Police's only public pronouncement on terrorism was on 10th March, 2008 during the inauguration of the anti-terrorism squad when he said, 'The creation of the new outfit is borne out of our mission to safeguard our environment against terrorism, even though the nation has not experienced terrorist attack; we don't have to wait until it happens before we start to prepare'" (*This Day* [Lagos], May 20, 2008). Despite the apparent reversal on the threat assessment, special Nigerian anti-terrorist squads were deployed to Lagos, Abuja and Port Harcourt (Panapress, May 14, 2008).

Nigeria is Africa's most populous nation with over 140 million people, roughly split equally between Christians and Muslims. The two groups usually live side by side peacefully, but there are occasional outbreaks of sectarian conflict. Tension heightened in 2000 after 12 mainly Islamic northern states began a stricter enforcement of Shari'a (Islamic law), alienating sizeable Christian minorities. Thousands were killed in sporadic riots across the country. In September 2007 the U.S. embassy in Nigeria said the country was at risk of "terrorist attack," and in 2003 Osama bin Laden named the world's eighth biggest oil exporter as ripe for jihad or Islamic holy war (Reuters, May 10, 2008).

A number of suspected jihadis have been arrested by police and the Nigerian State Security Service (SSS) in recent years, but the cases have dragged on in the courts and there have been no convictions. No conclusive evidence of al-Qaeda's presence in Nigeria has been made public. Five Islamist militants with suspected links to al-Qaeda are on trial in the capital, Abuja, for plotting attacks on the government (Voice of America, December 9, 2007). The men were arrested in November 2007 by the SSS in the mainly Muslim north of Nigeria. Three of them have also been charged with training in Algeria with the Salafist Group for Preaching and Combat (GSPC) between 2005 and August 2007. The GSPC renamed itself al-Qaeda in the Islamic Maghreb (AQIM) in January 2007.

The northern part of Nigeria has witnessed some Islamist violence in the past. There are several armed Islamist groups throughout the northern region, but whether they are linked to bin Laden's al-Qaeda is not clear. These groups include the Hisbah, the Zamfara State Vigilante Service (ZSVS), Al-Sunna Wal Jamma ("Followers of the Prophet," also known as "the Nigerian Taliban") and others. To understand Nigeria's militant Islamist movement it is necessary to briefly look at the origins of some of the groups, their composition, leadership, areas of operation and sources of financing/support:

• The Hisbah are an Islamic vigilante group that support adherence to Shari'a, which several states in northern Nigeria have adopted in recent years (the civil code, covering wills, marriage, and so forth, has been in force across the Nigerian federation since 1979). These groups do not usually carry firearms, but are more likely to carry sticks and whips as well as knives and curved weapons with a blade known as a "barandami" [1].

The Hisbah groups are sponsored by state governments in the north that practice Shari'a, and draw their membership from the army of unemployed in those states. They were considered instrumental in influencing the outcome of the 2003 elections.

• Another Islamist group that operates in the northern part of Nigeria is the Zamfara State Vigilante Service (ZSVS). The ZSVS wear red uniforms and have been described as a "ragtag volunteer army" that patrols Zamfara state arresting anyone suspected of violating Islamic law. The group reportedly carries pistols along with homemade machetes and whips. The governor of Zamfara state has been the driving force directing the ZSVS and organizing its funding [2].

• Al-Sunna Wal Jamma was formed sometime around 2002. Its objective is the establishment of Nigeria as an Islamic state; its adherents are predominantly Maiduguri university students from the northeastern part of Nigeria. Some 200 members apparently took up arms for the first time in December 2003, possibly in response to the attempt by the governor of Yobe to disband the group.

The porosity of the Nigerian border, economic hardship and religious tensions combine to make these Islamic groups vulnerable to recruitment into dangerous terrorist networks, threatening the security of the country.

So fervent is its adherence to a fundamentalist notion of Islam that locals have dubbed it "the Taliban" in recognition of the group's admiration for the former Afghanistan government, toppled by Coalition forces in 2001. Indeed, Al-Sunna Wal Jamma once replaced the Nigerian flag with the Afghan flag on a state building briefly occupied during an altercation with police.

The porosity of the Nigerian border, economic hardship and religious tensions combine to make these Islamic groups vulnerable to recruitment into dangerous terrorist networks, threatening the security of the country. The alarm raised by Police Chief Mike Okiro regarding threats to the Nigerian nation by al-Qaeda extremists might not be backed by intelligence reports, but in Nigeria, particularly in the Muslim north, there are various armed Islamist formations with agendas similar to that of Osama bin Laden.

Originally published in *Terrorism Monitor*: Volume 6, Issue 12 on June 12, 2008.

Notes

1. See Nicholas Florquin and Eric G. Berman, "Armed and Armless; Security in the ECOWAS Region," Small Arms Survey, Geneva, 2005.

SOMALIA

Weapons and Tactics of the Somali Insurgency
By Andrew McGregor

After being driven from the Somali capital of Mogadishu to the port city of Kismayo by Ethiopian troops in late December, Islamist leader Sheikh Sharif Sheikh Ahmed urged "Islamic Courts fighters, supporters and every true Muslim to start an insurgency against the Ethiopian troops in Somalia" (Shabelle Media Network, December 30, 2006). In mid-January, the Islamic Courts Union (ICU) reorganized into an insurgent group with the name Popular Resistance Movement in the Land of the Two Migrations, or PRMLTM (Qaadisiya.com, January 19, 2007). The insurgents are dedicated to removing the Ethiopian-imposed, but internationally recognized, Somali Transitional Federal Government (TFG) as well as expelling all foreign troops from Somalia. According to TFG President Abdullahi Yusuf, "Those who throw grenades at night are definitely the remnants of the Islamic Courts and we can defeat them" (Shabelle Media Network, January 14, 2007). The government estimates that 3,000 Islamist fighters are still active in Mogadishu. In light of these threats, it is important to assess the tactics that insurgents will use in their operations against TFG, Ethiopian and other foreign troops deployed to Somalia.

Tactics

Modern Somali combat tactics are typically based on the use of the "technical," an armor-plated pick-up truck equipped with an anti-aircraft gun, used for firepower and battlefield mobility. Insurgents have largely abandoned the use of the technical in urban Mogadishu, where civilian vehicles attract less attention from Ethiopian patrols. ICU technicals in Mogadishu were returned by the Islamists to the clan militias that had originally donated them. Nearly 100 technicals in Kismayo were driven out of the city when the Islamists abandoned it on January 7. The technicals are, in any case, no match for Ethiopian armor. Insurgents are active mostly at night when the police, TFG troops and Ethiopians retreat to their compounds, but daytime attacks are not uncommon.

Somali insurgents prefer three types of operations against allied (TFG/Ethiopian) positions:

1. Mortar or rocket assaults on allied positions are the most common form of attack, occurring on an almost daily basis in Mogadishu. The mortar is usually transported to a residential neighborhood by car or pick-up truck before deployment. Typically, a small number of rounds are launched before the target is engaged with automatic weapons fire, while the mortar is withdrawn. Firefights can last a few minutes or several hours, with government or Ethiopian forces generally reluctant to emerge from their positions until the firing has stopped. As the gunmen withdraw, retaliatory allied rocket or artillery fire targets the neighborhood from which the mortar fire came. TFG/Ethiopian troops may conduct a house-to-house search for weapons in the neighborhood the next day. At one

point, TFG soldiers began to confiscate cell phones from people in the street, fearing that they might be used to direct mortar attacks (SomaliNet, February 21, 2007).

2. Assassinations are the second most common tactic. Politically-inspired killings of government officials or police officers are often carried out in a "drive-by" fashion by gunmen in a car. Bombs may be used for significant targets, although it is much more common for a hand grenade to be tossed through a house or car window. A TFG spokesman claimed that assassinations are a long-standing technique of the Islamists: "Before Islamists took control of the capital, specific individuals were being assassinated and when they clutched control of the capital, assassinations halted. Now that they were defeated, killing has restarted" (Shabelle Media Network, January 28, 2007).

3. RPG and automatic weapons fire on TFG/Ethiopian convoys is rare in comparison, but offers the insurgents the best opportunity to kill allied troops outside their well-defended compounds. In a February 8 daylight RPG attack on an Ethiopian convoy, the grenade missed the convoy entirely and took out a civilian Toyota, killing two people. Ethiopian troops can overreact to such situations. On January 20, 2007 for example, a man fired a pistol at an Ethiopian convoy in a north Mogadishu market. While the man slipped away, Ethiopian troops opened fire on the market crowd, killing four and wounding many others. In early January 2007, there were two instances of gunmen in cars or pick-up trucks attacking allied convoys or positions with RPGs and automatic weapons, but this tactic has been little used since (although passing cars may still lob a grenade into army positions).

The insurgents' targets include police stations, the presidential compound, the Defense Ministry, hotels housing TFG, Ethiopian or AU officials (such as the Banadir Hotel, Hotel Kaah and the Ambassador Hotel), TFG/Ethiopian army compounds (including the Difger Hospital, commandeered for military use), the seaport (where Ethiopian troops are quartered) and the airport (the PRMLTM threatened to shoot down aircraft using the airport, but so far only mortar attacks have been carried out). Insurgent losses during operations in Mogadishu appear to be remarkably small. Those killed or wounded are apparently recovered before pulling out. No insurgent has been taken prisoner in the course of an operation in Mogadishu. Nearly all insurgent attacks occur in the Mogadishu region, with a small number of attacks in the port city of Kismayo. This does not, however, indicate a state of peace in the rest of the country, where clan fighting and battles between tribal militias and government forces claim as many lives as the insurgency.

A spokesman for the PRMLTM recently threatened the use of suicide attacks against AU peacekeepers: "We promise we shall welcome them with bullets from heavy guns, exploding cars and young men eager to carry out martyrdom operations against these colonial forces" (Banadir.com, February 25, 2007). So far, suicide attacks have been rare in a population little inclined to such methods. Iraq-style bombings directed at masses of civilians have also failed to appear in the Somali insurgency.

As the Ethiopians entered Somalia in December 2006, Sheikh Yusuf Mohamed Siad

"Indha-Adde," the ICU defense chief, made an appeal for foreign assistance: "The country is open to all Muslim jihadists worldwide. We call them to come to Somalia and continue their holy war in Somalia. We welcome anyone, who can remove the Ethiopian enemy, to enter our country" (Shabelle Media Network, December 23, 2006). At the time, TFG Prime Minister Ali Muhammad Gedi claimed that 4,000 foreign fighters had joined the ICU. While several scores of foreigners have been arrested at the Kenyan border, the prime minister's tally seems to have been greatly exaggerated. There is no evidence yet that foreign fighters are involved in the current clashes in Mogadishu, although TFG military commander Saed Dhere accused unnamed foreign countries of financing the attacks (SomaliNet, February 24, 2007).

Despite disarmament efforts, arms can be found everywhere in Mogadishu. When the Islamists withdrew from the capital, they abandoned large stocks of arms that were then plundered by looters (Shabelle Media Network, December 28, 2006). Incredibly, the Bakara and Argentina arms markets in Mogadishu remain open, selling hand grenades, RPGs, machine guns, anti-aircraft guns and the ubiquitous AK-47 assault rifle. Several warlords who turned in their arms during the government's disarmament campaign (including Mohamed Dheere, Muhammad Qanyare Afrah and Abdi Nur Siyad) have been observed stocking up on new RPGs, heavy machine-guns and other weapons (*Terrorism Focus*, February 27, 2007). The AK-47 remains the insurgents' most common weapon, many of these having been seized from the police.

Counter-Measures

Deputy Defense Minister Salad Ali Jelle claims that the insurgents always target the civilian population in Mogadishu in order to create a perception of instability for foreign consumption (Shabelle Media Network, February 7, 2007). The insurgents actually do not target civilian areas so much but display ineptitude in finding the proper range with their mortars, leading to widespread destruction of civilian areas and large losses of life compared to the relatively few casualties they inflict on the government compounds. Further casualties are created when allied forces lash out blindly with artillery and rocket fire when they come under attack from residential neighborhoods. The wounded have difficulty reaching already overwhelmed hospitals due to continuous weapons fire or roadblocks erected by allied forces. Nearly half of the wounded perish after they finally reach medical care.

Although Mogadishu's Islamist insurgents may be willing to start a large-scale insurgency, their lack of training on most weapons more powerful than an AK-47 restricts the effectiveness of their attacks on allied positions.

Religious and community leaders in Mogadishu have begged both sides to stop the devastation created by these endless rounds of attacks and counter-attacks. Sheikh Ali Haji Yusuf urged the formation of local security forces until the government can establish security in Mogadishu. The sheikh's call was apparently heeded; in the evening of February 21, 2007 vigilante forces discovered and beat a team of gunmen attempting to deploy a mortar from their car to fire at government positions in Mogadishu. Some gunmen have found new careers as vigilantes for hire in different neighborhoods.

Mogadishu police retired to their compounds several weeks ago after a series of assassinations and have rarely emerged since, leaving control of the streets to gunmen, vigilantes, criminals and the well-armed security forces of Mogadishu's business community. The TFG claims to have developed new teams of counter-terrorism specialists, but these appear to have had little effect so far.

Conclusion

Although Mogadishu's Islamist insurgents may be willing to start a large-scale insurgency, their lack of training on most weapons more powerful than an AK-47 restricts the effectiveness of their attacks on allied positions. Just before the Ethiopian invasion, large numbers of students were handed arms from Islamist stockpiles. Predictably, Ethiopian regulars and warplanes quickly routed these inexperienced would-be jihadis on open ground. Mogadishu is another story. Here, TFG and Ethiopian troops have shown distaste for urban operations. TFG forces rely on Ethiopian firepower, while the Ethiopians are already in the process of withdrawal.

The first of 8,000 AU peacekeepers are scheduled to arrive on March 2, 2007 Uganda asserts that its contingent will include counter-insurgency veterans and is well trained in countering suicide attacks (Banadir.com, February 25, 2007). AU peacekeepers will have to be more aggressive than the Ethiopians to contain the Mogadishu insurgency, although such tactics might reinforce popular perception of the peacekeepers as an occupation army. TFG soldiers and police will also be certain to stand aside while AU troops do the heavy work. With time, the effectiveness of the insurgents will improve, leading to the possibility of intense fighting as long as the TFG refuses to include the Islamist leadership in the national reconciliation process, as urged by Ethiopia, the United States and the European Union.

Originally published in *Terrorism Monitor*: Volume 5, Issue 4 on March 1, 2007.

The Leading Factions Behind the Somali Insurgency
By Andrew McGregor

The U.S.-supported Ethiopian invasion that expelled Somalia's Islamist government in December 2006 is rapidly deteriorating into a multi-layered conflict that will prove resistant to resolution. Resistance to Ethiopian troops and the Ethiopian-installed Transitional Federal Government (TFG) is inspired by nationalism, religion, economic factors and clan loyalties, yet all of these motivations are part of a constantly shifting pattern of allegiances in which the only common characteristic is a desire to expel foreign troops from Somalia. Local warlords and clan leaders who were deprived of power by the Islamic Courts Union (ICU) are now scrambling to reassert control over their small fiefdoms in Mogadishu, while many former ICU gunmen have transferred their allegiance to clan militias.

Fighting in the Somali capital of Mogadishu has created over 300,000 civilian refugees. Thousands more (nearly all from the Hawiye clan that dominates the capital) have been killed as residential areas become battlegrounds. Only one overwhelmed hospital is open as Ethiopian troops are using other hospitals as barracks. The Somali TFG is exacerbating the situation by imposing bureaucratic delays on the delivery of relief aid arriving in Mogadishu. Unable to resist the Ethiopian incursion, the ICU dissolved December 27, 2006, returning its stockpiles of weapons and vehicles to the clans and militias who had donated them. Since then, a number of leading elements in the resistance have emerged.

The Hawiye

The Hawiye (one of Somalia's four major clans) provided important support for the ICU in the south-central region of Somalia, which includes Mogadishu. Hawiye members (especially those of the powerful Habr Gidir Ayr sub-clan) dominated all of the ICU's decision-making bodies. Former ICU leader Sheikh Hassan Dahir Aweys is a member of the Habr Gidir Ayr (one of four major sub-clans of the Hawiye). The Hawiye sub-clans have fought each other for years in Mogadishu, but there are signs that opposition to Ethiopian/TFG forces is beginning to unify formerly antagonistic groups.

Now operating from Yemen, Sheikh Aweys claims that U.S. government support for the Ethiopian occupation and the resulting civilian deaths is motivated by a need to exact revenge for the deaths of U.S. troops in Somalia in the early 1990s. The former ICU chairman insists that Ugandan and other African Union troops will receive the same treatment as the Ethiopians. According to the sheikh, negotiations with the TFG are impossible until all foreign troops are removed from Somalia (Qaadisiya.com, April 15, 2007). On April 13, 2007 a sub-committee was formed from Hawiye representatives and Ethiopian officers in order to negotiate the terms of a cease-fire (HornAfrik Radio, April 13, 2007). A spokesman for the Hawiye cease-fire committee lashed out at the United States for its support of the Ethiopian invasion (Shabelle Media Network, April 7, 2007).

The TFG is dominated by the Darod, another of the four major clans. The Hawiye suspect that the TFG is dedicated to the advancement of the Darod and the elimination of the Hawiye. Elders of the Hawiye clan pin responsibility for the devastation of Mogadishu on the TFG and have asked for an international commission to investigate the circumstances of the conflict (Radio Shabelle, April 15, 2007; Radio Banadir, April 14, 2007). Hawiye elders also accuse the TFG of recruiting only Darod into the army. To deflect such criticism, TFG Prime Minister Ali Muhammad Gedi recently appointed a notorious Hawiye warlord to the post of Somali chief of police (Garowe Online, April 18, 2007).

TFG President Abdullahi Yusuf Ahmad is from the Majerteen sub-clan of the Darod. He commanded Darod forces in battles against the Hawiye in the 1990s. The Hawiye believe that the Ethiopians are set on installing a Darod-dominated government intent on eliminating their clan. Claims of "ethnic-cleansing," "war crimes" and "genocide" are increasingly used by the Hawiye to describe Ethiopian actions in Mogadishu. Relations between the Hawiye and the Darod clans were irreparably poisoned by the massacres of Darod by the Hawiye in Mogadishu after the overthrow of Somali dictator Siad Barre in 1991. Given this history, the arrival of President Yusuf and his well-armed veteran Darod militia was especially alarming to the Hawiye, who now fear retribution for the massacres of 1991. The intense fighting of the last month began when the president announced plans to forcibly disarm non-government militias in Mogadishu.

Deputy Prime Minister Husein Mohammed Farah Aideed has angered his comrades in the TFG by visiting the Eritrean capital of Asmara, where he accused Ethiopia of planning "genocide" in Somalia. Aideed, a former U.S. Marine, leads a militia drawn from the Habr Gidir Sa'ad sub-clan of the Hawiye. Notorious for changing sides, Aideed created a controversy earlier this year when he suggested Somalis and Ethiopians use a common passport. Having survived the resulting firestorm, Aideed appears to have made a strategic decision to now oppose the Ethiopian invasion.

Shabaab

Shabaab (Youth) once served as an ICU-controlled elite militia. The group was formed in August 2006 from a core of fighters who played an important role in last year's defeat of the Anti-Terrorist Alliance, a U.S. supported coalition of Somali warlords (Somaliland Times, August 12, 2006). The group became known for its ruthless methods that often discredited the ICU in international opinion.

After Sheikh Aweys fled to Yemen, leadership of Shabaab passed to his former aide, Adan Hashi Ayro, a U.S.—and UN-designated terrorist and radical Islamist who is reported to have trained in Afghanistan prior to the September 11 attacks. U.S. spokesmen claimed that a January 8, 2007 airstrike by U.S. gunships wounded Ayro. The roughly 30 year-old Shabaab leader released an audiotape in March denying rumors of his death: "I will fight the troops who are enemies of my religion and who have invaded my homeland ... and I am certain I will remove them by force soon" (Garowe Online, March 7, 2007). The Shabaab leader has several disputes with his own Habr Gidir Ayr sub-clan.

Mukhtar Robow ("Abu Mansur") is another prominent Shabaab leader, accused by the United States of providing logistical support to al-Qaeda (U.S. Department of State, African Affairs Fact Sheet, January 25, 2007). Other Shabaab leaders include Afghanistan veteran Ahmad Abdi Godane and Ibrahim Haji Jama ("al-Afghani"), who is reported to have fought in Kashmir as well as in Afghanistan. "Al-Afghani" is wanted in the quasi-independent state of Somaliland, where he was sentenced last December to 25 years in prison on terrorism charges (*Somaliland Times*, December 9, 2006).

Typical of many Salafi militant groups, Shabaab offers an alternative to clan- or tribal-based movements, drawing on a wide base of recruits. The typical Shabaab gunman is a poorly-educated youth in his late teens or early twenties who has grown up in the midst of Somalia's violent rivalries. Unlike former ICU colleagues who have found work with the re-emerging clan militias, the Shabaab fighter holds a rather inflexible and radical interpretation of Islam that compels him to undertake dangerous missions in the cause of creating an Islamist Somalia. This is a fairly new development in Somalia, where allegiance to ideology has tended to take second place to family and clan loyalties when under pressure. Many Shabaab fighters are reported to have undergone military training in Eritrea (Voice of America, January 6, 2007).

Shabaab fighters are often referred to as "the masked men" due to their habit of drawing red scarves across their faces during assaults on TFG and Ethiopian troops. The masks protect their identity not only from government forces, but also from Mogadishu residents, many of whom are bitterly unhappy about the civilian carnage resulting from Shabaab's poorly-aimed mortars and the brutal retaliation of Ethiopian artillery on the residential districts that Shabaab uses as launching points for its reckless assaults. Many Mogadishu neighborhoods have hired vigilantes to prevent their use

... the Shabaab fighter holds a rather inflexible and radical interpretation of Islam that compels him to undertake dangerous missions in the cause of creating an Islamist Somalia. This is a fairly new development in Somalia, where allegiance to ideology has tended to take second place to family and clan loyalties when under pressure ...

as firing-points by Shabaab fighters. Shabaab leader Adan Hashi Ayro claims that the mortar shells raining down on Mogadishu homes are fired by Ethiopian troops. Although Shabaab once numbered several thousand fighters, it probably does not field more than several hundred men at the moment.

In early April 2007, U.S. Assistant Secretary of State for African Affairs Jendayi Frazer claimed that Eritrea and the "global jihadist network" were supporting Shabaab (Shabelle Media Network, April 7, 2007). Eritrea denies accusations from the United States that it is supporting and supplying the Somali insurgency, but there is little doubt that Asmara takes delight in the predicament of Ethiopia, a bitter enemy of Eritrea since the two countries fought an inconclusive but bloody border war in 1998-2000 that claimed 70,000 lives. A Hawiye spokesman insisted that clan leaders have no contact with Eritrea or the former ICU leadership (Radio Shabelle, April 9, 2007).

The Popular Resistance Movement

Another resistance group formed in January 2007 is al-Harakah al-Muqawamah al-Sha'biyah fi al-Bilad al-Hijratayn (The Popular Resistance Movement in the Land of the Two Migrations, PRMLTM) (Qaadisiya.com, January 19, 2007). Led in the Banadir region by Sheikh Abdikadir, the movement has issued warnings to African Union peacekeepers that they can expect no different treatment than the Ethiopians. The PRM has since claimed responsibility for a March 12 attack on a Ugandan convoy. On March 21, an Ethiopian offensive against Habr Gidir strongholds in south Mogadishu was ambushed by hundreds of masked gunmen. The Ethiopians withdrew after a firefight lasting several hours, leaving their dead behind to suffer mutilation and burning before being dragged through the streets. The PRM claimed responsibility for the ambush (The Associated Press, March 22, 2007).

Other Resistance Factions

Responsibility for a March 6 assault on the Mogadishu airport and a March 16 mortar attack on the presidential palace was claimed by the Tawhid wa'l-Jihad Brigades in Somalia (Unity and Struggle), apparently in response to the alleged rapes of Somali women by Ethiopian troops. The group promises a series of suicide attacks.

The Young Mujahideen Movement in Somalia is another group that has claimed attacks on Ethiopian troops, including an April 19 suicide bombing that allegedly involved the use of chemicals (SomaliNet, April 21, 2007).

Al-Qaeda in Somalia?

TFG Prime Minister Gedi maintains that the relentless shelling of north Mogadishu is designed to clear out "terrorist groups." Using the now familiar language of those seeking U.S. military support, Gedi referred to "al-Qaeda operatives" while insisting that only terrorists opposed the government: "there are no Hawiye people involved in the conflict" (Somaliweyn Radio, April 21, 2007). The TFG seems well aware that clan warfare rarely brings the type of U.S. support that can be expected by allies in the war on terrorism. According to a Hawiye spokesman, Ethiopian officers insisted during a meeting with the Hawiye cease-fire committee that the attacks on Ethiopian positions in the capital were being carried out by al-Qaeda, a suggestion the Hawiye rejected. The spokesman added that the Hawiye community would prefer death over giving allegiance to President Abdullahi Yusuf (Radio Shabelle, March 23, 2007).

... Ethiopia's attempt to establish a weak Somali government that owes its existence to Ethiopian power has been a failure. On the other hand, the descent into chaos means Somalia no longer represents a threat to Ethiopia's territorial integrity.

After a battle on April 23, 2007 between two Darod sub-clans for control of the southern port of Kismayo, Prime Minister Gedi denied that there was any clan struggle for the city, blaming the fighting there on "al-Qaeda-linked terrorists from Mogadishu," whom he alleged were also responsible for the deteriorating relations between Somaliland and Puntland (Shabelle Media Network, April 23, 2007).

Statements of support from al-Qaeda's Ayman al-Zawahiri, foreign volunteers and diaspora returnees (not necessarily al-Qaeda affiliated) appear to have had little influence on the fighting so far. Scores of these poorly-trained fighters have been detained at the Kenyan border or picked up in Ethiopian security sweeps.

Conclusion

Ethiopia will never support a strong central government in Mogadishu that might ultimately prove capable of pressing Somali claims in the Ogaden region. Thus far, however, Ethiopia's attempt to establish a weak Somali government that owes its existence to Ethiopian power has been a failure. On the other hand, the descent into chaos means Somalia no longer represents a threat to Ethiopia's territorial integrity. If Ethiopia can manage to extricate its troops from Somalia in the near future, this might be interpreted as a victory in Addis Ababa.

Somali life is shaped by a unique social system that aids the survival of the individual, but in turn promotes schisms and hinders the creation of enduring alliances or devotion to ideological causes. Foreign occupation is possibly the only factor capable of uniting Somalis, but there are signs that resistance to Ethiopian/African Union troops may soon exist simultaneously with a Hawiye/Darod clan war. If the situation is allowed to deteriorate to that point, it may be years before peace can be re-established in Somalia.

Originally published in *Terrorism Monitor*: Volume 5, Issue 8 on April 26, 2007.

Expelling the Infidel: Historical Look at Somlai Resistance to Ethiopia
By Andrew McGregor

The U.S.-supported Ethiopian invasion of Somalia has an unsettling resemblance to the British-supported Ethiopian incursions in the early years of the 20th century. In both cases, the Western powers became involved because of perceived strategic considerations, while their proxy, Ethiopia, went to war as a result of Somali resistance to Ethiopian domination of the ethnic-Somali Ogaden region. Last December's invasion succeeded in bringing the Ethiopia-friendly Transitional Federal Government (TFG) of President Abdullahi Yusuf Ahmad to power in Mogadishu. Although the Islamists have been dispersed for the moment, there are signs that a guerrilla campaign is in the making.

Like the late 20th century, the late 19th century witnessed an international Islamic revival, spurred in part by the military occupation and economic domination of Muslim nations by the Western world. The Egyptian withdrawal from its short-lived occupation of the Somali coast in the 1880s and the failure of the Ottoman Empire to press its claims on the region opened the region to the advances of Britain, Italy, France and Ethiopia. In Somalia, there was a rare shift in public affairs as religious leaders became involved in traditionally secular Somali politics, using their unique position to transcend traditional clan divisions. The most notable of these leaders was Sayyid Muhammad 'Abdullah Hassan, who led his "dervishes" in a 21-year struggle against foreign domination.

Introducing Political Islam

As a young man in Mecca, Muhammad adopted the austere teachings of the Salihiya sect of Islam. Like today's Somali Islamists, Muhammad rejected foreign influence and enforced the strict observance of Islamic law. The uses of alcohol and tobacco were forbidden, as was the use of Qat, a narcotic leaf widely consumed in Somalia. In Somalia's devastated economy, the Qat trade continues to be one of the most reliable ways for entrepreneurs to make money. The prohibition of the trade by the Islamic Courts Union (ICU) damaged local support for these modern Islamists only weeks before the Ethiopian invasion (*Terrorism Focus*, November 28, 2006). Sayyid Muhammad was a harsh critic of Somalia's dominant (but relatively tolerant) Qadiri Sufi order, who in turn called the renegade holy man "the Mad Mullah," the name by which he is best known to history.

Like many modern Islamist leaders in Somalia, Muhammad cut his teeth as a political militant in the Ogaden region, preaching resistance to the Christian Ethiopians who were steadily occupying the area. One of Muhammad's greatest strengths was his mastery of oral poetry, a powerful social and political tool in Somalia, where a man could be ruined by an effective attack in verse or a tribe brought to war by skillful alliteration. At first, the British imperialists who occupied his native northwestern Somalia tolerated Muhammad's preaching, believing that adherence to Sharia law would help bring order to the wild tribesmen of the interior. It was not long, however, before Muhammad turned his attention to the British because of their support for Ethiopia. By 1899, he had broken with British rule and enraged the Ethiopians with a ferocious but ultimately unsuccessful attack on their forces in the Ogaden. With Britain's colonial army forced to concentrate on the concurrent war in South Africa, British authorities invited Ethiopia to join the campaign against this troublesome preacher.

Sayyid Muhammad grew concerned that the Ethiopian and Western Christians sought to destroy Islam in Somalia, a fear shared by Somalia's modern Islamists. In the period 1901-1904, the dervishes repulsed four Anglo-Ethiopian expeditions, although their own losses were often severe. Sayyid Muhammad's stern and often ruthless measures in dealing with rivals cost him the opportunity of uniting the Somalis against foreign rule.

Somalia's social structure is also a major obstacle in the development of a unifying Islamist cause. Muhammad never quite succeeded in overcoming the reluctance of Somalia's many clans and subsections to join a movement that was not directly devoted to enriching or empowering their own group. Military success brought supporters, while failure led to desertions. The problem persists to this day, accounting in large part for the quick collapse of the ICU when an Ethiopian victory became obvious in December 2006.

The Ethiopian and British Campaigns

The first Ethiopian campaign against Muhammad was a disaster. A massive army of 14,000 men chased the dervishes around the near-waterless Ogaden in 1901, its numbers shrinking daily from heat, hunger, thirst and disease. With typical Somali fractiousness, some Ogaden Somalis accompanied the Ethiopian forces against their would-be liberator. To the British authorities, the lesson was obvious, and it was decided in typical colonial fashion that Somalis must fight Somalis. Thousands of tribesmen were recruited under Indian NCOs and British officers to destroy Muhammad's army. Similarly, the United States engaged Somali warlords under the guise of the "Anti-Terrorist Coalition" to depose of the Islamists last summer. The strategy was a complete failure, with the warlords being driven from most of the country.

A second Ethiopian expedition to the Ogaden in 1903 killed only a few of Muhammad's men, while suffering terrible losses of their own from lack of food and water. In familiar language, the dervishes were at one point characterized as "terrorist thugs," and joint British/Ethiopian campaigns continued until the devastating loss of 7,000 dervishes at the 1904 battle of Jidbaale. During these four campaigns, Ethiopian troops were accompanied by British advisers. There are reports that British SAS units are now acting as advisers to Kenyan border forces in an effort to trap fleeing Islamists (*Sunday Times*, January 14, 2007).

> *Somalia's social structure is also a major obstacle in the development of a unifying Islamist cause. Muhammad never quite succeeded in overcoming the reluctance of Somalia's many clans and subsections to join a movement that was not directly devoted to enriching or empowering their own group.*

After the defeat at Jidbaale, Sayyid Muhammad agreed to settle peacefully in Italian Somaliland, but within months he and his followers were again raiding the Ogaden and British territory in an attempt to drive out the "infidels." Ethiopia had dropped out of the fighting, leaving Britain to carry on alone. Today, there is a danger of U.S. forces meeting the same fate, as Ethiopia is seeking only a brief occupation and most African Union states (except for Uganda) are very reluctant to commit peacekeepers to a conflict they view as intractable. As Under Secretary of State for the Colonies in 1908, Winston Churchill pointed out the enormous expense involved in holding this deeply impoverished wilderness and the unlikelihood of British-led Indian and Somali troops ever providing security in the interior. Churchill suggested withdrawing to the coast and leaving the barren interior to the dervishes. It was two years before this policy was implemented, but the withdrawal did nothing to end the fighting.

A strong blow was dealt to Sayyid Muhammad's movement when two defectors succeeded in obtaining a letter in 1908 from the leader of the Salihiya movement in Mecca condemning Muhammad as a heretic and an infidel. Despite this, Muhammad's call for an anti-colonial jihad continued to spread and his quick-moving horsemen dominated the desert

The United States, like Britain, often tends to regard militant Islam in any form as "fanaticism," directed by irrational religious impulses. Too frequently, however, foreign intervention is the fuel that allows political Islam to grow in an otherwise hostile environment.

wilderness. As the First World War broke out in Europe, fierce fighting continued in Somalia, almost unnoticed by the outside world. The conflict continued as Sayyid Muhammad grew older and ever more corpulent, no longer able to perform the feats of horsemanship for which he was once known, but still able to use his poetic oratory to inspire his dervishes. Sayyid Muhammad's army was finally broken by a combined infantry and Royal Air Force assault on their fortresses in the Somali desert in 1919. Most resistance collapsed with Muhammad's death from influenza in 1921.

Conclusion

The dervish/Islamist war with Britain was a direct result of the empire's cooperation with Ethiopia, which sought to use British support to solidify their rule of the Ogaden region. Although Ethiopian Prime Minister Meles Zenawi speaks of the importance of joining the "war on terrorism," it was threats from the modern Somali Islamists that they intended to "liberate" the Ogaden that brought Ethiopia to war. There are signs that Ethiopia is taking advantage of its occupation to round up members of the Oromo and Ogaden rebel movements (Garowe Online, January 13, 2007). Others have been intercepted trying to flee into Kenya (Ethiopian News Agency, January 8, 2007).

With growing opposition to his government at home and international criticism of his regime's human rights abuses, Zenawi has strengthened himself by achieving the inviolable status that comes with being a "vital partner" in the U.S. war on terrorism. His power base in the Tigrean-dominated army has improved through U.S. funding, training, intelligence cooperation and the practical (if limited) experience of mobile warfare gained through the invasion of Somalia. The war is also seen as an antidote to recent defections in the officer corps to the Oromo Liberation Front (an Ethiopian resistance movement). The Ogaden National Liberation Front (ONLF) declared on January 7 that "the ONLF will continue to resist the presence of Ethiopian troops in Ogaden and we shall resist the use of our territory as a logistical and planning center for Ethiopian occupation troops in Somalia" (ONLF Statement on Ethiopian Occupation of Somalia, January 7, 2007). With political unrest in his own country, Zenawi cannot spare the best units of his army for long.

Despite an al-Qaeda video released on January 4, 2007 urging Muslims to go to Somalia to fight the Ethiopians ("the slaves of America"), there is little indication that any have done so. Somalia has always provided an inhospitable environment to foreign adventurers. Popular support for the Islamists was not an expression of approval by Somalis for international terrorism, and Ethiopian/American suggestions that al-Qaeda fugitives had usurped the leadership of the Somali Islamists seem highly unlikely in light of the traditional patterns of Somali power structures.

The United States, like Britain, often tends to regard militant Islam in any form as "fanaticism," directed by irrational religious impulses. Too frequently, however, foreign intervention is the fuel that allows political Islam to grow in an otherwise hostile environment. TFG Minister of the Interior Hussein Aideed (a former U.S. Marine) provided the Islamists with a rallying point by urging Somali integration with Ethiopia, including the use of a single passport (Shabelle Media Network, January 7, 2007). Sharif Hassan Sheikh Adan, the TFG speaker, does not share President Abdulahi's pro-Ethiopian position, stating "I believe that the security created by the [Islamic] Courts during their six-month rule cannot be recreated by Ethiopian troops, even if they stay in Somalia for another six years" (Garowe Online, January 13, 2007).

Despite their desperate position, Somalia's Islamists remain defiant: "If the world thinks we are dead, they should know we are alive and will continue the jihad against the infidels in our country" (Shabelle Media Network, January 7). Their words are a modern echo of Sayyid Muhammad's verse: "And I'll react against the malice and oppression unleashed upon me, Yes, I am justified to smite, to sweep through the land with terror and fury, And I'll go out to make the country free of infidel influence" (Quoted in Said S. Samatar: Oral Poetry and Somali Nationalism, Cambridge, 1982, p.192).

Originally published in *Terrorism Monitor*: Volume 5, Issue 1 on January 18, 2007.

UN/African Union Peacekeepers in Darfur Unlikely to Succeed
By Andrew McGregor

Despite optimistic predictions, the expected deployment of the "hybrid" United Nations-African Union peacekeeping force in Darfur (UNAMID) is in peril. It now seems there will be no peace to keep and no mandate capable of imposing it. Sudan is insisting that African troops comprise most of the 26,000 troops projected for UNAMID. The peacekeeping force of 9,000 African Union troops (AMIS) is already unpopular in Darfur, condemned by civilians for failing to protect them, reviled by rebels for alleged cooperation with the Sudanese army and paid as little heed as possible by the government in Khartoum. For their part, the peacekeepers are poorly equipped, rarely paid and suffer from serious transportation and communications deficiencies. Will UNAMID succeed where AMIS has failed? There are many reasons to think not.

• Failure to start afresh: Integrating AMIS troops into UNAMID will prove to be a major mistake. In a perfect world, AMIS peacekeepers would provide the new troops with the benefit of their experience in Darfur. In reality they will quickly infect the newcomers with the "live-and-let-live" methods the demoralized AMIS soldiers use to survive their mission. Night patrols are nearly unheard of, and the troops are generally unwilling to do anything risky or provocative. The massacre of 10 African Union (AU) peacekeepers at Haskanita on September 30 was a shocking warning to AU troops to keep their noses out of the conflict.

• Bigger is not better: UNAMID appears to be little more than a bigger AMIS. Tripling the size of the existing force will only multiply existing logistical problems. There are no roads, water is in short supply in most areas and nearly all supplies will need to be flown in. Most of UNAMID's energies will be spent supplying their own outposts. The U.S. company Pacific Architect Engineers Inc. (owned by the Lockheed-Martin Corp.) has been awarded a $250 million contract (without competitive bidding) to build five camps in Darfur and Kordofan for AU troops (The Associated Press, October 16, 2007).

• AU Mismanagement: As with the AU peacekeeping mission in Somalia, AMIS funds seem to evaporate before they reach the troops in the field. The frequent disappearance of valuable fuel stocks from AMIS stores is no doubt related to the infrequency of pay. Senegal has threatened to withdraw its troops from AMIS over reports that the troops at Haskanita did not have enough ammunition to defend themselves (Daily Telegraph, October 2, 2007). Rwanda has also threatened to withdraw, citing the inaction of Nigerian commanders.

• Inadequate air-support: The wounded at Haskanita had to wait 18 hours for relief to arrive by road. UNAMID needs 24 transport and light tactical helicopters, but rejected the sole offer of six Cobra attack helicopters and four Huey transport craft from Jordan because the aircraft "did not meet UN requirements." Sudan is demanding the right to approve the nationality of all UNAMID pilots, virtually ensuring there will be no further offers of helicopters. No Western nation will pledge their troops if air evacuation of wounded troops is unavailable. 60 major transport trucks are also needed—none has been pledged.

• "Hybrid" force not so hybrid: So far pledges of troops from non-African countries have been given the cold shoulder by Khartoum and the AU. Most of the African troops pledged so far do not meet minimal UN standards. A team of 400 Swedish and Norwegian engineers has been ready to deploy as early as this month, but are still waiting to hear back from the AU regarding their offer. Equipped with a dozen armored personnel carriers instead of the ubiquitous Land Cruisers, the force would be responsible for building roads and bases, an essential part of the mission. The Norwegians have one requirement that so far has not been met: the provision of enough helicopters to offer 24 hour evacuation of wounded troops. Unwelcome in UNAMID, European troops are joining a European Union (EU) peacekeeping mission that will deploy in neighboring Chad.

Khartoum has not raised any objections to Chinese participation in the mission. The People's Liberation Army (PLA) will supply a 315-man team of multi-purpose engineers (with a medical and "force protection" unit) to help build the needed infrastructure. A Chinese firm has also begun sinking wells in South Darfur to radically increase the amount of available water (*Sudan Vision Daily*, November 7, 2007; Xinhua, September 22, 2007). The Chinese contribution is part of a new effort to become involved in African peacekeeping missions; in the Western Sahara Major General Zhao Jingmin has become the first Chinese officer to take command of a UN peacekeeping mission (Xinhua, September 17, 2007). Chinese oil facilities in Kordofan have recently come under attack from Darfur rebels who demand China and other foreign countries abandon their operation there until a peace agreement has been signed. China may have something of a conflict of interest in their deployment; China remains the largest arms supplier for the Khartoum government (The Associated Press, May 8, 2007; July 5, 2007).

Sudan claims that criticism of UNAMID's African composition is intended to "send a message that Africans are not capable." UNAMID's commander, Nigerian General Martin Agwai disagrees: "I'm an African ... but the reality is not many African countries can provide troops that can self-sustain themselves for six months." The leader of the SLA, one of the largest rebel groups, simply calls the idea of an all-African force "racist." According to rebel leader 'Abd al-Wahid al-Nur, "it seems to be that the international community wants to compromise the life of our people in order to please the Khartoum regime" (Reuters, September 22, 2007). Some of the African officers bring their own political baggage—the Rwandan Deputy Commander of UNAMID, Major General Karenzi Karake, has been accused of war crimes by Rwandan exiles (New Times, September 16, 2007). 3,000 experienced Egyptian soldiers are also expected to join the force, but Egyptians are best remembered in the area for their slave raiding and ruthless taxation measures during the period of Egyptian rule in the 19th century.

• No mandate for resettlement: The rebels want a force that will restore their lands. UNAMID's mandate only allows the force to "encourage" resettlement. If the displaced have no expectation of resettlement they will continue to supply fighters to the rebellion. Khartoum has its own interpretation of the modified agreement on the Chapter 7 mandate from the United Nations. According to the Sudanese government, no action can be taken for the physical protection of refugees without the permission of Khartoum.

• The Janjaweed wild card: The Sudan government is losing control of some parts of the Janjaweed. Many are dissatisfied with what they see as broken promises from Khartoum, some going so far as to cross over to the rebels. 800 heavily armed Janjaweed recently massed outside the government-held town of Nyala to press demands for unpaid wages (Sudan Tribune, October 9, 2007).

• Collapse of the Government of National Unity (GNU): Sudan's southern rebel party, the Sudanese Peoples' Liberation Movement (SPLM), pulled out of the coalition government in October because of the government's failure to implement the terms of the SPLM peace agreement with Khartoum. The Darfur rebels had expected to find a sympathetic hearing from southern politicians in negotiations with the coalition government, but must now negotiate with the ruling Arabist/Islamist party in Khartoum. One major rebel faction pulled out of the October 27 peace talks in Sirté (Libya) because of this. Tensions are running high between the former GNU partners; an adviser to Sudanese President al-Bashir accused the SPLM of trying to "torpedo the Sirté negotiations" (Agence France-Presse, October 25, 2007). With the danger increasing of renewed north-south violence, commanders from Darfur's rebel Justice and Equality Movement (JEM) have been meeting with southern military officials to create a united front against Khartoum.

Chinese oil facilities in Kordofan have recently come under attack from Darfur rebels who demand China and other foreign countries abandon their operation there until a peace agreement has been signed. China may have something of a conflict of interest in their deployment; China remains the largest arms supplier for the Khartoum government.

• No connection to the ICC: The UN says the peacekeeping mission "is distinct" from the enforcement of International Criminal Court indictments of war criminals in Darfur. Individuals under indictment will continue to operate in Darfur as they please.

• National peace talks for an international conflict: The conflict has become multinational (following the traditional political geography of the region), drawing in Chad and the Central African Republic. There are nearly 200,000 displaced persons on the Chadian side of the border with Darfur, enmeshed in a web of violence fuelled by a seemingly inexhaustible supply of weapons. The success of peace talks limited to Darfur is unlikely.

UN projections now suggest UNAMID's full deployment will not happen until mid-2008. Even this may be optimistic; in the AU's ongoing peacekeeping mission in Somalia, many of the pledged units failed to appear, pleading lack of transport among other reasons. Only the Ugandans actually deployed, though they were forced to pay costs that should have been covered by the AU. Banditry (including attacks on humanitarian convoys) will continue even through a ceasefire. Any such attack could easily provide an excuse to resume hostilities. With 16 active rebel factions there is every chance of a ceasefire violation.

The Darfur conflict shows every sign of intensifying with little chance of an effective ceasefire any time soon. It is time for UNAMID's planners to return to the drafting table and create a capable international force before it is too late.

Originally published in *Terrorism Monitor*: Volume 5, Issue 21 on November 8, 2007.

Darfur's JEM Rebels Bring the War to Khartoum
By Andrew McGregor

Last weekend's daring raid on greater Khartoum by Darfur's rebel Justice and Equality Movement (JEM) has shaken the regime and effectively disrupted the already morbid peace process in West Sudan. Though often referred to as a Darfur rebel group, JEM in fact has a national agenda, much like John Garang's Sudanese Peoples' Liberation Army (SPLA), which always maintained it was a movement of national liberation rather than a southern separatist group. Until 2006, JEM was also involved militarily in the revolt of the Beja and Rashaida Arabs of Eastern Sudan against Khartoum.

The Zaghawa tribe that straddles Darfur and Chad dominates the JEM leadership, marking a major challenge to traditional Arab superiority in Sudan (*Terrorism Monitor*, March 7, 2008). While some of the leaders of Darfur's badly-divided rebel groups have fought the rebellion from the cafés of Paris, JEM leader Khalil Ibrahim has remained at the front, forging a disparate group of refugees, farmers and ex-military men into the strongest military force in Darfur and the greatest threat to the Sudanese regime.

Greater Khartoum consists of the capital, Khartoum, the city of Omdurman on the western side of the White Nile, and the industrial suburb of Khartoum North on the north side of the Blue Nile. Khartoum itself is protected by broad rivers to the west and north, making assaults from these directions extremely difficult. Despite decades of warfare in Sudan's provinces, Khartoum has not experienced any fighting in its streets since 1976, when Libyan-trained Umma Party rebels—also from West Sudan—fought running gun-battles in a failed attempt to overthrow the military government.

Khartoum has increasingly become an island of prosperity surrounded by a vast and impoverished hinterland that now calls for an equitable distribution of the national wealth.

The once dusty and decaying Sudanese capital has undergone an astonishing transformation in recent years due to growing oil revenues and massive investment from the Gulf, Malaysia and China. Khartoum has increasingly become an island of prosperity surrounded by a vast and impoverished hinterland that now calls for an equitable distribution of the national wealth.

Across the Desert to Khartoum

On May 8, 2008 the Sudanese Armed Forces (SAF) reported they had learned of "preparations made by rebel Khalil Ibrahim to conduct a sabotage attempt and a publicity stunt through infiltrating the capital and other towns" as well as noting that "groups riding vehicles" were headed east from the Chadian border (Sudan Tribune, May 8, 2008). A JEM commander reported that the column consisted of 400 vehicles and took three days to reach Khartoum (Agence France-Presse, May 11, 2008). Notably absent from the attack were forces from the Sudan Liberation Army—Unity (SLA-Unity), another Darfur rebel group that has operated in a military alliance with JEM for the past two years.

A government spokesman claimed that the armed forces met the rebel column in Kordofan, at a point 75 miles west of the capital, where a portion of the rebel force made a run for Omdurman after most of the column had been stopped by a government attack.

JEM claims to have hit the Nile north of Omdurman, seizing and looting the Wadi Saidna Air Force base, 10 miles north of Khartoum. This claim has not been verified, but eyewitnesses reported seeing an attack on the base (Sudan Tribune, May 11, 2008).

On Friday night, May 9, Khartoum's embassies received calls from the government warning them of a possible rebel attack on Khartoum (Agence France-Presse, May 10, 2008). Despite the incoming reports of a JEM column heading east across the desert, Sudanese President Omar al-Bashir continued performing the umrah (the minor pilgrimage) in the holy cities of Saudi Arabia. With Bashir in Saudi Arabia, the acting president was First Vice President Salva Kiir Mayadrit of the SPLA, who maintains he was in constant contact with al-Bashir until his return late on May 10.

Assault on the Suburbs

On May 10, some 150 armored pick-up trucks reached the outskirts of Omdurman. With helicopters in the air, security personnel poured into the streets, setting up checkpoints and securing potential targets. The bridges linking Omdurman to Khartoum across the White Nile were blocked.

Despite bold claims from JEM spokesmen that their forces were "everywhere in the capital," it appears that few, if any, of the rebels managed to penetrate much farther than the suburbs of northern Omdurman, where their burning pick-up trucks could be seen after the battle. Claims by rebel commanders that their troops had seized the bridges and entered Khartoum appear to have been wishful thinking or an attempt to unnerve the regime.

Throughout the attack, media-savvy JEM field commanders were on the phone to major international media sources, giving progress reports with the sound of gunfire and explosions in the background. A commander called Abu Zumam claimed his forces had entered Omdurman and were preparing to seize the National State Radio building (Radio Omdurman). Another JEM commander named Sulayman Sandal was also in constant contact with media. As the government counter-attacks began to drive JEM fighters from the city, Commander Sulayman insisted: "This was just practice. We promise to hit Khartoum one more time unless the [Darfur] issue is resolved" (The Associated Press, May 11, 2008). The commander claimed JEM forces had initially seized all of Omdurman, but were beaten off due to the inexperience of JEM troops in urban warfare (Agence France-Presse, May 11, 2008).

Sudan's official news agency SUNA claimed that JEM's "military commander" Jamal

Hassan Jelaladdin was killed on the outskirts of Khartoum in the morning of May 11. SUNA also reported the deaths of Muhammad Saleh Garbo and Muhammad Nur al-Din, described as the leader of the attack and the JEM intelligence chief, respectively (SUNA, May 11, 2008). JEM reported that no one by these names were in the rebel ranks, but claimed Jamal Hassan had been captured and summarily executed after his vehicle broke down (Sudan Tribune, May 12, 2008).

What Were the Targets?

JEM spokesman Ahmad Hussein Adam declared that Wadi Saidna air force base was targeted because it was "the base from where all Sudanese military planes go to Darfur" (Agence France-Presse, May 10, 2008). Heavy civilian losses were reported in Northern Darfur in the weeks preceding the raid on the capital. JEM recently accused Khartoum of recruiting 250 Iraqi pilots to carry out bombing missions in Darfur following combat losses and a reluctance by Sudanese pilots to continue bombing civilian targets (Sudanjem.com, May 4, 2008).

State radio facilities head the list of desirable targets on any coup-leader's target list—in this case Radio Omdurman was no exception. JEM may have anticipated that the residents of Khartoum were only awaiting a sign to rise up against the government, but there appeared to be no verifiable instances of tri-city residents offering material support to the rebels. With residents confined indoors by a curfew, parts of the city were remarkably quiet.

When the bridges across the Nile were secured by Sudanese security forces it became impossible to complete JEM's objectives. There does not appear to have been any backup plan for this fairly predictable circumstance. When asked by the BBC how he plans to deal with this problem in his promised return to the capital, Khalil Ibrahim responded; "I am not empty handed. I took a lot of things from Khartoum—a lot of vehicles, ammunition and money" (BBC, May 12, 2008). There are reports that a large quantity of weapons and ammunition were seized at the Wadi Saidna air base.

According to VP Salva Kiir, the rebel targets in the capital included Radio Omdurman, the military headquarters and the presidential palace beside the Blue Nile (Sudan Tribune, May 13, 2008).

Mopping Up

When the JEM attack crested in the suburbs of Omdurman many fighters found themselves without any means of escaping the city. Some surrendered while others were reported to have doffed their camouflage gear in favor of civilian clothing. Gunfire continued throughout the weekend as security forces tried to flush out hidden JEM fighters. Reports of gunfire in the center of Khartoum were apparently the result of edgy security men firing on a group of civilians hiding in a building (BBC, May 12, 2008). When the fighting had stopped, government forces stated 400 rebels and 100 security men had been killed.

Security forces reported seizing 50 rebel pick-up trucks while battered prisoners were repeatedly displayed on state television. With continuing reports that Khalil Ibrahim had gone into hiding in Omdurman after being injured when his truck was hit by gunfire, Sudanese state television broadcast his photo for the first time, encouraging viewers to report any sightings. A reward of $125,000 for information leading to the JEM leader's capture was later doubled to $250,000.

Despite the lack of any public support in Khartoum for the rebels, security forces quickly decided that the attack must have relied on a fifth column within the city. This prompted mass arrests of Darfuris in the capital, especially those of the Zaghawa tribe (Sudan Human Rights Organization statement, Cairo, May 13). Some Darfur groups reported the arrest and beatings of thousands of Darfuri laborers working in the capital (Al Jazeera, May 13, 2008). Other reports claim dozens of Zaghawa in the city have been executed (Sudan Tribune, May 13, 2008). A JEM spokesman described the arrests as "ethnic cleansing" (Sudan Tribune, May 10, 2008).

Sudan's leading Islamist, Hassan al-Turabi, was detained for questioning by security forces due to his former association with JEM (see Terrorism Monitor, June 17, 2005; July 1, 2005). Khalil Ibrahim was once described as a follower of the controversial al-Turabi, but there appear to be few, if any, ties remaining between the two. Turabi and several other members of his Popular Congress Party (PCP) were quickly released after questioning.

The Role of the Army and Security Forces

The majority of the rank-and-file in Sudan's army comes from the African tribes of Darfur and Kordofan. They are typically led by Arab officers from the Northern Province of Sudan. Most of the fighting in the capital appears to have been done by government security services and police rather than the military. VP Salva Kiir notes that the army did not intervene until it became clear the rebels had been repulsed (Sudan Tribune, May 13, 2008). Some mid-level army commanders are reported to have been arrested after the attack.

Reacting to public criticism of the military's failure to stop the assault long before it reached Khartoum, a presidential adviser claimed that the military had intentionally drawn the rebels "into a trap" (Sudan Tribune, May 13, 2008). Sudanese Defense Minister Abdel-Rahim Muhammad Hussein was roundly condemned by members of parliament who called for an inquiry as to how JEM forces could reach the capital (Al-Sharq al-Awsat, May 14, 2008; Sudan Tribune, May 14, 2008). While some MPs called for his resignation, the Defense Minister blamed the U.S. embargo for the lack of surveillance and reconnaissance aircraft.

After returning to Darfur, Khalil Ibrahim thanked the neutrality of the Sudanese army, which "welcomed him" (Sudan Tribune, May 13, 2008). This statement alone will create chaos in the security structure as the government seeks out real, potential and imagined collaborators.

Reaction of the SPLA

JEM frequently states its commitment to the 2005 Comprehensive Peace Agreement (CPA) signed by the southern Sudanese Peoples' Liberation Army (SPLA) and the ruling National Congress Party (NCP). At the same time, it is vehemently opposed to the idea of southern separation—the CPA calls for a referendum on southern separation in 2011, a position that has interfered with JEM efforts to forge stronger ties with the SPLA. Regarding any attempt to overthrow the government as interference in implementing the CPA, the SPLA's military commanders offered Khartoum the use of SPLA troops still under VP Salva Kiir's command.

Proxy War with Chad?

In March 2007, N'Djamena and Khartoum signed yet another in a series of worthless peace agreements after an attack by Sudanese-supported rebels nearly deposed the Zaghawa-based government of President Idriss Déby. Khartoum has accused Chadian forces of mounting a diversionary attack on the SAF garrison at Kashkash along the Chad/Sudan border "meant to support the attempt of sabotage of the rebel Khalil Ibrahim" (Sudan Tribune, May 10, 2008). The SAF claimed to have successfully repulsed the Chadian troops, forcing them to pull back across the border.

On his return from pilgrimage, Bashir severed relations with Chad and laid the blame for the raid on the "outlaw regime" in N'Djamena: "These forces come from Chad who trained them ... we hold the Chadian regime fully responsible for what happened." Perhaps unwilling to admit the military potential of the Darfur rebels, Bashir claimed: "These forces are Chadian forces originally, they moved from there led by Khalil Ibrahim who is an agent of the Chadian regime. It is a Chadian attack" (The Associated Press, May 11, 2008). The SAF claimed that most of the prisoners were Chadian nationals. A Chadian government spokesman quickly denied any official involvement in the attack (Agence France-Presse, May 10, 2008).

Chadian officials reported that uniformed Sudanese security forces broke into all the offices of the Chadian embassy in Khartoum, seizing documents and computers (Sudan Tribune, May 11, 2008). The Sudanese Foreign Ministry claimed: "We have evidence there was communication between [the rebels and] the government of Chad and the embassy of Chad in Khartoum" (Agence France-Presse, May 11, 2008).

China Stays Aloof

Though China has natural concerns over the effect of a regime change in a country that is now one of its largest foreign oil suppliers, the reaction from Beijing was supportive but muted. JEM has made clear its opposition to China's oil operations in Sudan, attacking Chinese oil facilities in Kordofan (Terrorism Focus, September 11, 2007). JEM is also angered by the Chinese supply of arms and warplanes to the Khartoum regime. China was one of the few non-African countries approved by Khartoum for participation in UNAMID, contributing a group of military engineers to the Darfur peacekeeping efforts. In a Foreign Ministry statement, China condemned the attacks but hoped "the Darfur armed rebel group could join in the political process as soon as possible and resume negotiation with the Sudanese government, for the early signing of a comprehensive peace agreement, to realize peace, stability and development in Darfur" (Xinhua, May 11, 2008).

What Next for the Regime? For JEM?

Khartoum declared negotiations with JEM to be at an end on May 14, but this will make little difference since JEM was already not part of the ongoing negotiations with other Darfur rebel groups. Presidential adviser Mustafa Osman Ismail promised government retaliation instead: "From this day we will never deal with this movement again other than in the way they have just dealt with us" (Xinhua, May 11, 2008). President Bashir has also claimed that Israel funded the assault, calling Khalil Ibrahim "an agent ... who sold himself to the devil and to Zionism" (The Associated Press, May 14, 2008). The government is demanding that JEM be declared an international terrorist organization by the United States and the UN (Radio Omdurman, May 13, 2008).

The raid on Khartoum was a reminder to the Northern Arab regime that it might all come crashing down one day and that their continued wealth and power is by no means guaranteed. After the raid, Khalil Ibrahim provided this justification for the attack: "The Sudanese government killed 600,000 people in Darfur and they are living at peace in Khartoum" (Al Jazeera, May 13, 2008). Whether the raid results in greater conciliation efforts and distribution of wealth to the provinces is yet to be seen. Past experience suggests that the government's response will be increased violence and repression. Large-scale retaliation against Chad is virtually inevitable. In the meantime Khartoum may have to deal with a sudden reluctance on the part of international investors to put their money into an uncertain situation.

Khartoum will undoubtedly implement measures to prevent a repeat of the attack, but JEM has also learned several important lessons in this operation. It is difficult to believe that JEM intended to hold and seize the city at this time, but the operation may lay the groundwork for a larger effort in the future. More plausible is Khalil Ibrahim's claim that he intends to exhaust and divide the Sudanese military by spreading the war far beyond Darfur (The Associated Press, May 13, 2008). According to the JEM leader, "This is just the start of a process and the end is the termination of this regime" (BBC, May 12, 2008).

Originally published in *Terrorism Monitor*: Volume 6, Issue 10 on May 15, 2008.

Oil and Jihad in Central Africa: The Rise and Fall of Uganda's ADF
By Andrew McGregor

In the midst of all the horrors generated in Central Africa by the Rwandan genocide of 1994 and the collapse of Zaire in 1997, a little known group of Islamist radicals has done its own part to contribute to the suffering. Based since 1996 in Bundibugyo, an impoverished and underdeveloped district in western Uganda, the Alliance of Democratic Forces (ADF) has killed thousands in its pursuit of an Islamic state in Uganda. Strangely enough, few of its rank and file are Muslims (or even Ugandans), and its leader is a convert from Catholicism. The movement was believed destroyed by the Ugandan Popular Defense Forces 1999 campaign, but seems to have enjoyed a revival after the discovery of oil in Bundibugyo. Now, however, there is word that the ADF is seeking peace talks with Uganda after a series of setbacks to enable the return of some 200 ADF fighters from the forests of the Congo to Uganda (*The Monitor* [Kampala], December 4, 2007).

The Allied Democratic Forces

Bundibugyo is a small district at the foot of the Rwenzori Mountain range along the border with the Democratic Republic of the Congo (DRC). It has a natural connection to the vast Ituri Forest, which has become a home for various regional insurgent groups. This mountainous area is the last region of Uganda to go without electricity and is notorious for the poor quality of its roads. Bundibugyo is currently enduring a bout of Ebola Fever that has killed 35 people (New Vision [Kampala], December 11, 2007). The ADF did not begin here, however, but started rather in the urban Muslim areas of Kampala and the towns of central Uganda.

The ADF has its origins in the evangelistic Tabliqi Jamaat movement of Uganda, a local offshoot of the larger Indian-Pakistani Tabliq movement founded in the 1920s. Tabliq means "to deliver (the message of Islam)." Muslims are a minority in mostly Christian Uganda, representing about 15 percent of the population. While the Indian-Pakistani Tabliq movement is usually non-political, the Ugandan Tabliqis claimed political persecution after they opposed the appointment of a new national mufti. Following a period of street-clashes and arrests in 1991, many in the Tabliq movement left for the wilds of the Rwenzori mountains where they were joined by radicalized prisoners released in 1993. The absence of Muslims in the higher ranks of President Yoweri Museveni's administration also contributed to the growing militancy of the Tabliq movement. According to the Ugandan government, the Tabliqis received funds and encouragement from the Sudanese embassy in Kampala, leading to the severing of diplomatic ties in 1995 (Islamism and its Enemies in the Horn of Africa, 2004).

The first major strike by the ADF took place in 1996, when the movement's fighters attacked Ugandan troops in Kasese District along the border with the Congo. At first most of the fighters had little more than machetes, but arms began to flow to the movement from external sources, most likely the Sudan or the DRC government of Laurent-Desire Kabila. During the 1990s, ADF militants carried out 43 bombings in Kampala and Jinja. Never well liked within Uganda, the ADF leaders found it simpler to recruit new fighters from the DRC by offering promises of money and education. Many children were seized on both sides of the border and incorporated into the ranks.

Once in western Uganda, the ADF formed an alliance with the National Army for the Liberation of Uganda (NALU), a rebel group that had become fairly inactive. NALU was formed in 1988 and split from the Rwenzori Movement in 1991 [1]. NALU tactics typically involved raids on small villages and attacks on civilians, including a 1998 suicide bombing on a Kampala bus that killed 30 people. Eventually the ADF was also joined by remnants of the Rwenzori separatist movement and a number of Idi Amin loyalists who were living in southern Sudan.

Kampala's campaign against the ADF was slow to develop but finally bore fruit in 1999. Borders were secured, roads brought under control, UPDF outposts placed on the high ground of the mountains, and self-defense units organized in the villages (IRIN, December 8, 1999). Despite this, the already impoverished Bundibugyo District was still forced to cope with over 100,000 displaced people.

ADF leader Jamil Mukulu was an associate of Osama bin Laden during the latter's stay in Sudan in the 1990s, before launching his first attack in Uganda in 1996. Mukulu is believed to have received training from al-Qaeda both in Sudan and Afghanistan (*The Monitor*, December 1, 2007). The ADF leader remains a shadowy figure, usually heard only on the cassette tapes the ADF distributes. Mukulu urges violence against non-Muslims and Muslims who fail to carry out jihad, including a heavy dose of invective against various international leaders: "Let curses be to Bush, Blair, the president of France—and more curses go to Museveni and all those fighting Islam." According to Lieutenant-Colonel James Mugira, Uganda's acting chief of military intelligence, "We think [Mukulu] will become the next bin Laden of Africa" (IWPR, June 6, 2005).

The ADF Attempts to Join the Global Jihad

On December 5, 2001 the ADF was added to the U.S. list of designated terrorist organizations. In the chaos that followed the entry of U.S. troops into Baghdad in 2003, reporters were able to obtain a cache of papers from the bombed-out ruins of Iraq's intelligence headquarters. Among the documents were a series of letters from the ADF's "chief of diplomacy," Bekkah Abdul Nasser, to Fallah Hassan al-Rubdie, the Iraqi chargé d'affaires in Nairobi. These 10-15 pages of English-language letters (translated into Arabic by the Mukhabarat) seek Iraqi financing to set up an African mujahideen front: "We in the ADF forces are ready to run the African mujahideen headquarters. We have already started and we are on the ground, operational." Another letter suggested the creation of an "international mujahideen team whose special mission will be to smuggle arms on a global scale to holy warriors fighting against U.S., British, and Israeli influences in Africa, the Middle East, and the Far East" (*Christian Science Monitor*, April

18, 2003; *Daily Telegraph*, April 17, 2003). There was no indication from the files that Iraqi funds were ever sent, or that the correspondence was even encouraged.

During a visit to Washington in 2004, Ugandan Defense Minister Amama Mbabazi emphasized that "Uganda's domestic terrorist groups have been subsidized and trained by al-Qaeda" (Afrol News, September 30, 2004). Uganda has been a beneficiary of the $100 million U.S.-financed East Africa Counterterrorism Initiative (U.S. Department of State, April 1, 2004).

By 2005, Ugandan officials were warning the ADF had regrouped and were receiving funding and training from other extremist groups. According to Captain Joseph Kamusiime, operations chief for the Ugandan anti-terrorism unit, the ADF had supporters in Pakistan, Afghanistan and Saudi Arabia, but its chief backer was Sudanese Islamist Hassan al-Turabi, leader of the National Islamic Front. In the early days after its creation in 1996, the ADF was reported to have received training at a camp run by Sudanese intelligence in Juba (Islamism and its Enemies in the Horn of Africa, 2004). By 2005 Ugandan intelligence estimated 650-1,000 ADF fighters to be in the Congolese bush, but other sources claimed many of these were only camp-followers.

ADF leader Jamil Mukulu was an associate of Osama bin Laden during the latter's stay in Sudan in the 1990s, before launching his first attack in Uganda in 1996. Mukulu is believed to have received training from al-Qaeda both in Sudan and Afghanistan.

Kamusiime described the ADF as part of a larger Islamist project: "The ADF ... is motivated by Islamic fundamentalists—more in line with al-Qaeda ideology like other African terrorist organizations with global reach, such as the Armed Islamic Group of Algeria, Egypt's Muslim Brotherhood, and Somalia's Al-Ittihad al-Islamiya" (IWPR, June 6, 2005).

A Struggle Going Nowhere?

The 2005 signing of the Comprehensive Peace Agreement between the Khartoum government and the rebel Sudanese Peoples' Liberation Movement/Army (SPLM/A) in southern Sudan ended the usefulness of the ADF and Lord's Resistance Army (LRA) to Khartoum as counter-measures against Ugandan support for the SPLM/A. The last major attack by the ADF occurred in March 2007, when 60 rebels crossed from the Congo into Bundibugyo to strike the new oil facilities. At least 45 guerrillas, including senior commander Bosco Isiko, were killed in a battle with the UPDF along the Sempaya River in the Semliki game reserve on March 27 (Radio Uganda, April 3, 2007; *The Monitor*, November 20, 2007). In the three months between April and June of 2007, nine ADF commanders were killed by the UPDF, effectively destroying the group's command structure (New Vision, June 19, 2007).

Seven captured ADF rebels were granted amnesty in November 2007 after undergoing "psycho-social counseling" by the Ugandan Red Cross and officers of the UPDF (*The Monitor*, November 21, 2007). Four Ugandans who aided the organization from the

Ugandan side of the border with the Congo were not so lucky—they have been charged with treason (New Vision, October 12, 2007).

Ugandan security services claim to have interrupted a plot to bomb last month's Commonwealth summit in Kampala. The plan, allegedly devised by ADF leader Jamil Mukulu, involved the use of state television vans to deliver bombs through security lines (*The Monitor*, December 1, 2007). Intended targets included the queen and about 45 other international leaders in attendance. Extensive searches of the vans by the Presidential Guards Brigade turned up nothing, but the security services claimed a success.

Conclusion

MONUC (Mission de l'ONU en RD Congo) has confirmed that the ADF has approached the UN mission to facilitate peace talks with Kampala. The initiative seems to have been spurred by a rift between Jamil Mukulu and his deputy Abdallah Kabanda (Monitor, December 4, 2007). MONUC is already demobilizing and resettling ADF rebels in the eastern Congo before a final operation to flush out remaining rebels in the region (New Vision, December 2, 2007). In a new complication for the Ugandans, Congolese dissidents are now crossing into Uganda to take refuge there from DRC/MONUC sweeps.

There is no question that some of the Ugandan estimates of ADF strength were exaggerated and the description of Jamil Mukulu by Ugandan intelligence as "the next bin Laden" seems calculated to draw U.S. military and financial assistance. Nevertheless, the ADF has been an integral part of a wave of violence that has denied security and development to millions of Africans in the Congolese-Ugandan-Rwandan border region. The collapse of this would-be international jihadi movement would be a welcome development in returning peace and security to this beleaguered part of Africa.

Originally published in *Terrorism Monitor*: Volume 5, Issue 24 on December 20, 2007.

Notes

1. The Bakonjo-Baamba people of Rwenzori made an abortive attempt at independence for the Rwenzori region in 1962. While the attempt failed, a small separatist movement lived on in the bush.

Part IV

South Asia

Gulbuddin Hekmatyar: From Holy Warrior to Wanted Terrorist
By Omid Marzban

During the last week of August 2006, officials in the northern Afghan province of Kapisa announced the arrest of five accused terrorists related to Gulbuddin Hekmatyar, the former leader of Hezb-e-Islami Afghanistan (the Islamic Party of Afghanistan). Hekmatyar, a key figure in the Afghan jihad against the Soviet invasion in the 1980s, is now believed to be at his most powerful state since the U.S.-led invasion in 2001. A high-ranking provincial official from the northern Parwan province, who declined to be named, told The Jamestown Foundation that the most recent government investigation shows that Hekmatyar is leading the insurgency in the northern and eastern parts of Afghanistan, while Mullah Omar and his al-Qaeda ally, Osama bin Laden, operate in the south and the west. It is believed that these three leaders form a triangle that has been labeled the "Triangle of Terror." Since Hekmatyar forms one of these three points, it is important to understand his background.

Hekmatyar's Background

Born in 1948 in Imam Saheb district of northern Kunduz province, Gulbuddin Hekmatyar is a Kharoty Pashtun who comes from the Ghilzai confederation. His father, Ghulam Qader, who migrated to Kunduz, is originally from the central Ghazni province. Hekmatyar has two wives (both Afghans from his tribe), six daughters and three sons. According to Hamayon Jarir, Hekmatyar's son in-law, one of his wives lives in Iran and the other lives in Shamshatoo refugee camp in Peshawar together with their sons and daughters [1]. After graduating from Sher Khan high school in Kunduz in 1968, Hekmatyar joined the Mahtab Qala military school in Kabul. Due to his political activities, however, he was expelled from the school two years later. He speaks Dari (Farsi), Pashto, English, Urdu and Arabic.

A high-ranking provincial official from the northern Parwan province, who declined to be named, told The Jamestown Foundation that the most recent government investigation shows that Hekmatyar is leading the insurgency in the northern and eastern parts of Afghanistan, while Mullah Omar and his al-Qaeda ally, Osama bin Laden, operate in the south and the west.

From 1970 to 1972, Hekmatyar attended the engineering department at Kabul University, but after being implicated in the murder of Saydal Sukhandan from the pro-China Shola-e-Jawedan Movement, he was jailed by the government of King Zahir Shah. As a high school student, Hekmatyar was a member of the communist People's Democratic Party of Afghanistan (PDPA) for four years. As a result of studying engineering at Kabul University, Hekmatyar's communist ideology was also affected by an extremist version of Islam, and he joined the Muslim Youths Movement (Nahzat-e-Jawanane Musalman). While at Kabul University, Hekmatyar's radicalism began to show its face: he was notorious for spraying acid on the university's female students [2].

Hekmatyar's followers addressed him as Engineer Hekmatyar even though he was unable to complete his degree as a result of spending almost two years in prison. In 1974, when King Zahir Shah's government was overthrown by the king's cousin, Daoud Khan, in a military coup, Hekmatyar was freed from prison. He then left the country and took refuge in Pakistan's bordering city of Peshawar together with Burhanuddin Rabbani, Qazi Muhammad Amin Waqad and other jihadi leaders. The radical leaders continued to work as members of the Muslim Youths Movement; they later, however, divided into various factions and parties.

Apparently, a failed uprising by jihadi leader Ahmad Shah Masoud of the Jamiat-e-Islami party in the Panjshir Valley against Daoud's regime in 1975 contributed to a split between Hekmatyar and Rabbani. It was, however, more Hekmatyar's desire for control that led to the disagreement between the two leaders. Waheed Mujda, who was a former member of Hezb-e-Islami, told The Jamestown Foundation that the main cause of Hekmatyar's clash with Rabbani was his idea of defeating the pro-Russian regime militarily, while Rabbani wanted to reach this goal politically. Strongly backed by the Pakistani government of Prime Minister Zulfiqar Ali Bhutto, Hekmatyar established Hezb-e-Islami Afghanistan in 1976. Later in 1979, another clash between Hekmatyar and jihadi leader Mawlawi Khalis evenly divided Hezb-e-Islami into two factions. Khalis established another faction called Hezb-e-Islami's Khalis faction.

Hekmatyar received most of the funding provided by Saudi Arabia, the United States and Pakistan to support the Afghan jihad against the Soviets; this made him the most well know and also the most controversial of the Pakistan-based mujahideen leaders. It was Hekmatyar who received anti-aircraft Stinger missiles from the U.S. government through Pakistan's Inter-Services Intelligence (ISI). "Hekmatyar's commanders in eastern Afghanistan were those who fired the first Stinger anti-aircraft missiles at Soviet warplanes," explained Mujda [3]. Indeed, it was Hezb-e-Islami Commander Abdul Ghaffar who hit the first Soviet helicopter gunship with an anti-aircraft Stinger missile in eastern Nangarhar province in September 1986 [4].

"Hekmatyar was indeed the key character in collecting money from anti-Soviet factions and countries to make the war continue, but since he was so selfish and hungry for power most of the jihadi leaders did not like him, though they needed him," said Mujda. Mujda quoted Mawlawi Khalis as saying "I pray to god to let Hekmatyar live among us in Pakistan, but I don't want him with us in Afghanistan because he would not let anyone, other than himself, become the country's leader." Hekmatyar was known as an anti-American figure among the Afghan jihadi leaders; ironically, the United States, through the ISI, was his biggest financial and military supporter. Hekmatyar most clearly expressed his anti-American credentials when he refused to shake hands with President Ronald Reagan in 1985 under the roof of the White House. Hekmatyar came under great pressure from Pakistani leaders to meet with Reagan, but his argument was that being seen shaking hands with the U.S. president would strengthen the Soviet claim that the war was not a jihad and was instead a U.S.-led campaign to win the Cold War.

Hekmatyar's power increased during the 1979-1988 war against the Soviet invasion of Afghanistan. His active Hezb-e-Islami intelligence service made him a hero among other fighters because his agents were able to penetrate the Afghan government; this allowed Hekmatyar to neutralize government initiatives. It was Hezb-e-Islami's intelligence service that gave Hekmatyar the power to resist against the Soviet's KGB and the Afghan government's security service, KHAD (Khedamat-e Etelea'at-e Dawlati).

Hekmatyar's power later became a great threat to Dr. Mohammad Najibullah, who was elected as the president of Afghanistan in November 1986. Feeling the threat, Najibullah, the former chief of KHAD, invited Hekmatyar to join the government, but Hekmatyar rejected Najibullah's request even though Najibullah agreed to give him 95 percent control of the regime. The withdrawal of the last Soviet soldier from Afghanistan on February 15, 1989, based on a UN resolution, provided more opportunity for Hekmatyar and his allied jihadi leaders to expand the insurgency to the country's bigger cities. In 1992, Najibullah's regime was overthrown and Sebghatullah Mujadeddi, the leader of the Afghan National Liberation Front, took power based on an agreement with the mujahideen forces in Pakistan. Mujaddedi transferred power to Burhanuddin Rabbani, the leader of Jameat-e-Islami Afghanistan, after a two months term.

Hekmatyar's followers addressed him as Engineer Hekmatyar even though he was unable to complete his degree as a result of spending almost two years in prison.

It was during Rabbani's rule when the various jihadi parties and factions, including Hekmatyar's Hezb-e-Islami, began to fight for more power. Hekmatyar played a key role in provoking the multi-factional war in the country. In 1996, Hekmatyar joined President Rabbani and his defense minister, Ahmad Shah Masoud, and became the prime minister, but it was too late for him to be able to establish control over the country because Taliban fighters had already established control on the edges of Kabul. In September 1996, after being in power for three months, Hekmatyar sought exile in Iran and the Taliban took power in Kabul. After Hekmatyar warned his former ally Pakistan in 2001 not to support the U.S.-led war against the Taliban and al-Qaeda, and after his negative position toward the U.S.-backed Afghan government, Hekmatyar was expelled from Iran. Since then, Hekmatyar has been living in hideouts and has been targeted by U.S., Afghan and Pakistani security forces.

His appearance on Al Jazeera television in May, and his pledge to fight foreign troops in Afghanistan and Iraq "under the banner of al-Qaeda," once again inspired fears among those who know Hekmatyar well.

Hekmatyar's Effect on the Afghan Insurgency

Hekmatyar is not blinded by a radical Islamic vision. For him, Islam is more about politics than it is about religion. In fact, this makes him more dangerous than Taliban leader Mullah Omar, who has surrounded himself with illiterate religious leaders. Hekmatyar, on the other hand, is more adept at military and political strategy. Additionally, Hekmatyar has led wars throughout Afghan territory and is completely familiar with the country's diverse geography, culture and beliefs.

"Hekmatyar's ability of imposing his inspirations, especially on the youth, is unbelievable," says Qazi Muhammad Amin Waqad, a former member of Hezb-e-Islami's leadership council and Hekmatyar's former deputy. "During the past few years, Hekmatyar has found an absolutely new Hezb-e-Islami by absorbing new members—most of them youths—who may not even know me," added Waqad [5].

Every week, Hekmatyar's Tanweer Weekly publishes in Shamshatoo refugee camp in Peshawar together with Estiqamat, a pro-Taliban magazine. In the August 10 issue of Tanweer, Hekmatyar again pledged to fight foreign troops in Afghanistan "till the last drop of blood moves in his body"—an expression always heard in Hekmatyar's speeches. By controlling this publication, Hekmatyar is able to recruit a tremendous amount of followers who are willing to die in order to kill a foreign soldier. Meanwhile, Hekmatyar uses his military experience to defeat the enemy (coalition and Afghan government soldiers), which for him are no different than the former Soviet army. In fact, among the three top insurgent leaders, who are located on each angle of the Triangle of Terror, Hekmatyar is considered the most powerful and the most dangerous for the current stability situation in Afghanistan.

Originally published in *Terrorism Monitor*: Volume 4, Issue 18 on September 21, 2006.

Notes

1. Author interview with Hamayon Jarir, August 22, 2006, Kabul, Afghanistan.
2. Author interview with Waheed Mujda, a former member of Hezb-e-Islami's Political Relations Department, August 25, 2006, Kabul, Afghanistan.
3. Waheed Mujda, August 25, 2006.
4. Ishtiaq Ahmad, Gulbuddin Hekmatyar, an Afghan Trail from Jihad to Terrorism, Islamabad: 2004.
5. Author interview with Qazi Muhammad Amin Waqad, former member of Hezb-e-Islami, August 20, 2006, Kabul, Afghanistan.

Combating the Ideology of Suicide Terrorism in Afghanistan
By Waliullah Rahmani

Although there was no record of Afghan suicide attacks during the Soviet invasion of Afghanistan and the pursuant civil war, suicide attacks in the country have steadily increased since the fall of the Taliban. Since January 2006, more than 85 suicide attacks in Afghanistan have killed or injured 700 people (BBC Persian, October 13, 2006). Recently, on September 30, a suicide bomber blew himself up in an entryway to the Afghan Interior Ministry, killing more than 12 people and injuring 42 others (Radio Farda, September 30, 2006). Since the September 30, 2006 attack, Kabul has suffered from at least one suicide bombing per week. Statistics show that this year alone, Afghanistan was hit by more suicide attacks than in all past years combined. With the absence of a historical tradition of suicide attacks, important cultural and sociological questions must be addressed. For example, what has convinced Afghans to adopt suicide attacks as a military tactic? When was this tactic adopted? Were there outside influences or examples that influenced Afghans? Most importantly, can this ideology of suicide terrorism in Afghanistan be combated?

Suicide Attacks: Low-Cost and High Profile

After the fall of the Taliban, there was a large-scale campaign to bolster the support of the Afghan government through the strengthening of the Afghan army and the presence of coalition forces. Initially, this made ground operations for the Taliban difficult. In recent months, however, the Taliban insurgency has adapted and has changed tactics to fit the new situation on the ground. Kabul-based Afghan analyst Fahim Dashti, the editor of Kabul Weekly, argued that the current surge in suicide attacks marks a "change in tactics by the Taliban." He stated that "suicide attacks have been executed to decrease the Taliban's causalities" and "to create fear" among the Afghan people. Dashti explained that by "killing civilians and causing insecurity, the Taliban want to motivate people against the foreigners in Afghanistan" (Radio Dari, May 12, 2006). The rationale behind this strategy rests on the assumption that the population will blame the U.S.-led coalition and the Afghan government, rather than the Taliban, for the lack of security in the country.

Mukhtar Pidran, an Afghan political analyst, told The Jamestown Foundation on October 2, 2006 that the Taliban needed to have an instrument for imposing their religious influence on people who resisted their position. "Insurgents brought suicide terrorism to Afghanistan since it had worked in Iraq. Mostly here [Afghanistan], people are illiterate and know less about the complicated issues of Islam like jihad [amaliyat istishhadi] or martyrdom and can therefore be easily duped into adopting them. Through their use of suicide attacks, insurgents have reaped great benefits. For example, a suicide attack that claims the lives of many people can put a group in the headlines of the international media." Pidram added, "This tactic is working in Afghanistan and is giving the Taliban and other insurgents a high-profile identity."

The "Islamic Theory" Behind Suicide Attacks

Abdullah Azzam, one of the masterminds behind Hamas, theorized suicide attacks and spent part of the 1980s in Peshawar supporting Afghan mujahideen who were fighting against the Soviet invasion. He found religious and Islamic justifications for using suicide attacks against Israel and in the greater Muslim world (Payam-e-Mujahid, September 27, 2006). The first suicide attacker in Afghanistan was in 1992 when an Egyptian fighter for Gulbuddin Hekmatyar in Kunar killed Maulvi Jamil Rahman, a Salafi leader who was against Hekmatyar and headed the Jamaat al-Dawat w'al-Quran wa Sunna group (Payam-e-Mujahid, September 27, 2006). Suicide attacks, however, increased in Afghanistan after the September 9, 2001 assassination of Ahmad Shah Masoud, the leader of the Northern Alliance who fought against the Taliban. It is believed that al-Qaeda leader Osama bin Laden ordered the assassination. In the first years of Afghan President Hamid Karzai's government, the Taliban rarely used Afghans as suicide bombers. Yet, since the end of 2005, suicide bombings have been widely exercised by Taliban insurgents.

Al-Qaeda and their allies in the Taliban have published books for their followers in which they call upon men to join the Taliban, al-Qaeda and Hekmatyar's Hezb-e-Islami— groups that are based on Sharia law. A series of books in which they argue for the legitimacy of their actions is called "Zad al-Salam," or the "Muslim Provision." These books are used in military training centers and give justifications for every military tactic based on statements from the Quran, Hadith and the Sunna. The fourth series of the "Muslim Provision," titled "Al-Amaliyat al-Istishhadiya Fil Islam Wa Hukm Aawan al-Tawaghiet Wa Junudahum," specifically focuses on suicide attacks. The 158-page book bases the legitimacy of suicide attacks in Buruj, a chapter of the Quran, which focuses on jihad, bravery and the toleration of difficulties. The author references suicide attacks to a part of Buruj which states that Allah prefers those Muslims who fight against threats to their religion. The author additionally links encouragement for joining jihad to committing suicide attacks. For example, he quotes a story about one of the Prophet Muhammad's companions who asked the Prophet whether a person would be martyred if he was slain fighting infidels. The Prophet answered, "He would enter Paradise." In response, his companion went to the scene of the war and fought until his death (Payam-e-Mujahid, September 27, 2006).

The main question that remains is how to curb suicide attacks in Afghanistan, which has increasingly become both a tactical ideology and a popular fear that may change the face of traditional Afghan culture.

These factors make clear that there are religious reasons driving the attackers to sacrifice themselves for the "benefits of others." The majority of Afghans who have attended religious schools in Pakistan or in other Muslim countries are easily indoctrinated by the religious propaganda issued in these madrassas. Unfortunately, many begin their studies at a young age and therefore their knowledge of Islam is confined to the often misguided teachings they receive.

Sociological Landscape of Afghan Suicide Attacks

Motivating an Afghan to perform a suicide attack is no simple task. The leaders of the Taliban and Hezb-e-Islami motivate insurgents in the name of "Afghanistan's occupation" and the obligation to perform jihad (*Terrorism Focus*, October 10, 2006). The creation of a Sharia-based Islamic government is the motivation that extremists use to rally the support of insurgents. They argue that infidels dominate the secular government of Karzai and are not properly pursuing Sharia (Afghan National Security Intelligence Report, October 4, 2006). One such way that insurgent leaders recruit fighters is by saying that the West is decadent and completely opposed to the implementation of Sharia. One Afghan intelligence agent reported that in many madrassas for Afghan students, videotapes are played that show women in the West wearing bikinis while walking in public andgoing to nightclubs (Azadi Radio, October 4, 2006). Students at these seminaries are taught that Afghan girls employed by NGOs are sexual bait for the Western male employees. By pushing these views about the United States and European countries, extremist groups motivate Afghans to engage in conflict against the coalition. Many of the people in the seminaries want to see Sharia implemented, at least outwardly such as in the national dress code (Armans.info, September 29, 2006).

Yet the main unresolved question is that of the domestic makeup of the suicide attackers. Since its formation in late 2001, the Afghan government has yet to create active diplomatic channels with other Islamic countries. It is alleged in other Muslim societies that Afghanistan is an "occupied country" and therefore it is necessary for Muslims to engage in jihad against the "occupation." These sentiments encourage Muslims to fight Western and government forces in Afghanistan.

Afghan MP and political scholar Qayum Sajjadi, in an interview with The Jamestown Foundation on October 7, said that there should be a difference between a country under "occupation" and a country that has "invited" foreign forces to help maintain stability. "The foreign diplomacy system in Afghanistan acts passively," said Sajjadi. "The diplomats should contact the Islamic countries to define their position about what is taking place in Afghanistan. Afghan diplomats should contact the people, media and governments of Islamic countries to explain the conditions in Afghanistan in order to prevent fighters from these outside countries from joining the Taliban. Afghan diplomats should argue that their constitution is Islamic and that their law is Islamic. This will remove the perception held in other Muslim countries that Afghanistan is a country under occupation." Unfortunately, Afghan elites and moderate clerics are not taking active roles in promoting the image of their country abroad. In Afghanistan's media and elite circles, for example, there is a lack of scientific discussion on the use of suicide tactics (Armans.info, September 29, 2006).

Conclusion

The main question that remains is how to curb suicide attacks in Afghanistan, which has increasingly become both a tactical ideology and a popular fear that may change the face of traditional Afghan culture. It is critical to propose methods for curbing suicide attacks so that they do not become culturally inured into Afghan culture.

The leaders of the Taliban and al-Qaeda are not experts in Islamic jurisprudence nor well-respected Islamic scholars, but rather a group that have the potential to resist even Islamic Sharia if it is necessitated by their political ambitions. Since Afghanistan was subjected to the rule of extremism for nearly the past three decades, it is very difficult to purify the Islamic jurisprudence from the extremists' ideology. Yet it is the essential need of Afghanistan to purify Islam of this ideology. The work of countering extremist ideology has been started in other Islamic countries by some scholars.

Aside from the purification of extremist Islamic ideology, the role of politics in the development of suicide terrorism in Afghanistan runs deep. The existence of madrassas or religious seminaries in Pakistan—a country that has used Islamism for its political objectives in Afghanistan and Kashmir—shows that a significant number of seminaries are used to indoctrinate and radicalize students. These seminaries are specifically operated for political objectives. The practical way to counter this is to open moderate seminaries in Afghanistan.

Another practical way to curb violence and suicide attacks is an active foreign policy that engages other Islamic countries in the Arab world. Good ties with Islamic governments will help connect people and will encourage them to share radio and television programs from their respective countries. This will also reduce the validity of the argument that Afghanistan is under occupation. Moreover, it is important to act upon a coherent strategy that introduces Afghanistan to the world as an Islamic and democratic country.

Finally, in domestic affairs, forming committees with the participation of real Islamic scholars is the only way to prevent Afghan citizens from joining extremist groups. Academic institutions, mosques and the media could be a great help in curbing suicide terrorism. Acting upon such a strategy, the Ministry of Haj and Awqaf could lead the mosques and clerics in the campaign against this violent ideology.

Originally published in *Terrorism Monitor*: Volume 4, Issue 21 on November 2, 2006.

Iranian Involvement in Afghanistan
By Muhamad Tahir

The Afghan media has published an increasing number of critical reports about Iran's secret contacts with insurgent groups in Afghanistan, specifically those groups fighting against the U.S. presence in the country. On September 5, 2006 for instance, the Pashto-language newspaper *Weesa* referred to unidentified local officials in Nimruz province who claimed that Tehran was financing and providing weaponry to Afghanistan's militant groups. In March 2006, the Afghan official news agency Bakhtar reported on the secret activities of Iranians, including officers belonging to the armed forces, in border towns inside Afghanistan. Bakhtar quoted a high-ranking Afghan border policeman in Herat province, General Mohammad Ayub Safi, saying that "in only the first quarter of this year [2006], more than 10 Iranian officials have been arrested in Herat who were allegedly involved in illegal activities." These developments show that Iran has been increasing its operations in Afghanistan in an effort to gain influence with the contending insurgent factions and to hasten the departure of U.S. troops from the country.

Tehran has a long history of close contact with militant groups in the region, especially with Shiite groups in central Afghanistan. According to Kabul-based analyst Ustad Faizullah Amini, who spoke to The Jamestown Foundation in December 2006, Iran has been against the Talibanization of Afghanistan, but the presence of U.S. troops at its doorsteps has changed the direction of its foreign policy. Now, Tehran is willing to cooperate with different groups to reach the shared goal of defeating the United States in Afghanistan. After the September 11 attacks, an unidentified official source in Tehran said that Iran's new policy in Afghanistan would be to play all available cards in its hand to defeat U.S. efforts there (Asia Times, February 14, 2002). According to Amini, this fear has led Iran to act fast, and cooperate with all anti-American forces in the region regardless of their religion and language. In addition to Amini, many other regional experts argue that the current escalation of violence in some parts of Afghanistan is a direct result of Tehran's new strategy.

Background of Iranian Involvement in Afghanistan

More than a decade ago, while mujahideen leaders were toppling the Moscow-backed Afghan leader Mohammad Najibullah, it was predicted that a strong Sunni fundamentalist regime in Kabul could come into conflict with Shiite Iran. This fear led Tehran to support groups such as the Shiite Hazara parties and the influential Tajik commander Ismail Khan in Herat province. When the Taliban finally gained control of Afghanistan, Iran referred to the development as a Sunni and U.S. plot to isolate Iran. The relationship between Kabul and Tehran took a more serious hit when Taliban forces killed seven Iranian diplomats who were serving in Mazar-e-Sharif in August 1998. This Taliban action led Tehran to announce its open support for all forces that would resist the Taliban and to increase its activities to bring anti-Taliban factions together. The most notable act by Tehran was to allow the influential Pashtun leader, Gulbuddin Hekmatyar, to be stationed in Iran.

Tehran gave thousands of Hazara leaders refuge, training and financial support to fight against the Taliban. Yet the involvement of the al-Qaeda network in the September 11 attacks and the impending U.S. invasion of Afghanistan led Iran to again re-shape its strategy in the region since it considered the U.S. presence in the region a much greater threat than the unorganized Taliban.

9/11 Changes Iranian Policy toward Afghanistan

Shortly before the 2001 invasion of Afghanistan, Tehran made some swift policy changes in the region, which were evidenced by comments said by the top political and religious leader in Iran, Ayatollah Khamenei. In his televised speech on September 26, Khamenei said, "The Islamic Republic of Iran will not offer any assistance to America and its alliance in their attacks [on Afghanistan]." He also accused the United States of seeking to establish itself in Central Asia—Afghanistan, Pakistan and the subcontinent—under the pretext of "establishing security."

Many regional experts argue that Tehran does not believe that a stable Afghanistan with a large, long-term U.S. troop presence is in its interests. Tehran worries that if both its neighbors, Afghanistan and Iraq, are stabilized, Iran will be sandwiched between two pro-U.S. governments. In such a situation, "If Iran has not been attacked, it will definitely be troubled by internal pressures, such as minorities, inspired by the developments in the neighborhood," said Dr. Mehmet Seyfettin, a regional analyst with the Ankara-based think-tank Center for Eurasian Strategic Studies, who was interviewed in December.

The difference between new and past Iranian policies is that now Iran is ready to cooperate and support any group, regardless of their religion and language, who can fight the U.S. presence in Afghanistan, according to Bahmen Karimi's column published recently in the local Afghan paper *Arman-e-Milli*. The columnist also argues that the escalation in fighting in the bordering provinces with Iran and in the Shiite populated central Afghan provinces is the direct result of the Iranian strategy. For instance, on October 2, 2006, *The Guardian* published an article stating that "military and diplomatic sources said they had received numerous reports of Iranians meeting tribal elders in Taliban-influenced areas, bringing offers of military or more often financial support for the fight against foreign forces." In addition, Afghan analyst Amini proposes that the armed groups who have been sidelined by the current central regime in Afghanistan create potential forces for any outsider such as Iran to harness and influence. He specifically points out some of the commanders of the former Northern Alliance, as well as Shiite forces in central Afghanistan, who feel ignored by the new administration. One of these is Abdul Rashid Dostum who, according to Aina TV on November 25, 2006, met with Iranian Ambassador to Afghanistan Reza Bahrami on November 24,

> *The difference between new and past Iranian policies is that now Iran is ready to cooperate and support any group, regardless of their religion and language, who can fight the U.S. presence in Afghanistan ...*

2006. The influence of Iran on the charismatic Tajik leader Ismail Khan is already widely known.

Multi-Layered Iranian Policy on Afghanistan

According to reports published in local Afghan newspapers, including Weesa, Iranian involvement is not limited to unofficial cooperation with militant forces, but in fact includes official efforts to influence the Afghan administration. Some regional experts argue that Iran is using the political tension between Afghanistan and Pakistan in its favor, leveraging the fact that Iran is the only route by which Afghanistan can maintain foreign trade. Afghanistan is becoming increasingly dependent on Iran for its transit trade route as a result of the tense Afghan-Pakistan relationship. Through this route, Afghanistan receives key imports such as electronic equipment, cars and spare parts— much of which originates in Japan. Food, clothing and other essential products are also supplied through Iran. This reality limits Washington's options to pressure Tehran since if Iran blocks its border, the Afghan economy could collapse.

In the meantime, the Iranian government is active in the financial sector as well. According to the Islamic Republic News Agency (IRNA), the chambers of commerce of the two countries have recently signed a number of documents, which are expected to make Iran a major player in the Afghan economy. Iran has become one of the largest donors in the reconstruction process in Afghanistan. An Iranian Foreign Ministry official puts the total amount of aid to Afghanistan since 2001 at about $600 million.

The Iranian media is also publishing provocative reports against the U.S. presence in Afghanistan, blaming Washington for not delivering what it promised to the Afghan people. The well-known Iranian newspaper Jamhur-e-Islami published an article on the fifth anniversary of the September 11 attacks questioning the legacy and intentions of the United States in Afghanistan: "The Afghan people do not see any improvement in their lives and welfare as it was promised to them. Moreover, they are forced to bow to the presence of foreigners on their land and suffer the shame of occupation. Now the Afghan people know that America's goal in attacking Afghanistan and occupying it was part of the global plan America pursues for domination of the Middle East."

Iran encourages students who have graduated in Iran to be more active in establishing religious schools in Afghanistan and to strengthen Afghan-Iran ties. The education attaché at the Iranian Embassy in Kabul was quoted by Weesa on November 6, 2006 saying that "Shiite students who have graduated from Iranian universities are the messengers of Iran in Afghanistan and they should play a more important role." The Iranian official called on the Afghan government to permit Iran to launch cable network offices that operate Iranian educational programs in order to curb U.S. cultural influence in Afghanistan. Iran has recently inaugurated its huge cultural center in Kabul, which works to promote Iranian culture and to spread official propaganda by organizing workshops and literary exchange programs. In opposition to these Iranian efforts, Western countries have done little in Afghanistan, which is a result of the extensive cultural, religious and linguistic differences. Iran has used this void to change the situation in Afghanistan in its own favor.

Conclusion

If the increasing violence—not only on the Afghan-Pak border, but also in the areas bordering Iran and in the central Shiite populated provinces—is taken into account, the view of the aforementioned Afghan analysts seems to carry value. Experts on the region believe that the insurgency in Afghanistan has many directions, one of which is leaning toward Tehran. Insurgent fighters in Afghanistan traditionally opposed to working with Iran may have also changed their policy in light of the mutual short-term interest of removing U.S. and Western influence from the country. Due to the strategic location of Iran and its importance to the Afghan economy, however, the Kabul administration has avoided speaking publicly about Iranian influence in Afghanistan, as they believe, as a result of political tension with Pakistan, Iran is Kabul's last significant open door to the world.

Origianlly published in *Terrorism Monitor*: Volume 4, Issue 21 on November 2, 2006.

Cheney Attack Reveals Taliban Suicide Bombing Patterns
By Brian Glyn Williams and Cathy Young

The information for this article came from a five-month study of suicide bombings from 2001 to 2007 in Afghanistan. No suicide bombing was listed in the study unless it was corroborated by numerous sources. Sources varied from coalition countries' press releases, open media, al-Qaeda/Taliban websites, U.S. military sources and Afghan news agencies. While the sample analysis of 158 attacks is not definitive, its overall findings are indicative of general Taliban targeting trends.

The recent suicide bombing attack on Bagram Air Base, which killed between 15-23 people during the visit of U.S. Vice President Dick Cheney, has highlighted the growing problem of suicide bombers in Afghanistan. While the United States has dismissed the Taliban's claims that they attacked Bagram in an effort to assassinate Cheney, the targeting of a U.S. base fits previous Taliban targeting patterns.

Prior to the Bagram incident, U.S. military and government sources routinely spoke of the "Iraqification" of the Afghan conflict. Recent statistics from U.S. and Afghan agencies seem to support this claim. While Afghanistan had 25 suicide bombings in 2005, in 2006 it experienced as many as 139 suicide attacks. Recent media images from Afghanistan of bombed buses, shattered markets and burnt out U.S. Humvees further support the notion that the carnage that has shredded the fabric of Iraqi society has come to the so-called "Forgotten War" in Afghanistan.

If taken at face value, these claims represent a disastrous, if unintended side effect of the invasion of Iraq and bode ill for the upcoming year. Yet despite the mounting evidence that the Iraqi invasion has destabilized Afghanistan via the sharing of Iraqi tactics with Afghan insurgents, the suicide bombing campaign in Afghanistan has its own specific dynamics. It is little noticed local characteristics that distinguish suicide bombing in Afghanistan from that in the Iraqi theater.

2007: Suicide Bombings ... or Suicide?

An analysis of the Taliban's 2007 suicide campaign makes some of these differences glaringly obvious. At first blush, this year's statistics seem to support the notion that suicide bombers are ramping up their attacks in an effort to cause as much Iraqi-style carnage as possible. While it is only seven weeks into the new year, there have already been 22 suicide bombings (or attempts) in Afghanistan. This seems to be a fulfillment of Mullah Hayat Khan's promise to use 2,000 suicide bombers to make 2007 "the bloodiest year" in Afghanistan (Al Jazeera, January 27, 2007). Yet a deeper analysis of the suicide bombing attacks carried out since January 1 reveals an altogether different picture.

Astoundingly, of the 22 attacks carried out this year, in 16 cases the only fatality has been the suicide bomber himself. In the 17th case, the suicide bomber succeeded in killing himself and one policeman. In two other cases, the suicide bomber was arrested or shot. This translates to 19 Taliban suicide bombers for one Afghan policeman, hardly an inspiring kill ratio for would-be-suicide bombers. In most of these cases, the suicide bombers attacked foreign convoys on foot or in cars and were unable to inflict casualties on their targets. Typically, the suicide bombers' explosives went off prematurely or their bombs failed to kill coalition troops driving in heavily armored vehicles.

In only three of the 22 cases for 2007 were there notable fatalities. In the first successful case, a suicide bomber killed two Afghan policemen and eight civilians (Camp Salerno, Khost, January 23, 2007). In the second case, three policemen were killed (Zherai District, Khost, February 4, 2007). In the third case, the February 27 attack on Bagram Air Base while Cheney was visiting, the bomber succeeded in killing 15-23 people (including two to three coalition soldiers). Such numbers hardly compare to Iraq where suicide bombers often carry out synchronized attacks that regularly kill anywhere from 60 to 130 people. Such uninspiring statistics beg the question: what are Afghanistan's suicide bombers doing wrong?

Taliban "Hard Targeting"

While the low death statistics certainly speak to the Taliban bombers' general ineptitude, part of the answer also lies in their targeting patterns that differ from those in Iraq. Iraqi suicide bombers from such jihadi groups as Ansar al-Sunnah and al-Qaeda in Mesopotamia frequently seek to inflict high casualty rates by attacking soft targets, such as crowded markets. Their objective is to cause as much bloodshed as possible, incite sectarian violence and destroy U.S. efforts to construct civil society in Iraq. Afghan suicide bombers, on the other hand, appear to have different objectives and have focused almost exclusively on hard targets (government, police, military). In 2007, for example, the Taliban have attacked foreign or Afghan military/police targets in 16 of their 22 bombings (in three cases the target was undetermined).

This in-depth analysis of 158 Afghan suicide bombings since 2001 shows that this is no anomaly and demonstrates an important point: in only eight of the 158 suicide attacks from 2001-2007 did civilians appear to be the direct target of Afghan bombers. Further scrutiny of these eight civilian attacks reveals an important fact. In two of these instances, the Taliban apologized for inflicting civilian casualties and in one case a Taliban spokesmen actually denied involvement. In four other cases the suicide bombers seem to have been targeting passing military convoys or governmental representatives in crowds; therefore, the high civilian casualties appear to have been unintended "collateral damage." In only two instances were civilians clearly the target of Afghan suicide bombers.

These findings tell us volumes about the Taliban's overall strategy in employing suicide bombing as a tactic. Far from imitating Iraqi insurgent tactics, the Taliban are trying to avoid losing the battle for the hearts and minds of the Afghan people by needlessly killing civilians.

Long-Term Taliban Strategy

While more targeted than the Iraqi suicide bombing campaign, the Taliban suicide bombing operations nonetheless share one key objective with their Iraqi counterparts: to disrupt the local "infidel proxy" government's efforts to bring security to contested provinces. In Iraq, this translates to fighting the Maliki government for Anbar Province. In Afghanistan, it means fighting the Karzai government for Paktia, Paktika, Khost, Helmand and, most importantly, Kandahar, the spiritual capital of the Taliban. Kandahar has been the scene of the greatest number of suicide bombings and is the key to understanding Taliban strategy. The Taliban movement sprang from Kandahar by offering the war weary Kandahari Pashtuns the one thing the mujahideen could not: security.

While more targeted than the Iraqi suicide bombing campaign, the Taliban suicide bombing operations nonetheless share one key objective with their Iraqi counterparts: to disrupt the local "infidel proxy" government's efforts to bring security to contested provinces.

While actively contesting the Karzai government for control of its natal territory, the current Taliban leadership does not want to be seen as destroying the local tribes' sense of security. The Taliban Shura knows from its own past experience that this would drive those Pashtun tribes sitting on the fence into the arms of the Karzai government.

For this reason, the Taliban merely aim to deprive the Karzai government and its International Security Assistance Force (ISAF) sponsors of their ability to offer the people security. The Taliban know all too well that NATO-backed efforts to lay roads, build schools, drill wells and outlaw banditry represent the greatest threat to their movement. For this reason, they have commenced an insurgent campaign that aims to disrupt ISAF's efforts to stabilize the south and bring security to the people.

Nothing in the Taliban/al-Qaeda arsenal seems to have been as effective as a shock weapon against the militarily superior Afghan National Army and ISAF/U.S. troops as suicide bombers. One cannot overestimate the psychological damage that this asymmetric tactic has had on ISAF troops who have handily bested their Taliban opponents in pitched battles. After Canadian ISAF troops delivering candy to children were targeted for suicide attacks, their skittish patrols began to attach speakers to their vehicles warning Afghans in Pashto to stay away. In a couple of instances, ISAF troops that have been targeted by suicide bombers have subsequently overreacted and shot innocent Afghan bystanders. Dutch ISAF troops, for example, have refused to be deployed in areas where suicide bombing is prevalent.

On many levels, the suicide bombing campaign does seem to have been successful. It has disrupted the coalition's efforts to interact with local populations and to win the race to bring security to contested provinces. Yet the Taliban are clearly playing a dangerous game, and this author's findings back up the Pentagon's claim that as many as 84 percent of the victims of suicide bombings in Afghanistan are civilians [1]. In several instances, Afghan suicide bombers have attacked foreign military convoys and succeeded in killing more than a dozen civilians and only one or two soldiers [2]. On other occasions, suicide bombers have killed or wounded innocent bystanders in mosques, hospitals, restaurants, or waiting for visas to partake in the Hajj. In the recent attack on Bagram Air Base, the vast majority of victims were once again civilians, and hundreds came to mourn their deaths. Not surprisingly, this has caused widespread resentment and protests in several Afghan cities.

Even in the best of circumstances, suicide bombing is not a precise technique and Afghanistan's feckless bombers seem far better at killing themselves and Afghan civilians than foreign troops. Far more coalition troops in Afghanistan have died from IEDs, gunfire, RPG attacks and other conventional methods than they have from suicide bombs. One Afghan study of the bloody 2006 campaign has found that suicide bombings in that year took 212 civilian lives, while leading to the death of only 12 foreign soldiers [3].

Conclusion

In light of the above, it seems clear that the Taliban will continue to employ suicide bombings in the upcoming year as a disruptive shock tactic. While the Taliban may get the occasional public relations coup, as in the seemingly coincidental attack on Bagram while Cheney was visiting, the main victims will continue to be the very people the Taliban are trying to win over, along with the suicide bombers themselves. As coalition troops continue to use close air support and superior artillery firepower to flush Taliban insurgents out of provinces like Kandahar, the real contest for the hearts and minds of the local population for 2007 may well hinge on the competing sides' "collateral damage" statistics.

Originally published in *Terrorism Monitor*: Volume 5, Issue 4 on March 1, 2007.

Notes

1. See "Afghan Suicide Bombings Take Mostly Civilian Toll," American Forces Press Service, September 3, 2006, http://www.pentagon.mil/news/NewsArticle.aspx?ID=679.
2. These instances include, among others: Kandahar, December 7, 2006; Kabul, September 18, 2006; Kabul, September 8, 2006.
3. See "Afghanistan's Record of Suicide Attacks in 2006," PakTribune, January 06, 2007, http://www.paktribune.com/news/index.shtml?165055.

Afghanistan's Drug Trade and How it Funds Taliban Operations
By Hayder Mili and Jacob Townsend

The opium economy in Afghanistan is a key component of the counter-insurgency campaign, yet remains one of the most difficult issues to tackle. It is a critical problem facing international efforts to create a functional government in Kabul that can prosecute counter-terrorism on its own territory. A successful counter-narcotics intervention would have the added benefit of undermining an important terrorist funding source in arenas as diverse as Chechnya, Xinjiang and Central Asia. While coalition and Afghan officials regularly acknowledge the power that the narco-economy has over their ambitions, it has proven exceptionally challenging to turn this into a national strategy that incorporates counter-narcotics into counter-insurgency and provides the resources for its execution.

According to the United Nations Office on Drugs and Crime (UNODC), opium production had a boom year in 2006, rising to 6,100 metric tons. This marked a 49 percent increase over 2005, yielding an estimated $755 million to farmers on the basis of a slightly decreased farm-gate price of $125 per kilogram of dry opium. With the national government's revenues at less than $350 million for 2006, the opium economy is a formidable financial power base beyond the state's control. Good weather conditions are expected in 2007, suggesting another huge harvest.

Any national counter-narcotics strategy for Afghanistan must begin with a preface noting the geographical variations of the country. In 2006, the southern province of Helmand accounted for 46 percent of Afghanistan's opium production. To the east of Helmand, Kandahar produced eight percent. In other words, the majority of Afghanistan's opium economy is built on production in two southern provinces. Of the remainder, 25 percent is produced in the northern belt close to the borders with Tajikistan, Uzbekistan and Turkmenistan, with lighter concentrations in the eastern and western provinces. Based on the UNODC's observations of recent opium planting, southern pre-eminence is likely to intensify further in 2007 [1]. The distribution of production correlates strongly with areas of ongoing insurgency/terrorism and coalition fatalities. Using NATO's divisions of Afghanistan, Regional Command South, which includes Helmand and Kandahar provinces, is where 62 percent of the country's opium is produced and where the coalition has suffered close to two-thirds of its combat deaths [2]. Basically, people are dying where poppies are thriving.

The difference between the relatively calm north and west and the militarized south and east should be reflected in approaches to counter-narcotics. Opium is undoubtedly a governance problem across the country. In the south and east, however, it is also strongly related to the Kabul government's most immediate existential threat—the Taliban-led insurgency—as well as to the funding of 139 suicide attacks in 2006 [3].

Farmers and Fighters

Out of Afghanistan's total opium production, 21 percent is trafficked northward through

Central Asia. Around 31 percent travels directly to Iran, which has suffered considerable human and financial costs in responding to both the direct drug traffic and the substantial opiate shipments arriving via Pakistan. The remaining majority of opiates leave Afghanistan across its 2,430 kilometer border with Pakistan. Harsh terrain, corruption and insecurity make it difficult or impossible to interdict opiate flows in most places.

In practice, it is challenging to differentiate between criminality, farmers' economic needs, insurgency fundraising and state complicity. Separating these factors conceptually, however, helps to formulate effective counter-insurgency tactics, highlighting the interactions between the drug trade and the Taliban. According to officials from the United Nations who interviewed Afghan law enforcement and coalition agencies in 2007, a symbiosis between the opiate trade and the Taliban continues, to the extent that some Taliban units simultaneously organize drug production and insurgent activities. In some regions, there has been a methodical process of fighting for territory while establishing relationships with opium cultivators that vary from symbiotic to despotic. Insecurity reinforces these relationships and this in turn makes the territory easier to penetrate by insurgents.

The feedback loops are evident in southern labor markets. A survey by the Senlis Council, a drug policy advisory forum, suggested that $200-600 per month was offered to work for the Taliban [4]. Law enforcement officials corroborated this in their report stating that the Taliban successfully recruits young locals to fight for $20 a day. These are not hardcore, dedicated and ideological fighters—they are unemployed men, some of whom are accustomed to a mercenary life. Although generally inferior to coalition troops and seemingly deployed in many circumstances as cannon fodder, they can be effective in ambushes and arranging Improvised Explosive Devices (IEDs). Taliban commanders have also used these "tier two" fighters to assist opium harvesting. Harvest time raises the stakes for insurgents in terms of maintaining territorial control. Traditional migrations for seasonal employment supply itinerant laborers who can be employed simultaneously as harvesters and protectors of opium. The Taliban can then take credit for providing local security and ensuring control of opium production.

According to the United Nations Office on Drugs and Crime (UNODC), opium production had a boom year in 2006, rising to 6,100 metric tons. This marked a 49 percent increase over 2005, yielding an estimated $755 million to farmers on the basis of a slightly decreased farm-gate price of $125 per kilogram of dry opium.

With the government and coalition unwelcome and subject to active (ambush) and passive (IED) attacks, areas of intense opium cultivation are the most difficult in which to demonstrate any reconstruction and development benefits. Alternative employment for mercenaries and alternative livelihoods for farmer-fighters cannot be delivered and those who might be attracted to such alternatives fear Taliban retribution. For example, the Pajhwok News Agency reported on October 30, 2005 that farmers in the Khan Nishin

District in Helmand province were being forced by the Taliban to cultivate poppies under threat of death.

Addicted to Poppy-Dollars

Law enforcement officers and UNODC officials interviewed by the authors in April 2007 believe that the "Taliban are completely dependent on the narco-economy for their financing." Where the Taliban are able to enforce it—mostly in the south and some eastern districts—they are said to levy a 40 percent tax on opium cultivation and trafficking. A low estimate of the amount that the Taliban earn from the opium economy is $10 million, but considering the tradition of imposing tithes on cultivation and activities further up the value chain, the total is likely to be at least $20 million [5]. There are also regular reports of cooperation between political insurgents and profit-driven criminal groups. One example is their collusion to throw small farmers off their land or to indenture them under debts and threats in order to maintain opium production. More detailed information provided to the authors describes arrangements whereby drug traffickers provide money, vehicles and subsistence to Taliban units in return for protection [6].

The synergy between politically-motivated warfare and economic logic is starkly visible and should drive the integration of counter-narcotics and counter-insurgency strategies. Of course, not all violence is linked to transnational jihadis. Across Afghanistan, profit-driven criminality is more pervasive than sympathy for or cooperation with insurgents, even if both benefit from and contribute to general lawlessness. When it comes to the Taliban, however, the centrality of the opium economy in their funding model is both a strength and a weakness. Reducing their financial power would undermine an important component of their recruitment model. It suggests a potential for turning the vicious circle of insecurity and economic stagnation into a virtuous one of coalition military superiority and job creation.

Dimensions of Counter-Narcotics

The failure to reduce opium cultivation in the early post-invasion years has directly augmented the Taliban's military strength. They have harvested the opium into weapons. The opiate trade and terrorism activity currently overlap to such an extent that some law enforcement actions fall under counter-narcotics and counter-terrorism simultaneously. So far, despite the millions spent and the various schemes that the coalition has attempted, opium production has increased, maintaining its importance as a source of terrorist funding domestically and internationally. As one Afghan diplomat lamented, "it makes no sense why the donors are blind to what they can see" [7]. An integrated approach to counter-

The synergy between politically-motivated warfare and economic logic is starkly visible and should drive the integration of counter-narcotics and counter-insurgency.

terrorism and counter-narcotics is required, taking account of the problem's three major dimensions.

First, proselytizing insurgent groups are treading a fine theological line in financing themselves through drug trafficking. Some drug barons linked with al-Qaeda, such as Badruddoza Chowdhury Momen, have argued that "it is a noble ... responsibility to spoil Western society with drugs" (Asian Tribune, May 19, 2006). This line of thought has a long tradition: in 1981, heroin trafficker and mujahideen leader Nasim Akhunzada published a fatwa stating that "poppy has to be cultivated to finance holy war against Soviet troops and their puppets in Kabul" (Eastern Review, January 1989). The difficulty is that most Muslim communities are intolerant of drug use, and to claim that flooding the West with narcotics is a form of jihad glosses over the millions of Muslims addicted to heroin and the associated HIV/AIDS infections. Furthermore, despite the apparently clear religious prohibition on the consumption of intoxicants, the issue appears divisive in the insurgency—as in Chechnya, Algeria and Somalia—because some Taliban are drug users themselves (*Dawn*, March 21, 2006).

These contradictions should be exploited in approaches to counter-narcotics operations. Ironically, it was the Taliban who in 2001 produced a successful opium clampdown, justified by religion. The same leaders are now protecting poppy growers from eradication. More than a third of the farmers surveyed by the UNODC who had never planted poppies responded that religion guided their decision. Fear of eradication was a negligible concern [8]. Insurgent justifications depend on potential supporters agreeing that the ends of jihad justify the inherently sinful means. Taliban spokesman Mohammad Hanif summarized the difficult argument for his organization last year when he opposed the cultivation of opium, but was "happy with any means of combating Western societies," including the production of heroin (RFE/RL, May 11, 2006).

Opium eradication is a promising counter-terrorism strategy if it can be executed without damaging the livelihood of the average opium farmer. For every leaflet and exhortation from the insurgents justifying opium, the Afghan government should be there to highlight the Taliban's hypocrisy and advertise the damage done to other Muslims.

Second, development programs that offset farmers' loss of income also need to provide some benefit to the pool of unemployed workers from which the Taliban recruit. Intervening in the opium economy means re-arranging a number of markets, including those for labor. At least, the under- or unemployed should not be left worse off, although, of course, the better outcome is a self-sustaining development trajectory.

Compensation to farmers is probably necessary. Options for delivering compensation are complicated by the tendency of some farmers to receive loans from traders and insurgents in anticipation of opium delivery, creating a debt burden that requires alleviation. A plan to pay at the end of the planting season is likely to be resisted more strongly. However, payment at the start of the season raises the risks of cheating and also the costs of monitoring since some crops may need to be checked twice. The United Kingdom's payments for not planting in 2002 and 2003 were unsuccessful as farmers (and politicians) pocketed funds and still produced opium. UN officials report that micro-credit programs have often been considered as an alternative to direct subsidies. Essentially, donors would take over the position that money-lenders currently occupy, with lower interest rates and a prohibition on using funds for opium cultivation.

Whatever the offsetting option chosen, the amount pumped into rural economies would need to equal that generated by opium production minus the value of producing licit crops and adhering to socio-religious rules. An eradication program supported by compensation and religious justification would trap the legitimacy of insurgents in a pincer maneuver. President Karzai's 2004 suggestion for a "jihad on drugs" showed the right intent, but the argument needs to be heard at the micro-level through anti-drug proselytizing by local religious leaders (Agence France-Presse, March 7, 2004). With the precedent of the Taliban's 2001 ban on opium cultivation and a strong effort by the Afghan government—with the help of foreign funds—to buffer the loss of income, incitements to rebellion will be weakened.

Finally, the geographical concentration of the insurgency indicates that counter-narcotics tactics need to vary with location. For example, eradication is difficult and possibly counter-productive in Helmand and Kandahar. Less than 10 percent of Helmand's poppy cultivation was eradicated in 2006, a figure subject to question in light of frequent reports that bribes are successful in avoiding eradication, particularly where government control is weak. Where security is already poor, teams of eradicators are likely to increase support for local insurgents, who by responding violently can demonstrate that they are protecting communities' interests. During counter-insurgency campaigns, policies of attraction are at least as important as those of attrition. This holds true for an integrated counter-narcotics component. In the north and west, there are relatively good prospects for reducing and holding down opium production through a comprehensive approach. Where Kabul and the coalition can exert a degree of effective governance, they can gain trust and promote credible programs. An additional angle that could be considered is a safe biological agent to eradicate and suppress poppy cultivation.

As of November 2006, Afghanistan's Counter-Narcotics Trust Fund had approved only two projects across the south [9]. Where territorial control is hotly disputed or in the hands of the Taliban, the best counter-narcotics policy is benign neglect toward cultivators and attempting to interdict traffickers. Priority districts for implementing comprehensive programs should be those that have a relatively strong coalition/government presence and adjoin to insecure or Taliban-controlled opium-producing areas. Where successful, these demonstrate to others nearby the intent and benefit of government efforts. Perhaps the best way to spread this news is to take participants from one district into adjacent non-compliant or less secure districts to share their experience.

Conclusion

A three-year commitment that integrates secured eradication and economic offsets is a promising alternative to the medium-term uncertainty of facing off against insurgents without attacking their local sources of funding. The current consensus that a decades-long project is required to turn farmers away from opium needs to be challenged by a strategy that views continuing production as a paramount security problem. The economic implications of opium eradication are huge for Afghanistan, but if the country can be secured then the development challenges of the national economy are no greater (or smaller) than those in other destitute states around the world. The difference is that Afghanistan will have removed the primary additional burden it faces: violent terrorist/insurgency activities funded by illicit narcotics.

Originally published in *Terrorism Monitor*: Volume 5, Issue 9 on May 10, 2007.

Notes

1. UNODC, Afghanistan Opium Winter Rapid Assessment Survey, Kabul, February 2007.
2. UNODC, Afghanistan Opium Survey, October 2006. For information on coalition combat deaths, see http://icasualties.org/oef.
3. Anthony Cordesman, Testimony to the U.S. House Armed Services Committee on "Stability and Security in Afghanistan," January 30, 2007.
4. Senlis Council Afghanistan, *Countering the Insurgency in Afghanistan: Losing Friends and Making Enemies* (London: MF Publishing, 2007).
5. Unofficial comments by international staff working in the region, April 2007.
6. Unofficial comments by international staff working in the region, September 2006.
7. Author interview, March 2007.
8. UNODC, Afghanistan Opium Survey, October 2006.
9. UNODC, Afghanistan Opium Winter Rapid Assessment Survey, Kabul, February 2007.

Shamshatoo Refugee Camp: A Base of Support for Gulbuddin Hekmatyar
By Omid Marzban

Two years after the Pakistani government banned it from publication, *Shahaadat Daily* newspaper, funded by Gulbuddin Hekmatyar, the leader of Hezb-e-Islami Afghanistan (Islamic Party of Afghanistan), is again available on the streets of Peshawar (Ariana Television, May 6, 2007). The daily has published articles that denounce the Afghan government and its major supporter, the United States. *Shahaadat* is the second newspaper, after *Tanweer*, which publishes articles that support Hekmatyar's declaration of jihad against the Afghan government and Western troops in Afghanistan. The paper prints new statements from Hekmatyar and serves as a vehicle for the leader's propaganda. Both Shahaadat and Tanweer are supported from Hezb-e-Islami's stronghold, the Shamshatoo Refugee Camp. According to Waheed Mujda, an Afghan analyst and a former member of Hezb-e-Islami Afghanistan, who lived in Shamshatoo during the 1990s, "Shahaadat restarted publication when Gulbuddin Hekmatyar ordered his followers to reinforce Islamic law and to strengthen Hezb-e-Islami activities inside Shamshatoo refugee camp" [1]. Located some 25 kilometers southeast of Peshawar, the capital of Pakistan's North-West Frontier Province (NWFP), Shamshatoo remains a bastion of support for Hekmatyar.

The Camp

Shamshatoo is a dusty and dry piece of land, surrounded by almost two-meter high clay walls. Inside the camp reside approximately 2,000 Afghan refugees. Almost all of them consider Gulbuddin Hekmatyar a hero. "Engineer Hekmatyar is a hero, his declaration of jihad against Americans shows that he is a servant of Islam," said a resident of the camp and a financial officer for the camp's administration, who went by the alias Haji Abdul Qahar [2]. Speaking to The Jamestown Foundation inside the camp, Qahar said, "Whoever lives or has lived in the camp is a supporter of Engineer Hekmatyar and a member of Hezb-e-Islami Afghanistan because this camp belongs to Hezb-e-Islami." Qahar, who was planning to visit Saudi Arabia a few days after his interview, apparently for umra, said, "whoever once became a member of Hezb-e-Islami will never quit following Hekmatyar because only those who become Hezb-e-Islami members believe in Hekmatyar's ideology with all their hearts."

Gulbuddin Hekmatyar did not return to Shamshatoo refugee camp after the pro-Pakistani Taliban rejected negotiations with him and refused to give him a role in their regime in 1996, but his thoughts are still alive with the residents of Shamshatoo and his statements continue to have a strong effect on the Afghan refugees living in the camp [3]. "I remember how Hekmatyar was speaking here in the mosque," says Ezatullah Menhaj, a young, 29 year-old resident of Shamshatoo. "Hekmatyar's words and his loyalty to Islam taught me to be a good Muslim. Wherever he is, I pray for his safety" [4]. Menhaj attended a school funded by Hezb-e-Islami Afghanistan in the 1990s. His comments demonstrate Hekmatyar's ability to influence the residents of Shamshatoo. "In one of Hekmatyar Sahib's statements [published] in Tanweer, I read that he said killing one American soldier is more rewarded by God than killing 10 Afghan soldiers," Menhaj explained. Asked whether he agreed with that statement, Menhaj said, "Yes, I do, because they [Americans] have come all the way from their country to occupy our country and joining in jihad against these infidels is farz (obligation) for us." In the August 10, 2006 issue of Tanweer, for example, Hekmatyar pledged to fight foreign troops in Afghanistan "till the last drop of blood moves in his body."

The Shamshatoo refugee camp has its own leadership and its own conservative Islamic rules. Watching television, listening to music, dressing in Western-style clothes and shaving facial hair are prohibited by the camp leader, Tooran Amanullah Khogman, who is extremely loyal to Hekmatyar [5]. Khogman is a former commander of Hezb-e-Islami, and he led party militants during the early 1990s in Charaasyab, south of Kabul [6]. Nevertheless, there is a girls' school in the camp, and even those who once allegedly poured acid on schoolgirls in Afghanistan now send their daughters to this school.

The History of the Camp

Shamshatoo is a Pashto word, meaning little male tortoise. "The place is called by the name of the animal because before the influence of refugees in the area, there were a lot of tortoises living there," explained Waheed Mujda, who was one of the first residents of the refugee camp [7]. The piece of land, once also called Woch Nahr, which means dried stream, was given to Hekmatyar and Hezb-e-Islami Afghanistan by the Pakistani government in 1979 when the anti-communist party was gaining strength. A dried steam, which is the basis of the area's name, still exists in the camp.

Hekmatyar, who fled Kabul in 1974 after spending almost a year in prison because of his membership in the Muslim Youths Movement, was given shelter inside Pakistan and was later recruited by Pakistan's Inter-Services Intelligence as an anti-Afghan government element. He first started his political and military activities in a small building in the Faqir Abad district of Peshawar. Later, because of a huge influx of Afghan refugees into the frontier province of Peshawar, and also because of security threats, the Pakistani government decided to move the bases of Afghan jihadi groups to the outskirts of the city. As part of this plan, the Jalozai Refugee Camp was given to Abdul Rasool Sayyaf, an anti-communist leader who later formed the party Ittehad-e-Islami, and Shamshatoo Refugee Camp was given to Hekmatyar. Waheed Mujda explained that the first building built in Shamshatoo was a mosque: "Like any other Afghan jihadi party at that time, Hezb-e-Islami established its base in Shamshatoo by building a mosque there."

Besides its military and political activities and despite its involvement in the war against the Russians in Afghanistan, Hezb-e-Islami granted social services—such as health care and educational facilities—to Afghan refugees in Shamshatoo. This social support network, which helped to make Hezb-e-Islami the biggest and the most influential party among jihadi groups in Afghanistan, aimed to attract more and more Afghans to the organization. Other activities, such as Hekmatyar's speeches to refugees and his regular publications, which were mainly based in Shamshatoo, played a significant role in making him a "hero" among the camp's residents.

Conclusion

Today, Hekmatyar's whereabouts are unknown. Nevertheless, his statements, newspapers and audio cassettes are still available in Shamshatoo and the surrounding area. Despite having gone underground, Waheed Mujda claims that Hekmatyar recently ordered his men to restore humanitarian services in the camp, including the funding of schools for the children in Shamshatoo [8]. According to individuals from the camp who declined to be identified, Hekmatyar maintains a leadership role in the camp through his representatives in Shamshatoo.

Just as he did during the jihad against the Russians and their appointed government in Kabul, Hekmatyar continues to exploit two key assets: providing humanitarian aid to the people and garnering positive publicity. For more than two decades, Shamshatoo has played a key role in this strategy. Furthermore, the camp demonstrates Hekmatyar's entrenched support in not only Afghanistan, but also Pakistan. It is unclear whether Hekmatyar still recruits fighters from Shamshatoo, but his popularity in the camp and the region displays his capabilities.

> *Just as he did during the jihad against the Russians and their appointed government in Kabul, Hekmatyar continues to exploit two key assets: providing humanitarian aid to the people and garnering positive publicity.*

It is also unclear whether Hekmatyar still receives support from state clients. The fact that Shamshatoo's finance officer, Haji Qahar, is able to make trips to Saudi Arabia, coupled with the nearly free reign of Hezb-e-Islami activists in Pakistani territory, raises further questions about the origins of Hekmatyar's bases of support.

Originally published in *Terrorism Monitor*: Volume 5, Issue 10 on May 24, 2007.

Notes

1. Author Interview, Waheed Mujda, May 8, 2007.
2. Author Interview, Haji Abdul Qahar, Shamshatoo Refugee Camp, Pakistan, April 2007.
3. For a profile of Gulbuddin Hekmatyar, see Terrorism Monitor, September 21, 2006.
4. Author Interview, Ezatullah Menhaj, Shamshatoo Refugee Camp, Pakistan, April 2007.
5. Author Interviews, Shamshatoo Refugee Camp, Pakistan, April 2007.
6. Ibid.
7. Author Interview, Waheed Mujda, May 8, 2007.
8. Ibid.

A Report from the Field: Gauging the Impact of Taliban Suicide Bombing
By Brian Glyn Williams

The following study is based on field research carried out in the summers of 2003, 2005 and the spring of 2007 in 15 Afghan provinces including: Paktia, Nangarhar (Jalalabad), Panjshir, Balkh (Mazar-i-Sharif), Takhar, Bamiyan, Kabul and Herat. Specific assistance was granted by the United Nations, the U.S. military, Hekmat Karzai's Center for Afghan Peace Studies as well as numerous NGO members and average Afghans who chose to remain anonymous.

In the aftermath of the toppling of the Taliban, Kabul, which has tremendous significance as a symbol of authority for those who aspire to rule Afghanistan, was the primary target of the Taliban's suicide bombing campaign. The initial sporadic attacks— which included an attack on a German International Security and Assistance Force (ISAF) convoy and foreigners in an antique-selling street known as "Chicken Street" that is popular with Afghanistan's rare "tourists"—rattled foreigners living in Afghanistan and presaged things to come. The United Nations, for example, subsequently forbade its workers from visiting Chicken Street. ISAF and U.S. convoys appeared to be on edge as they moved through the streets as early as 2003, long before the real suicide bombing campaign began. The initial wave of bombings from 2002-2005 was the Taliban's way of "throwing down the gauntlet" and demonstrating that the Hamid Karzai government could not uphold its promise of security to the people in the capital.

Nevertheless, for most Kabulis who have a much higher threshold for violence than Westerners who have not lived through two-and-a-half decades of war, life went on. Kabul's population skyrocketed; restaurants and modern steel and glass buildings sprang up; "Roshan" cell phones began to appear in the hands of young women who wore head scarves instead of burqas; traffic jams materialized; and Kabulis threw themselves into taking advantage of the new climate of security to rebuild their lives. Between 2003 and 2005, Afghans, including General Rashid Dostum who was the target of one such bombing, unanimously dismissed the suicide bombings as being the work of "die hards," "foreigners," "Arabs" and, most importantly, "Pakistanis" [1]. Many claimed that the Afghan Taliban, for all its faults, would not engage in suicide attacks and President Karzai himself proclaimed that the "Sons of Afghanistan" would never carry out such "un-Islamic" actions.

Today, however, there is a perceptible shift in opinion in Kabul that stems from the fact that Kabul has been the target of more than two dozen suicide attacks since 2005. Nevertheless, progress in the capital, which in and of itself is a bubble removed from the provinces, especially those in the south, has continued apace despite the fact that these random attacks are clearly beginning to take their toll. Among the many stoic Kabulis, there is a palpable sense of fear and acceptance of the fact that fellow Afghans are increasingly responsible for the carnage that takes its toll primarily on civilians. A driver in Kabul, for example, had the disconcerting habit of pointing out to his passenger the spots where suicide bombings had taken place in recent months [2]. He seemed to be consumed by the fear of becoming a victim himself.

His fear is shared by many Kabulis, especially those who work for Western companies that appeared to be benefiting the most from post-Taliban development [3]. Some Westernized Afghans make a point of consciously mixing up their schedules so as not to have predictable travel patterns that could be picked up by Taliban spies. It is rumored that Afghan governor Abdul Hakim Taniwal was sent pictures of his movements by the Taliban before he was killed by a suicide bomber in Gardez in September 2006 [4]. Urban myths of suicide bombers are not surprisingly widespread. One such story describes a taxi driver who picked up a passenger for a journey from Kabul to an outlying city only to find out that his passenger was a suicide bomber wearing an explosives-filled vest. Luckily for the taxi driver, his passenger failed to see any ISAF targets on their journey.

Foreigners also seem to have reacted to real or perceived threats by adopting a heightened sense of awareness and many have adopted robust security procedures. The few Western-style restaurants and clubs in the city are protected by sand-bagged entrances and guarded by soldiers with metal detectors. Foreigners rarely utilize taxis or walk the streets. While a few travel freely around Kabul on foot or by taxi, many foreigners working for NGOs are forbidden from doing so.

The greatest obstacle facing Western researchers in Kabul is getting out of the city to the south of the country along the newly paved Kabul-Kandahar highway. Traveling the highway by car is an open invitation for becoming a target of a Taliban suicide bombing or kidnapping [5]. Astoundingly, foreigners traveling between the capital and Afghanistan's second largest city have to rely on air transport due to the insecurity on this vital section of the Afghan "ring road" (a road that, ironically enough, was rebuilt with Western aid money). Average Afghans consider it foolhardy to travel to such "hot zones" as Gardez and villages around Jalalabad without any protection. Coalition convoys traveling on these provincial roads are increasingly wary of road-side pedestrians using cell phones when they pass for fear that they are passing on their itineraries to militants. Coalition troops have even found that children using remote-controlled toy cars on the road are doing so to test the strength of their electronic counter-measures designed to scramble bomb wiring and IED transmission signals.

Signs of Hope

While there is little that someone on foot or driving in a "soft-skinned" vehicle can do to save themselves from a determined suicide bomber, the Karzai government and its coalition supporters have made some headway in defeating them. Coalition troops and the National Directorate of Security have, for example, broken up numerous suicide cells (usually a trainer, bomb-maker, spotter and the bomber himself). Additionally, average Afghans have prevented suicide bombings on numerous occasions by apprehending bombers themselves [6].

The following account recorded by the United Nations Mission in Afghanistan (UNAMA) of Afghans proactively preventing a suicide bombing is certainly heartening: "On March 4, Zabul Province, Qalat District, at approximately 1520 hours local, shopkeepers in the bazaar area identified, arrested and subsequently severely beat a man carrying a BBIED [Body-Borne Improvised Explosive Device]. After being handed over to the ANP [Afghan National Police] and receiving treatment at the hospital, the man claimed to be part of a three-man suicide team that had entered Qalat City" [7]. A reliable source that chose to remain anonymous told the most harrowing story of a suicide bomber who pulled up to a gas station driving a vehicle-borne improvised explosive device. When the gas station attendant saw the suspicious wiring in the car, he and another worker jumped the bomber, fought with him to prevent him from detonating his device in a gas station filled with civilians and eventually subdued him.

While the Karzai administration can be faulted for often failing to provide security for those who stand up to the Taliban, many clearly continue to do so regardless of the cost. For example, in the Pashtun areas of the southeast, a fatwa-decree written by 30 ulema/religious scholars in Khost proclaimed that "suicide is strongly prohibited by Islam. Nobody is allowed to assassinate himself by any means. Allah says 'don't kill yourselves.' Abi Horrira says that the Prophet, peace be upon him, says 'The one who jumps down from a mountain and kills himself will be put in hell forever'" [8].

Civilians are not the only ones who remain vigilant. The ANP has saturated the capital with thousands of heavily armed policemen. Entry to the capital has now been channeled through police checkpoints and ANP members have set up road blocks throughout the city where they carry out random searches of vehicles. As the front-line defense in the war against suicide bombers, the ANP, who man dangerously exposed positions, have suffered the brunt of the Taliban's attacks. They often sustain more casualties than the Afghan National Army.

There are other signs of hope that distinguish the campaign in Afghanistan from that of Iraq—most notably, the reluctance of Afghan insurgents to target the United Nations. The United Nations, which has a long history of neutrality in Afghanistan, stemming from its period of relief work during the Afghan Civil War and the Taliban period, is perhaps one of the most exposed organizations

There are other signs of hope that distinguish the campaign in Afghanistan from that of Iraq—most notably, the reluctance of Afghan insurgents to target the United Nations.

in Afghanistan. There are arguably more white UN vehicles on the road on any given day than coalition military vehicles. Unlike Iraq, however, where the UN has been deliberately targeted, the Taliban appear to have recognized the UN's neutrality. They appear to accept its positive role as a mediator and source of assistance in improving the lives of average Afghans (even the Taliban's). For this reason, it appears that they avoid targeting its vehicles and bases with suicide attacks [9].

The ethnic-sectarian strain to the suicide bombing campaign in Iraq, which often supersedes the targeting of foreign troops, is also completely absent in Afghanistan. While the Taliban and al-Qaeda have been involved in anti-Shiite suicide bombings in the North-West Frontier Province and Federally Administered Tribal Areas in Pakistan, this trend has not appeared in Afghanistan. Even though the ANP presence in the Shiite Hazara regions around Bamiyan (not to mention the Panjshir Valley, and the plains of Turkistan) was minimal, traveling appears safe [10]. Although there have been suicide bombings in areas with pro-Taliban Pashtun pockets in the north and west, such as the recent bombings in Kunduz and Herat, there have been no deliberate attacks on the Shiite Hazara areas to date. For both logistical and strategic reasons, the Taliban appear to have largely focused its suicide terrorism operations on the Pashtun belt and the symbolically important capital despite their history of oppression against Hazaras and, to a lesser extent, minorities of the north.

The Taliban's much-hyped campaign to employ "hundreds" if not "thousands" of suicide bombers against Afghanistan in Spring 2007 has not come to pass. Furthermore, with the death of Mullah Dadullah, the operational Taliban commander who has made the most use of suicide bombing, there is cause for hope even though many people continue to live their lives under the shadow of this new and unpredictable threat.

Originally published in *Terrorism Monitor*: Volume 5, Issue 10 on May 24, 2007.

Notes

1. Author interviews with Afghan citizens and with General Rashid Dostum, Kabul, Afghanistan, 2003 and 2005.
2. Author interview with driver, Kabul, Afghanistan, April-May 2007.
3. Author interviews with Afghan citizens, Kabul, Afghanistan, April-May 2007.
4. Author interview, Kabul, Afghanistan, April-May 2007.
5. Author's personal experience in attempting to travel by car to Kandahar, Afghanistan.
6. The media widely reported the case of one Afghan who heroically subdued a suicide bomber attempting to enter a U.S. base in January 2007. See Mark Sappenfield, "The Afghan Guard Who Stops Suicide Bombers," *Christian Science Monitor*, March 8, 2007.
7. UNAMA Field Report, March 4, 2007.
8. "Sentence Judgment (Fitwa) of the Religious Scholars of Khost Province," November 21, 2006.
9. The recent case where a UN vehicle carrying Nepalese soldiers was hit by an IED was said to be related to drug cartels in the region and not to the Taliban.
10. Author's personal evaluation from traveling in the Shiite Hazara regions around Bamiyan, the Panjshir Valley and the plains of Turkistan.

The Taliban Fedayeen: The World's Worst Suicide Bombers?
By Brian Glyn Williams

Suicide bombing statistics from Afghanistan alarmingly demonstrate that, if the current trend continues, 2007 will surpass last year in the number of overall attacks. While there were 47 bombings by mid-June 2006, there have been approximately 57 during the same period this year. Compounding fears of worse carnage to come, Afghanistan's most lethal single suicide bombing attack to date recently took the lives of 35 Afghan police trainers near Kabul. When considering the expanding use of Improversied Explosive Devices (IEDs) and the discovery of the first Iraqi-style Explosively Formed Projectile (EFP) in Afghanistan in May (i.e. a more deadly form of IED that has killed high numbers of soldiers in Iraq), it is understandable that critics of the war in Afghanistan discuss it in alarmist tones. Approximately 80 percent of U.S. casualties in Iraq come from IEDs, and members of the U.S. and Afghan military who were interviewed for this study believed that the absence of mass casualty suicide bombings and EFPs were the two factors that made Afghanistan less dangerous than Iraq. A deeper investigation of the wave of suicide bombings that have swept the country in 2006 and 2007 paints a less bleak picture.

Missing the Target

An analysis of the attacks carried out in the last two years reveals a curious fact. In 43 percent of the bombings conducted last year and in 26 of the 57 bombings traced in this study up to June 15, the only death caused by the bombing was that of the bomber himself. Astoundingly, approximately 90 suicide bombers in this two year period succeeded in killing only themselves. This number exceeds 100 when you factor in those who succeeded in killing only one person in addition to themselves. There was one period in the spring of 2006 (February 20 to June 21) when a stunning 26 of the 36 suicide bombers in Afghanistan (72 percent) only killed themselves. This puts the kill average for Afghan suicide bombers far below that of suicide bombers in other theaters of action in the area (Israel, Chechnya, Iraq and the Kurdish areas of Turkey). Such unusual bomber-to-victim death statistics are, of course, heartening for both coalition troops— who have described the Afghan suicide bombers as "amateurs"—and the Afghan people—who are usually the victims of the clumsy bombings.

These statistics also represent a uniquely Afghan phenomenon that warrants investigation. In the first portion of this study, it was demonstrated that a part of the reason for this low kill ratio lies in the Taliban's unique targeting sets (*Terrorism Monitor*, March 1, 2007). As Pashtuns with a strong code (Pashtunwali) that glorifies acts of martial valor and badal (revenge), the Afghan suicide bombers are more prone to hit "hard" military targets than callously obliterate innocent civilians in the Iraqi fashion. On the rare occasions where there have been high casualty bombings of Afghan civilians, they tend to have been carried out by Arab al-Qaeda bombers [1].

The Taliban's selective targeting is a calculated decision on the part of the Taliban shuras (councils) to avoid inciting the sort of anti-Taliban protests that led thousands in the

Pashtun town of Spin Boldak to chant "Death to Pakistan, Death to al-Qaeda, Death to the Taliban" following a particularly bloody suicide bombing in that frontier city (BBC, January 18, 2006). Taliban spokesman Zabiyullah Mujahed recently claimed, "We do our best in our suicide attacks to avoid civilian casualties. These are our Muslim countrymen, and we are sacrificing our blood to gain their freedom. Their lives are important to us, of course. But fighting with explosives is out of the control of human beings." Then he made an interesting admission that speaks to other factors that might explain the Afghan suicide bombers' failure rate. He stated, "We have a problem with making sure they attack the right targets, avoiding killing civilians" (BBC, June 21, 2007).

Clearly, there is more to the Taliban bombers' stunning failure rate than simply "hard" targeting difficulties and an obvious reluctance to slaughter the Afghan constituency that the Taliban is trying to win over. Members of the Afghan police, government and National Directorate of Security (NDS) who were interviewed about this trend during the months of April and May 2007 offered a surprisingly unanimous explanation for the Taliban bombers' poor showing [2].

> *... there is more to the Taliban bombers' stunning failure rate than simply "hard" targeting difficulties and an obvious reluctance to slaughter the Afghan constituency that the Taliban is trying to win over.*

The cause for the Afghan suicide bombers' underwhelming performance, they claimed, lay in the ineptitude of the people that the Taliban were recruiting as fedayeen (suicide) bombers. Afghan officials continually told stories of lower class people who had been seduced, bribed, tricked, manipulated or coerced into blowing themselves up as "weapons of God" or "Mullah Omar's missiles." Afghan NDS officials also spoke of apprehended bombers who were deranged, retarded, mentally unstable or on drugs.

Such claims should, of course, be accepted with caution for two reasons. First, the targets of suicide bombings are prone to speak in disparaging tones regarding the mental state and motives of those who carry out bombing attacks against them. They tend to describe them as mindless, insane, fanatical, drugged or brain-washed. Second, in his ground-breaking work *Understanding Terror Networks*, Marc Sageman has refuted the long-held notion that suicide bombers are impoverished, voiceless dupes tricked into killing themselves. Rather, he has shown them to be politically and religiously motivated. They are conscious actors who, like the multilingual and educated September 11 attack team, do not need to be brainwashed. Certainly, in the Afghan context there are bombers who fit the Sageman profile. Several Taliban leaders have carried out bombings, and the al-Qaeda team that scrambled on short notice to launch the symbolically important mass-casualty bombing at Bagram Air Base during Vice President Dick Cheney's February 2007 visit was clearly comprised of professionals [3].

Nevertheless, interviews and field work conducted in Afghanistan for this study revealed considerable evidence that the "duped, bribed, brainwashed" paradigm applies to a growing percentage of the bombers being deployed in the Afghan theater [4]. Afghan police told of numerous incidents where citizens in Kabul reported finding abandoned suicide vests in the city. They seemed to signify a last minute change of heart in several would-be-bombers. In one case, they told of a mentally deranged man who threw his vest at an Afghan patrol, assuming it would explode on its own [5]. Several of the bombers apprehended by the NDS were carrying mind altering hallucinogens or sedatives, which they had been told to take in order to calm their fears during their last moments of life. Others, including a Taliban bomber who was arrested while pushing his explosives-laden car toward its target after it ran out of gas, appear to be inept beyond belief [6]. Recent media and think-tank reports have also mentioned the utilization as suicide bombers of an Afghan war invalid who was blind, another who was an amputee and one who was a disabled man whose only motive was to make money for his family (*Terrorism Monitor*, November 18, 2004; *New York Times*, October 21, 2005). Coalition troops who have spoken of seeing bombers blow themselves up far from their convoys have characterized it as the act of drugged or mentally unstable bombers.

While this might explain some of the Afghan suicide bombers' failures, there also appears to be a financial motive behind several of the bombings that offers further explanation. UN representatives spoke of a bomber who entered a Kabul internet cafe in 2005. Instead of setting off his bomb in the middle of the cafe where it would do the most damage, he went into a bathroom to set it off, killing only two people [7]. There are many such examples of Afghan suicide bombers seemingly with a conscience or reluctance to inflict mass casualties. The fact that a number of them are doing it simply for payments for their families might explain this [8].

Research in the Pashtun areas to the southeast of Kabul reveals an even more disturbing trend than the employment of suicide bombers who are mentally unsound, using drugs or working solely for money payments: the use of child bombers.

Afghanistan's Child Bombers

Local villagers interviewed for this study—living in front-line provinces such as Khost, Paktika and Paktia—have reported that Taliban recruiters were active in their areas. Many parents have lost their young impressionable sons to those who prey upon them [9]. Parents often learn of their tragic fates only when the Taliban arrive at their homes to hand out their sons' "martyrdom payments." Villagers are, of course, outraged by such tactics, but there is often little recourse in light of the Taliban's dominance in the countryside. In one case, a powerful tribal chieftain in Khost province who discovered that his son had been recruited by Taliban commander Jalaluddin Haqqani for a "martyrdom operation" managed to get him back (after threatening to attack the Taliban with his tribe); unfortunately, this is an exception, as is the recent case of a captured 14 year-old suicide bomber who was personally pardoned by President Hamid Karzai, who announced, "Today we are facing a hard fact, that is a Muslim child was sent to madrassa to learn Islamic subjects, but the enemies of Afghanistan misled him toward suicide and prepared him to die and kill" [10].

Such recruitment for madrassa training of young bombers is even more widespread on the Pakistani side of the border. There have been several widely reported instances of the

Taliban recruiting school children to be suicide bombers in the Federally Administered Tribal Areas and the North-West Frontier Province (NWFP). In one notorious instance, Taliban soldiers arrived at the Oxford High English medium school in a tank and began to recruit young boys by asking them to fulfill their "jihad duty" and engage in an "adventure." According to eyewitnesses, "The militants came to town with a mission, and wanted to convert us to their cause.'They said that jihad was obligatory and those who heed the call are rewarded,' the principal said. 'As many as 30 students from each of the four government schools in Tank enlisted.' A similar number have also joined from private schools. The ages of those taken are between 11 to 15 years." According to one of the teachers involved, the students who were recruited without their parents' permission were subsequently trained as suicide bombers (BBC, June 12, 2007). The age of these bombers would explain why one of the courses in Taliban suicide camps teaches students how to drive a car.

In a similar case, two Pakistani teenagers who left school to train as suicide bombers without their parents' permission claimed, "We were told to fight against Israel, America and non-Muslims," said Muhammed Bakhtiar, 17, explaining why he wanted to become a suicide bomber. "We are so unhappy with our lives here. We have nothing. We read about jihad in books and wanted to join...We wanted to go to the Muridke madrassa so we would have a better life in the hereafter" (MSNBC, March 28, 2007).

While Mullah Nazir, a powerful Taliban leader in Pakistan's Waziristan provinces recently made an unprecedented request for the Taliban to stop recruiting children, a recent video of a suicide bomber ceremony in the region would seem to indicate that his appeal has been honored in the breach (Daily Times, June 19). In the video that was obtained by ABC, boys as young as 12 are shown "graduating" from a suicide bombing camp run by Mullah Dadullah Mansour, the successor to his brother, the recently slain Mullah Dadullah (ABC News, June 22, 2007).

As disturbing as this video is, it pales in comparison to the discovery Afghan security officials recently made in eastern Afghanistan. In an incident that caused tears of fury among local villagers, a six year-old street urchin approached an Afghan security checkpoint and claimed that he had been cornered by the Taliban and fitted with a suicide bomber vest. They had told him to walk up to a U.S. patrol and press a button on the vest that would "spray flowers" (Daily Mail, June 26, 2007). Fortunately, the quick thinking boy instead asked for help, and the suicide bomb vest was subsequently removed.

While this case is obviously an extreme example, it fits the trend and certainly goes a long way in helping to explain why almost half of Taliban suicide bombers succeed in killing only themselves. Many Taliban bombers come from small backwater villages and have to be taught how to drive on strange roads, travel beyond their locale or country and then hit fast moving, armored coalition convoys with improvised explosives. Even at the best of times, suicide bombing is a task that involves considerable resolve, determination, focus and a degree of intelligence. Clearly, such vital ingredients are often missing in the Afghan context, where many of the bombers appear to be as much victims as perpetrators.

Commenting on the bombers' failure rate, U.S. military spokesman Lieutenant Colonel Paul Fitzpatrick explained the lack of ambiguity that U.S. military personnel have about the bombers who commit suicide instead of suicide bombings. "Certainly there are a fair number of failed attempts, and that's OK. I hope they don't get better" (*St. Petersburg Times*, November 23, 2006). While some have engaged in relativism in efforts to compare the coalition's "collateral damage" losses from close air support to the Taliban's "collateral damage" from suicide bombing, the coalition clearly has the moral high ground when the enemy has resorted to deploying children as "living weapons."

Originally published in *Terrorism Monitor*: Volume 5, Issue 14 on July 19, 2007.

Notes

1. The bomber who killed 20 people in a mosque in Kandahar in 2005 was an Arab. The bomber in the Spin Boldak bombing of 2006 which killed 26 civilians was also said to be an Arab and the Taliban later denied responsibility for the unusually bloody bombing. Similarly, al-Qaeda leader Abu Laith al-Libi has been accused of being the mastermind behind the February 2007 large suicide bombing at Bagram Air Field during Vice President Dick Cheney's visit that killed 22 civilians. Most recently, NDS officials in July arrested an Arab member of al-Qaeda who was planning to use suicide bombers to assassinate Afghan officials.
2. Author Interviews, Kabul, April 2007.
3. In one case a mullah drove a vehicle-borne improvised device into a bus. Most recently, the Kunduz bombing of May 2007 was carried out by a mullah named Jawad from Baghlan province.
4. Marc Sageman's excellent work has more applications for elite, transnational al-Qaeda-style bombers than the impoverished, illiterate Afghans who seem to make up the majority of the bombers in recent years.
5. Author Interview in National Directorate of Security Headquarters, Kabul, April 2007.
6. Story relayed to author by Craig Harrison, Director of UN Security in Afghanistan, UNAMA Compound, Kabul, April 2007.
7. The media erroneously reported that the bomber had set the bomb off in the middle of the café.
8. As in other "zones of jihad," including Chechnya and Iraq, it appears that Arab financiers are offering payments ranging from $11,000 to $23,000 for those who carry out bombings.
9. Author's findings while carrying out research in the region in April 2007.
10. This story was conveyed to the author in Gardez, Paktia province by Tom Gregg of the UNAMA, on the morning after a suicide bomber hit the town. Local Pashtuns interviewed after the bombing called the attack "obscene" and "un-Islamic."

Farah Province: The New Focus of the Taliban Insurgency
By Waliullah Rahmani

With the war in Afghanistan steadily spreading to the north and east of the country, a new front for the Taliban insurgency has opened in the previously secure western regions. The seizure of districts in Farah province by the Taliban and the expansion of insecurity, criminal activity, kidnappings and corruption to the western provinces of Afghanistan are growing concerns.

In November 2007, three districts of Farah province, including Khake Safed, Gulistan and Bakwa, all fell briefly into the hands of the Taliban (Hashte Sobh, November 6, 2007). Parts of the Herat-Kandahar highway that runs through Farah and Nimruz provinces are seized by the Taliban on a daily basis. The insurgents stop buses and search the passengers in order to find government employees or officials.

Lack of Coordination Impedes the Anti-Taliban Effort

The Taliban's tactic of capturing districts for only a few days or even hours is enabled by a lack of coordination between NATO forces, the Afghan National Army (ANA) and Afghan national police. A security official in Farah province declared that after ANA and NATO forces retake control of a district, they fail to make provisions for its future security. The Afghan national police are not able to protect these districts alone because they are poorly equipped, suffer from poor morale and are limited in numbers (Hashte Sobh, November 18, 2007).

In each district of the western provinces the maximum number of police is typically only 20 or 30. For a district with a population of more than 30,000 people, it is impossible to control even a district headquarters, much less the rest of the province. A TV cameraman who declined to be named recently visited some of the Farah districts and described the situation: "I saw how miserable the police were. They didn't have enough food. The police officers were saying that after three or four hours' battle their weapons don't work well" [1].

The Taliban's tactic of capturing districts for only a few days or even hours is enabled by a lack of coordination between NATO forces, the Afghan National Army (ANA) and Afghan national police.

Abdul Rahman Sarjang, the police chief of Farah province, said that the police there have limited facilities. Police often go unpaid and are largely incapable of tackling better-armed Taliban forces. "The coalition forces do not fight either. The management bodies in the province are weak. When the Taliban seized six police vehicles, the coalition forces actually did not react. Forty-five Afghan police officers and soldiers have been killed over the past few days" (Hashte Sobh, November 21, 2007).

Iranian Interference

Since the rise in security problems in southwest and western Afghanistan, many circles within the country and without have pointed to the Islamic Republic of Iran as a leading force in supporting the insurgents in Afghanistan. Following the recovery of Iranian-made weapons in Afghanistan, there are suggestions that the Islamic Republic is trying to bring down the international forces in Afghanistan, especially those belonging to the United States (Pagah, November 12, 2007). Mawlawi Wakil Ahmad Mutawakil—former foreign minister of the Taliban—has said that the Islamic Republic might support the Taliban in the border provinces because the Taliban and Iran share a common goal of forcing the withdrawal of foreign forces from Afghanistan (Kabul Direct Monthly, October 21, 2007). The police commander for the western provinces of Farah, Badghis and Herat, Colonel Rahmatullah Safi, claims that Taliban insurgents are trained and armed inside Iran before crossing back into Afghanistan (PakTribune, June 20, 2007).

The defense minister of Afghanistan, Abdul Rahim Wardak, has said that the current insurgency in some parts of Afghanistan (including the western provinces) is supported by (unnamed) foreign interests. Meanwhile, a recent analysis says that the expulsion of Afghan refugees from Iran in large numbers is connected to the insecurity in Farah, Herat, Nimruz and Badghis provinces. Iran may be interfering in Afghanistan to put pressure on the Kabul government and foreign forces in order to gain the political leverage needed to lessen international pressure on its nuclear program (Wessa, October 3, 2007).

Opium Cultivation

Farah and the other western provinces of Afghanistan are central to the production and export of narcotics and opium to Iran and Europe. Autumn and winter are the most important seasons for opium cultivation, which is likely a leading factor in the timing of the Taliban's expansion of the war into the western provinces. The Taliban are highly dependent on the narco-economy for their financing. Some analysts following the situation in the west and southwestern provinces relate that "currently the major traffickers help the Taliban to destabilize the region in order to cultivate more opium. The only forces who enjoy the insurgency economically are the traffickers whose interests are in insecure areas under the control of the Taliban. These traffickers contribute to the Taliban financially because of their interests. The Taliban can destabilize the region by using the financial resources of the drug traffickers or the narcotics mafia" (author's interview with two analysts based in the Western provinces). Opium produced in Helmand province is smuggled through the western districts of Bakwa, Delaram, Kashrud, Bala Bulok, Gulistan and Sinadand into Iran and on into Europe. Smugglers contribute to the insurgency to remove any threat to their operations from law enforcement agencies [2].

Leading Insurgents

The insurgents active in Farah, Herat, Nimruz and Badghis provinces are local Taliban with close ties to the insurgents in Helmand province. Mawlawi Abdul Hamid is a leading local insurgent in the Zirkoh area of Shindand district of Herat province. Some commanders from the Bomadi tribe are also active in the western provinces of Farah and Nimruz. One leading insurgent who is not affiliated with the Taliban is Sakhi Momin.

Inside Farah and Nimruz provinces the Taliban are mainly led by Mullah Bismillah and Mullah Baz Muhammad, who are in close touch with the Taliban in Musa Qala province. Although they are not high profile commanders of the Taliban, they have played an important role in coordinating Taliban operations in the western provinces.

The most dangerous stronghold of the Taliban in western Farah province is the village of Shaiban in the Bala Bulok district. Many attacks in the western provinces are planned and organized in Shaiban, which is dominated by members of the Alizai tribe. The Alizai of Shaiban were transferred to the area over a century ago from the Musa Qala district of Helmand and still maintain close ties with the Musa Qala insurgents [3].

Using a Western Front to Spread Taliban Influence Northwards

The war is expanding into the western provinces of Afghanistan, with Farah and Nimruz provinces as the focus of the insurgents. Most of the fighters in these areas are local in origin and are centered in the Bakwa district of Farah province (Pajhwok Afghan News, November 19, 2007). There are signs that the Taliban are intent on connecting areas they control in Bakwa with the Parchaman and Taghor districts. If the Taliban succeed in doing this they will be able to provide support to other insurgents across the western provinces [4]. In the neighboring Herat province, the pro-Taliban Norzai tribe is creating a stronghold for the movement in the Adraskan district. Another center for Taliban activity is developing in the Qara Jangal area of Badghis province, just north of Herat. Heavy fighting has taken place in Badghis province for several months now. Afghan MP Hashim Ortaq recently described Qara Jangal as the most important place for Taliban efforts to expand the war into northern Afghanistan (Kabul Direct Monthly, October 2007).

NATO and ANA forces are beginning to concentrate in Badghis in order to prevent such expansion, but much of the region is mountainous and difficult to control. The struggle to control Badghis, Herat and Farah provinces will play an important part in determining the future of the Afghan conflict. Opening new fronts will increase the pressure on international forces and possibly cause political dissatisfaction with the war in the NATO countries deploying troops in Afghanistan. Iran's role in fuelling further fighting in the region has important international implications.

Originally published in *Terrorism Monitor*: Volume 5, Issue 23 on December 10, 2007.

Notes

1. Author Interview, November 27, 2007.
2. Author interview with Dad Norani, an Afghan researcher from western Herat province, December 8, 2007.
3. Ibid.

4. Ibid.

The Haqqani Network and Cross-Border Terrorism in Afghanistan
By Imtiaz Ali

There has been an increase recently in alleged missile strikes inside Pakistani territory by U.S. forces operating across the border in Afghanistan. The attacks come at a time when there is a growing call in the United States for strikes on Pakistani territory to take out al-Qaeda safe havens believed to exist in the tribal agencies along the Afghan border. NATO military commanders in Kabul have time and again expressed their dissatisfaction with the performance of Pakistani security agencies in stopping the infiltration of armed Taliban groups like the "Haqqani Network" from Pakistan's tribal areas into Afghanistan. Despite the fact that U.S. authorities have consistently expressed their respect for Pakistan's sovereignty, they are simultaneously growing impatient with the growing strength of the militants on the Pakistani side of the border. According to U.S. officials, the cross-border activities of these militants have a direct impact on U.S. operations in Afghanistan.

Attack on Lwara Mundi

A March 12, 2008 missile attack targeted a home in the town of Lwara Mundi in North Waziristan, killing two women and two children. Pakistan quickly registered a protest with the Coalition forces in Afghanistan, deploring what an official called "the killing of innocent people." However, U.S.-led Coalition officials in Kabul said that the target of the precision-guided missile was a safe house of the Haqqani Network based in the border region of the North Waziristan agency (*Daily Nation* [Lahore], March 14, 2008). Just a day after Pakistan lodged its protest over the attack in Lwara Mundi, another missile attack on March 16 left as many as 20 killed, including a number of foreign fighters, when a house was targeted in Shahnawaz Kheil Doog village near Wana, the regional headquarters of South Waziristan. It is believed that the missiles were fired from two U.S. unmanned aerial vehicles (UAVs) in the belief that the house was being used as a training camp for terrorists (*Daily Post* [Lahore], March 14, 2008). Though a U.S. Central Command spokesman would only say the missiles were not fired by any military aircraft—Predator UAVs are operated by the CIA—U.S. forces took responsibility for the earlier "precision-guided ammunition strike" on Lwara Mundi but made it clear that the target was the Haqqani Network (*Daily Mail* [Islamabad], March 14, 2008; Agence France-Presse, March 13, 2008; Reuters, March 17, 2008). A spokesman for Coalition forces in Afghanistan said that Pakistan was informed after the attack, not before. The spokesman made it clear that U.S. forces will respond in the future as well if they identify a threat from across the border in Pakistan's tribal belt (*Daily Times* [Lahore], March 14, 2008). Though the Pakistani tribal region has been a center of concern since late 2001 when hundreds of al-Qaeda fighters took refuge there, the lawless belt between Pakistan and Afghanistan is now receiving attention for the growing activities of the Haqqani Network, a Taliban group that has been spearheading the insurgency against U.S.-led NATO forces in Afghanistan.

A Profile of the Haqqani Network

The "Haqqani Network" is a group of militants led by Jalaluddin Haqqani and his son, Sirajuddin Haqqani. Jalaluddin, who is said to be in his late 70s, is a noted Taliban commander with a bounty on his head and a place on the U.S. most-wanted list. Jalaluddin Haqqani is considered to be the closest aide of Taliban supreme leader Mullah Omar and was a noted mujahideen commander in the 1980s resistance against the Russian occupation of Afghanistan. He rose to prominence after playing a leading role in the defeat of Muhammad Najibullah's communist forces in Khost in March 1991. After the Taliban's takeover of Kabul in 1995, the senior Haqqani joined the Taliban movement and rose to the top echelon of power in the regime. He remained a minister during the Taliban government and a top consultant to Mullah Omar. The senior Haqqani has rarely been seen in public since the collapse of the Taliban regime in Afghanistan in late 2001, when he is believed to have crossed into Pakistan's Waziristan Tribal Agency to evade the advance of Coalition forces. There are continuous rumors that he is seriously ill or has even died. However, his son, Sirajuddin Haqqani, alias Khalifa, has not only filled the void created by the absence of his veteran jihadi father, but his well-organized group, known as the Haqqani Network, has emerged as the most dangerous and challenging foe for the Coalition forces in Afghanistan.

The Haqqani Network is based in the Dande Darpa Khel village near Miramshah, headquarters of the North Waziristan Tribal Agency. The town is about 10 miles from the Afghan border. Sirajuddin, believed to be in his early thirties, has a $200,000 bounty on his head. He belongs to the Zadran tribe of Afghanistan, which also has roots on the Pakistani side of the border. Residents in Dande Darpa Khel say that the junior Haqqani grew up in this small and remote town of North Waziristan, once the operational headquarters of his father's jihadist activities. It is said that he attended the now defunct religious seminary that his father founded in the early 1980s in the town of Bande Darpa Khel. Though he could not be considered a religious scholar, Sirajuddin certainly sharpened his jihad skills under the guidance of his father. Considered to be the leader of a new generation of Taliban militants on both sides of the border and a bridge between the Pakistani and Afghan Taliban, NATO officials have recently declared him as one of the most dangerous Taliban commanders in the ongoing insurgency in Afghanistan (*Los Angeles Times*, March 14, 2008). He is suspected as the mastermind behind the deadly attack on Kabul's only five-star hotel in January 2007, which left eight people killed, including three foreigners (*Daily Times*, March 4, 2008). A U.S. military spokesman at Bagram Air Base described Sirajuddin's role in a series of devastating suicide bombings: "We believe him to be much more brutal and much more interested in attacking and killing civilians. He has no regard for human life, even those of his Afghan compatriots" (The Associated Press, February 21, 2008). The United States has offered a $200,000 bounty for Sirajuddin, who is expanding his operations from east Afghanistan into the central and southern regions.

Sirajuddin has evaded capture several times despite attempts by Pakistani security forces to arrest him at his house and seminary in Miramshah in North Waziristan. In 2005 Pakistani officials raided his headquarters in Dande Darpa Khel, the religious seminary and residential compound used by his network. The raiding party seized huge caches of weapons and ammunitions but Sirajuddin again escaped arrest (*Dawn*, September 15, 2005).

Sirajuddin is also reported to have taken credit for a suicide-truck bombing in Khost on March 3 that killed two NATO soldiers and two Afghan civilians (Xinhua, March 13, 2008). The attack on a government building involved a truck loaded with explosives, drums of petrol, mines and gas cylinders. A Taliban videotape of the bombing was released on March 20, including a statement from the German-born suicide bomber, Cuneyt Ciftci—also known as Saad Abu Furkan—"The time has arrived to give sacrifices to Islam. Since we lack resources to fight the enemy, we will have to turn our bodies into bombs" (Newkerala.com, March 20, 2008).

On the Pakistani side of the border, Sirajuddin's influence has been growing as a "revered jihadist commander." He strongly opposed Maulvi Nazir's campaign against Uzbek and other foreign militants waged earlier this year by the militant tribal leader in South Waziristan (*Terrorism Monitor*, January 11, 2008). He is reported to have played an important role in stopping the fighting between Maulvi Nazir's tribal militia and Uzbek militants in Wana and the surrounding area in March 2007. Sirajuddin took part in a tribal jirga, attempting to sort out differences between combatant foreigners and local militants, but the talks collapsed when Maulvi Nazir asked for the surrender of all foreign militants residing in the region bordering Afghanistan (*Dawn*, March 24, 2007). In late January, two arrested members of the Haqqani Network revealed that up to 200 suicide bombers had infiltrated into Pakistan's cities in preparation for the current wave of bombings (*Khabrain* [Lahore], January 28, 2008).

Two months ago, one of Sirajuddin's most important commanders, Darim Sedgai, was reported killed after being ambushed by unknown gunmen in Pakistan, though spokesmen for the Haqqani Network claim that Sedgai is recovering from his wounds (The News [Karachi], January 28, 2008). Coalition forces in Kabul confirmed the killing of Sedgai, who was known as a powerful commander of the Haqqani Network, overseeing the manufacture and smuggling of improvised explosive devices (IEDs) into Afghanistan.

As the Haqqani Network has risen to the first rank of the Taliban insurgency it can be expected that U.S.-led Coalition forces in Afghanistan will continue to target Sirajuddin Haqqani and the rest of the network leadership.

These activities led U.S. forces to post a $50,000 reward for information leading to his death or arrest. A native of the North Waziristan agency, Sedgai was a follower of Jalaluddin Haqqani and fought under his command with the mujahideen in Afghanistan. Until his reported death in January 2008, Sedgai was an important leader of the Haqqani Network and was considered to be a close friend of Sirajuddin Haqqani (Pajhwok Afghan News, January 28, 2008).

Conclusion

Afghan officials as well as Coalition forces in Kabul have cited Sirajuddin's use of North

Waziristan as operational headquarter for his alleged cross-border terrorist activities as one example of Pakistan's inability to eliminate terrorist sanctuaries in its tribal areas. Though the Pakistan government regards these claims as baseless, it is known that two years ago Sirajuddin issued a circular urging militants to continue their "jihad" against the United States and the Karzai government "till the last drop of blood." But in the same statement he pointed out that "fighting Pakistan does not conform to Taliban policy ... those who [continue to wage] an undeclared war against Pakistan are neither our friends nor shall we allow them in our ranks" (*Dawn*, June 23, 2006). There are signs that this is no longer the policy of the Haqqani faction of the Taliban.

As the Haqqani Network has risen to the first rank of the Taliban insurgency it can be expected that U.S.-led Coalition forces in Afghanistan will continue to target Sirajuddin Haqqani and the rest of the network leadership. With such strikes now occurring on Pakistani soil the Haqqanis are emerging as a serious domestic problem for Islamabad. How it chooses to deal with the Haqqani Network threat will provide a test case for Pakistan's role in the ongoing war on terror.

Originally published in *Terrorism Monitor*: Volume 6, Issue 6 on March 24, 2008.

Dostum: Afghanistan's Embattled Warlord
By Brian Glyn Williams

While the resurgence of the Taliban is the focus of interest in the Pashtun south of Afghanistan, the year started with a different story in the north that many are depicting as one of the greatest challenges to Hamid Karzai's government. Namely the surreal confrontation between General Abdul Rashid Dostum, the larger-than-life Uzbek jang salar (warlord)—who was once described as "one of the best equipped and armed warlords ever"—and one of his former aides [1].

In a move that many critics of the situation in Afghanistan saw as epitomizing the Karzai government's cravenness in dealing with brutal warlords, the Afghan government backed away from arresting Dostum after he beat up and kidnapped a former election manager and spokesman in Kabul on February 3, 2008 (*International Herald Tribune*, February 4, 2008). As his house was besieged by Ministry of the Interior police, Dostum appeared on the roof, defiantly waving his fist.

While many critics of President Karzai's policy of appeasing warlords called for making an example of Dostum, Karzai limited his response to removing Dostum from his largely symbolic post of "Commander in Chief" of the Afghan Army. Karzai's decision *Dostum's power base lies in the* not to prosecute Dostum for his brazen *northern provinces of Jowzjan, his* assault in the Afghan capital was *home district, as well as Saripul,* depicted as "timid and hesitant" (Asia *Balkh, Faryab, Baghlan and Kunduz.* Times, April 9, 2008; RFE/RL, February 3, 2008). Glib calls for "removing" warlords like Dostum, however, display a lack of understanding of the complex issues involved in Karzai's delicate balancing act in a country faced with a mounting Taliban insurgency.

The Missing Historical Context

Dostum's power base lies in the northern provinces of Jowzjan, his home district, as well as Saripul, Balkh, Faryab, Baghlan and Kunduz. These provinces make up an Uzbek-dominated steppe and hill region known as Afghan Turkistan since it was conquered by the Pashtun-Afghans in the 19th century. Independent Turkistan was subdued only after the Afghans made an alliance with the Uzbek ruler of Faryab, who sent his horsemen to fight alongside the Afghans against fellow Uzbeks [2].

While a later Afghan ruler, Amir Abdur Rahman, broke the spine of the Uzbeks' final resistance in 1881 by blowing their elders and khans out of cannons, subsequent leaders were not as strong as the "Iron Amir" [3]. Instead of using force, they were forced to resort to the traditional Afghan ruling policy of "divide and rule" to dominate the Uzbek khans. Whenever a local khan grew too strong, the Afghan wali (governor) undermined him by promoting his rivals [4].

In the 1980s, as the resistance of the mujahideen increased, the Pashtun Communist leader Najibullah took the unprecedented step of arming ethnic Uzbeks to fight the Islamic rebels. The guns empowered an Uzbek commander from the backward province of Jowzjan: Abdul Rashid Dostum. Dostum proved to be skilled in rallying Uzbek and Turkmen mujahideen to both the government's cause and his own. By the late 1980s his army of pro-Communist government horsemen had pacified the north.

By 1992 President Najibullah had come to see the writing on the wall as the Soviet Union collapsed and his funds dried up. He began to send out feelers to Pashtun elements in the mujahideen and started to remove non-Pashtun commanders in the north. In 1992 Dostum betrayed Najibullah and joined the moderate Tajik leader Massoud in toppling the Afghan Communist government.

Despite assisting Massoud and the mujahideen in capturing Kabul, Dostum—more of an ethno-opportunist than a Communist—was pointedly excluded from the new government on the grounds that he was a "Communist." The Uzbeks claimed it was because the dominant Pashtuns and Tajiks defined him as a ghulam (a medieval Persian term used to describe Turkic slave warriors).

In frustration Dostum returned to the north and helped create the Jumbesh-i-Milli Islami (Islamic National Party), which eventually became the dominant Turkic party of the five provinces he controlled. But Dostum's autonomous realm was not recognized by the mujahideen government. When Massoud attacked his northern realm, Dostum responded by besieging Kabul in January 1994.

Hundreds of civilians died in this short-lived attack which, however, paled in comparison to the number of civilians killed by Hekmatyar, Massoud and the Hazara leader Mazari, who fought for the capital from 1992 to 1996. Nonetheless, Dostum's troops earned a well deserved reputation for raping and pillaging and Dostum had a difficult time enforcing his rule over his wild troops, colloquially known as gilimjans (carpet thieves).

For the most part Dostum remained confined to the north and had no aspirations to rule Kabul like the other warlords. From 1992 to 1997 he ran a secular mini-state based in Mazar-i-Sharif and the surrounding provinces. According to one account, "Dostum was also benign. Women enjoyed freedom to go to school, go out without the burqa and to wear high-heeled shoes, in sharp contrast to their oppression by the Taliban elsewhere in the country." Mazar-i-Sharif's university, the last in Afghanistan, had 1,800 female students (Observer, October 21, 2001).

As Mullah Omar's Taliban forces overran the rest of the country after 1994, Dostum led his Uzbek and Turkmen forces in defending this last pocket of secularism. Dostum seemed to be invincible until he was betrayed in May 1997. Once again the Pashtuns had relied upon the policy of divide and rule to overcome Uzbek resistance. On this occasion, Dostum's Uzbek commander in Faryab, Abdul Malik, went over to the Taliban with his forces in the middle of a battle. At this moment the leader of the Pashtun community of Balkh and Mazar-i-Sharif, Juma Khan Hamdard, attacked from the east and destroyed Dostum's forces.

As always, the disunited Uzbeks were their own worst enemy. Juma Khan Hamdard's troops subsequently welcomed their Pashtun Taliban brothers into Mazar-i-Sharif and strict sharia law was enforced. A furious Dostum was forced to flee to Turkey, where he remained in exile until April 2001.

Dostum the "Tank Crusher"

Dostum's old ally and rival, the hard-pressed Massoud, clearly valued Dostum as a leader and tried to convince him to return to Afghanistan to fight the Taliban. But his reputation was severely damaged in 2000 with the publication of Ahmed Rashid's book Taliban: Militant Islam, Oil and Fundamentalism in Central Asia. In this best-seller, which became an unofficial manual for U.S. troops in Afghanistan, Rashid relates a second-hand story of Dostum using a tank to impose discipline on one of his own troops caught plundering. Using language that resentful Uzbeks claim is tainted by Turcophobia, Rashid defined Dostum in colorful terms as a neo-Genghis Khan:

"He wielded power ruthlessly. The first time I arrived at the fort to meet Dostum, there were bloodstains and pieces of flesh in the muddy courtyard. I innocently asked the guards if a goat had been slaughtered. They told me that an hour earlier, Dostum had punished a soldier for stealing. The man had been tied to the tracks of a Russian-made tank, which then drove around the courtyard crushing his body into mincemeat, as the garrison and Dostum watched" [5].

With those words the legend of Dostum the "tank crusher" was born. As the story was told and retold it took on a life of its own. Subsequent writers, many of whom had the oblique aim of criticizing U.S. policy in Afghanistan, competed to embellish the episode, often pluralizing the number and type of victims (Times, October 11, 2004; The Times [London], September 29, 2004; Washington Post, February 23, 2002). The story would eventually shape Coalition governments' policies and lead to calls for Dostum's arrest.

But even as Rashid's Taliban began to cast Dostum and his "pillaging" people in a negative light, Dostum decided to return to Afghanistan to make one last stand against the Taliban.

An Embattled Warlord: Dostum in Post-Taliban Afghanistan

For five months Dostum led a desperate horse-mounted guerrilla war against the Taliban in the barren Hindu Kush Mountains of central Afghanistan. When he heard about the 9/11 attacks he promptly offered his services to the U.S. Central Command. While his small band of less than 2,000 cheriks (horse-mounted raiders) was considerably smaller than other factions of the Northern Alliance, it was Dostum's group that actually went on the offensive. In November 2001, Dostum and U.S. Special Forces broke out of the Hindu Kush Mountains and destroyed the Taliban army of the north. Within days Dostum was greeted across the north as a liberator.

But at the Bonn Conference of 2001, organized to create a government for post-Taliban

Afghanistan, Dostum was sidelined, much as he had been after overthrowing the Communist government in 1992. Dostum responded by running for president in 2004, garnering 10 percent of the vote, roughly the proportion of the Uzbek-Turkmen population of Afghanistan.

Dostum then resurrected his Jumbesh Party, which became an outlet for expressing the grievances of the Uzbeks and their Turkmen kuchuk kardeshler (little brothers). At this time Dostum criticized Karzai—a Pashtun—for such policies as reaching out to the Taliban and arming Pashtun militias. Dostum also hid weapons for future use against the resurgent Taliban and a neighboring Tajik warlord named Ustad Atta.

It was at this time that Karzai returned to the tried and true policy of divide and rule to weaken Dostum. Malik, the commander who had betrayed Dostum in 1997, was encouraged to return to the north, where he created a political party to compete with Dostum's Jumbesh (RFE/RL, April 21, 2006).

Karzai also placed a governor in Faryab who called for Dostum's arrest for war crimes— Dostum's troops were accused of killing as many as 200 Taliban prisoners in 2001, a number inflated in some accounts to as many as 3,000. Dostum, however, checkmated Karzai when his Jumbesh followers rioted and drove the unpopular governor out of Faryab in 2004.

The Karzai government responded to these failures by trying to woo the Turkmen—many of whom resent being the Uzbeks' "little brothers"—away from Dostum. To add a quintessential Afghan twist to the whole affair, it was at this time that a Turkmen Jumbesh spokesman began to criticize the Karzai government for its campaign against Dostum. That spokesman was none other than Muhammad Akbar Bai, the aide who was beaten by Dostum in February 2008.

Dostum versus Akbar Bai

In the 2004 presidential election, Bai, a Turkmen, was plucked from obscurity by Dostum and made manager and spokesman for his campaign. Bai was chosen by Dostum largely for his knowledge of the United States and the English language, as Dostum belatedly realized that he needed to counter his image as a "tank crusher." Bai learned his English while serving a jail sentence in the United States from 1989 to 2003 for drug dealing and tax evasion (IWPR, February 6, 2007).

The two fell out during the parliamentary election of 2005. In January 2007, Bai turned on his patron and publicly claimed that Dostum was hiding weapons and "misused his power in northern provinces and destroyed Uzbek and ethnic Turkmen" (Pahjwok News Agency, January 8, 2007). Dissidents across the north rallied to Bai. Then, in what was seen as a deliberate provocation, Bai established a rival party known as the Turkic Islamic Council in Sheberghan, Dostum's home town. In response, the local Jumbesh youth wing ransacked the party's headquarters, claiming Bai was working for the Karzai government as a "new Malik" to divide Turkmen and Uzbeks as the 19th century Afghan amirs and the Taliban had done.

As the quarrel weakened Dostum, who was facing a financial crisis as well, Karzai felt the moment was right to move against him. Karzai appointed Juma Khan Hamdard, the Pashtun commander who had attacked Dostum alongside the Taliban in 1997, as governor of Dostum's home province of Jowzjan. When the Jumbesh Youth rallied to protest Hamdard's appointment, his security forces gunned down and killed over a dozen of them in Sherberghan.

Hamdard also seems to have been tipped off about the location of Dostum's weapon caches by Bai, recovering the largest stash of explosives in post-Taliban Afghanistan (Asia Times Online, May 30, 2007). Reeling from these setbacks and unable to defend his followers even in Sheberghan, Dostum had to find a way to maintain his nam (a Dari word meaning name or reputation) and prevent defections.

It was in this context that Dostum and his followers attacked Akbar Bai in a calculated display of power, sending a message to the Uzbeks and Turkmen of the north that he was still in charge. Bai's bold challenge to his authority was finally answered and the Turkmen leader was forced to turn to Karzai, a Pashtun, for protection. In one bold stroke Dostum reunified his power base and intimidated his challengers.

For his part, Karzai, a master of Afghan provincial politics, knew that he could not move forcefully against Dostum despite the widespread calls for his arrest. Dostum still had the key support of other Northern Alliance warlords, not to mention the support of his own Turkic qawm (tribe) and the well organized Jumbesh Party. As the Taliban make inroads in the strategic northern provinces, having a bulwark like Dostum—who still builds schools for women and supports secularism—serves Karzai's purposes, so long as he is not too strong.

So while Karzai would like to remove Dostum, who is perceived as a warlord relic, he realizes that this would destabilize the north, where Dostum is defined by many as a liberating hero. And the north is one of the few areas in Afghanistan that has seen comparative security and progress. For this reason, while the story of Dostum's assault on Akbar Bai is already being embellished and will certainly contribute to his tank-crusher name in the West, among the Turkic people of the north his authority remains largely unchallenged, at least for the time being (ABC.net, February 5, 2008).

Originally published in *Terrorism Monitor*: Volume 6, Issue 8 on April 17, 2008.

Notes

1. Tom Cooper, "Afghanistan Without the Soviets," Part 3, *Air Combat Information Journal*, October 29, 2003.
2. Jonathan L. Lee, *The Ancient Supremacy. Bukhara, Afghanistan and the Battle for Balkh, 1731-1901* (Leiden: Brill Academic Publishers, 1996) 76-86.

3. Ameer Abdul Rahman Khan, *Taj ul Tawreeq*, vol. II (Bombay, 1905).
4. G. Whitney Azoy, *Buzkashi. Game and Power in Afghanistan* (Prospect Heights, IL: Waveland Press, 2003) 89, 98, 101.
5. Ahmed Rashid, *Taliban: Militant Islam, Oil and Fundamentalism in Central Asia* (New Haven: Yale University Press, 2000) 56.

Afghanistan's National Army: The Ambiguous Prospects of Afghanization
By Antonio Giustozzi

Over the last few years the Afghan National Army (ANA) has often been presented as a success story. This certainly holds some truth, at least in comparison with Afghanistan's national police, which is widely seen as a complete failure. The ANA is reasonably well behaved and quite popular throughout most of Afghanistan. Its initial difficulties in retaining troops within the ranks seem to have been addressed to some extent and both the desertion and absence-without-leave (AWOL) rates are down from the high levels of 2002-2006. AWOL rates in particular have declined dramatically from about 33 percent in 2006 to a relatively low 8 percent in 2008 [1]. This appears to be the combined result of a presidential decree turning absence-without-leave into a crime, a widespread media campaign, rising unemployment and rising food prices, which force even less than enthusiastic recruits to stick to the ANA. The number of infantry battalions now stands at 36, while the army as a whole numbers 37,000 men: Still substantially short of its personnel projections, but way above the 22,000 which it numbered at the end of summer 2007 [2]. These relative successes have turned the ANA into one of the pillars of the much touted "Afghanization" strategy. The term "Afghanization" itself is used with some ambiguity within the NATO-led International Security Assistance Force (ISAF), sometimes implying a gradual withdrawal of foreign troops; at other times it implies the gradual shift of the weight of the fighting from the international contingents to the Afghans. A number of European countries seem to lean toward the first interpretation, while Washington clearly opts for the second [3].

Difficulties in Operating Independently

To the extent that Afghanization is meant to allow a withdrawal of foreign troops, the ANA still has several weaknesses. The main one is its extreme dependence on embedded trainers. Five years on, not a single battalion has graduated from the embedded training program, even though the original plan was for two years. A number of battalions, perhaps as many as 12, are considered to be led by sufficiently skilled officers capable of operating without advisers [4]. However, as the insurgency grew into a relatively large conflict through 2005-2007, the ANA has grown dependent on close air support, administered through the embedded training teams. The ANA does not have any personnel trained to handle close air support, nor does it seem bound to develop such skills in the foreseeable future [5]. The fighting tactics that ANA officers have been learning from their trainers are largely based on American tactics; the infantry's main task is to force the enemy to reveal itself, allowing the air force to wipe it out with air strikes. There is little evidence that ANA units would be able to control the battlefield without such air support, or that they are learning the necessary skills.

The ability of the ANA and the Afghan Ministry of Defense (MoD) to plan and conduct complex operations on their own has not yet been tested; the few autonomous operations carried out by ANA units are simple ones, usually with back-up from foreign units and always with the embedded trainers present [6]. Tight international sponsoring of the ANA also means that it is usually not operating in very small units, which would be most effective in engaging and pursuing the insurgents in the absence of overwhelming air support. Usually the task of engaging the insurgents in close combat is left to the special forces of various foreign contingents. Several ANA officers complain about the fact that the training received by the infantry battalions is too "conventional" [7]. By not practicing effective counter-guerrilla tactics, the necessary skills are not being developed, and it will not be possible to rapidly produce such skills in the event of a substantial change in the involvement of foreign troops in the war.

Another dubious aspect of Afghanization is the limited logistical capabilities of the ANA. Although its logistical units are now being developed, the ANA's difficulties in recruiting skilled staff casts some doubts about the future efficiency of its logistics once the foreign contingents hand over these responsibilities to the ANA.

Ethnic Fault Lines

With regard to its long-term viability, another problematic aspect of the ANA is represented by its internal ethnic fault lines. Since 2005 both the MoD and the Americans have securely guarded any data about the ethnic composition of the ANA, but there is evidence that a genuine ethnic balance has not yet been achieved; even more worryingly, although a point was initially made that units would be ethnically mixed, it is now obvious that they are not. Tajiks are still overrepresented, particularly in the officer corps. According to one estimate, 70 percent of the battalion commanders are Tajiks [8]. This figure is in stark contrast with the Afghan army of the pre-war period, where the overwhelming majority of field officers were Pashtuns and ethnic minorities were mainly relegated to logistics and administration.

Recruitment to the army is not going well in a number of Pashtun regions affected by the insurgency, mainly because of a campaign of intimidation carried out by insurgents against the families of soldiers, which discourages potential recruits from joining and has forced a number of soldiers not to re-enlist.

Recruitment to the army is not going well in a number of Pashtun regions affected by the insurgency, mainly because of a campaign of intimidation carried out by insurgents against the families of soldiers, which discourages potential recruits from joining and has forced a number of soldiers not to re-enlist. The situation is compounded by the habit of the MoD to deploy only predominantly Tajik units to the war zones of the south and southeast, presumably to avoid the risk of "fraternization" and to enhance the cohesion of the units. As a result, there are very few Pashtuns fighting against the insurgency within the ranks of the ANA. Although friction between ANA units and the local population or even between ANA and locally recruited police is reported, there is no evidence that this is a driving factor in the insurgency. However, such friction and the fact that many soldiers and officers do not speak Pashto must certainly limit the cooperation that these units are able to enlist locally, particularly in remote rural areas. Even the few Pashtuns who serve in these units are usually not from the region where they are deployed, but from other Pashtun-populated regions. Therefore, they lack local knowledge even if they can understand the language spoken by the villagers.

These characteristics of the ANA units deployed in the south, southeast and east are compounded by the unreliability and ineffectiveness of the police, which in principle should contribute local knowledge to the counter-insurgency effort. Locally recruited police forces are more often than not militias in disguise, which fight for their own agenda and are locked in local rivalries. These forces do not effectively cooperate with the ANA and are not reliable sources of information [9].

Perhaps more relevant in the long term is the risk of ethnic tension compromising the unity of the ANA, once foreign troops have been withdrawn or their presence substantially reduced. Given battalions that are largely ethnically homogeneous and with many within the officer corps having a background in ethnically-based political factions, the stage seems set for serious trouble in the event of a foreign withdrawal. Moreover, the army, whose size is now planned at 80,000 but may grow further, is already unaffordable for the revenue-stripped Afghan state and will one day have to be downsized, raising the prospect of serious disgruntlement among officers.

Conclusion

At some point ISAF will have to allow the ANA to be tested on the battlefield in conditions resembling those which it will meet in the event of a withdrawal of foreign forces. Apart from being a test of Afghanization, such a trial—if successfully passed—would also enhance the credibility of the ANA and the legitimacy of the government, as well as increase the leverage of Kabul in any negotiations with the Taliban. The test could, for example, consist of leaving the ANA alone to manage a province or region without external support. The fact that such a test has not been attempted yet in more than six years of international tutoring might reflect a relative lack of confidence in the capabilities of the ANA, or the fear of the political consequences of a failure.

Originally published in *Terrorism Monitor*: Volume 6, Issue 9 on May 1, 2008.

Notes

1. Video Teleconference with Major General Robert W. Cone, Commander of Combined Security Transition Command – Afghanistan, Stars and Stripes, Mideast Edition, March 26, 2008.
2. American Forces Press Service, April 7.
3. Author's personal communications with diplomats in Kabul, April 2008.
4. A. Giustozzi, "Reconstructing the Defence Sector," in Eden Cole, Alex Dowling, and Candace Karp, eds., *Deconstructing the Afghan Security Sector* (Geneva Center for the Democratic Control of the Armed Forces, 2008); A. Giustozzi, "Auxiliary force or national army? Afghanistan's 'ANA' and the counter-insurgency effort, 2002-2006," *Small Wars and Insurgencies* 18, no. 1 (March 2007):.45–67.

5. Author's personal communication with a senior American officer and a NATO diplomat, Kabul, April 2008.
6. Author's personal communication with British army officers and journalists, London, November 2007; personal communication with military attaché, Kabul, October 2007.
7. Author's personal communication with military attaché, Kabul, April 2008.
8. Author's personal communication with UN official, Kabul, April 2008.
9. Author's personal communication with British, Dutch and American officers and diplomats, 2007-2008; personal communication with senior Ministry of the Interior official, Kabul, October 2007.

Gulbuddin Hekmatyar's Return to the Afghan Insurgency
By Muhammad Tahir

The Hezb-i-Islami Afghanistan (Islamic Party of Afghanistan, or HIA), sidelined from Afghan politics since the fall of the mujahideen regime to the Taliban in the mid-1990s, has recently reemerged as an aggressive militant group, claiming responsibility for many bloody attacks against Coalition forces and the administration of President Hamid Karzai.

Led by 61-year-old Gulbuddin Hekmatyar—a charismatic engineer, former premier and mujahideen commander once favored by Washington—the HIA most recently claimed responsibility for the April 27 attack on a military parade in Kabul from which President Karzai escaped unharmed, but took the lives of three Afghan citizens, including a member of parliament (Quqnoos, May 25, 2008). The Taliban, however, has also claimed responsibility for this attack, leading some to suggest that the attack was a joint operation between the Taliban—which has a weak presence in the north—and Hekmatyar's followers. Though an apparent attempt to kill President Karzai might appear counterproductive to proposed negotiations between Karzai's government and Hekmatyar, these proposals, including the possibility of joining the government, have so far all come from the government side (Tolo TV, September 27, 2007). In this sense Hekmatyar's attack may be viewed as a display of force intended to soften the government position before talks commence.

These offers of talks by the central government indicate the strengthening power of Hekmatyar. Though his name has been largely absent from the Afghan political scene over the last few years, Hekmatyar is now in a position to bargain with the government, conditioning his cooperation on the departure of foreign troops from Afghanistan, the establishment of an interim government followed by general elections (Ariana TV, February 14 and May 8, 2008; Pakistan Observer, May 10, 2008).

Hekmatyar's Political Base

Born in 1947 in the Imam Sahib district of the Kunduz province of northern Afghanistan, Hekmatyar is a Pashtun, belonging to the Kharoty faction of the Ghilzai tribe. His political career began in 1970 when he adopted a leftist ideology while a student at the engineering faculty of Kabul University.

As a member of the leftist People's Democratic Party of Afghanistan, his first act of violence was the killing of a member of a rival wing, leading to his imprisonment in 1972. The seizure of power by Daud Khan from King Zahir in 1973 helped him to escape to Pakistan, where in 1975 he became one of the founding members of the HIA (*Terrorism Monitor*, September 21, 2006).

During that period the anti-Pakistan policies of the Kabul regime and an emerging Pashtun nationalism in Afghanistan helped Hekmatyar catch the eye of the Pakistani leadership and especially the attention of its secret service, Inter-Services Intelligence

(ISI), which was increasingly displeased by the efforts of the Kabul regime to turn Pakistani Pashtuns against Islamabad. The Soviet occupation of Afghanistan in 1979 and the agreement reached by Pakistan and the Western powers to block the further expansion of the Soviet Union brought Hekmatyar into an advantageous position, as the majority of financial support from the international community to Afghan resistance groups began flowing through him.

Hekmatyar used the Afghan refugee camps of Shamshatoo and Jalozai as recruitment bases for his group (Aina TV, April 22, 2008). In these camps, the HIA distributed rations provided by the West for Afghan refugees while also forming a social and political network that operated everything from schools to prisons.

On the other hand Hekmatyar was always accused of spending more time and resources fighting other mujahideen groups than doing battle with the common enemy, not only during the 1979-1989 Afghan resistance against Soviet occupation, but also after the fall of Najibullah Ahmadzai's communist government to the mujahideen in 1992. Hekmatyar's bombardment of the capital in 1994, for instance, is said to have resulted in the deaths of more than 25,000 civilians (Aina TV, May 23, 2007). As a result of this bloodshed, relatively modern-minded residents put up no resistance against the entrance of the fanatically religious Taliban to Kabul in 1996, which eventually led Hekmatyar's foreign supporters—such as Pakistan and Saudi Arabia—to turn against him, preferring to lend their weight instead to the Taliban.

Disgraced by his former allies, Hekmatyar went to Iran in 1997, sharing with its rulers a common hatred of the Taliban. But almost six years of isolation in Tehran lost him his power base back home, as the majority of his former party members abandoned their resistance or changed sides and joined the Taliban.

The Iranians may have regarded him as a potentially useful Pashtun card to have up their sleeve, but in practice he turned out to be more of a liability. Following the fall of the Taliban in 2001, he was not even invited to the Bonn Conference where the foundation of the new Afghan government was being laid. In Hekmatyar's view, this left no alternative but to oppose the new government. Hekmatyar paid a high price for his opposition to the new Afghan government, as intensive pressure from the United States and the Karzai administration led the Iranian government to expel him in February 2002 and freeze his accounts. On February 19, 2003, the U.S. State Department designated him a global terrorist.

While his former allies joined the Afghan government in one form or another, Hekmatyar reportedly lives today in an unknown location in southeastern Afghanistan, somewhere close to the Pakistani border. This location in his decades-old power base has brought him some advantages, as today he is one of the last of the former mujahid leaders to refuse to join the government and who still talks about removing foreign troops from the country by force. In a recent and rare interview, Hekmatyar expanded on his demands:

"We want all foreign forces to leave immediately without any condition. This is the demand of the entire Afghan nation. Naturally, if it is within their power, they will never leave Afghanistan and Iraq. They will only leave if staying becomes extremely expensive as compared to leaving. No imperial power leaves its domain willingly—they leave under compulsion. The English left the subcontinent, Africa and Asia only when they were forced to leave. What have the Americans got out of their occupation of Afghanistan and Iraq? What they wanted from the occupation was to have control of the Central Asian and Iraqi oil and to firmly establish Israel in the Middle East. Islamic renaissance shall be suppressed and al-Qaeda will be eliminated. Please tell me which of these objectives they have achieved?" (CBS, May 6, 2008; Shahadat, May 19, 2008)

A Shifting Power Structure

The problem of dealing with Hekmatyar is the question that now dominates the local Afghan press. Despite clear opposition by his Western allies, particularly those in Washington, Karzai is increasingly left with no other option than to engage with Hekmatyar in one way or another.

According to the local press, during the last year there have been several occasions when Karzai has offered to open talks, suggesting that present opponents of the government could take official posts such as deputy minister or head of department. Hekmatyar was not named personally for these posts, but there is little doubt that he was one of the "opponents of the government" that Karzai was referring to (Tolo TV, September 29, 2007).

President Karzai may have many reasons to soften his approach toward Hekmatyar, but one of them is surely Hekmatyar's increasing involvement in violent activities, the most recent being the attack of April 27, 2008. The Taliban claimed responsibility for the attack but more than one local newspaper suggested that while the Taliban is an obvious suspect, the attack seems more the act of organized and experienced militants, most probably assisted by high-ranking Afghan officials in penetrating a supposedly secure area (Kabul Weekly, April 30, 2008; Tolo TV, April 27, 2008).

From the security perspective, the timing of Hekmatyar's re-emergence is highly critical, as today Taliban and al-Qaeda fighters are increasingly being cornered by Coalition forces.

HIA members—who, according to Deputy Speaker of Parliament Sardar Rahmanoglu, today occupy around 30 to 40 percent of government offices, from cabinet ministers to provisional and other government posts— are better placed than the Taliban to cause harm to the government or its members (Aina TV, April 22, 2008).

However this is not the only event that signals the re-empowering of HIA and Hekmatyar. An HIA spokesperson has recently claimed responsibility for many other attacks against the government and foreign troops. These include shooting down a helicopter containing foreign troops in the Laghman province (Pajwak News Agency, January 2, 2008), forcing a U.S. military helicopter to make an emergency landing after being shot in the Sarubi district of Kabul (Pajwak News Agency, January 22, 2008) and blowing up a Kabul police vehicle in March, which the spokesperson claimed took the lives of 10 soldiers (Pajwak News Agency, January 22, 2008; AIP, March 8, 2008).

Hekmatyar still maintains his bases in Afghanistan and Afghan refugee camps in Pakistan, such as in the crowded Shamshatoo camp in the North-West Frontier Province (NWFP) of Pakistan. There, the HIA runs madrassas, has set up bases for the governing council of the party and publishes its weekly journal, Tanweer, which commonly employs jihadist slogans against the Karzai administration and foreign troops in Afghanistan (Ariana TV, December 12, 2007; Monthly Kabul Direct, October 2007).

From the security perspective, the timing of Hekmatyar's re-emergence is highly critical, as today Taliban and al-Qaeda fighters are increasingly being cornered by Coalition forces. Some elements of the Taliban are disorganized and frustrated, especially after the death of commander Mullah Dadullah last year. The HIA, under the leadership of an experienced guerrilla strategist, is becoming an attractive proposition for not only the Taliban fighters, but all of those opposing the Karzai government and the presence of foreign troops in Afghanistan. Many Taliban fighters were attached to Hekmatyar's forces in the past in one form or another, so many are basically returning to their former leader, though the numbers involved are unclear.

On the other hand, the HIA is already well-placed within the government, being able to encircle President Karzai politically. As Hekmatyar's former Deputy Qazi Muhammad Amin Waqad notes: "The party has two to three [Cabinet] ministers, five governors, a deputy minister and many other high ranking officials" (Monthly Kabul Direct, October 2007).

Conclusion

These realities leave no alternative for President Karzai but to try to bring Hekmatyar under the umbrella of the government. If he manages this, he will also gain a measure of legitimacy and popularity among the Pashtun tribes, a popularity he currently lacks. This would then help Karzai to win the support of the religious circles of the Pashtun tribes against the Taliban (Daily Cheragh, June 28, 2007).

Not only does Hekmatyar not trust the government's intentions behind the peace talks, but he places as a condition of his cooperation with the government the departure of foreign troops from Afghanistan (Hasht-e Sobh, May 19, 2008). Due to the reality on the ground, President Karzai is unlikely to accept such a deal.

In addition, President Karzai has other serious obstacles to the appointment of Hekmatyar to the administration. Some of his government partners, such as former President Burhanuddin Rabbani and current Parliamentary Speaker Yunus Qanuni, are unlikely to welcome such a move, given almost three decades of hostility with Hekmatyar (Hasht-e Sobh, May 5, 2008). Short of pursuing the military option, the government may seek the mediation of influential regional players like Pakistan or Saudi Arabia in reaching a deal with Hekmatyar (Monthly Kabul Direct, October 2007). With Hekmatyar having emerged as a legitimate threat, Karzai needs to act quickly if he does not wish to see the emergence of another serious security challenge to the central administration.

Originally published in *Terrorism Monitor*: Volume 6, Issue 11 on May 29, 2008.

Rotation of Coalition Forces Brings New Hope to Helmand Province
By Waliullah Rahmani

With the onset of a wide operation against the Taliban in Garmsir district of Helmand province, once again the lawless Helmand province has become the focus of national and international circles. On April 30, 2008 the U.S. Marines announced they had recaptured Garmsir district from Taliban control and entered governmental buildings (BBC Persian.com, April 30, 2008). As of June 2008, at least 10 insurgents have been reported killed or injured every day during the Marines' operations in different areas of Helmand.

The return of U.S. forces to this volatile southern province has been accompanied by rumors in Helmand and Kabul that the U.S. forces will eventually be replaced by British troops who were in charge of Helmand for the past two years. Such a development would be generally unwelcome in the province. Meanwhile, the redeployment of U.S. troops to Helmand has brought hopes for the betterment of security and easing of the insurgency in at least parts of this neo-Taliban-dominated province. These developments in Helmand over April-May 2008, however, need to be examined so that there can be a clear vision of where Helmand stands and to distinguish the status of the leading players there.

The General Situation of Helmand

Following U.S. operations in Garmsir district and raids by NATO forces on Musa Qala and other areas of Helmand, there have been reports that violence has eased in the center of neo-Taliban power. An aware resident of the Nawamish area of Helmand province told Jamestown that in comparison to last year, the movement of the Taliban in Helmand for now is very low and few in numbers. On the condition of anonymity, the resident said that by the start of the spring and good weather, people were expecting more attacks and violence from the Taliban, but stressed that this year the situation in the province has changed [1]. Meanwhile, another source who did not want to be named told Jamestown that the general mood and morale of the Taliban is very weak in comparison to last year. He admitted that even in Musa Qala district, once called the Taliban's "university of terror," the insurgents are weak and have lost their power to maneuver [2]. This assessment was confirmed by an Afghan MP from Helmand province, who says that the Taliban's tactic of attack and escape has seen only limited use since the start of 2008 and they have not been successful in putting serious pressure on government forces or international troops. That said, the Taliban are in control of some districts of Helmand and have recently divided into two groups as well. Reports confirm a rift within the local Taliban and say that in comparison to last year, the Taliban's ability to coordinate in Helmand is in question.

Rift within the Helmand Taliban

Among the public in Helmand's Lashkar Gah district there are rumors of a wide rift between the different Taliban groups. In interviews with Jamestown, many residents of Lashkar Gah admitted this rift and said that a high-ranking Taliban official who had recently joined the government was killed by his former comrades. These residents point out that the murder of this influential former Taliban leader—who still had many loyalists among the neo-Taliban of Helmand—caused deep divisions between two groups of insurgents (Author's interviews with Laskhkar Gah residents and individuals).

Meanwhile, an Afghan official, on condition of anonymity, admitted the gap between the Taliban forces. He named the murdered influential Taliban leader as Haji Abdur Rahman who had joined the government and was based in the city of Laskar Gah. He said that recently Haji Abdur Rahman had been on a trip to Marjah district, where he wanted to solve some problems among the Taliban. On his way back to Lashkar Gah city—the provincial capital—a group of Taliban killed him together with his associates.

Meanwhile, there are reports of changes in the Taliban administration of Helmand. The neo-Taliban forces have set up provincial administrations for every province of Afghanistan. For Helmand, the Taliban announced a governor, district chiefs and judges. During the last few years, the Taliban governor of Helmand was someone named Mullah Abdur Rahim Akhund who was appointed to control Helmand

The Taliban's main base of power is now in some districts of Helmand province which were gained by the insurgents during the last two years.

and lead the Taliban insurgents there. But now the Taliban have announced the replacement of Mullah Abdur Rahim Akhund with a new governor named Mullah Mistari Akhund. Although the names are fictitious, some sources confirm these changes among the top officials of the local Taliban.

The Taliban's Power Base in Helmand

The Taliban's main base of power is now in some districts of Helmand province which were gained by the insurgents during the last two years. On March 3, 2008 Amrullah Salih of the National Security Department of Afghanistan confirmed that four districts of Helmand province are still under the control of Taliban insurgents; namely, Deshu, Khanshin, Baghran and Washir (Tolo TV, March 3, 2008). In his March 3 speech in Afghanistan's parliament, the head of the National Security Department of Afghanistan never mentioned the Taliban's control over Garmsir district, which is now controlled by U.S. forces.

Two months after Amrullah Salih's comments, some sources maintain the Taliban still control these provinces. One official said that the districts of Washir, Barghran, Khanshin and Nawzad are not under the control of the Afghan government [3]. Nawzad district has a variety of passages to the western Farah province where insurgent activity has increased in the last year. The districts of Khanshin and Deshu are located on the border of Afghanistan and Pakistan and have many ways into the neighboring country's territory. Khanshin also has routes to the insurgents' bases in the southwestern province of Nimruz.

The Taliban in Helmand can resist government and Coalition forces partly because of the support they receive from either Pakistan or the neighboring Nimruz and Farah provinces. An Afghan MP from Helmand, Niamathullah Ghafari, told Jamestown that whenever the Taliban feel themselves to be under pressure, they escape to Farah, Nimruz or Pakistan. According to Ghafari, the Taliban's control over these four districts of Helmand is due to the fact that they have never been confined to these districts [4].

The Taliban's Chain of Command

In Helmand the Taliban are reported to be controlled by Mullah Berader Akhund, the deputy of Mullah Omar. Although it is not confirmed whether Berader is directly engaged in the planning, coordination and implementation processes of the insurgents' operations against the government and international forces, it is clear that he has been given the power to be the core commander of the Taliban in the provinces of Helmand, Kandahar and Oruzgan.

Aside from Mullah Berader, some residents of the Nad Ali district of Helmand province say that they have heard Mullah Naqib Akhund is back at the frontlines in Helmand. This claim has not been confirmed, as it was recently announced that Mullah Naqib was injured and arrested by government forces and was supposedly in prison. The other well-known commanders of the Helmand Taliban are said to be the aforementioned former Taliban governor of Helmand, Mullah Abdur Rahim Akhund, and his replacement, Mullah Mistari Akhund.

Helmand Public Opinion of Afghan and International Forces in Helmand

The majority of Helmandis appear to be optimistic about the performance of the Afghan National Army (ANA) in Helmand province. The ANA forces have been widely welcomed by different groups of Helmand citizens who are supportive of these forces [5]. Some people said that the National Army forces were doing their duty in accordance with Afghan culture and traditions. Many people, however, were negative regarding the performance of that part of the Afghan Police forces called the "Helping Police." These police forces were deployed during the last two years, but it is reported that the new governor of Helmand province has removed most of the so-called "Helping Police," whom the people claim are mostly drug addicts and members of criminal groups.

Meanwhile, Helmand MP Niamathullah Ghafari told Jamestown that most of Helmand's citizens are happier with the Afghan forces than the British troops. He added that the people also have a good opinion of the U.S. forces.

According to Ghafari, many Helmandis know that four decades ago the Americans built a great deal of infrastructure in Helmand. They point to the work done by Americans in Lashkar Gah city, including the U.S.-built school and hospital and the U.S.-built Bughra dam. On the other hand, many still have negative impressions of the British occupation of Afghanistan, particularly during the period of the Second Anglo-Afghan War (1878-80).

In what was once called the center of the Taliban insurgency in Afghanistan, there are at most 3,000 Taliban insurgents still in the field. The current situation in Helmand is expected to improve in comparison to that of the last two years. There are expectations that with the redeployment of U.S. troops and nearly 6,000 Afghan National Police and ANA to Helmand, the insurgency and related violence will ease in the near future.

Originally published in *Terrorism Monitor*: Volume 6, Issue 12 on June 12, 2008.

Notes

1. Author interview with a Nawamish district resident.
2. Ibid.
3. Ibid.
4. Author interview with Ghafari.
5. Author interviews with many residents of Lashkar Gah city.

BANGLADESH

The Bengali Taliban: Jamaat-ul-Mujahideen Bangladesh
By Wilson John

The April 30, 2008 sentencing of four cadres of the outlawed Jamaat-ul-Mujahideen Bangladesh (JMB) to 26 years of hard labor for throwing bombs at a local court in 2005 returned the focus to Bangladesh's struggle against pressing odds to contain the rise of Islamic extremism (Daily Star [Dhaka], May 1, 2008).

The government has been hunting down JMB leaders and cadres ever since the group carried out an audacious series of blasts in 63 districts out of a total of 64 across Bangladesh, planting 458 locally-made bombs while distributing leaflets that declared, "We're the soldiers of Allah. We've taken up arms for the implementation of Allah's law the way the Prophet, Sahabis [companions of the Prophet] and heroic Mujahideen have done for centuries ... it is time to implement Islamic law in Bangladesh" (Bangladesh Observer, August 18, 2005). In the crackdown that followed, two top leaders of the group, Shaykh Abdur Rahman and Sidiqul Islam (alias Bangla Bhai), were executed in 2007; several hundred cadres have also been arrested from different parts of the country. Many of these have since been given tough sentences by a judiciary which was once high on the list of JMB's potential targets.

Though the crackdown was ordered by the Bangladesh Nationalist Party (BNP) government under pressure from the Bangladesh Army and public outrage, it was the caretaker government run by the Army which saw the increasing clout of groups like JMB as a direct threat to its authority. The Army is deeply skeptical of political parties like the BNP, its rival Awami League (AL) and the ultra-conservative religious party, Jamaat-e-Islami (JeI), which aligned with the Pakistan Army during the independence struggle and opposed the creation of Bangladesh [1].

Political Connections

JMB drew its ideological and political support from JeI—both executed JMB leaders Abdur Rahman and Bangla Bhai were active members—which was the reason why the BNP government, which relies on JeI support, dragged its feet in taking a strong action against religious extremist groups despite credible evidence [2]. Both Rahman and Bangla Bhai were members of Islami Chhatra Shibir (ICS), the student wing of JeI, during their college days and maintained close contacts with JeI leaders [3].

In fact, Bangladeshi intelligence agencies warned the government back in 2003 about JMB and the threat it posed to the state (Daily Star, August 28, 2005). The group was banned in February 2005 after a key leader—a university professor and ideologue, Dr. Mohammad Asadullah al-Ghalib—revealed the group's plans to overthrow the civilian government through violence (New Age [Dhaka], February 28, 2005).

Set up in 1998, JMB is one of several extremist and terrorist organizations in Bangladesh waging a fratricidal war against the young nation-state with the aim of establishing an Islamic state. This type of political violence has existed since 1971, when largely Bengali East Pakistan wrested independence from Punjabi-dominated Pakistan. Though substantive evidence of the JMB's links with global jihadi groups like al-Qaeda has yet to surface, JMB's transnational terrorist linkages—ideological and material—are evident.

Creation of the JMB

JMB's founder and spiritual leader was Shaykh Abdur Rahman of Jamalpur district in Bangladesh. Abdur Rahman studied at Madina University and worked as a translator and interpreter at the Saudi Embassy in Dhaka before traveling to Afghanistan to take part in jihad (Daily Star, August 28, 2005). He most likely followed in the footsteps of the 3,500-strong batch of recruits dispatched to terrorist training camps by Harkat-ul Jihad al Islami (HuJI), an al-Qaeda-friendly Deobandi group. His association with HuJI, widely regarded as al-Qaeda's South Asia arm, could also be noted from his reported links with two foreign—likely Arab—trainers who came to Bangladesh in 1995 to train militants from the Bengali-related Rohingya, a Muslim ethnic group fighting for independence from Myanmar (Al Jazeera, April 2, 2007). Rohingyas formed the backbone of the Bangladeshi terror groups often known as the Bangladesh Taliban and had considerable presence in the Korgani town of Karachi, one of HuJI's key operational headquarters from where it assisted al-Qaeda and other groups.

These trainers had come to Bangladesh on the invitation of Asadullah al-Galib, a professor in Rajshahi University and head of the militant Islamist Ahle Hadith Andolan Bangladesh (AHAB). Al-Galib was a close ally of Abdur Rahman and part of the triumvirate—Abdur Rahman and Bangla Bhai being the other two—which ran JMB till 2005. Arrested in February 2005, al-Galib today awaits trial in scores of terrorism cases. The foreign trainers coached the Rohingyas for the Afghan jihad first and then trained local recruits for five to six years. In 1998, after returning from

JMB has a clear political agenda: It aims to capture power through armed revolution and run the country by a Majlis-e-Shur (Central Committee) under Islamic laws. The group also wants to rid Muslims of "anti-Muslim" influences, particularly those related to women, an ideology it shares with the Taliban.

Afghanistan, Abdur Rahman and al-Galib decided to launch their own militant outfit in Bangladesh, calling it Jamaat-ul-Mujahideen Bangladesh. There are also reports that one of Rahman's close associates, Faruq Hossain (alias Khaled Saifullah), was a HuJI leader and had learned bomb-making in the terrorist training camps of Afghanistan (Daily Times [Lahore], January 24, 2005; Daily Star, March 2, 2006). The contours of the outfit were decided at a 1998 meeting the duo had at Chittagong, the nerve center for extremist activities in Bangladesh (Al Jazeera, April 2, 2007). The first meeting of the JMB commanders was held in early 2002 at Khetlal in Joypurhat, but a series of arrests of some senior leaders, including Abdur Rahman's younger brother, Ataur Rahman—who was being groomed as the military commander of the group—forced JMB to go underground and expand their activities across the country (New Age, October 2, 2005).

The Political Agenda

JMB has a clear political agenda: It aims to capture power through armed revolution and run the country by a Majlis-e-Shur (Central Committee) under Islamic laws. The group also wants to rid Muslims of "anti-Muslim" influences, particularly those related to women, an ideology it shares with the Taliban. Abdur Rahman, however, denied any linkages with the Taliban and said in a May 2004 interview: "We are called part of al-Qaeda, Taliban or [an] Islamist militant organization. We are not like that ... If the people of Bangladesh give us the responsibility of running the nation, we will accept it ... We would like to serve people in line with Hilful Fuzul (a social organization founded by the Prophet Muhammad) to serve the destitute" (Daily Star, August 28, 2005).

Before the crackdown, the JMB was led by a seven-member Majlis-e-Shura, comprising its top leadership, including Abdur Rahman and Bangla Bhai. The group had 16 regional commanders and 64 district heads, besides hundreds of operational commanders. The cadre was organized in three tiers (Star Weekend Magazine [Dhaka], December 5, 2005). The first tier was known as Eshar, where the 200 members were full-timers and reported directly to the Central Committee. The second tier was Gayeri Easher and had about 10,000 members. The third tier was Sathis or Sudhis (assistants) consisting of younger foot soldiers. For operational requirements, the group divided the country into nine divisions—one division each in Khulna, Barisal, Sylhet and Chittagong, two each in Dhaka and Rajshahi (The Independent [Dhaka], September 22, 2005).

Training for Terror

A close ally of the group is the Jagrata Muslim Janata Bangladesh (JMJB), considered to be a more radical and violent wing of JMB. The leadership, structure, objectives and operational methodology of JMJB were similar to that of the JMB. Both groups had strong bases in the northwestern districts—Rajshahi, Naogan, Joypurhat, Natore, Rangpur, Bogra—and the southern districts of Bagerhat, Jessore, Satkhira, Chittagong and Khulna. At the height of its activities, the group had networks in 57 districts working through madrassas and educational institutions and at least 10 training camps at Atrai and Raninagar in Naogaon, Bagmara in Rajshahi and Naldanga and Singra in Natore. The recruits were trained with the help of video footage of warfare training at al-Qaeda's now defunct Farooque camp in Afghanistan, pro-Taliban videos and recorded speeches of Osama bin Laden. Recruits are also spurred by motivational speeches, leaflets and graffiti written and distributed across the country.

The JMB also had a suicide squad called Shahid Nasirullah Arafat Brigade; members had an "insurance policy" from the group (UPI, March 2, 2006). Bomb-making was a specialized task that was stressed during training, most of which takes place in open fields, mosque grounds and in wooded areas.

The group relies on the following sources of funding: Robbery and extortion, illegal tolls or taxes on traders and other businessmen in the areas they control, donations from local patrons, expatriate Bangladeshis and charities and NGOs based in West Asia. A joint 2005 report prepared by Bangladesh's Special Branch, National Security Intelligence (NSI) and Defense Forces Intelligence pointed out that 10 Islamic charities and NGOs were promoting and funding extremist groups like JMB [4].

The massive crackdown and the harsh sentencing of JMB leaders and cadres since August 2005 have crippled the group considerably. But recent arrests of younger cadre members, media reports of regroupings in remote areas of Gaibandha District of north Bangladesh [5] and a continuing manhunt for the new leader of the JMB, Maulana Saidur Rahman—a former JI leader—raises fears about the possibility of JMB's renewed attempts to make a comeback in a country that is vulnerable to the increasing spread of al-Qaeda ideology (*Gulf Times* [Kuwait], October 2, 2007; Daily Star, January 19, 2008).

Originally published in *Terrorism Monitor*: Volume 6, Issue 10 on May 15, 2008.

Notes

1. A detailed analysis of the nexus between JeI and extremist groups like JMB can be found in Hiranmay Karlekar, *Bangladesh: The Next Afghanistan?* (New Delhi: Sage Publications, 2005). See also *Terrorism Monitor*, January 13, 2005.
2. Selig Harrison, "A New Hub of Terrorism?" *Washington Post*, August 2, 2006. Also see Maneeza Hossain, "The Rising Tide of Islamism in Bangladesh," Hudson Institute, *Current Trends in Islamist Ideology*, vol. 3, February 16, 2006; Ajit Doval, "Islamic Terrorism in South Asia and India's Strategic Response," *Policing* 1, no. 1 (2007).
3. For a good reference to the politics of extremism in Bangladesh, see Liz Philipson, "Corrupted Democracy," *Himal Southasian*, August 2006.
4. Chris Blackburn, "Terrorism in Bangladesh: The Region and Beyond," Paper presented at the Policy Exchange Conference in London on November 14, 2006; *New Age*, September 22, 2005.
5. A report prepared by Dhaka-based NGO The Bangladesh Enterprise Institute; "Trend of Militancy in Bangladesh and Possible Responses," quoted "a suspected militant commander, Mustafizur Rahman Shahin, who was arrested in Pabna, as saying that some 5,000 operatives are active across the country." See also *The New Nation*, February 29, 2008; *Bangladesh Today*, February 29, 2008.

INDIA

India's Intelligence Services Struggle with War on Terrorism
By Wilson John

A diffuse but highly networked group of terrorists, driven by a dangerous cocktail of extremist ideology and a simmering sense of anguish and revenge, currently pose a serious threat to India's economic and social structure. The militants exploit gaping holes in India's counter-terrorism architecture and strategy as well as the nation's ambivalent policies toward religious minorities, particularly the 150-million strong but largely impoverished Muslim community.

What has complicated the Indian intelligence agencies' task since the flowering of al-Qaeda and a global jihadist movement after 9/11 is the alacrity with which various terrorist groups and their support structures have reworked their strategy and operational methods to effectively dodge a series of worldwide bans. The most dramatic change in the Indian context has been the realignment of terrorist forces, with prominent groups like the Lashkar-e-Tayyeba (LeT) and Jaish-e-Mohammad (JeM)—proscribed by the United States and other countries, including Pakistan—stepping back to allow Harkat-ul Jihad al-Islami (HuJI), an al-Qaeda ally with a pan-South Asian presence, to lead the terror campaign in India (Rediff.com, May 25, 2007).

> *The militants exploit gaping holes in India's counter-terrorism architecture and strategy as well as the nation's ambivalent policies toward religious minorities, particularly the 150-million strong but largely impoverished Muslim community.*

Other changes have been noticed in the structure and *modus operandi* of India's terrorist groups. The new recruits to the cause are local men: young, educated and without previous involvement in extremist activities. These men form the nucleus of groups throughout India who tap into the local criminal-hawala network of couriers and handlers to move money and explosives—often locally acquired—to carry out terrorist strikes [1]. The group carrying out the operation typically disengages and disappears after striking, leaving hardly any trace of its existence. Since the simultaneous explosions in Delhi in 2005, investigating agencies frequently encounter red herrings left by the terrorists to confuse the investigation and allow greater time to disband and escape.

Changing Circumstances

Two critical aspects in the growth of Indian terrorism are the mounting evidence pointing to the involvement of the HuJI in terror attacks and the alliance of this group with the Students' Islamic Movement of India (SIMI), a banned network of young Muslim activists who openly claim Osama bin Laden as their idol (The Hindu, April 3, 2007). For a long time India's federal and state investigating agencies did not see the link as a serious development, continuing instead to rely on past experience by focusing on LeT and JeM activists.

One of the primary reasons for this poor assessment was the inability of the intelligence agencies and the whole cornucopia of coordinating agencies at state and federal levels to think beyond the entrenched "conventional wisdom" of analyzing terrorist groups through ideological prisms, thereby completely missing the possibility that these groups might work together for a common goal. This has happened not only in India but even in Pakistan, where one such coalition of terror groups called Brigade 313 was involved in assassination attempts on President Pervez Musharraf (Newsline, August 2004; Asia Times, July 14, 2004).

Equally restricting has been the reluctance, and even refusal, to share information among the intelligence and security agencies. Along with an inept information-sharing architecture at the national level, this reluctance has proved to be the most critical flaw in counter-terrorism intelligence operations (The Hindu, October 30, 2001). The problem came to the fore recently when police in the Karnataka state of southern India arrested one Riyazuddin Nasir on charges of vehicle theft. Nasir would have been let out on bail for these minor charges but for a single intelligence official in Delhi who decided to search the database for connections with terrorist activities. Nasir was found to be a HuJI operative and one of India's most wanted men (The Hindu, February 12, 2008).

Failure to Cooperate

It is not really difficult to see where the problem is—an intelligence structure that has yet to emerge from its debilitating colonial legacy and a complementary stranglehold of bureaucracy. The structure and operational philosophy of state police and intelligence units have not changed much since British days—they are mostly structured as agencies to protect law and order and spy on rivals rather than act as investigative and intelligence units. Criminal investigators are usually inserted into terrorism investigations only after an incident takes place. There are no independent anti-terror units carrying out both intelligence and investigations into terrorist groups at the state level.

It is not really difficult to see where the problem is—an intelligence structure that has yet to emerge from its debilitating colonial legacy and a complementary stranglehold of bureaucracy.

At the top of the intelligence pyramid is the National Security Council Secretariat (NSCS), headed by an all-powerful, politically-appointed National Security Advisor (NSA), who often has much more than terrorism on his mind. Intelligence operations within the country are carried out by the Intelligence Bureau (IB) and its wide network of officers and men, all reporting to the Ministry of Home Affairs. The ministry is headed by a cabinet minister and one or two ministers of state—besides a secretary and other senior officials—who often get tempted, at least close to the elections, to utilize the IB for assessing the electoral chances of their party while spying on their rivals. EM

Rammohan, a former member of the National Security Advisory Board, notes: "Instead of concentrating on security issues, they are busy chasing the Opposition so that the ruling party is kept in power. Is that the job of the IB?" (Outlookindia.com, July 31, 2006).

External intelligence is the responsibility of the Research and Analysis Wing (RAW), working directly under the Cabinet Secretary but reporting to the NSA for all practical purposes. RAW keeps a sharp eye on the activities of terrorist groups with bases in foreign countries. According to former IB joint-director Maloy Krishna Dhar, RAW's reluctance to share information with IB is legendary (Rediff.com, August 17, 2006). There have also been instances where personality clashes have deterred effective coordination between the NSA and RAW chiefs [2].

The second set of intelligence agencies are the military ones, led by the Directorate General of Military Intelligence (DGMI) with a network of field offices and forward posts in the border areas as well as representatives in diplomatic missions. Since the DGMI has been historically part of the Army, the Air Force and Navy have individual intelligence units collecting and collating information relevant to their operations and bases. The Defence Intelligence Agency (DIA), created in 2002 to correct this anomaly, is entrusted with the task of coordinating the whole spectrum of military intelligence but is presently short-staffed, poorly funded and burdened with an ambitious and expanding circle of objectives [3].

Paramilitary organizations like the Central Reserve Police Force and Border Security Force maintain their own intelligence units to support counter-insurgency operations in Kashmir and elsewhere. Their intelligence operations have often been stymied by the Army's reluctance to share intelligence tapped from its wide network of informers and sources. Other government agencies providing physical security, like the Special Protection Group, Central Industrial Security Force and National Security Guards, all maintain their own intelligence units.

At the bottom of the pyramid are the state police, whose intelligence networks remain the primary source of information and main agency for implementing action on the ground. The most critical element in this structure is the investigative branch of the local police forces. These go by various names, such as the Criminal Investigation Department, the Special Branch or the Crime Branch. There is no uniformity in responsibilities or operational duties. Typically these units carry out the investigation and prosecution of terrorist, hawala, arms and counterfeit cases, placing them in the unique position of being able to detect the emergence of terror networks or coalitions.

Unfortunately they remain the weakest link in the intelligence chain as these units carry the burden of acting as colonial-style law enforcement agencies and not as modern units capable of organizing preventive measures based on intelligence collection. These forces are commonly afflicted with poor morale and problems related to accountability, pay and training. Even in metropolitan centers like Delhi and Mumbai, the police-criminal nexus and pervasive corruption have rendered effective intelligence from federal agencies worthless. There was clear intelligence available about terrorist attacks in Mumbai at least a month before the July 2006 commuter train blasts. This intelligence was not followed up on, nor were preventive measures put in place at railway stations. A week after the Mumbai blasts, Prime Minister Manmohan Singh was quoted by the media as saying that "past responses have been inadequate in dealing with these problems that are of a different intensity, magnitude, scale and scope" (The Tribune [Chandigarh, Punjab], July 21, 2006).

Reforming the Intelligence Structure

Of the several steps taken in recent years to overcome these outstanding difficulties, two held great promise. One was the creation of the National Technical Research Organization (NTRO), with a focus on collecting technical intelligence (TECHINT), cyber intelligence and cyber counter-intelligence [4]. Beginning with RAW's Aviation Research Centre (ARC) assets, NTRO is rapidly expanding and strengthening its intelligence capabilities to fulfill this mandate. On the other hand, the NTRO mandate adds one more agency to the mix, as the IB, RAW and the Army's Signals Directorate will continue to maintain autonomous TECHINT units.

The second step was the establishment of a Multi-Agency Centre (MAC) and a Joint Task Force on Intelligence within IB as a hub of India's counter-terrorism effort. The mission objective was to run an umbrella organization comprising state-level units called SMACs and the development of a national counter-terrorism database supported by state-level police-intelligence Joint Task Forces and inter-state Intelligence Support Teams (The Hindu, February 12, 2008). Conceived after the pattern of the CIA's Counter-Terrorism Center, the MAC was to be responsible for the joint analysis of intelligence flowing from different quarters and coordinating relevant follow-up actions (Rediff.com, April 6, 2003).

Five years after MAC was approved, it is today composed of a skeletal staff and five SMACs, using a database hosted on a bare-bones computer system designed in-house, with no real-time links to state police forces or other intelligence agencies. There is no sign of the development of the comprehensive database on terrorists on which the entire counter-terrorism information grid was to be built. Senior intelligence officials have pointed out that the interrogation reports of 16,000 Islamist terrorists caught between 1991 and 2005 could prove to be a goldmine of actionable intelligence (The Hindu, February 6, 2008). These inadequacies can be overcome by beefing up the present staff strength and widening the recruitment base to include the qualified technical personnel needed to develop, integrate and man the information grid. But progress is delayed due to unseemly bureaucratic wrangling over funding for an additional 140 positions at MAC. Added to this problem is the Indian Army's refusal to depute officials to the agency, citing disciplinary and administrative problems (The Hindu, February 12, 2008).

Conclusion

Difficulties like these and the tepid response of the state governments to a 2007 Supreme

Court directive ordering improvements in the functioning of police and intelligence agencies continue to bedevil India's attempts to fashion an effective counter-terrorism strategy. Meanwhile terrorist groups continue to display a marked advantage in adapting to newer technologies and modes of operation, allowing them to function more quickly and quietly than the Indian intelligence community.

Originally published in *Terrorism Monitor*: Volume 6, Issue 6 on March 24, 2008.

Notes

1. Hawala is an alternative remittance system with both legitimate and illegitimate uses.
2. Author's interview with a senior RAW official.
3. Author's interview with an official from the Defence Intelligence Agency, New Delhi, in 2007.
4. From B. Raman's lecture on National Security and Armed Forces Command Structure, organized by the Forum for Strategic and Security Studies, New Delhi, on October 16, 2007. Raman is a former senior RAW official who gives details of various intelligence operations in his recent book, *Kaoboys of RAW* (New Delhi: Lancer Publishers, 2007).

The Geostrategic Implications of the Baloch Insurgency
By Tarique Niazi

Pakistan continues to grapple with insurgent violence in its southwestern province of Balochistan, which is bounded by the country's tribal belt in the northwest, Afghanistan in the north and Iran in the west. In the northwest, Pakistan's Federally Administered Tribal Areas (FATA) has also been a hotbed of violence, where Taliban militants have humbled Pakistan's otherwise unbeatable armed forces in a three-year active conflict. On November 8, 2006 they dealt the Pakistan Army the deadliest blow yet, in which 42 soldiers were killed in one strike. Similarly, Afghanistan to the north continues to simmer with the Taliban's violent attacks that have registered a four-fold increase from 130 a month last year to 600 a month since the September 5 Pakistan-Taliban peace deal in North Waziristan (*Dawn*, November 13, 2006). The Taliban are alleged to have some operational bases in Balochistan, in addition to those in Pakistan's tribal north. In the west, Sistan-Balochistan, also known as western Balochistan, is up in arms against the Iranian government. On December 15, 2005, a daring assassination bid was mounted against a motorcade of Iranian President Mahmud Ahmadinejad on the Zabul-Saravan Highway, in which one of his bodyguards was killed (*Terrorism Monitor*, February 23, 2006). Pressure is, therefore, mounting on Islamabad to solve the situation in Balochistan before it spirals out of control.

Pakistan's Military Buildup in Balochistan

Pakistan has been watchful of Balochistan's violent surroundings, especially since the U.S.-led invasion of Afghanistan, which delivered Kabul from the Taliban's dogmatic theology and strict social order. Yet the Taliban, however repugnant, were Pakistan's guardians of its northwestern frontier with Afghanistan and its southwestern border with Iran, freeing up Pakistan's military resources to allow it to fortify its eastern border with India. Since the Taliban's toppling in 2001, Pakistan feels that its western border is now exposed to "hostile intentions." It has since moved fast to build up its military presence in Balochistan, planning a host of garrisons all across the province, especially in its resource-rich, but Islamabad-wary, bits of Dera Bugti, Kohlu and Khuzdar.

In parallel with army establishments, Pakistan, for the first time, began to build naval defenses in Balochistan to safeguard its nearly 1,000-kilometer coastline. One such defense installation is the Jinnah Naval Base at Ormara, which is the Pakistan Navy's (PN) second-largest base after its flagship naval port in Karachi. The Jinnah Naval Base has displayed Balochistan's paramount naval importance that has long been envied by regional powers, including the former Soviet Union and India. Yet the Jinnah Base is ancillary to the development of Pakistan's ultimate naval defenses in Balochistan's coastal town of Gwadar, which sits along the Arabian Sea coast. Pakistan, in collaboration with China, is building one of the world's largest deep seaports in Gwadar. General Pervez Musharraf, then Pakistan's president, and the visiting Chinese Vice Premier Wu Bangguo laid the foundation of the Gwadar Port on March 22, 2002, exactly four months after the

U.S.-led invasion of Afghanistan (*China Brief*, February 15, 2005). The first two phases of the $1.6 billion port has since been completed. Musharraf will visit it on November 16, ahead of Chinese President Hu Jintao's visit to Islamabad on November 23, 2006.

The Baloch, who are weakly represented in the military government in Islamabad, were opposed to the planned militarization of their province and "colonization of their natural resources," which include 29 trillion cubic feet of natural gas, six billion barrels of oil and about a 1,000-kilometer coastline (*Terrorism Focus*, September 6, 2006). They raised their voice against Islamabad's moves to "occupy their land." Islamabad dismissed them as "miscreants," "saboteurs" and "terrorists," responding with a large-scale military deployment to crush opposition. The conflict that ensued pushed Oxford-educated Baloch leader Nawab Akbar Bugti, who was internationally acclaimed as a statesman, especially in neighboring Afghanistan, Central Asia, the Middle East, India and Iran, to become involved. Nawab Bugti first called on his political reserves to persuade Islamabad against advancing on Balochistan's constitutionally protected "provincial autonomy." He, instead, offered a negotiated settlement of the dispute over appropriation of Balochistan's natural resources by reconciling federal claims of "eminent domain" with constitutionally protected "provincial autonomy." Islamabad agreed. Two parliamentary committees were formed to work out a settlement (Daily Times, July 31, 2005). When one of the committees announced its recommendations, Musharraf did not accept them and turned to military means to resolve the conflict.

Nawab Bugti's Assassination and its Aftermath

Early this year, government troops targeted Nawab Bugti in his house with artillery fire, in which he escaped unhurt (*Terrorism Focus*, September 6, 2006). He then collected his followers and took to living in the mountains, which is a centuries-old Baloch tradition of protest, called "pariris" (i.e., when all avenues of peaceful resolution of grievances are exhausted, violence becomes justified). On August 24, 2006 an intercepted telephone call tracked him to his mountain retreat (The News, August 27, 2006). For three days, a fierce battle raged that killed him and 21 Pakistan Army commandoes (The News, August 31, 2006). On September 1, 2006 when he was laid to rest, most of Pakistan (except for central Punjab province) was shut down to mourn his passing and to protest his assassination. The "official" Pakistan, however, was jubilant after eliminating its chief antagonist.

Within hours of Nawab Bugti's assassination, reality began to sink in for Islamabad. The backlash to his murder swept the country and shook the government. Many government leaders, except Musharraf, publicly grieved for the slain Nawab. Most importantly, former Prime Minister Nawaz Sharif, whose power base is the majority province of Punjab, called Musharraf a "killer" (PakTribune, August 28, 2006). As the Punjab dominates Pakistan's civil and military establishment, Sharif's outrage resonated with the country's elite. Above all, Punjab is the largest beneficiary of the federation, which instinctively makes it wary of centrifugal forces, especially since the fall of East Pakistan in 1971, which became the independent country of Bangladesh. Similarly, retired military leaders, who generally echo the views of serving officers, unanimously condemned the assassination and feared that "another East Pakistan is in the making." They rejected the military solution to the insurgency in Balochistan and urged Musharraf to make peace with Baloch nationalists. Musharraf took their counsel, but in reverse. Within 10 days of Nawab Bugti's assassination, he signed a peace deal with the Taliban in North Waziristan on September 5 (*Terrorism Monitor*, October 5, 2006). Observers find it ironic to see Musharraf cut his losses and run from the tribal north, leaving it in the hands of the retrogressive Taliban, only to crush a progressive nationalist movement in Balochistan, which is allied with the democratic federal forces, such as the Pakistan People's Party (PPP) of former Prime Minister Benazir Bhutto.

In doing so, he played on the military's general apprehension about the weak defenses in Balochistan, where the overwhelming majority of the Baloch and Pashtun population identify themselves with their own "Vatan" (i.e., native land of Balochistan) rather than with "Pakistan." This apprehension was amplified by the growing Indian presence in Afghanistan, Iran and Tajikistan since the removal of the Taliban government in Kabul. Pakistan blamed Indian consulates in Jalalabad and Kandahar in Afghanistan, and Zahedan in Iran, for insurgent violence in Balochistan (*Terrorism Monitor*, May 18, 2006). Pakistan specifically accused India of training and arming the militants of the Balochistan Liberation Army (BLA) for sabotage in the province. In the same vein, Pakistan accused Afghanistan of being India's conduit for cash flow and military supplies to the BLA (*Terrorism Monitor*, May 18, 2006). Yet, what unnerved Islamabad the most was India's military buildup next door in Iran and Tajikistan. In Iran, it was building the Chahbahar Port to rival the Gwadar deep seaport that came to symbolize the summit of the Sino-Pakistan strategic partnership. As a major power of the Indian Ocean, India's move into the Persian Gulf caused deep unease in Islamabad. Pakistan had not yet come to terms with the Indian presence in Iran, especially when it discovered that New Delhi was building an airbase in Tajikistan, which is its second base on foreign soil after its base in Sri Lanka (*Terrorism Monitor*, May 18, 2006). This base can bring northwestern and southwestern Pakistan (the tribal north and Balochistan) under India's air cover.

Balochistan in Revolt

The internal dynamics in Balochistan, especially after the slaying of Nawab Bugti, became all the more dangerous for federal unity. At the Nawab's funeral in Quetta on August 29, 2006 hundreds of youth tore down a portrait of Pakistan's founding father Mohammed Ali Jinnah, who is revered in the country so much as to be mentioned only by his title of Quaid-i-Azam (The Great Leader). In Karachi, which is home to two million Balochs, protesters ripped the Pakistani flag off a wedding hall and dragged it through the streets while stomping on it before they set it on fire (Reuters, August 27, 2006). Such expressions of outrage were simply unheard of in Pakistan. Many ignored these outbursts as spontaneous venting of grief until the Baloch National Jirga met in Quetta on September 21, 2006 and called for revisiting the accession of Balochistan to Pakistan (The News, October 16, 2006). The jirga, which was convened for the first time in 130 years, moved the International Court of Justice (ICJ) to help end Pakistan's occupation of Balochistan (The News, October 16, 2006). Earlier, the Balochistan National Party (BNP), a major nationalist grouping, resigned its seats in provincial and federal legislatures, dismissing them as no longer relevant. These events left most Pakistani shaken and unsure of Balochistan's future in a federal Pakistan. Musharraf further shocked them with his blunt admission on October 23, 2006 that the "federation is weaker today than it was seven years before" when he came to power (The Nation, October 24, 2006). Earlier, he rushed his prime minister to Balochistan on October 13-14 2006 to rally Baloch sardars for a pro-government Baloch jirga, which he called in Islamabad on November 8 to counter the Baloch National Jirga; the latter jirga was described as the most devastating fallout of Nawab Bugti's assassination (The News, October 16, 2006). The prime minister's two-day visit only revealed that no notable Baloch sardar was willing to attend the pro-government jirga, although Musharraf claims to have the support of 72 out of 75 Baloch sardars (The Nation, November 13, 2006). With this revelation, the government dropped the idea of the jirga, and instead decided to have "tribal elders" meet Musharraf in Gwadar when he visits the deep seaport there on November 16, 2006 (*Dawn*, November 4; The Nation, November 13, 2006).

Conclusion

Balochistan's strategic significance and natural endowment makes it a critical province for Pakistan. Strategically, Balochistan bridges Central, South, Southeast and East Asia on one end, and Central Asia, the Persian Gulf and the Middle East on the other. Regional states, especially India, cannot reach the energy and trade markets of the Caspian Sea region without transit through Balochistan, which Pakistan denies to India despite repeated pleas on New Delhi's behalf by Washington. India absorbs punitive freight costs by routing its trade goods through the Persian Gulf and the Middle East, even for shipments to Afghanistan. Since 2001, New Delhi has made great strides in reaching out to Baloch leaders, whose National Jirga has now made it a party to the arbitration of their "Accession to Pakistan Pact" in the ICJ (The Nation, November 13, 2006).

India is also wary of the Sino-Pakistan naval port on the Arabian Sea, which has raised Beijing's profile in the Indian Ocean. India is even more concerned over Taliban-inspired "militant groups" who operate in Indian-administered Kashmir. As the Taliban are widely believed to have their operational bases in Balochistan, they equally worry India's allies in the region, especially Afghanistan and Iran. Afghanistan resents Pakistan's patronage of the Taliban, which have become the largest threat to its stability since their regrouping in 2003. Iran is also unhappy with Islamabad's policy toward the Taliban due to the group's anti-Shiite theology and the subversive operations of the Taliban's allies, such as Jandallah, in Iran's Sunni-dominated province of Sistan-Balochistan.

Besides these external dynamics, Pakistan is not helping its cause either with its continued military repression of the Baloch national movement, the latest manifestation of which is the alleged abduction by its security forces of 6,000 Baloch youth who have been kept in illegal detention for years (The Nation, November 8, 2006). Although none of Pakistan's neighboring countries threatens Pakistan's integrity, every Pakistani's worst fear, however, is that Islamabad's repressive push in Balochistan will cause the province to revisit their accession to Pakistan.

Originally published in *Terrorism Monitor*: Volume 4, Issue 22 on November 16, 2006.

Asfandyar Wali: Profile of Pakistan's Progressive Pashtun Politician
By Hassan Abbas

On January 10, 2007 Pakistan's secular and Pashtun nationalist Awami National Party (ANP) won a critical electoral battle in Bajaur Agency. The ANP is led by the seasoned politician Asfandyar Wali Khan. The election struck a blow to pro-Taliban elements in the region, and also marks the revival of a party that appeared to be hibernating during the recent Talibanization process. The Pakistani military's hidden alliance with religious political parties made it difficult to effectively tackle the Taliban threat in the aftermath of the September 11 attacks in the United States. After 2003, the military opted for a show of brute force in Pakistan's tribal belt, which created more problems than it solved. The ANP was routed in national and provincial elections in 2002 because anti-Musharraf and anti-American sentiments were at their peak leading to support for the religious alliance Muttahida Majlis-e-Amal (MMA). The mistakes committed by the United States in Afghanistan in terms of not providing enough financial resources for reconstruction and overwhelming dependence on military options to tackle extremists also contributed toward the marginalization of the liberal and progressive forces in the region, including the ANP.

Nevertheless, the potency of Pashtun nationalist forces should not be underestimated. Given their checkered history and traditional support base, they are potentially an effective and viable political force to challenge the religious extremists in the North-West Frontier Province (NWFP) and the adjacent Federally Administered Tribal Areas (FATA). This analysis profiles Asfandyar Wali and his party, which has shown determination in reversing the radical Islamist political trends in the Pashtun-dominated areas of Pakistan.

Background: History of the Awami National Party

The ANP was formed in 1986 through the merger of several left-leaning political parties. Khan Abdul Wali Khan (the father of Asfandyar Wali) was elected as its first president. Wali Khan, son of the legendary Pashtun political leader Khan Abdul Ghaffar Khan, died in 2006. Ghaffar Khan was known as Bacha Khan and as "Frontier Gandhi" because he was a close associate of India's leader Mahatma Gandhi. A believer in non-violence, Ghaffar Khan was an ardent supporter of the idea of a united, independent and secular India. To achieve this goal, he founded a political movement known as Khudai Khidmatgar (Servants of God), also commonly referred to as the Surkh Posh (Red Shirts), during the 1920s. It became a powerful force in the Pashtun-dominated region. The Pashtuns and tribal elders of the region, however, voted to join Pakistan in 1947, as the idea of the nation of Pakistan proved to be quite attractive to the Muslim identity felt among the majority of Pashtuns. Geographic disconnection with the newly emerged independent India also led many Pashtuns to opt for Pakistan, despite being adherents of Ghaffar Khan who was aligned with the Indian National Congress. Ghaffar Khan was thrown in jail by the newly formed state of Pakistan, yet Pashtun nationalism continued to remain very relevant to the politics of the area.

Ghaffar Khan, who had briefly championed the cause of Pashtunistan (an independent state for Pashtuns) in 1947, spent most of his life either in jail, on house arrest in Pakistan, or in exile in Kabul. He died in 1988 and was buried in Jalalabad, Afghanistan as per his wishes. His name is highly respected and popular among Pashtuns on both sides of the border.

Wali Khan was no different. Despite being called a traitor by some (due to his family's links with India and their brief campaign in 1947 for an independent Pashtunistan), he was an important political leader in his own right. He was a strong proponent of provincial autonomy and a leading light in the National Awami Party (NAP), a national political party with leftist inclinations. In the 1970 elections, NAP, led by Wali Khan, did well in the NWFP and in Balochistan province, earning a place in the ruling coalitions in both of the aforementioned provinces. These governments, however, were short lived as Wali Khan was again jailed and his party barred from politics by the federal government on the controversial pretext of conspiring against the state of Pakistan.

n summation, when the ANP emerged in 1986, the party was neither new to politics nor led by any armchair politician. Since then, it has participated in five national and provincial elections. It continued to have a presence in the National Assembly (except in 2002) and always had a fair representation in the NWFP assembly. For instance, in the NWFP legislature, out of a total of 80 seats, the ANP secured 10 seats in 1988, 23 seats in 1990, 18 seats in 1993 and 32 seats in 1997. In the 2002 elections, the ANP could manage only seven seats in an expanded assembly of 124 as a result of the fallout from U.S. involvement in Afghanistan.

Who is Asfandyar Wali?

Asfandyar Wali, the elected president of ANP, is also heir to the legacy of Ghaffar Khan. An astute politician, he has been an elected senator since 2003. Previously, he served in the NWFP provincial assembly (1990) and two national assemblies of Pakistan (1993, 1997).

He holds an MBA and was a political activist associated with the Pakhtun Student Federation during his college days. His home, Wali Bagh in Charsadda, was an ideal nursery for political training since this has been the headquarters of Pashtun nationalist forces for more than half a century. The political upheavals that his family faced groomed him further. During the 1990s, the ANP lost some of its credibility due to corruption scandals that it had been associated with while in the government. The party, however, was then run by Naseem Wali (wife of Wali Khan and stepmother of Asfandyar Wali). Therefore, Asfandyar's reputation escaped this stigma since he was not in the driver's seat of the party's decision-making process. Since then, some notorious and corrupt ANP leaders were sidelined (and in some cases removed from party positions) by Asfandyar Wali when he took over the party leadership in 2000.

In terms of political orientation, the ANP is a nationalist Pashtun party that aspires to make Pakistan a truly democratic state. It also pushes for provincial autonomy and social justice. It was one of the very few political forces in Pakistan that was openly critical of how the Afghan resistance against the former Soviet Union in the 1980s was labeled as a jihad and sponsored from Pakistan (with the help of U.S. and Saudi money). Framing the conflict in religious terms meant increased influence of Islamic parties and decreased relevance of secular parties like the ANP. The ANP remained critical of Pakistan's pro-Taliban policies in the pre-9/11 phase. Their warnings, however, fell on deaf ears.

In the present political context, the ANP is actively challenging the NWFP religious alliance MMA and is critical of Musharraf's policies in the tribal belt. Despite official obstacles, Asfandyar visited Pakistan's tribal areas in November 2006 to hold political consultations with his supporters to the dismay of pro-government tribal elders (*Dawn*, November 18, 2006). If Afghan President Hamid Karzai respects and trusts anyone in Pakistan, it is the ANP and Asfandyar Wali. The idea of a regional Pashtun peace jirga (that was discussed at the September 2006 Bush-Musharraf-Karzai meeting in Washington) was a brainchild of the Asfandyar-Karzai dialogue. Asfandyar had articulated his support of this idea when he visited Washington in early 2006. The Pakistani government, however, is wary of this concept despite its commitment to the United States to undertake such an exercise since it fears that such an arrangement may lessen the Pakistani government's direct role in the Pashtun areas. Islamabad, therefore, is now backtracking by delaying and modifying the spirit of the regional jirga idea.

In Pakistan, it is difficult to challenge the military-intelligence establishment. Asfandyar, however, continues to do so, and argued that the Pakistani government, instead of introducing new political or economic reforms in the tribal areas, has turned the region into a battlefield by using it as "a sanctuary for their guests" (Daily Times, September 28, 2006). Responding to Pakistan's recent proposal to fence and mine the Pak-Afghan border in an effort to control the Taliban's movements, he bluntly called it a conspiracy to divide the Pashtuns.

An Interview with Asfandyar Wali: A Way Out

In a telephone interview with Asfandyar Wali on January 13, 2006 he argued that a Pashtun peace jirga involving Pashtun nationalists, civil society actors and religious players from both sides is the last hope for the region. He interpreted the recent ANP victory in the Bajaur elections as a bright spot in the overall troubling scenario and made a case for allowing liberal political parties to operate and function in the tribal areas. This can only happen, he emphasized, if the Political Parties Act of Pakistan is extended to FATA.

In reference to the causes of conflict in the tribal areas, he lamented the fact that only pro-government *maliks* (tribal elders who are on the government payroll) are engaged and *mushiraan* ("people's" maliks who are financially independent) were completely ignored. This led to a failure in resolving the crisis in FATA. Furthermore, he thinks that Pakistan should have distinguished between the pre-9/11 foreigners who are by now well settled in the area and the post-9/11 foreigners that came in to find a sanctuary.

He also believes that fundamentalist forces are now battling for influence and territory in

Sind and Punjab provinces. He was very confident that the "ANP is in a position to take on MMA in NWFP and tribal areas, but we are not in a position to take on the establishment." When asked what his expectations are from the international community and the United States, he replied: "the international community should ensure a level playing field for all political forces in the region." Elaborating on this further, he narrated a humorous Pashto proverb that can be roughly translated as: "I don't need any charity, but please chain your dog."

Conclusion

Critics of ANP argue that supporting Asfandyar and his party might lead to the cessation of the NWFP from Pakistan and even to the unification of Pashtun areas in Pakistan and Afghanistan. This is unlikely since the Pashtuns of Pakistan are well entrenched in the political system and have been integrated socially and culturally into the national fabric of the country. Another relevant criticism fired at the ANP is its provincial or nationalist identity. Since its inception, however, the ANP has always had some representation in the National Assembly and the Senate of Pakistan and has never called for a separate homeland. What it has asked for is more provincial autonomy, which is within the restraints and provisions of the federal constitution of Pakistan.

The ANP as a political party, however, needs better organization. To be able to pursue its liberal and progressive agenda it will have to join hands with other secular forces in the NWFP as well as in other parts of Pakistan. The Bajaur by-election was a test case for the ANP. The seat was vacated by Haroon ur Rashid, an MMA representative who resigned his seat in protest against the bombing of a madrassa in which 80 people were killed (Daily Times, January 15, 2007). The ANP won because the MMA boycotted the election and other political parties (the Pakistan Peoples Party and the Muslim League-N) supported its candidate. Still, it was a success since a member of Pakistan Muslim League-Q, supported by President Musharraf's followers, was also a candidate.

The ANP as a political party, however, needs better organization. To be able to pursue its liberal and progressive agenda it will have to join hands with other secular forces in the NWFP as well as in other parts of Pakistan.

The crux of the matter is that Asfandyar Wali and the ANP are potentially capable of reversing the Talibanization trend in the tribal areas provided that the Pakistani establishment recognizes the high stakes involved, such as the growing influence of religious extremists in the region and the increasing number of suicide attacks within Pakistan itself. One may also hope that U.S. Secretary of Defense Robert Gates' policy statement declaring "success in Afghanistan is our top priority" leads to significant financial investment in the development of Afghanistan, crippling the appeal of the Taliban in the region (The Nation, January 18, 2007). Secretary of State Condoleezza Rice's announcement that President Bush would ask Congress for $10.6 billion in aid for Afghanistan will, if approved, be a step forward for peace and stability in the region.

Originally published on *Terrorism Monitor*: Volume 5, Issue 2 on February 1, 2007.

Pakistan's Radical Red Mosque Returns
By Farhana Ali and Mohammad Shehzad

The reopening of Pakistan's Lal Masjid (Red Mosque) in Islamabad in October 2007 after a government siege in July is a direct threat to the country and to the world community fighting religious extremists and international terrorist networks. Three months after clashes between homegrown militants and the Pakistani army, whom many believed eliminated part of the extremist threat in the capital city, the use of the mosque for Friday prayers and inflammatory speeches against General Pervez Musharraf is evidence of a violent trend that the army may not be able to control.

To Pakistan's surprise, the army's raid against the mosque in the summer did little to silence the extremists' chant for an Islamic revolution. Rather than crush the militants, the government's siege provoked extremists throughout the country to seek vengeance on behalf of those who were killed during the nine-day standoff in July. Soon after the radical mosque reopened, extremist cleric Maulana Aziz delivered a sermon that called on his followers to start a revolution. He noted, "The nation should be ready for jihad because only jihad can bring a revolution ... The students of schools, colleges and universities should spread in the nook and corner of Pakistan and work for bringing Islamic revolution." In retaliation for the death of Aziz's brother and the students of the Red Mosque during the siege, Aziz further stated that those who were killed "were dear to Allah. That's why they have embraced martyrdom [which] has boosted our morale. Every mosque in the country is Lal Masjid."

Echoing Aziz's desire for martyrdom, the call for jihad by local groups and by al-Qaeda in its recent videotapes and communiqués prove that the Red Mosque affair is far from over. On the jihadi website Murasil al-Buraq, a September 20 statement entitled, "A Call for Jihad by the Lion, Sheikh Osama bin Laden," launched by al-Sahab Productions, contained a message warning the Pakistani public and its armed forces that jihad is the only answer. The voice of al-Qaeda's "grand strategist," Dr. Ayman al-Zawahiri, offered praise for a number of Pakistani clerics, particularly Abd al-Aziz Ghazi, the cleric of the Red Mosque who was killed by Pakistan's armed forces. Seeking revenge for his death, al-Qaeda urged the Pakistani public and the army to rise against Musharraf for his "submissiveness" to the United States.

The recent video also recognizes the tribes of Waziristan, an area in Pakistan's tribal belt identified with religious extremism, Pashtun nationalism and an al-Qaeda safe haven. Al-Qaeda applauds the tribal leaders and clerics in the province for their "great stand in the face of international *kufr* (disbelief)," a reference to the United States and its allies. In a strong show of support for the tribal lords, al-Qaeda states, "O Allah, Pervez [Musharraf], his ministers, his 'Ulama and his soldiers have been hostile to your friends in Afghanistan and Pakistan, especially in Waziristan, Swat, Bajaur and Lal Masjid; O Allah, break their backs, split them up and destroy their unity" [1].

On another website, Ana al-Muslim, a jihadi known as "Al-Saqr 99" posted a new 80-minute video entitled "The Power of Truth," in which the al-Qaeda leaders denounced

Musharraf for killing Ghazi. Al-Qaeda further discredits the Pakistani leader as someone who "does not deserve the honor of defending Pakistan because [it] is a Muslim land whereas the forces of Musharraf are hunting dogs under Bush's crucifix" [2]. In a similar message posted on July 11, 2007 al-Zawahiri called Musharraf's order against the Red Mosque a "despicable crime." Consistent with previous recordings, al-Qaeda urges Muslims inside Pakistan to facilitate an armed rebellion against the country's rulers for their participation in a war against the international terrorist movement.

Yet how much support does bin Laden have among Pakistanis? In a poll conducted by Terror Free Tomorrow, al-Qaeda has a 43 percent approval rate, the Taliban has 38 percent, and support for local extremist groups fall between 37 to 49 percent. Overall, bin Laden has a 46 percent approval rating with Musharraf falling behind at 38 percent—an astonishing figure, according to Ken Ballen, the director of the polling agency, because it reflects that the Taliban and al-Qaeda "are more popular than our allies like Musharraf" (CNN, September 12, 2007). Despite the apparent support for the terrorist movement, most Pakistanis (i.e., 75 percent, according to the poll) rejected suicide bombings (CNN, September 12, 2007).

While most Pakistanis disagree with suicide terrorism, a determined, dedicated and decisive al-Qaeda in Pakistan has adopted the tactic to launch attacks against targets inside both Pakistan and Afghanistan. Through a wave of suicide bombings, al-Qaeda and local jihadis have proven the lethality of their attacks inside Pakistan, which have mostly been directed at the Pakistani armed forces, paramilitaries and the police. Borrowed from the Iraqi insurgents, the use of suicide as a weapon of choice has had deadly consequences. In the first half of 2007, there have been more than two dozen suicide attacks in Pakistan. From January to March 2007, suicide bombings have accounted for 67 percent of civilian casualties, compared to 41 percent in 2006 (Criterion, July-September 2007). From 2003 to 2006, at least 150 tribal elders in Waziristan have been murdered, most presumably by the Taliban, who have publicly criticized many elders for siding with Pakistan in its war against the militants (*Christian Science Monitor*, June 8, 2006).

Unprecedented in Pakistan's history, suicide terrorism is an emerging trend that has gained popularity among militants after the Red Mosque event and the breakdown of a peace agreement between the tribal lords of North Waziristan and the Pakistani government. Pakistan has witnessed a new trend in suicide terrorism—female fidayeen are being prepared to carry out suicide attacks against U.S. interests. On the website of an extremist group, Jamaat-ud-Da'wa, 200 women are committed to striking U.S. targets: "If the U.S. tried to attack Iran or Pakistan like Afghanistan or Iraq then we will kill the Americans through suicide attacks. We will tie bombs with our body and stop the Americans from entering Iran and Pakistan."

One report suggests that suicide bombers recruited to perpetrate attacks against Pakistan's symbols of power are rooted in "the cause of Islam and targeting those who are damaging their religion" (*Dawn*, July 21, 2007). Through indoctrination by a senior cleric, young single males are promised paradise. In Voice of Islam in June 2007, an interview with a new Taliban recruit indicates his willingness to commit a suicide operation because he is "interested in women of that world." A September 9, 2007 report by the United Nations, entitled "Suicide Attacks in Afghanistan," explores the suicide phenomenon in Afghanistan and Pakistan, noting that the "tribal areas [of Pakistan] are an important source of human and material assistance for suicide attacks in Afghanistan," and suggests that most suicide attackers are poor, under-educated or uneducated, recruited from madaris and male.

Therefore, the steady rate of suicide bombings, motivated by al-Qaeda's resurgence in the tribal belt, reinforces Musharraf's claim to the world community that he alone is capable of battling a formidable foe. Chairman of the Department of International Relations at Karachi University, Dr. Moonis Ahmar, told the author in August, "Musharraf sends the message that without me, there is no future." In public statements, the general has acknowledged, however, that the fight against terrorism and extremism needs the support of the entire nation (Daily Times, September 2, 2007). On the other hand, there is growing speculation that his counter-terrorism strategies used against al-Qaeda can be used to counter the "Pakistani" Taliban's ascendancy in the tribal belt. According to the Afghan interior minister and other experts, Pakistan's war is directed against foreign militants, with little effort expanded to contain the Taliban [3].

One of the key challenges to Pakistan is that a resurgent Taliban allied with al-Qaeda—which can maneuver, regroup and rearm—destabilizes Pakistan's internal security, its relationship with its Afghan counterpart and further nurtures the perception among the international community that Pakistan is a refuge for terrorists. Pakistani journalist Ahmed Rashid's recent statement, "Taliban bases and sanctuaries in Pakistan are at the heart of the problem," points specifically to Quetta as the Taliban base and safe haven (Current History, January 2007; Yale Global Online, May 23, 2006). The exploitation of the porous border between Afghanistan and Pakistan, which Ahmed considers the "world's [new] terrorism central," inhabited by Pashtun tribes, has refocused attention in Washington and Islamabad [4]. The penetration of the tribal belt by al-Qaeda—once an ally of Pakistan's intelligentsia—and the Taliban is publicly acknowledged by the Pakistani military. According to Pakistan's military spokesman, Major General Shaukat Sulat, "We don't deny the Taliban come and go, but that is not the entire truth" (*Washington Post*, January 21, 2007). Whatever the truth may be, greater U.S. engagement in Afghanistan creates risks for Pakistan. After the U.S. assumed control of NATO forces in Afghanistan, the Taliban said 2007 will be "the bloodiest year for foreign troops" and have indicated a ready supply of at least 2,000 suicide bombers for their spring offensive against the United States (Reuters, February 4, 2007).

With the Taliban-al-Qaeda merger in the tribal belt, Pakistan's general will need to rethink his current strategy in the war against terrorism. In recent weeks, the army's heavy-handedness against the militants has resulted in civilian deaths in the northern areas and contributed to Musharraf's growing unpopularity (*Christian Science Monitor*, October 12, 2007). Liked or not, while in charge of a country that is seen as the citadel of Islam and the only Muslim nuclear power, he will continue to be a strategic ally in the U.S.-led war on terrorism. Pakistan will continue to garner international attention so long as al-Qaeda, the Taliban and homegrown extremists threaten the state's grip on power and as long as Pakistan is viewed by Western countries as fueling the fire of violent jihad.

Origianlly published in *Terrorism Monitor*: Volume 5, Issue 20 on October 25, 2007.

Notes

1. On September 20, 2007 a jihadi website posted a message entitled, "Remove the Apostate, al-Sahab Production Presents 'A Call for Jihad' by Sheikh Osama bin Laden," with links to a 23-minute, 36-second message from bin Laden.
2. From http://www.muslm.net/vb, a popular spot for statements and discussions by jihadi group members in Iraq and elsewhere in the Muslim world. The video referenced is dated August-September 2007 and includes statements from al-Zawahiri about the Red Mosque affair. Various reports make this point. See A. Jalali, "The Future of Afghanistan," *Parameters* 36, no. 1 (Spring 2006): 8; BBC, August 2007; Pakistan Security Research Unit (PSRU), September 22, 2007.
4. Based on author's discussions with a senior U.S. government official, who spent weeks along the Afghan-Pakistan border, who noted that a solution to the problem requires more than military might. He strongly advocated the need to understand the cultural and human terrain; that is, to better understand the tribal belt, the U.S. government would need to spend time with the Pashtun tribes to learn about their deeply rooted cultural history and beliefs as well as become familiar with the people currently supporting the insurgents.

The Road to Lal Masjid and its Aftermath
By Hassan Abbas

It is clear that most Pakistanis wanted Lal Masjid (Red Mosque) leader Maulana Abdul Rashid Ghazi to be held accountable for his vigilantism and for trying to enforce his extremist version of Islam on society. The public's views have changed, however, now that it has become obvious that the government used indiscriminate force during the operation and since its claims about the presence of foreign militants inside the mosque complex have not been independently verified. The following important questions remain unanswered: why did the government act so benignly for the past six months and allow a problem to augment into a major crisis; who was Abdul Rashid Ghazi and how did he manage to smuggle a huge cache of weapons into the mosque complex; was intelligence flawed or were intelligence agencies involved in the plot; and why did President Pervez Musharraf choose a time for the crackdown that coincided with the meeting scheduled for all of Pakistan's opposition parties in London?

While people search for answers to these critical questions, Pakistan is witnessing an unabated terrorism cycle—having experienced a suicide bombing or a bomb blast each day since the July 10, 2007 military operation against the mosque. Tragically, those who died in the Red Mosque operation are now being proclaimed as shaheed (martyrs), and a debate has ensued in Pakistan between what the media are calling "religious extremists" and "liberal fascists." A week before the operation, ordinary Pakistanis were stunned that the government was not acting to resolve the crisis; today, a week after the deadly operation, Pakistanis still have few clues as to the new crisis that is unfolding. Furthermore, Musharraf's legacy seems frozen between these two weeks.

History of the Red Mosque and its Former Caretakers

The foundational stone of the Red Mosque was laid in 1965 by Maulana Abdullah—the father of the militant clerics Abdul Aziz and Abdul Rashid Ghazi—a year after the birth of Pakistan's capital city, Islamabad. Maulana Abdullah, a Deobandi Muslim, was appointed as the mosque's imam by Pakistani President Ayub Khan (The News, July 8, 2007). The mosque was called "Lal" after Lal Shahbaz Qalandar, a revered Sufi saint buried in Pakistan's Sindh province.

During agitation led by religious parties against Prime Minister Zulfikar Ali Bhutto in 1977, Abdullah successfully mobilized the masses in support of the protests. By virtue of this contribution, he gained the favor of General Zia ul-Haq, the military dictator who dislodged Bhutto. Zia's tenure was a key time for religious groups to expand, and Abdullah earned additional gratitude for volunteering in the Afghan war of 1979-1989. As a reward, he was allocated land in the prized and posh E-7 sector of Islamabad to establish Jamia Faridia, a seminary. Arab financing also helped Abdullah build an institution where many orphans and poor children received religious education (The News, July 17, 2007). Abdullah's agenda changed, however, as he became involved in sectarian politics and started to support the newly emerged Anjuman Sipah-e-Sahaba (Soldiers of the Prophet's Companions)—an anti-Shiite terror outfit. General Zia was hardly perturbed, as he was focused on the Afghan jihad and could not see how these fissures would destabilize Pakistan in the future.

In the process, Abdullah motivated thousands of people for jihad in Afghanistan in the 1980s, and in collaboration with the Inter-Services Intelligence (ISI) he continued to provide fodder for the Afghan theater. In 1989, he attracted the limelight when at the time of Benazir Bhutto's electoral success, he issued a fatwa declaring women's role in politics as un-Islamic. Around 1992, he established Jamia Hafsa, a seminary for women, adjacent to the Red Mosque. Funds were not an issue because the ISI was gracious toward him due to the role he had played in Afghanistan. His warm feelings toward Arab-Afghans also became obvious when, in response to the U.S. missile attack on a suspected Osama bin Laden hideout in Afghanistan, he said, "America is like a thief who attacked the unarmed civilians ... [those] who make friends with Christians and Jews will become like them" (The Nation, August 22, 1998). Abdullah had just returned from Afghanistan and had started to campaign for the enforcement of Sharia in Pakistan. In his attempts, he crossed a few lines, resulting in his assassination at the Red Mosque in 1998.

This was a moment of transformation for his son Abdul Rashid Ghazi, who had been uninterested in all radical issues up to that point. Ghazi had an interesting background. He had earlier refused to enroll himself in Jamia Faridia and completed his masters in history in 1988 from the Quaid-i-Azam University in Islamabad, a reputable academic center. Afterwards, he joined the Ministry of Education in Islamabad as an officer, and later he served in the United Nations Educational, Scientific and Cultural Organization as an assistant director. At no stage in his career did he show any signs of extremism (Daily Times, July 8, 2007). Rather, he married into a modern family and was comfortable in his relatively secular lifestyle. In fact, his father was so angry with his lifestyle that he handed over all his property to his other son, Abdul Aziz. At the time of Abdullah's assassination, this same elder brother became the imam of the Red Mosque.

Developments, however, changed drastically after Abdullah's assassination. Ghazi decided to join his brother as his deputy in the Red Mosque. In about a year, he became a hard line cleric, vowing to impose a Talibanized Sharia in Pakistan. Pakistani intelligence agencies had also found a new agent who was willing to offer cooperation (Daily Times, July 8, 2007). Within walking distance of ISI headquarters, the Red Mosque complex attracted many heroes from the Afghan theater of conflict. It was understandable when the two brothers took a strong pro-Taliban stance and called Musharraf a traitor for his policy of cooperation with the United States in the aftermath of the September 11 attacks. Intriguingly, the state also overlooked the Red Mosque's potential threat when it showed its street power for the first time in 2003, by organizing riots in the capital city after the killing of Azam Tariq, the leader of the now banned Sipah-e-Sahaba. The seminary students of Jamia Faridia ransacked cinemas, restaurants and gas stations in the capital, yet Musharraf's government remained silent.

Encouraged by this response, the Red Mosque issued a controversial edict in 2004, declaring that Pakistani Army soldiers who died fighting tribal militants were not martyrs. News about Ghazi's links with al-Qaeda was flashed in the media at the time of the arrest of Osama bin Laden's driver (*Dawn*, July 6, 2007). The government was unmoved even by this development.

The final episode of the drama began earlier this year in 2007, when female students of Jamia Hafsa forcefully took control of a children's library adjacent to the Red Mosque complex and started vigilante actions in the city, trying to enforce their version of religious morality. Music shops were attacked, police were kidnapped and fatwas were issued to coerce the media. The government finally reacted and started negotiating with the Red Mosque administration, but to no avail. Abdul Aziz meanwhile threatened the government with a spate of suicide bombings around the country in the case of a military operation (*Terrorism Focus*, June 5, 2007).

Finally, both brothers forced the government's hand when they mishandled the soldiers of a paramilitary force surrounding the complex, leading to the deaths of 21 people on July 3. Abdul Aziz was caught fleeing the scene in a burqa and Ghazi took over the command of the complex. Around 1,200 students of the mosque and seminary surrendered, and those inside took up positions with their arms. Even then, the government procrastinated. People were upset at this turn of events while newspapers, electronic media and civil society groups all encouraged the government to enforce its writ. One could understand why it would be difficult to do the same in the tribal belt, but failing to do so in the heart of Islamabad was incomprehensible. Leading columnist Ayaz Amir aptly called it "a drama to beat all dramas" (*Dawn*, July 6, 2007).

Delay in effectively tackling the defiant stance of the Red Mosque not only complicated the crisis, but gave ample opportunity to Ghazi to entrench his forces militarily, start an effective media campaign and draw sympathy from segments of society by claiming that he and his comrades were merely asking for the enforcement of religious laws in the country.

Delay in effectively tackling the defiant stance of the Red Mosque not only complicated the crisis, but gave ample opportunity to Ghazi to entrench his forces militarily, start an effective media campaign and draw sympathy from segments of society by claiming that he and his comrades were merely asking for the enforcement of religious laws in the country.

Meanwhile, the government began claiming that Ghazi had many militants from various banned outfits holed up inside the complex who had taken hundreds of women and children hostage. Public opinion started to change, and demands for ensuring the safety of women and children were heightened. In the midst of this, Pakistani security forces suddenly began the operation, which lasted for the next 15 hours. Ghazi, with an ample supply of cell phones, gave last minute interviews to all major news channels, telling millions of people on live television that he bravely decided to lay down his life for the cause of Islam rather than bow to the dictates of the state. He called Musharraf a tool in the hands of the United States.

On the other hand, the government blocked the media from showing footages in the hospitals where casualties were taken. Journalists were only allowed to show ambulances rushing to the scene. Apparently, very few came out alive and it is unclear how many were killed inside the mosque complex. The government's figure of 100 dead (including 10 soldiers) leaves a few hundred unaccounted for. Graves were hastily dug around Islamabad, and people were buried at night, which encouraged rumors of a massacre and a cover up.

At the end of the day, Ghazi's stature rose in the eyes of the people, and the government's credibility collapsed further due to the way that they handled the issue—first with delay, then in getting bogged down in unnecessary negotiations, and finally in the inability to explain why its intelligence agencies failed to monitor what was transpiring inside the mosque complex for so long. The government has not explained its actions regarding why Ghazi and his brother were not stopped previously when they had challenged the government's policies so persistently. Critics believe that the two brothers were, in fact, being supported in their endeavors by elements within the intelligence agencies.

The Consequences

Since the July 10, 2007 operation, more than 100 people have lost their lives in bombings and suicide attacks in various parts of the country, including in Islamabad. Clearly, these strikes are revenge attacks—a deadly response from the sympathizers of the Red Mosque. Few in Islamabad realize that there are 88 more seminaries in Islamabad where 16,000 students are enrolled (Daily Times, July 7, 2007).

If developments in early July 2007 are any indicator, Pakistan is increasingly becoming an ungovernable state. Divisions within society about the direction of the state are becoming intense and if this confusion and cycle of violence continues, then cracks might appear within the military establishment as well. As before, Musharraf is making all the right statements, but implementation of his policies remains an acute issue. He is becoming increasingly unable to arrest developments inside Pakistan.

Originally published in *Terrorism Monitor*: Volume 5, Issue 14 on July 19, 2007.

Tribes and Rebels: The Players in the Balochistan Insurgency
By Muhammad Tahir

As the violence on Pakistan's northwest frontier dominates the headlines, a lesser-known insurgency has gripped Pakistan's southwestern province of Balochistan. Bomb blasts and rocket attacks have become almost daily events in this region: A ten-week period in 2008 saw 76 insurgent-linked incidents reported, claiming the lives of 14 people and wounding 123 (South Asia Terrorism Portal: Balochistan Timeline 2008).

The troubled history of Balochistan dates back to the independence of Pakistan in 1947, beginning as a reaction to the annexation of the princely state of Qalat—later joined to three other states to form modern Balochistan—by Pakistani authorities in 1948. The annexation led to the first Baloch rebellion, which was swiftly put down. The security situation in the region remained fragile as rebellions erupted in 1958, 1973, and most recently in 2005.

Unlike previous anti-government insurrections, it is currently hard to pinpoint one person or group for orchestrating these incidents as there are today several groups in Balochistan potentially interested in challenging the government. The most immediate suspect is the Taliban, who are unhappy with Pakistan's cooperation with the United States in its war on terror. The Taliban is active throughout Balochistan, particularly in Quetta and the Pashtun belt of the province, bordering with Afghanistan.

Though the Baloch have a long history of mistrust of the central government of Pakistan, the federal government has its own interpretation of the current tensions, claiming that the hostile situation is provoked by Baloch nationalist leaders who consider large-scale initiatives to develop the region as a threat to their influence.

However, despite the Islamist presence, the prime motivators of the current insurgency remain Baloch nationalists, who live in the remote mountains of the province and believe they have been deprived of their rights and revenues from the considerable natural resources of their province. The nationalists believe these revenues are appropriated by the federal government with little return to the province (Ausaf, February 7, 2006).

The Baloch claim to have been native to the region since 1200 BC. Today, there are an estimated eight to nine million Baloch, living in Iran and Afghanistan as well as Pakistan. Their language consists of three main dialects: Balochi, Brahwi and Saraiki. The Balochistan province of Pakistan is one of the important Baloch settlements in the region, located at the eastern edge of the Iranian plateau and in the border region between southwest, central and south Asia. It is geographically the largest of the four provinces of Pakistan and composes 48 percent of the nation's total territory.

Though the Baloch have a long history of mistrust of the central government of Pakistan, the federal government has its own interpretation of the current tensions, claiming that the hostile situation is provoked by Baloch nationalist leaders who consider large-scale initiatives to develop the region as a threat to their influence. President Pervez Musharraf even accused the leading tribal chiefs of the Baloch tribes of Bugti, Marri and Mingal of playing a direct role in the mounting insurgency (Daily Dunya, August 25, 2006; *Dawn*, July 21, 2006).

The Baloch Tribes

• The Bugti tribe is one of approximately 130 Baloch tribes, with approximately 180,000 members dwelling mainly in the mountainous region of Dera Bugti. The tribe is divided into the sub-tribes of Rahija Bugti, Masori Bugti and Kalpar Bugti. For decades this tribe has been dominated by the Rahija Bugti family of Akbar Khan Bugti, a prominent Baloch nationalist. Before he took the chieftainship at 12 years of age in 1939, his father and grandfather were leaders of the tribe.

Unlike some other traditional Baloch tribal families, the Akbar Bugti's family was considered moderate, as Akbar's grandfather, Shahbaz Khan Bugti, was knighted by Britain, and Akbar Bugti himself was educated at Oxford and held several of the most powerful political positions in the country: governor, chief minister of Balochistan and federal interior minister. Until his death in 2006 in an air and ground assault by Pakistani security forces, Akbar Bugti was also chief of the Jamhuri Watan Party, established in 1990 (Bakhabar, August 27, 2006).

The issue of royalties and the ownership of gas fields—discovered in Akbar Bugti's hometown of Dera Bugti and providing 39 percent of the country's total requirement—remained the main cause of conflict between the tribal chief and the government. Pakistani officials claim that Akbar Bugti was paid around $4 million annually in royalties, but used these resources to blackmail the state and build a state-within-the-state (Khabrain, August 6, 2006). Islamabad's response, such as supporting rival Kalpar Bugtis—who denounced Akbar Bugti's chieftainship—and deploying troops in Dera Bugti, led Akbar Bugti and his followers to take arms against the government.

Akbar Bugti's son, Nawabzada Talal Akbar Bugti, has rejected Prime Minister Gillani's offer of negotiations conditional on laying down arms, saying that the Baloch people will only do so after they have achieved their rights and gained complete autonomy (ANI, April 3). Another son, Jamil Akbar Bugti, is currently fighting a freeze on his assets on the placement of his name on Pakistan's exit control list (APP, March 28, 2008). A grandson, Nawab Sardar Brahamdagh Khan Bugti, is a major leader of Baloch militants.

• The Marri is another major Baloch tribe, based in the Kohlo district of Balochistan. Their chief, Nawab Khair Bakhsh Marri, was branded by President Musharraf as the "troublemaker Sardar" (tribal chief). The Marri are also divided into sub-tribes: the Gazni Marri, Bejarani Marri and Zarkon Marri, with Khair Bakhsh Marri belonging to the Gazni faction. The total population of the Marri tribe in Balochistan is reportedly around

98,000 and the nature of their relationship with the government is historically hostile—they have integrated little into the political structure of the country.

Unlike the leader of the Bugti tribe, the chieftain of the Marri is said to be closer to the communists, his sons graduating from schools in Moscow. Unable to withstand the Pakistani military, he and dozens of his followers took refuge in Kabul in 1979, remaining there until Russia withdrew. Khair Bakhsh Marri remains committed to an armed struggle for no less than full independence for Balochistan despite losing dozens of followers and relatives, most recently his son Balach Marri, who reportedly led a rebel group of the Baloch Liberation Army (BLA) (Balochistan Express, November 22, 2007).

• Ataullah Khan Mingal, leader of the Mingal tribe and another trouble-maker in Musharraf's eyes, has played a dominant role in the political history of Baloch in the region. Unlike the other tribes, the Mingals have given little military resistance, although Ataullah never denounced the anti-government armed resistance.

The party in which he began his political career was the National Awami Party (NAP), led by Pashtun nationalist Wali Khan. Following the elections of May 1972, in which the party swept Balochistan, Atualla Mingal took power as the first chief minister of Balochistan. His role in the NAP-led London Plan—a secret meeting of Pashtun and Baloch nationalists in London, allegedly to prepare ground for declaring the independence of the North-West Frontier Province (NWFP) and Balochistan—is the peak of his nationalistic political career, which led to his imprisonment in 1973. Subsequently the federal government began large-scale military operations in Balochistan to crush the nationalists (BBC Urdu, February 11, 2005).

Following his release from prison in the late 1970s, Atualla Mingal went into exile in London, returning in the mid-1990s to establish the Balochistan National Party (BNP), which brought his son Akhtar Mingal to power as chief minister of Balochistan. Mingal junior was jailed by Musharraf in September 2006 on charges of terrorism, due to his alleged involvement with the recent Baloch insurgency against the Pakistan government.

Tribal Leaders and Insurgent Groups

Since Musharraf came to power in 1999 there have been other goals besides independence that have drawn Baloch nationalists together. The most influential Baloch leaders—Akbar Khan Bugti, Khair Bakhsh Marri and Atualla Khan Mingal—have had a variety of reasons to be suspicious of the government's involvement in the area, which they viewed as an attempt to de-seat them from tribal chieftainship. Government moves have included state support to rival factions within the tribe and the deployment of military forces into the region (Bakhabar, August 27, 2006). Nevertheless, no tribal chief is ready to tie himself to insurgent groups publicly, though military sources remain skeptical that the authoritarian tribal chiefs are ignorant of who is firing rockets in their territory.

Currently at least five insurgent groups are publicly known in Balochistan, including the

Baloch Republican Army (BRA), Baloch People's Liberation Front (BPLF), Popular Front for Armed Resistance (PFAR), Balochistan Liberation Army (BLA), and the Balochistan Liberation Front (BLF), the last two being the largest and most widely-known.

Balochistan Liberation Army (BLA)

The BLA's political stance is unequivocal: They stand for the sole goal of establishing an independent state for Baloch in the Balochistan province of Pakistan. The roots of the BLA date back to 1973, during the period of resistance against military operations in Balochistan and the discovery of the secret NAP-led London Plan.

Though the movement did not become public until 2000, some sources claim that the BLA was a Russian creation and came into being during the Afghan war, propped up as a reaction to Pakistan's anti-Soviet involvement in Afghanistan (*Dawn*, July 15, 2006). Those supporting this claim point to the Moscow education of the alleged leader of BLA, Balach Marri, and the time he spent in Russia and Afghanistan.

The number of BLA activists is not known, but Pakistani military sources suggest that there are currently 10,000 Baloch insurgents involved in separatist activities, of which 3,000 are active in the insurgency. The government implicates India and Afghanistan in supporting the movement. President Musharraf reportedly presented a damning file regarding these allegations to President Karzai during his visit to Afghanistan in late February 2006 (The News [Islamabad], April 16, 2006). Despite these allegations and regardless of any possible outside support, the nature of the BLA's activities has a local focus, with no foreign nationals being arrested with proven involvement in the Baloch insurgency.

Baloch Liberation Front (BLF)

The BLF, like the other Baloch insurgent groups, recently re-emerged as a potential threat in the region, claiming responsibility for deadly and frequent attacks on government installations. The BLF has so far escaped state accusations of organized terrorism, although its operations seem far bigger than those of other factions. The seventh article of its charter—from the pro-Marri nationalist website sarmachar.org—describes the struggle as a holy duty of all Baloch and asks for moral and financial, if not military, participation. The tenth article says: "The independent state is a matter of life and death for Baloch." This organization, describing itself as an army of volunteers, also offers a complete program for a post-independence state, ranging from education and health policies to issues of foreign policy and internal and external security.

Some reports suggest that the BLF was established in Damascus in 1964 by Baloch nationalist Juma Khan Marri, who in the 1970s and 1980s was seen actively meeting with the communist regime in Moscow and Kabul. The BLF played an active role in the resistance against military operations in 1973, which continued until the collapse of

Zulfikar Ali Bhutto's regime. These clashes reportedly took the lives of 3,000 soldiers and around 5,000 Baloch rebels.

It is not clear on what scale the BLF currently operates and who leads it, though Akbar Bugti once described it as an autonomous organization that operated independently of tribal chiefs (Newsline, February 2005).

Conclusion

Regardless of the number of Baloch insurgents, the nature and scale of their activities since 2000 have marked their emergence as a major threat toward regional security, with Pakistan's new government—elected on February 18, 2008—apparently recognizing this threat. Soon after the election, the victorious politicians began signalling the adoption of a softer approach to ease tension in Balochistan. The election was boycotted by the Baloch nationalist parties in response to ongoing military operations in Balochistan that began in 2005.

As a first step to change the tense atmosphere, the Pakistan People's Party (PPP) has hinted at accommodating some Baloch nationalists under its political umbrella and has accepted their demand to stop military operations in the region. The nomination of Aslam Raisani, an independently elected Baloch member of parliament, for the post of provisional chief minister in Balochistan by the PPP is another signal directed at winning hearts and minds in the province.

It is unclear whether these policies and the appointment of Raisani as a chief minister may bring a major breakthrough, but soon after his nomination, Raisani hinted at taking a completely different approach toward the crisis from the military-based policies of the Musharraf regime. Recently he was quoted by local media saying that the so-called rebel Baloch are his own brothers and if he could not make them agree to lay down their arms, he will step down (Daily Zamana, March 9, 2008).

The question of an independent state remains a tricky issue, but some moderate Baloch voices say that independence is no longer a priority for the Baloch majority, as they are struggling to survive due to the devastating effect of hostilities on the local economy. The economic structure of Balochistan is where the future of the region begins. Involving local Baloch in the large-scale economic projects proposed for the province will be a major step in winning their confidence; otherwise there is no reason to believe that the tense political situation in Balochistan will not deteriorate further.

Originally published in *Terrorism Monitor*: Volume 6, Issue 7 on April 3, 2008.

Sino-Pakistani Defense Relations and the War on Terrorism
By Tariq Mahmud Ashraf

Concurrent with Pakistan's often tumultuous military relationship with the United States is a growing and highly amicable economic and military relationship with China that poses vital questions regarding Pakistan's future approach to the War on Terrorism. While suspicion of American motives runs high in Pakistan, China has made major inroads in the South Asian country, including a free-trade deal, assistance in power development, the implementation of a five-year trade and development plan and a strategic partnership meant to address deficiencies in Pakistan's military technology and increase cooperation against Islamist terrorist cells (Xinhua, April 3; The Associated Press of Pakistan [APP], April 17, 2008).

Discussions on defense and security issues were an important part of this week's state visit to China by Pakistani President Pervez Musharraf (APP, April 14). Pakistan and China are involved in major co-production projects involving the manufacture of JF-17 Thunder fighter aircraft—similar to American F-16s, which Pakistan continues to purchase from the United States—and F22P naval frigates. The latter project involves the construction of four frigates, three in China and the last in the Karachi shipyards. The project involves important technology transfers—unavailable from the United States—that will allow Pakistan to build major warships on its own (*Dawn*, April 5, 2008; *China Daily*, April 5, 2008).

Changes Brought by the War on Terrorism

Beijing has major stakes in the war against terrorism. It has clearly enunciated that Pakistan is as central to its national security interests as Israel is to Washington. In strategic terms, the infusion of a U.S. military presence into Central Asia, Pakistan and Afghanistan has seriously upset China's security calculus on which its Western strategy is predicated (*China Brief*, February 28, 2002). China also worries about the possible expansion of a U.S. military presence closer to China's doorstep [1].

While U.S.-Pakistani defense ties date back to 1954, Pakistan and China have had strategic ties since the 1962 Sino-Indian conflict, in which the United States rushed to support India. These relations crystallized after Pakistan's disillusionment with the United States for its lack of support during the 1965 Indo-Pakistan war. Since then, Pakistan's relationship with the United States has seen several ups and downs while its ties with China have been

Two major consequences of the U.S.-led War on Terrorism have been the positioning of sizeable U.S. military forces in proximity to China's southwestern frontier and the involvement of Pakistan, China's time-tested South Asian ally.

steady, consistent and expanding. China has been Pakistan's largest defense supplier with Beijing viewing Pakistan as a useful counterweight to Indian power and influence in the region [2].

Two major consequences of the U.S.-led War on Terrorism have been the positioning of sizeable U.S. military forces in proximity to China's southwestern frontier and the involvement of Pakistan, China's time-tested South Asian ally. These developments served to not only checkmate the spread of Chinese influence and precipitate a rollback of Chinese efforts at strategic expansion in the region but also tilted the regional balance of power decisively in Washington's favor virtually overnight [3].

Near airbases that were used by the U.S. Air Force until 2004-2005, China is now the major force behind the construction of a major civil/naval port at Gwadar, along the coast of Balochistan province. China's navy will have full use of the port once finished and a rail line, a fiber-optic line and a petroleum pipeline will run from Gwadar to the Karakoram highway that connects to China (APP, April 12, 2008).

These developments are taking place in an environment that sees China's relations with the United States as somewhat unstable, but relatively positive at the moment. Both countries want success in the war against terrorism but have different policies and interests in some areas, such as the war in Iraq and China's call for Taiwan reunification.

In the wake of the global wave of horror that swept the world after 9/11, both China and Pakistan expressed their support for the United States differently and with varying motives and reasons. While China needed time to formulate its policy afresh, Pakistan probably had no way out but to acquiesce and join the U.S. bandwagon, though this has not been without benefit to Islamabad. There is no denying the fact that the presence of U.S. forces on Pakistani soil contributed to the de-escalation of the 2002 Indo-Pak military stand-off and generated strategic dividends for Pakistan.

New Government, New Policy

While the War on Terrorism continues unabated, recent internal developments in Pakistan have raised fresh questions regarding Pakistan's continuing support for this war. With the pro-Musharraf forces having been routed, the new democratically elected government is bound to have a fresh look at its foreign policy, especially in the context of its relations with both the United States and China.

Interestingly, Pakistan's unstinting support of the War of Terrorism does not seem to have impinged negatively on its relationship with China. In fact, Pakistan and China have been cooperating in parallel on their own counter-terrorism efforts. In this context, the moves of the Pakistani government in recent years to clamp down on Uyghur settlements and on religious schools used as training grounds for militant Islamists are relevant, as is the Red Mosque incident (Daily Times [Lahore], June 26, 2006). When tensions over Islamic extremism developed between China and Pakistan after Islamic vigilantes kidnapped several Chinese citizens, Musharraf responded quickly and very strongly (People's Daily Online, October 12, 2004; Pakistan Times, October 14, 2004). Many believe that his decision to use military force against the extremists at the Red Mosque in Islamabad stemmed largely from the incident with the Chinese citizens, which had greatly embarrassed his regime. In his visit to China, President Musharraf declared that

Pakistan would extend its full support to China in its battle against "East Turkistan" (Uyghur) terrorists (Pakistan Times, April 9, 2008).

Pakistan has in the past been very helpful to China in controlling the separatist Uyghur movement in Xinjiang. Not only did the Pakistan military kill Hasan Mahsum—the leader of the East Turkistan Islamic Movement (ETIM)—in October 2003, but in August 2004, Pakistani and Chinese armies conducted a joint anti-terrorism exercise in the province (*China Daily*, December 24, 2003). The conduct of this military exercise clearly indicated the Pakistani government's acceptance of China's desire to stamp out separatism in Xinjiang—even though the Uyghurs are generally considered fellow Muslims—and its apparent agreement with China's declarations that the separatists are Islamist terrorists in league with al-Qaeda.

Directions for the China/Pakistan Security Relationship

A visualization of the future brings three vital questions to the fore: Would Pakistan's new government move away from its support for the War on Terror and tilt toward China? Could the Pakistani armed forces expect to get the desired military weapons and equipment from China that they can obtain from the United States? What role will the Pakistan Army's leadership and the Inter-Services Intelligence (ISI) play during this policy review?

• Firstly, even though the newly elected government has been described by most as "secular" and "liberal," it is going to find it difficult to distance itself from Islam because of the underlying strength of religious feeling among the masses and the widespread anti-American sentiment that prevails. On the other hand, its economic woes and security predicaments preclude it from distancing itself from the sole super-power. As such, the new government will likely adopt a middle-of-the-road path designed to keep both the Americans and the masses appeased. Walking this tightrope is not going to be easy, however, and will require skillful manipulation. On the external front, Pakistan trusts China much more than it does the United States, as Islamabad perceives Washington to have left it in the lurch once too often while China has been steadfast in its commitments. Once again, however, the imperative of staying in the U.S. camp will play a major role in the formulation of foreign policy but this will be done with the tacit approval of the Chinese, whom no Pakistani government can afford to alienate even in the slightest.

• Secondly, notwithstanding the enormous economic strides that China is making, its military weapons technology is nowhere near what the United States and the West are able to field. Since a budget-constrained Pakistan is limited in what it can afford to purchase, the best option for it would be to procure limited amounts of quality equipment from the United States and the West with the quantity factor being made up by purchasing cheaper, although less modern, Chinese weaponry in greater numbers. As with the foreign policy option discussed earlier, Pakistan's defense procurement is also expected to be two-pronged without either the United States or China being relegated in importance.

• Thirdly, much is being said about the role of the Pakistani military in the future foreign and defense policies of Pakistan, with some analysts conjecturing that the Pakistan Army is likely to be split into pro-United States and pro-China camps. This possibility appears farfetched because of a multitude of reasons: Firstly, since Pakistani-U.S. military ties date back several decades, most of the senior leadership have all been trained in the United States and have a soft spot for the West; secondly, a very limited number of Pakistani military personnel have been trained in China and most of these are still at the middle leadership level; thirdly, with the election of the new government, it can be expected that legislation would be put in place to obviate the chances of the military assuming power again in Pakistan; and fourthly, the fact that most soldiers, airmen and sailors realize that even the best weapons that China can provide do not technologically compare with what can be obtained from the United States and the West.

While there is no doubt that Pakistan's relations with both China and the United States are at critical junctures and any change in either is bound to impact the other, an objective analysis of the prevailing situation and the realities on the ground leads one to the following conclusions:

• Pakistan's new democratically elected government will continue to support the United States in the War on Terror. It will simultaneously strive to ensure that the Uyghur separatists from Xinjiang are neither afforded any help nor safe havens on Pakistani soil.

• Pakistan will adopt a middle-of-the-road foreign policy aimed at accommodating the needs and requirements of both China and the United States. Under the present circumstances, Pakistan cannot afford to distance itself from either.

• Since financial constraints dictate that Pakistan resort to a suitable quality-quantity mix in its military weapons, it will continue to rely on the United States for quality while depending on China for quantity.

• With the foundations of democratic order having been laid in Pakistan, one could surmise that the role of the military in affairs of state would gradually reduce. As regards the ISI, since it is a military-operated institution, one might expect its role on the international scene to be reduced correspondingly with an increased element of civilian control over its activities.

Originally published in *Terrorim Monitor*: Volume 6, Issue 8 on April 17, 2008.

Notes

1. Jing-dong Yuan, "The War on Terrorism: China's Opportunities and Dilemmas," Center for Non-Proliferation Studies, Monterey Institute of International Studies, September 25, 2001.
2. Lisa Curtis, "Security Challenges Involving Pakistan and Policy Implications for the Department of Defense," Testimony delivered before the Armed Services Committee, U.S. House of Representatives, October 10, 2007.

3. Mohan Malik, "Dragon on Terrorism: China's Tactical Gains and Strategic Losses Post September-11," Strategic Studies Institute, U.S. Army War College, Carlisle, PA, October 2002.

Part V

The Caucasus and Central Asia

Azerbaijan Increasingly Caught Between Salafism and Iran
By Anar Valiyev

After the collapse of the Soviet Union, Azerbaijan became a battleground for many religious groups, sects and radical organizations. Being a predominantly secular society, Azerbaijanis cautiously watched the appearance of new religious movements. Neighboring countries such as Iran, Turkey as well as the Arab Gulf countries consider Azerbaijan as a strategic arena to expand their influence, often through religion. As a result of the absence of a strict policy toward religious groups, Azerbaijan became a haven for various religious organizations that preach opposite and contradictory ideas. Moreover, representatives of various sects clash with each other over influence in the country. For the past couple of years, the struggle between Shiites supported by Iran and Salafis (mostly supported from the North Caucasus and the Arab world) has intensified.

Salafis Encroach on Azerbaijan's Shiites

Azerbaijan is a Muslim country where roughly 75 percent of the population is Shiite, with the remainder Sunnis. The decades of co-existence between the two branches of Islam in Azerbaijan created a fragile balance that neither mainstream Shiites nor Sunnis wish to break. Moreover, Soviet repression against all branches of Islam put the Shiites and Sunnis of Azerbaijan in similar predicaments, providing them with shared experiences. Meanwhile, after centuries of development, Islam in Azerbaijan became a culture and tradition rather than strictly a religion. Although most Azerbaijanis zealously call themselves Muslims, they hardly observe any pillars of Islam. Local people visit sacred places called pirs, along with graveyards of "saints," rather than mosques, where they give money and offer sacrifices. The official corrupted clergy do not discourage such behavior since it benefits them in various ways, including financially.

The appearance of Salafis in the country, however, broke this delicate balance. Salafis first started to preach against the pirs and saint worship, calling such practices acts counter to Islam. They do not recognize the official Shiite clergy and accuse them of conducting an Iranian policy. Moreover, they consider Shiites as heretics and call for purifying Islam in Azerbaijan. In many instances, Salafis employ violence in order to bring attention or to show their adherents the "right" path. Thus, for the last couple of *In many instances, Salafis employ violence in order to bring attention or to show their adherents the "right" path.* years, Salafis have attacked pirs and destroyed them in several instances, angering the local population. However, despite the population's hostility, the number of Salafis is increasing every year. By unofficial accounts, the number of Salafis reached 25,000 by the end of 2006, while 15 years ago they were non-existent in the country (Nezavisimaya Gazeta, April 2006; RFE/RL, August 10, 2007).

The northern region of Azerbaijan remains one of the areas where the Salafi movement has found promising ground. The media has reported several times on the existence of a Salafi extremist organization called the "Forest Brothers." The organization was involved in distributing religious literature, attacks on law enforcement officials and the murder of several policemen in Gusar region of Azerbaijan and in the capital (Day.az, March 29). Occasionally, law enforcement agencies report on attacks on police by "Wahabbis" who refuse to comply with Azerbaijani laws. On September 26, for example, two police officers were wounded by a member of a Salafi organization. Authorities immediately started another crackdown on Salafi cells in the region. Anti-terrorist groups arrived in the region from Baku and began intensive searches for suspects. A number of people belonging to Salafi cells were subsequently detained and arrested (Turan News Agency, September 27, 2007).

At the same time, every month police and Ministry of National Security officials conduct searches in the homes of Salafis for forbidden literature and illegal weapons. In April 2007, for example, 16 Salafis were arrested for illegal propaganda (Day.az, April 18). Many Azerbaijani Salafis sympathize with the Chechen cause and some have even been involved in military actions there (*Terrorism Monitor*, July 1, 2005). The first Salafi missionaries arrived in Azerbaijan from the North Caucasus in the mid-1990s, with the majority coming from Chechnya and Dagestan where Salafism had influence (*Terrorism Monitor*, July 1, 2005)

.
In Azerbaijan, there are diverging views among the public whether Salafism is a threat to the country. While law enforcement agencies repeatedly warn of the Salafi danger, other government agencies do not consider it much of a threat. Hidayat Orujev, the head of the State Committee for Working with Religious Organizations (SCWRO), believes that "there are few Wahabbi cells in the country, and they do not represent danger" (Day.az, September 27, 2007). Indeed, most of the time law enforcement agencies as well as the media inflate the danger posed by Salafis, often sensationalizing and hyping crimes where Salafism may have played a role.

It is also important to mention that the police respond intolerantly to adherents of Salafism. In the Zagatal region of Azerbaijan (a hotbed of the Salafi movement in Azerbaijan), for example, police allegedly burned and shaved the beards of Salafis. Many Salafis are brutally beaten and humiliated, and forced to come for "beard" check-ups at the police department every day (Turan News Agency, September 11, 2007). It appears that these harsh practices help to incite Salafis to undertake attacks against security services.

Overall, the government is playing a dangerous game with Salafis in Azerbaijan. The government does not, for instance, forbid Salafi preaching or close Salafi mosques. They do, however, prevent Salafism from expanding unchecked. Many analysts believe that the government artificially inflates the Salafi threat to distract the population away from its own inadequacies, and in fact employs Salafi adherents to irritate Iran and help curb Iranian influence in Azerbaijan.

Iran Monitoring Salafi Expansion in Azerbaijan

Salafi expansion in Azerbaijan is being closely monitored by Iran. The Iranian government and clergy are actively seeking ways to expand its influence over Azerbaijan and halt further Salafi incursions. Besides humanitarian assistance in refugee camps, exporting religious literature and TV broadcasting, Iranian authorities create and support radical organizations in the country. A branch of the Hezbollah organization that was closely related to the Iranian special services was active in Azerbaijan in the second half of the 1990s [1]. This branch was accused by the government of assassinating the famous academician Ziya Bunyadov in 1997 and was neutralized after unprecedented pressure by the authorities.

The failure of Hezbollah, however, did not stop other pro-Iranian terrorist organizations from emerging. In January 2007, Azerbaijani authorities announced the arrests of a group of 17 people headed by Said Dadashbeyli. The radical organization, called the Northern Army of the Mahdi, was formed with a purpose to fight against the United States and Israel, and to create a separate Sharia-ruled country. Allegedly, the heads of the organization kept secret contacts with the Iranian Revolutionary Guards Corp. Thus, one of the leaders of the organization met with a member of the Corp in Iran's Qom city where he was allegedly offered financial support. Meanwhile, the members of the Northern Army of the Mahdi received military training in Iran (Turan News Agency, January 15). The group has also been accused of racketeering, armed assault, treason, drug dealing and a coup attempt. Some newspapers pointed out that U.S. intelligence agencies actively participated in neutralizing this radical organization (Yeni Musavat, January 29). According to these reports, the U.S. government is concerned that the Iranian special services are expanding their influence in Azerbaijan, possibly in order to gain leverage over the United States should Washington attempt to attack Iran.

A further sign demonstrating Iran's influence in Azerbaijan is an incident that occurred in mid 2006. Journalist Rafig Tagi published an article in Senet newspaper titled "Europe and Us." The article claimed that Islam did not bring any positive developments to "progress," and his argument divided Azerbaijani society. Immediately after publication, Iran-supported rallies and protests were organized in some Shiite-dominated villages of Azerbaijan. During the rallies, protesters called for the murder of Tagi. Meanwhile, Grand Ayatollah Fazel Lankarani of Iran issued a fatwa calling for the deaths of Rafig Tagi and Samir Sadaqatoglu, the editors of the newspaper. Authorities jailed the journalists, fearing possible assassinations and a spark of terrorism by Iranian-supported organizations. This case was used by Iranian authorities and the clergy to show their influence over the religious situation in Azerbaijan and the ability to affect government policy.

Conclusion

At the present stage, radical Shiite and Sunni groups do not pose a serious threat to Azerbaijan. The tradition of secularism in the country is strong. Nevertheless, the situation could change. Azerbaijani government agencies do not have a unified approach to handling religious organizations in the country. Meanwhile, there is a hidden competition between the state committee and the official clergy for control and registration of religious organizations.

At the same time, police use brutal force in dealing with many radical organizations, rejecting the process of negotiation. Unfortunately, none of these agencies look at the social aspects that cause people to join radical organizations. Identity crises, dissatisfaction with the current regime, existence of an ideological vacuum and poverty are the main reasons that bring youth to radical organizations in Azerbaijan. As time passes, it is believed that more and more young people will join potentially violent groups in the country. If this trend continues, sectarian violence could break out and lead to more instances of terrorism in Azerbaijan.

Originally published in *Terrorism Monitor*: Volume 5, Issue 19 on October 11, 2007.

Notes

1. Arif Yunusov, *Islam in Azerbaijan* (Baku: Friedrich Ebert Foundation, Institute of Peace and Democracy, 2004).

The Islamist Underground in Southern Kyrgyzstan
By Igor Rotar

The 2005 uprising in the Uzbek city of Andijan was only the first symptom of renewed tensions in the Ferghana Valley. The region has seen an increase in inter-ethnic tensions and in operations by Islamist radicals. Groups such as Hizb-ut-Tahrir (HuT), the Islamic Movement of Uzbekistan and Akramiya are threatening to destabilize sections of the valley. In Kyrgyzstan, Islamist radicals are becoming especially active. Alexander Kniazev, a political scientist from Kyrgyzstan, summed up the situation for The Jamestown Foundation in the following way:

"The south of Kyrgyzstan was not only the cradle of the 'Tulip Revolution' that occurred in that country, but is also now a place of anarchy following the removal of the old central government. This lack of real authority, along with persistent inter-ethnic tensions, makes it a prime location for an Islamic revolution. The Kyrgyz section of the valley is currently the most problematic, and if war starts here, it will eventually involve the rest of the Central Asian countries. During the 1920s, Ferghana was divided between Uzbekistan, Tajikistan and Kyrgyzstan, but to this day the various parts of the valley remain as inter-connected parts of a greater whole. A crisis in any of the components creates a chain reaction that can lead to cataclysms in the nearby territories, potentially creating further instability in nearby countries."

Such a grim evaluation stems from the mass disorders that occurred in southern Kyrgyzstan in August after one of the most famous local imams, Muhammadrafik Kamalov, was killed by the country's security services. The official explanation states that Kamalov was caught transporting two terrorists from the Islamic Movement of Uzbekistan in his car. The men in question were responsible for attacks on Kyrgyz and Tajik border control posts in May 2006. When ordered to pull over, the imam refused and was killed along with his passengers by Kyrgyz security personnel fire.

Kamalov preached in the municipal mosque in the city of Karasu and thousands came to hear him. Karasu is located on the Kyrgyz-Uzbek border and is considered the Central Asian capital of the HuT movement. HuT, an international Islamic organization, has as its main mission the unification of Muslims globally into one caliphate. According to their ideology, Western democracy is seen as improper for Muslims, and countries such as the United States, Great Britain and Israel are considered creations of the devil. HuT has been banned in many Arab countries, as well as in Germany, Russia and in the Central Asian states. Kamalov's mosque was famous as a sort of club for those in favor of an international caliphate and his parishioners included not only people from Kyrgyzstan, but also similarly minded individuals from neighboring Uzbekistan.

An ethnic Uzbek, Kamalov was a pupil of the famous Uzbek imam Abduvali Mirzoev. Mirzoev gained fame for his independence from the Uzbek government and he preached in the Andijan municipal mosque where he argued for the creation of an Uzbek Islamic state. His views were similar to the Hanafi Mazhab school of Islamic teaching, which is widespread in Saudi Arabia. Thus, Mirzoev opposed pilgrimages to holy places and excessively fancy weddings and funerals. By these views, he fit the "Wahhabite" label as understood by all of Central Asia. In 1995, he was abducted by Uzbek special services, and his subsequent fate remains unknown. Sadykdzhan Kamalov, Muhammadrafik's brother and a former Kyrgyz mufti, told the author in an interview for this article that "the fact that my brother was Mirzoev's pupil and an influential theologian angered the Uzbek authorities. Though there is no direct proof, there are persistent rumors that his murder was linked to the Uzbek special services."

The story of Muhammadrafik Kamalov's involvement in the Islamic Movement of Uzbekistan is confusing and unclear. For example, videocassettes currently distributed in southern Kyrgyzstan show the most recent speech of Tahir Yuldashev, the leader of the Islamic Movement of Uzbekistan, attacking HuT sharply. It should be noted that many of the so-called Wahhabites are also opponents of HuT. Therefore, it is hard to determine just what sort of relationship the slain imam had with Islamic organizations in the region. Nonetheless, it is known that Muhammadrafik Kamalov hated Islam Karimov for the treatment of Mirzoev, making it likely that the imam sympathized with all the enemies of the Uzbek president.

It should be noted that many of the so-called Wahhabites are also opponents of HuT. Therefore, it is hard to determine just what sort of relationship the slain imam had with Islamic organizations in the region.

Regardless of whether the imam was actually connected with the Islamist underground, many of the faithful in southern Kyrgyzstan and the nearby areas of Uzbekistan see the death of Kamalov as an example of the government's assault upon an independent-minded Muslim. Consequently, the funeral of the renowned theologian became a massive anti-government demonstration, with Kamalov being declared "a victim of governmental terror" and a shakhid (martyr). For almost two hours, a crowd of 5,000 people carried the coffin around the city and chanted "Allah Akbar" and "Shakhid Muborak" ("Congratulations upon a martyrdom!") (Ferghana.ru, August 8, 2006).

"The situation in southern Kyrgyzstan is ready to boil over—the faithful are angered by the killing of a famous religious authority," Sadykdzhan Kamalov, who is currently the director of an international Islamic center, told the author earlier this fall. "The nerves of the locals are stretched to the breaking point and mass protests may break out following the smallest provocation by the government. It seems to me that certain forces have decided to simply cause an explosion in the south of the republic."

On the Road to a Caliphate

Up until two years ago, it was rare to see a woman in the southern Kyrgyz towns wearing the Islamic head scarf and even rarer to see one in full, all-concealing Islamic dress. Yet, today the majority of the female residents of the region wear styles "befitting a righteous

Muslim woman." According to Shamsybek Zakirov, the advisor to the head of the Kyrgyz religious affairs agency, "This 'fashion' for Islamic garments is a direct result of the propaganda undertaken by Hizb-ut-Tahrir and the Islamic missionary organization 'Tablig.' Many Kyrgyz citizens are trained in the Pakistani headquarters of this organization, and today, having returned home, they preach Islam among the Kyrgyz population."

Women wearing the hijab are not the only achievement of the Islamists. In recent times, attacks on Christian missionaries have been increasing in the region. "There is lynching," Alexander Shumilin, the director of the Union of Baptists of Kyrgyzstan, declared. "For example, around 100 men from a local mosque burst into a Christian prayer house in the village of Karakuldzha in the south of the republic. They broke two of pastor Zulumbek Sarygulov's fingers and knocked him unconscious. Having told him to 'get out of our village,' they flung him out of the building. The fanatics then piled all of the Christian literature they found in the yard (including several dozen Bibles) and burned it. They even wrote 'house for sale' on the gates of the building being used as the church. This pastor's life is still in danger, and he is being constantly threatened with death if he does not leave the village. While this incident is the most disgusting, it is not the only such occurrence, with Christians being beaten in many other villages of southern Kyrgyzstan" (Forum18.org, September 27, 2006).

Even the authorities admit that a significant part of the population of Kyrgyzstan's south rejects secular laws and lives according to Sharia norms. Shamsybek Zakirov noted that "Hizb-ut-Tahrir, Akramiya and the Islamic Movement of Uzbekistan are only a few of the radical organizations that function in south Kyrgyzstan. They grow like mushrooms after a spring rain and every day there are more of them. There are so many that we don't even know all their names."

Socialism the Islamic Way

Today, no one in Kyrgyzstan will deny that Kyrgyz citizens participated in the Andijan uprising. The citizens that took part were probably members of the Kyrgyz wing of the Akramiya organization that took the lead during the events in Andijan. "It's no secret that we have Akramists here in the south. Almost all of them are local Uzbeks. They knew of the uprising and left for Andijan several days in advance," said the head of the Osh human rights organization The Rays of Solomon, Sadykdzhan Mahmudov. Apparently, Akramiya has been active in the region for years. "In 1998, people who told the faithful that they shouldn't go to mosques and should instead pray at home appeared. This denial of the mosque is one part of Akramiya's teaching," Zakirov explained.

One of the key ideas of Akramiya is the creation of Islamic business-communities, a sort of Islamic form of socialism. Such communities in Andijan had a high level of social benefits, with the Muslim businessmen of the city agreeing that the minimum wage in the city should be $50 a month, a level roughly 10 times the general Uzbek wage, and swore not to pay their workers less than this amount. The Akramists also organized "community credit unions" that religious Muslims could draw on for help in developing their businesses. If the enterprise succeeded, the entrepreneur decided how much he wanted to return to the credit union. It is notable that the Kyrgyz security services have recently uncovered a number of business-communities run on the Andijan model. The Akramists, however, do not just want to build "Islamic socialism" peacefully since a veritable arsenal of weapons has been discovered among the Uzbek members of Akramiya arrested in Osh in August 2006.

The Kyrgyz-Uzbek Knot

The situation in southern Kyrgyzstan is exacerbated by the increasing tensions between the indigenous population and the Uzbeks, who account for roughly 40 percent of the population of this part of the Ferghana Valley. "Bloody conflicts between Uzbeks and Kyrgyzs can occur again," says Kadyrdzhan Batyrov, the director of the Uzbek Community of Dzhalal-Abad Oblast and a member of the Kyrgyz parliament. "Following the recent coup, the country has suffered from a power vacuum. With no real guarantee of their rights in place, Uzbeks of Kyrgyzstan feel defenseless before those 'revolutionary-thugs' that have realized that they can now act with impunity."

Batyrov is one of the richest men in Kyrgyzstan and has used his money to establish the University of National Friendship (Universitet Druzhby Narodov) in Dzhalal-Abad, which has become a popular learning institution for local Uzbeks. The millionaire came into conflict with the current authorities in May 2006 when Uzbeks demanded that their language be given national status during a demonstration. The government in Bishkek rejected these demands, and in early July 300 or so Kyrgyz captured several of Batyrov's homes and 12 hectares of his land. "I have no doubt," Batyrov explained, "that this attack on my property was instigated by the government. They're trying to punish me for standing up for Uzbek rights." It is quite possible that the businessman is right, since in September 2006 the local courts suddenly decided that he privatized the land in question illegally.

The killing of the influential businessman and head of the Osh municipal Uzbek National Center, Aybek Alimzhanov, on October 15, 2006 marked a new stage in the evolving conflict. The police have suggested that Alimzhanov's business rivals killed him, but the local Uzbeks feel that the case has obvious ethnic overtones. Alimzhanov's supporters have sent an open letter to Kyrgyzstan President Kurmanbek Bakiev, saying, "We are deeply concerned that the dark forces trying to destabilize the republic might be able to steer the current wave of crime into becoming an inter-ethnic conflict" (Ferghana.ru, October 18, 2006). It seems naive to dismiss these incidents as being a purely local issue. In 1990, Uzbek-Kyrgyz riots, prompted by previous calls for an official recognition of the Uzbek language, led to more than 300 deaths.

The correspondence between rising inter-ethnic tensions and the activities of Islamic radicals cannot be ignored. This has been deeply troubling to the Kyrgyz government, and, according to Kyrgyz Prime Minister Felix Kulov, the new year might see a group of extremist religious preachers attempt to foment an inter-ethnic conflict in the Ferghana Valley (Interfax, June 15, 2006).

Originally published in *Terrorism Monitor*: Volume 4, Issue 23, November 30, 2006.

Kyrgyzstan's Manas Airbase: A Key Asset in the War on Terrorism
By John C. K. Daly

The collapse of communism in the USSR in 1991 and the September 11 terrorist attacks in the United States a decade later offered the Pentagon basing possibilities impossible even to conceive of during the Cold War. The chief beneficiaries were Uzbekistan and Kyrgyzstan, which were catapulted from being the "back of beyond" of the "Evil Empire" to potential front-line states in Washington's and NATO's attempt to develop a new military footprint in former Soviet republics. Since relations between Uzbekistan and the United States soured after the events in Andijan in May 2005, Kyrgyzstan has emerged as Washington's sole front-line state for confronting terrorism in Afghanistan. The Manas airbase is critical to U.S. counter-terrorism strategy in Central and South Asia. A December 6, 2007 "incident" at Manas—when a U.S. serviceman fatally shot a Kyrgyz civilian at a truck checkpoint at the base—now threatens Washington's sole remaining military facility in the former Soviet Union, with no immediate resolution in sight.

Although U.S. interest in Central Asia predates the war on terrorism, it has been intensified by Washington's renewed counter-terrorism strategy. Impoverished, agrarian Kyrgyzstan has suddenly found itself wooed by the Russian Federation, the United States and China, which shares the Kyrgyz border with its restive Xinjiang province. Russia and the United States have airbases in Kyrgyzstan, while China has been eyeing the republic's rich natural resources. A new "Great Game" is indeed afoot. The crown jewels in this game are two military airbases in Kyrgyzstan—the U.S. facility at Manas established in December 2001 and, less than 30 miles away, Russia's facility at Kant that was leased only a year later in 2002.

Early Interest in Manas

The burgeoning U.S. interest in the tiny republic dates from the end of communism and was well advanced before the September 11 attacks. Beginning in 1995, the United States began to participate in the NATO Partnership for Peace (PfP) training exercises with Kazakhstan, Kyrgyzstan and Uzbekistan, the first exercise being August 1995's Cooperative Nugget exercise at Fort Polk, Louisiana. Cooperative Nugget exercises were also held in 1997 and in March and May of 2000. Both Kazakhstan and Kyrgyzstan participated in Cooperative Nugget exercises in Germany and Colorado.

In December of 1995, Kazakhstan, Kyrgyzstan and Uzbekistan formed the Central Asian Battalion, or Centrazbat, creating a regional peacekeeping unit. Troops from the United States, Kazakhstan, Kyrgyzstan, Latvia, Georgia, Russia, Turkey and Uzbekistan participated in the first set of Centrazbat exercises held in September 1997 in Uzbekistan and Kazakhstan. Five hundred U.S. 82nd Airborne Division members took part in the exercises, which began with a parachute drop from U.S. Air Force C-17 transport aircraft. Additional Centrazbat exercises were held in 1998 and 2000.

Another NATO PfP program, involving Central Asia, was Cooperative Osprey, the first exercise of which was held in North Carolina in August 1996, where U.S., Dutch and Canadian troops joined with 16 PfP countries, including Kazakhstan and Kyrgyzstan, in training exercises. Then, in March 2001 in Nova Scotia, six NATO members, one being the United States, joined 13 PfP countries, including Kazakhstan and Kyrgyzstan, in Cooperative Osprey training exercises. The same month, 12 U.S. servicemen participated in Operation Balance Night to train 150 Kyrgyz servicemen to resist armed incursions of Islamic fundamentalists from neighboring countries under bilateral agreements signed between Kyrgyzstan and U.S. CENTCOM in June 2000 (UPI Hears, March 3, 2001).

Manas Chosen for Operations in Afghanistan

The September 11 terrorist attacks in the United States bumped the Department of Defense's interest in Central Asia into high gear. On December 16, 2001, the U.S. Air Force in Europe sent the 86th Contingency Response Group from Ramstein Air Base in Germany to "kick in the door" of a new base. This unit set up security and air traffic control and began negotiating with airport and government officials on the base's footprint (Airman, February 2005). Manas was chosen for its 14,000-foot runway, which was originally built to handle Soviet bombers but could handle U.S. C-5 Galaxy cargo planes and 747s in their 1,000-mile flight to Afghanistan. Of Kyrgyzstan's 52 airports, Manas was the only one with a lengthy runway and the only one capable of supporting international flights. An adjacent 32-acre field was designated as the site of a tent city for U.S. personnel.

In February 2002, U.S. troops quietly began joint military exercises in Kyrgyzstan. This was the first prolonged stay of U.S. forces who trained Kyrgyz Special Forces border guards to cope with insurgents, notably those of the Islamic Movement of Uzbekistan, which had in 1999 ensconced themselves in southern Kyrgyzstan. Manas quickly proved to be a useful base for Afghan operations, as its 90-minute flying time to the war theater dwarfed the six to eight hours flight time from other potential launching areas, such as ships or U.S. bases in Saudi Arabia. Besides the U.S. forces involved in Operation Enduring Freedom, Manas hosted personnel from France, South Korea, Spain, Denmark, Norway, Australia and the Netherlands. Spanish, Dutch, Danish

While Kyrgyzstan's civil society is relatively tranquil compared to Afghanistan's in the wake of the Soviet-Afghan war, it is not immune to the terrorism roiling the region.

and Norwegian C-130s flew cargo missions; France contributed six Mirage 2000s and two C-135 re-fuelers; Australia sent two Boeing 707 refueling aircraft; and Spain offered HT-211 Super Puma rescue helicopters. Within about six months of September 11, the Pentagon established 13 bases in nine countries in and around Afghanistan. By October 2001, U.S. combat aircraft had flown over 900 sorties and logged more than 4,200 combat hours (Department of the Navy, Naval Historical Center, July-August 2002).

Threats to the Airbase

While Kyrgyzstan's civil society is relatively tranquil compared to Afghanistan's in the wake of the Soviet-Afghan war, it is not immune to the terrorism roiling the region. In September 2003, three Kyrgyz citizens were convicted for trying to organize a terrorist attack on the airbase, while on July 8, 2004 militants attacked Manas. Kyrgyz National Security Service Chairman Kalyk Imankulov stated, "The National Security Service believes that the Islamic Movement of Uzbekistan might have been involved in attempts to commit terrorist attacks at the Ganci airbase at Manas International Airport near Bishkek" (Jane's Intelligence Watch Report, July 9, 2004).

In addition to the threat of terrorism, Kyrgyzstan's Tulip Revolution, which flared up in February 2005 and culminated in President Askar Akayev fleeing the country the following month, worried Washington that the new Kyrgyz government might abrogate basing rights in Manas. Then U.S. Secretary of Defense Donald Rumsfeld visited Bishkek in early April 2005 to shore up Kyrgyz support for the continued U.S. presence at Manas. The situation only worsened, however, as events in neighboring Uzbekistan also affected the airbase. On May 13, 2005, Uzbek troops fired into a crowd of protesters in Andijan in the Ferghana Valley who were protesting the trial of local Islamic activists. While Tashkent maintained that 187 people, mostly "terrorist organizers," died during the Andijan unrest, human rights groups averred that the toll was far higher. Washington's equivocal response to the incident led the Uzbek government on July 29, 2006 to inform Washington that it was abrogating the agreement permitting the U.S. military to use the Karshi-Khanabad airbase under terms of the bilateral Status of Forces Agreement (SOFA), giving the Pentagon 180 days to end its activities there. A further irritant in U.S.-Uzbek relations was the issue of 450 refugees from Andijan who fled to Kyrgyzstan and were eventually airlifted to Romania. After the loss of Uzbekistan, Manas moved to the forefront of U.S. military efforts to maintain aerial operations over Afghanistan. The loss of Karshi-Khanabad was significant—just 60 miles from Afghanistan in Qashqadaryo Province near the border with Tajikistan, the base's 416th Air Expeditionary Group averaged 200 passengers and 100 tons of cargo per day on C-130H missions, supporting Operation Enduring Freedom with scores of flights each month.

Given the half-decade of the U.S. presence at Manas, disputes have inevitably arisen between Kyrgyzstan and the United States about personnel, hardware and money. On September 5, 2006 Air Force Major Jill Metzger went missing from Manas before she was scheduled to return to the United States after shopping in a mall in Bishkek. Only three days later, she turned up. Metzger claimed that she had been kidnapped; the incident is still under investigation, but in the aftermath, U.S. military personnel at Manas were confined to the base (Stars and Stripes, September 27, 2006). In the interim, members of the 376th Air Expeditionary Wing continued their re-supply efforts to Afghanistan and on September 17 unloaded 43,000 pounds of food, water and building supplies at Bagram Air Base outside Kabul.

On September 26, 2006, a collision between a Kyrgyz TU-154 passenger plane and an Air Force KC-135 Stratotanker on the airfield at Manas International Airport further strained relations (Air Safety Week, October 9, 2006; Gazeta.ru, December 22, 2006). Kyrgyz Transport Minister Nurlan Sulaimanov said the incident was caused by darkness and the U.S. jet being parked in the wrong spot on an uneven runway, commenting that a government commission has concluded that the "blame for the incident at the Manas International Airport rests with the crew of the American plane" (Stars and Stripes, November 16, 2006). U.S. personnel at Manas continued to carry out their duties. In October and November, they exceeded Air Mobility Command's standard of 95 percent for the Logistics Departure Reliability rate (Air Force Print News, October 30, 2006).

The Tulip Revolution also raised the rent for the Pentagon's use of Manas. Under the December 4, 2001 basing agreement, Manas cost a little over $2 million a year. Bakiyev's new administration sought to increase the amount to $100-200 million annually; presently, discussions continue on the topic (Kommersant, June 2, 2006). The Bush administration allegedly promised Kyryzstan $150 million immediately and $15 million annually afterwards, but the new agreement was never signed (Journal of Turkish Weekly, December 18, 2006). Whatever the final rent, Manas has proven useful far beyond situations in the Central Asia region; in July, C-17s based there were used to evacuate U.S. citizens from Lebanon, then under assault by Israel (Air Force Print News, July 26, 2006).

Conclusion

Despite what may happen in the long-term, it is clear that the United States will remain at Manas in the near future. In October 2006, the base received 7,256,000 gallons of fuel. In November, the U.S. troop transit rate through Manas tripled (DefendAmerica.com, November 11, 2006). Also in November, troops began winterizing the base (UPI, November 27, 2006).

The shadowy "Great Game" continues in Central Asia, as on October 4, 2006 Russian Deputy Prime Minister and Defense Minister Sergei Ivanov met Kyrgyz Prime Minister Feliks Julov in Bishkek. Russia insists that, while U.S. forces use Manas for supporting Operation Enduring Freedom in Afghanistan, their Kant facility is maintained under Kyrgyzstan's membership in the Shanghai Cooperation Organization and the Collective Security Treaty Organization. Kant is a bargain, costing the Russians only $4.5 million annually to support its 500 personnel there (RFE/RL Kyrgyz Service, October 5, 2006).

Nevertheless, new events have placed pressure on U.S. access to the base. On December 6, U.S. guards at Manas shot and killed Aleksandr Ivanov, an ethnic Russian Kyrgyz citizen at the airbase's entry gate. The U.S. military shot Ivanov, who the Kyrgyz government insisted was behaving correctly, twice in the chest with a pistol. Ivanov worked for the Aircraft Petroleum Co. (AKI Press, December 7, 2006). The United States claims that the victim was armed with a knife and was behaving aggressively (Kommersant, December 7, 2006). The incident has roiled the top levels of the Kyrgyz government, with President Kurmanbek Bakiyev calling for U.S. military personnel to be stripped of their diplomatic immunity (Iamik.ru, December 22, 2006).

Washington should learn from its equivocal tactics in 2005 in Uzbekistan, and if it does not address what it regards as a minor incident in the December 6, 2006 death of Ivanov, insisting instead that under a 2001 agreement with Kyrgyzstan U.S. servicemen come under U.S. jurisdiction, it might well lose its last base in the former Soviet Union.

Origianlly published in *Terrorism Monitor*: Volume 5, Issue 1 on January 18, 2007.

Uzbek Terror Networks: Germany, Jamoat and the IJU
By Cerwyn Moore

Three months after the arrests of three men in Germany, little is known about the network involved or the reasons behind a plot to use "massive bomb attacks" against targets in Germany. Reports immediately after the arrests pointed toward a U.S. airbase, nightclubs and the airport at Frankfurt as targets the plotters had considered. More recently, reports have indicated that the men intended to strike at both the U.S. and Uzbek Embassies in Germany. Along with a statement by a group called the Islamic Jihad Union, the reports point to the re-emergence of a terror threat from post-Soviet Central Asia.

Of course, the list of potential targets implies that the cell aimed to kill and maim civilians in a series of spectacular attacks, which have the hallmark of an al-Qaeda-inspired campaign. Two subsidiary aims may have been to damage transatlantic relations between Germany and the United States, and to undermine the U.S.-led war on terror in Afghanistan and Iraq. Germany continues to run a military base in Termez, on the Uzbek-Afghan border, as part of its role in NATO operations in Afghanistan, while the U.S. Ramstein airbase in Germany is a major military hub, providing support for operations in both Afghanistan and Iraq while housing the largest U.S. military hospital outside of the United States.

Elsewhere, German newspapers have begun to unfold a U.S. intelligence operation code-named "Alberich," which led to the arrests in Sauerland, some 60 miles east of Düsseldorf. The intelligence-led operation began in October 2006, when U.S. security agencies began intercepting suspicious emails and telephone calls between individuals in Germany, Turkey and Pakistan. It ended with the arrest of two German men, Fritz Gelowicz and Daniel Martin Schneider, both converts to Islam, and a third man named Adem Yılmaz, also in his 20s but of Turkish origin (Der Spiegel, September 13, 2007). Moreover, statements made by German officials after the arrests indicated that the men had trained in Pakistan, focusing attention on al-Qaeda affiliates in Central Asia such as the Islamic Movement of Uzbekistan (IMU). Nonetheless, it was the little known Islamic Jihad Union (IJU), described as an offshoot of the IMU, which laid claim to the foiled plot.

Central Asia: The Rise of the Islamic Movement of Uzbekistan

In recent years the IMU, a radical Uzbek group generally thought to have formed around 1996, appears to have played an important role in the continuing violence in Central Asia. Since the end of the Cold War, the Uzbek government has been involved in countering internal dissent and a rising tide of religious extremism, as the civil war in Afghanistan led to a resurgent interest in Islam. Throughout this period, Uzbek authorities employed harsh measures to counter internal dissent, whether from radical Islamic groups like the IMU or pan-Islamic groups such as Hizb ut-Tahir (HuT). Internal dissent and regional instability led fledgling radical groups to operate underground, locate themselves in neighboring countries or support regional movements. For instance, a number of Uzbek fighters participated in the Tajik civil war between 1992 and 1997, as well as the Afghan civil war. In 1999 a failed assassination attempt on Islam Karimov led to further accusations against HuT, although Islamic radicals (including the IMU) were later accused of planning the failed attack.

In late 1999, a lack of support in Uzbekistan and the measures deployed by the Karimov government forced the IMU, then led by Juma Namangani, to re-locate to Taliban-controlled Afghanistan. The group gained some financial support from Osama bin Laden and the fledgling al-Qaeda network, leading the IMU to establish a training camp in the tribal region of Waziristan between 2000 and 2001. After 9/11 and the subsequent U.S. invasion of Afghanistan, the operational capability of the IMU was severely undermined. Although Juma Namangani was reportedly killed in a U.S. bombing raid, remnants of the IMU and its senior leadership under the command of Tahir Yuldashev appear to have moved to Pakistan's tribal areas. Throughout 2002 surviving members of the IMU formed a loose alliance which led to the creation of the Islamic Movement of Turkistan (IMT), the Uzbekistan Islamic Jihad, and the Islamic Union Jihad. Even though none of these groups could coordinate a sustained terror campaign, they focused upon surviving as small clandestine groups.

The spread of Uzbek-led terrorism was not, however, focused solely on attacking the regime within Uzbekistan, nor were the popular demonstrations against the economic mismanagement of the country by the Karimov regime isolated. Instead, a series of events including bomb attacks in April 2004, the trial of 15 suspects following the bombings and a subsequent series of coordinated attacks in July 2004, including suicide bombings at the Israeli and U.S. Embassies, were part of a campaign against the Uzbek authorities, corrupt policing, and the Karimov government. Interestingly, the attacks on U.S. and Israeli targets occurred

> *The spread of Uzbek-led terrorism was ... part of a campaign against the Uzbek authorities, corrupt policing, and the Karimov government.*

shortly after the death of the spiritual leader of Hamas, Sheikh Ahmed Yassin on March 22, 2004, leading some reports to suggest that the suicide bombings were attempts by radical Islamic groups affiliated to al-Qaeda to respond to Israeli policies in the Middle East. Meanwhile, popular dissent aimed at the Karimov regime manifested itself in a large-scale May 2005 demonstration in front of the U.S. embassy. The protest was forcibly dispersed.

In more recent years, the deployment of considerable numbers of Uzbek volunteers, their involvement in a series of confrontations with Pakistani troops and indigenous tribal groups throughout 2006 and the establishment of Tahir Yuldashev as a key figure in the Taliban-al-Qaeda nexus, provide evidence of a resurgent IMU.

Jamoat: From the IMU to the IJU

In the trials that followed the events and arrests of 2004, the Karimov authorities indicated that a radical Jamoat group (jamoat is the Uzbek version of the Arabic jama'at, or "community") had been operating in Tashkent, Bukhara and Samarkand since 2000 (Tass, April 9, 2004). Indeed, trial proceedings indicate many of the arrestees were charged with membership in a group called "Jamoat," or the Jamoati Tablig organization (Novoye Pokoliniye, January 28, 2005). By 2002 it appears that remnants of the IMU had split, creating a series of factions affiliated to, but not controlled by, the IMU. Trial proceedings indicate that the underground group was led by Farkhad Kazabkhayev, and although it did not formerly have a name, the group operated with a radical Islamic agenda, seeking to establish a system of Islamic caliphates under the banner of the IJU.

In April 2004, the IJU accepted responsibility for the attacks in Tashkent and central Bukhara, while in June 2004 a second statement promised to undertake further attacks against the Karimov regime. Although the group remained distinct from al-Qaeda and may have remained a splinter group with different aims from those of the IMU, some of the group's members had been trained by Arab instructors in a camp in Pakistan's Waziristan region, creating a shared experience and shared belief in the continuation of jihad. The trial proceeding from the events of 2004 also pointed to a number of other figures like Najmideen Jalolov, who may have played a role linking the Jamoat with the network that facilitated the movement of small amounts of weapons and men to training camps in Pakistan (The Associated Press, July 27, 2004). Other sources, including Uzbek officials, mention a "Great Emir" based outside of Uzbekistan who, along with a series of lesser "emirs," was in charge of the Jamoat operations.

It is not clear whether the "Great Emir" refers to Yuldashev, but the 2004 trial proceedings indicate that the group had met members of the East Turkistan Islamic Movement (ETIM), a Uyghur separatist movement active in the Xingjiang region of China. Other meetings were attended by Uyghur fighters loyal to Abu Muhammad and alleged Uzbek Jamoat leader Ahmad Bekmirzayev. Subsequent trial proceedings in Kazakhstan against militants involved in the April and July 2004 attacks in Uzbekistan also charged the defendants with membership in the Jamoat Mujahideen, otherwise known as the Community of Holy Warriors. The proceedings thus indicate that the network comprised of members from Kyrgyzstan, Uzbekistan and Kazakhstan who sought to use violence to challenge the Karimov regime and promote radical Islam in the region.

In effect, this culminated in the events in Andijan in which a peaceful demonstration against the arrest of 23 businessmen quickly escalated. On May 13, 2007 the Uzbek secret police arrested demonstrators and relatives of the 23 arrested men, which sparked further opposition, the storming of a local police station by the protesters, the seizure of weapons from local government offices and an attempt to storm the prison, all of which left scores dead. Again, reports indicated the involvement of small numbers of radicals, including fighters from Kyrgyzstan who were operating under the banner of the IJU (Tass, September 15, 2005).

Thus, it appears that the IJU is an umbrella term used to link a network of affiliated

Jamoat groups from Central Asia, comprised of Kyrgyz, Uzbek and Kazakh radicals, linked to, but not formerly associated with, the IMU. The key themes linking the network with regional radical organizations include a shared interest in jihad, common channels of funding, violence directed against anti-Islamic Central Asian authorities, links to criminal networks and a broadly conceived goal of establishing an Islamic caliphate, although the network draws on informal indigenous groups, clan and familial associations and a more specific agenda targeting the Karimov regime.

Concluding Remarks

First and foremost, it appears that a loose affiliation of indigenous Jamoat groups with a shared anti-Karimov agenda formed in 2000, which has since linked itself to regional groups and affiliates, especially after the U.S. invasion of Afghanistan. Secondly, the group comprises some former IMU members and may have gained financial support from al-Qaeda. Although the group remains distinct from al-Qaeda, it is part of the broader Salafi-jihadi movement. Thirdly, over the last three years, on each occasion when the IJU has announced forthcoming operations, bombings or foiled attacks have followed, demonstrating an attempt to operate as a functioning terror network. In April 2007 the IJU announced that it would step up operations abroad, leading German officials to issue a warning and increase security around its embassies. Finally, and indeed more generally, it appears that Tahir Yuldashev and the Central Asian groups have re-organized following the U.S. invasion of Afghanistan and now play an important role in the emerging generation of Salafi-jihadi networks willing to operate in Europe.

Originally published in *Terrorism Monitor*: Volume 5, Issue 21 on November 8, 2007.

Part VI

Europe and the Americas

Current Trends in Jihadi Networks in Europe
By Lorenzo Vidino

The terrorist related events that took place during the summer of 2007 in Europe—the doctors' plot in Great Britain, the dismantling of various cells in Italy, Austria and Spain, and, finally, the September 2007 arrests in Germany and Denmark—have confirmed that Europe is a key staging ground for jihadi activities. Although large differences exist from country to country and within various subgroups in the ever-evolving underworld of jihadi networks in Europe, it is possible to identify some current trends that, in one way or another, are common to the whole continent.

Independent, or Part of a Network

During the last few years, commentators have been fascinated with homegrown networks in Europe and, clearly, small groups of European-born, self-radicalized, violence-prone Islamists have sprung up in most European countries. Yet, the panorama of jihadi networks in Europe is quite complex and, for a more accurate analysis, could be described on a continuum. At one extreme, one can identify quintessential homegrown groups such as the Hofstad Group in the Netherlands: small domestic clusters of radicals that have developed no ties to external groups and act in complete operational independence. At the opposite side of the spectrum are cells that respond to the traditional model used by al-Qaeda-affiliated groups in the 1990s: compartmentalized cells inserted in a well-structured network and subjected to a hierarchy whose heads are often outside Europe. That is the model to which various cells of the Algerian GSPC (today Al-Qaeda in the Islamic Maghreb) belong.

In between these two extremes, there is a whole spectrum of realities, positioned according to the level of autonomy of the group. The most recurring model seems to be that of the cell dismantled by Danish authorities on September 4, 2007: a small group of young men, most of them born and/or raised in Europe, who knew each other either from the neighborhood or from the mosque. Their radicalization *In contrast to the situation before the September 11 attacks, today most European jihadis do not travel out of the continent for training or to fight.* took place in Europe and only one or two members of the group traveled out of the country (Pakistan, in this case) to link up with foreign-based, well-structured groups ideologically or operationally affiliated with al-Qaeda. The knowledge acquired by the cell after this linkage obviously makes it more dangerous.

Traveling for Jihad: Primary and Secondary Fields

In contrast to the situation before the September 11 attacks, today most European jihadis do not travel out of the continent for training or to fight. Nevertheless, a small but significant number of them still opt for short stints in places where they can join training camps or guerrilla units. Pakistan/Afghanistan and Iraq are the two primary destinations. The former seems to attract recruits mostly from Northern Europe (Great Britain, in particular), while militants from Spain, Italy and France seem to travel mostly to the latter (*El Periodico*, May 6, 2007; *Le Monde*, December 16, 2004).

Noteworthy is the presence of European militants in two lesser known fields of jihad: Somalia and Lebanon. A few dozen European volunteers have been arrested by Ethiopian and Somali governmental forces among the Islamic Courts Union's (ICU) fighters since December 2006. Several of these militants possess Scandinavian passports, and, according to intelligence sources, Sweden is considered the hub for the flow of money from Europe to the ICU (Sveriges Radio, January 30, 2007). Italian authorities have also monitored the visits of several ICU-linked preachers who are traveling to various Italian cities in order to fundraise and recruit among the country's Somali population (L'Espresso, February 5, 2007). Reportedly, Swedish and British fighters were killed by U.S. missiles and Somali army operations (BBC, June 3, 2007). A smaller number of Western volunteers, mostly from Denmark and Australia, have allegedly fought with Fatah al-Islam in the Nahr al-Barid refugee camp in Lebanon (*The Australian*, September 13, 2007).

The Muslim Ghetto Subculture: Jihad and Rap

Europe today is witnessing the growth of a disturbing new subculture that mixes violent urban behaviors, nihilism and Islamic fundamentalism. Many young, often European-born Muslims feel a disturbingly intense sense of detachment from, if not sheer hatred for, their host societies and embrace various antagonistic messages. While some turn to Salafism, others adopt an indefinite blend of counter-cultures, ranging from hip hop to Islamic fundamentalism. Many youngsters from the Muslim-majority ghettoes of various European cities adopt several behaviors typical of Western street culture, such as dressing like rappers, smoking marijuana and drinking alcohol, yet watching jihadi videos and having pictures of Osama bin Laden on the display of their cell phones [1]. Any individual who attacks mainstream society becomes a hero to these teens, be it Abu Musab al-Zarqawi or the late American rapper Tupac Shakur.

> *Europe today is witnessing the growth of a disturbing new subculture that mixes violent urban behaviors, nihilism and Islamic fundamentalism.*

This hybrid street culture is particularly influenced by African-American gangster culture and music. Bands such as Fun-da-mental and Blakstone in the United Kingdom, Medine in France, and Zanka Flow (Moroccan-based, but hugely popular in the Netherlands) combine radical Islamic concepts with hip hop sounds, jargon and attitudes. An aspiring star in the jihadi rap underworld is Mohammed Kamel Mostafa, the son of former Finsbury Park imam Abu Hamza, who has recently formed a rap duo called Lionz of Da Dezert. Using the stage name of al-Ansary, Mostafa raps about jihad and killing infidels. "I was born to be a soldier," read the lyrics of one of his songs. "Kalashnikov on my shoulder, peace to Hamas and Hezbollah, that's the way of the lord Allah. We're jihad. I defend my religion with the holy sword" (Agence France-Presse, March 1, 2006).

While the phenomenon affects only a minority of European Muslims, its dimensions and repercussions are more than noteworthy. In London, city officials are worried about the growth of an extremely violent gang commonly known as the Muslim Boys. Operating in the southern areas of the British capital, the gang is composed of several hundreds of members and is active in criminal activities ranging from robberies to drug trafficking. The members of the gang are mostly British-born black youth originally from the Caribbean or Africa who converted to Islam in British penitentiaries and bond over their newfound faith (Evening Standard, February 3, 2005). Yet, their interpretation of Islam is perverted. The gang members do not respect the most basic tenets of Islam, and their appearance and slang more closely resemble that of American ghetto culture than that of practicing Muslims. Tellingly, a gang member admitted to a reporter from the Evening Standard: "I pray twice a day: before I do crime and after. I ask Allah for a blessing when I'm out on the streets. Afterwards, I apologize to Allah for what I done [sic]." The gang is also involved in "forced conversions," compelling black youth at gunpoint to convert to Islam and join them; two years ago, they executed a 24-year-old for refusing to convert.

The Expansion to the Countryside

Radical Islam in Europe has traditionally been an urban phenomenon. Muslim immigrants have historically settled in large and mid-size cities and, as a consequence, radical mosques and jihadi activities have also been largely confined to urban settings. Yet, during the past few years, there has been a noticeable expansion of radical activities to rural areas. The phenomenon is particularly evident in southern European countries, where large numbers of North African immigrants are employed, seasonally or permanently, in agriculture. Wandering imams, often linked to the Tablighi Jamaat and small makeshift mosques run by radicals, have popped up in small country towns and villages in Spain, Italy and France, spreading Salafism among the local Muslim communities. Taking advantage of the absence of other mosques and the limited surveillance of the small local police forces, Salafists have managed to establish a presence in rural areas of Piedmont, Campania, Provence and southern Spain [2].

In some cases, Salafist networks have taken advantage of the isolation provided by the countryside to create small fundamentalist communes, as in Artigat, a bucolic village of less than 1,000 residents in the French Pyrenees. When French authorities dismantled a Toulouse-based network that was smuggling volunteers to Iraq, they uncovered links to a 60-year-old Syrian man who was leading an Islamist commune in Artigat (Le Parisien, February 15, 2007). Living completely isolated from the outside world, the commune's five families lived under a strict self-imposed Islamic code and preached a radical interpretation of Islam to their children and to the visitors who would come occasionally from the city (mostly Toulouse) to spend time in a "pure Islamic environment."

Eastern Europe?

While not already an established trend, there are indications showing that radical Islam is spreading, albeit at a slow pace and with significant differences from country to country, to Eastern Europe. The presence of radical networks in Bosnia, many of them leftovers from the conflict of the 1990s, is well known. Although less grave, Wahhabi influence, propagated mostly by a wide network of Saudi-sponsored mosques, is on the rise in other areas of the Balkans with significant Muslim populations such as Albania, Kosovo and Serbia's Sandzak region (B92 Radio Serbia, June 6, 2006).

Various Islamist groups have been reported to be actively spreading their propaganda to other Muslim populations throughout Eastern Europe. Hizb-ut-Tahrir, for example, organized a large conference in Ukraine in August, targeting mostly Crimean Tatars (Kommersant-Ukraina, August 13, 2007). Yet, even countries with little or no native Muslim population have seen a tiny, yet growing, presence of Islamist activities, particularly among their Arab and Pakistani student population. During the last few years, authorities in Hungary, Romania and Bulgaria have arrested individuals who were either promoting radical Islam through websites and publications or funneling money to terrorist organizations. Additionally, in October 2006, Czech authorities issued a terror alert after uncovering information of an alleged plot to kidnap and kill Jews in Prague (Der Spiegel, October 6, 2006)

The attractiveness of Eastern European countries for jihadis has increased significantly with the inclusion of many of them in the European Union. Some Eastern European countries, with their understaffed and often corrupt intelligence and law enforcement agencies, easy access to black market weapons and forged documents, and possibility of traveling to Western Europe without border controls, can constitute ideal bases of operation. An interesting related phenomenon is the suspicious spike in marriages between Bulgarian and Romanian women and North African men reported in Italy and Spain immediately after the entrance of the two Eastern European countries in the European Union. In all likelihood, the majority of these artificial marriages involve individuals with no connections to terrorism who simply want to acquire a European passport to stay and work in Western Europe. Nevertheless, the possibility that terrorists could use the same scheme should also be considered.

Conclusion

Jihadism is a global movement whose characteristics mutate rapidly. While today some of the abovementioned trends are still in a developing phase or can be noticed only in some European countries, it is likely that they will be replicated with greater intensity and in more countries in the near future.

Originally published in *Terrorism Monitor*: Volume 5, Issue 20 on October 25, 2007.

Notes

1. The information is based on author's observations throughout Europe.
2. The information is derived from a variety of sources, including "Indictment of Abdelillah El Kaflaoui," Tribunal of Turin, May 7, 2005; *Libero*, October 18, 2007; author's private intelligence sources.

Europol Reveals Trends in Jihadi Terrorism in Europe
By Thomas Renard

Terrorist activities in Europe increased dramatically in 2007, according to the annual report published by Europol, the European Union's criminal intelligence agency [1]. Terrorists carried out—or attempted to carry out—583 attacks last year, a 24 percent increase from the previous year. Accompanying this increase in terrorist activities was an increase in counter-terrorist operations: 1,044 individuals were arrested for terrorism-related offenses, a 48 percent increase compared to 2006.

Most terrorist attacks were claimed or attributed to separatist groups in the Basque country, Spain (Euskadi Ta Askatasuna, or ETA), or in Corsica, France (Fronte di Liberazione Naziunale di a Corsica, or FLNC). ETA and FLNC were responsible for 517 attacks, constituting 88 percent of all terrorist actions. Arrests among separatist groups were also responsible for the large increase in arrests in the European Union (EU) in 2007. Spain saw a seven-fold increase in arrested suspects compared to 2006, while France registered a 68 percent increase. In total, arrests among separatist groups represented more than half of the total arrests.

Islamist terrorism was statistically much less significant. Only four attacks were recorded: Two failed bombings in the United Kingdom (the Glasgow attacks), and two foiled plots in Germany (the Sauerland cell) and Denmark (the Glasvej case). The number of arrests could indicate a general decrease in jihadi activities. Indeed, EU police forces arrested 201 jihadi suspects, 56 fewer than in 2006. However, it should be mentioned that these numbers do not include arrests in Great Britain, which refuses to communicate precise statistics, although Britain did indicate a 30 percent increase in jihadi arrests. Including the British data could result in an increase of the arrests between 2006 and 2007.

Despite the comparatively low number of attacks, Islamist terrorism is still perceived as the main threat to European security. The reason for this assessment cannot be measured in number of attacks or arrests; it is an estimate of potential damages. "Most investigations into failed and foiled Islamist terrorist attacks in the EU in 2007 showed that Islamist terrorists continue to aim at causing indiscriminate mass casualties," claims the report. "This is not only observed in the choice of targets but also in the methods and explosives used."

Several European countries are currently—or were until very recently—at a very high level of terrorism alert. This was the case, for instance, in France, the UK, Spain and Belgium. On April 22, Gerard Bouman, head of the Algemene Inlichtingen-en Veilgheidsdienst (AIVD—Dutch domestic intelligence), confirmed that the threat of jihadi terrorism is growing in the Netherlands [2], especially since the release of the Islamophobic movie "Fitna" by Dutch extreme-right politician Geert Wilders (The Associated Press, April 22, 2008).

The Europol report underscores several interesting trends in Islamist terrorism in Europe:

• First, "although the majority of all arrested suspects for Islamist terrorism continue to be North African citizens, the member states reported a high number of arrested suspects with the nationality of the country of arrest." This seems to confirm a growing threat of homegrown terrorism that has been observed for several years.

• Second, this increase in homegrown terrorists is partly the result of an increase in quantity and a "new quality" in jihadi propaganda in Europe (*Terrorism Focus*, February 20, 2008). It is now widely recognized that propaganda on the internet has a central importance in recruitment. Hence, some recent developments appear particularly worrisome. For instance, al-Qaeda's media arm, al-Sahab, now offers English subtitles or translations. In order to target some specific audiences, certain jihadi websites have recently decided to translate jihadi material into other languages, such as German, despite some apparent

> *Second, this increase in homegrown terrorists is partly the result of an increase in quantity and a "new quality" in jihadi propaganda in Europe (Terrorism Focus, February 20, 2008).*

difficulties in using the language correctly (Die Welt, February 8, 2008). Similarly, the website al-Ikhlas recently launched two new forums in French and Italian [3].

Recruitment constitutes an important part of jihadi activities in Europe and arrests related to this activity have increased. The observed developments in propaganda and recruitment suggest that al-Qaeda is taking roots in Europe and could potentially become stronger in the near future. On April 18, 2008 European ministers of justice reached agreement on a law that would condemn, among other things, online propaganda and recruitment (Agence France-Presse, April 18, 2008). This new law—which must still be approved by the European Parliament—should facilitate EU cooperation with internet providers and, eventually, allow the identification of cyber-terrorists. According to Gilles de Kerchove d'Ousselghem, the EU counter-terrorism coordinator, there are approximately 5,000 jihadi websites that contribute to the radicalization of European youth.

• Third, propaganda and recruitment serve multiple purposes. Some would-be jihadis are recruited by local cells to carry out operations in their own countries. Some are "self-recruited" through the media, and constitute a "new generation" of terrorists [4]. Some limit their support to financing terrorism. Others, finally, decide to join the jihad abroad, in Iraq—which remains the main destination for European fighters—in Afghanistan, or, increasingly (according to French intelligence), in Somalia.

• Fourth, the remaining core leadership of al-Qaeda in Pakistan still largely commands, controls and inspires jihadi terrorists in Europe. Europol, however, recognizes the rising importance of groups isolated—or more autonomous—from al-Qaeda's core leadership, and their potential threat to European security. "This expansion of the 'al-Qaeda franchise' has the potential to constitute a threat to the EU's security," claims the report. "It could provide al-Qaeda with access to new centers of support which it can motivate and exploit."

• Fifth, the report emphasizes the strategic importance of Iraq, Afghanistan and Pakistan for European security. Should the situation in Iraq improve or the war terminate, Iraqi fighters—European or not—could relocate to other places and continue to wage jihad. Former Iraqi fighters could, for instance, carry out operations in Europe, establish new cells, or teach their know-how to young, would-be terrorists. In other words, there is a risk that the Iraqi generation will follow a similar path to the 1980s Afghan generation.

The problem with Afghanistan and Pakistan is more imminent. European citizens receive training in Pakistani tribal areas camps, either to go fight in Afghanistan, or to bring jihad back to Europe. "Al-Qaeda and affiliated pro-Taliban groups in Pakistan and Afghanistan are increasingly recognized as one of the main drivers of Islamist extremism and terrorism in the EU," says the report. This statement underscores the European dilemma in facing terrorism. On one hand, EU members recognize that their domestic security is related to the evolution of the situation in Afghanistan and Pakistan. On the other hand, however, they refuse a greater commitment in those regions for various other reasons, including electoral concerns.

Finally, a last interesting trend relative to Islamist terrorism in Europe concerns judicial sentences. In 2007, one-third of jihadi terrorist suspects were acquitted, while only one-fifth of separatist terrorists were discharged. This seems to indicate two things. First, the strong emphasis on Islamist terrorism by security services has led to a certain "paranoia" and abusive arrests that could ultimately hurt European efforts in countering radicalization. However, it should also be emphasized that some individuals were acquitted due to a lack of evidence, but could still be related to terrorism. Second, the better records in jailing separatist terrorists prove that European intelligence agencies have a greater knowledge of separatist groups and more effective strategies to counter them than is the case with Islamist terrorism.

Although a large part of the Europol report is dedicated to Islamist terrorism, it also includes other chapters on separatist terrorism, left-wing terrorism, extreme-right terrorism, and single-issue terrorism. Four points concerning those other forms of terrorism are worth a quick highlight:

• Attacks by separatist groups continue to overwhelmingly outnumber any other form of terrorism.
• ETA activities remain largely based in Spain, with logistical support in France. However, Portugal noticed an increase of Basque activities within its borders.
• ETA is starting to use propaganda videos in order to recruit among youth. This confirms that terrorist groups copy successful strategies developed by other groups, in this case al-Qaeda's   model.
• Extreme-left terrorism is regionally in decline. However, these activities increased in Italy. Moreover, French Interior Minister Michèle Alliot-Marie declared recently that left-wing groups constitute a resurgent threat to domestic security (Agence France-Presse, February 10, 2008).

Looking at the number of attacks, separatist groups are more active than jihadi terrorists.

However, jihadi groups are still perceived as the main threat to European security due to their potential for damage. Moreover, it appears that the Islamist threat is growing. Al-Qaeda is taking roots in Europe, seducing an increasing number of EU citizens, although the influence of the core leadership remains important. In terms of counter-terrorist strategies, the EU as a whole—as well as EU members individually—are taking some steps to increase their efficiency. Nevertheless, they are still better at fighting separatist movements than at countering jihad.

Originally published in *Terrorism Monitor*: Volume 6, Issue 9 on May 1, 2008.

Notes

1. "TE-SAT 2008 – EU Terrorism Situation and Trend Report," Europol, April 2008.
2. "Jaarverslag AIVD 2007," Algemene Inlichtingen-en Veiligheidsdienst, April 2008.
3. "Islamist Website Al-Ikhlas Launches French, Italian Forums," MEMRI Islamist Websites Monitor Project, April 4, 2008.
4. Marc Sageman, "The Next Generation of Terror," *Foreign Policy*, March/April 2008.

BOSNIA-HERZEGOVINA

Foreign Jihadis Face Deportation in Bosnia-Herzegovina
By Anes Alic

After roughly 15 years of neglect, Bosniak (Bosnian Muslim) politicians and the country's Islamic community, each for its own reasons, have nearly simultaneously adopted a harsher approach toward former Islamic fighters who fought on the Bosnian side during the 1992-1995 war.

Since the end of the war, Bosniak officials have avoided dealing with the issue of these former fighters, but after much arm-twisting on the part of the international community, it seems the issue will have to be addressed and these Islamic warriors will inevitably be deported to their countries of origin.

Islamic fighters recently have found themselves in the spotlight in Bosnia, not necessarily because they present a direct or potential terrorist threat to the country or its foreign installations, but largely due to their criminal activity and the influence they have among young Bosnian Muslims, who are increasingly gathering around the growing Wahhabi movement (a fundamentalist form of Islam prevalent in Saudi Arabia).

In 1993 the Bosnian Islamic Community banned the Wahhabi movement as well as the practice of fundamental Islam in Bosnian mosques. The ban came at a time during the war when foreign fighters began recruiting moderate Muslims to their cause. However, the Wahhabi movement has since spread dramatically, even in largely secular Bosnia, since the U.S.-led invasions of Afghanistan and Iraq.

Since the ban in 1993, the Bosnian Islamic Community has done nothing to prevent Bosnian Muslims from taking up radical Islam. Nevertheless, since emboldened Wahhabis began making attempts to occupy the Islamic Community's administrative units and mosques this spring, including one in Sarajevo just several meters from its headquarters, the moderate Muslim leaders were forced to react.

The grand mufti of Bosnia, Mustafa Ceric, embarked on a series of visits to world capitals with a message. The main financiers and ideological leaders of the Bosnian Wahhabi movement are based in Western Europe, primarily Austria, as well as Saudi Arabia, according to the mufti. He has also pleaded with world leaders to take steps to prevent the activities of radical

Islamic fighters recently have found themselves in the spotlight in Bosnia, not necessarily because they present a direct or potential terrorist threat to the country or its foreign installations, but largely due to their criminal activity and the influence they have among young Bosnian Muslims, who are increasingly gathering around the growing Wahhabi movement (a fundamentalist form of Islam prevalent in Saudi Arabia).

Islamic groups there before they are imported to Bosnia. As for Bosniak politicians, they have neatly swept the radical program under the rug for years, not necessarily because they wish the militants to remain in Bosnia, but because any action against them could cost the politicians Bosniak nationalist votes.

Under international pressure in early 2006, the Bosnian government formed a commission tasked with reviewing how some 1,500 people—most of them fighters who came to Bosnia from Muslim countries during the war—gained Bosnian citizenship. Under similar pressure, the government has ordered the commencement of the deportations.

In July 2007 the international community's newly appointed high representative, Slovak diplomat Miroslav Lajcak, stepped up the pressure on local authorities, particularly the security minister from the Bosniak Party of Democratic Action (SDA), Tarik Sadovic, to move ahead with the deportations [1]. Sadovic had stalled over alleged technical difficulties, arguing that he was not authorized to sign the deportation orders and had attempted to place the onus of the move on his assistant. However, after Lajcak threatened to fire Sadovic by saying "it's either them or you," the minister gave orders to speed up the deportations. Soon afterwards the Bosnian government announced preparations for the deportation of the first group of 48 people originating from 11 African and Middle Eastern countries.

On September 30, 2007 a man identified only as Hattab72 published footage on YouTube threatening SDA leader Sulejman Tihic, Haris Silajdzic (the Bosniak member of the state's rotating presidency) and Grand Mufti Ceric over the Wahhabi deportations. Hattab72 accused the three of betraying all human and religious principles and ordered them to take care of "the brothers who are being extradited without any reason," threatening that otherwise he would release video footage that would destroy them politically.

"Anyone should see that you sell this country piece by piece, Muslim by Muslim; you betray everything that can be betrayed ... And be aware that Allah has the power and that you will face Him and answer for the betrayal of Islam and Muslims," Hattab72 threatened. The message threatened action by the time of Ramadan Bayram, in early October 2007, but the deadline passed and no attacks were made.

So far, the commission has revoked some 620 citizenships in cases where procedures were clearly violated (e.g. false personal data, falsified documents, fictitious addresses, unreported criminal histories, etc.). According to the initial plan, these violators would lose their status and be deported to their countries of origin with no right to appeal. However, this action would not be taken should the violators face potential ill treatment in their countries of origin. To date, only two former combatants have been deported from Bosnia, both last year.

Among the first group slated for deportation was Tunisian-born Karray Kamal bin Ali, alias Abu Hamza, the alleged ringleader of the Wahhabi movement in Bosnia and the mastermind of the recent incidents between his supporters and moderate Bosnian Muslims. Abu Hamza gained Bosnian citizenship during the war due to the fact that he fought with and was commander of the Mujahid unit and married a Bosnian woman. In mid-May this year, his citizenship was revoked because of false information in his citizenship application.

According to police information, Abu Hamza was part of a 15-20 member group of Egypt's militant Gama'a al-Islamiyya that arrived in Zenica and Travnik in the summer of 1992. While living in Bosnia, Abu Hamza used seven names and falsified Yemeni and Libyan documents, commission sources revealed to Jamestown.

However, Abu Hamza has managed to postpone his deportation to Tunisia—where he was sentenced in absentia to 13 years in prison—after being arrested only a week before the deportation date for his involvement in a shooting in a village near the central Bosnian city of Zenica. Abu Hamza and three associates were arrested on June 9 after an attack on a house owned by Zijad Kovac in which three members of Kovac's family were wounded.

In the car Abu Hamza was driving at the time of his arrest, police found a Kalashnikov assault rifle used in the attack and a hand grenade. Of Abu Hamza's co-conspirators, some were members of the local Wahhabi movement while others were common criminals who served their sentences with Abu Hamza in Bosnian prisons.

Abu Hamza became known to the Bosnian public after he murdered Egyptian Hisham Diab, alias Abu Velid, in Zenica in 1997. After managing to evade arrest for three years, Abu Hamza was finally captured in Germany in 2000 and deported to Bosnia. After being sentenced to seven years in prison he was released in January 2007.

The motive for the attack remains unclear, since nothing was taken from the house, nor could the owner or the house be linked with the radical Muslims. Zijad Kovac is a distant relative of Zahid Kovac, a Zenica prosecutor at the time when Abu Hamza was tried for the murder of Abu Velid. Because of his involvement in the attack, Abu Hamza managed to delay his deportation and secured a stay in Bosnia to face trial on the new charges.

After his release from prison in January, Abu Hamza became a close confidante of Jusuf Barcic, a former Bosnian Muslim cleric and later radical Islam cleric and self-proclaimed sheikh. Barcic served a seven-month prison sentence for domestic violence in Zenica at the same time that Abu Hamza was serving his sentence. When Barcic died in a car accident in early May 2007, Abu Hamza assumed his role as an aggressive preacher calling for a return to traditional Islam. However, Barcic's short career as leader of Bosnia's Wahhabis clarified long-sought answers about the group, such as who their financiers and real leaders are.

At times Barcic himself answered many of these questions during his sermons, all of them recorded and published on the internet. It became clear that Barcic and his movement were supported and financed by the Vienna-based radical Islam cleric

Muhammad Porca, who among other things donated the car in which Barcic met his end.

Porca, a former Bosniak imam, runs the Islamic Community's administrative unit in the Austrian capital, and moderate Muslim leaders in Bosnia believe he is a key financial and ideological supporter of radical forces in Bosnia. Some Bosnian Islamic Community officials also accuse Porca of organizing and financing visits to Bosnia for radical Muslims from Germany and Austria, a high-ranking federal anti-terror squad source close to the investigation of Wahhabi movements told Jamestown.

One such radical is Nusret Imamovic, a naturalized Austrian citizen living between Vienna and the northern Bosnian village of Gornja Maoca, near the city of Brcko. Imamovic founded a small Wahhabi community in Gornja Maoca, where journalists and non-Wahhabis are not welcome. Children there do not attend the public schools, but are instead given lectures held by Imamovic in accordance with a Jordanian school program. While in Vienna, Imamovic is said to frequently visit Porca's offices and attend his sermons.

Imamovic became better known to the Bosnian public when he and six other Wahhabis, three of them Austrian citizens, assaulted Bosnian Serb Mihajlo Kisic in Brcko in 2006. After a short trial, the seven were given symbolic sentences on parole and some of them returned to Vienna. Among the seven was another Wahhabi cleric, Effendi Nedzad Balkan (also known as Ebu Muhammed), a Vienna-born Serbian Muslim, the leader of Vienna's Sahaba Mosque and the alleged financier of the Serbia-based Sandzak Wahhabis.

Connecting these radicals and following their movements from Bosnia to Vienna, it may have caused little surprise when a Bosnian man was arrested in Vienna in early October 2007 after attempting to enter the U.S. Embassy with a backpack of explosives. The man was Bosnian refugee Asim Cejvanovic, a 41-year-old with a history of mental illness. During questioning, Cejvanovic named another Bosnian man, Mehmed Djudjic, as the one who gave him the explosives and instructed him to enter the embassy.

Unlike Cejvanovic, Djudjic can be linked to radical Muslims. His relatives told Bosnian media that he turned to traditional Islam after a 2003 car accident, and when visiting Bosnia he would spend much of his time with members of the radical Wahhabi movement. Djudjic was seen in Bosnia in April 2007 attending Barcic's funeral (Oslobodjenje, October 6, 2007).

With a lack of evidence in the case, Djudjic has been released from custody, while Cejvanovic has been transferred to the prison hospital. After the release, Djudjic gave an interview to Bosnian media saying that he is not a Wahhabi, even though he is accompanied by them sometimes. "As for Cejvanovic's claim, I have nothing to do with the explosives. After all police found explosives in his apartment and I believe that his attempt was well organized." Djudjic also said that Cejvanovic is not mentally ill but just a violent person (Slobodna Bosna, October 25, 2007). In their statements, Austrian police and prosecutors downplayed the incident, saying there is no political or terrorist motivation behind the attack. Sarajevo's Federal Television said in its "60 minutes" political program, however, that the case is actually being investigated and even controlled by U.S. intelligence (FTV, October 7, 2007).

As far as Vienna is concerned, it is not an accident that the Austrian capital is the base for Bosnia's Wahhabi movement, which has a 15-year history there. During the war Vienna was a major logistical and financial center for the Bosnian government, and hosted several Islamic aid agencies that collected funds used for arming the Bosnian Army and transferring foreign fighters and weapons at a time when Bosnia was under an arms embargo.

The biggest financier of Bosnian Muslim defenses during the war was the Vienna-based Third World Relief Agency (TWRA), established by a Sudanese native, Al-Fatih Ali Hassanein. Some $350 million in donations from Islamic countries flowed through the TWRA's accounts, half of which was used for financing the Bosnian government. In 1996, Austrian police raided TWRA's offices and bank accounts in Vienna and the investigations showed that the majority of the cash originated in the Middle East, with Saudi Arabia as the largest contributor.

Related to the TWRA's activity in Vienna, the Bosnian citizenship commission found that nearly 100 Islamic fighters were granted Bosnian citizenship through the embassy in Vienna. Some were recommended by TWRA while others were able to obtain diplomatic passports.

In 2002, the Intelligence-Security Service (FOSS) of the Federation of Bosnia and Herzegovina notified the prosecutor's office and the Interior Ministry of suspicions that several persons including some embassy personnel in Vienna and the Bosnian Foreign Ministry, as well as Ali Hassanein, were involved in international organized crime. The case was never prosecuted.

There is no doubt that incidents such as that at the U.S. embassy in Vienna are working to create a negative image for Bosnia in the West. Despite the fact that there have never been any terror attacks in Bosnia and no evidence of any Bosnian involvement in terror attacks, the country's loose policies for granting citizenship during the war ensures the issue comes up frequently in international terrorism trials. The Bosnian Islamic Community, the citizenship revision commission and the international community have only now started to address the long delayed problem of dealing with Bosnia's foreign jihadi community.

Originally published in *Terrorism Monitor*: Volume 5, Issue 21 on November 8, 2007.

Notes

1. The Office of the High Representative is an ad hoc international institution with close ties to the European Union. It is responsible for implementing civilian aspects of the Bosnia-Herzegovina peace accord.

Islam, Jihadism and Depolitization in the French Banlieues
By Anouar Boukhars

A growing number of French citizens fear that France faces "a Muslim problem." The global ravages of Denmark's cartoon jihad, triggered by offensive cartoons of the Prophet Muhammad as a terrorist and lecher, coupled with the recent alleged plot to blow up U.S.-bound airliners have made more people fear not only Europe's homegrown radicals but Islam itself, a religion increasingly seen as posing a direct threat to Western liberal democracy. In France, fear of Islam and its extremist elements is not a new phenomenon. The 1995 bombings in the Paris metro alarmed the French to the threat of Islamist extremism [1]. The French authorities' subsequent sweeps revealed the nexus between drugs, crime and radical Islamism and the discrete patterns of terror networks like the "gang of Roubaix," a collection of militants of Algerian descent led by Christopher Caze, a 25-year-old convert who had traveled to Bosnia to work as a hospital medic only to return as a dangerous jihadist. The dreadful events of September 11 heightened this fear of radical Islam. The main culprits are, of course, the Muslim youth of the suburbs, suspected of sympathizing with jihadis.

The feeling that France is under siege has been propelled by a wave of xenophobia and populism already spreading across the European continent. The series of terrorist attacks on the Madrid rail system and London's underground and bus system, compounded by France's restive Muslim enclaves, have invoked troubling questions about the roles of race, Islam and ethnicity, and highlighted the challenges to European states' integrationist models. In the French context, ethnicity, culture and Islam tend to be conflated and are portrayed as the main causes of social and economic marginality. The youth of the suburbs are usually "equated with thieves" and labeled as "veilers" (*Le Monde*, November 7, 2005). This "symbolic ghettoization" of poorer neighborhoods known as cités or quartiers difficiles in the political discourse and the media has hyped the threat of illusory concepts like communitarization or communalism of ethnic ghettos living parallel lives to French uniqueness and the ideology of the republic; in reality, French Muslims are far more depolicitized and individualistic.

This "symbolic ghettoization" of poorer neighborhoods known as cités or quartiers difficiles in the political discourse and the media has hyped the threat of illusory concepts like communitarization or communalism of ethnic ghettos living parallel lives to French uniqueness and the ideology of the republic; in reality, French Muslims are far more depolicitized and individualistic.

Yet the 2005 November riots in France were neither an Arab intifada against French republican ideals nor Muslim jihad against Europe. In fact, neither Islam nor Islamism—with its three different types (jihadi, missionary and political)—instigated the riots. There were no Palestinian or other Islamic green flags, nor were there any anti-Semitic arson attacks against Jewish synagogues, schools, or cemeteries. Arafat-style keffiyehs were noticeably absent as well as the usual suspects: the bearded provocateurs [2]. There were no shouts of "Allahu akbar!" erupting from the rioters. Most importantly, the riots did not spread outside the suburbs nor did they extend to the universities where students feel the same grievances and resentments against the system [3]. The spontaneity of the riots and lack of radical religious leaders contrasts with the theories of self-segregating Islamic communities fueled by Islamic radicalism and other simple cultural arguments that abound in media commentaries and popular discourse.

Interestingly enough, neither the politically-minded Islamist organizations, like the Union of Islamic Organizations of France (UOIF), nor missionary Islamists, like the Tabligh or the Salafis, managed to calm the rage of male youth rioters, aged between 12 and 25 years old [4]. Shortly after the outbreak of the spontaneous riots, the leaders of UOIF rushed to defuse the crisis hoping to prove their influence over second generation migrants and hence score points with the authorities and the public at large. They failed to accomplish either objective. Appeals for calm in the mosques on November 4, 2006 fell on deaf ears as did the "Anti-Riot Fatwa" issued on November 6, 2006 by UOIF. The failure of one of France's largest Islamic groups to lower tensions and break the chain of violent events speaks volumes about the disconnect of political Islamist movements with the social base they claim to represent. The UOIF lost the deprived French banlieues because of the leadership's failure to develop a discourse attuned to the realities of the Muslim enclaves. French-born Muslims denounced the structural weakness of the UOIF and their deliberate marginalization from decision making and leadership positions within the movement. The UOIF structure suffers from an over concentration of power in the hands of foreign-born leaders, such as the case of the 47-year-old Tunisian, Mohammed Ateb, who is at the same time a representative of the UOIF in Bourgogne region, imam of the Dijon Mosque, president of the regional administration council of CRCM and editor-in-chief of a magazine [5]. The resignation in June 2005 of Farid Abdelkrim, the only member in the administration council born in France, is a direct result of this growing disenchantment with the leadership's political orientation (*Le Monde*, December 13, 2002).

The UOIF and other political Islamist organizations thought that by taking advantage of existing possibilities to participate in a political system usually fraught with politically motivated resistance that they would maximize their influence with the authorities and attenuate fears of politically minded religious groups. Yet the groups' calculus, as well as those of the authorities who co-opted them, backfired. The UOIF's image was severely tarnished in the suburbs because of the perception that the group was co-opted by the authorities at their own expense. The UOIF's low-profile critical posture vis-à-vis the French law banning the hijab in state schools in 2004 and the Danish cartoons of the Prophet Muhammed in 2006 has given the impression that the organization's leadership has succumbed to the French authorities. This loss of faith in political Islamists, exacerbated by political under-representation and the disengagement of French Muslims from the institutional space, has created a dangerous void and an organizational vacuum similar to that of the 1980s when several movements of Muslims strove to provide social organizations for Muslim deprived neighborhoods.

The vacuum created by the failure of political Islamism and the decline of the associative network of the movement of young Muslims in French suburbs paved the way for the emergence of increasingly disturbing phenomena like the random violence of the November 2005 riots and the radicalization of a segment of indignant Islamic youths, angry at their social and economic exclusion and outraged over the bloodshed in Iraq, Lebanon and Palestine. While it is true that there is little evidence of widespread religious radicalism, there are signs that Salafi groups that focus on a punctilious adherence to morals and to the strict dictates of dogma and preach an irrevocable break with family, local authorities and society are on the ascendance.

Abdel-Hâdî Dûdî, the imam of the al-Sunna al-Kebira Mosque in Marseille, is the icon of the Salafi movement in France. A graduate of al-Azhar University in Egypt and a former mentor of Ali Benhadj, a former high school teacher known for his militant views of the role of political Islam, Abdel-Hâdî Dûdî belonged to the Algerian Salafi movement that helped create the Front Islamique du Salut (FIS) in 1989. Condemned to death by the Algerian regime for his involvement in Mustafa Bouyali's Armed Islamic Movement (MIA), he took refuge in France with the tacit approval of the Algerian authorities. It is Abdel-Hâdî Dûdî's teachings that birthed and fermented the Salafi movement in Marseille [6]. His influence spread rapidly with the endorsement he received from Rabî'al-Madkhalî, the foremost authority in Shaykhiste Salafism in France [7]. According to the International Crisis Group, the conversion of Abdel-Hâdî Dûdî from radical political Salafi into apolitical Shaykhiste Salafi is in line with the transformation that the Salafi movement underwent in the second part of the 1990s. The first return of French students from Saudi Arabia in 1995 contributed to the development of a quietist Salafism strongly influenced by Saudi theologians, namely those that belonged to the madkhaliste current, named after Rabî'al-Madkhalî [8]. The arrival of Saudi preachers on French soil at the end of the 1990s strengthened this movement (*Le Monde*, February 22, 2005).

The rise of the ultra-strict but quietist Salafi Islamism has laid the groundwork for a re-Islamization that delinks Islam from ethnic cultures and disconnects the religious from the political in a way that reflects individualist concerns. The movement's success can be attributed not only to the failures of political Islam in Algeria and France, but also to the emergence of a modern trend of the culture of the self in the suburbs whereby cynical, disempowered and alienated young French Muslims opt out of politics to become social, political and moral isolationists, paralyzed by their

> *The rise of the ultra-strict but quietist Salafi Islamism has laid the groundwork for a re-Islamization that delinks Islam from ethnic cultures and disconnects the religious from the political in a way that reflects individualist concerns.*

disdain for society. Rather than organizing the Muslim community into a model of citizenship consecrated to fighting social exclusion and Islamophobia and strengthening Muslim social cohesion, Salafism activates the depoliticization of the religious.

Salafists, as French scholar Olivier Roy correctly pointed out, play on the deculturation and individualization of youth, and provide a substitute cultural paradigm and a new Islamist tradition that is similar to the model of the "born again" in that it does not promote a return to traditional Islamic customs but a (re)Islamization of individuals within a de-territorialized ummah disconnected from traditional cultures and societies. Unlike political Islamists who aspire to create a model of integration through citizenship, contemporary Salafis advocate the creation of a new and purely Islamic religiosity that focuses on salvation, moral values and self-realization while maintaining a general aloof attitude toward the social and political issues that triggered the riots in France.

Yet since neither pietistic movements like Salafis or Tabligh nor politically minded Islamist groups like UOIF are capable of or interested in organizing a Muslim youth underclass, the banlieues have slid into a dangerous confusion and organizational vacuum where political and social demands have been increasingly expressed through rioting and, to a lesser extent, through jihadism. Jihadism in France is increasingly a product of the diaspora, a marked shift from the past when violent Islamism was strictly linked to foreign Islamic militants who internationalized and externalized their long-running disputes with their authoritarian governments into France with a wave of terrorist bombings. Since the mid-1990s, a high percentage of French jihadists were born in France, detached from any given culture and stimulated by a "de-territorialized" Islam that promises the uprooted Islamic diaspora a transnational Islamic identity forged in anti-imperialist discourse. This global jihad obsesses no longer about the creation of particular Muslim states but at a mythical final battle between the ummah and the forces of Western evil. "The issue for jihadis," as the ICG noted, "is not Western licentiousness but Western imperialism" [9].

Rioting and Salafi-Jihadism result from serious problems of political representation in contemporary France rather than from a religious radicalization of the new Muslim generations. Undoubtedly, the discovery and disruption of terrorist networks in France reveals an unsettling picture about the scope of France's homegrown radicals. Yet the point of connection between al-Qaeda and the destitute banlieues of France no longer comes via Algeria nor does it come from the "communitarization" of the banlieues. Instead, it comes from France, where a small proportion of disenfranchised French born Muslims embrace transnational jihadism in the name of a holy war against global imperialist aggression.

Originally published in *Terrorism Monitor*: Volume 4, Issue 18 on September 21, 2006.

Notes

1. The attacks carried out between July and November 1995 killed eight and injured around 150.
2. Olivier Roy, "The Nature of the French Riots," Social Science Research Council, November 18, 2005.
3. Ibid.

4. The UOIF was founded in 1983 by Tunisian intellectuals, namely Abdallah Benmansour and Ahmed Jaballah, to serve as the French branch of the Islamic Tendency Movement, which would later became known as Ennahda of Rachid Ghannouchi. The UOIF leadership would assume another direction under the leadership of the more moderate Moroccan Fouad Alaoui and Lhaj Thami Breze.

5. Samir Amghar, "L'Union des organisations islamiques de France: la gestion politique de l'islam," *Maghreb-Machrek*, no. 182 (2005).

6. "La France face à ses musulmans: Émeutes, jihadisme et dépolitisation," International Crisis Group European Report, no. 172, March 9, 2006.

7. Shaykhiste Salafism stands for an apolitical and non-violent version of Islam that draws heavily from the fatwas of Saudi theologians. Like Salafiyya 'ilmiyya, it is fundamentalist in its doctrinal outlook, eschews politics and is primarily concerned with the preservation of the Islamic faith and moral order in society.

8. It was quietest because it was heavily influenced by the teachings of Sheikh Rabî'al-Madkhalî and two of his contemporaries—Ahmed Ramdanî al-Jaza' irî and Sâlih al-Fawzen. All three condemn political Islam as a perversion of religion and preach an apolitical, puritanical and backward-looking wave of new fundamentalism. See also International Crisis Group European Report, March 9, 2006.

9. International Crisis Group European Report, March 9, 2006.

An Inside Look at France's Mosque Surveillance Program
By Pascale Combelles Siegel

France's counter-terrorism strategy is to disrupt terrorist networks before they are able to engage in violent action. Thus far, the strategy has worked since the last terrorist attack on French territory dates back to 1996. In the past few years, despite increased threats emanating from al-Qaeda and the Algerian Salafist Group for Preaching and Combat (recently renamed Al-Qaeda in the Islamic Maghreb), French intelligence services have successfully thwarted a number of plots and disrupted several cells recruiting French volunteers to fight in Iraq. Since radical mosques have played a critical role in the radicalization process of terrorists in the past, the Renseignements Généraux (RG), the French internal intelligence service, have been monitoring mosques, their clerics and their sermons since the mid-1990s. This article explores the current process of monitoring mosque sermons and assesses the program's strengths and weaknesses.

Large Scale Monitoring

The section of the RG called Milieux Intégristes Violents (Violent Fundamentalist Environment) is in charge of monitoring all 1,700 mosques and Muslim places of worship throughout France. Through their monitoring, they have identified radical mosques in almost every corner of French territory, with the exception of four, predominantly rural, régions (Corse, Poitou-Charentes, Basse-Normandie and Limousin) [1]. Every Friday, sermons are collected through unidentified means, and they are centralized and analyzed. The RG use their analysis to determine which imams are preaching a radical Salafi brand of Islam, or if they are assisting terrorist activities by helping recruitment or granting material support to an operational network.

The RG use a set of pre-determined indicators to assess the degree of radicalism of a particular imam or preacher. The full list of indicators remains confidential, but it includes, among others, open calls for jihad, anti-Western rhetoric or anti-Semitism.

The RG use a set of pre-determined indicators to assess the degree of radicalism of a particular imam or preacher. The full list of indicators remains confidential, but it includes, among others, open calls for jihad, anti-Western rhetoric or anti-Semitism. When such indicators are noticed, the RG may increase their surveillance to assess whether the professed rhetoric masks a violent engagement and to identify those individuals who might be involved in terrorist networks and who use the mosque to meet and recruit like-minded fellows.

The number of established Salafi mosques in France of concern to authorities is statistically low (Le Nouvel Observateur, February 2, 2006). In 2006, then-director of the RG, Pascal Mailhos, estimated that 80 out of the 1,685 mosques and places of worship in France were of concern to his services (4.7 percent of the total number). Mailhos further indicated that 40 of those 80 mosques were "under constant pressure" from radical Islamist networks (2.3 percent of the total). He also noted that half of those were resisting radicals' pressures, but that half had fallen into the hands of radical imams (1.1 percent of the total number) (Spyworld, November 24, 2005). It is also worth noting that religious practice is low among French Muslims. According to El Watan, only 10 percent of an estimated five million French Muslims attend a mosque regularly (El Watan, December 27, 2004). However, because any one of these mosques could breed or protect a terrorist network, French intelligence services consider each and every one of these radical mosques a potential threat.

Repressive Arsenal Designed to Elicit Moderation

Monitoring mosques to prevent radical imams from preaching radical Islam works because intelligence and judicial processes are intimately linked in France. In the mid-1990s, the French parliament passed a law authorizing the administrative expulsion of foreign imams who preach a radical and violent brand of Islam. When the RG identify a radical imam, they inform the local brigade criminelle (criminal police). According to the standard procedure, the brigade criminelle summons the offending preacher and threatens to expel him unless he moderates his preaching [2]. The relationship between the RG and the local brigade criminelle is generally good and efficient. During the past 10 years, both services have learned to work together and since 2005 their cooperation has been institutionalized into regional cells. Both services exchange information on a daily basis and handle each other's requests quickly.

This arsenal gives imams and preachers incentives to moderate their discourse. If they want the local city council's assistance to fund their activities, they need to cooperate with the RG and the police. As a police officer remarked, often the imam is summoned by authorities and reminded of the law. "That's enough" to convince him to moderate his discourse. This mechanism is useful because a large proportion of imams operating in France are of foreign origin. They can therefore easily be expelled to their country of origin.

Unresolved Problems

Despite increased surveillance and a repressive legislative arsenal adequate to suppress immediate threats, religious extremism continues to progress. First, in poor suburban areas, young Muslim males in a precarious social situation can fall prey to a new brand of radical imams who can arouse their anger and stir them into violent and nihilistic actions. According to Eric Denécée, senior researcher at the Centre Français de Recherche sur le Renseignement, these imams are often foreigners and reside in France illegally; they are not integrated into the social fabric; they reject the French social contract; and they are not fluent in French [3]. These imams preach their own brand of radical Islam based on the "systematic rejection of French secularism, anti-French racism and obsessive anti-Semitism" [4].

Second, the RG monitors the mosques and places of worship of which it knows. Although "L'Islam des caves" prevailed in the 1980s is largely a thing of the past, not all preachers operate in well-established and recognized mosques [5]. In particular, in difficult suburbs there are still preachers who operate in semi-hidden places of worship to dispense their teachings below the radar of the state surveillance system. Little is known of what is said in these mosques. Another difficulty in the surveillance system is to monitor what is said after the official sermons have ended. Supporting terrorism is not an open activity, even in radical Salafi mosques. These hidden activities involve a small group of attendees who might get to know each other at the mosque, but may plot their activities afterwards with or without the knowledge of the local preacher. Monitoring these activities requires infiltrating the actual network operating around the mosque.

Third, the pressure placed by the state surveillance system and the constant repression of radical clerics who preach intolerance and entice violence do not necessarily guarantee that moderation ultimately prevails upon radicalism. Assessing the respective influence of the mainstream Muslim community and of the more radical clerics over the main Muslim community is difficult. Established clerics who seek to represent the Muslim community have a vested interest in moderating themselves in order to gain the support of local communities and their elected representatives. Moreover, law enforcement authorities have at their disposal sufficient repressive mechanisms (notably the threat to expel trouble-makers) to stir imams into moderation.

Nevertheless, a large number of mosques in France are not affiliated with any of the representative organizations of French Muslims. The "Grande mosque de Paris" (Paris Grand Mosque) controls 14 percent of the French mosques. L'Union des Organisations Islamiques de France (French Union of Islamic Organizations), which is loosely affiliated with the Muslim Brotherhood, controls 13.5 percent. The Fédération Nationale des Lieux du Culte Musulman (National Federation of Muslim Places of Worship) controls seven percent (El Watan, December 27, 2004). This state of affairs leads some researchers to the conclusion that community leaders only exert "partial control" over their followers. According to Eric Denécée, the radical clerics "are those who influence the Muslim community, not the Muslim institutions or the Mosquée de Paris who only have partial control of their followers" [6].

Finally, French authorities appear to reluctantly use the procedure of expulsion. According to the testimony of the Préfet de Police de Paris, Pierre Mutz, before the French parliament, the authorities expelled 11 imams in 2005 out of 30 mosques classified by the RG as "radical." Although the law enabled the authorities to expel all 30 clerics, the government chose to expel only half of the culprits. It appears that the French authorities are using this legislative disposition as much as a carrot to stir the clerics toward moderation than as a stick when they have strayed.

A Larger Definitional Problem

Apologists of the French counter-terrorism strategy will point to the role played by previous Salafi clerics in the radicalization process of past terrorists to justify the extensive surveillance of mosques throughout the country. Three problems, however, remain.

Mosques do not constitute the only channel of religious radicalization in France. Radical discourses are now conveyed through satellite televisions, which are increasingly available to French Muslims. The internet, with numerous jihadi-friendly websites available in both Arabic and French, allows the dissemination of a radical Salafi discourse that preaches hatred of the West, rabid anti-Semitism and anti-French racism. Finally, libraries and publishing companies specializing in Islamic studies also participate in the dissemination of radical Salafi material. On these three fronts, French law enforcement authorities are ill-equipped to monitor and curb the expansion of radical Salafi ideology disseminated via these channels. Actions against satellite channels or websites located outside of France are difficult or impossible. The French government forbade French satellite companies from offering Hezbollah's television channel al-Manar, but cannot stop Arabsat from carrying the same channel. Similarly, the Préfet de Police of Paris testified before parliament that current jurisprudence does not allow his services to take action against libraries selling forbidden books.

The monitoring of mosques is designed to identify individuals who may become terrorists and engage in violent actions against French state interests or against the French population. It is conceived as a preventive measure designed to either identify and neutralize individuals who might become terrorists, or to suppress the ideology susceptible to motivate those individuals to pursue violent action. Although such monitoring may be necessary as a means to prevent terrorist actions, it is not currently leveraged to support a widespread effort to counter the radical violent Salafi brand of Islam. Suppression and repression has been a successful strategy for the past 10 years, keeping France free of terrorist attacks amid mounting threats. Nevertheless, it is not a strategy against a violent ideology that uses whatever channel is available to make itself available to those pre-disposed to find it. The constant monitoring of radical preachers should be used to inform a solid, coherent, well-argued alternative discourse to a violent, intolerant brand of Salafi ideology.

Systematic monitoring of mosques in France has served the country well so far, helping disrupt several terrorist plots and actions in France and outside. However, as currently structured, the current system under-utilizes the wealth of information collected and does not participate in a larger counter-propaganda effort against the violent radical interpretation of Islam.

Originally published in *Terrorism Monitor*: Volume 5, Issue 16 on August 16, 2007.

Notes

1. A "région" is an administrative district in France. There are 22 régions in France.
2. "Lutte contre le terrorisme: L'engagement de la PP," *Liaisons*, no. 87 (December 2005-January/February 2006).
3. The mastering of French by foreign imams operating in France seems to be a widespread problem. According to the Renseignements Généraux (RG), out of a poll of 1,000 imams, 360 were fluent in French, 315 were moderately proficient in French and 350 had no proficiency in French. For the RG, this is a "major source of concern for the future."

4. Eric Denécée, "Le développement de l'Islam fondamentaliste en France: aspects sécuritaires, économiques et sociaux," Paris, Centre Français de Recherche sur le Renseignement, rapport de recherche no. 1, September 2005.
5. The term "Islam des caves," which can loosely be translated as "Basement Islam," refers to the widespread practice of preachers holding sermons in the basements of high-rise buildings in predominantly Muslim suburbs during the 1980s.
6. Denécée.

The Threat of Islamist Terrorism to Germany
By Anouar Boukhars

The al-Qaeda threat to Germany over its forces in Afghanistan coupled with the recent arrest of four Arab men accused of supporting al-Tawhid—a terrorist organization believed to have links to al-Qaeda—have convinced German authorities of the rising jihadi threat to Germany. Even though the terrorism threat level in the country remains less critical than in other European countries involved in Iraq, law enforcement officials warn that in the eyes of jihadis, "Germany is classed as one of the so-called crusaders, the helpers of the United States and of Israel" [1]. The 2005 annual report on the protection of the constitution warns that Germany's involvement in Afghanistan, the deployment of its marines in Somalia and its training of Iraqi officers make it part "of the Islamist terrorists' theater of operations" [2]. Yet, while Germany is by no means immune to home-grown terrorism, it is still a fact that the ideologies that spawn terrorism or radicalism elsewhere in Europe have not found fertile ground in the country's Turkish immigrants who make up three quarters of the Muslim population [3].

According to the International Crisis Group report on Germany, Islamic activism, with the exclusion of the Islamische Gemeinschaft Millî Görüs (Islamic Community of the National Vision, IGMG), appeals far less to the Turkish Muslim element than it does to the rest of the Muslim minority. The few jihadi suspects apprehended so far are of Arab origin or were German converts [4]. Despite the scare of Islamist ideologues exporting their creed to a marginalized Muslim minority, the federal Verfassungsschutz (Office for the Protection of the Constitution), the equivalent of Britain's MI5 and the U.S. FBI, puts the number of the supporters of the 28 Islamist organizations that operate in Germany at 32,100, a slight increase from 31,800 in 2004. The number of supporters of Turkish Islamist groups stands at 27,250. The Islamische Gemeinschaft Millî Görüs gets the largest share of support with around 26,500. Arab Islamist groups claim 3,350 supporters. The Muslim Brotherhood tops this list with around 1,300 supporters; the Lebanese Hezbollah comes second with 900. As for Jama'at Tabligh, it has about 500 members, and Hamas 300 members [5].

Yet despite the fact that intelligence agencies have found little evidence of the association of Islamists with social unrest or jihadism, local and federal authorities are highly distrustful of Islamism in both its moderate and its radical forms. The Verfassungsschutz keeps a close eye on all Islamist groups, including non-violent ones whom it accuses of fostering radicalization. "Their wide range of Islamist-oriented educational and support activities, especially for children and adolescents from immigrant families, are used to promote the creation and proliferation of an Islamist milieu in Germany ... which could also form the breeding ground for further radicalization," the 2005 annual report on the protection of the constitution warns [6].

This radicalization, however, failed to manifest itself during the French riots of 2005 and the 2006 Muhammad caricatures affair. Civic unrest or a spillover of violence did not occur. There is no doubt that there are radical Islamists that warrant close surveillance. It is estimated that the Hilafet Devleti movement has 750 members. The banned Hizb ut-Tahrir al-Islami (Islamic Liberation Party) has about 300 members [7]. Hezbollah and Hamas count no more than a few hundred members. German officials put the number of supporters of the Iraqi Ansar al-Islam/Ansar al-Sunna and a handful of "non-aligned mujahideen" in the low hundreds. One to two percent of Islamists (400-600) are believed to be "ready to commit violence," but so are foreign leftist extremists, who are estimated to number 17,290 in Bavaria alone, and foreign extreme nationalists (8,430 members). All are described as potentially violent [8].

Notwithstanding the small numbers of radical Islamists, state officials lump all Islamists together as quintessentially undemocratic, oppressive and anti-Western. There is a tendency to conjure the worst case scenarios in which non-violent Islamists, who are believed to deceptively project themselves as victims of state paranoia and Islamophobia, turn into terrorists or at the very least troublemakers who instigate civic unrest. Yet stigmatizing non-violent Islamists through exclusionary policies, aggressive surveillance and indiscriminate mosque raids will unfortunately do nothing to isolate radical Islamists and eliminate their alien threats. While it is true that non-violent Islamists can become radicalized, this radicalization is not automatic. Indiscriminate crackdowns and arbitrary humiliations might drive non-violent Islamists into the hands of the radicals.

Indeed, Germany is pondering the specter of "an enemy within," a fifth column of disaffected Islamic parallel societies that threaten its "Germanness." Ever since the discovery of the Hamburg-based terrorist cell at the heart of the September 11 attacks, there has been a growing fear about a perceived Islamist wave sweeping across Germany, seeking to re-Islamize its Muslim minorities, deepening their presumed status of "extraterritoriality" and expanding their "culture-based crime." Warnings about the transformation of Germany and the rest of Europe into an anti-Christian, anti-Western "Eurabia" and the emerging dawn of "the darkness of a new barbarism" that threatens to overtake the symbols of the nation and subjugate a destructively passive and self-doubting population, are rampant in political and media rhetoric (Spiegel Online International, January 25, 2007; Der Spiegel, February 6, 2006). The fear of the "unwanted Germans" living fraudulently and infiltrating the citadels of Germanness prompted a bishop emeritus of Germany's Independent Lutherans to express his anxiety in striking terms: "I fear that we are approaching a situation resembling the tragic fate of Christianity in northern Africa in Islam's early days."

Warnings about the transformation of Germany and the rest of Europe into an anti-Christian, anti-Western "Eurabia" and the emerging dawn of "the darkness of a new barbarism" that threatens to overtake the symbols of the nation and subjugate a destructively passive and self-doubting population, are rampant in political and media rhetoric (Spiegel Online International, January 25, 2007; Der Spiegel, February 6, 2006).

The Discomfort of Strangers

The rhetoric about the rising tide of fundamentalism overtaking Germany engenders only more fear and paranoia of the young, alienated Muslims that are poor, ill-educated and tempted by crime and radical Islam. The 2006 Pew poll found Germans as the most concerned in Europe about Islamic fundamentalism, with 82 percent of the general public saying that they are very (40 percent) or somewhat (42 percent) concerned. Some 58 percent expect "a coming conflict with the Muslim population" and 42 percent believe that Islamic terrorists blend in with the Muslim population [9]. The International Helsinki Federation for Human Rights 2004 report on intolerance and discrimination against Muslims in the European Union found that more than 80 percent of Germans surveyed in 2004 associated the word "Islam" with "terrorism" and "oppression of women" (IHF Press Release, Vienna, March 7, 2005).

A substantial number of Germans admit to being preoccupied with anything Muslim. A German judge, Christa Datz-Winter, has only recently provoked a public outcry by a ruling that confounded even Muslims when she cited the Quran in deciding a case of domestic violence. Der Spiegel magazine was quick to feature the story on its cover with the sensational title, "Mecca Germany: Silent Islamization." The ruling convinced many of the need to defend the country from an alien cohesive body of Muslims that are imbued by separatist beliefs and guided by a supposedly totalitarian Sharia that rigidly controls people's consciences and bodies (Der Spiegel, February 6, 2006).

Some critics of the perceived collaborationist posture of the judicial system in the name of cultural sensitivity urge the government to adopt more aggressive policies to protect German culture and recognize a cultural invasion by an anti-modern, medieval force (Perlentaucher, January 24). Any accommodation toward religious faith is seen as a dangerous betrayal of the values of the enlightenment and an appeasement of an Islamist foe whose rise is said to resemble the rise of the Third Reich (Die Zeit, March 18, 2004; Welt am Sonntag, July 24, 2006). This hard-line exclusionary rhetoric that begins with getting the Muslim monolith in line with the universalist and static secular culture of the superior "real Germans" leads inevitably to "cultural fundamentalism." There is a disturbing belief that good Muslims are the ones who do not practice their religion and suppress their Muslim identity. The emphasis on Muslims' loyalty to Germany's "fundamental principles and values" is the right of every country, but requirements of ideological conformity (are you truly with us or against us?) with moral dilemmas are difficult to comprehend and even violate the German constitution which stipulates "freedom of faith and of conscience, and freedom of creed, religious or ideological" (Expatica, January 11, 2006).

The Loyalty Test

The new citizenship test for Muslims, introduced by the German state of Baden-Wuerttemberg in 2006, is supposed to find out if a person shares German principles and values and acts as a social contract between Germany and its citizens. The irony of the test is that many Germans would fail to pass it. As Lale Akgün pointed out in an editorial for the Berlin newspaper Taz, "the current German pope would fail due to his opinions on homosexuality and sexual equality." Volker Beck, a Green Party politician, claimed that even Interior Minister Heribert Rech and many conservative politicians in the CDU would not pass the test (Expatica, January 11, 2006).

Given that a large number of Muslims in Germany were denied easy access to citizenship until very recently, their existence in Germany is increasingly becoming conditional upon the espousal of particular beliefs and fidelity to values that even the most patriotic Germans might not know or agree with. Yet it is counter-productive to threaten potential ostracism through naturalization and a foreigners' law as punishment for the "sin" of refusing to adopt an imposed ideological uniformity on moral dilemmas that looks more like absolute assimilationism than integration.

The Path Ahead

Pressures from within (Islam) and without (globalization and European integration) have made Germans feel apprehensive about their national identity and culture. The country is visibly struggling to mitigate the potentially explosive mix of nationalism and fear of the Muslim "stranger," while defining citizenship for its marginalized and disenfranchised immigrants. The issue is no longer the building of defensive citadels of "Germanness" since the country has finally come to grips with the reality that the Gastarbeiter (guest workers) are there to stay. The challenge for Germany today is to define what kinds of values are essential for the country's secular model of society and what are negotiable.

Originally published in *Terrorism Monitor*: Volume 5, Issue 7 on April 12, 2007.

Notes

The author would like to thank Jonathan Laurence for allowing him to draw heavily on his excellent report, "Islam and Identity in Germany," International Crisis Group, March 14, 2007.

1. German Federal Ministry of the Interior, "2005 Annual Report on the Protection of the Constitution." For the full report, see
http://www.verfassungsschutz.de/download/SHOW/vsbericht_2005_engl.pdf.
2. Ibid.
3. About 75 percent of the 3.2 to 3.4 million people of Muslim background in Germany come from Turkey or are of Turkish origin. The rest are: 200,000 Bosnian/Herzegovinian, 100,000 Iranian, 80,000 Moroccan, 70,000 Afghan, German Converts and 800,000 citizens (mostly former Turkish nationals). Around 95 percent are of non-Arab origin. This diverse population can be divided along ethnic lines: religion (Sunnis, 80 percent), (Alevites, 17 percent), (Shiites, three percent), degree of religiosity and political status. The German Conference on Islam (DIK), Federal Ministry of the Interior. See also the excellent report "Islam and Identity in Germany," International Crisis Group, March 14, 2007,
http://www.crisisgroup.org/home/index.cfm?l=1&id=4693.
4. ICG report.
5. "2005 Annual Report on the Protection of the Constitution."

6. Ibid.

7. Ibid.

8. "Islam and Identity in Germany."

9. "Muslims in Europe: Economic Worries Top Concerns About Religious and Cultural Identity," Pew Global Attitudes Project, July 6, 2006.

Catalonia: Europe's New Center of Global Jihad
By Kathryn Haahr

The strengthening of Islamist groups, combined with an increase in jihadi networks and activities in and around Barcelona, underscores Catalonia's status as a European center for al-Qaeda-associated terrorism operations. Statements by al-Qaeda leaders that emphasize Spain's unique "status" within the Global Salafi-Jihad, coupled with disclosed terrorism trends for Spain in 2007, reveal that the culture of global jihad has consolidated in Spain's northern autonomous region. Once seemingly disparate Salafi Islamist groups and neophyte militant Muslim grassroots networks have coalesced into radicalized Islamist collectives throughout Catalonia to pose a national threat to Spain, as well as to Western interests in Europe, North Africa and the Middle East.

Current Perspective of Islamist Activities in Catalonia

According to Spanish counter-terrorism officials, the Spanish Confederation of Police and various terrorism experts, Catalonia has become the "principle focus" of the development of jihadi terrorism in Spain and, more specifically, the largest jihadi recruitment center in Europe (La Vanguardia, June 3, 2007). "The study about the imprisoned terrorists in Spain—more than 300 since the end of the 1990s—shows that Catalonia is unquestionably the epicenter of jihadi activities in our country," stated Fernando Reinares, the main researcher and director of the Global Terrorism Program of Elcano Royal Institute and the adviser for anti-terrorism policies in the Interior Ministry between 2004 and 2006. Reinares believes that the analysis about Muslim extremism shows Catalonia as the meeting point for jihadis, and he clarifies that if the study had been made on the basis of the number of detentions instead of imprisonments, the percentage would be even higher. According to officials and various studies, the majority of Islamist terrorists in Spain now regard Muslim communities throughout Catalonia as "safe-havens" for building their Islamist ideological support bases, logistical and terrorism financing and recruitment of suicide jihadis for the insurgencies in Iraq and Afghanistan, as well as for potential targets in Spain and elsewhere in Europe.

According to the Spanish Confederation of Police, the three cities of Badalona, Santa Coloma de Gramenet and Sant Adria de Besos form the "most important triangle of jihadi recruitment in Europe" (El Pais, May 30, 2007). Every month, approximately three to five Muslim residents of Catalonia travel to Iraq, Chechnya and Afghanistan for terrorism training (El Periodico de Catalunya, September 9, 2006). After their training, the jihadis return to form sleeper cells in preparation for terrorist attacks, many of which have installed themselves in the jihadi triangle—there is a high concentration of Muslims in the three cities. Spanish counter-terrorism officials observe that many recruits come out of Catalonia due to the strong influence of Salafi Islamism and the susceptibility of young, marginalized and predominantly foreign-born Moroccan men. Many of the jihadi recruiters are foreign-born, typically from France and Belgium, and they reportedly travel throughout Spain on recruitment missions. After Catalonia, the other recruitment mills for militant Islamists are in Madrid and the Spanish enclaves Ceuta and Melilla (*Terrorism Monitor*, May 4, 2006; *Terrorism Monitor*, February 15, 2007).

A March 31, 2007 news report from Informativos Telecinco recently filmed the apartment of a detained jihadi recruiter in the city of Reus, where police found tapes of Osama bin Laden as well as training videos. According to the security services, Moroccan Mbark El Jaafari had trained an estimated 32 jihadi suicide bombers. National Police sources noted that the new recruitment strategy that El Jaafari employed was to "Westernize" his young recruits in order to better integrate them into Catalonian society; he encouraged them to wear jeans and modern dress and to refrain from growing long beards. The next step was to remove them from their cultural and sociological context by sending the trainees to smaller towns (places where they were not recruited), where a "sponsor" would find them employment. Eventually, the "trainees" would travel to Iraq, Algeria or Afghanistan. The favored "trainees" are apparently those who serve in the Moroccan or Algerian military services.

Synopsis of Counter-Terrorism Operations in Catalonia

Since 2001, an estimated 31 percent of the imprisoned Islamist terrorists in Spain have been captured in Catalonia, and most are Moroccans. Catalonia is home to around 300,000 Muslims, of which 100,000 are Moroccan immigrants. Officials estimate that the real number of Maghrebi immigrants is likely more than one million. Major counter-terrorism operations have taken place almost every year since 2001. In Operacion Tigris right after the March 11, 2004, Madrid train bombings, the national police detained around 20 Islamist terrorists in Catalonia, Madrid and other regions of Spain. As a result of information obtained in this operation, police in 2005 arrested five Islamists in Catalonia, all of whom were connected to the March 11 bombings. In 2006, the Guardia Civil detained two dozen North African Muslims, primarily in Vilanova I la Beltru, who had been working as part of a recruitment ring to send "kamikazes" to Iraq; one of these suicide bombers, Algerian Belgacem Bellil, killed 28 people by targeting the Italian base in Nasiriya in November 2003 (El Periodico de Catalunya, May 29, 2007).

In May 2007, Spanish counter-terrorism officials detained 15 Islamists—13 Moroccans and two Algerians—involved in recruiting jihadis for insurgencies in Iraq, North Africa and Afghanistan; 13 of them were detained in Catalonia alone. The raid was a result of two counter-terrorism operations in 2006—"Chacal" and "Camaleon" (EuropaPress.es, May 28, 2007; La Vanguardia, May 31, 2007). The Spanish government believes that these individuals formed part of al-Qaeda's Maghreb branch in Spain. One of the 13 Catalonian Islamists, Taoufik Cheddadi, is the imam of the Santa Coloma de Gramenet y Mollet mosque. Judge Baltazar Garzon is in the process of determining if there is enough proof to incarcerate the 13 Catalans (La Vanguardia, May 31, 2007).

Salafi Islamist Groups and Networks in Catalonia

Since September 11 and the ongoing revelations emerging from terrorism trials in Madrid, Spanish security officials observe an increase in the number of cells and networks associated with al-Qaeda and other Salafi organizations, notably: Al-Qaeda in the Islamic Maghreb (AQIM; formerly known as the GSPC), GICM, Hizb-ut-Tahrir al-Islami al-Magrebi (Party of Islamic Liberation of Morocco, HUT), Takfir wal-Hijra, the Armed Islamic Group (GIA), al-Adl wal-Ihsane (Justice and Charity), and the Jama'at al-Da'wa wal-Tabligh (La Vanguardia, January 29, 2007; La Vanguardia, May 31, 2007; La Vanguardia, June 3, 2007; El Pais, November 3, 2006; El Periodico, June 3, 2007; El Mundo, June 22, 2006). State security officials are particularly concerned with two Moroccan Islamist groups, which in the last year have been preaching radicalized messages in their sermons: al-Adl wal-Ihsane and HUT. Both groups have been detected in dozens of mosques and oratory sites, and officials worry that their sermons will have an impact in radicalizing young Muslims. HUT proves to be a useful case study of a group that denounces radicalization but in practice proselytizes subversion—many of their statements are anti-government. HUT came to the attention of security agents in 2003 in the town of Salt, when they discovered a concentration of jihadis who espoused al-Qaeda's ideology. According to Moroccan specialist Abdala Rami, HUT divides its international territories into wilayas (provinces), of which Spain pertains to the European province [1].

Catalonian Jihadi Models

The predominant Catalonian "jihadi model" follows a similar pattern to that observed in Madrid, Valencia and Andalusia (La Vanguardia, June 3, 2007). According to this jihadi model, radical Sunni terrorist groups (such as al-Qaeda and AQIM) establish regional operational cells and networks for the purpose of recruiting jihadis and to support other terrorism activities, such as organizing criminal activities in support of terrorism financing. These Islamists tend to be predominately foreign-born, from North Africa or other parts of Europe, and undertake specific terrorism missions, such as the establishment of jihadi recruitment rings. These groups recruit recent immigrants to Spain. Spanish police sources believe that jihadis recruited in Catalonia are training in al-Qaeda terrorist training camps in Mali, Mauritania and Niger. According to a senior official of the Guardia Civil, al-Qaeda's new base in the Sahel represents a threat to Spanish interests (El Pais, February 11, 2007).

An emerging characteristic of the jihadi model is that of informal, Salafi-inspired groups that are not formally linked to any one terrorist organization. Rather, these individuals tend to organize themselves around a commonly shared ideology of global jihad, one in which the religion of Islam is molded to serve their violent objectives. At times, small groups of "independently" inspired radical Muslims appear in villages and towns throughout Spain, especially in agricultural areas, to troll for recruits. Spanish terrorism expert Dr. Javier Jordan calls this phenomenon "grassroots jihadist networks," which are groups that are not formally linked to al-Qaeda but share its ideology. These individuals tend not to come from overseas, but operate exclusively within Spain; some are converts, hence the concern about home-grown terrorists. These groups recruit young Muslims into jihad after they have settled in Spain, as opposed to relying on foreign jihadis (El Periodico, September 9, 2006) [2].

The presence of a multitude of Maghrebi Islamist groups operating in Catalonia demonstrates the appeal that the Salafi agenda has with the North African immigrant community, especially with Moroccans. While these distinct terrorist groups and Islamist political parties are not formally associated with one another, they all share al-Qaeda's message of global jihad and preach the five commandments in mosques and other prayer sites. Groups such as AQIM ask their believers to not only sacrifice their lives for the jihad, but to proselytize; security officials worry that these Salafi messages are already radicalizing Muslims in Catalonia, as well as in other regions of Spain. AQIM, for example, recently urged the Moroccan government to clean the Spanish enclaves of Ceuta and Melilla of impurities (this follows Ayman al-Zawahiri's December 2006 proclamation that al-Qaeda should liberate them) (*El Pais*, May 21, 2007; *El Pais*, July 27, 2006). This type of rhetoric certainly appeals to Muslims all over Spain to coalesce and become one active body of jihadis striving to fight infidels.

Trends

Catalonia is emblematic of other regions of Spain, notably the Spanish enclaves of Ceuta and Melilla, Alicante and Castille, wherein grassroots jihadi communities (as in a systems-of-systems model) exist, operate and become stronger. AQIM's new name and mission of international jihad will appeal to an increased number of Muslims (foreign and Spanish citizens) in grassroots communities desiring a vehicle through which to legitimize their political, religious and social grievances. The appeal of Islamist ideologies (espoused by various political parties and other Islamist entities) has the potential to marginalize in a significant way the already existing divergences between multi-ethnic and moderate Muslims who have lived in the Catalonia territory for decades, and the militant Islamists now increasing their religious and social footprint in the region. A study by Islamic specialist Jordi Moreras on the Catalan town Ciutat Vella in 1999 documents the re-orientation of the main mosque and various sites of prayer to Pakistani influences (such as imams of Pakistani origin). What is noteworthy about this study is that the congregations tend to be fundamentally Maghrebi. Counter-terrorism experts should consider exploring the ethno-cultural dynamics and their subtle overt and non-overt manifestation as a way of mapping the developments in Catalonian Islam.

> *AQIM's new name and mission of international jihad will appeal to an increased number of Muslims (foreign and Spanish citizens) in grassroots communities desiring a vehicle through which to legitimize their political, religious and social grievances.*

Terrorism experts concur that Barcelona is a possible target for terrorist groups. Based on a study of recent al-Qaeda threats and attacks perpetrated by jihadis, the country's high-speed train (AVE), the national high court in Madrid and many tall, singular buildings in Barcelona are probable targets. Several Interpol reports also mention this possibility (*La Vanguardia*, May 9, 2007). The absence of threat information from terrorists complicates counter-terrorism efforts. According to Spanish police sources, the difficulty in recruiting moles to penetrate Islamist cells makes it extremely difficult to conduct surveillance and implement other counter-terrorism measures. Sources note that one of the main problems is the scarcity of speakers of key Islamist languages—Arabic, Berber and Urdi. Another factor is the lack of a deep understanding of the cultural variables that characterize distinct ethnic Muslim communities. Without collaboration from the Muslim community, security agents will remain challenged in not only preventing terrorist operations from occurring, but in engaging in predictive intelligence operations such as identifying the members of terrorist groups and their networks.

Originally published in *Terrorism Monitor*: Volume 5, Issue 11 on June 7, 2007.

Notes

1. HUT is principally active in Barcelona and its surroundings. Its leaders tend to be Libyan and its militants Moroccan. For an in-depth assessment of HUT, please refer to, Javier Jordan and Sol Tarres, "Movimientos Musulmanes y Prevencion del Yihadismo en Espana Hizb ut-Tahrir," Jihad Monitor Occasional Paper, no 9, April 21, 2007.
2. Fernando Reinares and Javier Jordan have conducted extensive sociological work on studying the profiles of Spanish jihadis.

The Pakistan Connection to the United Kingdom's Jihad Network
By James Brandon

The start of 2008 have seen increasing international interest in the connections between jihadis in the UK and their counterparts in Pakistan. Attention has focused on how such groups and individuals could link up and cooperate to carry out attacks in Europe, South Asia or the United States. This concern has now reached its highest levels. On January 29, 2008 then Pakistani President Pervez Musharraf said that flaws in the British counter-terrorist strategy were hurting global efforts to contain Islamic terrorism (*The Guardian*, January 29, 2008; *Dawn*, January 29, 2008). In particular, he referred to the UK's decision not to ban Hizb ut-Tahrir, a global group that aims to re-establish the caliphate and which has been blamed for radicalizing several individuals who carried out attacks after leaving the group (Independent, January 28, 2008). He also suggested that the UK's policy was excessively focused on preventing imminent attacks rather than defeating al-Qaeda's ideology. While Musharraf's accusations may have been partly intended to deflect attention from Pakistan's own problems, there is increasing evidence that networks linking jihadis in Britain and Pakistan have evolved to survive government crackdowns, threatening the security not only of Britain, but also that of its allies.

Background to the British Jihad

The Pakistan-UK axis has long been central to jihadist movements worldwide. The UK is home to at least 600,000 people of Pakistani origin, many of whom come from areas like Kashmir, which have played a central role in Islamic militancy. During the 1990s, several factors conspired to create a radical pan-Islamist identity among British Muslims, notably the entrenchment of Jamaat-e-Islami and Muslim Brotherhood activists in mosques and Islamic organizations and the arrival of radical preachers from the Arab world. Conflicts in Kashmir, Bosnia and elsewhere were widely interpreted by many Muslims as a conflict between Islam and Christianity, furthering the process of radicalization. However, the enthusiasm that this factor aroused for jihad was tempered by the idea of a "covenant of security" that radical Islamist preachers said existed between them and the British government and which initially prevented attacks against the UK. Inevitably, this restriction compelled British jihadis to export their violence abroad—often in the direction of Pakistan. In the mid-1990s, Mohammed Sohail, a Pakistani professional, created the Global Jihad Fund to channel donations from British Muslims to jihadis in South Asia.

In the late 1990s, Babar Ahmad, presently fighting deportation to the United States, allegedly used the Azzam.com website to spread pro-jihadist propaganda and to channel money, equipment and volunteers to the Taliban through Pakistan [1]. Separately, Dhiren Barot—also known as Isa al-Hindi—a Hindu brought up in the UK, converted to Islam and fought in Kashmir in 1995, writing of his experiences in The Army of Medinah in Kashmir, an influential book for would-be jihadis (BBC, November 7, 2006). In 1994, Ahmed Omar Saeed Sheikh, born to a middle-class Pakistani family living in the UK, travelled to Pakistan where he attended a training camp run by Harkat ul-Mujaheddin (BBC, July 26, 2005). In 1999, he attended an al-Qaeda training camp at Khalden in Afghanistan. In 2002, he kidnapped and killed Wall Street Journal reporter Daniel Pearl. Richard Reid, "the shoe bomber," a London-born convert to Islam, and his co-conspirator, Sajid Badat, are also said to have travelled to Pakistan or Afghanistan to collect detonators prior to Reid's attempt to down a trans-Atlantic airliner in 2001 (Telegraph, December 27, 2001). In some cases, Islamist groups had well-developed networks. During the late 1990s, al-Muhajiroun, a British radical Islamist group whose members were predominantly South Asian, sent several hundred British citizens to train in Pakistan. Following 9/11, the group openly arranged for several dozen British Muslims to travel via Pakistan to fight U.S. forces in Afghanistan. In many cases, these individuals did not work directly with al-Qaeda but with a range of other local groups; it is likely that this remains the case with present-day jihadis making the same journey.

Pakistan's Connection to the Transit System Bombings in London

The July 7, 2005 bombings in London in which four bombers killed 52 people marked the moment at which the idea of the "covenant" between the UK and its radical Islamists broke down. There were, however, substantial similarities between this attack and previous actions by British jihadis abroad. Three of the four bombers were of Pakistani origin and at least two of them travelled to Pakistan—and possibly Afghanistan—shortly before the bombings. There they apparently met senior al-Qaeda figures, recorded their political testaments and received instructions in bomb-making. In a video released after the bombings, Ayman al-Zawahiri said that the two visited al-Qaeda camps while in Pakistan. This and subsequent attempted attacks indicate that, while the covenant no longer exists and the formal networks of the 1990s have been replaced by looser webs of contacts and family members, a trip to Pakistan nonetheless remains an effective way for British jihadis to acquire military training and mental indoctrination into al-Qaeda's ideology.

Two weeks after the July 7 bombings, four men—this time of East African origin—attempted to carry out more suicide attacks on the London transport system. Again, there were clear links to Pakistan. In December 2004, the leader of the group, Muktar Ibrahim, an Eritrean, travelled to Pakistan with £2,000 in cash, a video camera and cold weather clothing. During his time there he is believed to have visited a training camp run by Harkat ul-Mujaheddin in Mirpur—an area of Pakistani Kashmir where many British Pakistanis originate—and received explosives training (Independent, July 10, 2007). This group is believed to have also been visited by Ahmed Omar Saeed Sheikh, Daniel Pearl's murderer. Ibrahim returned to the UK in March 2005, assembled the bombs and distributed them to the other three would-be bombers he had met in radical circles in London (TimesOnline, July 10, 2007). Before attempting to carry out their attacks, the bombers also travelled to the Lake District, a mountainous area of the UK, where they climbed mountains in an attempt to replicate some of the experiences of jihadist training camps.

Targeting Muslim Troops in the British Army

In January 2007, police broke up a plan by several Pakistani men in Birmingham to kidnap and behead a British Muslim soldier in the city (BBC, January 29, 2008). The group had planned to videotape the execution and post it online in order to cause panic and make Tony Blair go "crazy" (Telegraph, February 15, 2008). The planned murder fit into the long-standing takfiri strategy of attempting to deter Muslims from assisting non-Muslim governments. Significantly, members of the group not only planned to carry out attacks in the UK, but also shipped military equipment to jihadis in Pakistan. Between 2004 and 2006, they shipped goods weighing almost a ton, including tents, outdoor clothing, night-vision binoculars, range finders, walkie-talkies, electronic bug detectors and split-finger gloves, which were useful for snipers (TimesOnline, January 30, 2008). Some of these shipments were sent to Islamabad and then forwarded to Mirpur.

Operation Crevice

In 2004, a major police action, "Operation Crevice," halted plans by another group to use fertilizer bombs to attack nightclubs in London. This plot centered around four men of Pakistani origin and one Algerian. Omar Khyam, from Crawley near London, was the group's leader. He first travelled to Pakistan for military training in January 2000 when he attended the training camp of al-Badr Mujahideen, a militant group in Muzaffarabad, close to Indian-controlled Kashmir (BBC, April 30, 2007). "They taught me everything I needed for guerrilla warfare in Kashmir; AK-47s, pistols, sniper rifles, reconnaissance and light machine-guns," said Khyam at his trial, adding that he believed that he had received training from Pakistan's Inter-Services Intelligence (ISI). Later in 2001, after briefly returning to the UK, he attended another training camp in the North-West Frontier Province (NWFP) near Afghanistan before crossing the border to meet Taliban members. In 2003, he traveled to Malakand, in Pakistan's NWFP, with £16,000 taken from his overdraft, together with some of the other plotters (BBC, April 30, 2007). It is believed that he met Abdul Hadi, a senior al-Qaeda leader; the meeting was arranged by contacts in Luton, a town near London with a large radical Islamic population and a large number of Muhajiroun supporters (BBC, April 30, 2007). Among the other targets discussed by the group were soccer matches and airliners.

Plot to Bomb Trans-Atlantic Airliners

In summer 2006, British police arrested 23 people over an alleged plan to bomb several trans-Atlantic airliners. Although 11 people have since been charged, none has been tried. At least one of the suspects is said to have attended meetings of the Tablighi Jamaat, a non-violent but highly conservative Islamic group whose followers in Pakistan are believed to be seen by al-Qaeda as ripe for radicalization (Telegraph, July 11, 2007). Other arrests were made in Pakistan. One of those detained was Rashid Rauf, who was accused by the Pakistani authorities of being linked to al-Qaeda and possessing bomb-making equipment (*The Guardian*, August, 14, 2006). Rauf, who has dual UK-Pakistani nationality, escaped from the Pakistani police in December 2007 and remains on the run. He is also said to have links to Jaish-e-Mohammed, a Kashmiri militant group (*The Guardian*, January 28, 2008).

Prosecution of the Bradford Cell

In July 2007, five British men of Pakistani origin aged 19 to 21—including four students from Bradford University—were convicted of downloading extremist Islamic literature and planning to travel to Pakistan to attend a training camp (BBC, July 26, 2007). Although their convictions were quashed this month on the grounds that they had not made any concrete plans to carry out terrorist attacks, it is clear that their radicalization occurred in the UK (TimesOnline, February 13, 2008). The group's actions seem to indicate that fighting abroad is still perceived as preferable to carrying out attacks on civilians in the UK.

British Muslims and Terrorist Fundraising

In addition to these high-profile plots, there have been a number of less dramatic cases that shed further light on the links between jihadis in Pakistan and the UK. Last month, Sohail Anjum Qureshi, a Pakistani-born dental technician living in the UK, was convicted of attempting to travel to Pakistan to join the Taliban (Metropolitan Police Service [London], January 9, 2008). He was arrested in October 2006 at Heathrow airport while boarding a flight to Islamabad. A sniper scope, night-vision equipment, two metal batons and £9,000 in cash was discovered in his luggage (BBC, January 8, 2008). The police believed that he had previously received training from al-Qaeda and that he intended to rejoin them or the Taliban. There is other evidence which suggests that fundraising networks are able to operate in the UK with relative impunity—especially if individuals are raising funds not directly for al-Qaeda but for less high-profile Pakistani jihadist groups. In 2006, the Indian government said that British Muslims had provided funds which were used to carry out the July 2006 Mumbai train bombings which killed over 200 people (TimesOnline, July 17, 2006).

Conclusion

There is substantial evidence that the connections between UK-based jihadis and their counterparts in Pakistan remain of importance to both groups. Funds from British-Pakistanis play an important role in sustaining a number of jihadist movements in South Asia. Training—both ideological and military—available in Pakistan is an important stepping stone toward violence for British radicals. However, it remains unclear precisely how these networks function. For example, it is uncertain whether would-be jihadis usually obtain introductions and directions to jihadist camps through contacts based in the UK, or whether such connections were made entirely in South Asia.

Funds from British-Pakistanis play an important role in sustaining a number of jihadist movements in South Asia. Training—both ideological and military—available in Pakistan is an important stepping stone toward violence for British radicals.

It seems beyond dispute, however, that the primary radicalization of such individuals generally occurs in the UK; primarily in mosques, social clubs, gyms and universities. In almost all known cases, British militants appear to have absorbed radical ideas in the UK before travelling to Pakistan to seek out relevant military training and carry out attacks there or in Afghanistan. Their reasons for going to Pakistan vary; many have family connections, others speak the local languages—others still are drawn to places like Peshawar where renowned jihadis like Abdullah Azzam and Osama bin Laden once lived. Other would-be jihadis have never travelled abroad. In 2005, Muhammad Abu Baker Mansha, a 21-year old from London, was convicted of planning to kill a British soldier who had recently returned from Iraq (BBC, December 22, 2005). Police who raided his flat found a blank-firing pistol in the process of conversion to fire live rounds, al-Qaeda propaganda and beheading videos. Mansha, however, never traveled to a training camp and had few contacts with known radicals; he is the prime example of how the internet has become a "virtual training camp," making travel abroad largely superfluous. At present, however, such cases of "self-radicalization" are rare. Travelling to training camps in Pakistan or Afghanistan continues to hold a talismanic significance for British jihadis and this may provide vital opportunities for the security services to intercept them before they strike in Britain or abroad.

Originally published in *Terrorism Monitor*: Volume 6, Issue 4 on February 22, 2008.

Notes

1. "Affidavit In Support of Request for Extradition of Babar Ahmad," http://www.usdoj.gov/usao/ct/Documents/AHMAD%20extradition%20affidavit.pdf.

Britain's Prison Dilemma: Issues and Concerns in Islamic Radicalization
By Raffaello Pantucci

The increasingly rapid tempo of arrests and convictions of terrorist plotters by the British security services has had the concurrent effect of increasing the number of terrorist prisoners now incarcerated in the United Kingdom's penal system. This influx of hardened terrorists into the system has started to alarm many in the Ministry of Justice and the Home Office who are concerned about the "disruptive impact of terrorists on prison regimes" (*The Guardian*, March 3, 2008). Fears are focused on two main concerns: clashes between groups of Muslim prisoners and others in the general prison population, and the potential for high-profile terrorist prisoners to radicalize susceptible imprisoned youths.

The Shoe Bomber and the Amir

These fears are not without some basis. It has been widely reported that "shoe bomber" Richard Reid was radicalized while serving a sentence for petty crime in Feltham Young Offenders Institution. The "amir" of the July 21 group—responsible for the attempted bombings of the London underground on July 21, 2005—Muktar Said Ibrahim, was similarly radicalized during a period of incarceration at either Huntercombe or Feltham Young Offenders Institution (BBC, July 29, 2005; Observer, July 15, 2007). Imams preaching extremism have been blamed for radicalizing impressionable young men—in 2002, imams at both Huntercombe and Feltham were suspended for such activities (Observer, July 15, 2007).

British authorities are also concerned by behavior seen in prisons across the Channel in continental Europe. The February 2008 conviction in Spain of 20 individuals for "Islamic terrorist activity"—though not on the original charge of plotting to drive a truck bomb into the main anti-terrorist courthouse—spawned from a plot that was led by Abderrahmane Tahiri, also known as Mohamed Achraf, and was concocted behind bars (Reuters Espana, February 27, 2008). Similarly, in 2005, French police arrested Safe Bourada, an Algerian who had served time in prison for plotting the 1990s metro attacks in Paris. Bourada was charged with leading a terror cell he had recruited while serving his sentence (Times, October 3, 2006; *Le Monde*, September 27, 2005).

Fears in the United Kingdom, however, date back to the Irish troubles, when many remember the role played by detainees in HM Prison Maze during the 1970s-1990s (BBC, October 23, 2007). Initially intended as a place of incarceration, the penitentiary slowly developed into a political rallying point, even going so far as to attract a visit by Secretary of State for Northern Ireland Mo Mowlam as a part of the peace talks. Furthermore, violence between different dissident groups often spilled over beyond the prison walls, with some 29 prison officers killed during the troubles (Observer, July 15, 2007).

Her Majesty's Prison Belmarsh

In particular, there are concerns about the prison population in HM Prison Belmarsh in Southeast London, where at least 151 of 916 prisoners attend Muslim religious services regularly [1]. One police official described the prison to Jamestown as Britain's own "madrasah," and there have been reports of guard intimidation: "When an officer confronts a Muslim prisoner ... he or she finds themselves surrounded by five or six other inmates" (Observer, July 15, 2007). Even more alarming, in July 2007, prison officers confiscated a laptop computer from prisoner Tariq al-Dour, who was convicted alongside Younis Tsouli, also known as Irhabi 007 (*Terrorism Focus*, March 4, 2008), for allegedly using a mobile phone to connect to the internet and building a terrorist-sympathetic website (Mirror, July 15, 2007). The scuffle surrounding the seizure of the computer led to a riot between prison officers and al-Qaeda sympathizers detained in the prison (Observer, July 15, 2007).

There are currently around 130 prisoners convicted or on remand for terrorist-related crimes in the British penal system, though this number is likely to increase as a number of high-profile cases reach conclusion (*The Guardian*, March 3, 2008). This is in a prison population of around 80,000, about 11 percent of which identify themselves as Muslims (BBC, August 3, 2007). Given that not all of these prisoners are held apart from the general population, the result is that convicted terrorists can be incarcerated with criminals detained for more petty crimes, a potentially dangerous combination. As Steve Gough, vice-chairman of the Prison Officers Association, put it: "The majority of the prison population is comprised of angry young men, disenfranchised from society. It doesn't matter if they are English, Afro-Caribbean, or whatever. These people are ripe for radicalization" (Observer, July 15, 2007).

Stories of radicals openly leading Muslim services have emerged. In 2006, the BBC learned that Khalid al Fawwaz, also known as Abu Omar, who is currently fighting extradition to the United States for charges pertaining to the 1998 embassy bombings in Nairobi and Dar es Salaam, led prayers amongst Muslim prisoners while being detained in 2003 at HM Prison Woodhill (BBC, May 4, 2006). In August 2007, the Prison Officers Association expressed concern that Abu Qatada, a Jordanian-Palestinian wanted on terrorism charges in eight countries, might have been preaching in HM Prison Long Lartin—officers were unable to understand exactly what Qatada was doing during "thrice daily communal prayers" (BBC, August 3, 2007). Reflecting prison officers' heightened awareness of this problem, Dhiren Barot, also known as Essa al-Hindi—mastermind of a series of plots including against potentially high-profile financial targets in the United Kingdom and United States—has complained that "any time the prison [official] [sic.] feels that I may have found a 'friend' that I may be 'overly' socializing with, more often than not the individual/s concerned are promptly shipped out to other establishments. Why? For irrational fear of 'sermonizing' or 'talent scouting' of course because they believe I have an arresting personality! The same goes for physical training with other inmates" [2].

The Dispersal Strategy

One solution that has been attempted is dispersal, whereby prisoners detained on al-

Qaeda-related charges are sent to prisons around the country to avoid their clustering and forming gangs in specific prisons. A particularly high-profile instance of this has been the decision to transfer prisoners Omar Khyam, the leader of a group of would-be terrorist bombers broken up by 2004's "Operation Crevice," Hussein Osman, one of the July 21 plotters and Dhiren Barot to HM Prison Frankland in Durham, England.

Clashes between the extremists and other prisoners in HM Prison Frankland have been frequent. In July 2007, Barot was assaulted by other prisoners with scalding water and boiling oil, leading to substantial burns and scarring (Observer, February 10; al-istiqamah.com, November-December 2007). Then in October 2007, Omar Khyam, who according to his lawyer has faced death threats from other inmates [3], assaulted another prisoner in a similar manner resulting in charges being brought against him (BBC, January 31, 2008).

Many prisoners charged with terrorist offenses have been spread over a number of prisons nationally, but concerns remain surrounding the possibility of deeper long-term radicalization or clashes between gangs of extremists and other prisoners. As the national commissioning plan for security prisons highlighted: "There is an urgent need to understand the custodial behavior of this group of offenders and its potential impact on other prisoners" (*The Guardian*, March 3, 2008).

Many prisoners charged with terrorist offenses have been spread over a number of prisons nationally, but concerns remain surrounding the possibility of deeper long-term radicalization or clashes between gangs of extremists and other prisoners.

Government Response

In a speech at King's College on January 17, 2008 Home Secretary Jacqui Smith announced that "with the Ministry of Justice and the Prisons Service we have set up an important program to understand and address radicalization in our prisons system" [4]. This announcement is something that the Prison Officers Association and others have long been calling for. Its delay was the product of a recent shake-up in the Home Office of the United Kingdom. Sparked by an immigration scandal, then-Home Secretary John Reid announced in the ensuing process that responsibility across the government for counter-terrorism would be moved to an Office for Security and Counter-Terrorism within the Home Office. Responsibility for prisons, formerly a Home Office role, would now be handed off onto the newly formed Ministry of Justice (BBC, March 29, 2007).

The Home Office has also introduced a four-strand counter-terrorism strategy known as "Contest," involving phases known as "Prevent, Pursue, Protect and Prepare." It was determined, however, that the "Prevent" aspect—which deals with "tackling the radicalization of individuals"—of the government's strategy would be led by the Department of Communities and Local Government. One can see how radicalization in prisons falls tidily between the cracks in these newly defined bureaucratic lines.

Conclusion

The potential risks from Britain's prisons would seem to be real, though not completely understood. While more rigid vetting has hopefully prevented extremist imams from preaching to susceptible and captive populations of incarcerated young men, the system is not foolproof. The bigger problems remain of how to handle a growing long-term prison population of hardened terrorists from proselytizing to fellow prisoners and how to prevent a repetition of some of the problems faced during the Irish troubles. When one considers that Britain's internal security service MI5 claims to have at least 2,000 terrorist plotters under surveillance, with possibly "double that number" that they do not know about [5], it seems inevitable that the problem of prison radicalization will be further magnified.

Originally published in *Terrorism Monitor*: Volume 6, Issue 6 on March 24, 2008.

Notes

1. HM Prison Belmarsh, "Annual Report of the Independent Monitoring Board," July 2006-June 2007.
2. "Eesa Barot's Letter to the Ummah," http://al-istiqamah.com.
3. "Abuse of Muslims in Frankland Prison," Help the Prisoners campaign pack, December 27, 2007, http://www.helptheprisoners.org.uk.
4. Home Secretary Jacqui Smith, "Our Shared Values – A Shared Responsibility," First International Conference on Radicalisation and Political Violence, January 17, 2007, http://security.homeoffice.gov.uk.
5. Jonathan Evans, "Address to the Society of Editors by the Director General of the Security Service," November 5, 2007, http://mi5.gov.uk.

The Next Generation of Radical Islamist Preachers in the UK
By James Brandon

In the last few years the British government has imprisoned, exiled or deported most of Britain's most high-profile jihadist preachers such as Abu Hamza, Omar Bakri and Abdullah Faisal. In 2006, it also passed laws prohibiting the "glorification" of terrorism to prevent new preachers from gaining similar prominence. However, as a range of fresh plots and convictions show, these measures have not yet halted jihadist recruitment. Within the last two years, several groups of would-be terrorists have been convicted of planning to kidnap and behead British Muslim soldiers in Birmingham, join jihadis in Pakistan and carry out terrorist attacks in the UK. Other cases currently being heard by courts or awaiting trial include alleged plots to bomb several trans-Atlantic airliners and set off bombs in restaurants. The growing evidence that many of these plotters have often been radicalized within the last two years suggests that extremists in the UK have adapted to anti-terrorism measures rather than being silenced by them [1].

Extremists' Changing Rhetoric

The 2006 Terrorism Act—arguably the most significant counter-terrorism measure taken by the British government since 2001—prohibited giving talks or producing and distributing material that might "glorify terrorism" or which could encourage others to commit acts of terrorism. This law has badly damaged extremists' operations, leading to a number of successful prosecutions and sharply curtailing extremists' abilities to incite violence. Many radical preachers are now so troubled by this law that they habitually begin and end talks with a (legally useless) disclaimer that they are not "inciting" violence or "glorifying" terrorism. Inevitably, however, some preachers have sought to use the new law as evidence of government plots against Muslims—and to use this to recruit fresh followers. For example, in one recorded talk entitled "Who is the terrorist?" (available on the main extremist website in the UK, Islambase.co.uk), "Abu Mujahidah," a radical preacher apparently based in London, attacks the new law as specifically targeting Muslims, telling listeners that wearing Islamic clothing will soon be made illegal: "Laws will be passed to say anyone who is heard publicly praying for the mujahideen, they will be arrested under the terrorism law … not only will they do that, they will [next] make an issue out of clothing."

The 2006 Terrorism Act—arguably the most significant counter-terrorism measure taken by the British government since 2001—prohibited giving talks or producing and distributing material that might "glorify terrorism" or which could encourage others to commit acts of terrorism.

But while the law has curbed overt jihadist rhetoric, many extremists have altered their preaching style rather than abandoning their arguments. For instance, many of the new generation of preachers, instead of explicitly calling for terrorist attacks in the UK, tell listeners that Islam is a conquering religion and that Muslims are obliged to strive for global domination. For example, a recent talk available on the sawtulislam.com website, which is apparently run by former members of al-Muhajiroun (an extremist group banned by the 2006 legislation), "Abu Othman" tells listeners that "[Muhammad] wasn't content. His eyes, my dear Muslims, were on the whole world; his eyes, my dear Muslims, were on conquering the Roman empire, the Persian empire, America, Britain, Australia—you name it. That was the vision of the messenger." The speaker also added that "we one day want to see in the UK the black flag of Islam over Ten Downing Street." While extreme, however, these statements do not explicitly contravene the new Terrorism Act or call for terrorist attacks—leaving the government powerless against such rhetoric.

Grassroots Work

In the 1990s and early 2000s, extremist groups openly sought to recruit followers by holding high-profile events in central London and other major cities. The last major extremist rally took place in London in February 2006 to protest against the cartoons of Muhammad published in Denmark. Led by Yassir al-Sirri, a leading member of Egypt's Islamic Jihad group, protestors burnt the Danish flag, chanted in support of Bin Laden and called on Muslims to bomb Denmark and the United States. As a result of the protests, four of the demonstrators were convicted—many of whom were former leading members of al-Muhajiroun (BBC, July 18, 2007).

Since then there have been no comparable protests and radicals have abandoned their former tactic of holding high-profile demonstrations. Instead, extremists now hold smaller-scale talks and run Islamic dawa or outreach stalls in the streets with the aim of appealing to potential recruits without attracting the attention of the security services. Similarly, whereas leading extremists such as Omar Bakri and Abu Izzadeen used to regularly appear on television and radio, the new generation of extremists deliberately shuns publicity and as a result is often successful in escaping detection for long periods of time. A typical example of this occurred when Usman Ali, a prominent former member of al-Muhajiroun, was banned from a mosque in southeast London in January 2007 by its trustees for praising the 9/11 attacks (*The Times*, September 21, 2007). This story was briefly reported by the BBC but Ali refused all media requests for an interview. Soon afterward, Ali was appointed as chaplain to a nearby hospital. The mosque's trustees warned hospital staff but with no effect (BBC, September 21, 2007). Eventually Ali was suspended after Muslim patients and staff complained about his extremist sermons in the hospital's prayer room. The BBC reported the story but Ali again dropped from public view. This case indicates how extremists who avoid the attention of the media and who air their ideas only among potentially sympathetic Muslims are able to continue preaching unhindered until their activities are reported to the authorities by their own co-religionists.

Increasing Localization

In keeping with the radicals' decision to keep a lower profile and avoid the attention of the security services and the media, extremist activity is becoming increasingly localized. Whereas terrorist recruiters formerly operated openly in prominent mosques—such as the

Finsbury Park Mosque, London's Regents' Park Mosque (London Central Mosque) and Birmingham Central Mosque, activity has shifted to lower-profile venues around the country. In many cases, extremists now use community centers, gyms and private homes for study circles and pro-jihadist talks, although this is by no means a new development; for example, Muhammad Siddique Khan, the leader of the 2005 London bombings, attended a gym known as the "Al-Qaeda Gym" (*The Times*, May 12, 2006). The recent discovery of alleged terrorist plots in Bristol, Exeter and High Wycombe also indicate how extremists are now operating not only in large towns with substantial Muslim populations, such as London, Leeds and Birmingham, but also in smaller cities with comparatively small Muslim populations. At the same time, however, such localization does not always imply that any intellectual or logistical fragmentation of extremist networks is taking place. In particular, the internet allows extremists around the UK to coordinate their activities, exchange pro-jihadist texts, videos and audio recordings. Analysis of British jihadist websites shows that the most popular writers are Muhammed al-Maqdisi, the Jordanian Salafi cleric, Yusuf al-Ayyari, a leader of al-Qaeda in Saudi Arabia killed in June 2003, and Abdullah Azzam, the Paletinian-born leader of the "Afghan-Arabs" in the 1980s. Osama bin Laden and Ayman al-Zawahiri are comparatively rarely mentioned, cited or quoted, while recorded talks by UK-based preachers such as Abdullah Faisal, Abu Hamza, Abu Qatada and Abu Bashir al-Tartusi are notably more popular. The growing importance of the internet partly explains why attending terrorist "training camps" abroad is no longer a necessary step on the road to jihad. In addition to helping radicals distribute Islamic texts and recordings, recent terrorism trials show that many potential terrorists have also used online texts detailing weapons use and explosives manufacture as a substitute for or supplement to receiving training in camps. For example, Sohail Qureshi, convicted of seeking travel to Pakistan to join jihadist groups either there or in Afghanistan, was found to have downloaded U.S. and Canadian army training manuals on guerrilla tactics and urban warfare before attempting to travel abroad (*The Times*, January 8, 2008).

Conclusion

The British government's counter-terrorism initiatives have done substantial damage to older terrorism networks based around veterans of jihadist conflicts in Afghanistan, Algeria and Bosnia. However, a new generation of radicals is now arising to take their place. In many cases, these men are brought up in the UK, speak fluent English and are better able to work around counter-terrorism laws and avoid conflict with the police than the older generation of largely foreign-born radicals. These new extremists are not just based in a few prominent mosques but are widely dispersed throughout Muslim communities around the country. Despite this dispersal, the internet allows extremists to remain in contact, to keep abreast of ideological, military and strategic issues affecting the worldwide jihad and to communicate with like-minded radicals around the UK and abroad. The recent arrest of two young white converts to Islam in two separate alleged bombing plots further highlights the continuing and broad appeal of these ideas (*Terrorism Focus*, June 10, 2008). British jihadist networks are rapidly evolving; the British security services must now find ways to evolve to tackle this new and emerging threat.

Originally published in *Terrorism Monitor*: Volume 6, Issue 13 on June 26, 2008.

Notes

1. This article is largely based on research carried out by the author while writing "Virtual Caliphate: Islamic Extremists and their websites," a report published by the UK-based Centre for Social Cohesion, June 2008.

UNITED STATES

Behind the Indoctrination and Training of American Jihadis
By Chris Heffelfinger

On July 26, 2007 a former Washington D.C. cab driver and resident of Gwynn Oak, Maryland was sentenced to 15 years in federal prison for providing material support to a terrorist group. Ohio-born Mahmud Faruq Brent, 32, admitted to attending training camps run by Lashkar-e-Taiba (LeT, Army of the Pure) in 2002, a Pakistani-based jihadi group established during the 1980s campaign against the Soviets in Afghanistan. After training at various locations in Pakistan, Brent returned to the United States, residing in Baltimore when he was arrested in August 2005. Brent told Tarik Shah—who pleaded guilty to conspiring to provide material support to al-Qaeda—that he had been up in the mountains training with the mujahideen [1]. Through Shah, Brent's training is linked to other cases of Americans who attended LeT-run camps in Pakistan. After Shah's arrest, he agreed to record conversations with Brent in cooperation with the FBI. In Shah's cell phone, along with Mahmud al-Mutazzim, another name Brent used, was the contact information for Seifullah Chapman, who also knew Brent (*Dawn*, July 26, 2007). Chapman, a former Marine, was part of the "Virginia Jihad Group," another informal network convicted of terrorism-related charges stemming from their training in Pakistan. He was sentenced in 2005 to a 65-year prison term.

As disturbing as these cases are individually, collectively they demonstrate an even more troubling trend of radicalized American Muslims—bound by Salafi ideology—receiving training overseas and returning to the United States for potential future operations.

The Virginia Jihad Group

Based out of Falls Church, Virginia, the informal jihadi group was led by Ali al-Timimi. A U.S. citizen, al-Timimi was sentenced to life in prison for soliciting others to levy war against the United States. Eleven people were charged in total in the case, and the prosecutors successfully argued that the network was part of the jihadi threat akin to al-Qaeda. Al-Timimi was born in Washington. D.C., his father a lawyer for the Iraqi Embassy. At age 15, he moved with his family to Saudi Arabia. While there, he grew interested in Islam, invariably the Salafi variety that is espoused by the Saudi religious establishment. After returning to the United States, he received a Ph.D. in computational biology from George Mason University (The Atlantic Monthly, June 2006).

In addition to his academic pursuits, al-Timimi was an Islamic teacher in the northern Virginia area. Yet, he was also involved with the Islamic Assembly of North America (IANA), a group based in Ann Arbor, Michigan that receives funding from Saudis to promote Salafi Islam in the United States, especially in the prison system (www.iananet.org). Naturally, al-Timimi's scholarly ties, more than anything, reveal his ideological proclivities. Establishing a center for Islamic education, al-Timimi contacted the well-known Egyptian-born Salafi Abd al-Rahman Abd al-Khaliq and translated his works into English. Abd al-Khaliq openly promoted the Salafi Islam prominent in the

Gulf, and privately encouraged more militant Salafism among his followers, telling them that "American troops were legitimate targets of the jihad."

Ties to Salafi Organizations

Ali al-Timimi's work for IANA—which included leading a five-person delegation to Beijing in 1995, where he defended female circumcision at an international women's conference—ties him into a much broader circle of Salafis, such as those in the Saudi Salafi establishment. Like many others who have been a part of that movement, he sought more militant teachings that condoned violence against Americans. Yet, the gateway to militancy often begins with seemingly benign teachings at austere mosques and Islamic centers. Commonly called Wahhabi, they call themselves Salafi, but for purposes of da'wa (proselytizing) and education, they do not emphasize their denomination. It is simply presented as "pure" Islam, and theirs is a purification movement.

A former chairman of IANA, Muhammad al-Ahmari, told the *New York Times* that, as of 2001, roughly half of his organization's funding came from the Saudi government, with the remainder primarily coming from private individual donations from the Gulf. IANA received at least $3 million from 1995 through 2002, which funded the distribution of 530 packages containing Qurans, tapes, lectures and other instructional Salafi educational material to prisoners in the United States. Part of the funds, however, also went to disseminating what is among the most militant Salafi material to date in the United States.

The group's webmaster, Sami Omar Hussayen, was a graduate student in Idaho when he posted two fatwas from Saudi Salafi-Jihadis Salman al-Awda and Safar al-Hawali, which incited jihad against Americans. Sami's uncle, Saleh Hussayen, is a high-ranking Saudi minister who gave at least $100,000 to IANA. He was also a director of a northern Virginia organization (the Safa Group) with—the U.S. government contends—around 100 front companies operating under it to launder money to al-Qaeda through the Isle of Man and Swiss bank accounts (*Washington Post*, October 2, 2003). Those raids, which took place in late 2001 and early 2002, have not yet come to trial. More inexplicable yet, Hussayen also came under scrutiny for a trip to the United States where, on September 10, 2001, he stayed at the same Marriott Residence Inn near Dulles Airport as three of the Saudi hijackers who crashed Flight 77 into the Pentagon.

Hussayen was questioned by the FBI, but there was no evidence he actually met or interacted with the hijackers. He was said to have feigned a seizure during the interview and taken to the hospital, where he was declared to be in good health. He returned to Saudi Arabia and to his post as Minister of Religious Endowments, overseeing the two holy mosques in Mecca and Medina.

From Ideology to Action

After conducting numerous case studies at the Combating Terrorism Center at West Point, research has demonstrated a pattern for radicalization among Americans who embrace jihad, whether foreign or U.S. born. The cases of the Lackawanna Six, the Portland Seven, the Virginia Jihad Group, as well as John Walker Lindh, Adam Gadahn and others demonstrate the need to travel overseas to receive training. In all of the above cases, the individuals traveled, or attempted to travel, to Pakistan or Afghanistan. As the base of al-Qaeda's leadership and the site of the first jihad, the area continues to be one of the primary destinations for mujahideen seeking training.

These individuals and others from the United States may have arrived at LeT camps, rather than at the al-Farouq camp or others that have been under bin Laden and al-Qaeda because they enjoy far less scrutiny. Founded shortly after 1986 as the military wing of the Center for Da'wa and Guidance, LeT initially helped Pakistani Mujahideen enter the Afghan jihad against the Soviet Union. In the 1990s, the focused their efforts on Kashmir and have two of their training camps in Muzaffarabad, the capital of the Pakistan-administered section of the disputed province (*Terrorism Monitor*, February 24, 2005).

LeT also claims to have trained thousands of combatants to join the mujahideen in Afghanistan, Kashmir, Bosnia, Chechnya, Kosovo and the Philippines [2]. Clearly, among American Muslims radicalized by militant Salafi Islam, LeT camps in Pakistan became a center for incoming mujahideen, as did bin Laden's guest house in Peshawar two decades ago.

Conclusion

These cases all suggest that ideology, above anything else, is the common identity among group members. Their belief and commitment to the Salafi movement and its aims to purify Islam, which is the foundation upon which bin Laden and other jihadi leaders have built their platforms, was the common factor that bound together these diverse individuals with various ethnic, national and linguistic backgrounds. Even a cursory look at the Brent case reveals ties to members of Ali al-Timimi's northern Virginia jihad group, and through them, a much larger world of official Saudi funding and militant Salafi influence. For nearly all the terrorism cases involving radical Islam, the subjects began their journey with the Salafi Islam offered by the Saudi establishment, its leading scholars and its prestigious institutions in Mecca and Medina.

Although they are clearly responsible for a portion of the radicalized Muslims now on a course for militancy, whether headed for a jihadi front in Iraq, Somalia, Lebanon, or in the United States or United Kingdom, those same individuals who have committed themselves to the cause cannot be effective without adequate training. Such individuals are encouraged—by Ali al-Timimi and Abu Musab al-Suri alike—to seek training in a place like Pakistan as an essential stage in their path to truly serving the jihad.

Originally published in *Terrorism Monitor*, Volume 5, Issue 15 on August 2, 2007.

Notes

1. See Criminal Complaint, "United States of America v Mahmud Faruq Brent, aka Mahmud al-Mutazzim," Filed in United States District Court, Southern District of New York, August 3, 2005.
2. Ibid.

INDEX

J

About the Authors

Abdul Hameed Bakier is an intelligence expert on counter-terrorism, crisis management and terrorist-hostage negotiations. He is based in Jordan.

Alison Pargeter is a Research Fellow at the International Policy Institute, Kings College London. She has published widely on Libya.

Anar Valiyev holds Ph.D. in Urban and Public Affairs from University of Louisville in Kentucky. His areas of interest include urban terrorism, public policy of post-Soviet countries, governance and democracy.

Andrew Black is the Managing Director of Black Watch Global, an intelligence and risk management consultancy headquartered in Washington, DC.

Andrew McGregor is the director of Aberfoyle International Security in Toronto, Canada.

Anes Alic is the Executive Director of ISA Consulting, www.isaintel.com.

Anouar Boukhars is a specialist on politics of the Muslim world. Dr. Boukhars is an assistant professor and director of the Center for Defense and Security Policy at Wilberforce University in Ohio. He is also editor of *Wilberforce Quarterly* journal.

Antonio Giustozzi is a Research Fellow at the Crisis States Research Centre at the London School of Economics. He is the author of several articles and papers on Afghanistan, as well as of two books, *War, Politics and Society in Afghanistan, 1978-1992* (Georgetown University Press, 2000) and *Koran, Kalashnikov and Laptop: The Neo-Taliban Insurgency, 2002-7* (Columbia University Press, 2007). His next book, *Empires of Mud: War and Warlords in Afghanistan*, will appear in 2009. He is currently researching issues of governance in Afghanistan.

Babak Rahimi received a Ph.D. from the European University Institute, Florence, Italy. Dr. Rahimi has also studied at the University of Nottingham and London School of Economics and Political Science, UK. He was a Senior Fellow at the United States Institute of Peace from 2005-2006, where he conducted research on Ayatollah Ali al-Sistani and Shiite politics in post-Baathist Iraq. He is currently an Assistant Professor at the Department of Literature, Program for the Study of Religion, University of California, San Diego.

Bestman Wellington is a Nigerian journalist, a small arms researcher and an analyst based in Port Harcourt, Rivers State, in the Niger Delta.

Brian Glyn Williams is assistant professor of Islamic History at the University of Massachusetts-Dartmouth.

Brian O'Neill is an independent political analyst based out of Chicago, and is a former reporter for the *Yemen Observer*.

Brynjar Lia is a research professor at the Norwegian Defense Research Establishment (FFI) and the author of a forthcoming biography on Abu Mus'ab al-Suri *entitled Architect of Global Jihad: The Life of Al-Qaeda Strategist Abu Mus'ab Al-Suri* (London: Hurst & Co Publisher, 2007). Among his previous books are *Globalisation and the Future of Terrorism: Patterns and Predictions* (London: Routledge, 2005) and *The Society of the Muslim Brothers in Egypt, 1928-1942* (Reading: Ithaca Press, 1998).

Cathy Young is a research assistant at the University of Massachusetts-Dartmouth.

Cerwyn Moore is a Lecturer in International Relations at the University of Birmingham.

Chris Heffelfinger is an independent researcher affiliated with the Combating Terrorism Center at the U.S. Military Academy, West Point. He is also the editor of *Unmasking Terror: A Global Review of Terrorist Activities* (Vols. I and II, The Jamestown Foundation).

Chris Quillen is a former analyst in the Counter-Terrorist Center at the Central Intelligence Agency.

Chris Zambelis is an associate with Helios Global, Inc., a risk analysis firm based in the Washington, DC area. He specializes in Middle East politics. He is a regular contributor to a number of publications, where he writes on Middle East politics, political Islam, international security, and related issues. He has lived and worked in the Middle East, East Europe and the former Yugoslavia, and Latin America. He is a graduate of New York University and holds an M.S. in Foreign Service from Georgetown University.

Christopher Boucek is a Postdoctoral Researcher at Princeton University and a Lecturer at the Woodrow Wilson School.

Fadhil Ali is a freelance journalist based in Iraq who specializes in Iraqi insurgent groups.

Farhana Ali is an Associate International Policy Analyst at the RAND Corporation. She has done extensive research on jihadist networks and religious extremism.

Geoff D. Porter is the North Africa analyst with Eurasia Group, a consulting firm that advises corporate, financial services and government clients on political risks in emerging markets. He is a fluent Arabic and French speaker who travels frequently throughout North Africa and has previously lived in Morocco, Tunisia and Egypt for extended periods.

Gregory D. Johnsen, a former Fulbright Fellow in Yemen, is currently a Ph.D. candidate in Near Eastern Studies at Princeton University.

Hassan Abbas served as the Sub-Divisional Police Chief in the NWFP from 1996-1998, and was the Deputy Director of Investigations in Pakistan's National Accountability Bureau from 1999-2000. Currently, he is a fellow at Harvard University's Kennedy School of Government and is the author of *Pakistan's Drift into Extremism: Allah, the Army and America's War on Terror* (Pentagon Press, 2005).

Hayder Mili is an independent researcher specializing in terrorism and security issues in Central Asia and the Caucasus.

Hussain Mousavi writes on the Middle East.

Igor Rotar is Central Asia correspondent for Forum 18 News Service.

Imtiaz Ali is a Pakistan-based journalist working as a special correspondent for the Washington Post. Before this he was a correspondent for the BBC Pashto Service for about six years. He joined the BBC in 2001, reporting on the U.S. attack on the Taliban regime in Afghanistan in the wake of the September 11 attacks. Before the BBC, he was a print journalist and worked with Pakistan's premier English daily publications, *The News* and *Dawn*. Since 9/11, he has reported extensively on the Taliban, militancy in the border regions and Pakistan's military operations against al-Qaeda operatives and their local supporters in the tribal areas of Pakistan. Mr. Ali was a Knight Journalism Fellow at the John S. Knight Fellowships Program at Stanford during 2006-2007.

Jacob Townsend is a research analyst at the Australian Strategic Policy Institute and has been a consultant on border control to the United Nations Office on Drugs and Crime.

James Brandon is a senior research fellow at the Centre for Social Cohesion in London. He is a former journalist who has reported on Islamic issues in Europe, the Middle East and Africa for a wide variety of print and broadcast media. He holds an M.A, in Middle Eastern Studies from the School of Oriental and African Studies (SOAS) in London.

James Briggs is an analyst based in Nigeria.

John C. K. Daly is a Eurasian foreign affairs and defense policy expert for The Jamestown Foundation based in Washington, D.C.

Kathryn Haahr is a foreign affairs and counter-terrorism consultant in Washington, D.C.

Lorenzo Vidino is an analyst at the Investigative Project on Terrorism and the Jebsen Center at Tufts University's Fletcher School of Law and Diplomacy. He is the author of the book, *Al-Qaeda in Europe: The New Battleground of International Jihad* (Prometheus Books, 2005).

Lydia Khalil recently returned from Iraq where she worked as governance policy advisor for the Coalition Provisional Authority in Baghdad. Prior to that, Lydia was appointed to the White House Office of Homeland Security. She has worked at home and abroad for the U.S. government, international organizations, private companies and think-tanks on a variety of Middle East political and terrorism issues.

Matthew Chebatoris is a freelance analyst and 12-year veteran of the U.S. intelligence community.

Mohammad Shehzad is an independent researcher in Pakistan with years of experience reporting on jihadi groups.

Muhammad Tahir is a Prague-based journalist and analyst, specializing in Afghan/Iran and Central Asian affairs, and is author of *Illegal Dating: A Journey into the Private Life of Iran* (BookSurge Publishing, 2006).

Omid Marzban has worked for Good Morning Afghanistan Radio Station and Radio Free Europe. He is based in Afghanistan.

Pascale Combelles Siegel is a Virginia-based independent defense consultant specializing in perception management.

Raffaello Pantucci is a Research Associate at the International Institute for Strategic Studies (IISS) in London. He is also the London correspondent for *HS Today*, a magazine looking at Homeland Security issues, and writes on terrorism issues for newspapers, magazines and journals on both sides of the Atlantic. Before joining IISS in 2006, he worked at the Center for Strategic and International Studies (CSIS) in Washington for three and a half years.

Ramzy Mardini was Special Assistant on Iranian Studies at the Center for Strategic Studies in Amman, Jordan and a former Iraq Desk Officer for Political Affairs at the Department of State. He has also served within the Executive Office of the President.

Reidar Visser is a research fellow at the Norwegian Institute of International Affairs and editor of the Iraq website http://www.historiae.org. His books include Basra, The Failed Gulf State: Separatism and Nationalism in Southern Iraq (Lit Verlag, 2005) and, edited with Gareth Stansfield, *An Iraq of its Regions: Cornerstones of a Federal Democracy?* (Columbia University Press, 2007).

Sherifa Zuhur is Research Professor of Islamic and Regional Studies at the Strategic Studies Institute at the U.S. Army War College. She is also the Director of the Institute of Middle Eastern, Islamic, and Diasporic Studies.

Tariq Mahmud Ashraf is a retired Air Commodore from the Pakistan Air Force. A freelance analyst on South Asian defense and nuclearization issues, he has authored one book and published over 70 papers and articles in journals of repute.

Tarique Niazi teaches Environmental Sociology at the University of Wisconsin, Eau Claire. He specializes in Resource-based Conflicts.

Thomas Renard is a consultant and expert on terrorism and insurgencies. He is a frequent contributor to *Terrorism Focus* and *Terrorism Monitor* and an occasional collaborator with *Le Soir*, the main French-speaking newspaper in Belgium. Some of his other collaborations include French-speaking journals *Défense et Sécurité Internationale* (DSI) and *Les Cahiers du RMES*. He has also launched his own blog: Le Front Asymétrique (http://lefrontasymetrique.blogspot.com). Mr. Renard holds a M.A. in International Affairs from the Elliott School of International Affairs at The George Washington University; and a M.A. in Journalism and a B.A. in Political Sciences from the Université Catholique de Louvain, Belgium.

Waliullah Rahmani is the Executive Director of the Kabul Center for Strategic Studies (KCSS), a newly established Kabul-based think-tank that provides analysis and research from the Afghan perspective on the region with Afghanistan as its primary focus. Mr. Rahmani is the Editor in Chief of Kabul Direct monthly. Before joining the KCSS he was employed by RFE/RL. An expert on Afghanistan, Iran and Islamic movements, Mr. Rahmani has written for a variety of Western publications.

Wilson John is a Senior Fellow with Observer Research Foundation, New Delhi, India.